WOMEN
WHO KILL

ANN JONES

BEACON PRESS

Boston

Beacon Press
25 Beacon Street
Boston, Massachusetts 02108-2892

Beacon Press books
are published under the auspices of
the Unitarian Universalist Association of Congregations.

02 01 00 99 98 97 96   8 7 6 5 4 3 2 1

Text design by Christine Aulicino

Library of Congress Cataloging-in-Publication Data

Jones, Ann, 1937–
    Women who kill / Ann Jones.
        p.   cm.
    Originally published: New York : Holt, Rinehart, and Winston, © 1980.
    Includes bibliographical references and index.
    ISBN 0-8070-6775-X
    1. Women murderers—United States—History.   I. Title.
HV6046.J66   1996
364.1'523'082—dc20   95–46961

In memory of my mother,
Berenice Rufsvold Slagsvol,
and of Bunny,
who was killed.

O race of Adam, blench not lest you find
In the sun's bubbling bowl anonymous death,
Or lost in whistling space without a mind
To monstrous Nothing yield your little breath:
You shall achieve destruction where you stand,
In intimate conflict, at your brother's hand.

—Edna St. Vincent Millay

There are no new arguments to be made
on human rights. . . .

—Elizabeth Cady Stanton

Pray for the dead,
but fight like hell for the living.

—Mother Jones

CONTENTS

ACKNOWLEDGMENTS

Thanks are in order, for during four years of research I have incurred many debts. I am grateful to librarians and archivists of many institutions: the Historical Societies of Fall River and Worcester (Massachusetts) and New Castle (Delaware) and of the states of Wisconsin, Minnesota, Delaware, and Massachusetts; the Pennsylvania State Library, the Library of Congress, the libraries of John Jay College of Criminal Justice, Cornell University, Rutgers University, the University of Massachusetts at Amherst, Smith College, and the law libraries of Columbia University and the University of Missouri; the San Francisco Public Library, the Ithaca (New York) Public Library, and the Forbes Library in Northampton, Massachusetts; the American Antiquarian Society (Worcester, Massachusetts) and the Board of Trade of New Castle, Delaware. I am indebted to the New York Historical Society and to librarian Barbara Shikler, who cheerfully searched stacks and on fruitless days took me to lunch; to Jane Williamson, who put the library of the Women's Action Alliance at my disposal; and to director Abby Schaeffer, who provided work space in The Writers Room. My debt to the New York Public Library is enormous. It offered me a desk in the Frederick Lewis Allen Memorial Room (where I have maintained a typewriter and a toothbrush since 1978), the services of its concerned and patient staff (particularly in the American History and Newspaper divisions), and its incomparable collections. There is simply no place quite the equal of "the Library." I couldn't have written this book anywhere else.

Carol Kramer of the New York *Daily News* and Sherry Brown of the Lafayette (Indiana) *Journal and Courier* provided information from their files, and the clerks of the Supreme Judicial Court of Massachusetts, the Hampshire County (Massachusetts) Court, the Worcester County (Massachusetts) Court, and the Kings County (New York) Court searched records for me. Dr. Donald B. Hoffman, chief toxicologist of the New York Medical Examiner's Office, pored over old cases and offered expert opinion. Only three institutions declined to aid me: the law libraries of Harvard and Yale and the Pennsylvania Bureau of Correction.

It was exciting to me to move out of my self-imposed isolation in libraries and into research on contemporary feminist problems, for other women working on these issues willingly gave me a hand. Betsy Warrior and Del Martin, who led the way in the concerns of battered women, generously advised me. Attorney Elizabeth Schneider, Kathleen Ridolfi, and Elizabeth Bochnak of the Women's Self-Defense Law Project offered enthusiasm, help, and stacks of information. (The Project, in consultation with attorneys across the country, is developing important theoretical approaches to legal representation of women facing criminal charges for defending themselves against physical or sexual assault.) Among others who helped in my research on battered women were Rebecca Allerton of the Tompkins County (New York) Task Force on Battered Women and JoAnn Dunn of the Lincoln (Nebraska) Task Force on Abused Women, Ruth Childers, Betty Evett, Marie de Jong-Joch, Bill Johnson, Mary McGuire, Bernadette Powell, Mary Randolph, Lucy Slurzberg, Cheryl Smith, Judy Sturm, Mary Thom, David Trevallion, and Carol Ann Wilds. Providing information on other topics were Sharon Wiggins, Susan Reed, Odette L. McCartny, and the New York City Department of Correction.

Several attorneys helped me ferret out information or clarify points of law: Fern Adelstein (student), David Burres, Linda Fidnick, John Gambs, Mark Gasarch, Martin Luster, Jay Seeger, Martin Stolar, and especially Susan Thon. Among many friends who offered information, advice, or help were Barbara Bader, Rayna Green, Linda Hamalian, Leo Hamalian, Marvin Kaye, Claudette Kulkarni, David Lowe, Harry Maurer, Elizabeth Meyersohn, John Clair Miller, Lynn Myers, B. J. Phillips, Pat Sackrey, Anne Summers, and Kathleen Swaim. Others who shared their own work with me included Margaret

Culley, Sarah Hoaglund, and Robin Morgan. Lynn Campbell, Elisa Evett, Jeffrey Hessing, and Mary Lea Meyersohn criticized sections of one draft or another. Jennifer Josephy, my editor, remained encouraging through it all.

And there are special debts: to Maynard Cat and Big Randolph, two gray friends who sat up many a long night with me and my murderers; to my literary agent and dear friend Frances Goldin; to Ann-Ellen Lesser, director of the Millay Colony for the Arts, who made it possible for me to work at the Colony, where this book was finished, then brilliantly dissected my manuscript; to Norma Millay, who offered me her sister's studio and her incisive criticism; to my Allen Room cronies—Jane Alpert, Susan Brownmiller, Nancy Milford, and Paula Weideger—who read, ripped apart, comforted, and challenged; and particularly to Susan Brownmiller, who set a model of feminist scholarship for me long before I met her and who became an unstintingly generous colleague; to Joan Silber, who read everything, put to rights many a clumsy passage, and listened to more murder tales than one could want to hear; and to Anne Bowen, who lived with me and this book from its inception and whose mighty intelligence informs every page.

For all their help, encouragement, and devotion, my friends are not to be blamed. I committed this book myself.

FOREWORD

Five years ago in a women's literature seminar, a student depressed by reading *The Awakening, The House of Mirth,* and *The Bell Jar,* complained: "Isn't there anything a woman can do but kill herself?" To lighten the mood I quipped, "She can always kill somebody else," and realized in the instant that it was true. I have been working on this book ever since.

It has caused embarrassment. Tell people you're writing a book about women who commit murder and they make some joke about "lady-killers" or walk away muttering "weird." For both the killer and the killed, murder is one of the few human acts that cannot be ameliorated or revoked; yet no one seems to take it seriously. Books about murder (with the exception of some serious attempts at understanding, such as Truman Capote's *In Cold Blood* and Norman Mailer's *The Executioner's Song*) fall mainly into two categories: bone-dry academic criminology aimed at diagramming criminal patterns, and presumably helping to prevent crime; and grimly amusing homicidal anecdotes in the vein popularized in this country by Edmund Lester Pearson. For the most part, academic criminologists ignore women while the popular crime writers describe "murderesses" in books with snappy titles like *Fatal Femmes* and *The Deadlier Species.* Yet almost anyone who stops to think about it realizes that women's homicides are "different." Unlike men, who are apt to stab a total stranger in a drunken brawl or run amok with a high-powered rifle, we women usually kill our intimates: we kill our children, our husbands, our lovers. This fact is not amusing. But that these homicidal patterns might be shadows of profound cultural deformities—and thus worthy of serious consideration—seems not to have occurred to many.

But joking, you will say, is merely a psychological defense against the undeniable fact that people—you and I—are capable of murdering and of being murdered. We laugh because we are afraid. True enough. And this book is mostly about fear: the fears of men who, even as they shape society, are desperately afraid of women, and so have fashioned a world in which women come and go only in certain rooms; and about the fears of those women who, finding the rooms too narrow and the door still locked, lie in wait or set the place afire.

But are such women a fit subject for serious historical (or herstorical) study? Historians often assume that women have not significantly acted, but have been acted upon. Women are history's great blob of putty. So we have books—accurate and valuable books—on how women have been defrauded and oppressed by medicine, psychology, capitalism, the law, the universities, and our own mothers. Other historians, believing that some women did act, and from enlightened self-interest at that, have given us women in the antislavery movement, in the suffrage movement, in the labor movement: women like the Grimkés, Anthony, Cady Stanton, Goldman, Eastman, Mother Jones, who have said and done great things on behalf of themselves and others. Yet our great women are few. This year more women will kill their children than will be appointed to the judicial bench. More women will kill their husbands than will sit in the halls of Congress. A baby girl born tomorrow stands a chance of growing up to stick a kitchen knife into an assaultive husband; but her chances of becoming President are too slim to be statistically significant. The story of women who kill is the story of women.

This book does not proceed in a straight line. It consists of a series of studies, mostly historical, approaching the subject of women and murder from different angles. They are intended to dispel some false notions and to examine the connections among women, society, and killing. My aim has not been to get through the topic but to get at it.

I have not sought out obscure cases since they are often fascinating in their own right but reveal little about their times. Instead, I write mostly about prominent cases that obviously hit a social nerve. I recount some individual cases such as the Borden parricide because they are historical landmarks or (like the cases of Ruth Snyder and Alice Crimmins) representative of broad social concerns; and I discuss groups of cases that cluster about a single prominent issue, such as infanticide in the colonial era or woman's self-defense in our own.

In presenting cases I have had to mediate between my sources and my readers. That has been complicated because where murder is concerned people not only forget things and misunderstand—as all of us do in the best of circumstances—but they also lie a lot. I compared as many different accounts as I could lay hands on and produced a version as close to the truth as I could get, though it is only fair to say that I have read and retold history as a feminist. Where circumstances make it impossible to penetrate to the "truth" I have said so. And I have made up nothing. Indeed, because murder can so easily be sensationalized or sentimentalized, I have taken some pains to stick to the bare facts.

Some definitions are necessary. I use the term *feminists* throughout the book to refer to women who identified themselves with and spoke on behalf of women's rights. Feminism encompasses a broad range of opinion, but usually I found it neither necessary nor useful to make distinctions since the general public tends to lump all feminists together. When I cite a viewpoint of a particular group or spokesperson, I name the group or person; but for the most part the term feminists should be taken to apply to women who supported or were thought to support women's rights. Often I use the term *social fathers* in the same broad way: to suggest those people (mostly male) in positions of power and influence within society who, acting individually or in concert, shape public attitudes and policy. I do not imply that society is run by a handful of powerful men; I use the term for rhetorical convenience and to suggest that certain social institutions—notably the law—are indeed largely determined by the influence of an upper-class, predominately white male, elite.

In reading recent books on women's history, I notice that it is the fashion, particularly among academic historians and literary historians, to disclaim any notion of male conspiracy in the oppression of women. It seems to be incumbent upon the author to say that readers who gain from the book the impression that men as a group have done something unpleasant to women as a group are entirely mistaken, for the author never intended any such thing. "For my part," I must say with William Lloyd Garrison, "I am not prepared to respect that philosophy. I believe in sin, therefore in a sinner; in theft, therefore in a thief; in slavery, therefore in a slaveholder; in wrong, therefore in a wrong-doer; and unless the men of this nation are made by women to see that they have been guilty of usurpation, and cruel usurpation, I believe very little progress will be made." If this book leaves the impression that men have conspired to keep women down, that is exactly the impression I mean to convey; for I believe that men could not have succeeded as well as they have without concerted effort.

A.J.
New York, New York
August 1979

INTRODUCTION

Peachie was small enough to hide behind a potted plant. She could cover the patrons in the bank with her .22, and she couldn't be seen from the street. But she couldn't see the street either, so when she heard the door open she had to wait for George Morelock to walk to the center of the lobby into her line of vision. "Stop right there," she said, and poked the gun at him when he turned and noticed her. But Morelock was hard of hearing and didn't seem to understand. He started toward her, and she warned him again; but he kept coming and she pulled the trigger, again and again. Some of the patrons screamed. Peachie and one of her accomplices ran out of the bank and into an off-duty policeman who had stopped by to make a deposit. They forced him to stretch out in the street as they fled, but the encounter delayed them. In a panic, the driver stalled the getaway car, and by the time they transferred to their second car, scattering money behind them, the police were in pursuit. A police bullet shattered the rear window; the car went out of control, caromed off a parked car, and crashed through a plate-glass window. The police picked up Peachie Wiggins and her two male companions and $70,157. All three bank robbers were charged with murder. They were convicted and in 1969 sentenced to die in the Pennsylvania electric chair. Peachie Wiggins was seventeen years old.

She spent two years confined alone, first in maximum security, then in the prison infirmary, because Pennsylvania had no death cell for a woman. Then, in a new trial, she and her friends were given life sentences; and Peachie joined the general prison population. Since then she has come up for commutation of her sentence twice, and both times it has been denied. She has escaped twice, returning once of her own volition, once when she was recaptured after three years of freedom. And each escape has brought a sentence of additional time. She is now serving sentences of life imprisonment for murder, indeterminate to twenty years for robbery, indeterminate to three years for conspiracy, indeterminate to two years for violation of the firearms act, indeterminate to five years for one escape, and indeterminate to two years for another. That adds up to a maximum term of life plus thirty-two years, and her chances for parole are slim. She is young. She is black. In the course of an armed robbery she killed a man. And she has repeatedly escaped from prison. She seems to be one of those women we've heard more and more about in recent years: one of the so-called new breed of violent female criminals.

In recent years, the female crime wave and its violent women have been alarmingly described in articles and books; but they were first widely publicized in 1975 through a book called *Sisters in Crime* by Freda Adler, a criminologist who rose to prominence on the strength of a logical fallacy. Noticing that a renewed women's movement paralleled apparently phenomenal increases in crimes by women, Adler mistakenly concluded that one trend caused the other. The rapid rise in crimes by women, she said, was merely the "shady aspect of liberation"; and as more and more "libbers" rushed to emulate the criminal example of men—the only "full human beings"—we would be awash in a sea of emancipated crime.

While some prisons planned new facilities for the expected influx of violent women, feminists in criminology and the criminal-justice system were quick to respond to Adler with convincing arguments. They maintained, and rightly, that Adler's figures were misleading precisely because women commit so few crimes. When the number of crimes is small, only a few more may account for a large percentage increase; but Adler cited those alarming percentage increases without recording the low absolute numbers. She pointed to a shocking rise of 277 percent in arrests of women for robbery between 1960 and 1972; but the 1973 *Uniform Crime Reports* of the FBI reported only 5,700 women arrested for robbery that year, compared with almost 95,000 men. Across the board women were arrested in 1973 for about 15.3 percent of all crimes committed—not a high rate, and certainly not an alarming one, for a group that makes up more than half the population. Adler's critics also noted that there has been *no* demonstrable increase in crimes of violence committed by women. The greatest increases in women's crimes have been in larceny and fraud, particularly welfare fraud; and these are not violent crimes but economic ones, easily attributable to the growing financial needs of poor women, most of whom have children to support. Other critics pointed to evidence that spreading drug addiction has increased economic crimes for women and men alike. In any case, the so-called new woman criminal was likely to be—like the old woman criminal—young, poor, and black or Hispanic.

Adler was quite right that the two phenomena—the women's movement and female criminality—go together, but not as she supposed in terms of cause and effect. It is simply that the presence of one prompts fear of the other. Agitation for women's rights always sparks enormous anxiety, among women and men alike, about the proper place of women in society, and because "take" in one element of society seems to mean "give" in another, about the safety of the whole social order. That anxiety manifests itself in many ways: in the fear that women are "unsexing themselves," which in turn produces campaigns to outlaw bloomers, to elevate a regressive "femininity" to "total womanhood," and to make abortion a criminal offense; in the fear that the family is disintegrating, which results in virulent attacks upon women's colleges, divorce, homosexuality, women in the work force, federally funded day care, and unisex bathrooms; and in the fear that women, released from some traditional restraints, will turn to unbridled evil, mayhem, and murder. Even the traditionally macho skin magazine *Oui* observed in 1975, "Women criminals today seem to spark a special fear, fantasy and overreaction in male society."

That overreaction to an imaginary wave of criminality is likely to take shape as a wave of law enforcement. It happens all the time. Every so often the law cracks down on bootleggers or prostitutes or gamblers or drivers who park in towaway zones. The crackdown is simply a wave of law enforcement, but it may appear to have been occasioned by a wave of crime. The classic example of a wave of law enforcement in American history is the Salem witch trials. Since we are no longer troubled by witches, we can easily see that the dark affliction of Salem grew from a profound cultural neurosis, a "group panic." At the time Salem had good political and economic reasons to be concerned for the safety of the established social order; but we, having lost the theological habit of mind, can see that Salem suffered more from the fear of witches than from witches themselves. Still, we have not lost the disposition that finds a simple scapegoat for the incalculable complex of factors—social, political, economic—that may rise against us, threatening change or destruction. That anxiety about the social order is profound and abiding, and it surfaces from time to time in American society in the same form it took at Salem: sudden notice of the crimes of women.

That, it seems, is what is happening today. In absolute terms, crimes by women are increasing roughly on a par with crimes by men. Crimes of violence committed by women—about 10 percent of all violent crimes—have not increased significantly in the last twenty years; according to some estimates they are declining. The rate of murders committed by women has remained steady at 15 percent of all murders for as long as anyone has kept records anywhere. But the rate of arrests for all crimes between 1967 and 1976 rose 15 percent for men and 64 percent for women. Among juvenile women, arrests increased 68 percent. Methods of keeping criminal statistics are so inconsistent and misleading that the actual "criminality" of women is impossible to calculate; yet the law has been cracking down. And that crackdown certainly has a good deal to do with the women's movement. Researchers for the National Prison Project of the American Civil Liberties Union reported in 1979 that although there "clearly . . . is not a 'new breed' of violent woman . . . there is almost certainly a new attitude toward women within the criminal justice system." As law-enforcement officials repeatedly told criminologist Rita Simon: "If it's equality these women want, we'll see that they get it."

To spare us the panic, criminology should be able to provide some helpful information about women and crime; but in fact criminology knows next to nothing about women, since it has concentrated all along on the doings of men. That focus is quite legitimate and not simply the result of sex bias; men in all countries in all periods of history have committed far more than their share of crimes, particularly violent crimes. Manfully, criminologists have chosen to ignore women rather than to deal with the dilemma these differential crime rates present. The intimation that women are less violent than men by *nature* leads to disquieting conclusions about the innate moral superiority of women, conclusions that men are no longer willing to accept; and the alternative suggestion that women may be less violent because of their socialization raises even more unnerving possibilities to improve society by bringing up men to be more like women. Nevertheless, despite the obvious perils of exploring this question too closely, the occasional intrepid criminologist in search of female criminality has come along in the anxious wake of feminist agitation, dragging his bucket of cultural common sense behind him. The ostensible "father" of modern criminology, Italian scientist Cesare Lombroso, with the help of his son-in-law William Ferrero, produced his definitive work on women, *The Female Offender,* in 1893, less than a decade after Ibsen's Nora slammed the door on European patriarchy. In America, William I. Thomas produced his first study, *Sex and Society,* under Lombrosan influence in the last days of the suffrage fight, and his second volume, *The Unadjusted Girl,* in 1923, just after the battle was won. And Otto Pollak's *The Criminality of Women,* still regarded as the definitive modern study, appeared in 1950, just as a disgruntled Rosie the Riveter was shuffled off to premature suburban retirement. These studies were followed by Adler's *Sisters in Crime* in the wake of the current wave of feminism. Each of these studies was produced during a period of profound unease about woman's place in society or out-and-out reaction against the women's rights movement; each presented "scientific" conclusions firmly mired in the prevailing cultural stereotypes; and each study, along with the attention paid to it, became an important part of the antifeminist backlash.

These curious circumstances, coupled with the fact that criminology is a fairly new discipline anyway, have left us with a small body of "expertise" that is fundamentally alarmist, reactionary, antifeminist, and wrong. Still the experts have had an undeniable impact, and among social scientists they are still taken with some seriousness. Cesare Lombroso is credited with starting it all. Trained in biological sciences, Lombroso was uncomfortable with the philosophical musings on crime and society of criminology's first eighteenth-century contributors, Jeremy Bentham, the English reformer and utilitarian philosopher, and Cesare Beccaria, the Italian economist and jurist. Troubled by shifting legal definitions of crime, Lombroso set out to find hard, unchanging, scientific categories. And where better to look for crime than to the criminals themselves? Lombroso had made several studies of men before he set out to distinguish what he called the "born female criminal" from the "normal woman," the nice, upper-middle-class Italian lady. Common sense and Lombroso's own experience told him that there were only these two kinds of women in the world—bad and good—but he seemed haunted by the fear that an apparently good woman might, at any unexpected moment, turn out to be bad. Thus, he devoted a large part of his career to marking once and for all the difference between them. For the good woman, Lombroso said, love was "a species of slavery." She gladly sacrificed her "entire personality" for her loved one, and if she lost him to death or to another, she nobly killed herself. Criminal women, on the other hand, were scarcely women at all: "female criminals approximate more to males ... than to normal women, especially in the superciliary arches in the seam of the sutures, in the lower jaw-bones, and in peculiarities of the occipital region."

Lombroso was not a man to rest on his preconceptions. He went on assiduously measuring bumps and protuberances, noting the heavy dark hair and weighty brows he found repeatedly (given the social prejudice of his time) among the Sicilian prisoners who filled Italian jails, patiently amassing all the data he needed to convert his biases to science. Once he had done that he was able to predict the future of any woman on the most slender evidence. In the case of nine-year-old Louise C., Lombroso never saw the child, but he did obtain her photograph and her history: "At three she was a thief, and laid hands on her mother's money, on articles in shops, on everything ... that came in her way. At five she was arrested and conveyed to the police-office, after a determined resistance. ... She shrieked, tore off her stockings, threw her dolls into the gutter, lifted up her skirts in the streets." Lombroso's colleague noticed in the child "no morbid peculiarity of face," but Lombroso, by looking at her murky photograph, could identify "the exact type of the born criminal. Her physiognomy is Mongolian, her jaws and cheek-bones are immense; the frontal sinuses strong, the nose flat with a prognathous under-jaw, asymmetry of face, and above all, precocity and virility of expression. She looks like a grown woman—nay, a man." Louise C.'s likeness is still there among Lombroso's yellowing pages—the likeness of a forsaken little girl.

To William I. Thomas more than biology was at stake. All young people, he said, respond to four human wishes: the desires for (1) new experience, (2) security, (3) response, and (4) recognition. Yet, when Thomas began discussing these universal wishes, they turned out to be not so universal after all. "Men crave excitement," he said, "and all experiences are exciting which have in them some resemblance to the pursuit, flight, capture, escape, death which characterized the earlier life of mankind. . . . 'Adventure' is what the young boy wants. . . ." Women, on the other hand, are supposed to possess "originally, from early childhood to death, some interest in human babies. . . ." So, without batting an inconsistent eye, Thomas found the "beginning of delinquency in girls" in "an impulse to get amusement, adventure, pretty clothes, favorable notice, distinction, freedom in the larger world which presents so many allurements"—in short, all those things that men naturally "crave" and that "people" wish for.

As a new "liberal" in the field of criminology, Thomas argued that offenders should be treated individually to rehabilitation, not punishment. Thus, women who were unadjusted in Thomas's terms—that is, women who wished for "freedom in the larger world"—were to be detained for indeterminate periods and psychologically adjusted to their original "interest in human babies." Happily, women, like children, were not intelligent enough to have a genuine moral life; so morality for a woman meant simply "the adjustment of her person to men." And since the "ordinary girl" did not have "imagination enough to think out a general attitude toward life," the wayward female could be set right—much like a wind-up toy—by forcible, mechanical "adjustment" to her traditional feminine role.

Pollak, like Lombroso and Thomas, took what he "knew" of woman's nature and found evidence to support his presuppositions, but while Lombroso tediously measured supraorbital ridges and cranial sutures, Pollak simply invented "masked crime." This concept of female criminality was based once again upon woman's aberrant sexuality, but it was verified this time not by data but by the absence of data. It was Pollak's contention that women fall out of the criminal-justice system because their crimes are seldom detected, reported, or prosecuted. Women commit at least as many crimes as men do, Pollak maintained, but women's crimes rarely find their way into the record books. On one hand, women manipulate men and instigate many of the crimes for which men pay. On the other hand, as shoppers and cooks, women enjoy plenty of chances to steal and poison on their own. Women who cleverly hide monthly menstruation and routinely fake orgasm, Pollak argued, can lie about anything; and all women are vengeful—ready to lie, cheat, connive, manipulate, and kill—because all have suffered the trauma of first menstruation which blasted forever "their hope ever to become a man."

Pollak's ingenious theory, which proved on the basis of no evidence whatsoever that women are every bit as violent and criminal as men, led to other equally speculative and equally significant theories. He picked up the popular nineteenth-century notion that male chivalry shields women from legal punishment; and by incorporating that old idea into his theory, he gave it the authority of science. It is now widely believed by the general public and by people working within the criminal-justice system that vast numbers of women get away with crimes through the operation of chivalry: they are not arrested, or not prosecuted, or not convicted, or not sentenced to pay the full price. And since chivalry presupposes guilt, women who are acquitted of criminal charges are not thought to have been exonerated but to have gotten away with something.

Observers of the criminal-justice system have long complained that it operates erratically. White, upper-middle-class defendants do seem to get a better break, partly because they can afford better lawyers, and partly because they come from the same social group as those who are administering "justice." But that advantage is the result of class bias, not of bias in favor of a single sex. Its principal beneficiaries in recent years have been Richard Nixon and the Watergate conspirators, and it would be difficult indeed to find cases of white courts extending such "chivalry" to lower-class women of color. Nonwhite and poor women, like men from the same social groups, are overrepresented at every phase of the criminal-justice process; so it would seem that chivalry, such as it is, is part of a much larger system of race and class prejudice that weights the scales of justice. Certainly chivalry is not a policy that operates consistently in favor of women, but it is a handy veil to obscure what is really going on between women and the criminal-justice system.

Since chivalry must be a matter of informal, personal discretion, its effects have not been measured directly, but there is a growing body of evidence to show that chivalry, if it ever existed, has long been dead. Arrest rates are climbing, and between 1967 and 1971 convictions of women in federal courts went up 62.4 percent compared with 20.3 percent for men. Between 1970 and 1975 the number of women in federal prisons alone increased by 81 percent. For many offenses women and men seem to receive the same sentences, but for offenses traditionally considered to be "masculine"—such as armed robbery and felony murder—women tend to receive *heavier* sentences than men. Women who receive shorter or suspended sentences generally do so for legal, and not chivalric, reasons: women's crimes are apt to be less serious and less violent, and the women are more likely to be first offenders and to have dependent children who would be punished by their mother's incarceration. But if women continue to be arrested and convicted at such great rates, more of them may have to be let off because in the final analysis the number of criminals is determined by the number of available cells.

In many states the law itself provides stiffer penalties for women. In Iowa, for example, a woman may be sentenced to five years for a misdemeanor, while a man may receive no more than a year. Other states have similar discriminatory statutes, and at least fourteen states provide indeterminate sentences for women which result in their being held longer than men convicted of the same offenses. Several states provide by statute that women must be sentenced to the maximum term for their crimes while men may be given lighter sentences. Under such a law in Pennsylvania in 1966 Jane Daniel's one- to four-year sentence for robbery was declared illegal and she was resentenced to the maximum ten years. Under the same law, when Daisy Douglas and her boyfriend, Richard Johnson, were convicted of robbery, Johnson, with a record of six prior burglary convictions, was sentenced to three to ten years, while Douglas, with only a few prostitution arrests on her record, received the arbitrary maximum sentence: twenty years. Daisy Douglas and Jane Daniel, in a joint suit, succeeded in having their sentences overturned by the Pennsylvania Supreme Court on grounds that the so-called Muncy statute requiring maximum sentences for women denied them equal protection under the Fourteenth Amendment; but two weeks later the Pennsylvania legislature reenacted the statute in slightly amended form. Other state courts have held that there is nothing wrong with discriminatory sentencing; the usual argument is that since women are "psychologically" different from men they are "more susceptible to rehabilitation" and consequently can be imprisoned longer for their own good.

The same paternalistic argument applies to female juvenile offenders. Criminologists have long known that juvenile girls are likely to be sentenced at an earlier stage in the "criminal" career and that girls receive longer sentences than boys; they say that the girls are being rehabilitated, even though most female juvenile offenders are incarcerated for offenses such as running away, truancy, or waywardness, that would not be considered crimes if they were committed by adults or boys. In fact, a great many of these girls, over the years, have been imprisoned for the crimes of men. A classic criminological study of five hundred delinquent Massachusetts women found in 1934 that one hundred of "the girls" had not "entered upon unconventional sexual practices voluntarily." A 1920 study of New York State delinquents found that nearly a quarter of them had been raped, including a number of girls between six and ten. In 1923 Thomas found that forty-seven girls in an Illinois reformatory had been raped by some member of their own family, and the court records revealed an additional seventy-eight cases, in forty-three of which the "delinquent" had been "wronged in this way . . . by her own father." In 1966, criminologist Gisela Konopka found incest among "delinquent" girls far "more frequent than is usually assumed," and Susan Reed, former deputy superintendent of Muncy (Pennsylvania) women's prison, estimates that at least one-third of women in prison today got their start in "crime" as incest victims.

Lombroso, Thomas, and Pollak, pedantically elevating their prejudices to scientific fact, would be mildly amusing if they had not been so influential. Today Lombroso with his talk of Darwinian atavisms is something of an embarrassment to his discipline, yet criminologists go on charting and measuring criminals and locating woman's criminality in her sexual nature; and even the most up-to-date studies go on finding that women criminals are masculine, psychologically maladjusted, or diabolically devious. Criminologists also perpetuate the notion that women and girls are spared through chivalry, so that when from time to time the crackdown against women comes, that wave of law enforcement seems to be only a concession to women of that equality they have been clamoring for all along. That these criminological studies themselves are part of the crackdown is too plain to be denied; at times the mask of scholarly detachment slips away and the man behind the scientist stands revealed. Lombroso inveighed against "masculinizing" education for women, diagnosed independent and intelligent women as "morally insane," and advised them to kill themselves. Thomas warned that any change in the social position of women would knock their precarious "adjustment" out of whack. And Pollak conceded that men, even in their "apparent state of social superiority," have always feared "the possibility of rebellion or revenge on the part of women."

The problem is not simply that the criminology of women is bigoted or even that, as one feminist critic has noted, it is "retarded." The problem is that it has never addressed the right questions. American criminology in general, following Lombroso's lead, has sought out crime in the criminal. Even those radical sociologists who rescued the criminology of men from Lombroso's calipers turned their attention only from the criminal's eyebrows to his neighborhood. The chief contest in American criminology has been between genetics and environment as the locus of criminality—between chromosomes and the violent subculture—but it has always been clear whose chromosomes and whose ghetto were under discussion. Unlike the classical criminology of Beccaria and Bentham, which defined crime as a legal entity, American criminology has never explored the philosophical relations between crime and society. In the case of women's crimes, however, since they have always been defined differently from the crimes of men, it is far more productive to ask: Who labeled that behavior a crime, and why? Ever since reformatories were established in this country, young girls have been imprisoned for "sexual misconduct"; and criminologists still interview incarcerated girls and conclude that sexual misconduct is one of the chief crimes of teenaged girls. It was feminists who asked, and who still ask, why the sexual activity of teenaged girls is a crime.

These are the questions the experts never ask: Why was it a crime for a servant to have an illegitimate child? Why is it a crime for a girl to run away from home? Why should a woman be sent to prison for "illegal motherhood"? Why is a black woman's larceny a white woman's kleptomania? Why is it a crime for a woman on welfare to have a lover? Why is it a crime to be raped by your father? In 1876 Susan B. Anthony was arrested and fined for voting. A twentieth-century psychiatrist has retroactively diagnosed Anthony as a masculine, sexually maladjusted woman. To the criminologist that would explain why she became a criminal. But it would not tell us why casting a ballot, a civic duty for a man, was a criminal offense for a woman.

Why people behave as they do, and why that behavior is considered criminal, are two separate questions, but in the case of women both questions have to do with woman's place in society. That place has always been hedged about with biases about woman's nature and her proper sphere, and by real barriers of the civil and criminal law. In addition, women have been deprived—often with legal sanction—of education and vocation, and even of legal recourse to claim their own supposed rights. In response to those conditions, many women adjusted; but others did not. Some went crazy. Some developed a political analysis of their situation and became feminists. Some turned to the ultimate act of prepolitical violence; they committed murder. Over the centuries, changes in law and custom have altered the patterns, yet surprisingly little; and the same social and legal deprivations that compel some women to feminism push others to homicide.

So it was with Peachie Wiggins. She set out to commit a robbery, not a murder, and at the moment she pulled the trigger she was a kid in a panic. Growing up in the ghetto, Peachie was a child of chance. Too poor to go without work, even as a youngster, and too smart to be a prostitute, she turned instead to burglary and receiving stolen goods. Now she says wryly that she was led into serious crime by Martin Luther King, Jr., for during the night of riots following his assassination, someone looted a sporting-goods store and passed some stolen guns to Peachie. One of them she used in the bank robbery. But that crime had nothing to do with the women's movement and everything to do with poverty, bad schools, slim chances, impossible hopes, and the slaughter of a dream on a balcony in Memphis. Criminologists could see Peachie as part of the subculture of violence, for her father, who had served time for murder, was murdered himself, and the little sister she tried to protect was murdered two years ago by her husband. But the notion that violence is commonplace in her community, even in her family, does not explain why at sixteen she thought she had to take care of her mother, her grandmother, her little sister, or why, in order to do it, she turned her powerful intelligence, ambition, and anger to armed robbery.

Peachie Wiggins's crime is not unique. There have always been some female armed robbers, from Rachel Wall, who was hanged in Boston in 1789, to Bonnie Parker. But Peachie's crime *is* unusual. By all odds she should have been a prostitute. Susan Reed, after seventeen years as a corrections officer, described the typical woman in prison today:

> She comes into the corrections system at about age twelve, having run away from home and been knocked up. Her child is taken away from

her and she's told that she's a terrible person. She's locked up for a year or two; then she gets out and spends her time, sometimes successfully, trying to get her child back. Then she's knocked up again and returned to custody for some petty offense; she is doped up on Thorazine to keep her docile and told again how terrible she is; her kids are taken away. By the time she's nineteen she probably has three kids and a heroin habit, and she's turning some tricks to support them. Then she's told that she's a lesbian because for eighteen out of every twenty-four months of her life since age twelve she has been locked up with other women, and her only contact with men has been when they've knocked her up in her time out. She'll go on in this life as long as she can take it, but her initial crime—the offense that got her into this life in the first place—was simply being female.

For such women the criminal-justice system is a revolving door that passes them from juvenile home to jail to prison and sometimes spits them out briefly into the outside world. For Peachie, however, there is no revolving door except the one she makes for herself by escaping when all hope seems gone.

She committed a felony murder, an extraordinary crime for a woman, and one for which she says she can never be sorry enough; but because that crime seems to be part of the new wave of postliberation crime heralded by criminologist Adler, the chances of her sentence being commuted, despite the positive recommendations of prison officials, are small indeed. After her last commutation application she was informally notified that the governor just hadn't been able to free her in an election year. So in a curious way Peachie Wiggins, an ambitious kid who wanted to keep her sister off the streets, pays dues in a Pennsylvania prison for a women's movement she only recently heard of. In a complicated, uneasy time, it is another of those elusive and unforeseen connections that bring us together, like it or not, in the bonds of womanhood.

Society is afraid of both the feminist and the murderer, for each of them, in her own way, tests society's established boundaries. Not surprisingly, the interests of feminist and murderer sometimes coincide: Gloria Steinem argues for Joan Little's right to self-defense just as Lucy Stone argued in another century for Lizzie Borden's right to trial by a jury of her peers. Nor is it surprising that the panic provoked by feminism and the alarm at female criminality coincide almost perfectly, as though according to some plan. A wave of attention to women's criminality follows thunderously on every wave of feminism and surely will continue to do so until we can grasp the truth that free people are not dangerous.

Dangerous people, on the other hand, may not be so very extraordinary as we think. Enid Bagnold wrote that "a murderess is only an ordinary woman in a temper." Despite its flippancy, the remark suggests the truth that murder is often situational: given the same set of circumstances, any one of us might kill. Florence Monahan, who knew many murderers during her career as warden of various women's prisons, wrote that "they are just average, every-day sort of women. . . . in most instances they are futile, ineffectual women who couldn't think of a better solution than to shoot their way out of a bad situation." Women who kill find extreme solutions to problems that thousands of women cope with in more peaceable ways from day to day. So we can learn a good deal about woman's changing position in American social life by considering whom she killed, when, why, and how her community regarded her crime. From the very beginning of the country, women on the raveling edge have outlined and made plain the fabric of society.

ONE

FOREMOTHERS: DIVERS LEWD WOMEN

1.

A seamstress named Margaret Nicholson waited by the garden entrance to the Palace of St. James's for the returning carriage of King George III. In her gloved hands she carried a "memorial"—a written petition to the king—and, concealed beneath it, a long knife. The carriage arrived, the king descended, and Margaret Nicholson pressed forward to deliver her memorial and a stroke of the knife; but the king was saved by his exceedingly fine manners. As he took up the paper he bowed deeply to Miss Nicholson and so avoided the blow. Soon enough, the king's attendant yeomen caught "her drift" and disarmed her. Under questioning Nicholson claimed she had not meant to kill the king but only to terrify him so that he would grant her petition. The paper, however, was blank. When her landlords testified that Nicholson mumbled to herself a good deal, the king clucked over the poor woman, magnanimously refused to press charges, and committed her temporarily to the custody of one of his messengers who, for lack of anything else to do with her, took her to his home in Half Moon Street. What else was the fellow to do? It was 1786, just a few years too late to pack her off to America, where for years England had been dumping her riffraff.

From the very beginning of colonization, England had seen North America as (among other things) a convenient refuse heap. Abrupt changes in England from a feudal to a commercial economy had produced an enormous class of rootless, migratory poor people who turned for survival to crime. For the most part, their crimes were fairly trivial matters of shoplifting or pickpocketing, but the seventeenth-century Englishmen of property were alarmed and saw to it that the law defined more than three hundred crimes, including even such petty offenses, as major felonies punishable by death. Soon the country seemed to be overrun with felons, but the American colonies provided an out. Enforced transportation of felons to the New World, argued supporters of the policy, offered three distinct benefits: it relieved England of its criminal population; it improved the character of the individual criminals by giving them employment; and it provided labor needed to sustain the colonies.

James I initiated the policy in 1615, when he empowered members of the Privy Council to reprieve ablebodied felons "fitt to be ymploied in forraine discoveries or other services beyond the Seas" and willing to be transported to the colonies. Within the year, the first twenty convicts had been reprieved and handed over to Sir Thomas Smith, governor of the East India Company, for transportation to the East Indies. For the next twenty years Smith received convicts from the crown and shipped them to Virginia. Over the years, cumbersome legal procedures were changed several times to make conditional pardoning a formality. Sheriffs handed over reprieved felons directly to merchants who carried them to the colonies and sold them as indentured servants for the seven-year term required by law. By the mid-seventeenth century, transportation of felons was a private enterprise, and a lucrative one.

Felons were brought in such numbers that colonial leaders feared for the health of society. Apparently the moral character of felons was not necessarily improved by moving them from one side of the Atlantic to the other. As one of the Georgia Trustees noted ruefully: "Many of the Poor who had been useless in England, were inclined to be useless likewise in Georgia." Colonial court records, strewn with cases of convict-servants who burned their masters' houses, stole their property, and murdered them, indicate that many people who had been criminal in England continued their criminal careers in America. In 1751, the Pennsylvania *Gazette* angrily commented on a recent series of convict robberies and murders:

> When we see our Papers fill'd continually with Accounts of the most audacious Robberies, the most cruel Murders, and infinite other Villainies perpetrated by Convicts transported from *Europe,* what melancholly, what terrible Reflections must it occasion! . . . In what can *Britain* show a more Sovereign Contempt for us, than by emptying their *Jails* into our Settlements; unless they would likewise empty their *Jakes* on our Tables?

And Benjamin Franklin, petitioning Parliament in 1767 or 1768 to stop transporting felons, claimed the convicts "continue their evil practices" and "commit many burglaries, robberies, and murders, to the great terror of the people."

Massachusetts Bay Colony restricted immigration in 1640 to keep out people of unorthodox religious views and vicious character. Connecticut followed in 1660, admitting only people of "honest conversation." The southern colonies badly needed agricultural laborers, but after a servant uprising in Gloucester County, presumed to have been fomented by convicts, Virginia thought her peace "too much hazarded and endangered by the great numbers of felons and other desperate villains sent hither from the several prisons in England," and in 1676 Maryland, too, passed "An Act against the Importation of Convicted Persons into this Province." But the trade in convicts had barely begun.

In 1717 Parliament passed "An act for the further preventing robbery, burglary, and other felonies, and for the more effectual transportation of felons" which provided that felons deserving to be whipped or branded could be sentenced instead to transportation for seven years. In other words, transportation was no longer an *alternative* to criminal punishment; it became the punishment itself. In addition, convicts under sentence of death could still choose to be transported, although their term of servitude was extended from seven to fourteen years. For the next sixty years the colonies enacted laws against importing felons, but England disallowed them all, since Parliamentary law superseded and nullified colonial statute. Franklin proposed in return to send American felons to Scotland and American rattlesnakes to the garden of George III. Only after the Revolution was the new nation able to stop convict transportation, producing a crisis in England as jails overflowed into the new, short-lived penal colony at Sierra Leone and the floating prison ships from which too many (like Dickens's Magwitch) escaped, until finally the twelve-year surplus of felons could be shipped out to the new Australian dumping ground at Botany Bay. But until the Revolution, England continued to transport her convicts to America; and Americans, it must be said, continued to buy their labor.

Other nations took up the policy. The Pennsylvania Assembly advised the governor in 1755 that "the Importations of Germans have been for some Time composed of a great Mixture of the Refuse of their People and . . . the very Jails have contributed to the Supplies We are burthened with." France had taken to exporting convicts even earlier, making transportation an official policy in 1682; and in 1719 the worst Parisian jails and hospitals were opened to the unsavory Scotsman, John Law, head of the Company of the West, charged with populating French colonies in the New World. Soon Louisiana was notorious as the last refuge of French whores and scoundrels.

By the time transportation ended with the Revolution, some thirty-five to fifty thousand convicts had been brought to America. Perhaps one-third of them were women.

Records are elusive and fragmentary, but bits and pieces suggest a picture. Nine female felons were shipped to Virginia in 1635. Such shipments continued throughout that century and the next. In 1692 Narcissus Luttrell recorded "that a ship lay at Leith, going for Virginia, on board which the magistrates had ordered fifty lewd women out of the houses of correction and thirty others who walked the streets after ten at night." Six shipments during 1719–21 brought more than 400 convicts to Maryland, one-third of them women. In 1723 Jonathan Forward, one of the most notorious contractors in the business, was paid £4 per head to transport 66 felons, almost half of them women. About one-third of a shipload of 70 convicts Forward brought from Newgate to Maryland or Virginia in 1730 were women. One-third of 32 felons shipped on July 17, 1731, and almost half of 118 felons shipped October 26, 1732, were women. In June 1758 the *Snow Eugene* brought to Maryland 51 men and 18 women "of His Majesty's Seven Years' Passengers." Perhaps the last person transported to America, in October 1774, was Mrs. Elizabeth Grieve, a con artist convicted of posing as cousin to the Duke of Grafton and thereby "defrauding divers persons."

Some of the women, at least, must have been glad to be transported, for justice in England was heavy-handed. Public hangings of women at Tyburn were regular and festive occasions in the seventeenth and eighteenth centuries. Mary Jones, whose case often is cited as an infamous example, was convicted in 1772 of stealing bread to feed her two children after her husband had been impressed into the navy. She was hanged. Women convicted of more "serious" crimes suffered accordingly. Coining shillings, which disrupted economic power balances, and murdering one's husband, which disrupted social power balances enough to be categorized as petit treason, were punishable by burning at the stake. Accordingly, Catherine Hayes was burned in 1726. Isabella Condon was burned in 1779, Phoebe Harris in 1786, Margaret Sullivan in 1788, Christine Bowman—the last person so punished—in 1789. The executioner had devised a little cord that fitted around the prisoner's neck. With it, he could humanely throttle the woman before the flames reached her, so that she was insensible or dead when she burned. Very often this garroting device did not work.

Women convicts who escaped death suffered in the prisons. English jails were notorious holes freely spreading disease and despair. Newgate Prison, in the summer of 1697, teemed with women convicts awaiting transportation. While authorities negotiated with the colonies in America and the West Indies, the women waited in Newgate until the stench became so great that neighboring residents complained to city officials. The shipment was turned down by most of the colonies, although New York said it would accept if the women were "young and fitted for labor." The stinking women finally were sent to the Leeward Islands.

What was a woman to do? Defoe's Moll Flanders was quite right in judging that "the market is against our sex just now; and if a young woman have beauty, birth, breeding, wit, sense, manners, modesty, and all these to an extreme, yet if she have not money, she's nobody. . . . the men play the game all into their own hands." The problem throughout the seventeenth and eighteenth centuries was largely a question of numbers: about 5 percent of upper-class English girls remained unmarried in the sixteenth century, but by the eighteenth century between 20 and 25 percent were spinsters. "There is no proportion between the numbers of the sexes," Defoe's heroine observes, "and therefore the women have the disadvantage." Upper-class spinsters might retire, as Mary Wollstonecraft observed, "with a small stipend and an uncultivated mind, into joyless solitude," but poor spinsters were driven by the lack of job opportunities into prostitution. For Moll's class, only two occupations for women were thinkable, and the requirements for each were clear: ". . . it was requisite to a whore to be handsome, well-shaped, have a good mien and a graceful behaviour; but . . . for a wife, no deformity would shock the fancy, no ill qualities the judgment; the money was the thing."

If a woman had money she could merge with a titled man who might become her manager or her albatross, but in either case, her vocation. Having "looks" but no money, she could become, like Moll herself, the "friend" of a number of men in rapid sequence, possessed of just enough temporary constancy to forestall naming her occupation for what it was. And such a woman, like Moll, would pick up along the way some helpful skills as con artist and cutpurse. Such a woman—again like Moll—was likely to be transported.

Even those women who bravely welcomed transportation as a second chance suffered on the arduous crossing of two months or longer. Chained together, confined to the hold, and furnished with little more than dry peas, salt pork, and gin, the prisoners sickened and died. Captains of convict ships wanted to keep their passengers alive, since money made from selling the convicts went into the captains' pockets. Still the convicts died in wholesale lots: 61 out of 153, 37 out of 108, 15 out of 50, 20 out of 61, 30 out of 87, 38 out of 95. For some reason, women seem to have fared better than men. More women survived the voyage, and while half the men died soon after landing, almost two-thirds of the women lived on. Some historians explain that the thoroughly dissolute male felons were "ridled with disease" when they were transported, but it is hard to imagine that the desperate, stinking women of Newgate were healthier.

Still, the women survived, except when their lives were taken by sacrifice. Like Iphigenia, women were sometimes killed to appease gods or men. In 1654, an old woman named Mary Lee, a passenger on the *Charity,* was hanged and thrown into the sea to assuage storms supposedly caused by "the malevolence of witches." In 1658 Elizabeth Richardson was executed for witchcraft on another ship bound for Maryland. In 1659 Katharine Grady, bound for Virginia, was declared a witch and hanged at sea.

Some of the women transported from England were poor people, driven by necessity to petty thievery. Some were girls who had been seduced and abandoned or illegitimate daughters not welcome at home, but most were London prostitutes, thieves, receivers, and shoplifters. Some were murderers. They were "a villainous and demoralized lot" according to one Lieutenant Clark, who kept a journal of his voyage on the *Friendship* with the first convict fleet sent to Australia in 1787. When the women were locked up at night, they broke through the wall that separated them from the men. Clark, who despised the "abandoned wretches," cheered up when they were transferred to other ships to make room for sheep and fodder taken aboard the *Friendship* at Cape Horn. "I am very glad of it," he wrote, "for they were a great trouble, much more so than the men." Of the sheep, he wrote: "we will find them much more agreeable shipmates than the women."

In the American colonies the frequent advertisements for runaway indentured servants (many of whom were convicts) described women well used to the world. Jane Shepherd: "about 5 feet 3 inches high, of a fair complexion, pretty fat and lusty, has black hair, and is about 23 years of age . . . she inclines much to smoking of tobacco, and her under-jaw teeth are black." Anne Young: "about 30 years old, pitted with the Small Pox, middling tall, and slender . . . has run away several times, and knows a great many noted men." Hannah Boyer: "a Convict Servant Woman . . . about 23 years of age. Pitted much with Small Pox, has a Scar in one of her Eye Brows, not very tall, but strong, fresh colour'd, robust, masculine Wench. . . . She had a Horse Lock and chain on one of her Legs."

Other women came to the American colonies under happier circumstances. From the first settlement of Plymouth Plantation and Massachusetts Bay, wives came with their husbands or followed close behind. The *Mayflower* brought twenty-nine women and seventy-five men in 1620, and almost every ship arriving in Massachusetts in the following decades carried some women and children. Some of these women came reluctantly; Madam Winthrop kept postponing the trip to join husband John in Massachusetts Bay until he grew quite out of patience. Others changed their minds after they arrived. Young Mistress Dorothy Bradford's fatal plunge from the *Mayflower* as it lay at anchor off the bleak Plymouth shore was almost certainly no accident. But the women who settled in Massachusetts (or died in the attempt) in the first half of the seventeenth century were unique: they were probably the only Englishwomen who came to America before 1650 of their own volition. Most women were tricked or coerced. They didn't emigrate. They were shipped.

The first consignment of ninety single women was sent to Jamestown, Virginia, in 1620 at the urging of Sir Edwin Sandys, erstwhile highwayman and treasurer of the Virginia Company. Unlike the Massachusetts plantations, Jamestown had been established by a band of rogues and bachelor adventurers. Sandys shared Captain John Smith's opinion that the lack of wives and family attachments in the plantation made it unstable and easy prey to "dissolucon." The women were supposed to "make the men more setled & lesse moveable who by defect thereof (as is credibly reported) stay there but to gett something and then return to England." When the women married, as they all soon did, their new husbands were required to defray the cost of their crossing to the tune of 120 pounds of good leaf tobacco. These young women reportedly came "upon good recommendation," and by 1621 when "an extraordinary choice lot of thirty-eight maids for wives" was sent, the price had risen to 150 pounds of tobacco. The men paid the sales price willingly; by 1622 all the maidens shipped—some 147 in all—were married. (By 1625, due to disease and Indian attacks, three-quarters of them were dead.)

How were these "young and uncorrupt" women persuaded to hazard a dangerous voyage to an uncharted country? Historian Carl Bridenbaugh found that the "means used to assemble them approached kidnapping." He cites the case of William Robinson, a chancery clerk, who was convicted in 1618 of counterfeiting the Great Seal of England. His racket was to use this false commission "to take up rich yeomen's daughters (or drive them to compound) to serve his Majestie for breeders in Virginia." Robinson was hanged, drawn, and quartered. What became of the yeomen's daughters is not noted. Owen Evans, a messenger for the Privy Council, ran a similar business. Pretending to have a royal commission, he extorted money for himself, or maidens for Virginia and Bermuda. Many a father must have been willing to sell his daughter rather than pay extortion to keep her. Superfluous daughters were the price men paid for the supernumerary sons who ensured continuation of the male line, and since England had become a Protestant country, fathers could no longer dump them in nunneries, which had been for Catholics—as Milton observed—"convenient stowage for their withered daughters." Customarily, superfluous daughters had to be bought husbands, through a substantial dowry, or supported in idle spinsterhood. In seventeenth-century England, where basic family ties were more practical than affectionate, rich yeomen must have welcomed the patriotic alternative of bartering a daughter for the good of the empire. Bridenbaugh concludes that the Virginia Company's methods of recruitment "were such as to give the Company a bad name." He writes: "Women were transported to America after 1629 in considerable numbers by ruses and devices which will forever remain obscure."

The French seem to have been less fastidious. Women shipped to Louisiana to become wives of French settlers were not individually "recruited" but dispatched in lots from overcrowded Paris prisons. In 1706 Louis XIV shipped twenty "girls" as a gift to the governor of Louisiana. The official report that they were "of unspotted reputation, and upright lives" was almost certainly a polite fiction. Later that pretense was dropped. In 1715 Governor Cadillac wrote home to the ministry: ". . . if I sent away all women of loose habits, there would be no females left, and this would not meet the views of the government." After a royal grant in 1717 assigned the job of populating Louisiana to John Law and his Company of the West, Law increased Louisiana's citizenry from a few hundred adventurers to several thousand by kidnapping, shanghaiing, and rounding up prisoners from jails. Between August 1717 and June 1721 he brought at least 7,500 "unfortunates" to Louisiana. Thousands of them were poor, diseased, or criminal women shipped from the notorious Salpêtrière prison.

Prostitute, criminal, servant, orphan, spinster—they all came to the New World. More often, as migration increased and the crossing seemed less like a step off the edge of the earth, women came of their own will, as indentured servants, transported free of charge to be sold by the shipowner for five to seven years' labor in the colonies. Often the self-indentured servant was treated as badly as the prostitute or felon, as a tract designed to discourage English emigration maintains: "The poor creatures who have been induced to *indent themselves* are in situations the most pitiable; they are treated by their *masters* in a similar manner *to the felons formerly transported* from *England* to *Virginia*." And the self-indentured woman, like her convict sister, was likely to be unhappy. With winter coming on, Elizabeth Sprigg wrote from "Baltimore Town" in September 1756 to her father in London, who had banished her into servitude for "undutifullness," to plead for clothing:

> What we unfortunat English People suffer here is beyond the probibility of you in England to Conceive, let it suffice that I one of the unhappy Number, am toiling almost Day and Night, and very often in the Horses

druggery, with only this comfort that you Bitch you do not halfe enough, and then tied up and whipp'd to that Degree that you'd not serve an Annimal, scarce any thing but Indian Corn and Salt to eat and that even begrudged nay many Neagroes are better used, almost naked no shoes nor stockings to wear, and the comfort after slaving dureing Masters pleasure, what rest we can get is to rap ourselves up in a Blanket and ly upon the Ground, this is the deplorable Condition your poor Betty endures. . . .

Poor Betty's condition was not unusual. Other servants in Maryland couldn't bear it. Anne Vaughan cut her throat with a pair of scissors and stabbed herself in the belly. Ann Beetle, beaten by her master, drowned herself. She was subsequently indicted by the coroner's jury for "wilfully murdering herself."

But despite hardship, women pressed by men and circumstance continued to come to the colonies—lawful wives, self-indentured servants, victims of kidnap and coercion, whores, thieves, con women, and murderers. They were America's founding mothers.

In the New World the Old Bailey could be forgotten. Marriageable women, who glutted the market in England, were a valuable commodity in the colonies largely because the work to be done, just to stay alive, was too great for any single person to handle. The men who bought and sold women as servants and wives took the profit, but many of the women came out better by the exchange than they would have done in England. Marriage in the New World was for many women the alternative to prostitution, crime, or slow starvation in the Old.

In the colonies, unlike Moll Flanders's England or continental Europe, a woman did not need a fortune to buy a husband. She would be bought. Writing his *History and Present State of Virginia* in 1705, Robert Beverley noted that the first settlers quickly "grew sensible of the Misfortune of wanting Wives." Modest women, he wrote, "if they were but moderately qualified in all other respects, might depend upon Marrying very well in those Days, without any Fortune. Nay, the first Planters were so far from expecting Money with a Woman, that it was a common thing for them to buy a deserving Wife at the price of 100 pound, and make themselves believe they had a hopeful Bargain." George Alsop of colonial Maryland noticed that any woman, beauty or no, could marry. "The Women that go over into this Province as

Servants," he wrote, "have the best luck here as in any place of the world besides; for they are no sooner on shoar, but they are courted into a Copulative Matrimony, which some of them (for aught I know) had they not come to such a Market with their Virginity, might have kept it by them untill it had been mouldy."

Often women married again. Life was harsh and early death commonplace, but a spouse was easily replaced. The first marriage in Plymouth Plantation united Susanna White, a widow of twelve weeks' standing, and Edward Winslow, a widower of seven weeks. It was not unusual for a person to marry three times, and many married four, five, and even six times. Men replaced one young wife, dead of childbearing, with another—often within a matter of weeks or days. Hardier women buried husbands and quickly took others. Women were so much in demand that they might continue to marry at any age. Loss of youth was more than compensated by the size of the estate an old woman, many times widowed, had accumulated. Thus, with only mild amusement, the Virginia *Gazette* for March 15, 1771, announced: "Yesterday was married, in Henrico, Mr. William Carter, third son of Mr. John Carter, aged twenty-three, to Mrs. Sarah Ellyson, Relict of Mr. Gerard Ellyson, deceased, aged eighty-five, a sprightly old Tit, with three Thousand Pounds Fortune."

Apparently a woman could get by even without that reputation for "modesty" usually required for marriage. Even a woman whose past as criminal or prostitute was known could marry and become a respectable citizen. Most of them must have done so. Despite the fact that hundreds of prostitutes had been shipped to Virginia, William Byrd scoured Williamsburg in November 1720 looking for a whore and couldn't find one. Probably they were all in retirement—at home with their husbands.

The demand for wives in the colonies was so great that the double standard of sexual behavior had to be set aside. "Fallen" women did not—as they did in Europe—stay down. The case of Ellinor Spinke of Maryland is instructive. When Ellinor testified in a lawsuit against Dr. Luke Barber, the doctor retaliated by calling her a whore. He claimed to have brought Ellinor to Maryland from England in the first place— one of a group of "rogues and whores from Newgate, some from Bridewell, and some from the whipping post." Ellinor, he charged, was "the impudentest whore of them all." Besides, he added for good measure, he had caught her in bed with Tom Hughes. Ellinor, however, had a champion in Henry Spinke, her husband, who promptly sued

Barber for slandering his wife. In the five years she had spent in the colony, Spinke said, Ellinor had maintained a good reputation "without the least blemish of immodesty that carping envy could suspect either in her behaviour, speech, or carriage." Since her good name had been tarnished by the doctor and "she blazed for a whore and a strumpet," the court awarded Henry Spinke thirty thousand pounds of tobacco in damages. Henry also argued that Ellinor had earlier lived an "honest, modest and civil" life in England, but since evidence on that score could only have been a matter of Ellinor's word against the doctor's, the court must have awarded damages on the basis of Ellinor's short-lived but respectable reputation in Maryland. (The decision was reversed on appeal and the parties ordered to split the cost of litigation, but that reversal was based on a defect in legal procedure and not in the character of Madam Spinke.)

Unfortunately, indentured servants were prohibited by law from taking advantage of the thriving marriage market. They could not marry until they had completed the terms of their indentures. This law and ill treatment by cruel masters spurred many women to deliver themselves from servitude by running away. Evidently they had a better life in mind, for many ran off in their mistresses' clothing. Mary Holland of Georgia fled in "a reddish stuff gown, green petticoat, white flowered bonnet, and large roll under hair, and carried a fine lawn apron and flowered handkerchief stolen from her mistress." Anne Barret of Virginia ran off with "a striped Holland gown, a quilted callimanco petticoat, several headdresses, ruffles, and aprons, and new pumps with red heels." But Sarah Wilson was the most ambitious of them all. A former attendant upon an attendant upon the queen, she was transported to Maryland and sold into servitude in 1771 for stealing jewels from the royal apartments. Having managed to bring along some of her loot, some court dresses, and a miniature of the queen, she fled to the Carolinas and set herself up as the Princess Susanna Carolina Matilda, sister to the queen. There she carried on comfortably for more than a year, gaily promising offices and promotions, and accepting in exchange "heavy contributions upon some persons of the highest rank in the southern colonies." In the end she was exposed and dragged back into servitude. There she disappears from history.

Sarah Wilson, a.k.a. the Princess Susanna Carolina Matilda, was an exceptionally enterprising woman, but on the whole, outlets for such enterprise in the land of opportunity—though far better than prospects in Europe—were still limited. Most transported women, lucky enough to survive prison and the Atlantic crossing, probably considered themselves doubly fortunate to marry respectably; but colonial life was both hard and dangerous, and many women who sold themselves once or twice as wives instead of repeatedly as prostitutes must have wondered if they had made the better bargain. Men claimed that America was "a paradise on Earth for women." No woman is known to have thought so.

2.

To Dorothy Talbye, Massachusetts was more like hell. She was a devout member of the Salem church and maintained a reputation "of good esteem for godliness," according to Governor Winthrop, but she quarreled with her husband and gradually grew depressed and melancholy. In her trouble, she listened intently (as all godly Puritans did) for the voice of God, who revealed to her that she should refuse to eat and prevent her husband and children from eating as well. The church elders admonished her time after time, but she wouldn't listen. She began to act with violence. In April 1637, when the Quarterly Court sat at Salem, she was ordered to answer charges of assaulting her husband, but she failed to appear. The three magistrates—among them the first Judge Hathorne, whose son would earn his page in history presiding at the Salem witch trials—ordered that:

> Whereas Dorethy the wyfe of John Talbie hath not only broak that peace & Love, wch ought to have beene both betwixt them, but also hath violentlie broke the kings peace, by frequent Laying hands upon hir husband to the danger of his Life, & Contemned Authority, not coming before them upon command, It is therfore ordered that for hir misdemeaner passed & for prvention of future evills that are feared wilbe comitted by hir if shee be Lefte att hir Libertie. That she shall be bound & chained to some post where shee shall be restrained of hir libertye to goe abroad or comminge to hir husband till shee manefest some change of hir course. . . . Only it is pmitted that she shall come to the place of gods worshipp, to enjoy his ordenances.

Apparently she chose not to visit the place of God's worship, having found her own line of communication with God, and the church elders decided to excommunicate her. She turned her back on them and would have walked away, but they held her by force and read the order casting her out. "Whereupon she grew worse," Governor Winthrop noted. In July 1638 the court pronounced her guilty of "missdemanour ageanst hir husband" and ordered her to be publicly whipped. After that "she reformed for a time, and carried herself more dutifully to her husband"—until in November she once again fell into "spiritual delusions," mistaking the instigations of the Devil for the voice of God. At his persuasion she decided to free from "future misery" her three-year-old daughter, to whom she had given the ominous name "Difficult." She broke the child's neck.

It was clear to Governor Winthrop and to her neighbors that Dorothy Talbye was possessed by Satan, and indeed she continued to the end to behave very badly. She would not confess her crime until the judges threatened to press her to death; she refused to stand up to hear their sentence and had to be set on her feet by force. And she never for a moment repented. When they hanged her in Boston in 1638 she snatched off the cloth that should have covered her face and tucked it under the noose to make the bite of the rope less painful. And even "after a swing or two," Winthrop wrote, "she catched at the ladder."

For Dorothy Talbye even dying was a struggle. Surely life had been so. When John Talbye died six years later he passed on to three surviving children an estate consisting principally of "twenty bushels Indian corne" and a "Cannoe." There was more, but not much: a barrel, a tub, an old ax, "aparrel and beding" worth ten shillings, and a spinning wheel that once must have been Dorothy's. The Talbye family was very poor indeed, and Dorothy Talbye, driven by hardship and her own piety, tormented by those who tried to "save" her, finally skidded into "melancholia" and "delusions"—as Winthrop himself could see.

Nevertheless, she had committed murder, and the penalty for that offense was clearly prescribed by God himself. "He that smiteth a man so that he die, shall be surely put to death," says Exodus 21:12. "Moreover, ye shall take no satisfaction for the life of a murderer, which is guilty of death: but he shall be surely put to death," says Numbers 35:31. "Whoso sheddeth man's blood, by man shall his blood be shed: for in the image of God made he man," says Genesis

9:6. Proverbs 28:17 commands that "a man that doth violence to the blood of any person, shall flee to the pit; let no man stay him." Exodus 20:13 says simply: "Thou shalt not kill." So said the Bible, and while colonial law in this matter followed the language of English Common Law—borrowing concepts not delineated in these scriptures, such as premeditation, malice, cruelty, self-defense, and accidental homicide— it remained substantially biblical. And where Common Law and scripture conflicted, early Massachusetts law followed the Bible. Under Common Law, manslaughter—defined as unpremeditated homicide committed in the passion of the moment—was not necessarily a capital offense, but Massachusetts law strictly followed Leviticus 24:17 and Numbers 35:20,21 and offered no out: "If any person slayeth another suddenly, in his ANGER or CRUELTY of passion, he shall be put to death."

Massachusetts law held that "If any person shall commit any wilfull MURTHER upon premeditate malice, hatred or cruelty, not in a man's necessary and just defense, nor by meer casualty, against his will, he shall be put to death." When quarrelsome John Billington, a notorious troublemaker, shot his neighbor in 1630 and became Plymouth Plantation's first murderer, the elders had some passing doubts about their *legal* right as colonial administrators to execute him, but they never doubted their *moral* duty to see the murderer hanged. Eighteen years later, when Allice Bishope cut the throat of her four-year-old daughter, Martha Clarke, the justices having "found the said Allice Bishope guilty of the said fellonious murthering of Martha Clarke aforsaid" hanged her too. For the law of God—and consequently the criminal law of Massachusetts—applied with equal sternness to men and women. Then, as now, women murdered much less often than men, but when they did they faced the same hangman.

It is not that the colonists believed in equality of the sexes. No man of the time imagined that women were of the same rank in the created order as he himself. Theology, social philosophy, and the poets confirmed what his own reason told him: that the great God who had made him just a little lower than the angels had made woman just a little lower still. Nevertheless, certain influences of religion and necessity combined to assure roughly equal treatment for both sexes under the criminal law.

The Society of Friends (Quakers) acknowledged the spiritual equality of women and men, and admitted women as religious teachers, while in Puritan colonies women were covenanted church members in their own right. God's law and Puritan social practice required wives to submit themselves to their husbands' governance, but a woman's soul was her own. Husbands might legitimately demand (as Dorothy Talbye's did) that wives not starve them; but husbands could not interfere in their wives' religious life. A man who kept his wife from church or neglected husbandly responsibilities would be admonished by a church committee and—if he defied the church by continuing his bad behavior—excommunicated. Even Governor Winthrop, who believed firmly that women should keep to womanly activities and who refused to dispute with Anne Hutchinson because of her sex, acknowledged his own wife's private spiritual life, committing her, somewhat ambiguously, when he left England for America, to the care of a God who loved her "much better [than] any husband can." And Governor Winthrop, having urged Dorothy Talbye's Christian duty upon her, could do nothing more than record the event of her execution. Each woman—like each man—was responsible for her own salvation; and Dorothy Talbye had chosen to be damned.

Civil authority, too, particularly in New England, recognized a degree of female autonomy that women were later to lose. For the sake of community stability, all single people under age twenty-one in Massachusetts Bay were required to live within a family, under the governance of its head. But the law specifically stated that "this act shall not be construed to extend to hinder any single woman of good repute from the exercise of any lawful trade or employment for a livelihood ... any law, usage or custom to the contrary notwithstanding." Throughout the colonies, women—single, married, and widowed— kept shops, managed taverns and inns, operated mills and distilleries. They wrote poems, doctored the sick, printed newspapers, founded religious sects, negotiated Indian treaties, established shipping lines and, at home with their children's help, developed the textile industry. Since the exigencies of colonial life demanded that everyone work, New England law and social practice aimed to preserve the community by saving individuals (like Dorothy Talbye) from the sin of idleness. Other colonists—the Dutch of New Amsterdam, the Germans of Pennsylvania, the Swedes of New Jersey and Delaware—brought their own traditions of hard work for men and women alike. During the seventeenth century and much of the eighteenth, women were engaged in every line of work known in the colonies, and manufacturing was carried on almost exclusively by women. In the Old World men were apt to "dispise and decry" women as "*a necessary Evil,*" said John

Cotton, one of the most respected colonial preachers; but in the New World women had become "*a necessary Good*; such as it was not good that man should be without." It is true of women, Cotton maintained, "what is wont to be said of Governments, *That bad ones are better than none.*"

In theory, women in the English colonies were still subject to the medieval law of *baron et femme* which held that a married woman was a *femme covert*—a woman literally *covered* by her husband and thus, for all practical and legal purposes, nonexistent. But that rigid doctrine of English Common Law was already being tempered in England by judgments under equity (chancery) law which adjusted old imbalances to protect (among many other things) the property rights of married women. And the colonists, to save their fragile plantations in the New World, bent the old laws even further to the side of fairness to meet the needs of the new place.

They learned from the Virginia Company's initial mistake that bachelor adventurers were an unstable and unsettled lot. Most colonies not only received shipped and shanghaied "maidens" but enticed other women to come by offering opportunities unknown in the Old World. Many colonies offered outright grants of land to women—married or single—as well as to men; and indentured servants, regardless of sex, usually received such land allotments at the end of their servitude. From the beginning Virginia offered equal pay for equal work in skilled trades such as weaving. In some colonies women could own and inherit property even when married; in others they could retain control of their property and bequeath it as they chose by establishing trusts or entering into antenuptial or postnuptial contracts with their husbands. Colonial divorce decrees often stipulated that a wife take her own property with her; colonial probate records and deed registries indicate that many women owned property and disposed of it as they saw fit. And as property owners, women could vote (at least in local matters), serve as jurors, and hold state offices. Law and practice varied widely from one colony to the next, with New England and such middle colonies as New York and Pennsylvania offering the most equitable treatment to women, the colonies of the Deep South offering the least. But as far south as Virginia the value of women was recognized and equitable treatment urged. In July 1619 the House of Burgesses petitioned the Virginia Company to allot land to their wives as well as to themselves "because that in a newe plantation it is not knowen whether man or woman be the most necessary."

Where women enjoyed a rough equity with men in the labor market and under the terms of the civil law, they were subject to equal treatment by the criminal law as well. Women who were valued as responsible, productive members of the community were also seen—when they turned to crime—as responsible criminals and punished accordingly. New England laws against fornication and adultery punished men and women alike; both partners in the crime were stripped to the waist and whipped in public an equal number of lashes, or both were fined or set on the gallows. When in 1643 in Massachusetts one James Britton confessed to adultery and named Mary Latham, "a proper young woman about 18 years of age," as his partner, they who had sinned together were executed together. Punishment for such crimes might vary with the times and with the known character and record of the criminal—but not with the criminal's sex.

Women, like men, were pilloried and set in the stocks. They were publicly whipped, often while being dragged through the streets "at the cart's tayle." They were maimed and branded and forcibly held under water. In Virginia they were dragged behind boats in the river and sometimes burned at the stake. All criminals were subject to punishments that today seem medieval. In 1639 the first official act of the new government of New Haven Colony was to try for murder, condemn, execute, and decapitate an Indian named Nepaupuck. Afterward in the marketplace they displayed his head on a pole. One hundred and fifty years later, Connecticut, which then included the former New Haven Plantation, was just as rigorous in the case of Hannah Occuish, charged with murdering a six-year-old girl in a dispute over strawberries. They hanged her in New London in 1787, when she was twelve years old.

The rigorous law and order of colonial America was thought to be the handiwork of God himself. Even in colonies mainly concerned with laying up earthly rather than heavenly treasure—such as Virginia, Maryland, Carolina—social order copied the order of God's creation. In Massachusetts Bay, which self-consciously tried to conform society perfectly to God's will, the order of creation was discussed endlessly. In mid-ocean Winthrop addressed the *Arbella* pilgrims on the topic:

> God Almighty in His most holy and wise providence hath so disposed of the condition of mankind as in all times some must be rich, some poor; some high and eminent in power and dignity, others mean and in subjection.

The purpose of this order, as the mean and subjected were often reminded, was "to show forth the glory of His wisdom in the variety and difference of the creatures and the glory of His power, in ordering all these differences for the preservation and good of the whole, and the glory of His greatness." Thus, it became the duty of all men, women, and children to honor God by cheerfully following the rules for their station in life—rules interpreted by the "high and eminent" magistrates and ministers but understood to come directly from God.

Foremost among the rules was the fifth commandment—honor thy father and thy mother—a law that governed congregations and towns as well as families. The Reverend John Cotton asked in his catechism for children: "*Who are here* [in the fifth commandment] *meant by Father and Mother?*" And the children learned to answer: "All our Superiours, whether in Family, School, Church, and Commonwealth." Cotton's illustrious grandson, Cotton Mather, interpreted the fifth commandment in the same way: "There are *Parents* in the *Common-Wealth,* as well as in the *Family*; There are *Parents* in the *Church,* and *Parents* in the *School.*" Society was built of these relationships of "parents" to "children," superiors to inferiors, the high to the mean, the eminent to the subjected. Many of these relationships took up only a part of life, amounting to what modern sociologists call "roles." But the most important relationships filled the whole of life, for they demanded full-time submission of one person to another: servant to master, child to parent, wife to husband. And within them the standards of behavior were established by God. These relationships might end in time: the servant might become a freeman, the child an orphan, the wife a widow. But they could not be changed.

The social order was maintained by seeing to it that people played their parts according to God's rules. That task required constant watchfulness, for people, left to themselves, quickly grow wild and shred the delicate social fabric. Over and over again in journals and histories and sermons, the elders sounded one theme: the need for restraint. "There is a strain in a man's heart," wrote John Cotton, "that will sometime or other run out to excess unless the Lord restrain it. . . ." And Winthrop argued that the differences among people provided God "the more occasion to manifest the work of His Spirit" by "moderating and restraining" the wicked "so that the rich and mighty should not eat up the poor, nor the poor and despised rise up against their superiors and shake off their yoke. . . ."

Massachusetts took the lead in legally restraining the mighty. Husbands were forbidden in the Body of Liberties to deliver "bodilie correction or stripes" to their wives, a rule unknown in English law but apparently rigidly enforced in Massachusetts. In cases of repeated abuse, magistrates could remove the wife from her husband's custody and order him to maintain her in a separate household. They could also grant annulment and divorce; and they most often did so upon the complaints of women. Similar laws protected servants who could be taken away from cruel masters and bound out to others, the proceeds going into the public till; and in some colonies masters were executed for raping their servants or slaves, or for beating them to death. Children too were legally safeguarded from both cruelty and neglect.

But it was not so much the excesses of the mighty that the magistrates—in all the colonies—feared. It was the rising of the poor and despised, the rising of the servants, the wives, and the children.

Patriarchal anxiety on this account runs like a dark warp through all the jottings and preachments of the founding fathers. They feared their children's disobedience, their servants' insolence, their wives' scolding—in short, the odious threat of democracy that Winthrop called "the meanest and worst of all forms of government." So they shaped the law to their fears, giving themselves the right to destroy those who seriously challenged them.

A woman's love for her husband was supposed to make her content to serve God through serving him. As Winthrop described the ideal marriage relationship: "The woman's own choice makes . . . a man her husband; yet being so chosen, he is her lord, and she is to be subject to him, yet in a way of liberty, not of bondage; and a true wife accounts her subjection her honor and freedom, and would not think her condition safe and free but in her subjection to her husband's authority." But John Cotton, arguing that authority itself must be restrained, pointed out the dangers of yoking wives too closely: ". . . it is good for the wife to acknowledge all power and authority to the husband, and for the husband to acknowledge honor to the wife; but still give them that which God hath given them, and no more nor less. Give them the full latitude that God hath given, else you will find you dig pits, and lay snares, and cumber their spirits, if you give them less; there is never peace where full liberty is not given, nor never stable peace where more than full liberty is granted." Both Winthrop and Cotton were speaking in these passages about civil government and its relation to the people, but they turned to the marriage relationship for analogy, as colonial clergymen so often did, because every citizen knew that pits could indeed be dug at home.

Everyone knew of the Talbye case. She had attacked her husband first, and more than once; if she had been strong enough to break *his* neck, she might not have killed her daughter. Other New England women were punished in the stocks or pillory for striking their husbands; Joan Miller of Plymouth was charged with "beating and reviling her husband and egging her children to healp her, bidding them knock him on the head, and wishing his victual might choake him." And only a few years later, in 1644, a man named Cornish was found in the river near Acomeniticus in Maine. Evidently he had been hit on the head and stabbed with a pole that still stuck out of his side. His canoe, weighted down with clay, was found sunk nearby. Cornish's wife, reputed to be a "lewd woman" and previously admonished for her "incontinence," was brought to the corpse, whereupon it "bled abundantly." A man named Footman, supposed to be her lover, was brought in, and the body bled again; but with no other evidence against him, Footman could not be convicted. Mrs. Cornish was charged with murder, tried by the mayor and other province officials, condemned upon "strong presumptions," and sentenced to die. To the end she denied the murder, but she confessed freely that she had "lived in adultery with divers," including one Roger Garde, the mayor. This accusation was backed up by witnesses and by the mayor's reputation as an unwed and "carnal man." He denied it, and Mrs. Cornish was executed.

Among the many colonial court proceedings never recorded or later lost there may have been other cases of wives convicted of murdering their husbands; but Mrs. Cornish just may have been the only husband-murderer in New England during the seventeenth century, when wives enjoyed some latitude and esteem. Certainly she was the only woman executed for this crime within the jurisdictions of Plymouth and Massachusetts Bay. Farther south, however, white wives were more likely to be confined by customs carried over from Stuart England, while both white and black women suffered their peculiar degradations under the growing practice of slave concubinage and rape. And while southern servant and slave women rarely could marry, southern free women rarely could divorce. Restricting women as they did, leaders of middle and southern colonies had reason to fear them, reason to punish rebellious wives and servants to the limit.

The outer limit was death for a wife who rose up against her husband and killed him, and for a servant or slave who rose up against her master. Here the colonial lawmakers fell back upon English Common Law, which defined the murder of husband or master as petit treason. Since the husband was "lord" of the wife, the Common Law said, her killing him was treachery comparable to murdering the king—though on a lesser scale. A Virginia judge defined the gravity of the crime: ". . . Other offences are injurious to Private Persons only, but this is a Public Mischief, and often strikes at the Root of all Civil Government." For this crime a man who killed his master or ecclesiastical superior was drawn to the place of execution and hanged. The punishment for a woman who killed her husband or master, however, was different. William Blackstone, the eighteenth century's chief apologist for the Common Law, reasoned that "as the natural modesty of the sex forbids the exposing and publicly mangling their bodies, their sentence . . . is to be drawn to the gallows, and there to be burned alive." English Common Law inherited the custom of burning women from the Druids and passed it on to the American colonies. So it was that in 1731, with little regard to her "natural modesty," Delaware burned alive one Catherine Bevan.

When Henry Bevan, a man of sixty or more, died at his home in New Castle, Delaware, the neighbors mumbled. Bevan had complained to them that he was being abused by his wife, Catherine, and their young servant, Peter Murphy. Some gathered from Bevan's hints that Catherine's relationship with the servant was not what it should be. Still, Catherine herself was more than fifty years old, and it seemed to be in the nature of such couples—too long together—to be quarrelsome. One of the guests invited to the funeral, however, was a local magistrate suspicious of Bevan's sudden death, suspicious of the sealed coffin, nailed shut before the mourners arrived. He ordered the coffin opened, and the mourners, looking in one by one, were "all surprized at the Dismal Spectacle." Henry Bevan was, as anyone could see, very badly bruised. The coroner's jury was summoned to view the body and quickly agreed that Bevan had died a violent and unnatural death. Catherine was arrested, and with her Peter Murphy, assumed to be her lover. Both denied that they had harmed Bevan, but when they were confined separately and given time to stew in their own guilt, Murphy did what was expected of him: he accused the woman.

His mistress had sent him to New Castle, he said, "to buy some Rats Bane, or, if he could not get that, some Roman Vitriol; and not being able to get Rats Bane he brought Vitriol, which she gave her Husband to drink dissolved in a Glass of Wine; but the old Man vomiting it up immediately, she feared it would not have the desir'd Effect, and therefore bad him the Servant beat his Master well, especially about the Breast, till he should grow so weak as that she might be able to deal with him, and leave the rest to her." According to Murphy's own confession, as reported in Benjamin Franklin's Pennsylvania *Gazette*: "He beat the old Man till he could not stand, and then laid him on a Couch, when his Wife twisted a Handkerchief round his Neck in order to strangle him; and at the same time sent the Servant away to some Neighbours who lived at a Distance, to tell them that her Husband was in a Fit, and she feared he would die in it, and desire them to come to the House immediately. The Servant returned before any Neighbours came; and she said to him, *I have had two hard Struggles with the old Man since you went away, and he had like to have been too strong for me both Times, but I have quieted him at last.*" So much Peter Murphy said over and over again. Catherine Bevan denied it all.

Murphy repeated his story at the trial, and he and Catherine Bevan were condemned for the murder of her husband. Murphy, found guilty of murder, was sentenced to hang, Catherine Bevan, guilty of petit treason, to be burned alive. Before the execution, Murphy admitted that he had lied about Catherine Bevan and "wronged her much; . . . she did not tie the Handkerchief round her Husband's Neck, and . . . the chief of his Evidence at Court was false." He maintained only that Catherine Bevan had "consented" to the murder and had been "the Promoter of all that happen'd." This charge Catherine Bevan also firmly denied, and by the time they reached the place of execution on June 10, 1731, neither she nor young Murphy—who had talked too much already—had anything more to say. Franklin's newspaper reported that the "Man seem'd penitent, but the Woman appear'd hardened." The paper also recorded, with that typical colonial detachment in the presence of death, the end of Catherine Bevan: "It was design'd to strangle her dead before the Fire should touch her; but its first breaking out was in a stream which pointed directly upon the Rope that went round her Neck, and burnt it off instantly, so that she fell alive into the Flames, and was seen to struggle."

Some years before, Cotton Mather had written: "The 'judgments of God,' seizing upon a few persons only, before our eyes, they should make us afraid, lest we be the next that those judgments do seize upon. . . . if the judgments of God single out one malefactor, to punish him, his voice is, let all be afraid!" The lesson to all offenders is " 'Tremble and repent, lest all of you likewise perish.' " The dying struggle of Catherine Bevan in flames must have been a powerful lesson. Some wives may indeed have repented of murderous intent; others may afterward have removed husbands with greater stealth; and after a time the law abandoned burning at the stake. So Catherine Bevan seems to have been the only white woman in the American colonies to die by judicial fire.

Black women were a different story. They suffered the punishment for petit treason not for killing their husbands but their masters, for the greatest threat to the colonial social order came from outside the immediate family—from indentured servants and especially from slaves.

From the start, servants and slaves were insubordinate. As early as 1639, only three years after the settlement of Hartford, a black servant murdered his master. In 1674 two white indentured servants, Robert Driver and Nicholas Feavour, were hanged in Boston for murdering their master with an ax. Cotton Mather, never one to let a moment pass unimproved, quoted one of the condemned men as saying that "his pride had been his bane" for he sometimes thought: " 'I am flesh and blood, as well as my master; and therefore I know no reason why my master should not obey me, as well as I obey him.' " Mather had warned servants before about that sin of pride they seemed so easily to fall into. "The Proud hearts of many *Servants,* make them discontent at their Servile State; The *Subjection* expected from them throws them into a very Grumbling Discontent," he said. This pride was "the very Sin that at first made all the *Devils* in Hell. The *Devils,* those proud Spirits, could not bear to be Servants in such a Station as God had ordered for them; and for this their *Pride,* the Almighty has *Cursed* them, and *Damned* them." There would be no reconciling Mather's divinely ordained social order and the reasoning of men and women who could not see why their masters might not just as well obey them. Admonishing servants, Mather quoted Colossians 3:23: "... *whatever ye do, do it heartily as unto the Lord....*" Servants and slaves heartily rebelled.

Every colony—even those in which slavery was an unpopular and *relatively* mild institution—wrote a slave code. Despite some variation among colonies, generally slaves were forbidden to carry arms, to drink liquor, to gather in groups larger than three or five, to preach to slaves from other households and never without a white man present. Slaves could not leave their master's yard without a written permit. They could not walk about at night without displaying a candle in a lantern. And they could not train dogs.

These rigorously enforced restrictions must have hindered slave conspiracies—though Gabriel Prosser, Denmark Vesey, and Nat Turner were still to come. But they probably didn't interfere much with simple, individual murder. Sometimes servants and slaves killed quickly in the heat of the moment or the spontaneous release of bottled rage. Robert Driver and Nicholas Feavour struck their master in the midst of an argument. And some newspaper accounts imply a sudden snapping: ". . . at Wallingford in Connecticut, a Negro Woman went up to the Chamber where two of her Master's Daughters lay, and made a Pass with a Knife at the Stomach of one of the Daughters, but her Ribs prevented the Knife from going into her Body; but she cut the others Throat, and she died immediately."

A black servant or slave who killed and was caught was quickly dispatched. Usually there was no jury trial but only a kangaroo hearing because servants who committed petit treason were held to have abrogated the very social bond that bestowed such few legal safeguards as they enjoyed. The Virginia *Gazette* in 1737 tersely summed up the fate of an ax murderer: "The Negro Woman who lately kill'd her Mistress in *Nansemond,* upon her Tryal confess'd the Fact, receiv'd Sentence of Death, and is since burnt." In 1769 it printed another curt report from Charleston, South Carolina: "On Friday last a Negro man and woman were burnt alive on the Green, near the Workhouse, being convicted, one of administering poison, and the other of having procured it." Another slave woman named Eve, who allegedly poisoned her master in Virginia in 1745, was burned alive "on the high hills of Orange County, adjacent to the old courthouse, and the smoke of the burning of Eve was visible over a large extent of country."

Crimes such as these poisonings were horrifying because they were unpredictable and because their obvious premeditation suggested black hostility whites would have preferred to overlook. Whites in the southern colonies with their large black populations had much to fear, and by the eighteenth century they made it a capital crime for blacks to "administer medicine" to whites. In consequence, some slaves must have paid with their lives for the sudden *natural* death of their masters.

Other servants and slaves undoubtedly murdered their masters undetected. It was just such a perfect crime that inspired the botched job and recriminations of slaves Phillis and Mark. In its motive and plan, their crime probably was representative of slave murders. It differs mainly in that we know more of it, for unlike southern slaves accused of petit treason, Phillis and Mark were tried before they were executed.

Phillis and Mark were among several slaves owned by Captain John Codman, who was known in Charlestown, Massachusetts, as "a thrifty saddler, sea-captain, and merchant." Captain Codman used his women slaves as house servants and put the men to work in his own shop or hired them out as common laborers. They didn't like him. In 1749 Phillis and Mark set fire to Codman's workshop, reasoning that its loss would force Codman to sell them to better masters. The plan was a desperate measure, for arson was also a capital crime in Massachusetts, and at least one black woman slave, Maria, was burned at the stake for it. The fire Phillis and Mark set destroyed the workshop, but Codman kept his slaves.

Six years later, on the last day of June 1755, Codman became ill after eating a bowl of water-gruel served by his daughter Betty. After "languishing" for fifteen hours, he died on July 1. The slaves were immediately suspected, and the very next day the coroner's jury declared that Codman had died "By Poison Procured by his negro man servant Mark." Arrested and questioned, Mark admitted only that he had obtained "powder" from the slave of a Boston doctor and given it to Phillis; he understood that she wanted it for killing three pigs.

Phillis, on the other hand, blamed Mark. The poisoning, like the earlier arson, was all his idea. He tried to persuade her to help him by telling her that "Mr. Salmon's Negros poison'd him, and were never found out, but had got good masters, & so might we." Besides, she said, Mark claimed that he had read the Bible through and found it was no sin to kill Codman as long as they did not spill his blood. In the end, according to Phillis, Mark had convinced another slave, Phoebe, to carry out the poisoning. "Phoebe gave me the first Powder," she claimed. "Then it was put into his Chocalate by Phoebe. The next was also put into his Chocalate by Phoebe on the next Wednesday morning. . . . the next Fryday . . . Phoebe put some into his Chocalate. . . ." For her own part, Phillis said that she had once put some arsenic into Codman's water-gruel but then "felt ugly and threw it away, and made some fresh, and did not put any into that." When Phillis was examined by Edmund Trowbridge, the attorney general, and a Mr. Thaddeus Mason, Esq., on July 26 and again on August 2, her entire testimony went like that.

> Quest: Who poured the Water out of the s^d [said] Vial into the Chocolate?
> Answ^r: Phoebe did, and Master afterwards eat it.
> Quest: Who pour'd the Water out of the Vial into the Infusion?
> Answ^r: Phoebe did. . . .
> Quest: Who put the Second Powder into the Vial?
> Answ^r: Phoebe put it in. . . .

But at last Phillis insisted that Codman had died of black-lead poison mixed into a porringer of sago by Mark himself.

The grand jury decided that Codman had been poisoned by arsenic; and the last lethal water-gruel, served by daughter Betty, had been prepared by Phillis. The mutual recriminations of Phillis and Mark amounted to a joint, if unintentional, confession. In August the grand jury returned a true bill against Phillis for petit treason and against Mark and Robin, the slave who had stolen the arsenic from his master's pharmacy, as accessories before the fact. Phoebe, who may have cooperated with the government, was not charged, but she seems to have been transported to the West Indies. Further implicated by the testimony of others who had helped or refused to conspire, Phillis and Mark were convicted by the Superior Court; and on the afternoon of September 18, 1755, they were executed at Cambridge. The Boston *Evening Post* reported that at the place of execution "they both confessed themselves guilty of the Crime for which they suffered, acknowledged the Justice of their Sentence, and died very penitent."

After Mark was hanged his body was taken down and hung in chains at Charlestown on the Cambridge Road. Oddly enough, when a certain Dr. Caleb Rea passed by three or four years later, he found the body still hanging there with the skin "but very little broken." The body of Mark, gibbeted as a lesson to deter other rebellious servants, became a local landmark. Twenty years after the execution, Paul Revere passed the body on his way to Lexington; and twenty years after that, describing his famous ride in a letter to the Massachusetts Historical Society, Revere still remembered passing the spot "where Mark was hung in chains." Of Phillis, however, nothing remained. Condemned for petit treason, she had been burned alive.

Who can say what the passersby learned from Mark in chains? Were masters spared because rebellious slave women recalled the reek of Phillis's burning skin, or Eve's, and cowered? Did husbands survive because vacillating wives remembered Catherine Bevan's struggle in the fire and turned, quite suddenly, squeamish? Magistrates of the time believed so and continued to enforce the letter of the law as example and deterrent to others. And indeed, the number of women who murdered husbands or masters seems to have been relatively small.

But among women there was a worse and far more common offense—a kind of alleged murder for which women were most often accused, convicted, and hanged. It was called "concealing the death of a bastard child."

3.

Bastardy was a problem from the first. Whether single or married, there were never enough women to go around, so that many men lusted after women who were not their legal wives. Many young married couples, later to become upstanding citizens, were fined or whipped for premarital fornication after they produced the presumptive evidence: a seven-month baby. Other sinners who didn't or couldn't marry one another were tried for fornication and adultery, sometimes on the evidence of witnesses, often on the circumstantial evidence of a bastard child. Bastardy itself was everywhere a crime, and an increasingly common one.

During the seventeenth century, when settlements were small and homogeneous, moral standards could be more easily enforced; cases of fornication and bastardy were severely punished. But by the end of the seventeenth century, all observers remarked a severe decline in public morals. Cities grew too rapidly and developed characteristic urban problems, including prostitution and general sexual laxity. Meanwhile, in the countryside, the absence of established social institutions produced a similar carelessness; where there was no one empowered to perform legal marriages, domestic relationships arranged themselves. The Reverend Mr. Woodmason, traveling through the South Carolina backcountry in the mid-eighteenth century, was shocked by the "aban-don'd Morals and profligate Principles" of the inhabitants. He report-ed that hundreds "live in Concubinage, swapping their Wives as Cattel."

The law, which severely punished bastardy on the one hand, en-couraged it on the other. It expressly prohibited the marriage of inden-tured servants during their term of service and provided that a servant who gave birth to a bastard would be publicly whipped and then bound for one year's or, in some colonies, two years' additional service to recompense her master for time lost from her work—even though she may have been absent for only a few days. Some colonies, such as Virginia, provided an optional fine of one or two thousand pounds of tobacco—a fine hardly within the means of an indentured servant. That law made servants' pregnancies worth their masters' while; and so many unscrupulous masters bound their servants to additional years by rape that the Virginia law quickly was changed to provide that a servant woman who bore a bastard fathered by her master or his sons would be sold away for an additional term of service with the proceeds of the sale going to the parish. The master received no rec-ompense for the loss of his servant. To the woman servant, the result was much the same. Still, she served.

Colonial leaders were concerned about bastardy on several counts. In the first place, bastardy was an economic problem, for every illegitimate child was a potential drain upon the community. Civic officials coerced the mother to name the father so that he could be as-sessed for child support if he was a free man, or bound out by the town if he was a servant. If a servant/mother refused to name the father, she could be held responsible for the child's support; she could be assessed a fine of one thousand or two thousand pounds of tobacco and—un-able to pay—bound out for an additional one, two, or even five years' service. Her bastard child, too, could be bound out for twenty-one years or thirty years or even lifetime servitude. Free men usually were fined and free women, in lieu of fines, publicly whipped twenty or thir-ty lashes. And free women and their bastards could also be bound into servitude to meet the town's expense. When Eve Sewell, a free white woman, bore a child in 1790 by a black slave, under Maryland law her white husband received an automatic divorce and both she and her child were sold into slavery. Secondly, civic leaders were worried about preserving the family, the cornerstone of society and one of its chief instruments of social control. The establishment of the sort of ad hoc family implicit in bastardy challenged traditional legal arrangements. So a child born beyond the confines of legal marriage was considered no child at all, its mother no mother at all, its father a cipher.

Religious leaders professed concern for the salvation of the mothers of bastards. Such "criminals" were always used as examples for the spiritual edification of others, but their individual souls—the ministers claimed—were also significant. So Cotton Mather (who turned out his own servant when she had a bastard) cataloged, supposedly for young women's edification, the sins the flesh is heir to. Beginning with disobedience to parents, the child falls into "uncleanness" commencing with "self-pollution" (masturbation) and regressing to fornication, adultery, double adultery, sodomy, buggery, incest, and bestiality. Mather cites a shocking case in point: "In the Southern Parts of this Country," he says, an animal gave birth to a monster with "something of an *Human Shape*" and a "Blemish in one Eye just like what a loose Lewd Fellow in the Town, was known to have." The "greater monster" confessed his paternity and was executed. This bizarre example of uncleanness hardly seems to apply to unwed mothers, but Mather used it in a sermon called "An Holy Rebuke to the Unclean Spirit" preached "on a Day when Two Persons were Executed for Murdering of their Bastard Children."

That was the greater sin: not to birth bastards, but to destroy them. Yet the laws that forbade servants to marry and extended the term of bondage for bearing a bastard compelled women to escape detection and additional servitude by getting rid of their live bastards and hiding those born dead. Laws that punished fornication with public whipping pressed women to remove the evidence of their sin. And slavery, which made a slave of a slave's child, gave many mothers a powerful impulse to "spare" their children by killing them. Attorney Theodore Sedgwick called bastardy "the only crime which good society never pardons. . . . Shame, ridicule, infamy, exile attend it," he said. There was "therefore every motive for such a mother to obliterate with the blood of her child, its sufferings and her own disgrace." In punishing bastardy, society ensured that many women would turn in desperation to murder.

Massachusetts leaders suspected that infanticide was a widespread problem, but in many cases it was difficult to get a murder conviction. Concealment of pregnancy and birth obscured evidence, and even when a dead baby was found and its mother identified, she might claim that the child was stillborn and that she hid it to avoid public shame or additional bondage. So in 1692, the Massachusetts General Court sought approval of the king's Privy Council to make "concealing the death of a bastard child" a capital offense, as it had been in England and Virginia since 1624. The "Act to prevent the Destroying and Murdering of Bastard Children" was widely reprinted in the next few years "to prevent Lives being lost thro' Ignorance thereof"; and because so many women *did* lose their lives to this law, it is worth reprinting again:

> *Whereas many Lewd Women, that have been Delivered of Bastard Children, to avoid their Shame, and to escape Punishment, do secretly Bury or Conceal the Death of their Children; and after, if the Child be found Dead, the said Women do allege that the said Child was born dead; whereas it falleth out sometimes (although hardly it is to be proved) that the said Child or Children were Murdered by the said Women their Lewd Mothers, or by their Assent or Procurement.*
>
> Be it therefore Enacted . . . That if any Woman be Delivered of any Issue of her Body, Male or Female, which if it were born Alive, should by Law be a Bastard; and that they endeavour privately, either by Drowning or secret Burying thereof, or any other way; either by herself, or the procuring of others so to conceal the Death thereof, that it may not come to light, whether it were Born Alive or not, but be concealed: In every such case the Mother so Offending, shall suffer Death, as in case of Murder. Except such Mother can make proof by One Witness at the least, that the Child whose Death was by her so intended to be concealed, was born Dead.

This law presumes guilt, not innocence. Under its terms prosecutors don't have to prove that the accused woman murdered her baby; she has to prove—through testimony of at least one witness—that she did *not.*

A woman bent upon avoiding public shame is unlikely to call in a witness, but the absence of a witness to the birth was construed as circumstantial evidence of guilt, clinching the case against the accused. As a Philadelphia judge advised the jury during the trial of Alice Clifton, "People determined upon the commission of the crime of infanticide, always are silent and alone for the purpose of concealment. . . ." Being silent and alone was enough to hang you.

When Alice Clifton, a sixteen-year-old slave, was tried in 1787, her owners John and Mary Bartholomew both testified about serious injuries she had suffered during her pregnancy, and two doctors testified that her child was born dead, probably as a result of these injuries. Still, Clifton had tried to conceal the birth; and she had no witness. The jury pronounced her guilty of concealment and the judge sentenced her to death. Luckily, the sentence was later respited by the Executive Council, which had begun to question the law's severity.

Everyone believed that one sin led to another. The Reverend Thomas Foxcroft, preaching at Rebekah Chamblit's hanging, warned his audience to "Take heed . . . that you do not *dishonour your own Bodies* by unnatural & impure Abuses; lest from *solitary* Filthiness you be left to pass on unto *social*; and from secret *Fornications* to secret *Murders*; and at length come to an untimely & shameful Death. . . ." The Reverend Eliphalet Adams, warning against the sin of "uncleanness" at Katherine Garret's execution, said, "They who have Committed folly of this Kind, are so often . . . tempted, in Order to *hide* their *Sin and Shame* from the world, to add Murder to their former Offence." But if women slid from fornication to infanticide, said the divines, they had only themselves to blame. The Puritans taught that the sinner who neglects God, God neglects. God has merely to withdraw his restraining grace, and the sinner plunges headlong to damnation. Colonial leaders and divines taught that in turning to "uncleanness," women asked God, in effect, for the rope to hang themselves. The colonial period was not given to sociological thinking; if civic leaders and clergymen understood how religion, social structure, and law combined to provoke desperate women to murder their illegitimate children, they did not mention it.

Instead, they talked about God, as Cotton Mather and Governor Winthrop did when Mary Martin—convicted of murdering her bastard child—was hanged at Boston in 1646. Martin was hanged, but she didn't die. She simply "hung in space" and then asked boldly "what they did mean to do." At that, wrote Winthrop, who recorded the whole unhappy story in his *Journal,* someone "stepped up, and turned the knot of the rope backward, and then she soon died." In this grotesque moment Mather saw the hand of God. He wrote that "there was this remarkable at her execution: she acknowledged her *twice* essaying to kill her child before she could make an end of it; and now, through the unskillfulness of the executioner, she was turned off the ladder twice before she died."

To Mather that tidy coincidence must have been a sign as compelling as any burning bush, a sort of cosmic symbol far more enlightening than any of the bare facts of Mary Martin's life. She was twenty-two when her father, a merchant in Casco Bay, Massachusetts, was ruined and returned to London, leaving Mary and a younger sister behind to fend for themselves. Mary went into service in the house of a Mr. Mitton of Casco. She was reputed to be a "very proper maiden . . . of modest behaviour," and Mr. Mitton was a married man. Nevertheless, Mitton "was taken with her, and soliciting her chastity, obtained his desire, and . . . divers times committed sin with her." The arrangement must have been more congenial to Mr. Mitton than to Mary, for within three months she left his house and the town; she placed herself in service to a Mrs. Bourne in Boston. Stricken with "horrible regret of mind," she begged God for deliverance, promising "that if ever she were overtaken again, she would leave herself unto his justice, to be made a publick example." Then she discovered that she was pregnant, and because she could not bear the shame, she concealed her condition.

Others suspected that she was pregnant, and asked her about it, but she denied the fact, and Mrs. Bourne took her at her word. At last, in the middle of the night, she gave birth to a girl "in a back room by herself." Afraid of discovery, she kneeled on the baby's head until she thought it was dead and then put it aside. But "the child being strong, recovered, and cried again." Martin took up the baby again and "used violence to it till it was quite dead." Then she hid it in a chest where it remained until a suspicious midwife began searching and found the baby's body, its skull fractured. Martin was brought before a grand jury and made to touch her dead baby's face—"whereupon the blood came fresh into it." She confessed and volunteered the information that she had previously had another illicit relationship. She was sentenced to die, led to the place of execution, and hanged—twice.

Women were thought to be particularly susceptible to the sin of uncleanness—and all that followed from it—because of their besetting sin: pride. A woman's pride in her appearance, said the ministers, would draw her into lustful company. The Reverend Mr. Foxcroft, who apparently had ransacked his Bible for appropriate texts, went on and on about it. "And let our young Women be admonish'd," he said, "by those Words of the Prophet":

> *Moreover the Lord saith, Because the Daughters of Zion are haughty, & walk with stretched forth Necks, and wanton Eyes; therefore the Lord will smite with a Scab the Crown of the Head of the Daughters of Zion: and it*

shall come to pass, that instead of sweet Smell there shall be Stink; and instead of a Girdle, a Rent; and instead of well set Hair, Baldness; and instead of a Stomacher, a girding of Sackcloth; and Burning, in stead of Beauty.—Remember also the Words of *Solomon; Favour is deceitful, & Beauty is vain.* How many that proudly valu'd themselves upon it, have been expos'd by it to such Temptations, as have been the Ruin of their Virtue, rob'd 'em of their Honour, cost 'em their Lives in the End, and destroy'd their precious Souls!

A woman's pride in her reputation would drive her to hide her illegitimate pregnancy. Abiel Converse of Chester, Massachusetts, daughter of a Minute Man, whose great-great-grandfather had sailed to America with Governor Winthrop in the *Arbella,* killed her child "to hide her misfortune." Sarah Smith of Deerfield, Massachusetts, whose husband had been captured by Indians more than two years before, killed her child "with intent to conceal her Lewdness. . . ." Even the servant Susanna who, being black, was not expected by the judge to possess "the same acute sensibility to dishonor as in the superior grades of society," nevertheless "felt in some degree the constraint of shame arising from her pregnancy. . . ." But Susanna, who had been a slave and was still an indentured servant, said that she killed her child "because she thought it would be happier out of the world than in it, where its mother had a hard lot, and it would have the same if alive. . . ." The Massachusetts court received the statement as evidence of Susanna's "derangement," while all across the South dozens, perhaps hundreds, of black women deprived their masters of slaves by killing their own infants. Such overweening pride was the sin of Satan himself and had to be punished.

And so it was, in public, to provide a warning, a supposed deterrent, and certainly a spectacle. Ministers cited Deuteronomy 17:13: "*And all the people shall hear and fear and do no more presumptuously.*" Most people heard. In 1701 "so many Thousands" gathered to see Esther Rodgers hanged at Ipswich, Massachusetts, "as was scarcely ever heard of or seen upon any occasion in any part of New England." The crowd was estimated at "Four or Five Thousand People at least. . . ." Katherine Garret was hanged at New London, Connecticut, in 1738, "surrounded with a Vast Circle of people, more Numerous, perhaps, than Ever was gathered together before, On any Occasion, in this Colony. . . ." About ten thousand people gathered to see Sarah Bramble hanged in New London on November 21, 1753. Even though the weather was bad, people came from twenty or thirty miles away.

Many of these hanged women were the first persons executed in their county or town; spectators had simply never seen the like before. Sarah Bramble was the first (and only) white person publicly executed in New London. Esther Rodgers was the first person sentenced to death since the Ipswich Courts had first convened more than sixty years earlier. The double hanging of Sarah Simpson and Penelope Kenny at Portsmouth, New Hampshire, in 1739 "drew together a vast Concourse of People, and probably the greater, because these were the first Executions that ever were seen in this Province." And people who saw the executions remembered. Simeon Clapp, in his nineties, told a Massachusetts antiquary about the hanging of Abiel Converse, which he had seen when he was a young man. At every execution the ministers preached vigorously: "Beware the Sin of *Pride.* . . . Pride has tempted many a young Woman to destroy the Fruit of her own Body, that she might avoid the Scandal of a spurious Child; and the monstrous Fact being detected, has brought her to yet greater Shame, by an infamous Execution, as a Murderer."

Still the women continued to "do presumptuously": Jane Champion, executed in Virginia, 1632. Margaret Hatch, executed in Virginia, 1633. Mary Martin, executed in Massachusetts, 1646. Elizabeth Emerson and Grace, "Negro," executed in Massachusetts, 1691. An unnamed woman, executed in Virginia, 1692. Susanna Andrews, executed in Massachusetts, 1696. Sarah Smith and Sarah Threeneedles, executed in Massachusetts, 1698. Esther Rodgers, executed in Massachusetts, 1701. Betty, "Negro," executed in Massachusetts, 1712. Rebekah Chamblit, executed in Massachusetts, 1733. An unnamed woman, executed in Virginia, 1737. Katherine Garret, executed in Connecticut, 1738. Elizabeth Maze and Elizabeth Twopence, executed in Virginia, 1739. Sarah Simpson and Penelope Kenny, executed in New Hampshire, 1739. Sarah Bramble, executed in Connecticut, 1753. Susannah Brazier and Catharine Peppers, executed in Virginia, 1774. Hannah Piggin (or Pigeon), executed in Massachusetts, 1785. Elizabeth Wilson, executed in Pennsylvania, 1786. Abiel Converse, executed in Massachusetts, 1787. Undoubtedly there are many more forgotten names in the back pages of colonial newspapers, sandwiched between the social news from the Court of St. James's and the reports of ox teams struck by lightning in the barnyard.

Why were these women so severely punished? Certainly they were not a danger to the public at large. Women who commit infanticide do not have to be restrained—like armed robbers, arsonists, or rapists—for the public safety. Many other people, guilty of crimes far more damaging to society, escaped the hangman. Just about the same time that Hannah Piggin and Abiel Converse were hanged in Northampton, Massachusetts, six leaders of Shays' Rebellion, convicted in the same jurisdiction of treason and sentenced to hang, were pardoned. Still others, guilty of far more brutal crimes, got off with light sentences. When Robert Thompson was convicted of assault in the same Northampton jurisdiction, he was whipped twenty stripes, set on the gallows for one hour, whipped nineteen more stripes, jailed for a year, and ordered to pay costs. He had beaten up his wife, Agnes Thomspon, and "dug out both her eyes with his thumb & a stick so she is entirely blind."

To Puritans infanticide was worse. Murder an unbaptized infant, they taught, and you murder its soul, for the unbaptized have no place in heaven. Yet, oddly enough, that theological point was rarely mentioned by the ministers charged with preaching execution sermons. One argued that infanticide is worse than other murders on the grounds of fair play: "In many if not most instances of murder, there is either some provocation, or injury received from the person murdered, or a prospect of considerable gain, or there is no relation by kindred blood, or the person is capable of making some defence." Since none of these conditions pertained, he concluded, infanticide is "a most horrid, monstrous, and unnatural crime."

Most clergymen condemned infanticide because it is a violation of divine authority. The Reverend Aaron Bascom instructed Abiel Converse on her execution day on this point:

> ... the evil of sinners lies in opposition to GOD, because sin is a violation of the divine law. All sins whatever that people commit, are a violation of GOD'S law; therefore, a contempt of his authority, and wholly opposed to him. All sins against society, against rulers, parents, Masters, and guardians; yea all sins of thought, word and deed, are violations of GOD's holy law; therefore express opposition, and enmity against him.
>
> That sinners are opposed to GOD, and hate him, is evident from plain facts.

The woman guilty of infanticide mocked God's authority in many ways. Through simple neglect of religion, she challenged God. By breaking the civil law, she scorned the authority of patriarchal leaders who were thought to be God's right-hand men. And she broke not just one but several laws—since fornication and bastardy had to occur before infanticide—and then covered up the crimes over a long period by secrecy and lying. Servants and slaves who killed their offspring scorned both their masters and the civil authorities, and through them, God.

Finally, all women who killed their babies violated what was—even then—taken to be the law of nature decreed by the God of Nature. During the trial of the bond servant and former slave Susanna, court-appointed defense attorney John Van Ness Yates defined *mother.*

> . . . what malice or revenge could have entered the bosom of a mother against her innocent and helpless offspring? A mother who, by every tie human and divine, was bound to foster and protect it? By that endearing title we had a certain pledge of her affection, not her hate. No matter whether the offspring was legitimate or not; the God of Nature had implanted this affection so strongly in her bosom, that neither time nor accident could alter or impair it.

The women who killed their children, then, were by definition "unnatural" and "monstrous"—more "hardened" than the "sea monsters, who draw out their breasts, and give suck to their young ones."

Now that birth control is more or less routine, infanticide seems an unrelated and horrifying event; but to colonial women, who had no alternative and whose offspring were very likely to die in infancy anyway, infanticide might be a desperate kind of birth control after the fact. Various means of contraception were known at the time, and coitus interruptus was widely practiced. Sarah Smith, who had two husbands and several lovers, may have known about such things, but no means of birth control was foolproof. Young unmarried motherless women like Mary Martin, on the other hand, probably knew nothing of birth control. And in some cases birth-control information wouldn't have helped. Alice Clifton, the sixteen-year-old slave, was "debauched" in an alley by a white man known as "fat Shaffer." Women in desperate circumstances then turned to infanticide. But in killing their infants they not only committed murder; they also asserted, symbolically at least, that a woman should not be punished for her sexuality, that she is entitled to some measure of control of her own body. Such statements challenge civil and divine authority most of all. In a patriarchal society, they are revolutionary.

In Chester, Massachusetts, a week after Abiel Converse was arrested for murdering her bastard child, a Mrs. Tyler, several years a widow and several months pregnant, ate rat poison for breakfast. She spent the day "in great agony" and, about sunset, she died. The editor of the county newspaper took a dim view of this "inconsiderate conduct," and the Reverend Mr. Bascom denounced her at the Converse execution as "an unclean and whorish woman [who] was led on by this abominable wickedness, to murder herself: deliberately, designedly, without hope of any mercy; and without desiring the good wishes or prayers of any friend whatever." Not even the Reverend Mr. Bascom.

It is hard to read the old sermons today without suspecting that men like the Reverend Mr. Bascom were more concerned with their own authority than with God's. Always they warned women to be docile and obedient. At the executions of women convicted of infanticide, the ministers harangued women about "uncleanness"; but they also warned them against the sins of lying, secrecy, anger, disobedience, hypocrisy, sullen discontent, idleness, and "gadding about" with other women. In a political context, these "sins" amount to resistance, rebellion, subversion, sabotage, coalition, and conspiracy. No wonder the preachers thundered: "The Apostle wou'd have the young women taught to be *sober, discreet, Chast,* Keepers at home, that the word of God be not blasphemed. . . ."

But women apparently were not keepers at home, for during the eighteenth century bastardy became such a common offense that penalties against it had to be reduced. In 1747 Benjamin Franklin's marvelous fictitious creation, Miss Polly Baker, prosecuted for bearing a fifth bastard, argued that she had done her civic duty in adding "to the king's subjects" and should have a statue erected in her honor. Franklin's satiric essay is a serious argument for distinguishing "sin" from "crime." By 1780 the Marquis de Chastellux could relate straightforwardly the story of a "deceived" Miss Dorrance in Voluntown, Connecticut, being well cared for by her family. And George Grieve, Chastellux's translator, who also had met the family, advised English readers that in America such a young woman was "pitied rather than blamed" and could "still retain all her rights in society and become a legitimate spouse and mother, though her adventure be neither unknown nor even dissimulated."

Court dockets were crowded with bastardy cases. At the Court of General Sessions of the Peace held at Springfield, Massachusetts, in May 1785, Mary Howard, a "singlewoman," appeared and "voluntarily confesse[d] herself to have been guilty of the Crime of Fornication, and that she . . . had a Female Bastard Child born of her Body on the twentieth day of January last past. . . ." Mary Howard was followed by six other women. Each made a similar confession. Each was fined six shillings and charged three shillings for costs—a little more than a week's wages for a skilled spinster. A woman who accepted her child and her shame could be rehabilitated, but a woman who took matters into her own hands could not. In the same month, the Superior Court meeting nearby at Northampton sentenced Hannah Piggin to die for concealing the death of her bastard child. It was almost as though women who committed infanticide were punished not so much for killing but for trying to put one over on the authorities.

Some women got away with it. They hid pregnancy under full skirts and aprons. And they labored alone and in silence. Esther Rodgers went out to the field in winter to give birth. Susanna Andrews left her parents' house in the middle of the night, went to an open field, and had twins. Katherine Garret gave birth in the barn, Sarah Three-needles in the pasture, and Alice Clifton—pleading a headache—bore her child in a second-floor bedroom while all the family ate midday dinner just below. Esther Rodgers, sentenced to die at age twenty-one for murdering her bastard, confessed that she had had another bastard when she was seventeen. She had smothered it, hidden it in her room, and buried it at night in the garden. No one, not even the father—a black servant in the same household—had suspected. When a dead baby was found in a well at Portsmouth, New Hampshire, authorities questioned Sarah Simpson and Penelope Kenny, who were suspected of having given birth. Both confessed that they had borne children, but one insisted she had thrown hers in the river, and the other led authorities to the spot where hers was buried. Simpson and Kenny were hanged, but the mother of the baby in the well was never found.

This sort of slipup troubled authorities. The Reverend William Shurtleff, who preached for the hanging of Simpson and Kenny, composed a "brief narrative" of this extraordinary case to accompany the printed text of his address. Baffled, he urged the reader particularly "to make proper and pertinent Reflections upon the *remarkable Discovery of their Crimes, and the Mysteriousness of Divine Providence in suffering a third Person ... as yet to escape....*" He knew that the guilty woman would be punished in the next world. Still, in *this* world, it clearly was possible for a woman to get away with murder.

Troubled and threatened, the civil authorities continued to execute women for concealment, and the ministers labored mightily to make of the condemned women proper and terrifying examples. Executions were postponed to give ministers time to prepare the condemned women for death. As Sarah Simpson waited to die, all the ministers of Portsmouth and many from neighboring towns were busy "making it their constant business to instruct her, as well as pray with her." Since Penelope Kenny, born in Ireland, had been brought up as a Catholic, the same ministers worked to convince her of "*her miserable and perishing Estate.*" Ministers worked for six months on Katherine Garret's "preparations," eight months on Esther Rodgers's. Cotton Mather noted in his *Diary* that he had spent "many and many a weary Hour . . . in the Prison, to serve the *Souls* of those miserable Creatures": Elizabeth Emerson and Grace, a black indentured servant, who were hanged together. Mather concentrated his efforts on the white woman; when he preached on hanging day he addressed his sermon strictly to "Elizabeth," referring to Grace only parenthetically as "thy Black Fellow-Sufferer." He wanted Emerson to say that she had brought her death upon herself through her own sinfulness. To save her soul, she had to say it. And if she said it—just incidentally—she would absolve the authorities, civil and religious, from responsibility.

After the ministers "prepared" Rebekah Chamblit, she admitted she had provoked God by hiding her sin. Esther Rodgers said that God had "justly" given her up to her "hearts Lusts, and ways of Wickedness" because she had "neglected God, refused his Counsil, and would not walk in his Ways. . . ." Sarah Simpson said that she had neglected God's duty in childhood and ignored opportunities to study religion.

During his execution sermon, Mather read a declaration that he said Elizabeth Emerson had written:

> I am a Miserable Sinner; and I have Justly Provoked the Holy God to leave me unto that Folly of my own Heart, for which I am now Condemned to Dy. . . . I believe, the chief thing that hath, brought me, into my present Condition, is my *Disobedience to my Parents*: I despised all their Godly Counsils and Reproofs; and I was always of an Haughty and Stubborn Spirit. So that now I am become a dreadful Instance of the Curse of God belonging to *Disobedient Children*.

Esther Rodgers, after eight months of preparation, spoke from the gallows:

> Here I am come to Dy a Shameful Death, and I justly deserve it. Young People take Warning, O let all take Warning by me; I beg of all to have a Care. Be Obedient to your Parents and Masters. . . . O Run not abroad with wicked Company, or on Sabbath day Nights. . . . If you do

not love God he will not love you; If you go on in Sin, You will provoke God.

Sarah Simpson advised young people to pay attention in church and not let their eyes wander. In the end, the condemned women produced dying declarations as correct as if they had been written by the ministers themselves.

But not just at first. At first Esther Rodgers refused to speak to the ministers who haunted her cell, and she wouldn't go to church. Rebekah Chamblit also kept her mouth shut, and a minister involved in her "conversion" admitted that her few remarks to the clergy had been, at best, "short." But she must have lost her temper at times, too, for in her declaration she apologized for any "rash Expressions" she had "uttered since . . . condemnation." Sarah Smith told nothing but lies. Cotton Mather, perhaps worn out by his labors for Elizabeth Emerson's conversion, called her a "Bloody *Murderer*" and told her that "there never was a Prisoner more *Hard-Hearted,* and more *Unfruitful,* than you have been." Simpson and Kenny denounced their sentences as "rigorous and unjust," applied for a reprieve, and made plans to escape. Eleanor White, awaiting execution in Freehold, New Jersey, broke out of jail and got away. The Reverend Mr. Adams, preaching on Katherine Garret's execution day, said she has been "Stupid & Obstinate and Insensible under this Sentence of Condemnation" and warned her to "*harbour no Grudge or Animosity.*" When first sentenced she had been "thrown into the utmost Confusion & Distress"; she had made "rash and unguarded" statements and blamed "all sorts of persons," so that the ministers were hard pressed "to allay this resentment."

Without the help of the ministers all of these women might have blamed "all sorts of persons" for their misfortunes. Mary Martin might have blamed her father, who deserted her, or the master who seduced or raped her. Young Alice Clifton, coerced by a white man, seemed to a doctor to have "lost herself much" in her trouble, but she told the doctor that she had killed her child on orders from the father, fat Shaffer. Elizabeth Wilson of Chester, Pennsylvania, accused the father of her twins of murdering them when they were five or six weeks old while holding her off at gunpoint. The story elicited sympathy in the Executive Council, which issued a stay of execution, but the order arrived twenty minutes after she had been hanged.

Yet even Elizabeth Wilson blamed herself, seemed penitent and resigned, and prayed on the gallows "that others might take warning from her, to shun those sins that brought her to [a] shameful end." At the same time she "once more declared her innocence of some things"—namely, the murders for which she was hanged. Simpson and Kenny also "*deny'd that they laid violent Hands on their Children; one* affirming that her Child was *dead born;* and the *other,* that hers dy'd *soon after it was born.*" But the help of the ministers made them "sensible" that they had not taken enough care to preserve their children's lives; and they agreed that they were "guilty of the *Breach of the Sixth Commandment by Omission, if not by Commission.*" Whether guilty of murder or not, most of the condemned women came to feel as Esther Rodgers did. "I find . . . a willingness in me to accept the punishment of my sins," she said, "and a readiness to glorify the Justice of God by suffering that Death I have deserved in hope of receiving his mercy to Eternal Life; . . . I submit to his pleasure. . . . [God] has made me to loath my self."

Some few condemned women held out. Sarah Bramble refused to attend the sermon preached ostensibly for her benefit on her execution day. Sarah Smith slept through the sermon and the public prayer. And portions of Rebekah Chamblit's published Declaration read more like a threat than a confession. "I have often thought," she wrote, "had I been let alone to go on undiscovered in my Sins, I might have provok'd Him to leave me to a course of Rebellion. . . ." If there were more cases of proud, angry, willful women, their histories surely would have been suppressed by ministers who published accounts of only their most successful conversions.

So the women were schooled for death. Each was preached a sermon based upon some terrifying text. Sarah Smith heard a discourse on Revelation 21:8: "But the fearful, and unbelieving, and the abominable, and murderers, and whoremongers, and sorcerers, and idolators, and all liars, shall have their part in the lake which burneth with fire & brimstone: which is the second death." Rebekah Chamblit had a sermon on Deuteronomy 22:21: "*They shall bring out the Damsel, and stone her with Stones, that she die, because she hath wrought Folly in Israel: So shalt thou put away Evil from among you.*" Then the condemned woman walked to the gallows—usually set up about a mile outside of town—accompanied all the way by ministers "mixing with words of Consolation, something of Terror and Caution." Her coffin was carried before her, and sometimes during this walk the woman wore the rope around her neck. The Reverend Mr. Adams reported that Katherine Garret "made apt and pertinent remarks, upon the sight of her Coffin, the taking off of her fetters, the putting the rope about her Neck & other such Occurrences." At the gallows the ministers prayed at length and read out the condemned woman's dying declaration. Sometimes the woman herself spoke to the crowd. Sarah Simpson displayed great "*Composure of Mind*" and Esther Rodgers "undaunted Courage and unshaken Confidence." Katherine Garret delivered a memorized prayer, then continued to pray in a "broken and Incoherent" way. Rebekah Chamblit, responding correctly to a minister's question, said, "*I feel I am in a miserable condition: and I can do nothing, of myself, to please GOD.*" She answered a few more questions, then "grew disordered and faint, and not capable of attending further to continu'd discourse."

Then the ministers withdrew, the executioner turned the woman off the ladder, she hung for a time, and died.

As the century ended, so did the public hangings. Many changes in social attitudes, a long time stirring, came together to produce changes in the punishment of women. For one thing, Enlightenment thinkers such as John Locke and the influential Italian jurist Cesare Beccaria taught that the purpose of punishment is not to deter others but to restrain and reform the offender. In 1651 Thomas Hobbes, expressing the older view, had written that "it is of the nature of punishment to have for an end the disposing of men to obey the law," but by 1690 Locke was insisting that punishment should be "proportionate to the transgressor" and should serve only "for reparation and restraint." Under the tempering influence of Enlightenment thinkers, public capital and corporal punishments were given up. England and America stopped burning women. Branding, mutilation, and dismemberment were relinquished as cruel and inhumane punishments. The offense for which women had been most severely penalized—concealing the death of newborn bastards—was recognized as essentially an offense against certain religious beliefs. And as the Puritans and Anglicans lost their hold on secular authority, even infanticide came to seem a less heinous offense. The number of religious sects multiplied with varied immigration, so that America finally stumbled into toleration.

On the other hand, the position of women in society rapidly declined. By the middle of the eighteenth century women and men were about equal in number. Women married later and less often; the number of women who never married or who did not remarry after being widowed rose steadily. Women lost value simply because they were no longer scarce. During the last half of the century, manufacturing began to move from the home to the newly invented shop or factory. At first women and children followed the work of textile production into the mills; later, men took on the skilled jobs in industry. But work removed from the home was not the same as work *at* home; and as "man's sphere" and "woman's sphere" diverged, men and women came to seem essentially different kinds of people. That undoubtedly made it easier, as the colonies became a new nation, to bar women from some occupations, to pay them less, to take away their right to vote, to deny them education, to remove them from state offices, and to strip married women of the rights they had held under equity law. When Abigail Adams warned her husband, then engaged in writing the Constitution, to "remember the ladies," he *laughed* at her demand for legal rights and reminded her of the informal privileges she enjoyed as a woman. Abigail, even as she called herself Lady Adams, knew she held the short end of the stick.

One of the "privileges" of some women—white women of certain social classes—was to be exempt from corporal punishment. In New Haven in 1699 the man employed to whip offenders refused to whip a woman; he was fined and discharged from the job, but no one could be found to take it on. A similar incident took place in Hartford in 1722. By mid-century the practice of whipping women for petty offenses was discontinued all over New England, although women were still whipped for more serious offenses such as adultery and repeated cases of bastardy. Even then, according to one observer, "females had it lightly" and "a severe whipping" was reserved only for "a great villain."

As attitudes changed so did the law, for its penalties could not be enforced. The burning of Catherine Bevan in Delaware in 1731 was widely publicized, including the grim detail of her falling into the fire alive. Perhaps because of lurking memories of that event, officials of York County, Virginia, did not prosecute a Mrs. Thompson, a white woman, when in 1769 she killed her sleeping husband with an ax. They pronounced her "deranged" and incarcerated her, for if they had convicted her they would have had to burn her. Previously Virginia had burned only black people, and that too was becoming abhorrent. Three years after the slave Eve was burned in Orange County, another slave, Letty, charged in the same county with poisoning a white man and a black man, was acquitted because "the horrible scene so recently enacted at the burning of Eve" was too hideous to repeat. When Sarah Kirk was convicted of murdering her husband in 1787, the Delaware legislature hurriedly changed the old law under which Bevan had been burned fifty-six years earlier. Kirk was hanged. Massachusetts changed the penalty for petit treason from burning to hanging in 1777, twenty-two years after burning the slave Phillis.

Except in cases of infanticide, where the church still firmly clutched the criminal law, it became more and more difficult even to hang women. In colonial Pennsylvania, which always had a relatively humane code, of fifteen women convicted of capital crimes after 1718, ten were pardoned or banished; and among the five who were hanged was Elizabeth Wilson, who died only because her pardon arrived too late. Even rigorous Massachusetts law—darkened by the shadow of Salem—finally yielded to changes in public opinion. The case of Bathsheba Spooner was the last straw. It was a remarkable case, for Spooner did not kill her child. The state did.

Bathsheba Spooner was the favorite daughter of one of Massachusetts's leading citizens, Timothy Ruggles, a distinguished lawyer and judge, brigadier general to Lord Jeffrey Amherst, and a lion of society. On the eve of the Revolution, Ruggles came out foursquare for the king and was forced to flee to Nova Scotia with his sons, leaving Bathsheba behind in a miserable marriage of his own arranging. In 1766, Ruggles had married off Bathsheba, then twenty, to Joshua Spooner, a retired merchant whose money seems to have been his only redeeming feature. Peleg W. Chandler, commenting on the case in 1844, noted that Spooner was "in Character a feeble man"—utterly unlike the commanding father who had "spoiled" Bathsheba. The Spooners were a mismatched pair, and Bathsheba, who according to all reports was beautiful, smart, well educated, high spirited, and a remarkable horse-woman, quickly came to despise her cloddish husband. After twelve years of marriage, she decided to kill him.

At first she enlisted the help of Ezra Ross, a soldier in Washington's army who—quite by chance—recuperated at her house after his first campaign, and with whom she contracted "an improper intimacy." But Ross was a respectable boy of eighteen and no cutthroat. Time and again he failed to act. At last Bathsheba hailed two former British soldiers passing in the road: James Buchanan, a thirty-year-old

Scotsman, and William Brooks, a twenty-seven-year-old Englishman. She asked the men to stay on during her husband's two-week absence; they ate and drank well at Joshua Spooner's expense, and eventually the talk turned to murder. When Spooner returned he ordered Buchanan and Brooks to leave, accused them of stealing a spoon, summoned a neighbor to guard him, and slept on the floor with his head on the money box. Buchanan and Brooks agreed to kill him.

A couple of weeks later, on the night of March 1, 1778, Joshua Spooner, beaten to death, tumbled headfirst into his own well. His widow broke open the money box, and in the presence of servants who later testified against her, divided the spoils among Buchanan, Brooks, and young Ezra Ross, who had stopped in that night—apparently by coincidence—only to be pressed into service as an assassin. The next morning Bathsheba reported her husband's absence, but searchers soon found his battered body in the well. Buchanan and Brooks turned up drunk in a nearby tavern wearing Spooner's clothes and some handsome silver shoe buckles bearing the initials *J.S.* They were arrested, and soon Bathsheba was charged with murder as the one who "did incite, move, abett, counsel and procure" the killing.

Levi Lincoln was appointed to defend Buchanan, Brooks, Ross, and Spooner. Later in his long, successful career, Lincoln became President Jefferson's attorney general and turned down an appointment to the Supreme Court, but at the Spooner trial he didn't have much to work with. He gave up on Buchanan and Brooks, who had confessed, urged Ross's youth and accidental involvement, and argued fervently that Mrs. Spooner was of unsound mind. Only a woman deranged, he contended, would have instigated such an obvious murder in company with such thoroughly unreliable rogues. Still, the jury returned a guilty verdict and the four defendants were sentenced to die. The whole trial—start to finish—took less than sixteen hours.

Quickly the men broke down. They wept and repented, wrote a confession blaming the "lewd" woman who had "seduced" them, and petitioned the court for a reprieve so they would have time to prepare for death. Bathsheba, on the other hand, appeared calm. Those who opposed her said she was "hardened" while sympathizers praised her remarkable fortitude; she did not break down. But she did advise the court that she was pregnant and asked for a postponement of execution, not to prepare herself for death but to give birth to a child that she claimed had been legally conceived.

Following standard procedure in cases in which a woman "pleaded her belly," the court appointed a panel of two male midwives and twelve "discreet matrons" to examine Spooner. They were charged with determining not only whether Spooner was pregnant but whether she was "quick" with child. It was a fine distinction but an important one. Quickening was the coming to life of the fetus, the point at which church authorities recognized it as a living being which it would be sinful to destroy. That crucial moment was thought to occur at about thirty to forty days for female fetuses, eighty to ninety days for males. Before quickening, the fetus was only a lump of protoplasm. Consequently, no church (not even the Catholic Church) objected to aborting a fetus before it quickened or to hanging a woman in the early weeks of pregnancy. In the eyes of the law, it was no crime to kill a child before its birth; only a child fully born into the world, separated completely from its mother, qualified as a person who could be murdered. But once a fetus had quickened it was supposed to have a soul; to kill it was to commit, if not a crime, at least a terrible sin.

In Spooner's case the distinction seemed moot; the examining jury found that she was not with child. The court wrote her off as a conniving woman, looking for a way out. Even when the male midwives and one matron reported that they had changed their opinion after a second examination, the judge ruled that she should die. She did, but when they cut her down, and in keeping with her last request performed an autopsy, they found a five-month fetus, male, perfectly formed.

Then, as the news passed among the thousands who had crowded to the execution, people "understood" the terrible thunderstorm that had attended it, the worst in living memory. Chandler described that "awful half hour":

> The loud shouts of the officers, amidst a crowd of five thousand people, to "make way, make way!" the horses pressing upon those in front; the shrieks of women in the tumult and confusion; the malefactors slowly advancing to the fatal tree, preceeded by the dismal coffins; the fierce coruscations of lightning athwart the darkened horizon, quickly followed by loud peals of thunder, conspired together and produced a dreadful scene of horror. It seemed as if the Author of nature had added such terrors to the punishment of the criminals as might soften the stoutest hearts of the most obdurate and abandoned.

Spooner, through it all, was calm though exceedingly feeble. Unable to walk, she was carried to her execution in a chaise, bowing graciously to old acquaintances who came to see her hanged. When she was told to ascend the gallows, she crawled up on her hands and knees. Not once did she ask for favor or quarter or the good wishes of any person, and her apparent contempt for public opinion made her all the more despicable in the eyes of her fellow citizens. Yet Chandler reported that when the fact of her pregnancy was made known "the terror, which her punishment was intended to produce, was neutralized by pity for her sufferings. Her appearance was so calm, and her end so peaceful, that it was forgotten how deeply her hands were stained with blood. The tragedy was long recited around the hearths of those who saw her die, and the obdurate wickedness of the heroine was almost disregarded in the admiration excited for her beauty, her energy, and her fortitude." The execution of Bathsheba Spooner was a public trauma. Twenty-eight women had been executed in Massachusetts before her, but more than half a century would elapse before another jury summoned the hardihood to convict a Massachusetts woman of murder—and only after the compulsory death penalty was replaced by the option of a prison term.

Juries that would not hang women for murder would not hang them for infanticide, a form of killing that came to seem not *more* serious but far *less* serious than the murder of an adult. Among the lower classes infanticide was considered a necessary evil, while within certain high-ranking circles it became merely the unfortunate sequel to a sexual peccadillo. Lawyers in kid gloves handled "everything" for women of high rank; courts did not require the women to appear, and newspapers did not print their names. During the early years of the new nation the change in attitude was completed. In 1837 the Edgefield, South Carolina, *Advertiser,* reporting a case of infanticide, commented: "The female is said to have previously sustained an excellent character, and her name is withheld to avoid adding a pang to the already lacerated feelings of her unhappy relatives, many of whom are very respectable."

No longer a responsible individual, possessed of civil rights and accountable legally and morally for her offenses and her soul, "the female" became a nonentity, a mere appendage of the father or husband whose name she bore, a name that had to be protected at all costs. The lady had arrived.

TWO

DOMESTIC ATROCITY

1.

Some time after the Revolutionary War American "ladies" and men stopped speaking to each other. Everyone noticed the odd silence, and European visitors remarked again and again on this conspicuous void at the heart of American society. One could always spot the foreign men at a party, they said, because they alone spoke to the married women. Except for these free agents, the men at any gathering clustered in conversation on one side of the room, the women sat in silent ranks on the other. In the 1820s, Frances Trollope noted the separation of the sexes at "supremely dull" evening parties in Cincinnati: "The gentlemen spit, talk of elections and the price of produce, and spit again. The ladies look at each other's dresses till they know every pin by heart." Wherever she traveled Trollope was struck by "this feature of American manners." "The women invariably herd together at one part of the room, and the men at the other," she wrote; and often at private balls "the gentlemen sat down to supper in one room, while the ladies took theirs, standing, in another. . . . Whatever may be the talents of the persons who meet together in society," she concluded, "the very shape, form, and arrangement of the meeting is sufficient to paralyze conversation." It was almost as if the two sexes had drawn sides, preparing for a competition or a war.

According to Englishman Edward Kendall, a careful and amused observer, the "separation of the sexes prevail[ed], in New England, through all the intercourse of society." Ladies were relegated to one side of the church and one tier of the theater; and they were banned altogether from levees given in honor of their own weddings. In New York City it was not "the fashion to invite the fairer part of creation" to dinner parties. Urbane Thomas Hamilton was surprised that he rarely met any ladies "on such occasions, except those belonging to the family of the host"—and even they were removed, like the dirty dishes, before the claret and Madeira. In Boston, where it was "still less the fashion, than at New York, to enliven the dinner-table with their presence," Hamilton saw almost no women at all. From Cincinnati, Trollope reported that on the rare occasions when men and women dined together, the men sat at one end of the table and the ladies at the other; and unless "several foreigners" were present, they did not converse.

Even more commonly, among classes that could not afford to employ servants, women were suffered to be present only to serve. Kendall reported a fact that seemed to him "ludicrous": that no man, at home or away, would willingly wait upon himself. "The sturdiest and grimmest wayfarer at the poorest inn," he said, "is . . . waited upon like a bashaw, but always by a female hand. . . . If he asks for breakfast or *supper*, it is not sufficient to place all the long list of requisite articles upon the table, but a female must attend him through his meal, to pour out his tea or coffee, and put milk and sugar into it. She must also cut him a piece of apple-pie, to eat after his tea—put it upon his plate—and, in short, do every thing but eat it."

It was the "want of [such] good female attendants, and of proper servants," said visitor Henry Duhring, that increased the "household duties" of American ladies. "Young women of the respectable families . . . ," reported another visitor, Captain J. E. Alexander, "were all actively employed in domestic occupations, for the want of good servants . . . in America imposes increased household-duties on the mistresses of families and their daughters of all classes." In short, women in every class seldom ventured out because they had to remain at home to attend the men of their own family—even when those men, in the company of other men, were elsewhere. And men of every social class were spending less and less time at home as the industrial revolution shook society like an earthquake and abruptly sundered the workplace from the private house.

Men went to factories, offices, countinghouses fourteen hours a day, and as their anxieties mounted they went more often to taverns, giving America international notoriety as a nation of tobacco-spitting drunkards. Men hustled to the marketplace, redoubling cities almost overnight. In 1800 there were only five cities of more than 10,000 people; by mid-century there were seven cities of more than *100,000* people. In 1800 only about 4 percent of the 5,300,000 Americans lived in cities; by 1840 the total population had more than tripled, and at least 11 percent of the people lived in cities—thousands of them in the filthy New York City slums that shocked visitor Charles Dickens. Yet more and more men fled the jammed cities and the overcrowded Eastern Seaboard to go west. In some eastern states a third of the people packed up and headed out. Many family groups found their way to Ohio and beyond, but most of the people venturing west were lone men who left behind them a surplus of women with whom nobody wanted to dine.

Men had to be out and about for they lived in times of staggering changes: political revolution, industrial revolution, the transportation revolution, the rise of business and the middle class, the growth of party politics and Jacksonian democracy, international war and bank war, depression and labor agitation, urbanization and western expansion, the rise of reformist religion, and for the first time in the history of the world the widespread distribution of good, cheap clocks.

And women? Women had to stay at home, for the home—as men began to take pains to explain—was woman's proper "sphere," domesticity her very reason for being. The popular marriage counselor William Alcott heartily advised that "young women should love domestic life, and the care and society of the young, because it is, without doubt, the intention of Divine Providence that they should do so." Since the "true sphere of women has been placed by Providence in their home," argued Henry Duhring, ". . . where, then, may women expect to feel the greatest enjoyments, or to meet with that degree of happiness which they are capable of, but in their home, in the circle of their parents or of their offspring, in the affectionate society of their husbands, and in all those tender cares which are the necessary consequences thereof?"

Woman's sphere and its intrinsic rewards were to be endlessly touted throughout the nineteenth century, yet it was clear to America's early visitors that the wife who remained in her sphere would enjoy precious little of the affectionate society of her husband. Trollope described in detail the innocuous day of "a Philadelphian lady of the first class": in the morning she makes pastry, in the afternoon she makes penwipes for charity with some ladies of the Dorcas society, and in the evening she "receives at tea a young missionary and three members of the Dorcas society." She sees her husband at the breakfast table where he reads the newspaper and again at dinner when he comes in, "shakes hands with her, spits, and dines" hurriedly, reads the paper, and goes out to a card game. In New York Harriet Martineau was told of the "enviable lives" of ladies whose husbands worked to exhaustion to support them in grand style; but it appeared to Martineau "that if the ladies prefer their husbands' society to that of morning visitors and milliners, they are quite as much to be pitied as their husbands."

Society ladies were not the only women abandoned in their sphere. In the Indiana wilderness, Morris Birkbeck came upon a "neat, respectable-looking female" spinning outside her cabin. Her husband was away on business for "some weeks," and since she had no family or companion, she was "quite overcome with '*lone*'" and urged Birkbeck to "sit awhile." He reported that "her husband was kind and good to her, and never left her without necessity, but a true lover of bear hunting. . . ." Captain Alexander, too, pitied the many women he saw in the West who were married to "incorrigible rovers" urged on by the "mad spirit of speculation." Although these women were "generally silent," he said, they "occasionally gave vent to complaints of want of society [and] said they felt deeply the melancholy occasioned by the dark woods around them." Anna Howard Shaw, sent in 1859 with four sisters and brothers and their sickly mother to settle a claim in the Michigan wilderness—while her father remained in Massachusetts for almost two years—concluded that her father "like most men" should never have married. And one woman in Wisconsin, with some of her children, starved to death while her husband went fishing.

In every class, the spheres of women and men became more and more rigidly divided. One writer observed that the points of contact between women and men were so few that if a man married a woman with "tastes, disposition, and character essentially different from his . . . he might become the father of a large family and die without discovering his mistake."

It was commonplace to excuse men for their neglect on the grounds that they were busy making money with which to support and protect their wives and children. Yet foreign visitors unanimously agreed that his family was the least of the American man's concerns and that greed and rapacity were his most common traits. Americans could not deny it. Henry Adams admitted that the American man "sacrificed wife and child to his greed for gain, that the dollar was his god, and a sordid avarice his demon." Author Thomas Nichols agreed that "the real work of America is to make money for the sake of making it," and explained the American's pervasive habit of mind: "Everything, whether for sale or not, has a money value. Money is the habitual measure of all things. I believe the American husband unconsciously values his wife in the Federal currency. . . ." Americans took umbrage at Talleyrand's remark that the average American would sell his favorite dog; but men bargained to buy wives, and in some cases, sold them.

Women, then, were not so much the *reason* for men's work as the *excuse* for it. They were also intended to be part of the reward. Duhring approvingly quoted an opinion of Oliver Goldsmith: "Women are not naturally formed for great cares themselves, but to soften ours. Their tenderness is the proper reward for the dangers we undergo for their preservation; and the ease and cheerfulness of their conversation, our desirable retreat from the fatigues of intense application." Yet American men seemed to resort less and less to that "desirable retreat." Instead, they resorted to their clubs, to the taverns, to the homes of their friends—anyplace where they could be in the company of other men. When Frances Trollope observed once again the "very singular, but eminently characteristic" practice of seating the gentlemen at supper in a private room while the ladies were left standing in the ballroom, she asked the reason for it and was told by everyone she asked that "the gentlemen liked it better."

It is not surprising then that some women came to believe that woman's sphere had been set aside not by Providence but by the gentlemen themselves. Harriet Martineau granted that God had appointed a "sphere of woman," but it was "bounded by the powers which he . . . bestowed"; and no one could say what those powers might be until women were given a chance to test them. But there was another more popular and "widely different" conception of the sphere of woman, she said. "The narrow, and, to the ruling party, the more convenient notion is that sphere appointed by men, and bounded by their ideas of propriety," and from that notion, "any and every woman may fairly dissent."

Sarah Grimké dissented on behalf of American women, denouncing "those who, having long held the reins of *usurped* authority, are unwilling to permit us to fill that sphere which God created us to move in, and who have entered into league to crush the immortal mind of woman." For their part, the "ruling party" or "those who held the reins" were stuck, to their embarrassment, with the doctrine of natural rights on which the nation had been founded; and they were harassed by the circulation of a little English book—Mary Wollstone-craft's *A Vindication of the Rights of Woman*—which suggested by its very title that the doctrine applied with equal force to women. That, of course, was out of the question. But if women were to have different and fewer rights than those men enjoyed, it must be because their God-given natures—the powers which *he* bestowed—were fundamentally different. To set aside the "vain question of equality" the "ruling party" insisted more and more loudly upon those differences that led to woman's "most happy inequality."

Martineau noticed it at once. It was a "prevalent persuasion," she said, "that there are virtues which are peculiarly masculine, and others which are peculiarly feminine. . . . It is not only that masculine and feminine employments are supposed to be properly different. . . . But it is actually supposed that what are called the hardy virtues are more appropriate to men, and the gentler to women." Duhring listed the manly virtues so useful in the "common daily struggles" in the marketplace: "knowledge, a penetration of judgment, a firmness of mind, a strength and even a boldness of character." These virtues, he insisted, are "not combined, in the same degree at least, with those charming qualities, so sweet, so attractive, nay, so irresistible, in women." Since the masculine and feminine virtues were so very different, it followed that women, for their own good, had better stay at home.

The thoroughly American author James Fenimore Cooper agreed that there was "something repugnant to the delicacy of American ideas in permitting a lady to come, in any manner in contact with the world." Luckily, as the century progressed, author Albert Mathews could assure his readers that the trend was toward greater divergence of the "discriminable" characteristics of the sexes. "As barbarism recedes," he wrote, "and educational refinement advances, the more man and woman are found to differ in essentials."

When Frances Trollope visited New York, she went to church one bright Sunday and found it stuffy and filled with women. The following Sunday she ferried across the Hudson to stroll in a beautiful wooded park overlooking the river at Hoboken. There she saw thousands of people scattered throughout the park—almost all of them men. The women were again at church. "It is impossible," commented Trollope, "not to feel . . . that the thousands of well-dressed men you see enjoying themselves" in the gardens of Hoboken "have made over the thousands of well-dressed women you saw exhibited" in the churches of New York "into the hands of the priests." She speculated that ministers held the devotion of women because "it is from the clergy only that the women of America receive the sort of attention which is so dearly valued by every female heart throughout the world." Together the ministers and the dutiful women upheld for the nation those moral standards which the men who wrestled in the marketplace disregarded. Ladies prayed. Men got and spent.

With the definition of different virtues, immiscible natures, distinct spheres, and separate social functions, the break between the sexes in America was complete. No wonder, then, that the ladies returning from church had nothing to say to the men who had spent another long busy day in the countinghouse or the tavern or the gardens of Hoboken.

Still, many girls dwindled into wives—often before they could fairly be called women. Girls usually married at fifteen or sixteen, mothers of eighteen were a common sight, and a bride of thirteen was not a rarity. Captain Marryat claimed that girls of the upper classes might "be said to throw down their dolls that they may nurse their children." Frances Wright complained that "laughing maidens" quickly were "metamorphosed" into wives and mothers, and the metamorphosis was not altogether pleasing. It startled Swedish Baron Klinkowström. The married woman's life was so "confined and restricted" to household duties, he wrote, that "after marriage the friendliest girl becomes silent and reserved." The "gay, lovable, free spirit" of the charming American girl "disappears completely when she marries." Fanny Kemble agreed that "married women are either house-drudges and nursery-maids, or, if they appear in society, comparative cyphers."

With her spirit went her looks. Wright noticed that the beauty of

American women was "on the wane at five and twenty." Nothing could be prettier to Thomas Hamilton than a "smiling damsel of New York" at seventeen, but "at twenty-two," he remarked, "the same damsel, metamorphosed into a matron, has lost a good deal of her attraction." Among the working class, hardships were greater; and Trollope reported that it was "rare to see a woman in this station who . . . reached the age of thirty, without losing every trace of youth and beauty." She repeatedly mistook young mothers for the grandmothers of their own children. Many observers blamed the rapid decline of American women on the climate, but others knew that women were overburdened with the "wifely and motherly occupation" that had become their "sole business."

With overwork and too much childbearing came bad health. Marriage "expert" and "physiologist" William Alcott noted the "undeniable fact" that even "in the very healthiest parts" of New England "nearly every adult female is more or less diseased." Catherine Beecher conducted a nationwide survey of the health of married women and found almost none in sound condition, while author Abba Woolson sniffed that the most energetic women of her day could scarcely "vibrate about the piazzas." Relatively robust visiting Englishwomen such as Harriet Martineau complained that married women were shut up in their houses—overheated by anthracite coal—and assigned tedious chores that involved no real physical exercise. Their idea of a healthful outing, she jeered, was a ride in a sleigh, seated with their feet on hot bricks while their faces were frostbitten and their ears assailed by rackety jingle bells. Curvature of the spine became an increasingly common female problem; and tight corseting caused permanently bent and broken ribs, cramped breathing, and a variety of "female" complaints. Fanny Kemble attributed women's ill health to "tight-lacing, want of exercise, and a perpetual inhaling of over-heated atmosphere," but plain-speaking Abba Woolson exonerated both the "abused climate" and "manifest overwork"; women's prevalent ill health, she said, was caused by the "state of public opinion." To be ladylike in America was "to be lifeless, inane, and dawdling."

There were psychological symptoms too—particularly the "languor" and "lassitude" which most foreign travelers noticed. Martineau called it "vacuity of mind" and charged that it led to widespread alcoholism among women, particularly of the upper classes. And that secret drinking, she argued, was a symptom of more serious social ills. To her it suggested "wide and deep subjects of investigation" because "if women, in a region professing religion more strenuously than any other, living in the deepest external peace, surrounded by prosperity, and outwardly honoured more conspicuously than in any other country, can ever so far cast off self-restraint, shame, domestic affection, and the deep prejudices of education, as to plunge into the living hell of intemperance, there must be something fearfully wrong in their position."

In exchange for their cloistered lives and hard work, women were accorded an exaggerated deference in *some* carefully delineated public situations. It was customary during travel, for example, for men to give up the best seats in coaches, trains, and steamboats to the ladies, a consideration which Martineau angrily denounced as "greater than is rational, or good for either party," particularly the ladies who were encouraged to behave like "spoiled children." Sarah Grimké also protested woman's "being treated like a spoiled child" in the coaches; and Captain Hall complained that on some trips the gentlemen passengers rearranged themselves so often for the comfort of a lady that he could have reached his destination faster on foot. American Thomas Nichols boasted loudly that "a lone woman, old or young, pretty or ugly, may travel from one end of America to the other, finding kindness, civility, and help from every man she meets." Martineau recognized this "indulgence" for what it was: merely "a substitute for justice."

In any case, married women "buried to the world" were unlikely to travel. They were far more likely to stay at home, maintaining "woman's sphere" in the houses of men who were increasingly described by foreign visitors as "cold, stern, unkind," vain, harsh, despotic, and tyrannical. By 1845 when Tocqueville observed American life, the two spheres of women and men appeared to be completely separate:

> In no country has such constant care been taken as in America to trace two clearly distinct lines of action for the two sexes, and to make them keep pace one with the other, but in two pathways which are always different. American women never manage the outward concerns of the family, or conduct a business, or take a part in political life; nor are they, on the other hand, ever compelled to perform the rough labor of the fields, or to make any of those laborious exertions which demand the exertion of physical strength. No families are so poor as to form an exception to this rule. If on the one hand an American woman cannot escape from the quiet circle of domestic employments, on the other hand she is never forced to go beyond it.

But the lines between the sexes were not quite so clearly drawn as they were made out to be, for many women did not marry. And thousands, both single and married, went to work. When the first yarn mill opened in Massachusetts in 1793, women who had been spinsters at home became factory workers. (In the textile industry women workers always outnumbered men.) As men "professionalized" many occupations, they arbitrarily barred women from work in health care, business, and the ministry that they had done before the Revolution; but women continued to work as teachers, seamstresses, and servants. And on the western frontier and in the slave states, both free and enslaved women did farm labor. Jane Swisshelm, publisher of the *St. Cloud Visiter*, noted that farm women routinely would "plough, harrow, reap, dig, make hay, rake, bind grain, thrash, chop wood . . . ," and "after working in the fields until meal time, come home, cook, milk and churn, while the men lounge around and rest." Millions of women, she said, were "condemned to the most menial drudgery, such as men would scorn to engage in, and that for one-fourth wages." This large group of working women was ignored by all the observers who insisted that American women were "never forced" beyond the confines of home. Timothy Dwight, usually a keen social observer, wrote in 1821–22 that "the employments of the women of New-England are wholly domestic. The business, which is abroad, is all performed by men, even in the humblest spheres of life." At that time, *thousands* of women were working in new textile mills, including many married women who worked under assumed names to prevent intemperate husbands seizing their wages. In fact, the economy of Dwight's native state of Massachusetts was rapidly coming to depend upon the factory labor of "surplus" women and girls.

Yet Dwight's false notion was so entrenched that facts couldn't budge it; for apparently in his eyes women were women only when they appeared in their separate sphere. Martineau observed that an American woman who had no "wifely and motherly occupation" had "nothing." Popular American writer Lydia Sigourney maintained that a mother held "a higher place in the scale of being" than a mere woman. By mid-century a Philadelphia newspaper could write: "A woman is nobody. A wife is everything." In the public mind, then, women were effectively separated into two classes: those who married and bore children, and those who worked and consequently were not really women at all.

The married woman's "quiet circle of domestic employments"

consisted mainly of the same hard and tedious work she had always done. While spinning and weaving moved to factories in the early decades of the nineteenth century, women at home continued to prepare and preserve food, make and repair clothing and linens, nurse the sick, mind the children, and—endlessly—clean. Until late in the century, simply doing the laundry—without running water or electricity—usually exhausted two full days.

It is no wonder that the dozens of volumes of advice to young ladies and wives and mothers emphasized the same topics: industry, order, punctuality, method, self-government, early rising, and—in the face of it all—inveterate cheerfulness. Young girls who might otherwise have entered domestic service took higher paying factory jobs instead, and left more and more wives to do the housework themselves. They in turn enlisted the help of their daughters, ostensibly to train them for their own future duties as wives. The advice books all agreed that young girls should be given some regular household responsibilities by the age of nine or ten, and that by age twelve "girls should begin to take turns in superintending the household—keeping account of weekly expenses,—making pudding, pies, cake, &c." To a large extent, then, the position of women and girls worsened in the early nineteenth century because the work of most of them did *not* change at a time when everything else was changing very rapidly.

Those other changes also made the position of women *appear* worse by throwing it into high relief. With industrialization men's labor became more specialized and varied. Women's work was still the same old thing. (At the end of the nineteenth century, economist Charlotte Perkins Gilman complained that housework was the only job that had not been modernized.) Increasingly men's labor was regulated by the time clock of industrial capitalism, but women's work remained irregular, seasonal, task-oriented, and never-ending. The country moved to a market economy with cash as the medium of exchange, but women, whose "domestic employments" were not defined as labor deserving pay, came up empty-handed and dependent.

That dependent state was further enforced by devastating changes in the legal system, made just after the Revolution under the influence of William Blackstone's new and bestselling *Commentaries on the Laws of England*. Generations of self-taught "Blackstone lawyers" dictated American jurisprudence throughout the nineteenth century; and they were all just as ignorant as Blackstone was of the chancery law system that had long tempered the inequities of Blackstone's beloved Common Law in both England and the American colonies. Under the old doctrine of the *femme covert*, which Blackstone almost single-handedly revived, married women legally died; they lost their property rights, their rights to contract and sue, and even the right to custody of their own children and possession of their own bodies. At the same time, the states, one by one, acted to correct an "oversight" in their constitutions; in 1798 New York inserted the word *male* in the section dealing with suffrage. New Jersey, in 1844, became the last state to add the qualifying *male* to *citizen*, and women who had been voting all along could not vote anymore. In addition, new systems of licensing and accrediting which governed entrance to schools, apprenticeships, and professions, hemmed women in their own sphere. Thus, the law and such quasi-legal arrangements did not simply accede to popular prejudice against women but became positive and deliberate instruments of constraint. After studying the law, Sarah Grimké concluded: "That the laws which have generally been adopted in the United States, for the government of women, have been framed almost entirely for the exclusive benefit of men and with a design to oppress women . . . is too manifest to be denied."

There were only two alternatives for women. Many acquiesced. Lydia Sigourney preached the popular wisdom that "the province of our sex, though subordinate, is one of peculiar privilege"; and counseled "the duty of submission, imposed both by the nature of our station and the ordinances of God. . . ." Tocqueville reported, in fact, that women "attach a sort of pride to the voluntary surrender of their own will, and make it their boast to bend themselves to the yoke, not to shake it off. Such at least," he added, "is the feeling expressed by the most virtuous of their sex; the others are silent." But Tocqueville—like Timothy Dwight—missed something; for only three years later, in 1848, those other "silent" ones issued their Declaration of Sentiments at Seneca Falls. From the early warnings of Abigail Adams and Judith Sargent Murray, some women had not been silent. Temperance workers protested the economic dependence that made married women subject to drunken husbands. Organizations of women workers sought respect and higher wages for women's labor. Women's voluntary associations tried to help the poor and "save" prostitutes. Antislavery leaders such as the Grimké sisters preached the rights of women as well, warning men to "take their feet from off our necks." And before mid-century, women came together in an organized national movement not just for suffrage but for a broad program of women's rights.

That sort of thing makes men nervous. When they could not persuade women to give up their own interests—as women abolitionists were convinced to put the slave's cause ahead of their own—men coerced women by force or ridicule. It is impossible to determine the extent to which women in the nineteenth century were subdued by physical force, but both Margaret Fuller and Elizabeth Cady Stanton thought that wife-beating was widespread. Emily Collins reported the case of a Methodist class leader and "worthy citizen" who regularly beat his wife, the mother of seven children, with a horsewhip "to keep her in subjection." Collins noted that "a husband's supremacy was often enforced in the rural districts by corporeal chastisement, and it was considered by most people as quite right and proper." On the basis of her work among the poor, Sarah Grimké charged that "brute force, the law of violence, rules to a great extent in the poor man's domicil." And indeed the law authorized husbands "to restrain a wife of her liberty" and to administer "moderate correction" in any case of "misbehavior." Wife murder became commonplace. One murderer, Guy Clark, of Ithaca, New York, hanged for beating his wife to death, died denouncing Frances Wright. To her "sentiments" on women's rights, which his wife "in a great degree embraced," Clark "attributed the cause of his raising his hand against [his wife], which resulted in bringing them both to a premature grave." New cases of wife murder appeared in the newspapers every week. Yet it was not until 1871 that Massachusetts courts ruled that a man had no right to beat his wife, and in the event of her death, might be charged with "manslaughter at least." And not until 1879 did the court rule that a verdict of murder in the first degree could be found against a man who had killed his wife by "beating, stamping and jumping upon her person, and kicking her upon vital portions of her prostrate body . . . at intervals during the day. . . ."

While men beat women at home, they ridiculed them in public. The jokes aimed at temperance women and "bloomer-girl" suffragists persist to our own day. They struck not just at avowed feminists, but at any woman who stepped out of her "wifely occupation." An 1860 cartoon in *Vanity Fair* depicted women salesclerks as "counter jumpers" in short hair and mustaches. And in 1866 a cartoon in *Yankee Notions* pictured a bestselling novelist "engaged in writing her last new sensational novel" while impatiently waving away a husband who holds a squalling baby, and ignoring three other screaming children. William Lloyd Garrison attributed this ridicule and derision of the women's rights movement not to "ignorance" but to "the natural outbreak of tyranny.... It is because the tyrants and usurpers are alarmed," he said. "They have been and are called to judgment, and they dread the examination and exposure of their position and character."

If men feared these women who refused to stay in their assigned sphere, they had as much to fear from the women who stayed at home. Those apparently domesticated women, deprived of all legal and political rights, were far more likely to resort to violence—and men *knew* it. Wives might at least fight back. In Lawrence, Massachusetts, Patrick Doherty's wife pulled out a pistol to stop him from beating her with a stick; he swung anyway and hit the gun, which went off and killed him. Or women might—as perhaps Mrs. Doherty actually did—take the offensive in the domestic battle. In Massachusetts in 1857, during debate over a legislative bill to grant a larger share of a man's estate to his surviving widow, an opposing senator argued that "wives were already too much disposed to rid themselves of their husbands." Citing several cases of women who allegedly murdered their husbands to get their property, he argued that increasing the widow's portion would only whet the wife's murderous inclinations. In the same year, in a remarkable sermon in defense of slavery, an Alabama minister described the typical wife's position: analogous to a slave's and, like it, ordained by God.

> Your service is very, very, very often involuntary from the first, and, if voluntary at first becomes hopeless necessity afterwards.... the husband may not ... love you. He may rule you with the rod of iron. What can you do? Be divorced? God forbid it, save for crime. Will you say that you are free, that you will go where you please, do as you please? Why ye dear wives, your husbands may forbid. And listen, you cannot leave New York, ... not leave your parlor, nor your bedchamber, nor your couch, if your husband commands you to stay there. What can you do? Will you run away with your stick and your bundle? He can advertise you! What can you do? You can, and I fear some of you do, wish him, from the bottom of your hearts at the bottom of the Hudson.

Bathsheba Spooner, with the help of her friends, had wished her husband to the bottom of the well. But there were other, more subtle ways of shaking off the yoke, ways more appropriate to woman's domestic sphere. Woman was thought to be "fitted by nature to cheer the afflicted, elevate the depressed, minister to the wants of the feeble and diseased...." For the wife whose duty it was to cook the meals and nurse the ailing, what could be simpler than poison? First one case and then another was reported. As agitation for women's rights increased, men (and antifeminist women) shrilled that the traditional marriage relationship, established by God, would be destroyed. Women would no longer respect, serve, and obey their husbands. They might even turn against them, as indeed it seemed some women were doing in a direct, personal, sneaky, and lethal way. The rights of woman were at issue, but the fear of woman was never far from the surface of any debate. The poisoning wife became the specter of the century—the witch who lurked in woman's sphere and haunted the minds of men.

2.

Lucretia Chapman, at thirty-five, was a tall, strong, rather plain woman and a very hard worker. She started teaching school at seventeen, and after marrying William Chapman in 1818, when she was twenty-two, she joined him in running a boarding school in Andalusia, Pennsylvania, which specialized in correcting speech defects. Neighbors and friends said the marriage was happy enough, but William Chapman—short, fat, and increasingly feeble—left more and more of the work to his younger wife. She managed the school and did the teaching, looked after the boarders, raised five children of her own, directed the hired help, and supervised all the workings—indoors and out—of household and school. It was a taxing life, but it began to change on May 19, 1831, when a stranger appeared at the Chapmans' door, penniless, asking to be accommodated for the night. Only five feet five, he was not tall; but he was dark and handsome and young—just twenty-two—and possessed of a romantic name: Don Lino Amalia Espos y Mina. Lucretia Chapman told him he could stay.

He was noble, highly connected, and fabulously rich—or so he said. He had been sent abroad for "finishing" by his grandfather, a wealthy Mexican nobleman who owned a silver mine. But as Espos y Mina's bad luck would have it, the noted English doctor with whom he was traveling suddenly died in a Parisian church, and the French authorities confiscated Mina's diamond-lined trunk along with the doctor's. Sympathetic friends (female) advanced Mina his passage to

America, where he hoped to meet a rich uncle, but when he arrived (wouldn't you know) the uncle had returned to Mexico. If only Mina could contact his grandfather (the silver-mine owner) or his mother in Mexico City (also fabulously wealthy) or his father (who just happened to be the governor of California), all would be well. Mr. and Mrs. Chapman, who were not above hoping for a return on a little Christian charity, assured the poor fellow of a temporary home. Within a week, both Lucretia and William Chapman wrote to the parents of their new lodger, expressing joy at having the pleasure of assisting him. In the furor of the weeks that followed, no one seemed to notice that the letters were never answered.

Peculiar problems arose because of Mina's "race." The Chapmans' hired woman Ellen Shaw didn't like "the Spanish" who—she thought—might do almost anything. She warned Lucretia Chapman about Mina, and in so doing she eliminated herself as a confidante and friend; and from that moment Ellen Shaw, who quit her job when she saw them "kissing," could be only what she finally proved: the star witness for the prosecution. And when it all came out in court, a witness for the defense would be chivalrous Colonel Cuesta, the Mexican consul to Philadelphia, a man too well bred to communicate to the lady, Lucretia Chapman, the conclusion he had reached after a few minutes' talk with Mina: the conclusion that Mina was a fake.

To Lucretia Chapman he was an exotic young man; she wrote his mother of her intention to "adopt" him as her own son. (He supposedly was, after all, heir to a silver mine.) Lucretia and Mina rode out in the buggy together, and coming home after dark, he laid his head in her lap and crooned love songs. Soon Mina was invited to stay on at the Chapmans'—for three years. He would study English with Lucretia. Although the $6,000 fee agreed upon was not due until Mina completed his studies, he and Lucretia fell to work at once. More and more often they were closeted together in the parlor with the English lessons or in Mina's room on the third floor, where he was frequently confined with mysterious "fits" that required the ministrations of Lucretia. Sometimes they went to Philadelphia together, and once they stayed away for three days. Mr. Chapman didn't like that a bit, but still—perhaps remembering the silver mine—he gave Mina a letter of credit to his tailor and sent them off to town again.

On one of those trips, less than a month after his arrival, Mina stopped at a drugstore to get the Spanish-speaking clerk to write a letter for him. (According to the Mexican consul, the uneducated Mina himself wrote Spanish according to no known system.) He came away with a letter directed to Mr. Chapman thanking him for his kindness to Señor Espos y Mina and hinting at the tangible forms the gratitude of his family might take. It was signed with the name Cuesta, the Mexican consul. Mina also came away from the drugstore with two ounces of arsenic.

The next day, June 17, William Chapman fell ill after dining heartily on pork and smearcase. When Dr. Phillips heard of his illness and called two days later, Chapman was much better. Phillips ordered that he be given the classic restorative: chicken soup. The next day, Monday, Lucretia Chapman bought a chicken from her neighbor and made soup, which William ate along with some of the chicken on the side. Suddenly he grew worse. Mr. Fanning, an acquaintance who came in to sit with him, offered to fetch a doctor, but Lucretia declined. When Dr. Phillips came round again on Wednesday, he was shocked to find Chapman "*in articulo mortis.*" On Thursday he died; on Friday he was buried; and four days later Mina went to town with Lucretia to order more new clothes. On July 5, 1831, twelve days after William Chapman's death, Mina and Lucretia were secretly married in New York City in a ceremony attested to by a certificate that Mina filled out himself.

That marriage was short and unhappy. On the very day of the wedding, Lucretia set off for Schenectady to fetch her sister, a Mrs. Green, who was to take over the Chapman house in Andalusia while she and her new husband went to Mexico City to claim his birthright. When Lucretia and her sister arrived at the Chapman house, they found some of Mina's friends carting away valuables—right down to the spoons—which they claimed Mina had given them. On July 18, Mina was called to Baltimore to see a sick friend named Casanova who, he said, wanted to give him $45,000. He gave Lucretia a solid-gold antique chain—a family heirloom, he said—and left Andalusia with her horse and wagon and all her money. Soon he sent back word that his wealthy friend had died, leaving him a fortune; but some slight legal technicality prevented his taking possession of the property at once. He wrote next from Washington to say that he was enjoying the company of an old friend—an English duke—and discussing the legal arrangements for his legacy with President Jackson who, incidentally, was eager to meet Mrs. Espos y Mina. The arrangements would take time, he explained; and his amorous letters came less often. Impatient Lucretia, left with only the golden chain, noticed that her neck was turning green.

On July 23 she went to Philadelphia to call upon the Mexican consul and on Mr. Watkinson, the tailor, who told her frankly that they thought Mina was an impostor. At home she ransacked his room and found a bill from a Philadelphia hotel for himself and two "ladies." For three days she was distraught; then she wrote to denounce him and demand the return of her horse and buggy. Even the gold chain, she complained, was phony. That letter never reached Mina. It was claimed by a man Mina had defrauded in Washington, turned over to the Washington police, and sent back to a local Andalusian busybody, Willis Blayney, who took it upon himself to investigate rumors that Lucretia Chapman had been swindled. Formerly Blayney had been a printer and worked for William Chapman; his sister had taught music in the Chapmans' school. But now he was the high constable of Philadelphia. One line at the end of that intercepted letter caught his eye: ". . . no, Lino . . . I do not believe that God will permit either *you or me* to be happy this side of the grave." Blayney took the letter to his superior, William McIlvaine, the recorder of Philadelphia, and in the mayor's absence, temporary head of the police.

Mina returned a few days later to hear Lucretia's accusations in person. He would go away, he said, as she demanded; but first he had one little secret for her ears alone. He whispered. And she took him back, explaining to her sister that he was not, after all, an impostor, but merely a "clever fellow." When Mina set off again supposedly to visit another wealthy friend in Massachusetts, he carried letters of introduction to Lucretia's relatives there, presenting him not as her husband—that was still a secret—but as her protégé.

Meanwhile, Constable Blayney and Mr. McIlvaine made inquiries. On August 28, a month after William Chapman's death, they called on Lucretia, not knowing that she had remarried; they wanted to put some questions to her concerning the man known as Mina. She denied that he was an impostor, denied that he had taken away her furnishings and her silverplate, denied that he had sold her horse and wagon in Baltimore. After her husband's death, she said, Mina went to Baltimore on business, then to Washington, and from there by train to New Orleans, again on business. The officials left after telling Lucretia that no train ran between Washington and New Orleans. A few days later Mina, visiting Lucretia's relatives in Massachusetts, sent her a $1,000 draft against a Philadelphia bank. It was forged. Lucretia went to see a lawyer.

McIlvaine continued to pry. People talked. On September 17 the *National Gazette*, a Philadelphia newspaper with nationwide circulation, hinted that William Chapman might have died of unnatural causes. Lucretia left town. On September 21 the body of William Chapman, three months buried, was exhumed at the order of the county prosecutor. By September 27 the Doylestown (Pennsylvania) *Democrat* reported that "the facts of the poisoning ... are said to be almost positive." And by that time, Don Lino Amalia Espos y Mina was already in the hands of the Boston police, charged with swindling.

During his short visit to Massachusetts he reportedly had married a young woman at Barre, made off with her property, and proceeded to Barnstable, where he passed himself off as *both* the son of a Mexican nobleman and the son of a West Indian planter, temporarily embarrassed by the theft of his pocketbook. With the help of "loans" he made his way to Boston, where he planned to collect from a merchant a $9,000 cash advance drawn against a forged letter of credit, and to marry "a young and respectable female" lured from Barnstable by "the offer of valuable presents." The young lady, who quit her job as a schoolteacher to marry the Mexican grandee, was Lucretia Chapman's niece. But before Mina could carry out his plans he was arrested; and within a few days, he was given into the custody of the diligent Mr. Blayney. Mrs. Chapman, shielded by relatives in western New York State, was harder to find, but Blayney and a $300 reward offered by the governor of Pennsylvania, flushed her out. In late November she was arrested in Erie County, Pennsylvania, and returned to Doylestown under arrest. She and Mina were charged with the arsenic poisoning of William Chapman. Ever resourceful, Mina quickly escaped from jail; but the sheriff caught up with him seven miles from town, brought him back, and chained his left leg to the floor.

The trial, which took place in February 1832, drew excited crowds. On the first day six hundred people packed into the hall, the largest in Doylestown, the county seat; the next day even more people pressed in, and the doors were twice burst open during the proceedings by the crush of people outside. Presiding Judge John Fox had men arrested for trying to climb in the windows. There were more people than had ever been in Doylestown before—and more reporters. The trial excited so much interest, all across the country, that the judge ordered journalists not to publish their accounts until it was over.

Actually, two trials were held, for Lucretia's attorneys moved early and wisely to separate the cases. Together Mina and Lucretia could only be seen as conspirators; separately Lucretia could be presented as a victim. And if she were a victim, then Lucretia deserved not the law's punishment but its protection. George Fitzhugh, the eminent southern sociologist of the time, explained the unwritten social deal: "So long as [woman] is nervous, fickle, capricious, delicate, diffident and dependent, man will worship and adore her. Her weakness is her strength, and her true art is to cultivate and improve that weakness. . . . In truth, woman, like children, has but one right and that is the right to protection." Certainly Lucretia Chapman had been fickle and capricious; and just as certainly her lawyers improved upon her weakness.

She was, they said, essentially a woman of good character, as a stream of witnesses testified; but she had been taken in by the wiles of Mina the swindler. Perhaps she was naïve and rather greedy, but in this she had been guided by her husband, who was similarly gulled. In yielding to Mina's amorous advances, she had been foolish and perhaps even sinful, yet it was in the nature of weak women to fall. She was rash and unwise to marry in haste, yet she had been propelled by her children's need for a provider. Admitting her faults, Lucretia's lawyers argued that she was not a criminal, certainly not a murderer. She was, they said, simply giddy, foolish, stupid, vain, and weak—in short, a normal woman. As such she should be shielded by the law's "chivalry." After all, she had already lost to the base impostor her "horse and carriage, gold and silver watches, breast-pins, finger-rings, medals, musical box, silver bells with whistle and cake basket"—perhaps even her husband.

But had William Chapman in fact been poisoned? That was the great issue of Lucretia's trial, argued at length by expert witnesses whose shaky science was left to the jury's evaluation. Dr. Phillips had thought at the time that Chapman came to his deathbed with cholera morbus. At the trial he agreed with other experts that Chapman suffered arsenic poisoning. Chapman's symptoms—vomiting, intestinal burning, chilled extremities—pointed equally to either diagnosis, so the postmortem examination became the only source of definitive evidence. Unfortunately, that exam was performed hurriedly in the graveyard on a corpse three months buried by two doctors who had never before examined an exhumed body. It was less than thorough, as the inexperienced examiners themselves admitted. They did not examine the heart or even the rectum, although medical opinion agreed that an inflamed rectum infallibly distinguished arsenic poisoning from cholera morbus. Instead, they reburied Chapman as quickly as possible without his stomach, which they sent to a chemist's laboratory. The chemists removed tissue and cooked it and dissolved it and mixed it with reagents—all without positive results, except for one brief burning test during which a beaker accidentally cracked and one chemist smelled the garlicky odor of arsine. He turned to his partner and asked, "Is somebody burning arsenic in here?" Was that enough evidence? The lawyers consulted their volumes of medical jurisprudence and came up at a standoff.

Odd and macabre bits of medical evidence were debated. When opened by the postmortem examiners, Chapman's body cavity smelled like pickled herring. Was that smell characteristic of arsenic poisoning, or might a corpse, for perfectly natural (if unpleasant) reasons, come to smell like a pickled herring? The experts couldn't agree. Chapman's body, at the time of the autopsy, also was remarkably well preserved. Since arsenic was known to be a preservative—even Mina claimed to have bought arsenic for use in taxidermy—could Chapman's condition be attributed to arsenic in his system? The pastor of All-Saints Church was called to attest to the remarkable preservative powers of the sandy soil in his graveyard. Besides, he said, the sexton, in consequence of being reprimanded for digging shallow graves, was digging them deep, and that alone helped to preserve corpses.

The prosecution argued that arsenic preserved the body. The defense argued that an amount of arsenic sufficient to preserve the body would also show up positively in the chemist's tests. The prosecution argued that Chapman might have thrown off the arsenic in the retching fits of his final illness. The defense maintained that negative tests meant no arsenic; no arsenic meant no poisoning. Lacking conclusive physical evidence, attorneys on both sides put to the jurors rhetorical questions that they were hardly equipped to understand. "If the death had been caused by cholera morbus," asked prosecutor Thomas Ross, "would the inflammation have been confined to the stomach and oesophagus? Would there not have been some inflammation in the intestines . . . ?" Who knew? Yet such scientific "fact" was to be determined by consensus of the jury. And in resolving the issue they must have been more confused than edified by the affair of the ducks.

Mr. and Mrs. Boutcher, who lived next door to the Chapmans, kept poultry. From them Lucretia bought the chicken to make the soup prescribed by Dr. Phillips. That soup and the chicken, according to various conflicting testimony at the trial, were carried up to Mr. Chapman either by Lucretia or her daughter Mary and returned to the kitchen either by Lucretia or her younger daughter, also named Lucretia. There the remains sat until the end of the day when a servant threw them into the yard. The next day Mr. Boutcher watched his roving flock of ducks coming home from the Chapmans. They seemed to him to be "worried." One by one, they keeled over. By the end of the day between twenty and thirty ducks had died; four that were too big to get through the fence into the Chapman yard survived. Mr. Boutcher testified that "it is not a common thing for ducks to fall over and die." He believed they had been poisoned.

Again experts could not agree whether the sudden wholesale demise of poultry was a natural event. Various opinions were offered, but by the time defense attorney Brown summed up his case, the topic had become a joke. He claimed to shed "a passing tear of pity" for the "unsuspecting ducklings" whose "rights of sepulture" had been "barbarously invaded" by the prosecution which had dug up the bones and brought them into court for some unexplained reason. Mr. Brown dismissed the whole matter as "quackery," and the jury could scarcely help smiling at his witticism. Still, Mr. Boutcher's ducks, like William Chapman, were suddenly dead—and no one could explain why.

Debated at the same time was the second great issue of the trial: If William Chapman died by poison, had Lucretia Chapman administered it? The prosecution waffled. Initially it fixed on the chicken soup as the vehicle of death for both Chapman and the ducks. Lucretia had prepared it with her own hands and—oddly—carried it to the parlor for "seasoning." Ellen Shaw, who followed her to the parlor, testified that Mina was there and appeared to help. That circumstance seemed damning, especially when the druggist testified to Mina's arsenic purchase of the day before; but the defense produced little Lucretia Chapman who said she had eaten some of the soup with her father and put the rest on the kitchen table, where it stood until late afternoon when the servant, Mary Bantom, threw it out into the yard. Would any woman, however depraved, asked the defense, leave a tureen of poisoned soup within easy reach of her children and servants? Quickly the prosecution produced a new theory—one separate bowl of poisoned soup had been given to Chapman while the soup tureen remained uncontaminated—but there was no bit of evidence to substantiate the hypothetical separate bowl. Suspicion fell upon the chicken itself, but testimony of servants and the child Lucretia—who said she ate the gizzard—was conflicting and inconclusive. In the end even the judge remained puzzled, but in charging the jury he removed the chicken soup (named in the original indictment) from consideration. "Here it has been supposed that the poison was put into the bowl of soup," he said, "but that cannot be. It seems to be impossible that Mrs. Chapman should have put poison into this, to have poisoned her husband with it, and then have placed it on the kitchen table; and suffered it to remain there several hours, exposed to the chance of being eaten by her servants, who dined at the table; or by her own children, whose dining room adjoined the kitchen. If Mr. Chapman was poisoned, as heretofore I have supposed, I look in vain for evidence to show distinctly *how* he was poisoned." At the very end of the trial then, as the judge charged the jury, the two central issues remained murky. Was William Chapman poisoned? And if so, by whom?

Some points were clearer—especially Lucretia's devotion to her young lover. Their letters were read in evidence at the trial. On the night of their wedding, Lucretia wrote to Mina from Albany, where she had stopped on the way to her sister's.

> MY DEAR LENA [*sic*],
>
> Very pleasant are the sensations which vibrate through my soul, when thus addressing you ("My dear Leno,") for the first time to call you *mine*! and till death shall separate us! how pleasing, how delightful! and you, *dearest* Leno, so young, so fond, so noble, and so truly grateful to your Lucretia! my soul would gladly dwell upon *you* till the time for writing would pass away.

Two days later she wrote, "It seems a long time to wait till next Wednesday, before I meet the fond embrace of him who is so dear to me, as is my young General Esposimina." But it was Mina who excelled at romantic composition. On July 25 he wrote to explain why he had to go to Washington and to express his feelings on the occasion:

> When I left Baltimore I really thought that I should lose my senses. My soul poured forth showers of tears. I looked upon the sky that stretched itself over Pennsylvania, & I re-echoed in my heart the sweet name of Lucretia Esposimina. The green fields, the verdant forests, the sweetly singing birds, every thing softened my heart to thoughts of love & I shed tears in torrents. Dear Lucrecia [*sic*], there is neither day nor night of pleasure for me when away from you. I neither eat, drink, or sleep. All is melancholy in my soul. I fear that I shall be hurried to the grave ere I see you & fold you in one long embrace.

There was much more in the same key, so that the translator who wrote the letter appended a note (probably at Mina's dictation) expressing his "hope of one day beholding a lady capable of inspiring such ardent affection." Mina always wrote loftily. He just didn't write often enough to suit Lucretia. By the end of July she had been told that he was an impostor, and when she wrote to charge him with it, she penned that one incriminating sentence: ". . . no, Lino, when I pause for a moment, I am constrained to acknowledge that I do not believe that God will permit either *you or me* to be happy this side of the grave."

The prosecution quoted that line over and over again, and they cited one compelling circumstance: why, when Lucretia knew that Mina was a criminal who had exploited her affections and stolen all her property, when she had denounced him and told him (before witnesses) to leave at once, why, when he whispered a single secret to her, did she change her mind? The prosecution argued that only the guilty secret of homicidal complicity could have bound her to him; and the defense could answer only that the notion was "ridiculous."

Where issues are blurred, attention centers on personality, or to use the nineteenth-century term, *character*. The question becomes: Is the accused the sort of person who could have committed the crimes charged? About Mina there could have been little doubt in the minds of the twelve good men and true. He was too flamboyant, dressed in frock coat and pantaloons and silk stockings with a gold stud in his embroidered shirt front. And he was too nonchalant, feigning indifference and nodding affably to his acquaintances. He aped gentility and mocked it. Here was Colonel Cuesta, a respectable Mexican bureaucrat, to testify that Mina was not the gent he pretended to be. And here was Israel Deacon, keeper of the penitentiary at Philadelphia, to testify that Mina, under the name of Celestine Armentarius (or Celestina Armentirus, alias Amalia Gregorio Zarrico), had been imprisoned there for more than a year, convicted of three charges of larceny for stealing a watch, a musical snuffbox, and some other trinkets from fellow lodgers at a Philadelphia boardinghouse. On the very day of his release he had knocked at the Chapmans' door. Surely Mina seemed a man who could have done—as Ellen Shaw feared—almost anything.

There were two ways of looking at Lucretia Chapman's character and both of them were made necessary by the horror of the crime she was accused of. Murdering one's husband was, as even the defense said over and over again, the single "most horrible and atrocious" crime imaginable. The woman who killed her husband committed the most "unnatural" of crimes: "treason to her husband—to her children—

and to her God." The woman capable of such an offense must be a
monster, a creature unknown to nature; and such indeed was the portrait of Lucretia Chapman drawn by prosecuting attorney Ross. There
was plenty of evidence in the servants' testimony that Lucretia was not
Mr. Ross's idea of a good wife: she told her husband she was ashamed
of him and that she "wished to God he was gone." Once, apparently,
she kicked him; and once—although testimony on this point was long
and conflicting—she told him to help their little daughter make the
bed. Ross argued that a woman who would "compel" a man "to make
the bed in which he sleeps" could only be "actuated" by "feelings of a
savage or a demon." Lucretia Chapman, he said, could not "have exhibited greater cruelty and indignity, . . . more absolute and tyrannical
dominion," if she had been "a household fiend." The prosecutor urged
the jury to convict Lucretia, for crimes such as hers, left unpunished,
"teach the wife in whose bosom the flame of impure passion brightens,
that there is a summary mode by which she can remove the only check
to licentious indulgence, and suggest means and materials for the com-
pletion of the gloomy edifice of crime."

That possibility did not bear thinking about, hinting as it did at
the presence of more—perhaps many—household fiends skulking in
parlors and kitchens, awaiting only the inspiration and the chance to
commit domestic atrocities. The jury could hardly accept the doctrine
of punishment as a deterrent of homicide without acknowledging that
women in large numbers might indeed murder their husbands if not
prevented. Surely it was far more reassuring to see Lucretia Chapman—and women—in a different light.

In fact, argued the defense, the very "malignity of the crime only
renders more improbable its occurrence." How could a crime so
"fiendlike and unnatural," so "deserving of utter abhorrence and exe-
cration," be committed by Lucretia Chapman, who was, after all, "a
female, with whose character we are ever accustomed to associate all
that is lovely in tenderness, affection, and fidelity." Far from being a
fiend, she was simply, as her attorneys presented her, "a woman—hapless, helpless, friendless, and forlorn."

Proof of her womanhood—and of her innocence—was her continuing "natural" love for her children; an unnatural fiend who had
killed her husband would certainly be incapable—by a "rule of human
action"—of loving children. It was true, said Lucretia's attorneys, that
she had been "infatuated"; she had fallen under a "spell that seemed
to have enchained the judgment"—rather like a dozing princess in a

fairy tale or a romantic novel. Lucretia, too, took this view of herself; in a letter from prison to Colonel Cuesta, read at the trial, she referred to Mina as the "cruel spoiler," alluding to the villainous Montraville who led Charlotte Temple, America's favorite literary victim, to disgrace and untimely death.

Surely Lucretia had been disgraced. Adopting the overblown style of Susannah Rowson, the creator of Charlotte Temple, Lucretia put her case in the letter to Cuesta:

> Ah! from what a height have I fallen! But yesterday, I had, and enjoyed all that heart could wish; blest with competence, surrounded with a lovely family, enjoying the society and smiles of a husband I loved: what more could I wish? what more had this world to bestow?
>
> But, alas! the *cruel spoiler* came! and in one hour, all, all is blasted!! All my hopes and prospects are vanished! and, O! my husband, who once would have stepped forth to protect me, and sympathize with me, is now no more! his head lies low under the clods of the valley, unconscious of the sufferings of his family! O! how enviable is his lot to mine! While my bleeding heart is torn with a thousand pangs by the death of the kindest, the best of husbands, as if this was not enough to complete my sufferings, in order to put the finishing stroke to them, and dart the last pang to my already too much agonized bosom, I am charged, am arrested, on the false, the cruel suspicion of "being thought accessary to the death of my husband." Was it not for conscious innocence, and the happiness of my dear babes . . . life would be intolerable. O that Heaven would plead my cause! and though I have acted very foolishly, very imprudently, yet may God in his infinite mercy, restore me again to my bereaved, my distressed little family. . . . I have been infatuated with a mysterious stranger; a base Imposter! I have been decoyed and duped by him; so, that without due consideration of consequences, which might result from such a step, (believing him, alas! to be a grateful friend to my deceased husband, self, and children,) I precipitately married the cruel monster; and plunged myself and fatherless children into irreparable ruin! The remorse, chagrin, and shame I felt, on account of having been so dreadfully duped in my marriage with that accomplished Villian [*sic*], are not to be described; for I very soon learned that he was a vile Imposter!
>
> . . . those who now have no compassion for me, if they but knew the truth of my story, their very souls would weep blood. While I write, my eyes are bathed in tears, and my heart is overflowed with sorrow, occasioned by my unparalleled sufferings! and O! my dear children! what will become of my poor, dear children!! Is there no redress for a heart-broken mother, who would now only wish to live for the sake of her children?

Prosecutor Ross put it less generously. "It is indeed painful," he told the jury, "to behold a woman, who had reached the meridian of life, with a family of young and interesting children around her, all dependant, in some measure, upon the good name of their mother for their future reputation, thus surrendering herself to the vilest excesses of criminal indulgence, and becoming a spectacle so odious and debasing to the moral sense of the community. Her counsel have not dared to excuse, or even palliate, this open and shameless exhibition of vice. . . ."

But there she sat in the courtroom: an ordinary-looking, jowly woman pushing forty—not homely perhaps, but certainly not pretty either. She wore a drab riding habit in cinnamon and black, a close-fitting cap, and a hood. Sometimes during the proceedings, particularly when her husband's last hours were described, she wept quietly into a handkerchief. Sometimes her rather heavy jaw seemed to tremble. But mostly, the newspapers said, "her deportment was calm" and ladylike. Directly behind her (despite the objections of the prosecutors) sat her five children who bore the name that she, through her womanly foolishness, had brought to ruin. The jury stepped out for a decent interval—about two hours—and then returned the verdict: not guilty.

Mina was not so lucky. At his brief trial in April the expert medical testimony was even more confused. The chemist, Dr. Mitchell, admitted that his earlier arsenic tests probably were "worthless" (he had never tested for arsenic before), but subsequent tests had convinced him that arsenic was the cause of death. On the other hand, the attending physician, Dr. Phillips, had decided that Chapman's symptoms were *not*, after all, consistent with arsenic poisoning. The only other new evidence was Mina's own statement, repeated by Constable Blayney, that he had been Lucretia's lover before Chapman's death and that *she* poisoned her husband's soup. In a matter of days he was pronounced guilty of two counts of murder and sentenced to die.

Throughout the trial he "generally displayed levity and indifference," according to the press, but "when the verdict was explained to him by his counsel, he evinced considerable agitation." As Celestino Almentaro, a poor soldier boy, he pleaded for permission to return to his family in Cuba. That didn't work. He asked for a stay of execution to arrange settlement of his "estate" upon a four-year-old daughter in Cuba. He mailed a letter asking for help to his father, a brigadier general in San Salvador. Finally, he "made a confession, fully implicating himself and his accomplice," Mrs. Chapman, now referred to in the press as simply "the woman." He was not a Mexican grandee after all, he confessed. Nor was he the son of a West Indian planter. He was neither Celestino Almentaro nor Lino Amalia Espos y Mina. He was *really*, he wrote, Carolino Estradas De Mina, the son of the military governor of Cuba. There followed another long, picaresque tale of slaves and beautiful maidens (some saved, some ravaged), warfare and pirates, jewels and gold—all in the most excessively inflated prose.

At last his adventures brought him to Philadelphia, where, in all innocence, he said, he was seduced by Mrs. Chapman, alias Miss Wilson, a hardened prostitute and criminal. "Here began the ruin of the unfortunate stranger," he wrote, referring to himself in the third person, "from the moment that he shewed his wealth to the accursed [woman] the foundation of his ruin was laid." It was she, he said, who for vague and contradictory reasons made up his Mexican identity, forged the letters, bought the arsenic, killed her husband by poisoning not his soup but his beer, and finally bribed all the witnesses to testify against Mina.

Mina's confession is a tour de force that marks him as no ordinary con man but a pathological one and—while his brief career lasted—a smart one. His standard gambit of luring women into marriage with the promise of riches, then selling off *their* property (as *any* husband *legally* could do) both exploited and caricatured the venality of American marriage and the dependent position of women. But these social arrangements were supposed to work for the comfort of all "upstanding" men, not the quick advantage of a fast-talking con. In killing William Chapman—or helping to—Mina breached that code and made plain that it was not the foolish wives but the vulnerable husbands who needed "protection" from the wily charlatan and the household fiend he incited. So in the end they hanged the stranger with a rope too short for the purpose; it did not snap his neck but held him kicking and choking a good ten minutes before he strangled. A few women attended the execution at Doylestown—and ten thousand men. Mrs. Chapman (she had resumed her former respectable name) was reported to be at home with her children.

3.

Mina was not the first man punished for a murder which may have been instigated by or committed by a woman. When a man and woman seemed to be accomplices in murder, men found it reassuring to pin the crime on the man and to ignore the woman's motives and her ability to act. Women, dead to the civil law, were in practice dead to the criminal law as well. The case of Ann Baker illustrates the connection. She was tried in Philadelphia in 1816 for second-degree murder, charged as an accessory when Richard Smith, her second husband, shot John Carson, her first husband, in the parlor of *her* house. That Smith had done the shooting was certain; there were several eyewitnesses, and he admitted it. The main issue of the trial was the question of whose wife Ann Baker Carson or Smith was on January 20, 1816, the day of the shooting.

For nine years or more, Ann Carson had been supporting herself and her four children by running a china shop, doing business legally as a *femme sole* (or single woman) during the long absences of her seafaring husband. She paid the rent on the house and shop, transacted all the business, paid all her husband's old debts, and—when she fell into debt herself—served time in jail because as a *femme sole* she could not claim that her husband was responsible. In 1815, having heard that Carson had died at sea, she married Richard Smith; three months later John Carson returned after four years' absence to take possession of his house, goods, chattel, and wife. When he ordered Smith out of the house, Smith shot him. Consequently, the issue at Smith's trial for first-degree murder was whether his marriage to Ann Carson was legal. If it was, then he, as her husband, owned the house and was entitled to defend it; at worst he might be guilty of manslaughter. If Smith's marriage was not legal, then John Carson legally owned his wife's house and was entitled to evict Smith; in that case the shooting would constitute first-degree murder. So the debate centered on which man had the exclusive right to the woman's "person" and to her personal property. The judge instructed the jury that the Smith marriage was not legal; and Smith, found guilty of murder, was sentenced to hang.

Ann Carson had no rights under the civil law to her property, her house, her children. She did not even have the right to choose which of the men would be her husband, for under the law the first husband, returning after a long absence, could decide whether she must still be his wife or not. The woman was a cipher. And so she was at her own trial as an accessory to the murder of John Carson. She apparently had helped Smith get a gun and had arranged several confrontations between the two men, including the fatal one. At that meeting Smith—whom Ann Carson knew to be armed—appeared so crazed when he burst into the room that the terrified servant snatched up a child and ran into the street; yet when John Carson told Smith to leave, Ann Carson told him to stay. The indictment charged that she "feloniously, wilfully, and of her malice aforethought, did incite, instigate, stir up, counsel, direct, advise, command, aid and abet . . . Richard Smith" in "felony and murder." But what reason could Ann Carson possibly have for wishing dead the drunken sailor who had left her penniless and then returned after four years (with $6.80 in his pocket) to possess her? Perhaps it was better not to inquire too closely. The prosecutor announced that he would not urge conviction because he didn't have enough evidence. The judge ordered the jury to acquit her, although he could not help observing that "certainly the prisoner was a bad woman." The whole trial took less than half a day and left Ann Carson with her life and her property.

At Albany, New York, in 1827, Jesse Strang was hanged for shooting John Whipple with a rifle, but the victim's wife, Elsie Whipple, charged as an accessory, was speedily acquitted at the judge's instructions. She had had an affair with Jesse Strang and gave him the money to buy the gun, but the judge found no evidence that she was involved in the killing. In Harpswell, Maine, in 1863, a young man named Thorn was convicted of murdering Elisha Wilson in his bed. Mrs. Wilson, Thorn's lover and accomplice, was not prosecuted. And in Rochester, New York, in 1857, twenty-year-old Sarah Littles escaped murder charges in the death of her estranged husband, Charles, a man described by all as a drunken, blasphemous, unfaithful, syphilitic ne'er-do-well. Sarah, who had been walking out with a new gentleman friend, led her husband to the deserted cliff above the Genesee Falls where the murder took place; afterward she apparently helped push the body over the edge, falling herself and acquiring some telltale injuries in the process; and then she helped carry home and hide her husband's hat and the bloody hammer. With that kind of evidence against her (plus a probably false but alarming rumor of incest), the court couldn't just let her go. She was convicted of second-degree manslaughter and sentenced to seven years in prison. Her brother, ex-convict Marion Stout, who had wielded the hammer, was hanged at Sing Sing, cursing her for "falsehood, contradiction and imbecility."

These cases were signs of things to come. The double standard of "justice," reinforced by the double standard of conventional morality, grew more entrenched as the century wore on. Radical feminists found themselves oddly aligned with conservative legal theoreticians in demanding equal justice, but their reasoned arguments were lost on high-minded and chivalrous patriarchs. Favoritism toward women under the criminal law was the trade-off men made for stripping women of rights under the civil law. Criminal Marion Stout might cry out against inequitable "justice" and find support from Susan B. Anthony, but the lawmakers—patriarchs all—seemed content with the bargain they had made. They rested comfortably in the knowledge that few men of the class that designed the criminal-justice system would ever fall under its wheels.

Always their question was the same: What motive could any woman have for killing her husband? The answer, for the typical nineteenth-century trial lawyer, was hard to come by, for he was doubly deluded. In the first place, the term "motive" was routinely taken to mean "cause." Inquiring into motive, lawyers sought the immediate event that had caused a woman to react by committing murder. Properly understood, however, a motive is not the *cause* of the homicide, but the cause *for the sake of* which the homicide is committed. In other words, a wife does not poison her husband *because* he is drunk, as lawyers would argue; she poisons her husband for the sake of a future life in which she will no longer have to contend with his habitual drunkenness and domination. Motive so conceived was particularly difficult for nineteenth-century lawyers to understand because of their equally mistaken notions about woman's nature; they did not take women to be reasoning, planning beings, able to act for the sake of some future state of affairs. That women might be capable of such self-determination and control was simply unthinkable. Assuming that women were passive creatures, lawyers usually looked for "motives" outside the woman's volition, in some other agency or force that caused her to behave as she did. They put the blame on menstrual tension, hysterical (i.e., womb-centered) disease, insanity, or a male accomplice. And over and over again they blindly asked: What *motive*?

They still asked that question about Hannah Kinney even after she had allegedly poisoned not one, but two husbands. At her trial in December 1840 for the murder of George T. Kinney, her defense attorney argued "a total absence of motive"; ". . . the relations between Mrs. K. and her husband were kind and affectionate," he claimed, "thus repelling all reasonable supposition of motive on her part to attempt the life of her husband." Witness after witness took the stand to testify that George Kinney had never been heard to say a word against his wife. On his deathbed he told her before witnesses that she had been "a good woman" to him. Since he had failed in the hosiery business, he was lucky that Hannah could support the family with her millinery shop and pay the expense of his heavy drinking and gambling. He told his friends that she never scowled. Certainly Hannah Kinney was a dutiful wife to George, but there was little evidence to indicate how she *felt* about him—except that once she was quite upset when he hit her.

Hannah Kinney was born Hannah Hanson about 1805 in Lisbon, Maine. At seventeen she married Ward Witham, a twenty-one-year-old of uncertain occupation. Witham tried farming and logging for a while, but when he came home in 1826 from several months in the woods, the neighbors told him that Hannah had replaced the hired boy with a hired man who became her lover. Hannah denied the charges but Witham insisted on moving the family to Dover, where he soon failed in the tannery business. Leaving his family behind—there were three children—he moved to Boston. He claimed that Hannah had disgraced his name once again; she called it desertion. After two years Hannah placed her children with relatives and set off after Witham, ostensibly to persuade him to support his family; but when she found him living in Boston as "a single man" she decided she could not live with him again and sued for divorce. She remained in Boston, supporting herself as a needlewoman and milliner, and boarding in the same house as Mr. George T. Kinney, a man who "was spoken of very highly by those with whom he was acquainted." Mr. Kinney quickly became her "valuable friend," but in 1832, just after her divorce was granted, she met again her cousin and childhood sweetheart, the Reverend Enoch W. Freeman, minister of the First Baptist Church of Lowell, Massachusetts.

For the next two years, florid letters and insipid verses passed between Lowell and Boston while the Reverend Mr. Freeman tried to persuade his congregation that a divorced woman—even one who reportedly had conducted herself in an "unchristian" manner on a visit to Lowell—was a fit object of matrimony. At last, in 1835, they were married; and exactly a year to the day later, the Reverend Enoch W. Freeman suddenly died. There was suspicious talk which Mrs. Kinney (then Sister Freeman) attributed to the jealousy of another woman who had wanted Freeman for herself, and to the anger of a church deacon whose improper advances she had spurned. There had always been "a secret complaining or conspiracy" carried on against her at Lowell, she said, so she may not have been surprised when the church committee suggested she leave town and neglected to pay the annual salary still owed to her husband. She blamed all the improper conduct charged against her on another woman who, she said, had the same name and looked just like her and "had often been seen" at Lowell; but she arranged to move back to Boston and marry her old friend Mr. Kinney, who—it was whispered—waited impatiently for her to return to him with the Reverend Mr. Freeman's money.

When Kinney's business collapsed, she supported him and her three children by running a millinery shop and taking in boarders. And then, as she explained in a memoir written after her trial, she discovered Mr. Kinney's secret "course of conduct": "He often appeared singular in his manners," she wrote, "and sometimes when I noticed these appearances, he would become angry, and absent himself from home for a day or two. . . . I expostulated with him, and he acknowledged all. He said frankly that he had practiced drinking and gambling too freely. When in the full exercise of his better judgment, he was humble, penitent, and fully aware of his lamentable propensities." Nevertheless, she concluded, "his faults were *mine to keep*; he was my husband." Hannah Kinney knew that she was not simply tied to a man of bad habits but that his habits were in some way *her* responsibility. William Alcott expressed the popular notion this way: ". . . woman is made to *supply*, in some measure, the defects in her husband's character—thus making him a more perfect man than he otherwise would be." A woman was never to correct or contend with her husband, but to make up in *her* behavior what he lacked and to influence him by "constant and unremitted kindness." Both religion and popular psychology dictated that the worse the behavior of the man, the better the behavior required of the wife. As another woman of the time noted bitterly: ". . . we must allow men to be impure, vile, wicked, and then welcome them to our hearts and our homes. *They* may be, and do, whatever they please—*we* must be pure, still, and bright for them." Hannah Kinney, however, kept her husband's faults very briefly. On

August 9, 1840, after drinking some herb tea, George Kinney died in great agony.

Arsenic was found in his stomach. The only issue at the subsequent murder trial of Hannah Kinney was: How did it get there? Three theories were debated. The defense argued that Kinney might have taken the poison himself because he was despondent over his extensive business debts and his "lamentable propensities," but that line of testimony oddly contradicted the picture of Kinney as a supremely happy husband and seemed, at best, flimsy. The second theory, far more compelling, was that he perished at the hands of his doctors. In the heydey of so-called heroic medicine, minor complaints were massively dosed with dangerous drugs; and feeble patients were bled, leeched, blistered, and poulticed without mercy. No doubt many died from such treatment, though medical "experts" could scarcely be expected to say so in court. During the few days of his final illness, George Kinney was treated by at least three different doctors who *all* prescribed one or more forms of opium, morphine, and laudanum. In addition, one of them gave him pills made of cayenne pepper and mucilage, while another applied mustard poultices to his abdomen and feet. Most suspiciously, one "irregular practitioner" treated him for secondary syphilis with some homemade "bowel pills"; the "doctor" denied that he ever used arsenic in his pills, but if he killed his patient, he certainly had every reason to perjure himself. Arsenic eating was a common "cure" for syphilis, and Kinney, who was known to prescribe for himself, might also have bought it over the counter in such popular tonics as "Swaim's Panacea." One of these treatments, or the combination of them, could have killed George Kinney, the defense contended. Certainly, they didn't do him any good.

The third theory—the one set forth in the indictment—was that Hannah Kinney administered the poison. But the police couldn't trace a purchase to her, even after a servant found a piece of paper in the kitchen with the word *poison* written on it. Kinney's friend Mr. Goodwin, who helped nurse him, noticed a white sediment and a peculiar sweetness in the sage tea that was the last thing Kinney took in. Goodwin tasted the tea himself to make sure it was not too hot for the patient, and later he became nauseated. The defense demonstrated that Boston water and Boston sugar characteristically left white sediment, and many things might have made Mr. Goodwin ill. The same bits of evidence were construed to suit each side: the prosecution thought it suspicious when Hannah Kinney told friends that Mr. Kinney died in just the same way Mr. Freeman had, and that she seemed beset by sudden death; but the defense reasoned that if she had killed one or both men she would hardly call attention to the similarity of their deaths.

So in the end it came down to the question of motive. The defense concluded flatly: "All the evidence shows there could have been no motive." But the prosecutor halfheartedly came up with one in his summation: "I shall suggest no imaginary motive, for it is not for me to draw the curtain of the soul," he began apologetically, "but, surely, if half is true that the counsel have told you; if, ruined in fortune, broken down in health, a drunkard and a gambler, the victim of a disease that loosened the marriage tie, that had no children to bind it; what is to restrain the jealousy of an infuriated woman, in its revenge, provided she have the heart to entertain it, and wants the moral principle to restrain its exercise?" That a woman might be jealous of the "other woman" from whom her husband presumably had caught a "loathsome disease" was something men could understand, even sympathize with, since it amounted to a competition among females for the coveted prize: the man. But no one breathed a word of the rage a woman might feel at finding herself bound for life to such a man, or the despair at knowing that indeed his faults were legally "hers to keep." After Kinney's death, Hannah Kinney's millinery shop by which she supported herself and her children was sold to help pay off his debts of $2,000; when "his" estate was finally settled, Hannah received $89. Her shop had been worth more than $800.

But was Hannah Kinney a woman wanting in moral principle? Her defense attorney told the jury, "If that woman is a murderer she is a moral monster, such as the world never saw! There is no sentence your verdict can impose, and no punishment the law can give, that is adequate to such a crime. No, gentlemen; human nature could not compass it, and human intelligence cannot believe it." The jurors looked at Hannah Kinney, a prepossessing and beautiful woman "of respectable rank in society" and couldn't believe it either. They took just three minutes to return a verdict of not guilty, and the crowd in the courtroom cheered.

Her brother mortgaged his horse and carriage to set her up in business again, and she was able to pay off the debt within the year. Still the story didn't die, and people turned against her. Trying to clear her name, she wrote a book describing the misfortunes of her life, including her first husband's desertion; but that prompted Witham to write a book about her, charging her with adultery, theft, lying, and slander. He did say, in justice to Mrs. Kinney, that she had never (to the best of his knowledge) attempted to poison *him*; but most people who had come around to the opinion that she was guilty as charged thought Witham had escaped only by luck. It was the price Hannah Kinney paid for going free on the pretext that she had no motive; just as her freedom was the price society paid to maintain the illusion that women had no reason to hate their husbands or marriage itself. The prosecutor spoke early in the trial about the increasing difficulty of convicting a woman. "Recent experience has shown," he said, "how difficult, if not impossible, it has been to obtain a verdict of condemnation, in cases of alleged murders by secret poison, when females have been the parties accused, and men were the persons murdered." Citing the cases of Lucretia Chapman, Eliza Norton, and Phebe Ann Floor, he asserted that, "There are some who think it was the SEX ONLY, of those defendants, which saved them from the punishment of the law." Men called that unequal justice "the law's chivalry" instead of what it was: a precarious prop of society's grand illusion that men loved and protected women, and that women, by nature, loved men. The arrangement saved men in general from the fear of household fiends; and it saved many women from "the punishment of the law."

But it could not save them from the punishment of public opinion; and it is that contradiction between the institutional pronouncement and the popular view that gives the game away. Everyone played along with the courtroom drama, but afterward, in kitchens and bedrooms, people talked. In courtroom orations, lawyers proclaimed that ladies had no motive for murder; but of course, everyone *knew*. Certainly there were always some champions of that nice Mrs. Kinney and that poor Mrs. Chapman, but the public mind, in a complicated recoil of fear and envy and embarrassment, set itself against them. On the day that Mina was hanged, one observer reported: "So strong was the excitement against Mrs. Chapman, that had she appeared upon the ground, it was the opinion of many that she would immediately have been put to death."

Still, in case after case, the pretense went on. By the time Ann Simpson was tried in Fayetteville, North Carolina, in 1850, the pattern was so well established that attorneys on both sides could argue *their* case by reading aloud page after page of a handy legal publication: *The Tri-*

al of Lucretia Chapman. The issues were exactly the same, and the story—by now—familiar.

On the evening of November 7, 1849, Alexander C. Simpson drank his after-dinner coffee and suddenly became ill. The doctors summoned the next morning treated him with calomel and opium and morphine and poultices on his stomach; and by nightfall he was dead. The doctors found white granules in his stomach, submitted them to the standard tests, and announced that Alexander Simpson had died of arsenic poisoning. They all appeared in court to state their unanimous expert opinion in the prosecution of Simpson's wife, Ann. The defense attorneys produced not a single expert witness to contradict them. Instead, they quoted the testimony of Dr. Phillips in the Chapman case to show that the symptoms of cholera morbus might be mistaken for those of arsenic poisoning. They quoted confused expert testimony from the Chapman case to show that the chemical tests in the Simpson case might have been inaccurate, unreliable, or contaminated by dirty vessels. And they quoted certain apparently contradictory parts of the testimony of Dr. Mitchell, head chemist in the Chapman investigation, to prove that experts are not completely trustworthy. The prosecution, finding its own experts disregarded, was forced to debate the merits of the experts in the Chapman case, so that in a curious and altogether confusing way, the question of whether Alexander Simpson died by poison came to depend upon whether a chemist had or had not found grains of arsenic in the stomach of William Chapman.

The second issue of the trial was whether Ann Simpson administered the arsenic to her husband. All the circumstances pointed to her. A druggist's clerk testified that on November 3 he sold an ounce of arsenic to Ann Simpson; he recorded the purchase because she charged it to her husband. A boarder reported that she prepared a special syllabub for her husband on the day he fell ill, and she poured him a special cup of coffee. At the table she sharply told the boarder, who had kept the cup himself, to pass it along to her husband. And after Alexander drank the coffee, Ann read his fortune in the cup: he would sicken, she said, and die. Another woman testified that shortly before Simpson's death, Ann visited a fortune-teller, complaining that her husband had hit her in the mouth. The fortune-teller, old Polly Rising—reported by some to be a witch—told her not to worry; her husband would not live another week, and then she would marry the man she loved.

That "man she loved"—who remained nameless throughout the

trial—provided Ann Simpson's motive, according to the prosecution. She had wanted to marry him in the first place, but since he possessed neither fortune nor promise, her family persuaded her to marry Simpson instead "to get a home." The lover apparently continued to visit her until Simpson discovered after three years of marriage that she "loved another." Husband and wife quarreled; he hit her; she went to visit the old woman; and in a week Alexander Simpson was dead. When she learned that she was suspected, Ann Simpson fled to Charleston and took ship to Havana, but after a year she came back and surrendered herself for trial. Some said she returned because she couldn't bear the separation from her lover.

The defense had ready answers. The arsenic was for rats. The boarder was misrepresenting ordinary events; his coffee was always kept separate from Simpson's because Simpson took his stronger and much sweeter. The fortune-telling was simply the innocent pastime of a "silly girl" and a "sillier old woman." And as to the motive, the state had "signally failed" to show one. In fact, said the defense, using the now familiar argument, there could be no motive because the crime itself was unthinkable:

> A wife is arraigned to answer to the accusation of the foul and unnatural murder of her husband; charged with the cold destitution of all the finer feelings of our nature—a woman's nature: with the hellish and fiendlike spirit, which would prompt her, under the guise of love, to extend the poisoned chalice to him, to whom all her affections were pledged, all of her obedience due, and upon whom all her hopes of human happiness ought to have been centered. A crime so monstrous, so revolting, so unnatural, that one is tempted to pronounce its impossibility.

Such crimes might have occurred "in other lands," the defense attorney contended, but never, "thank God, hitherto in North Carolina." Only a "monster" could commit such a crime, but here in the courtroom "lay" a "weeping girl"—who, throughout the trial, seems to have been more or less collapsed in her mother's arms—and not "the unnatural monster busy fame has painted." Ann Simpson had her faults, of course, as her attorneys were quick to admit. She was "giddy, and thoughtless, and volatile, and indiscreet," but these "errors of youth and of temperament" a Christian would "contemplate with sorrow, and pardon."

In other ways Ann Simpson was an admirable young lady, her attorneys said. For example, when some "busy Iago" aroused her husband's jealousy with an unfounded charge against her, Ann Simpson was "kind, noble, generous, forgiving." One of her attorneys, Robert Strange, compared her to "the humble chamomile: . . . though trodden under foot, she rises up beneath that tread a fragrant and healing balm to him who has oppressed her." He himself, he claimed, had come to fancy Ann Simpson as his "own daughter pursued by a band of cruel and relentless enemies. . . . I feel as if I could throw my arms about her," he continued, "and exclaim, 'God help thee, poor innocent, they shall not hurt thee, but at the sacrifice of my life!' " He urged the jurors to feel the same. "I beg you, gentlemen," he said, ". . . that you may be able to do her justice, to fancy her your own daughter, and ask yourselves what you would think of a jury, who . . . should find her guilty?"

The paternal attitude that attorney Strange asked the jury to assume hardly seemed compatible with disinterested justice; yet he returned again and again in his long summation to Ann Simpson's need for a champion. "Hitherto we have been wont to see ruffians, and negroes, and the outcasts of society, brought to yon bar," he said. "But now, something which has assumed the name of justice, as if disdaining an ordinary victim, has gone forth into one of the most respectable families in our county, and dragged from thence a being, almost a child, fair and beautiful, in the very bloom of womanhood. . . . Is there no chivalry left amongst us that will enter the arena . . . and defend this young creature from destruction?" Only ten years earlier, in the trial of Hannah Kinney, Massachusetts Attorney General J. T. Austin argued that it was the duty of the jury to protect society. He asked: "If the secret poisoner, who can carry the agent of death on his finger nail, and infuse it into drink or food, may escape unpunished, where is our security?" And he answered: "Here, gentlemen, is our only protection—in a jury of twelve honest and intelligent men, who in a case of proper proof will come up boldly to the point, and execute the law of the land, painful, terrible though it be." If the Kinney jury did not "come up boldly to the point," they at least had been reminded of their duty. But in the Simpson case, attorney Strange, influenced no doubt by the passage of a decade in which the ideal of ladyhood had steadily gained ground and by southern society, which prided itself on its greater chivalry, told the jury flatly that it was their duty to protect not *society* but the *defendant because* she was a lady. Strange compared Ann Simpson to a snow-white dove that had flown for safety into the bosom of the jury. Would they "cast her forth a prey to her enemies"? Or would they "cherish and protect her"?

They would protect her indeed. A few hours after Strange's impassioned summation, they returned a verdict of not guilty. The jurors may have been persuaded by other considerations, but on the face of it, they seem to have put justice behind chivalry and to have found their duty not in deliberation but in protection of yet another "weak and fragile woman, 'hapless, helpless, friendless, and forlorn.' " In a moment remarkable for how closely it shaves the truth, attorney Strange argued that the jurors should not be influenced by their own "fears" or "any notions of expediency for striking terror into the married women of the land. . . . Gentlemen," he asked, "are you such poltroons as to hang a woman, lest your wives may poison you?" They were not.

4.

Alleged poisoning became the crime of the century; and acquittal for lack of motive became almost routine. William L. Sayer, a reporter who covered the trial of Rosalie Thyng in New Bedford, Massachusetts, in 1876, looked back on the case years later to lament the "waste of chances for sensational manifestations." To Sayer, the story had all the makings of a Borgia legend. Rosalie Wordell, a beautiful twenty-one-year-old "girl," was forced by her "previous misconduct" into marriage with George H. Thyng, a much older man who might still have been legally bound to a first, and apparently never divorced, wife. After delivering a seven-month child, Rosalie became pregnant again, although George could barely support them. Rosalie, it seemed, continued to pine for her sweetheart, Del Brownell, while George took an uncommon interest in a pretty neighbor, the widow Rebecca Field. When George fell sick, Rebecca came in to nurse him; and just when he seemed about to recover completely, he died in the most sudden and hideous manner. Months passed before suspicious relatives ordered the body exhumed and found it laced with arsenic. A neighbor claimed he had bought arsenic at Rosalie's request; but others testified that he had been paid to say so.

Still, the reporter complained, very little was made of these dramatic details in the courtroom. Even the attorney general suddenly "took sick" on the day he was to sum up for the prosecution; a good politician, he didn't want to identify himself too closely with the side that must—inevitably—lose. His assistant summed up; the judge gave brief instructions; and the jury brought in the acquittal in no time. By 1876 it was almost standard procedure. To William Sayer it was humdrum. The disgruntled reporter charged that the whole trial was "exceedingly matter of fact"; even "two of the ablest lawyers of the day failed to give the case even a tinge of morbid romance."

Reporter Sayer's idea of a good romantic story involved mass poisonings, secret societies, "deep, dark intrigues . . . where love and passion and jealousy rage in the hearts of men and women—particularly women." He hoped to make of Rosalie Thyng a reincarnation of one of the "resentful young Italian matrons" whose story he quotes with great relish from a nameless "authority." Investigation of an "epidemic of poisoning cases" in mid-seventeenth-century Italy, he reports, revealed

> that most of the unhappy marriages were speedily dissolved by the sickness and death of the husband; and further inquiries resulted in the discovery of a secret society of young matrons, which met at the home of an old hag, by name Hieronyma Spara, a reputed witch and fortune teller, who supplied those of them who wished to resent the infidelities of their husbands, with a slow poison, clear, tasteless, and limpid, and of strength sufficient to destroy life in the course of a day, week, month, or number of months, as the purchaser preferred.

Sayer, reminiscing from the "safe" vantage point of 1909, believed that poisoning was a crime "of the mediaeval ages" or at least "three hundred years ago. . . . Murder by poisoning," he said flatly, "does not often appear in the courts."

But in the nineteenth century it did. And murder by poison was particularly feared because there was no way to see it coming or to defend against it. The prosecutor at Ann Simpson's trial called poisoning the "most horrid and detestable" crime because "it is usually committed in secret, and so insidiously, that no forecast can prevent it—no manhood resist it." The masculine term was not accidental, for although poison was the weapon of the oppressed (slaves of both sexes used it on their masters), it was associated with women. "This method of causing death has seemed always to have been a favorite one in the female mind," said one nineteenth-century commentator, citing cases beginning in 200 B.C.: Greek and Roman women conspired "extensively" to poison, and "very many young married ladies" in seventeenth-century Italy, while in France a whole government Chambre de Poison had to be set up to handle the problem, and even in the nineteenth century itself "in two years there were five hundred and forty-one deaths from poison in England and Wales alone." To nineteenth-century men these stories must have been more frightening than romantic. It is no wonder, then, that Ann Simpson's uneasy defenders dismissed as mere silliness her conspiracy with old Polly Rising who apparently—like the old hag in William Sayer's story—told her how to get rid of her husband. Nor is it any wonder that Ann Simpson's prosecutor betrayed a deeper fear of the old woman's influence. "When we see a wretch like this," he said, "imposing her infernal sorceries upon either the folly of the wicked, or the credulity of the simple, one almost regrets that the ancient mode of trial for witchcraft has passed away." In the courtroom, that masculine ambivalence—the fear of female vengeance *and* the compulsion to overlook it—meant (as we have seen) that a woman who pretended to have no motive was likely to go free. The mere thought of widespread poisoning of men by conspiratorial women was too threatening; and the last thing any nineteenth-century patriarchal judge wanted to find in his courtroom was the reincarnation of a "resentful Italian matron."

Nevertheless, there were some women who pushed the law's protection past endurance. The chivalry accorded to females did not extend to witches, or even, in some cases, to "real" women, for the law's "protection" was meant to preserve a certain social innocence, not to respond to the real complaints of women as a class.

Certainly no one wanted to confront the grievances of Jane Swett, who had—if ever any woman did—an undeniable motive to kill her husband. At nineteen she married Charles Swett, a factory worker of seventeen, who "got religion" and set himself up as a Freewill Baptist minister. He developed several bad habits thought unbecoming to a clergyman, so he moved to Kennebunk, Maine, and began to practice medicine, a field in which he had no training but some little experience helping his father, who was a horse doctor. After thirty-one years the couple was still married, and "Doctor" Swett still had his bad habits: he was addicted to alcohol, morphine, and women. Laura Stevens, the Swetts' only surviving child, who married a young carpenter to escape from her parents' home, kept track in her diary of her father's drunken spells: drunk 111 out of 265 days, drunk 81 times in less than 6 months, drunk on Laura's wedding day. Once he came home without his horse, having forgotten where he left it; more often the horse came home without him, and Jane Swett had to go looking for her husband along the roadside in the middle of the night. Jane intercepted "indecent" letters her husband wrote to a Mrs. Hutchings and other women. Neighbor Rebecca Newbegin told her that the doctor had made "improper advances" and continued to call upon her. Daughter Laura saw him in town with a prostitute and begged him to come home. He contracted venereal disease, and Jane refused to sleep in the same room with him. When he was drunk, he sometimes tried to have sexual relations with his daughter. Drunk or sober, he was often violent. An adopted daughter, Sarah, fourteen years old, was terrified of Charles Swett and hid whenever he came home; she was afraid he would hit her as he so often hit his wife. Jane Swett was also afraid of her husband and sometimes persuaded a friend of his to stay at the house for her protection. She was afraid, too, that if Charles Swett continued his bad habits, he would squander the last of their property. She talked him into giving her the deed of a house they owned and tried unsuccessfully to sell it to get the money to "get away." And still she tried to help him. When he came home roaring drunk and plunged headfirst from the haymow into the horse crib, she pulled him out before he suffocated.

But she also fought back, as all the neighbors testified. She locked him out of the house when he was drunk; she fetched the horse from the saloon, leaving him to stagger four miles home through the snow; she broke into his office to find letters from other women; once, when he pulled her hair, she hit back with a piece of wooden molding and drew blood; once she went after him with an ax, though she said it was only to break in the door; and once when he came home with a woman and a bottle in the wagon, she threw the bottle at him and knocked him cold. (She was aiming, she said, at the wagon wheel.) And finally, on September 23, 1866, she put morphine in the whiskey bottle he had hidden in the barn and killed him.

He came home drunk late the night before and passed out on the sofa in the living room. At 4:00 A.M. he awakened everyone when he "sneaked" out to the barn for a drink from his hidden bottle. Three hours later he made another trip. Jane Swett sent Sarah to the barn to find the bottle and then to fetch the paper of morphine she had previously taken from her husband's supply. In Sarah's presence, Jane

Swett poured the morphine into the half-pint of whiskey remaining; Sarah took the bottle back to the barn. In half an hour Charles Swett went to the barn, drained the bottle and broke it, and returned to the living room sofa. In fifteen minutes he was comatose. Jane Swett sent for a doctor and told him what she had done, but his stomach pump was broken and another could not be found. She said that if her husband died, she had killed him; she went upstairs and took the rest of the morphine herself, but she vomited and survived to stand trial for murder.

Her defense was that she had not meant to kill him, but merely to reform him by making him literally sick of his drunkenness. He had tried to reform himself by taking the pledge of the Good Templars Temperance Society, but he soon fell back into old habits. For about two years she had occasionally laced his liquor with morphine to make him vomit; he knew that she did so and told her, in a sober moment, that she was "quite right." Jane Swett's attorneys pointed out that if this story were true, she could not be convicted of murder because no malice was involved in Swett's death. Nor could she be convicted of manslaughter, for technically manslaughter had to result from the performance of an *illegal* act, and administering morphine was not in itself illegal. If the jury believed Jane Swett's story, then they had to acquit her. Unfortunately, the only witness who said he had heard Charles Swett approve his wife's method of curing intemperance was Charles Swett's best friend and drinking companion, a man so thoroughly dissolute that he could not be believed.

The prosecution, on the other hand, called for a murder conviction, blaming Jane Swett not only for her husband's death but also for his miserable life. She admitted that she never loved her husband but had been compelled by her parents to marry him. This "ill starred marriage," said the prosecutor, consisted of "uninterrupted quarrels, and violence, originating . . . with her, whose sex ought to make her blush to relate them." Here was no fragrant, downtrodden chamomile, but "a woman of ungovernable temper and fiendish passions, violent, abusive, outrageous, easily moved to anger and desperate deeds, living with her husband on terms disgraceful to a civilized and christian community. . . ." Cursed with such a wife, Charles Swett soon lost his "high hopes" and "holy purpose." "Soon his noble aspirations . . . cooled," said the prosecutor, "his native impulses [were] degraded, and he [fell] from his high calling [the ministry], first into drunkenness and finally . . . into gross licentiousness. In a word, he traveled the downward road *just as might have been expected of most men in his sit-*

uation." She scolded him, "beat and abused him," provoked him to infidelity through her own "fiendish passion" of jealousy, and at last plotted his death. Her guilt was compounded, the prosecutor argued, by her husband's depravity, for even worse than murdering an ordinary person was murdering one whose soul was so obviously "unprepared" to meet its maker. Jane Swett seemed a monster indeed.

Still there was no getting around the fact that Charles Swett was not a great loss to his family or his community. The jurors, torn in sympathy and apparently confused by the legal technicalities of the manslaughter charge, deliberated ten and a half hours before returning the verdict: guilty of manslaughter. Almost immediately eleven of them signed an informal note to the judge asking for a merciful sentence. The sentence prescribed by law could have been a fine of $1,000 or a prison term of up to ten years. The judge, considering "circumstances" he did not specify, sentenced Jane Swett, fifty-one years old and in bad health, to six years in prison at hard labor.

The prosecutor complained of the "unexpected mildness of the verdict" and attributed it to the law's chivalry:

> The privilege of sex, though unknown to the law or to justice, has in this country and age been nearly as potent as that of clergy in medieval times, and has in fact shielded almost every woman tried in the land from capital conviction and execution, however manifest and aggravated in many cases their guilt has been. To misplaced sympathy for this prisoner as a woman and simply because she is a woman ... she is largely indebted for her escape from the gallows. It must also be conceded that she succeeded in blackening the memory of her husband quite effectually.

Here, then, was the predictable reaction to the law's chivalry: if a woman escaped hanging, it must be *because* she was a woman. In fact, the trial of Jane Swett offered no evidence that she *intended* to take her husband's life and a good deal of evidence that she tried to save him. But a snow-white dove in need of the jurors' protection she was not; she had held her own against Charles Swett for more than thirty years. And since she had such good reason to kill him, it was hard to believe she hadn't tried.

One could never be quite sure of the truth. At the trial of Elizabeth Van Valkenburgh in 1845 for the murder of her husband John, the evidence went strongly against her. She was known to have had arsenic in her possession; her husband suddenly sickened and died just after his physician declared him fully recovered from a lingering illness; arsenic was discovered in the body; and Elizabeth ran away twice and was captured only after being injured in a fall from the haymow in the barn where she was hiding. More damaging to her case was the fact that she, like Jane Swett, had every reason to wish her husband dead. Here were the same women's grievances that men were unable or unwilling to hear. John Van Valkenburgh was an irresponsible drunk who, far from supporting his family, consumed what little property they had, physically abused his wife and children, and forcibly prevented them from leaving him. Quickly the jury convicted her and the judge sentenced her to hang.

Then, in a backwash of guilty sympathy, ten of the jurors petitioned the governor for clemency; and citizens throughout Fulton County, New York, petitioned to have her sentence commuted, arguing—as Jane Swett did later—that she had tried only to make her husband sick to cure him of intemperance. Governor Silas Wright, although moved to sympathy by her sex and poverty, found no new evidence in these petitions and upheld the sentence of death. The clergymen gathered to prepare Elizabeth Van Valkenburgh for hanging.

On January 22, 1846, two days before she was to die, she dictated a confession and signed it with her mark. She was born in Vermont in 1799, the document said, orphaned at five, married at twenty, and mother of four children in six years. In 1833 her first husband died "from dyspepsia and exposure." She said, "There is no foundation for the report that I had in any way hastened his death, nor did such a thing ever enter my mind." A few months later she married John Van Valkenburgh, a man "addicted to liquor" who "misused the children." She bore two more children, and her life with Van Valkenburgh became intolerable. Her two oldest sons offered to buy her a place "at the West" and to provide for her and the younger children, but her husband wouldn't let her go. She got some arsenic from a friend and killed the rats in the house. Then, when her husband returned after weeks of being "in a frolic," she put the rest of the arsenic in his tea. He was very ill. That was in January, and when on March 10 the doctor pronounced him well again, she got some more arsenic and made him a hot toddy. Within a week he was dead.

Elizabeth Van Valkenburgh said in her confession that her husband's final sufferings so terrified her that "if the deed could have been recalled" she would have done so. And seized by the compulsion to confess, she described in curious detail the recipe for the lethal "decoction with brandy": ". . . I poured boiling water on it [the arsenic] in a tea-cup, and after it had settled, mixed the water without the sediment with brandy. This mode of preparing it was intended to prevent its swimming on the surface and being discovered." On the next day, the day before her hanging, Elizabeth amended her confession. She had reflected upon it during the night, she said, and found "some particulars . . . untrue." She "should have stated" that she also gave arsenic to her first husband by mixing it in his jug of rum. She had been "provoked by his going to Mr. Terrill's bee." She confessed: "I had threatened that if he did go, he should never go to another, and as he did go notwithstanding this, I put in the arsenic as I have said." She admitted—as though it explained everything—"I always had a very ungovernable temper."

One suspects that there was more to it: that Mr. Terrill's bee was only the last straw in a load of domestic grievances that included too many children too fast, too much work, too little money, and a husband who *would* go partying, who *would* keep his jug of rum. But the laws that deprived women of rights and made them dependent upon men made them subject to tyranny. Many women enjoyed the kindness of benevolent husbands, but their welfare was "protected" only by the character of their particular husbands, not by the law which could as well bind women to drunken, brutal, and abusive men. The standard argument held that women did not need the protection of law because they enjoyed the protection of their husbands; but feminists said that the facts of the matter were quite different. Margaret Fuller countered that many women had no husbands, and that married women, as often as not, needed protection *from* their husbands. Sarah Grimké said that many women felt that "in the dominion . . . unrighteously exercised over them, under the gentle appellation of *protection*, . . . what they have leaned upon has proved a broken reed at best, and oft a spear." And Susan B. Anthony, who rescued more than one woman from a disastrous marriage, claimed that "the sufferings of the sober, virtuous woman, in legal subjection to the mastership of a drunken, immoral husband and father over herself and children, not only from physical abuse, but from spiritual shame and humiliation, must be such as the man himself can not possibly comprehend. . . ."

Since the temperance movement had failed to reform the seemingly enormous population of drunken husbands, feminists campaigned to reform the institution of marriage and secure for married women some rights to their property and the custody of their children. In 1848, after a twelve-year struggle, New York became the first state to pass a married woman's property act. In the same year the first woman's rights convention at Seneca Falls took up the issue in its Declaration of Sentiments: man has made woman, "if married, in the eye of the law, civilly dead. He has taken from her all right in property even to the wages she earns." In 1850 the Ohio Woman's Convention charged that "those laws which confer on man the power to control the property and person of woman" were "only the modified code of the slave plantation." And by 1851 the Second Worcester Woman's Rights convention passed a resolution calling for woman's suffrage: "We do not seek to protect woman," it said, "but rather to place her in a position to protect herself."

Newspaper editors and sermonizing ministers grumbled more and more about "mannish" and "unsexed women . . . who would step out from the true sphere of the mother, the wife, and the daughter, and taking upon themselves the duties and business of men . . . upheave existing institutions and overturn all the social relations of life." The enormously influential Mrs. A. J. Graves warned the American woman to "regard home as her appropriate domain. . . . Well ordered families are the chief security for the permanent peace and prosperity of the state, and such families must be trained up by enlightened female influence acting within its legitimate sphere." Nevertheless, women began in the 1830s to associate themselves in groups dedicated to all sorts of causes: antislavery, temperance, moral reform, "social purity," church missions.

By the end of the 1830s thousands of women's groups existed and "woman's sphere" had been expanded to take in many segments of public life. At the same time, popular notions of marriage and the home were challenged on other fronts. Utopian communities experimented with radical new forms of marriage or, as in the Oneida Community, did away with it altogether. The Shakers took up celibacy, the Mormons polygamy; and Charles Knowlton issued an underground best-seller on birth control methods. William Alcott, Catherine Beecher, Harriet Beecher Stowe, and scores of other experts countered with volumes of advice on wifely conduct, domestic science, and cookery. The home, which was only just coming into its own as a haven from the outside world, became the subject of endless discussion; and during the 1840s marriage came increasingly under attack. By midcentury the declarations and resolutions of the woman's rights conventions added to the small but powerful body of feminist literature—by Mary Wollstonecraft, Harriet Martineau, Sarah Grimké, and Margaret Fuller—which discussed these issues.

At the same time, a product of the same social ferment, there flowered and disappeared a little body of literature: fictional accounts of women murderers. Most likely these little pamphlets were intended primarily to make money, for murder is always a popular subject; and published accounts of notorious murder trials apparently sold very well, especially in the absence of local newspapers. Their authors publicized them as absolutely true accounts of the most "cruel, heart-rending, attrocious, [sic] cold-blooded and horrible crimes and murders" and incidentally as "thrilling and interesting" narratives. But these tales are particularly curious because they are not factual reports of real cases—as they pretend to be—but fanciful creations of the men who wrote them. Predictably, the themes of these stories resemble one another; and they also echo certain flights of oratory heard in courtrooms. They betray the same notions of women and the same abiding fears that surfaced again and again in real courts of law.

Fictional murderesses are naturally "fiendish." During their homicidal careers they violate every principle of woman's "nature." They choose as victims the very people they "by all natural laws" should most cherish: husbands and children. Ann Walters strangles her baby and poisons her husband; Pamela Lee poisons her second husband to get the money to go kill her first husband; and Mary Jane Gordon, one of the busiest murderesses, kills her baby, her husband, and, for good measure, her father. The women's motives—greed, lust, and gratuitous cruelty—are "masculine" impulses far beneath the "higher nature" of woman. Mary Thorn poisons a whole family to steal $500; Mary Jane Gordon opens a temperance rooming house to murder and rob wealthy travelers; Ann Walters also waylays travelers in her tavern and, dressed in men's clothing, she leads a gang of male highway robbers; Ellen Irving, wearing men's clothes and false whiskers, becomes a cardsharp, robber, and murderer of sixteen men. The meanest of the lot, Walters takes "no delight whatever in anything but acts of the most bloodthirsty and inhuman nature"; she bites and burns a baby to death for no reason whatever, and at the end of her life of crime, she has a whole cellar full of skeletons. The women use extraordinarily varied means of killing, and although most of them use poison at least once, they often choose singularly "unladylike" means: they shoot, stab, strangle, and slit throats. And all of them rush about in the middle of the night lugging cumbersome bodies to the river or to secret graves.

Such acts were judged by the authors of the stories just as they were by prosecutors in real courtrooms; they seemed "doubly shocking and attrocious [sic] when . . . committed by one of the female sex, which sex have always been esteemed as having a higher regard for virtue and a far greater aversion to acts of barbarity, even in the most abandoned of their sex, than is generally found in men of the same class." But the authors "reported" these cases as cautionary tales to warn against "youthful folly, reckless revenge, and ultimate ruin" and "to rescue from impending ruin thousands now ingulped [sic] in crime." Certainly for women readers, the lessons were clear. Most of the murderesses suffer agonies of remorse before dying, usually by suicide. Had they been content with domesticity, they might have enjoyed "the meridian of woman's glory, basking in the full enjoyment of a husband's love, surrounded by . . . little children, trying to lisp the sacred name of Mother, while the warbling birds are pealing forth their gentle notes as they skip from limb to limb through the sunny grove around the smiling cottage home." But no, not content with that blissful sphere, they became monsters. They had to be condemned for "the safety of society, the protection of . . . sacred homes." "You had a kind and loving husband, and all the means necessary to ensure happiness," says the fictional judge to Pamela Lee. "How can your guilty soul find repose, while your eyes rest on the fearful vision of your unnatural cruelty—your hands dripping with innocent blood."

For male readers the moral of the stories is a confused pastiche of fear and false consolation. On the one hand, the stories are a "warning to all [men], both old and young, not to allow themselves to be drawn by the fair pretensions of such females, so that they may avoid the unmerciful grasp of delusion lying in wait for them." But how was a man to distinguish "such females" from any others? After all, Mary Thorn is "beautiful" and Pamela Lee "like the bird in spring"; Mary Jane Gordon's only apparent failing is a rather "haughty" attitude, while Ann Walters's "tender looking countenance" conceals her "real character" altogether. Nevertheless, the stories hint at some guidelines, notably—in anticipation of Freud or remembrance of the Puritans—the murderess's childhood and her sexuality. Thorn and Lee are orphans; Gordon, Irving, and Walters have criminal fathers, and Walters—the worst of the lot—also has a witch for a mother. All of the women are sensual and "depraved," and Gordon seems to be bisexual to boot.

All women, of course, were *either* good or bad, for "in the female character there is no mid-region; it must exist in spotless innocence, or else in hopeless vice." But here was some reassurance for fearful men: it might be possible after all to tell the true woman and the monster apart, though perhaps not just by looking them over. Thirty years earlier, Parson Mason Locke Weems, the prolific author of little moral tales, had joked about justice deluded by a pretty face; his fictitious account of the trial of Mrs. Rebecca Cotton for killing her husband with an ax made an amusing and instructive story.

> Mrs. Cotton came off clear; nay, more than clear, she came off conqueror. For, as dressed in modest black she stood at the bar in tears, with cheeks like rose-buds wet with morning dew, and rolling her eyes of living saphires [*sic*] pleading for pity, their subtle glances seized with ravishment the admiring throng; the stern features of justice were all relaxed, and both lawyers and jury, hanging forward from their seats with fondly rolling eyes, were heard to exclaim, "*O Heavens what a charming creature.*"
>
> "*Yes,*" replied a bystander, a baptist, "*if she had not been such a murderer.*"
>
> "*A murderer!*" quoth one of the jury very angrily, "*a murderer sir! 'tis false. Such an angel could never have been a murderer.*"
>
> Thus beauty ... prevailed against justice. And thus did this self made widow force her way through the sacred nettings of the law, even as a beetle drives through the slender webbings of a spider; not only extricating herself but enthralling her enemy.

The jurors acquitted the murderess and one of them married her; so justice in this case had to await the hand of fate.

By 1850 the husband-killing woman—the household fiend—was no longer a joke. She had become a social problem, and for *every* husband, potentially a personal one. The question was how to spot her in advance. By the end of the century the new "science" of criminology would confirm that sensual women were likely to be criminals, thus reassuring men—as these mid-century fictions did—that the murderer and the true woman (appearances notwithstanding) were completely different kinds of people. Even, some said, different species: fiends and angels.

The early feminists didn't think so. In a sophisticated attack on marriage, divorce, and property laws, they argued all along that the institution of marriage bound women in desperate circumstances. Even after the Civil War, when the more conservative American Woman Suffrage Association campaigned exclusively for the ballot, the radical Stanton-Anthony wing of the movement continued to attack marriage. In 1868 *The Revolution*, the official publication of their National Woman Suffrage Association, editorialized:

> The ballot is not even half the loaf; it is only a crust—a crumb. The ballot touches only those interests, either of women or men, which take their root in political questions. But woman's chief discontent is not with her political, but with her social, and particularly her marital bondage. The solemn and profound question of marriage . . . is of more vital consequence to woman's welfare, reaches down to a deeper depth in woman's heart, and more thoroughly constitutes the core of the woman's movement, than any such superficial and fragmentary question as woman's suffrage.

Their analysis of marriage led the radicals to conclude that the very structure of the institution might make the people within it murderous.

> The institution of marriage is either the greatest curse or the greatest blessing known to society. It brings two people into the closest of all possible relations; it puts them into the same house; it seats them at the same table; it thrusts them into the same sleeping apartment; in short, it forces upon them an intimate and constant companionship from which there is no escape. More than this, it makes any attempt at escape disreputable: the man or woman who seeks to loosen or break the tie which he or she finds intolerable, is frowned upon by society. The fracture of the galling chain must be made at the expense of the reputation of one or both of the parties bound together. There is no hope for two people shackled in the manacles of an unhappy marriage, but a release by death; and no wonder that each desires deliverance, and longs for the death of the other.
>
> Yet what can be more horrible or more degrading to human nature than such a situation. Can anything be more demoralizing than this position of two people living under the same roof, forced into daily and almost hourly companionship, each of whom secretly desires the death of the other.

That the number of people who find marriage intolerable is not small, the annals of crime prove. Wife murders are so common that one can scarcely take up a newspaper without finding one or more instances of this worst of all sins; and none but God can know how many men and women are murderers at heart.

They predicted that as long as "men and women marry in the same old hap-hazard way, learning nothing from each other's experience" the result would be "what one might expect, confusion, misery and crime."

Conservatives counterattacked, turning the argument upside down and using it against all claims to any women's rights, including suffrage. Marriage, they said, was instituted by God, not man; and "woman was created to be a wife and a mother" and "to make home cheerful, bright, and happy." Therefore, any woman who tried to alter woman's sphere or to step out of it in any way—whether by voting or by poisoning her husband—must be "unnatural." A woman living "an independent existence, free to follow her own fancies and vague longings, her own ambition and natural love of power, without masculine direction or control, . . . is out of her element, and a social anomaly, sometimes a hideous monster, which men seldom are, excepting through a woman's influence." In short, it was woman as monster who threatened the institution of marriage—and not the other way around.

This conservative argument, backed by the full force of religion and masculine "reason" and soon bolstered by the sciences of criminology and psychology, overwhelmed the tentative and sometimes inconsistent insights of the radical feminists. And when social anthropologists proclaimed the patriarchal nuclear family the most highly evolved and "civilized" form of social organization, feminists seem reactionary and barbaric indeed. So, by the end of the nineteenth century, almost everyone had been converted to the "domestic mythology"; and even once-radical feminists campaigned for woman suffrage on the grounds that it would strengthen the American family.

One holdout was Dorothy Dix, whose own experience as a wife and as a reporter of murder trials convinced her that restrictive marriage bred homicide; well after the turn of the century she argued in her courtroom reportage for liberalized divorce laws. "Undoubtedly there are women with whom men find it impossible to live," she wrote, thinking of Mrs. Brouwer, whose husband fed her arsenic and ground glass, "and there are men who are simply insupportable as husbands, and if these victims of unhappy marriages knew that death was the only thing that could relieve them of their burdens, it would make the poison bottle a far greater temptation than it is now. . . . there is good reason to apprehend that many of the fifty thousand couples who agree to disagree and part amicably in this country every year would be driven to rid themselves of the matrimonial partners of whom they have wearied by foul means if they could not by fair." The indictments of marriage would continue, but long before the nineteenth century closed there appeared—just as *The Revolution* had said "one might expect"—the predicted monsters: not mere fears or fictions this time, but real domestic fiends who made of woman's sphere a tight little circle of death.

5.

In May 1871 Horatio Nelson Sherman of Danbury, Connecticut, returned home from a week-long bender in New Haven feeling sick. His wife, Lydia, nursed him with hot chocolate but he grew worse, suffering from vomiting and intense, burning pains in his stomach. He sent for Dr. Beardsley and said that he was having one of his "old turns"— another bout of withdrawal from alcoholic poisoning, which Beardsley always generously diagnosed as recurrent cholera morbus to be treated with morphine and brandy slings. But this time Beardsley disagreed. He took Lydia Sherman aside and asked her what she was giving her husband. "Only what you have prescribed," she said. Beardsley called in two consultants, and while they puzzled over the case, Sherman died on May 12. Suspecting the worst, the three doctors called for a postmortem to which Lydia Sherman readily agreed. They found arsenic. Someone suggested that sixteen-year-old Ada, Sherman's daughter by a previous marriage, had died rather suddenly on New Year's Eve. The doctors disinterred her body for examination and found more arsenic. They exhumed the body of one-year-old Frankie, another of Sherman's children who died shortly after Lydia entered the household. More arsenic. Then, in what some took to be an excess of zeal, the authorities exhumed the body of Lydia Sherman's previous husband, old Dennis Hurlburt. He too had died quite suddenly, leaving his farm and his fortune of $10,000 to his wife. And he too was full of arsenic.

The authorities inquired further into the history of Lydia Sherman, who had come to Connecticut from New York. Her first husband, Edward Struck, died there in May 1864 after a short illness diagnosed as consumption. He was followed on July 5, 1864, by three of their children: six-year-old Martha, four-year-old Edward, and nine-month-old William. On March 9, 1866, twelve-year-old Ann Eliza Struck died, and on May 19 her eldest sister Lydia, eighteen years old. That death left the senior Lydia Sherman all alone, for Edward Struck's older children by his earlier marriage had already left home. One of them asked the New York district attorney to have the bodies of his family exhumed. The Bureau of Vital Statistics had attributed the deaths in the Struck family to consumption, remittant fever, bronchitis, and typhoid; but there now seemed reason to doubt these diagnoses. Lydia Sherman, however, was already in the hands of Connecticut authorities. When she went on trial on April 16, 1872, for the murder of her third husband, Horatio N. Sherman, the newspapers were content to leave New York out of the case and call her simply "The Borgia of Connecticut."

She said that she hadn't killed Sherman. As in the case of Hannah Kinney, the evidence of arsenic poisoning was too strong to be challenged; so the defense argued that Sherman might have come by the arsenic by accident. Several family members, including Sherman himself, had used arsenic to poison rats in the house; and one rat had been seen to run into the well. Or perhaps Sherman had committed suicide; he was in debt, depressed with intemperance, and recently had lost his first wife and two children. The suggestions of accident and suicide were all too familiar in cases of this kind, and given what everyone knew of the other victims, not at all convincing. So the defense concentrated on arguing that Lydia Sherman had no motive to kill her husband.

It didn't work. The prosecution produced Sherman's brother, a man who had spent many weeks in the household, overheard many domestic quarrels, and advised Lydia Sherman to get a divorce. He testified that the couple, although married only a few months, didn't sleep together. Sherman borrowed more than a thousand dollars from her—part of the inheritance from Dennis Hurlburt—supposedly to pay his debts; but instead he used it to go on one spree after another, leaving Lydia at home to care for and support his four children and his previous wife's mother, Mrs. Jones. Both Sherman and Lydia wanted Mrs. Jones to leave the house, but she wouldn't go until she was paid $78 owed her for the piano. Lydia gave her husband the $78 to pay his debt to his mother-in-law and get rid of her, but Sherman went off on a binge and Mrs. Jones remained, still talking about her $78. Lydia gave her husband another $100; he paid off Mrs. Jones, then sold the piano for $350 and went on another binge—a big one. Apparently, he had married Lydia for her money, and he was spending it at a remarkable rate. Surely any juror—even the most romantic champion of the ladies—might find a motive for murder in the issue of hard cash. And the jurors, like everyone else, knew that if Lydia Sherman were acquitted in this trial, she would immediately be seized for trial for the murder of Dennis Hurlburt; in that case the evidence of her guilt would be far more compelling since she had been entirely alone in the house with him until he died with an arsenic residue in his stomach.

Yet during the trial, Lydia Sherman, who apparently had poisoned three husbands and six or eight children, still seemed to be—somehow—an ordinary woman. She was born in Burlington, New Jersey, in 1824, orphaned at nine, and taken into the house of an uncle. At sixteen she joined her older brothers in New Brunswick, New Jersey, and became a "tailoress." At the Methodist class she met Edward Struck, a carriage blacksmith, and married him. Lydia was about twenty years old; her husband was a widower with six children, the youngest four years old. He worked in Yorkville and came to her on weekends until they could afford to set up housekeeping in Yorkville, where their daughter Lydia was born. When he got a better job they moved to Elizabeth Street in Manhattan, on the edge of the notorious Five Points slum, and Lydia gave birth in quick succession to two sons, named for good Methodists John Wesley and George Whitfield. In less than three years the family moved to Carmansville, where Lydia bore four more children, three girls and a boy. Trying to support his large family, George Struck moved them to 125th Street and joined the police department in Manhattanville. There, after eighteen years of marriage on the edge of desperation, the Strucks came into their "trouble."

A drunken and apparently deranged man threatened a hotel bartender with a knife; and a detective who happened upon the scene, unable to subdue the man without the help of a policeman, shot him.

When Officer Struck arrived by streetcar a few minutes later, the man was dead. At the inquest, however, several hotel employees testified that Struck had been outside when the altercation started, afraid to go in. Lydia believed her husband's story, but his superiors did not and discharged him. He fell to brooding, slid deeper into depression, and at last refused to get out of bed. Struck's former employers tried to coax him back to work; his friends tried to cheer him; but he refused to see anyone or to dress himself. The police captain who had been his superior urged Lydia to send him to a lunatic asylum. Struck himself, unable to support the children, told Lydia to "place them out." She did not want to part with her children, but she could not care for them *and* her husband. Finally, she said in the confession she wrote in prison, she took the advice of another police officer to "put him out of the way." He died very quickly of arsenic.

Lydia Struck still had at least six children at home and nothing whatsoever to live on. She found the smallest children the biggest burden. "I thought that I could not get along and support them," she wrote, "and I came to the conclusion that it would be better for them if they were out of the way. I thought the matter over for several days. I was much discouraged and downhearted." Torn and hopeless, she gave a little arsenic to four-year-old Edward and six-year-old Martha Ann, and then she sent for the doctor because she was "afraid they would die." They did, and so did the baby, William, whom she forgot to mention in her confession.

Lydia got work sewing and nursing, and the older children found work; but then fourteen-year-old George Whitfield, employed by a painter, developed "painter's colic" and was told he could not work again. George kept "continually growing worse" and Lydia "got discouraged." She put arsenic in his tea and he died the next day. Lydia, by then well acquainted with the doctor, got full-time work as a nurse through his recommendation. Her oldest daughter, Lydia, eighteen, worked in a Harlem dry-goods store; but there was no one to look after Ann Eliza, who suffered through an unusually hard winter with recurrent chills and fever. Lydia, "downhearted and much discouraged," poisoned her too. "I thought," she said, that "if I could get rid of her that Lydia and myself could make a living." But just as Lydia Struck got her family down to size so that she and daughter Lydia could get by in the world, young Lydia died of natural causes.

The elder Lydia worked at nursing, took a job as a domestic in Sailorsville, Pennsylvania, and returned to New York to work in a sewing-machine store on Canal Street. There she met a customer who hired her to care for his invalid mother in Stratford, Connecticut; and in Connecticut, after eight months of caring for the old woman, Lydia was recommended by the storekeeper to old Dennis Hurlburt as a "good woman" who would keep his house for him. He hired her as a housekeeper, married her within a few days and died a few months later, leaving her money and a farm too large for her to maintain alone. Then Horatio Sherman came to call. His wife had died and he wanted to hire the widow Hurlburt as a housekeeper and nurse for his baby. He upped the offer to marriage and she, after a proper courtship, accepted. Apparently she was quite taken with him, for even before the wedding she gave him money to pay his debts. But the marriage did not work out as she had hoped. "I felt so bad," she said, that "I was tempted to do as I had done before."

At first she tried to consolidate her position within the Sherman family: she poisoned baby Frankie in hopes that once he was dead his grandmother Mrs. Jones (the mother of Sherman's first wife) would go away. Then she poisoned Sherman's daughter Ada, who at sixteen took so much of her father's attention away from his new wife. Only when it became apparent that no matter what Lydia did, Horatio Sherman would go on drinking, abusing her, and spending her money did she top off his brandy bottle with arsenic. Years before, after all her little children died, Lydia told her grown son John Wesley, who had been giving her money for their support, to keep his wages for himself. "I was alone in the world," she said, "and could take care of myself." And that is what she did until she made the mistake of marrying Horatio Sherman, who threatened to squander the little advantage she had gained. Having blundered into that marriage, she cleared the decks again to get out—in the only way she knew.

When Lydia Sherman appeared in court she was dressed in "a neat black alpaca dress, trimmed with silk velvet, a mixed black and white woollen shawl, white straw hat, trimmed with black velvet and brown plume" and "a thin lace veil." She looked younger than her forty-eight years, and one reporter described her face as "not exactly prepossessing" but surprisingly "not repulsive" either. She politely declined a chair and stood through the reading of the long indictment with "perfect calmness." When her sister and brother-in-law entered the courtroom, she smiled, kissed them "heartily," and wept. The jury found her guilty of murder in the second degree and the judge sentenced her to be imprisoned for life at Wethersfield. Bad as she might be, she still *looked* like a woman; and American society had passed beyond the "barbarity" of hanging women—at least in New Haven. Besides, it seemed unlikely that America would ever see such a monster as Lydia Sherman again.

In the summer of 1886 some of the officers of the fraternal United Order of Pilgrim Fathers in Boston began to suspect that a new Lydia Sherman might be loose in their midst. The order, an organization of working-class women and men, held social gatherings and monthly entertainments; but its chief purpose was to provide its members with low-cost life insurance. One of many mutual assessment and cooperative societies that brought life insurance to the working class in the 1870s and 1880s, it was the only one to which the relatives of Sarah Jane Robinson belonged. And the relatives of Mrs. Robinson seemed to die at a great rate.

In August 1886, Dr. Emory White, medical director of the Governor Prescott Colony of the Order of Pilgrim Fathers, was called to Mrs. Robinson's to attend her twenty-three-year-old son William, an insured member of the order. While at work in a commercial warehouse, William was struck between the shoulder blades by a falling empty box, and although he thought little of the accident at the time, he later became nauseated and vomited. His symptoms grew worse after he drank some tea at dinner that tasted "bad." Dr. White knew that William's sister Lizzie had died only six months before, and he had heard of other deaths in the Robinson household; he resolved to watch the course of William's illness carefully. When William grew worse, Dr. White sent a specimen of his vomit to the famous chemist and toxicologist Dr. Edward Wood at Harvard, and he discussed his suspicions with officers of the Pilgrim Fathers and of the police. Chief Parkhurst, on the advice of another suspicious doctor, was already looking into the death only a few weeks before of Mrs. Robinson's nephew, Tommy Freeman. He dispatched officers to watch round the clock for two days until the word came back from Professor Wood that William Robinson's stomach was full of arsenic. "The old woman dosed me," William said and died. Sarah Jane Robinson, age forty-nine, was arrested for the murder of her son.

The authorities did not stop there. Acting on the suggestion of the Order of Pilgrim Fathers, they exhumed the bodies of Mrs. Robinson's other insured relatives: her daughter Lizzie, who had died in February; and her brother-in-law, a laborer improbably named Prince Arthur Freeman, who had died in June 1885. The examinations in both cases found arsenic and inspired the police to dig further. The body of Freeman's wife, Annie, Mrs. Robinson's sister, who had died in February 1885, was found to contain arsenic. So was that of seven-year-old Thomas Arthur Freeman, Annie and Prince's son, who had died in July 1886. Mr. Winslow Litchfield, the superintendent of the Garden Cemetery, warmed to his work; having buried all of Mrs. Robinson's connections, he now, as he said in court, "took them pretty much all up." He took up her husband, Moses Robinson, who had died years before in 1882, and again the examiners found arsenic. For good measure he took up the body of Oliver Sleeper, Mrs. Robinson's landlord until his sudden death in 1881, and again arsenic was found. With that, the investigation stopped, leaving Sarah Jane Robinson with seven or eight murders to her credit; some of the crimes seemed purposeless, but many seemed to have been committed for the sake of the insurance money that the Pilgrim Fathers so vigilantly watched over.

She was brought to trial for the death of her son William, and the prosecution was bound by standard evidentiary procedure to refrain from mentioning the other murders of which she was suspected. Consequently it presented its case piecemeal and left out altogether the most damning bits of circumstantial evidence against Mrs. Robinson: the rate at which her relatives died and the accuracy with which she publicly predicted the death of each one. The weakness in the Commonwealth's case was compounded by the incompetent attorney general; his questions were "slow, rambling, and ... pointless," and according to the press, his cross-examination of Mrs. Robinson was the work of a windbag. After six days of hearing testimony and twenty-four hours of deliberating, the jury could not reach a decision. Unwilling to let the "Massachusetts Borgia" go free, the government indicted her for the murder of Prince Arthur Freeman. In this case, they argued, they should be allowed to introduce testimony about the death of Annie Freeman, for Annie was killed only to remove a beneficiary and make certain that the insurance for which Prince was then killed would be made over to Mrs. Robinson. The murder of Annie, the Commonwealth maintained, was only part of the scheme to murder Prince; and the jury should be allowed to hear about it. The judge agreed, and Mrs. Robinson went on trial again—this time for a murder in two parts.

The first part, according to the prosecution, began in late February 1885, when Annie Freeman, Mrs. Robinson's forty-two-year-old sister, fell ill with pneumonia at her home in South Boston. A nurse was called to look after her, and Prince's mother came in to help. Under their care she grew steadily better; soon, they thought, she would be well. But Mrs. Robinson had a premonition that her sister would never get up again; and after she dismissed the nurse and took full charge herself, Annie Freeman died, as Mrs. Robinson had predicted, on February 27. The prosecution called several witnesses to attest to the sudden bad turn Annie's illness had taken. Others testified that even before Annie died, Mrs. Robinson was enlisting the aid of friends to persuade Prince to come and live with her, making the insurance over to her for the care of his two children. She was afraid that Prince would go to live in South Boston with his sister, Mrs. Melvin, who, according to Mrs. Robinson, was only trying to get his insurance. Mrs. Robinson's daughter Lizzie took Prince's children home as soon as their mother died; and within a week Prince followed to make his home with his sister-in-law.

After a few weeks, Prince's one-year-old daughter Elizabeth died, for Mrs. Robinson had already tired of looking after her relatives. She said—in the presence of several witnesses who appeared against her at the trial—that Prince was a lazy, good-for-nothing fellow who would be better off dead. Somebody, she said, should "give him a dose and put him out of the way."

One night at supper with Lizzie and her friend Belle Clough, Mrs. Robinson had one of her little spells, looking startled and rather faint; her dead husband appeared to her, she said, and told her that Prince would soon die. On June 17 she sent Prince over to Charlestown to visit his mother; she told him he might not live to see her again. Five days later Prince ate breakfast at Mrs. Robinson's, started to walk to work, and vomited in the road. He was sick all day, but he needed his wages too badly to leave his work. That evening he took to his bed with Mrs. Robinson nursing him. She sent Lizzie and Belle Clough to call upon an officer of the Pilgrim Fathers and make sure the insurance was in order. The next day she sent them to summon Mrs. Flora Stanwood, another officer, who called upon Freeman. Mrs. Robinson told her that she sometimes went without food on the table to make the payments to the Pilgrim Fathers; if anything happened to Prince, she would need the insurance money to raise the boy. Mrs. Stanwood pitied her, paid the small assessment due on Prince's account herself, and handed over the receipt. The account was in order. After that Prince worsened quickly, and by Saturday night he was dead.

The Order of Pilgrim Fathers duly paid over to Mrs. Robinson the sum of $2,000, and she quickly spent it, though not on little Tommy Freeman. First she paid off some of her creditors; it seems she had mortgaged her furniture four or five times under different names. Then she bought herself some new clothes, moved to a larger flat in suburban Somerville, and took a trip to Wisconsin to visit her brother. When she returned she spent the last part of the insurance money to take out a new policy with the Order of Pilgrim Fathers on the life of her daughter Lizzie, who died less than six months later. That left no money for the care of Tommy; he became simply a liability. The prosecution was not at liberty to discuss the murder of Tommy since it had not been a step in the plan to acquire Prince's insurance money, but merely a loose end. Still, the prosecutors did manage to remind the jury that Tommy, too, was dead.

The government's case was circumstantial but highly incriminating, and the defense responded with the predictable but confusing arguments that (1) Prince died of natural causes, and (2) someone else murdered him. Prince's job at the Norway Iron Works was to remove the scale from pieces of steel after the steel had been bathed in a trough filled with sulfuric acid solution. The defense contended that he was a victim of industrial pollution, poisoned by inhaling the fumes that rose from that acid bath. But toxicology and pathology had become much more exact in the half-century since Lucretia Chapman's jury struggled to understand medical evidence; and when Harvard experts testified that Prince Arthur Freeman's death was caused by arsenic poisoning and not by fumes of vitriol, no juror presumed to second-guess them.

As a second line of defense, Mrs. Robinson's attorneys cast about for another murderer. Perhaps Prince was murdered by Dr. C. C. Beers, an elderly mesmerist and quack doctor who specialized in curing alcoholism and drug addiction with his medicine, marketed at six dollars a bottle—a ten-cent concoction of strawberry syrup and tartar emetic that made patients vomit and very nearly die of "sheer exhaustion." Though married, he was a long-time suitor of Mrs. Robinson and may have killed in jealousy or in the hopes of wheedling some of the money for himself. Certainly he knew all about poisons. Or perhaps Thomas Smith had a hand in it. He met Mrs. Robinson in his official capacity as chaplain for the Pilgrim Fathers, and by the time

William died he was calling upon her almost daily. Both Beers and Smith were indicted as co-conspirators in the deaths of William and Elizabeth Robinson, but the state, unable to find evidence that they were involved, did not proceed against them. On the stand both men contradicted each other and Mrs. Robinson; but Smith seemed innocuous and Beers a fool inching into senility. Neither seemed a likely killer.

For her part, Mrs. Robinson denied everything. She was simply a poor woman who suffered unduly the loss of first one and then another member of her ill-fated household. And now there were those who accused her—good, God-fearing woman that she was—of being the author of her own suffering. Offered another chance to speak before she was sentenced, she said again, "I am innocent." But the jury did not believe her, and the judge sentenced her to death.

Yet Sarah Jane Robinson, like Lydia Sherman, was as ordinary-looking as a bread crust. Dressed for court in a simple black dress, with her dark hair parted in the middle and brushed smoothly down at the sides in an old-fashioned style, she was a quiet, self-possessed matron. Through hours and hours on the stand she proved herself to be alert, rational, intelligent, consistent, articulate—and much smarter than the people's elected prosecutor. Mrs. Nichols, the minister's wife, told reporters that Mrs. Robinson was "a woman of tears. . . . She shed tears in the church, shed tears on the street," but Mrs. Nichols, like everyone else who observed Mrs. Robinson's low spirits, attributed them to "her bereavements."

Psychologists could not fit her into any of their categories of insanity. Dr. Charles Follen Folsom, the famous specialist in "mental diseases" from Harvard Medical School, could not find "that her mind showed any deviation from that of an every-day sort of woman, although a clever, intelligent one." Ironically, as the months passed between her trials, she became even more "an every-day sort of woman." She was pale, haggard, wild-eyed, and frantic when first arrested; but after months in jail, she was well rested, better fed, and obviously in much better health. The reporters admired her composure, and gradually as the months dragged on they gave up their sensational headlines about "The Borgia of Somerville" and began to write with compassion of "Mrs. Robinson's Ordeal." Yet throughout the ordeal, all the changes in Mrs. Robinson's appearance and manner were for the better. Those changes suggested that Sarah Jane Robinson's greater ordeal was her life.

Mrs. Robinson was born Sarah Jane Tennant about 1839 in

Northern Ireland; her Scotch-Irish parents were poor and died when she was about fourteen. With her little sister, Annie, then about nine years old, she was sent in the care of a ship's captain to her older brother in Cambridge, Massachusetts. There she made dresses, a trade she had learned in Ireland, and when at nineteen she married Moses Robinson, a machinist, she found it necessary to go on working. The Robinsons lived in that wretched condition known as "humble circumstances" while Sarah Jane gave birth to eight children, two of whom died in infancy, one in early childhood. Sarah's sister, Annie, also lived in the household until she married a man named McCormick, and again after his death until she married Prince Arthur Freeman. Moses Robinson took to running an express service; the two boys William and Charley went to work, William on the horsecars and Charley in a store; daughter Lizzie took over the housekeeping and care of the younger girls, Emma and Grace; Sarah Jane worked for a dressmaking company. Still, it was hard to make ends meet. The family moved often, from one tenement to another, sometimes just ahead of the collectors.

Then Oliver Sleeper, the Robinsons' feeble old landlord, became sick, and after Mrs. Robinson's nursing, he was pronounced dead of heart disease. Mrs. Robinson submitted a bill of $50 to the estate for her nursing services, and when she was given instead a remission on her rent, she sold the remission for ready cash. The executors threatened to prosecute her for fraud but settled the matter out of court. They were more concerned about the loss of $3,000 in cash which Sleeper was known to have had on hand a month before his death and which could not be found. If Mrs. Robinson took the money, no one knows what she did with it; but she may well have needed it (as she later needed Prince's insurance money) to pay off the creditors to whom she had mortgaged many times over every stick of movable property.

Less than a year later, in July 1882, just after being served an eviction notice for failure to pay rent, Moses Robinson suddenly died at the age of forty-five. His life was insured by the Pilgrim Fathers for $2,000, but the member to whom Moses had made some of his payments absconded; Sarah sued the order for the money she expected, but the case was still undecided when she was arrested. Moses was the only family member insured at the time of his death and thus, if insurance was the motive, the only possible victim; but in killing Moses, Sarah killed a wage-earner, and although his death might have brought her money, it cost her some as well. Still, it was not the week-ly wages Sarah required; she could scrape by well enough with her sys-tem of frauds and false mortgages. But periodically she needed a large amount of money to bail herself out and launch anew. Presumably, she saw in her sister's illness the chance to bring into her household another insured man, and one to whom she was scarcely attached. First Annie and then Prince Arthur Freeman died within the year, bringing Mrs. Robinson $2,000.

It was not enough. At the time of Prince's death, the household crammed into a small three-bedroom tenement flat consisted of Mrs. Robinson, four of her children, her brother-in-law, his child, and usu-ally one or two boarders. Occasionally, she retrenched. She dispatched ten-year-old daughter Emma in August 1884; and she did away with Tommy Freeman in July 1886. In addition, she persuaded Lizzie to enroll in the Pilgrim Fathers, making her insurance payable to Wil-liam. As housekeeper, Lizzie was a valuable member of the household, but she talked of marrying Fred Fisher and moving to Cambridgeport; and the creditors were pressing again. On the day Lizzie got sick, Mrs. Robinson hired a servant to fill her place, though it took Lizzie three more weeks to die. Her insurance of $2,000 went to William who, at his mother's insistence, joined a new chapter of the Pilgrim Fathers and named his mother as beneficiary. William spent $100 on his sis-ter's funeral and paid $100 down on a wagon and team; the rest of the money was unaccounted for when Lizzie returned to Mrs. Robinson in a dream and said she had come for brother William. His death should have brought his mother another $2,000 and a streamlined family con-sisting of only herself, her favorite son, nineteen-year-old Charley, and her favorite daughter, six-year-old Grace. Perhaps that would have been enough. According to Charley, she was good to her children. "Mother always seemed to like us," he said, "and we all cared the world for her." But Sarah Jane Robinson, worn out by poverty and thirty-five years of hard work, killed to get the money for subsistence in "humble circumstances"—more money than she and all the wage-earners in her household could get by their labor, though they all worked a twelve-hour day, six days a week. When that was not enough, she attacked the problem from another direction by eliminat-ing almost all the dependent members of the family. If there is shrewd calculation in such long-range plans as her elimination of Annie to get at Prince, there is also a desperate necessity in picking off one insured worker after another. In the circle of poverty, no person's work was as valuable as life insurance; and even that lump—the sum of a person's life—was never, in the long run, enough.

At the time, Sherman and Robinson—the poison fiends, the modern Borgias—incarnated the worst fears of men. Yet in retrospect they seem to be predictable products of their situations: of the confluence of hard times in big cities where men worked long hours for low wages and women worked for less; of marriage as a binding but often affectionless institution that spawned more children than it could embrace; of a society too bent upon acquisitive individualism to assist the ill and indigent; of a society too dominated by frightened men to offer education and position to clever, aggressive, lower-class women. Given those circumstances, another Robinson or Sherman was likely to come along, as Tillie Klimek came out of the Polish ghetto of Chicago a generation later. Indicted in 1922 for poisoning three husbands for their life insurance—a fourth lay dying of arsenic in the hospital—she was also suspected of killing several of her children, some cousins, and a boyfriend who had refused her marriage offer, and of helping her cousin Nellie Koulik rid herself of one or two husbands of her own. Tillie Klimek was denounced in the newspapers as the "Polish Borgia" and "Mrs. Bluebeard." But like Robinson and Sherman—and their English counterparts Betty Eccles, Mary Ann Cotton, Mary Anne Geering, Sarah Freeman, and others—she was an ordinary working-class woman with few chances and small hope.

Women were expected to be self-sacrificing. They were supposed to give up everything—their lives if need be—for the welfare of their husbands and children; but such sacrifices, wept over in the dime novels, were not considered *truly* heroic. Maternal self-immolation was thought to be a simple instinct, not a choice; and since self-sacrifice was thought to be "natural," self-interest was condemned as unnatural and monstrous. The best thing—perhaps the only thing—for society to do with these murderous female "fiends" was to lock them up, throw away the key, and above all *forget* about them. So the governor of Massachusetts—a state that had not hanged a woman since its nasty experience with Bathsheba Spooner—locked away Sarah Jane Robinson, commuting her death sentence, and she, like Lydia Sherman before her and Tillie Klimek after her, spent the rest of her natural life quite contentedly in prison. She died in 1906, professing eagerness to rejoin her family and confessing nothing.

6.

If women who put themselves first merely to survive were thought to be monstrous, what was society to make of women who acted selfishly simply for fun and profit? There are murders and murders. Certainly it is one thing for a penniless woman to kill a hopelessly insane husband, an invalid child, or a baby that can't be cared for, and quite another thing for a fairly well-to-do matron to seek out people to murder for the sake of getting more money and apparently some pleasure from the acts of homicide and butchery. Cases of this sort are rare and difficult to understand; yet if marriage is woman's only career, it can just as well become her business.

As the century turned, an industrious Norwegian immigrant, imbued with the thoroughly American drive to make money, devised her own get-rich-quick scheme. Her sister said she was "money mad" and "would do anything for money"; and indeed she parlayed an initial capital investment of virtually nothing into a profit estimated at $51,000 before her disappearance or death in 1908. Her business was marriage and murder.

Belle (neé Bella) Paulson emigrated from the village of Selbu, near Trondheim, Norway, in 1883 when she was twenty-three, and joined her older sister and brother-in-law, who had paid her expenses, in Chicago. She did sewing and laundry work until she married Mads Sorenson, a watchman, and set up housekeeping. According to neighbors, Belle always had a "deep affection for her own and other children," but having none of her own for several years after her marriage, she took in foster children. About 1890 she adopted eight-month-old Jenny Olson, and six years later she began to bear children of her own. Her first daughter, Caroline, died only five months after birth in 1896, and her first son Axel died in infancy in 1898. Both died of severe inflammation of the lower intestine, a characteristic of acute colitis and of poisoning; and both were insured. Belle's second child, Myrtle, born in 1897, and her fourth child, Lucy, born in 1899, survived.

For a dozen or more years the family scraped by, shuffling from one cheap flat to another, trailed by ill luck, poverty, and fire. First the confectionery, which Belle and Mads had bought less than a year before, burned to the ground in 1896. The Sorensons moved out to the fringe of blue-collar homes in suburban Austin, but two years later their house was severely damaged by fire. Both buildings were insured, and although the exploded kerosene lamp which Belle said started the fire at the store could not be found in the wreckage, the insurance companies paid up. The insurance windfalls must have helped the family get by, but apparently they didn't help enough. Then, too, life on the raggedy edge of a well-to-do suburb can make an ambitious woman raise her sights.

On July 30, 1900, Mads Sorenson died suddenly in the arching convulsive rigor characteristic of strychnine poisoning—on the one and only day that his two life insurance policies with two different mutual benefit associations overlapped. Belle said she had given him a "powder" because he had a cold. The death certificate said that he died of an enlarged heart; and when Sorenson's suspicious family had his body exhumed a month later, examiners indeed found the heart enlarged and proceeded no further. A more complete postmortem could have cost the Sorenson relatives another $300; and no one seems to have told them that an enlarged heart may be one of the consequences of strychnine poisoning. Still, the neighborhood children teased Belle's daughters about the suspicious circumstances of Sorenson's death. Belle took the $8,500 in life insurance, bought a run-down farm fifty miles away near La Porte, Indiana, and moved with her surviving daughters—Jenny Olson, Myrtle, and Lucy—into the big brick house. Some of her new riches she invested in improvements to the property, repairing fences, painting outbuildings, planting shrubbery and flowers, until she had what she liked to call "the prettiest and happiest country home in northern Indiana."

In April 1902, Belle married Peter Gunness, a recently widowed younger man whom she met on a visit to her North Dakota cousins. With his young daughter Svenveld, Gunness moved to Belle's farm, and there less than nine months later he died in such a bizarre way that the coroner and many of the neighbors talked of murder. But at the inquest Belle had an explanation. Peter, sitting next to the stove, had reached down to pick up his shoe and jarred the stove in such a way that a large stone crock of hot water overturned, scalding him, and a sausage grinder that had been drying on the top shelf of the stove fell down and struck him right between the eyes. The testimony of twelve-year-old Jenny seemed to corroborate this odd story, and Peter Gunness's death was declared an accident. Unconvinced, Gust Gunness hurried down from Minneapolis, kidnapped his brother's child, Svenveld, and hid her on a Minnesota farm. Belle collected the

$2,500 life insurance, gave birth to a posthumous child, Philip, and hired a man to help her run the farm.

Belle's arrangements with that hired man and the others who followed him never seemed to work out well because Belle—who by all accounts was a sensuous woman—would sleep with the hired man who in turn would begin to think himself master of the place; and then Belle would have to set him straight about that. The relationships ended abruptly. Peter Colson packed up one day and moved back into town. Olaf Lindboe went to Norway "to see the King crowned" in July 1904 without finishing the plowing. And Henry Gurholt left the following July right in the middle of digging the new privy hole. Only Ray Lamphere hung around, even after she fired him, until she had to prosecute him for trespassing and charge him with insanity. Some time in 1905, about the time that Henry Gurholt disappeared, Mrs. Gunness stopped looking for a hired man and placed an ad in one of the Norwegian newspapers that circulated throughout the Midwest.

> WANTED—A WOMAN WHO OWNS A BEAUtifully located and valuable farm in first class condition, wants a good and reliable man as partner in the same. Some little cash is required for which will be furnished first-class security.

Almost immediately the procession of Norwegian men to La Porte began—all of them hoping to contract an alliance with the rich Norwegian widow. Belle Gunness was in business.

She went out of business on the night of April 27, 1908, when her farmhouse burned to the ground; the charred bodies of Belle and her three youngest children, Myrtle, eleven, Lucy, nine, and Philip, five, were found in the debris. The troublesome hired man Ray Lamphere was charged with arson, and, when the bodies were more closely examined, with murder. Apparently the victims had first been poisoned and their bodies stacked in the cellar like cordwood; then the house had been fired. The woman's head, which had been cut off, was missing.

Searchers were still looking for the rest of Belle Gunness ten days after the fire when Asle Helgelein, a persistent Norwegian farmer from Mansfield, South Dakota, came to La Porte looking for his brother Andrew, who had visited the widow Gunness after answering an ad and courting her by mail. One question led to another, and on May 5 the searchers began to dig up a rubbish pit in the Gunness chicken yard, which had been filled in only a day or two after Andrew Helgelein collected $2,900 in cash at a La Porte bank. They found Andrew a few feet down, neatly cut up and packaged in old grain sacks. In a second rubbish pit, a few feet away, they found the skeleton of Belle Gunness's foster child, Jenny Olson, who at Christmastime 1906, when she was sixteen, had supposedly gone off to school in California without saying good-bye to anyone. Under the skeleton was an old mattress, then a layer of dirt, then—in putrid gunnysacks—the dismembered body of a large man with a big, dark mustache who would later be identified as Ole Budsberg, a Norwegian farmer who left Iola, Wisconsin, in March 1907, to marry a rich widow.

Just at first no one could accept the evidence suggested by the discovery of the corpses. Some said the bodies must have been planted by mysterious strangers, unknown to Mrs. Gunness. The district attorney first advanced the strange but popular theory that the corpses had been corpses all along—that Mrs. Gunness simply received cadavers from Chicago and buried them on her farm—though just why a respectable Indiana widow would choose to become a sort of Chicago dead-body fence escapes imagining.

The next day, while a curious crowd watched, searchers dug into an old privy vault and found more sacks containing the pieces of another body; they thought this one might be a woman, but it was impossible to tell because it had been treated, like most of the others, with quicklime. In another rubbish pit in the chicken yard, about three feet down, they found another man, and beneath him, the bones of two more men and the rotten shreds of old gunnysacks. One of these men may have been hired man Olaf Lindboe, whose brother warned him to take care of the $300 cash and the gold pocket watch he had when he went to La Porte in 1904. Another may have been Henry Gurholt, who had $400 when he left Scandinavia, Wisconsin, in May 1905 to work for Mrs. Gunness; his last letter home was written on the Fourth of July, 1905. Another of the bodies was thought to be that of John Moo, a forty-year-old Norwegian farmer from Elbow Lake, Wisconsin, who arrived in La Porte on December 24, 1906, drew $1,100 in cash from the La Porte bank on the day after Christmas, and was never seen again. But it was impossible to identify the bodies. They had been cut up and packaged—a sack for each arm removed from its socket at the shoulder, a sack for each leg sawed off at mid-thigh, another sack for the head and one for the torso—and they had been sprinkled with lime. Little but bones remained, and they were apt to fall away under the shovel.

Rain held up the digging on the next day, and officials laid out the recovered bodies—too fragile to be moved to town—in the little red carriage shed. Reporters by the score could find no words to describe the stench. When the digging resumed the following day, more bodies and sacks almost destroyed by quicklime were found about three feet down in another rubbish pit in the chicken yard. Thousands of onlookers hunched expectantly against the drizzling rain to see more bodies brought up, but that one—the tenth—was the last. Digging went on sporadically for days: suspicious "soft spots" were probed and newly cultivated earth under the lilac bushes was turned over. For weeks there was talk of taking up the concrete foundation onto which Belle had moved her barn a couple of years before; and plans were made to dig up the cellar and the yard of the house she had owned in Austin, Illinois—though such excavations cost the taxpayers money. Neighbors suggested that the sheriff drag the lake just below the Gunness chicken yard, particularly to search for a large reeking box many of them had noticed floating a year or two back. But it was mostly just talk; soon, the searchers stopped looking. It almost seems as though they were afraid of finding more.

And who could blame them? As relatives of missing persons—the sons of Ole Budsberg, the brothers of Olaf Lindboe, Henry Gurholt, and John Moo—came to La Porte to identify the dismembered corpses, others wrote to tell the sheriff of relatives who had gone to La Porte and never returned. Tonnes Peter Lien, for one, left Rushford, Minnesota, for La Porte on April 2, 1907, carrying $1,000. His brother wrote to ask if a large silver pocket watch inscribed *P.L.* was found in the ruins. It was. The watches of at least eleven men—and their razors—were found in the ashes of the house; the bodies of only eight or nine men were found in the yard. And when all the reports were in, at least a dozen men, known to have gone to marry an Indiana widow, remained unaccounted for.

Perhaps Belle Gunness, too, remained unaccounted for. The dead woman in the cellar, burned past all recognition, seemed too small to be Belle. At Ray Lamphere's trial for arson and murder the coroner had a blunt explanation: roast meat shrinks. But the women in attendance, knowing *how much* roast meat shrinks, thought it unlikely that Belle Gunness, who weighed well over two hundred, could have cooked down to a mere seventy-three pounds. A woman's head found in the cesspool did not seem to be Belle's, but it lacked the lower jawbone, which the local dentist needed to make a positive identification. Then, three weeks after the fire, a professional placer miner hired to sift the ashes in search of the gold in Belle Gunness's teeth, came upon the dentist's handiwork: a few false teeth, still attached to the stump of a real tooth that anchored them. The teeth had been through a fire, but dentist George Wasser, who made tests with a Bunsen burner, thought they had burned in a fire much less hot than the one that charred the kerosene-soaked bodies. And still no jawbone was found— only, belatedly, Belle's bridgework.

Lamphere's defense attorney, H. W. Worden, argued that Belle staged her own death and left town with the profits of her unholy business. Certainly she had every reason to flee, the defense argued. Embarrassing questions had been raised when she prosecuted Lamphere for trespassing and insanity; Jenny's friends and her suitor were too concerned about her long absence; and Asle Helgelein clearly was not satisfied with the explanation she sent him of his brother's disappearance. Worden maintained that Belle, fearing discovery, lured an unknown woman to her farm, poisoned her with strychnine, and threw her head into the cesspool to prevent identification of the corpse, and that she poisoned the children, stacked all the bodies in the basement, set fire to them and to the house, and left. She hoped to give the impression that she and her children had died in their beds, and she might have succeeded had the fire burned long enough to consume the bodies and the telltale fact that four people who slept in different bedrooms on the second floor fell in one tidy heap in the cellar. The defense produced witnesses to testify that Belle bought a big can of kerosene only a few days before the fire and that she drove to her farm with a stranger, a blonde woman smaller than herself. And a neighbor and two children testified that they saw Belle driving near her farm *after* the fire.

In fact, the defense argued, Belle set Lamphere up. Her obviously false testimony at his sanity hearing—contradicted by several other witnesses—indicated that she had it in for him. Belle spent the very day of the fire in town dictating a will to her attorney (she left her property to a Norwegian-American orphans' home) and telling him and several other people that she was afraid Ray Lamphere would kill her. She rented a safe-deposit box at the bank and left her new will in it. Then, too, the defense raised the troublesome issue of Belle's money. On the day she "died," Belle had only $700 on deposit in a La Porte bank—and she had deposited it that very afternoon. If Belle Gunness had been murdering men for their money, where was the money? Had it been consumed in the fire? Or was it tucked in Belle's familiar pocketbook—traveling?

The prosecution countered that Belle Gunness was indeed afraid of Lamphere, and for good reason. Their theory was that Lamphere—suspicious—surprised Gunness just after she murdered Helgelein, helped her get rid of the body, and then began blackmailing her. More than once, after having one too many at the local tavern, Lamphere boasted to the bartenders that he knew enough about his "sweetheart" to keep her "on her knees." The prosecution's blackmail theory, however, raised two still tantalizing questions: If Lamphere was extorting money from Gunness, where was it? And—more to the point—why didn't she kill *him*?

The jury pondered these conflicting theories for twenty-six hours and came to a strange conclusion. They found Lamphere *not* guilty of the murders, but guilty of arson; and they announced their unsolicited opinion that the body in the cellar was that of Belle Gunness. Many people still didn't believe it, but even Lamphere came around, at least temporarily. "I thought Belle Gunness was not in the fire," he told a reporter, "because all the money she must have had wasn't shown up. But after hearing the evidence it looks to me as if that must have been her body in the fire." Yet when Lamphere died in prison in 1909, it was reported that he believed Belle Gunness to be alive and living not far from La Porte. Even a minister's tale a few years later that Lamphere had confessed the murders to him couldn't lay Mrs. Gunness to rest. For years people all over the country looked with suspicion at Scandinavian women and positively identified Belle Gunness in this town and that.

Yet the first of these positive identifications may have helped Gunness get away. On May 8, three days after Andrew Helgelein was unearthed, Mrs. Flora Belle Heerin, widow of a wealthy Chicago industrialist, traveling to New York City with her mother, was dragged off a train in the middle of the night at Syracuse. Several hours elapsed before Mrs. Heerin was able to establish her identity apart from Mrs. Gunness, and during that time the police—certain that they had Gunness in hand—refused to let her wire news of her detention to her sister who awaited her arrival in New York: Mrs. Charles Rockefeller. Mrs. Heerin sued the Syracuse police and the railroad for false arrest. After that, though citizens and police *saw* Belle Gunness everywhere, they rarely tried to arrest her. If the real Belle Gunness left La Porte after the fire, she certainly could have traveled freely while the spurious Belle Gunness remained under highly publicized arrest in Syracuse. And after the false arrest of Mrs. Rockefeller's sister, Belle Gunness could have traveled almost at will. Gunness could not have anticipated the fortuitous detention of Flora Belle Heerin. So she may have chosen to leave town in disguise; after all the murders she had committed, she had a wealth of male identities at her disposal. In any case, no one would have looked for Belle Gunness until it seemed possible that she was missing. She "died" on April 27. Not until May 4, when the first buried victims were unearthed, did anyone suspect that Gunness might still be alive. In the meantime, she had more than a week to travel undeterred and to read in the newspapers the sad story of the death of a "well to do widow" and her children in a tragic fire.

The discovery of the chopped-up bodies in Belle Gunness's chicken yard changed everything. It caused a terrific stir. To see her burned-out lair, the open graves, the makeshift morgue in the carriage shed, thousands of people flocked to La Porte and paid enterprising livery men a dime for the wagon ride out to the place. (The return trip cost a quarter; Belle Gunness was not the last greedy entrepreneur in La Porte.) On the first Sunday after the victims were found in the chicken yard, ten thousand people came to La Porte, almost doubling the town's population; on the following Sunday, fifteen thousand people visited the farm. The Lake Erie and Western Railroad scheduled special Sunday excursion trains from Indianapolis. Interurban cars and automobiles came from Michigan City and Chicago. At the farm the crowds trampled the fields, stripped the leaves from the trees, picked bricks from the ruins. The Gunness place became "a Mecca for curiosity seekers," according to the Chicago *Tribune*, and not a bad place for a picnic. Vendors hawked their wares: candy, ice cream, and picture postcards of Andrew Helgelein's dismembered body. The crowd included "women in smartly tailored gowns who came all the way from Chicago with their husbands in costly automobiles, old men and old women . . . and hired men galore from all the farms in northern Indiana. . . . Members of churches mingled with the demimonde in struggling for views of the pits from which the bodies were taken." In the crush, babies were neglected and people on crutches were pushed aside. "Women clawed at the little red carriage house" where the bodies were laid out. "They stuck their fingers in the cracks and wrenched in an attempt to pry them apart far enough to see inside. . . . Men boosted each other to the window in the end of the structure and gazed at the bodies until others behind pushed them from their places to make room for other gazers." At last Sheriff Smutzer gave in; he opened the carriage-house doors and let the spectators file by to gape at the reeking skeletons.

The town made a business of it. For reporters and other overnight visitors, cots lined the halls of La Porte's hotels, and spare rooms were let in private houses. An enterprising writer hurried into print with a pamphlet detailing forty-two grisly murders Gunness supposedly had committed. Reporters joked in print about "The Port of Missing Men." Crammed La Porte restaurants peddled tubs of chili con carne as "Gunness Stew." To the *Trib* reporter, booming La Porte presented "the appearance of a fair or big convention" marred only by fear of an invasion of pickpockets. All in all, the gathering was "an organized feast of the morbid and curious, believed to be without parallel in the United States." On that first rollicking Sunday, Sheriff Smutzer, who had stationed *two* men to guard the ashes in the cellar, was appalled. He had spent the week painstakingly unearthing rotten bones of murdered men with his own shovel. On Sunday he looked around at the crowd and told a reporter, "I never saw folks having a better time."

And so the folks domesticated the fiend and turned her truly psychopathic butchery into a titillating joke. Faced with an apparently genuine monster, the public turned her grisly farm into a tourist attraction, a sort of circus ground, and Gunness herself into a sideshow draw, last appearing as the headless woman—not a monster but a freak.

No one joked about Lucretia Chapman, Ann Simpson, or Hannah Kinney. No one joked even about Sarah Jane Robinson or Lydia Sherman. But Belle Gunness was something more and worse and different. The family poisoner was thought to be a woman askew. Something out of whack at the very center of her nature caused her to kill by stealth those whom she most should honor. She was by popular definition, then, unnatural and a monster. But aside from her poisoning of long-time husband Sorenson, Belle Gunness was nothing of the sort. She was, above all, an entrepreneur. As such, she was intelligent, original, energetic, persistent, ambitious, thoroughly American, and distinctly "masculine." And Belle's particular sort of murder was decidedly "male." She was a sort of female Landru and flimflam man rolled into one: Bluebeard with a profit motive. In part she used her sex to attract and kill. She knew woman's assigned role by heart; to Andrew Helgelein she wrote, "My dear Andrew: I am lonesome; I need help. I need a good strong man to help me. . . . I put my confidence in you. I would depend on you more than any king in the world. How happy we will be when I see you. Come as soon as you can. . . ." Helgelein, Budsberg, and Moo disregarded her instructions to bring cash, but after a day or two with Belle, each man went to the La Porte bank to convert his savings into ready money.

But the main part of Belle's attraction was not some sirenlike sensuality; it was good acreage, a big chicken yard, and a thirteen-room brick house. Like any good confidence man, Belle appealed to the greediness of others. She matched her suitors' desire to exploit her with plans of her own, and most often, she won. To men her story may have been frightening, but it was intelligible, for Belle Gunness merely applied to the domestic sphere the "cutthroat" tactics of the business world. It is not surprising then that Belle Gunness, with her axes and knives and her chicken yard full of skeletons, resembled those fictitious villains of earlier nineteenth-century cautionary tales—Mary Jane Gordon, Ellen Irving, Pamela Lee, Mary Thorn, Ann Walters— much more closely than she resembled any *real* woman; for those female arch-villains were simply the creations of male imagination limited to its own terms. Paradoxically, Belle Gunness was precisely what men imagined a vicious female criminal would be, and because that model was so outrageous, Gunness seemed to be—at the same time— not an unnatural and monstrous woman, but an absolute *freak* of nature.

Women might see Belle's crimes differently. Using sex and property to attract her victims, Belle reversed at one stroke the familiar tales of young ladies despoiled by the vile seducer and powerless women manipulated by the man of property. Her crimes speak powerfully to the vengeful, man-hating part of every woman. Later generations of men—always trying to distinguish the dangerous woman from the harmless—have emphasized Belle's sexual "hold" on her victims and have pictured her as a sex kitten. The cover painting for a 1955 paperback book about Belle, for example, depicted a young, buxom blonde wearing a black lace negligee and bearing an uncanny resemblance to Jane Russell. But Belle Gunness was not what men would make of her. She was almost fifty years old. She weighed almost 250 pounds. She was a housewife turned psychopath.

The weekend circuses in the Gunness farmyard and all the cartoons and jokes masked some profoundly disturbing anxieties. Public officials, like the private citizens who picnicked at graveside, behaved in oddly inappropriate ways; Sheriff Smutzer reluctantly became a sort of ringmaster for the Gunness show, and in Chicago, under the orders of a federal district attorney, the police launched a sweeping campaign to arrest all the proprietors of matrimonial agencies. Clearly it was time for the patriarchs to reassert some old truths. The Reverend Mr. M. H. Garrard, minister of the La Porte Christian Church, took the task upon himself. He told a reporter that he was "thoroughly disgusted . . . with the way women have flocked into the courtroom to have poured into their ears all the filth connected with the notorious trial" of Ray Lamphere. First there was Gunness herself, and now this horde of harpies. "It is a strange thing that women, under no compulsion whatever, are found in large numbers in every notorious trial everywhere, and the dirtier the trial the more women usually will be found in attendance." Still the women pushed their way into the courtroom.

On Sunday, November 23, 1908, while the Lamphere trial was still in progress, the Reverend Mr. Garrard preached a sermon on the evil of women attending trials. God, he said, "gave woman a peculiar nature and set her in the home." Woman gained "power" through "sympathy, purity . . . and love"—three "feminine" virtues that must have rung slightly flat in the ears of La Porte townspeople; but to them, even in the presence of proof to the contrary, the conventional wisdom was wisdom still. The Reverend Mr. Garrard concluded stirringly and closer to the truth than he could have wished: "I say to you that if woman is to conquer she must do it with these [feminine] weapons. If she does it in other ways, . . . instead of being [man's] complement, as divinely intended, she becomes his worst enemy." Four days later the Lamphere jury announced that although apparently no one had killed her, Belle Gunness was finally, definitely, officially dead.

THREE

SPOILING
MAIDENS

1.

Luckily for men, the monstrous women were exceptional. The great mass of women were mere babes, children really, permanently simple and infantile, but on the whole rather charming. That at least is how the biologists explained the vast differences between men and women when science supplanted religion as Victorian gospel. As the nineteenth century waned, women and men seemed as distant from one another as ever, but now the reasons for that estrangement were sought in scientific research rather than religious preachment. The law of nature replaced the law of God as rationalization for the law of men. The justification changed but the ladies remained the same pretty, foolish, harmless, and despised creatures they had been for a hundred years.

Thanks to Darwin and his popularizers, science was able to "prove" what earlier had only been suspected: that men indeed had larger brains than women, that they had higher levels of metabolism and energy, that they were altogether more highly evolved, more nearly perfect. There were some rather embarrassing findings—such as the fact that woman's brain in proportion to her overall body size was a good 6 percent heavier than man's—but such inconclusive results, obviously derived from erroneous formulas, were scarcely worth quibbling about and best left alone. Eminently objective biologists and anthropometrists agreed about the results of the research they planned and interpreted: white men led the evolutionary vanguard while children, Negroes, and women slouched in a retrograde clump at the end of the parade. The conclusive finding was this: woman was "simply a lesser man, weaker in body and mind,—an affectionate and docile animal, of inferior grade."

Not that men complained of this shoddy creature they had devised for themselves. Inferior she might be, but her affectionate nature and docility made her a welcome household pet—much like a spaniel or a well-broken pony. If men could not condescend to love women, they could at least love the "devoted affection" women naturally felt for them. That at least was the opinion of "Professor" Orson Fowler, the enormously influential popularizer of phrenology, who wrote at great length on the relations between the sexes, codifying the popular notions of his time and recycling them as scientific facts. "Ask any number of sample men what female quality they prize most," he wrote, and "nearly all will answer—'Give me the woman who *affiliates* with, and dotes on, me. . . .' " In fact, he said, a wife who did not "thus assimilate and identify herself" with her husband was "not worth much to any man."

To the popular French writer Jules Michelet, whose works on love and life were republished in America, woman's chief charm was her tractability. That, combined with her "Byzantian" education, gave every "man of modern times, fresh in intellect, in learning, in conceptions," the chance to play Pygmalion to his ignorant teenaged bride. The girl's natural "affection and gratitude" would lead her into "an innocent error" (which her husband need not bother to correct): that all the knowledge he possessed originated with him. "You have the credit of everything," Michelet exclaimed to his male readers. (He seemed to think that women did not read.) "It is you who have made all living things, all science. . . . for, being her creator, you are also the creator of the world; the world and God are both lost in you."

While woman's dumb devotion gratified a husband, it raised problems for the man who had no wish to become one. Professor Fowler explained that the same principle that made wives "cling" like demented leeches to their husbands made it "so extremely difficult" for any man to get " 'shake of' a woman whose affections were once allowed to fasten." Like a duck, which takes most anything it sees as its mother, a girl who engaged her affections could not be detached. "Either prevent their concentration," Fowler warned, "or else consummate them in marriage." For this reason as well as compelling questions of pedigree and property, a man contemplating marriage in respectable society was expected to secure the consent of a young lady's father before addressing the lady herself. Only a bounder would seek the lady's affection before the father's permission.

But what if the poor, docile, affectionate female had no father to give either permission or protection? As Margaret Fuller pointed out, thousands upon thousands of women muddled along without the guardianship of father, brother, or husband. And too often such women, lacking male guidance, attached their undying affections to men who had no intention of marrying them. Seduced and betrayed like their lamented fictional prototype, poor Charlotte Temple, they were cut off from family and friends. Usually unable to support themselves (and perhaps their illegitimate children as well), they had no choice but to hang on for as long as possible to the men upon whom they depended. Mistaking that necessity for undying affection, Fowler describes such a woman:

> Behold her clinging, even to her betrayer, with a devotedness bordering on madness! Rendered a complete wreck in mind and body, by arts however diabolical, one would expect her to arm herself with fiendish vengeance, and drink his heart's blood; yet behold how fondly she embraces him, still delighting to serve him, even to the utmost that complete devotedness can possibly devise! She keeps sleepless vigils, night and day, over his sick bed; seizes every opportunity to load him with perpetual kindness; closes her ears to whatever may be uttered against him; is blind to his faults, though as palpable as Egyptian darkness; and pertinaciously defends him, though as black with crime, committed even against herself, as a devil incarnate! She is utterly regardless of self, and patient under all the misery she suffers, because they are inflicted by him, yet devoted still. Completely wrapped up in him, she meekly endures any and every torture he inflicts!

And what if the man tired of all her doting affection and threw her out or left her for another woman? Novelists, journalists, preachers, and moral reformers agreed that her only options in that event were prostitution or suicide. The latter was the nobler choice.

Feminists took up the cause of the despoiled maiden, protesting against the double standard that punished her and allowed her victimizer to go free. At the National Woman's Rights Convention in Cleveland in 1853 Ernestine Rose drew a thunderous response when she addressed the issue:

It is time to consider whether what is wrong in one sex can be right in another. It is time to consider why if a woman commits a fault, too often from ignorance, from inexperience, from poverty, because of degradation and oppression—aye! because of designing, cruel man; . . . why such a being in her helplessness, in her ignorance, in her inexperience and dependency—why a being thus situated, not having her mind developed, her faculties called out; and not allowed to mix in society to give her experience, not being acquainted with human nature, is drawn down, owing often to her best and tenderest feelings; in consequence also of being accustomed to look up to man as her superior, as her guardian, as her master,—why such a being should be cast out of the pale of humanity, while he who committed the crime, or who is, if not the main, the great secondary cause of it,—he who is endowed with superior advantages of education and experience, he who has taken advantage of that weakness and confiding spirit, which the young always have,—I ask if the victim is cast out of the pale of society, shall the despoiler go free?

"No, No!" shouted her audience. But their enthusiasm led feminists straight into a crooked issue. What feminists wanted was to get rid of the double standard of sexual conduct, but anyone who advocated pardoning errant girls (in that era of stifling high-mindedness) was standing on a shaky platform. So the call for equal treatment was taken to mean not that women should be forgiven but that men should be punished too—a policy with scant chance of success in a man-made world. Moral reformers—men and women—demanded legislation to punish seducers for ruining maidens. Other kinds of property were protected against theft and damage; why not women? In the subsequent debates about antiseduction legislation almost everyone lost sight of the fact that women (although treated as such by the law) are not *property*. To campaign for antiseduction laws was to acknowledge that a woman's chastity was a *thing* of value, the *only* thing that gave her value in the man-made commodity market. At the heart of the seduction issue lay profound questions of woman's nature and her sexuality, but nineteenth-century feminists could not bring up matters that could not be spoken, matters that could scarcely be imagined. Only the Claflin sisters, Tennessee and her sister Victoria Woodhull, whose frankness on sexual matters made them notorious, argued that female chastity and virtue (from the French *vir* meaning *man*) were not synonymous.

Men were all too happy to admit that seduction was vile—though unlike the ladies, they really didn't intend to do anything about it. Professor Fowler condemned seducers as the "worst Beings on Earth. . . . Blasted be that fiend, in human shape, who does this wicked deed!" he wrote. "Hurled, ay, even *hunted* from society; scorned by man and spurned by woman; uncheered by one ray of love!" Like many feminists, he argued that "Society has an undoubted right to inflict on [the seducer] any and all the punishments it may rightfully inflict on any." Even "hanging *forever*" would be too good for such a villain, he contended, but the actual penalties he proposed were mere wind: "Indians should be paid to torture him in this life, and the prince of satanic torturers throughout the next." Even the Devil himself, Fowler unwittingly suggests, wouldn't bother to punish the seducer without a bribe.

Certainly the issue was not a simple one for the class of men who made—or failed to make—laws. On one hand, as Fowler reminded men, they should guard women's virtue because it was more valuable to *them*, the fathers and husbands of women, than to the women themselves. "When *she* is defiled," he asked, "what becomes of *your* domestic happiness?" Every "darling girl" seduced and betrayed·was some "father's idol" and would have become some other man's excellent wife. On the other hand, the ideal purity of the respectable home— with the virgin daughters and the affectionate though passionless wife—was maintained at the expense of the real sexual abuse of prostitutes. So, in a curious unacknowledged way, the seducer performed a kind of social service in recruiting the public body of fallen women which hedged the virtue of respectable lady-wives. This was no small task; since the working life of a prostitute—before she succumbed to ravaging disease—was universally estimated at five years, thousands of new "girls" were needed each year to replace the dead. Then, too, every man was himself a potential seducer. So, men declined to pass laws against seduction and, in true sporting fashion, resolved to let each man guard his own nest. George Lippard, one of the most popular and influential novelists of the day, passed the final responsibility on to God. Although he was outraged that society forced young factory girls to work "sixteen hours for as many pennies," he did not hold the social fathers responsible for their ruin; to one of his poor fallen heroines he says, "If the pure blossom of your virgin soul has been trampled into the mire of temptation and crime, why, God be merciful to you, and may you rather be dealt with by His justice than by the tenderest mercy of man!" This do-nothing policy kept women dependent upon men for their protection and so drove women in search of nests— where they could be married or seduced, as a gentleman preferred.

It was not that men could not do anything. Some argued even then that morals could not be regulated by legislation—a contention hardly likely to stop a determined Victorian moralist—but in its report to the New York State Assembly in 1842 a judiciary committee responding to petitions for the suppression of licentiousness maintained that since all civilized nations safeguarded the "sanctity of the marriage institution" through civil and criminal law, the enactment of laws against adultery and seduction would not be a departure from the legislature's principles but "in fact . . . a restoration of its own powers and duties." And that argument was largely beside the point because New York was the only state that did not have laws against adultery on its books at the time. It was seduction that was the sticking point. The "Act to prevent licentiousness" introduced by the committee aimed mainly at adultery, although it did provide a three- to five-year prison term for any man convicted of inveigling or enticing a girl under eighteen. If the seduced woman was over eighteen, *both* she and her seducer were guilty of fornication and subject alike to a $200 fine and a two-year prison term. The proposed law seemed oddly punitive of the seducer's victim, but in any case, it didn't pass. Why, after all, should men change an arrangement so comfortable and flattering to themselves—particularly when they had taken such pains to design it?

If respectable men did nothing, they said a great deal. They joined Fowler in a chorus of outrage at the vile seducer and pity for his hapless victim—who was, nevertheless, ostracized. But their pity was only a mask of their contempt for women. Feminists argued that girls and young women were an easy prey to the skilled rake because of their *social conditions*: poor education, enforced inexperience of the world (called respectability), financial dependence, and ingrained deference to men. Men, on the other hand, thought that women were easily seduced because of their *inferior development.* So eager were the poor, docile, affectionate creatures to throw themselves at the feet of some man—any man—that they were only prevented from abandoning themselves willy-nilly by the gentleman's sense of fair play. "Does the noble lion pounce upon the feeble lamb because he *can*?" asked Fowler. Certainly not. All women, Fowler concluded, repeating the popular notion, "can easily be seduced, yet are not worth the effort."

Many men apparently made the effort, however, and early in the

nineteenth century seduction, white slavery, and wholesale prostitution were recognized as "social problems." To relieve them, women
did what they could. During the 1830s women in New York—home to
an estimated ten to fifteen thousand prostitutes—organized two
groups, the Female Benevolent Society and the Female Moral Reform
Society, to eradicate prostitution. They established shelters and employment agencies for prostitutes who wanted to change their line of
work, and they campaigned in their publications for laws to do away
with the double standard by punishing men as well as women. By
1840, 555 similar organizations across the country joined New York in
the American Female Moral Reform Society. The best thinkers among
the moral reformers and other feminist allies knew that what was
needed was not more protection for women, but *less.* Stop "protecting" girls from education, experience, decent jobs—and they would
hold their own against men. The reformers urged young women, even
wealthy young women, to prepare themselves for jobs rather than to
consider marriage as their only possible career. Concurrently they
campaigned for higher wages for working women. They found an ally
in Walt Whitman, then a young journalist, who argued in his editorials in the Brooklyn *Daily Eagle* that the below-subsistence wages of
women—"from *fifty cents* (!) to two dollars per week"—sowed "a public crop of other evils." Lucy Stone put the issue bluntly: "Women
working in tailor-shops are paid one-third as much as men. Some one
in Philadelphia has stated that women make fine shirts for twelve and
a half cents apiece; that no woman can make more than nine a week,
and the sum thus earned, after deducting rent, fuel, etc., leaves her just
three and a half cents a day for bread. Is it a wonder that women are
driven to prostitution?" When the moral reformers started watching
the houses of prostitution and printing in their newspapers the names
of men who frequented them, the reformers were denounced in press
and pulpit as crazed "Amazons." Still they were not deterred, but they
had to wait until 1910 for legislation to curb the interstate traffic in
girls and women.

Meanwhile, Professor Fowler noted that men continued to "recount their female conquests—obtained by whatever strategems and
false promises . . . —as exultingly as Indian warriors powwow over
their scalps. . . . Even those whose consciences prevent actual indulgence, often go far enough to see that they could go farther, and then
boast of their power over woman's passion, and jeer at the 'easy virtue'
of her sex." And even those men who did not go that far had the grati-

fication of knowing, like Fowler, that they could if they wanted to. It was, after all, "woman's *own* natural frailty" that made her a natural victim. Men who devised this image of woman had no intention of changing the picture. It is no wonder then that some women, seduced and betrayed, struck back.

In New York in the autumn of 1843, Amelia Norman sought out Henry Ballard one day and broke her parasol over his head. She had reason to be angry with him. Some two and a half years before, Ballard, a fashionable merchant, had bribed another girl to introduce him to Norman, a sixteen-year-old motherless New Jersey girl, a servant in New York since age thirteen. Ballard took Amelia Norman to restaurants and theaters and then to a house of prostitution on Mott Street, where he "seduced" her. He kept her confined in Brooklyn for a time, then moved with her from one boardinghouse to another, always as husband and wife, always under an assumed name. When she became pregnant, he took her to an abortionist—twice. Before the year was out Ballard seduced another young girl and dumped Norman in a cheap room on Canal Street. In the summer of 1842, when she was seventeen, she gave birth to a child; and Ballard moved her to a new "boarding house"—a Five Points brothel—and abandoned her there.

Amelia Norman chose not to follow the career Ballard had set up for her. She found a job ironing shirts in Joel Behrend's wholesale shirt store and in August 1843 went to live with the Behrend family. She could support herself; but from that time on, she tried to persuade Ballard to help support the child. He told her to get her living as other prostitutes did. She met another of Ballard's cast-off girls, and together they went to his store asking for child support. He called the police, charged her with vagrancy and prostitution, and tried to have her sent to Blackwell's Island penitentiary. After that, she hit him with her parasol. And then on the night of November 1, 1843, she followed him up the steps of the fashionable Astor House Hotel and struck him with a knife, once, in the chest, just above the heart. The blade only glanced off a rib and Ballard survived, but Amelia Norman was brought to trial for assault with intent to maim and assault with intent to kill.

On the face of the evidence, a dispassionate observer could reach only one verdict. Norman had provided herself with a knife, waylaid Ballard and followed him, aimed the knife blow at his heart, and stated afterward that she wished she had killed him. As the district attorney contended, the prisoner "committed a premeditated assault upon

Mr. Ballard, with intent to take his life—for which the Jury were bound to find her guilty." Yet the trial went on for a week, and at the end of it the jury deliberated for eight minutes and returned a verdict of not guilty. Amelia Norman went home with "a highly respectable lady" and then to "the bosom of the family" of Mrs. Lydia Maria Child, one of America's most famous "lady-authors" and an outspoken abolitionist who had campaigned for Norman's release and sat by her side during the trial. Up in Concord, feminist theoretician Margaret Fuller—who did not altogether approve of fallen women *or* of the sentimental Mrs. Child—nevertheless praised her for taking up this worthy cause.

Amelia Norman had become not just another criminal defendant but everybody's heroine. Mrs. Child took her up as an example of woman's finer nature violated by base sexuality; the moral reformers used her as a case in point in their crusade for antiseduction legislation. Unfortunately, they worked at cross purposes—the reformers pushing for social change, Mrs. Child pushing for Amelia Norman's personal redemption. And even these positions were decidedly ambiguous, for the moral reformers' emphasis on immediate antiseduction legislation obscured their long-term demands for equitable social standing—education, jobs, wages—and a single standard of sexual conduct; while Mrs. Child's effort to rehabilitate Amelia Norman implied that woman's sin, like man's, was forgivable and not, as the double standard dictated, graven in stone. Calling for social change, the reformers touted the most conservative and least practical plank in their platform: antiseduction laws. And Mrs. Child, trying to restore one soiled individual to pristine purity, or at least to self-respect, implied a single sexual standard for all. The two sides were closer than they knew, but in that dazzling confusion, who could see? They could agree on nothing but their disapproval of Amelia Norman's rash act. The moral reformers stated flatly that they did not "encourage in any circumstances the violation of one commandment of the decalogue because another has been violated, and no human statutes exist through which to seek redress." But they pressed the argument voiced in another case of seduction: that "every one who justifies or in any degree palliates the act of him who slays a seducer, *by so doing accuses and condemns the law* for not affixing a penalty to seduction. . . . Taking this view," the editors of the *Advocate of Moral Reform* maintained, "we cannot but hope that the expression of public sentiment in [the Norman case] will have some weight with the Legislatures of the several States."

It was the law that was on trial—or rather the lack of a law against seduction. Feminists pointed out that an equitable society would not need such legislation. When women had the education, the worldly experience, and the financial independence of men, they could fend for themselves. Until then, the reformers and a good many feminists said, the law was obliged to redress their grievances. More and more cases of the evils of seduction and its aftermath were brought before the public as the demand for such protective legislation increased. The same issue of the *Advocate for Moral Reform* that summarized the Norman case also presented other cases culled from newspapers across the country. These, the paper said, were typical: The Philadelphia *Gazette* reported that a young woman in Bradford County, Pennsylvania, seduced by her minister, became insane and so did her mother; the young woman's father, given the "fatal intelligence" of this disaster, dropped dead. The Rockville (Maryland) *Journal* reported the case of a man who seduced a widow and her fifteen-year-old stepdaughter, then killed the girl's illegitimate child. And the Cincinnati *Commercial* sadly announced that one General Beardsley, "a good citizen and beloved of all," had shot his daughter's seducer and turned himself over to the authorities. Even worse than these sad cases, argued the moral reformers, was the case "of more common occurrence"—the case of the young virgin fallen to prostitution, disease, and death. This is how reformers described the typical instance:

A youth fascinating in person, but without friends or home, save such as a cold world furnishes for a hard earned equivalent, falls in the pathway of the seducer. He is skilled in the black art, and at once determines to make her his prey. Not suspecting danger, she permits him to follow her from day to day. Her heart is uncorrupted, and he soon secures her affections. She confides implicitly in his assertions, her mind soon becomes absorbed with "love's young dream," and she awakes from this dream, deserted and ruined, to weep over her folly, with no word of human sympathy to soothe her grief—or glimmering ray of hope in earth or heaven. She is cast off by her employers, and, perhaps sick and destitute, seeks a shelter in the Alms House, where she must be supported, with her offspring, at the public expense. In her new situation she is introduced to a school of vice. Her hold upon a virtuous life is broken, and she listens to proposals from those old in sin, at which she once would have shuddered. A few brief years pass, during which her influence mingles with the broad current, from whence come the desperadoes that infest society: the inmates of our prisons and the victims of the scaffold. We next find her in the hospital, stretched upon a bed of pain, bloated, diseased, and loathsome to the sight. The room where she has been laid down to die, contains some 40 or 50 inmates in a similar condition, placed on narrow beds a few feet apart, with sunken eyes, ghastly countenances—often interspersing their groans with horrid blasphemies, till one after another falls into the embrace of the king of terrors.

That was a sad picture—more accurate and less sentimental than it sounds to a modern reader—and one that would draw a tear or a tirade from Amelia Norman's defense attorney, Lydia Maria Child, or Professor Fowler himself. But it did not produce law.

Nor did the fact that many so-called seductions were, in fact, cases of kidnapping and rape. The Philadelphia *North American* dispatched another story of "Shameful Outrage" concerning one C. W. Hepburn, who "seduced" a fourteen-year-old girl named Kensinger away from the home of her foster mother. The details of the story are these: another young girl was paid to persuade the Kensinger girl, by some ruse, to walk with her to the home of one Amanda Barney, alias Mrs. Simons. There the Kensinger girl was kept in "close confinement," and there Hepburn was "introduced" to her and "finally succeeded in accomplishing his base purpose." Hepburn and Mrs. Simons moved frequently to avoid detection, taking with them the Kensinger girl and one or two other girls whom they had "seduced" by the same means. Still, legislators did nothing; they even seemed to want to *know* nothing. Like the newspapers, they persisted in calling rape "seduction" and coercive seduction "feminine frailty." The *Advocate* noted acidly of its opponents: "In their philosophy, like that of the 'supersubtle Venetian,' the great desideratum is 'not to leave undone, but keep unknown.' If any mention, however guarded, is made . . . of some peculiarly horrible outrage on female purity, they are shocked, not at the *crime,* but its *exposure!*"

But when Amelia Norman stuck a knife into Henry Ballard, she ripped the familiar script to pieces. She did not take laudanum or slink off to die painfully in a whorehouse as seduced-and-abandoned maidens were *supposed* to do; and by the time she did make a halfhearted suicide attempt in jail, moral reformers and Mrs. Child had determined to make of her a cause célèbre. If men who made and enforced the laws would not protect Amelia Norman and her like from seduction, at least they would be forced to hear her story. Men who did not wish to learn would at least be compelled to listen. But the reformers had not counted on the deliberate obtuseness of the men in power who talked more than they listened and—luckily enough for them—got it all wrong.

At the trial of Amelia Norman in January 1844, attorney John A. Morrell, appointed by the court to defend her, announced that he had "left home, family, office and profession" to attend to the case because he was so filled with "virtuous indignation" at the "simple tale of the young and unfortunate victim." Then he put on trial not the law, but one Henry S. Ballard—"the coward, philosophical profligate, seducer!" Despite the district attorney's repeated reminders that Amelia Norman, and not Henry Ballard, was on trial, Morrell thundered: "I say he is on trial, and she is not—the community are the judges. The God of Heaven directed the blow, in order to bring this man before the court, jury and people. The people all ask for this seducer, who comes to the domestic hearth and tears away the beloved child." It pleased Morrell that the Norman case had been "the means of bringing *one scoundrel* before the public. . . . We have got him there," he said, "and let us hold him fast." And what was to be done to punish the scoundrel? Attorney Morrell would call him names in the courtroom, and reporters would call him names in print, in a sort of ritual public humiliation. Apart from that, attorney Morrell suggested only one punishment: "Let me tell that Ballard," he blustered, "that he had better go to Texas as soon as possible—for any man who should hereafter see him in the street, or elsewhere, addressing a virtuous female, it would be his duty as a man, as a citizen—a duty which he would owe to his God—to tell that female she was talking or walking with a vile, philosophical, coward seducer." Amelia Norman's other attorney, David Graham, lamented in his closing speech the "want of law to protect female virtue, and the absence of all criminal enactments to punish the base and villainous seducer—while property, and every other thing of value, were protected by laws." Yet he hastened to add that the highly respectable ladies who rallied round Miss Norman in the courtroom had "no connection whatever with the Moral Reform Society"; Mrs. Child—"one of the pillars of the literature of the age"—and her friends wished only to reform Miss Norman, not society. The jury, which could not in any case make new laws, could at least bend the existing ones; they made amends to poor Amelia Norman by pronouncing her not guilty while the audience in the courtroom applauded.

The apparent victory of Miss Norman and Mrs. Child—which Mrs. Child spoke of as an instance of the "occasional triumph of the moral sentiments over legal technicalities"—was in fact no victory at all, though it did save Norman from doing time in Sing Sing. Ballard had not been significantly punished (in some circles his romantic aura was enhanced), and should he take Morrell's hint and exile himself to

Texas he would find more innocent young girls to seduce. Amelia Norman, on the other hand, though publicly branded a fallen woman, got off—leaving her champions nothing to complain of. If existing laws could be applied to make amends to girls like Norman, where was the need for new legislation? The righteous patriarchs—judges, attorneys, jurors—could take the credit for protecting (however belatedly) the unfortunate girl. They could complacently gaze upon their own magnanimity, for the girl had fallen through her own fault. They could even bask in the gratitude of the "real" ladies like Mrs. Child who wrote of them: "When the poor girl returned to her cell, after her acquittal, some of the judges, several of the jury, her lawyers, and the officers of the prison gathered around her to express congratulation and sympathy. There was something beautiful in the compassionate respect with which they treated this erring sister, because she was unfortunate and wretched." At the same time these men could create the illusion that there was a fundamental difference between themselves (the "real" men filled with righteous indignation and compassion) and the vile, cowardly seducers, who socially, economically, and sexually exploited women. And they could avoid mentioning the double sexual standard altogether. All in all, the public scapegoating of the seducer seemed to please almost everyone, while changing nothing.

Only a year later, however, the moral reformers had begun to catch on. When Virgil Knapp seduced and impregnated seventeen-year-old Sarah Decker, he gave her some oil of tansy, an abortifacient, which she drank at his instructions, thinking it was "medicine." After several hours of agonizing convulsions, she died, asking that Knapp not be punished. Apparently Knapp had not meant to kill the girl, and although he was widely thought to be morally responsible for her death, he did not seem to be legally so. The American Female Moral Reform Society seized upon this case to renew the call for antiseduction legislation, and this time they were joined by Horace Greeley's New York *Tribune*. The *Tribune* noted that everyone was asking what was to be done with Knapp, but it thought the question of what to do with legislators "who persist in permitting the blackest crimes to go unpunished" was far more important. "If there are to be no legal penalties for Seduction," the *Tribune* argued, "we do not see why Knapp should be punished at all. . . . If Seduction is not a crime, he is no criminal; for he clearly did not mean to take his victim's life. He is as innocent to-day as thousands who enjoy the highest honors of the land, and less guilty than those who from year to year defeat, by juggling and trick, the passage of laws to punish Adultery and Seduction. Let not this one villain be made a scape-goat for the sins of Libertines in general; but let our laws be so amended as to provide suitable penalties for all who lure the innocent to ruin by false promises, and then we need not ask what is to be done with any particular offender."

Still, the lawmakers did nothing. Most women who were seduced and abandoned disappeared quietly into disgrace. But many others, like Amelia Norman, struck back.

2.

Mary Moriarty, in 1855, stuck a knife into John Shehan on a Memphis street corner. Mary Harris, abandoned in the Midwest, took a train to Washington in 1865 and shot Adoniram Burroughs in the corridor of the Treasury building. Fanny Hyde, in a Brooklyn factory in 1872, shot her employer George Watson as he was walking downstairs to lunch. And Kate Stoddart carefully laid out Charles Goodrich in the basement of his Brooklyn brownstone in 1873 after she shot him three times in the head. All of these women were arrested and charged with first-degree murder.

Their stories are almost interchangeable. Like Amelia Norman and like the typical seduced-and-abandoned maiden sketched in the pages of the *Advocate,* all of these women were young, poor, friendless, and innocent.

Mary Moriarty left her elderly parents and came to the United States some time around mid-century, along with a million other Irish immigrants. Her ship docked at New Orleans, and a river packet carried her up the Mississippi to Memphis and Mrs. O'Hara's boarding-house. Among the boarders chambermaid Moriarty discovered John Shehan, once a childhood playmate in Ireland, now a laborer on the Mississippi levees. He asked her to marry him, but when she found she was expecting a child, he still hadn't arranged for the ceremony. At Moriarty's request the Catholic priest spoke to Johnny and elicited a solemn vow to marry her; but the child was born and died, and still Johnny put her off. She lost her job at Mrs. O'Hara's and sifted down to Mrs. Young's boardinghouse, then to Colonel Coleman's, finally to the United States Hotel, where fewer questions were asked. Johnny Shehan left town for a few months on a bender and came back broke. He promised marriage again and borrowed ten dollars from her, supposedly to pay "his board." (Her wages were thirty-three cents per day for a twelve-hour workday.) They made wedding plans, and soon Mary discovered that she was pregnant again. On the evening of September 1, 1855, after dinner had been cleared away at the United States Hotel, Mary walked out with Johnny to discuss their wedding; but he told her that he had no mind to marry her. She tried to persuade him, and he tried to pull her into the bushes. She stabbed him twice in the chest, shouting, "Do you mind that, Johnny?" He turned and ran to his boardinghouse, and there, within forty-five minutes, he bled to death. Mary Moriarty was pursued by witnesses; when they caught her, she was still holding the knife.

Mary Harris, one of many children in a poor Irish family in Burlington, Iowa, was put out at age nine to live with and work for a woman who owned a fancy goods store. One of the customers, Adoniram Burroughs, who kept a store nearby, began to stop in daily. He enjoyed "fondling" the child. When his own business failed, he took over as bookkeeper in the store where Mary worked. Later he wrote her love letters, reminding her of the "stolen kisses" they had enjoyed in the back room of the store—when he was in his late twenties, and she was about ten. Following Michelet's advice, "he proposed to mold and fashion her mind by the superior force of his own age, experience, and will, in order that she might at a future period make him a suitable wife." This technique was successful, for she "learned to love" him although at first she hadn't liked him at all.

When Mary was thirteen her father objected to Burroughs's attentions; Burroughs went to Chicago and for the next four or five years wrote love letters to Mary, until he persuaded her to come to Chicago. She found work and lodging there with two respectable milliners, the Misses Devlin, who understood from Burroughs's conduct that the couple was engaged. The wedding was set for June 1863, but Burroughs went off to Washington to seek a better job, and the marriage was repeatedly postponed "for lack of means." Then, in September 1863, Mary read in the newspaper that Burroughs had married Miss Amelia Boggs, a well-to-do Chicago woman. For months she tried to sue him for breach of promise, but the lawyers dallied with her, saying they could not find him to serve a writ. (Breach of promise was a tricky claim in any case; in the mouth of an Irish shopgirl, given the prejudices of the day, it was ludicrous.) Twice she went to Washington looking for him herself; on January 30, 1865, she entered the Treasury building, where Burroughs worked as a clerk, waited an hour in the corridor, and when he emerged from his office at the end of the day, she took a Sharpes four-barrel pistol from her pocket and shot him once in the back. She fired again as he ran away down the hall, but that shot passed over his head as he fell, bleeding to death. She lowered her green veil and walked calmly away, but she was arrested by a guard as she left the building.

Fanny Windley was born in Nottingham, England. When she was four her mother died; at eight she got a job; at ten she came to the United States and went to work in a factory; at fifteen she took a job in a Manhattan hairnet factory owned by George Watson, a forty-five-year-old family man with five children. One day, four months later, when the other workers had gone, he locked her in his office and "seduced" her. As long as she worked there, he wouldn't leave her alone; but when she tried to leave, he threatened to blackball her. He impregnated her and gave her some unidentified medicine to induce abortion. As friends put it, her "flesh fell away"; she lost thirty pounds and her health failed. Then, when she was eighteen, she met a young man named Hyde. She got Watson to promise with his hand on the Bible that he would leave her alone, and she married Hyde. When Watson came after her again, she told her husband. Watson promised Hyde that he would leave Fanny alone. But he didn't. So on January 26, 1872, when George Watson left his third-floor office, he found Fanny Hyde waiting on the landing with a gun. She shot him once in the head, killing him instantly, and a few hours later surrendered herself to the police.

Elizabeth King, the second daughter of Isaac King of Plymouth, Massachusetts, left home early to earn a living by her needle. She worked in Boston, Philadelphia, and Providence, learned the bonnet business in Middleboro, New Hampshire, and went to New York when she was in her early twenties. Her family lost track of her; she started going by the name Kate Stoddart (or Stoddard) for reasons she never explained. She went to work making hats, sometimes in factories, sometimes taking the work home to her rooming house. Employers liked her because she was a good worker, though a slow one; they gave her all the most difficult styles at piecework rates. Apparently lonely, she answered a matrimonial ad placed by Charles Goodrich, a forty-two-year-old former lumber dealer with an interest in some newly built Brooklyn brownstones. She fell in love with Charley, and on May 20, 1872, they were married; she went to live with him in his bare, new Brooklyn house, but they kept the marriage a secret because Charley said it would interfere with some property negotiations he had under way with his brother. To the neighbors the ashy blonde woman was a shadowy figure. Some thought she looked ill and frail; and indeed she was—after Charley gave her medicine to induce abortion. Then, one night in February 1873, she returned from working in Manhattan to find herself locked out of the house. A friend of Charley's, pretending to be a watchman, took her to the unfinished house next door where Charley had dumped her belongings. Their marriage, it seemed, was not binding, for it had been performed by one of Charley's friends masquerading as a clergyman; and now Charley had decided to marry someone else. She wrote a letter to his father, complaining of his ill treatment of her; the father passed it on to Charley. Still, on the night of March 20, 1872, Lizzie King—or Kate Stoddart, as she would be called in the record books—went back to Charley's house to persuade him to marry her. He refused. So in the morning, as he was building up the fire in the kitchen, she shot him three times behind the ears. She laid him out in his stocking feet with his head resting comfortably on his shoes, washed the blood from his face, clipped a curl of his dark hair for her locket, and disappeared. The next day, Charley's brother found the body. Four months later a policewoman found Kate Stoddart crossing on the Brooklyn ferry.

All four of these women were young; and all of them had worked since childhood for subsistence wages in jobs that carried no possibility of advancement. Beyond that drudgery they had nothing to look forward to but marriage; and they were doubly impelled toward marriage by all that they had been taught about their natural destiny as women. In finding a husband, none of them enjoyed protection or guidance. Mary Moriarty and Kate Stoddart were completely on their own. Mary Harris's father could not keep her away from Burroughs because he could not provide for her himself; and apparently, by the time he discovered the relationship, Burroughs already had a hold of several years' standing on Mary. Fanny Hyde's husband—scarcely more than a boy himself—had no power short of violence to keep Watson away from Fanny, and (like Mary Harris's father) he could not take her away because he could not support her. Fanny Hyde did try to get her husband and her brother to take action against Watson; only when they failed her, did she shoot him herself.

With the exception of Mary Moriarty, who trusted an old friend, these women turned to men older, better educated, wealthier, and more powerful than themselves—men desirable as husbands, but desiring only to seduce. When they discovered their mistake, all of the women tried to save themselves, or their reputations, by fair means. Moriarty tried to hang on to Shehan by paying his expenses. She called upon the church just as Harris called upon the law and Stoddart upon her "husband's" father to remind the man of his obligation. Hyde married another. But none of these plans worked, and all of the women grew desperate, either because the men would not marry them, or would not let them go. Each woman gave her seducer one more chance to make amends; and then she killed him. None of them denied the crime; and only Kate Stoddart tried halfheartedly to avoid arrest. All of them said they were sorry. One by one they were brought to trial. Their cases were so similar that their trials echoed the same themes.

At the trial of Mary Moriarty in 1855, her defense attorney, Milton A. Haynes, appealed eloquently to the men of the jury who, as men, must "admire and love what is good and what is beautiful" and "hate and despise what is bad, and wicked." He left no doubt, as he retold Moriarty's story, that Shehan the vile seducer was bad and wicked, while Moriarty had responded only to that "great law of nature which has declared that woman shall be obedient unto, love and cherish the man." Killing this evil man who betrayed her, then, was no crime; in fact, as Haynes described it, the murder was almost an act of divine retribution. "It seems to me," he said, "that an unseen and invisible hand of some good angel from regions above reached this dagger down to Mary, at the moment she required it, and whispered to her 'strike!' and when she did strike an unseen hand guided her blow, and the angel of mercy, at the throne of Jehovah at that moment dropped tears of pity, which fell upon the book of fate and blotted out the record of her crime forever." The attorney general vainly reminded the jurors that the knife had come not from heaven but from the United States Hotel. Still, defense attorney Haynes appealed to an unwritten law. "You have all taken a vow as jurors," he reminded them, "and that is, *that you will 'a true verdict give, according to the evidence.'* It is the *evidence* upon which you are to found your verdict, and not the law; for really there is not much law in it, except natural law, and divine law, and that higher law of man—Nature—which makes him *rebel* against oppression, and by opposing, end it. The law of homicide need not be discussed in the case."

Haynes acknowledged that Tennessee had no statute authorizing the killing of seducers, but he put to the jury a hypothetical case: "If this girl's father or brother had killed John Shehan for seducing and ruining this girl by a base vow and promise to marry her, are there twelve men to be found in Tennessee who would be base enough as a jury to render a verdict to hang that father or that brother for it?" The jurors set aside the laws "written in books," and by following the laws written "upon the breasts of men" found Mary Moriarty not guilty. Agreeing upon the verdict took them two minutes.

But that was the South, where many a man single-handedly enforced an unwritten law. And both the defendant and the victim in this case were the poorest Irish immigrants, a class unlikely to threaten society as long as they kept their quarrels to themselves. Nevertheless, the case must have been disturbing to men. After all, Mary Moriarty was *not* her father or her brother. The unwritten law provided that *men* defend the honor of their families; it said nothing about women defending themselves. And this allusion of attorney Haynes to rebelling against oppression—surely that was man's work alone. Was there not something foolhardy in turning a confessed killer into the streets again? The prosecutor in the case of Amelia Norman argued that setting her free would be tantamount to giving twelve thousand prostitutes license to kill their seducers in the public streets. Although that predicted disaster hadn't come to pass, acquitting Moriarty seemed a vaguely dangerous precedent. Luckily, by the time Mary Harris came to trial in Washington, D.C., a decade later, her attorneys—although they continued to allude to the higher law—had devised a far more sophisticated defense: insanity. It seemed the perfect plea, for it illustrated once again the mental frailty of woman, and by helping female defendants get off, it undercut demands for antiseduction legislation. It was a useful tool, in other words, for keeping woman in her place.

Then, as now, neither lawyers nor doctors were very clear about defining insanity. Outside the courtroom, lawyers and doctors were at odds; as medical professor James Hendrie Lloyd noted in 1887, "The medical definition has sometimes been stretched so wide that it includes cases which shock the common-sense of the most intelligent, while the legal tests have been made so narrow and unscientific that it is difficult to include in them some of the most patent cases of insanity." Inside the courtroom, lawyers and doctors vied to impose the definition of their own discipline upon the criminal law. The general public—which still regarded insanity as punishment for sin—was puzzled.

In the eyes of the law, insanity usually meant a defect of reason so that the insane person was unable to tell right from wrong or to understand the nature and consequences of his act. The trial of Daniel M'Naughton in England in 1843 firmly established the rule in both English and American law that criminal insanity existed when a person was "labouring under such a defect of reason, from disease of the mind, as not to know the nature and quality of the act he was doing, or if he did know it, that he did not know he was doing what was wrong."

Unfortunately, reason was only one of the mental "faculties" identified by the psychology of the day; the emotions and the will had also to be considered, and psychologists began to find that they were just as subject to derangement as the reason. Some defined a condition in which a man's will was so impaired that he could not help doing what his reason and emotions told him to be wrong; this theory, popularized as the "irresistible impulse," quickly passed into the law of seventeen states. Other experts, like Isaac Ray, the leading psychiatrist of his day, postulated a condition called *moral mania* in which the reason was intact but the emotional propensities warped. The term *moral mania* or *moral insanity,* as it soon became known, was confusing, however, for faculty psychologists could not decide which faculty housed the moral sense. Some experts argued that moral insanity was a defect of the will, while others maintained that irresistible impulse actually sprang from deranged passions. Trying to clarify the options in 1887, Dr. Lloyd could not even enumerate them all: "With some [moral insanity] is purely an 'emotional' insanity, with others it is 'instinctive,' with others it is a sort of *abulimia,* or loss of will, as in the 'impulsive' varieties, etc."

Where women were concerned all this hopelessly snarled psychological theory was irrelevant, for all of it was about men. Psychologists themselves had little to say about women, for they had not bothered to inquire into their cases; but popular wisdom told a great deal. In the first place, reason, the traditional seat of malfunction in the insane, was thought to be weak and shaky in the healthiest women. Secondly, the emotions—particularly love—governed women and even in so-called normal women might reach insane proportions. Professor Fowler noted that women gifted with a large "faculty" of amativeness (there is no end to the confusing proliferation of terms advanced by the various "sciences") "literally idolize the opposite sex" and "love almost to insanity." Isaac Ray commented, "With women it is but a step from extreme nervous susceptibility to downright hysteria, and from that to overt insanity." Thirdly, the moral nature, such as it was, was usually thought to be an instinctive part of the emotional life. Women were conceded a finer moral "nature" than men, but women could not have a genuine moral "life"—with decisions and choices—because they were so deficient in reason. "Morality" in women consisted mainly in chastity, which could be forever lost in an instant to any man who set out to steal it away. A woman, then, already deranged in *all* of her faculties, was almost by definition insane.

On some points, the psychological experts did agree. In any type of insanity, presumably whether it affected men or women, two factors could be isolated: the underlying condition that predisposed the person to insanity, and the precipitating event that brought it on. These causes were itemized in lists that varied little from one expert to another. An international congress of 1867 listed, among other predisposing conditions, "great difference of age between parents; influence of sex; of surroundings; convulsions, or emotions of the mother during gestation; epilepsy; other nervous diseases; pregnancy; lactation; menstrual period; critical age; puberty; intemperance; venereal excess; and onanism." Among the "exciting causes" given were "trouble, and excessive grief; intemperance; excessive excitement, of whatever kind; epilepsy; disordered functions of menstruation; pregnancy; parturition; lactation; fevers; injuries to the head or spine; and overwork." Of all these factors, the only inescapable one for man is puberty, listed as a predisposing condition; but *every* phase in the life cycle of woman is listed as *both* a predisposing condition and a precipitating cause. Almost naturally insane, a woman might easily be a natural criminal. And that, said Dr. Ray, is precisely the case: "In the sexual evolution, in pregnancy, in the parturient period, in lactation, strange thoughts, extraordinary feelings, unseasonable appetites, criminal impulses, may haunt a mind at other times innocent and pure."

Of all the causes of insanity in women, the most fateful was thought to be menstruation. Even in "normal" women it was regarded as a disease. In a chapter on woman's "sickness," the knowing Frenchman Jules Michelet described the *normal* menstrual cycle as a "trage-dy" making every woman for "15 or 20 days out of 28 (we may say nearly always) . . . not only an invalid, but a wounded one." Henry Putnam Stearns, superintendent of the asylum at Hartford and a lec-turer on insanity at Yale, offered a scientific explanation:

> . . . in a general way the sexual system in the female exerts a much larger influence on the whole physical and mental economy, than in the male. A very intimate sympathy exists between it and both the stomach and the brain. This becomes especially manifest at the period of puberty, and continues until after the cessation of menstruation. The whole moral na-ture appears to come into existence and activity when the child becomes a woman, and thereafter, for thirty or thirty-five years, the whole person is largely affected one fourth of the time by the functional activity of the pelvic organ.

His colleague Thomas Smith Clouston of the Edinburgh asylum and university agreed; the connection between uterus and brain is so inti-mate that "the occurrence of absolutely normal menstruation is at-tended with great risk in many unstable brains."

The horrors of *abnormal* menstruation can scarcely be imagined. They were thought to afflict chiefly unmarried women—perhaps be-cause married women were occupied by all the predicted ills of preg-nancy, parturition, and lactation. In any case, whenever there was frustration of "all those instinctive yearnings for . . . husband and chil-dren; all the outgoing of longing for all that is implied in home, the care of it, and all connected with it," there the gynecologist (another new scientist) was bound to find a "nervous, capricious, irritable, and hysterical" woman suffering from "uterine derangement of one kind or another." Women who tried to study or to follow a profession diverted blood to their brains in the mental hyperactivity that characterized the insane; menstruation ceased and disease resulted. And any woman who tried to avoid motherhood, woman's "supremest function," was sure to end in disease.

Physicians generally agreed that menstruation could trigger such nervous ailments as "neuralgia, migraine, epilepsy, and chorea," as well as impulses toward "kleptomania, pyromania, dipsomania," ho-micide, and suicide. Clouston was convinced that in cases of dysmen-orrhea or amenorrhea "the organic instinct of reproduction becomes transmitted morbidly into instinctive impulses to kill, steal, etc." He, and other experts, reported cases of women who, while menstruating painfully, "did all sorts of impulsive acts." He knew of a perfectly nice young woman who ate dirt and pinched children. Dr. Halliday Croom reported the case of a woman who ate the bristles of her hairbrush every month and tried to steal the hairbrushes of others. Isaac Ray thought menstruating women were apt to kill their children. And then there was the case of Mary Harris, who killed Adoniram Burroughs.

From the moment Harris read in the newspaper of Burroughs's marriage, she was "seized with an attack of physical disease with which she had never before been disturbed, and which, at regular periodical intervals . . . continued to visit her" up to the time of her trial. "From that time forth," her attorneys maintained, "her character and her physical condition were all changed." Formerly "cheerful and happy—bird-like," she "became moody, melancholy, depressed, and exceedingly quiet." She slept little and often spent the night crying; on the coldest winter nights she got out of bed and huddled upon the floor. And periodically, at times thought to coincide with her menstruation, she fell into little fits of violence; she tore up books and clothing, spread preserves on the carpet, hit a customer with a weighted pincushion, struck her friend and employer Jane Devlin with a window brush, and once—when Jane said she wished to hear no more of Mr. Burroughs—chased her with a carving knife. She lost weight and grew haggard.

Such was her appearance when Dr. Calvin M. Fitch was called in to see her in late September. Conveniently enough, physicians thought the connection between nervous debility and uterine lesion to be so intimate that the presence of one condition indicated the other. So, when Dr. Fitch saw that Harris's "eye was wild," he knew immediately that there was something wrong with her uterus. Dr. Fitch saw his patient about once a month for the next three months, and although his five-minute visits gave him no time to perform a physical examination, he diagnosed the ailment as "severe congestive dysmenorrhea, arising for the most part as a consequence of the irritability of the uterus." Dr. Fitch said, "Such uterine irritation always affects the nervous system. In some instances it develops into insanity; and indeed a disturbance of the uterus—uterine irritability—is with females one of the most frequent causes of insanity." Still, Dr. Fitch treated not the nervous symptoms but what he took to be the physical cause of her condition. "I attribute the wildness of the eye merely to the pain and irritability consequent upon her physical condition," he testified, "believing that just as soon as the uterus was allayed the whole thing would pass off." He could not remember what, if anything, he had prescribed for her (he recorded only whether his patients paid their bills); but the standard remedy would have been opium or morphine. At the trial, Fitch and other medical experts agreed with "every medical man in the world, and every book ever written on that subject . . . that this disease is a constant physical cause of periodical, or, as it is more properly termed, paroxysmal insanity."

If that was not enough, Harris was also found to be suffering from the most common cause of "moral insanity": "disappointed affection." And according to Dr. Fitch, the combination of the two causes—uterine irritation and disappointed love—would "produce a very much greater effect than either would induce alone."

The effect of disappointed love was further intensified by the "moral shock" of some strange goings-on just before Adoniram Burroughs married Miss Boggs. Harris received a letter signed by a Mr. Greenwood asking her to meet him at a certain address. The handwriting looked quite familiar and prompted Jane Devlin, Harris's employer, to make inquiries at the address given and at the post office. The writer almost certainly was Burroughs; the house was a notorious place of assignation. Burroughs's socially prominent older brother did his best to cover up the already obscure "Greenwood affair"; but the defense maintained that Burroughs wanted to use Harris's visit to the house to impugn her character and relieve himself of the moral obligation to marry her. Whatever his intentions, his conduct was sure to have presented a "moral shock" to any respectable young lady.

That double insanity, then, was the Harris defense. Her attorneys maintained, "She was insane from moral causes, aggravated by disease of the body. . . . A pure, virtuous, chaste, delicate little girl, not more than twenty years of age at this time, whose frame is wasting and whose spirits are gone, whose heart is broken, in a paroxysm of insanity has slain the man who has brought upon her all this suffering." Attorney Joseph Bradley assured the jury that the prisoner at the bar, who sat swathed in dark veils, "is not guilty of any crime towards God or man, although she has been the instrument of taking the life of another." After five minutes of deliberation, the jury agreed, and Mary Harris went free.

When Fanny Hyde came to trial in Brooklyn in 1872, her attorneys pulled out all the stops. They appealed to the unwritten law, saying to the jury, "Gentlemen, if you go home to-night and your daughter tells you that some villain has ruined her, you will not wait, the instinct of your nature will not permit you to wait a moment until you have avenged her dishonor in the blood of her seducer." Secondly, they argued that Fanny Hyde's crime was justifiable homicide, for she had killed in self-defense. She had not lain in wait for George Watson, but rather "she met deceased at the head of the stairs, and when she went up stairs and reached the top he suddenly seized on her with violence, in an indecent manner and insisted upon her accompanying him to an improper place; and they had a struggle. . . . and then it was that she shot him." And, for good measure, they argued that Fanny Hyde was insane.

Summing up for the defense, attorney Samuel Morris traced the beginnings of her insanity to her seduction at age fifteen. He said that since then "her health had become broken and she a wreck, that she was suffering from disease at the time, that her mind was at the time affected, under great strain, the sense of some great wrong pressing upon it, great grief, and all these things existing at the time; add to that this assault made upon her by this man, and, like the touching of the match to the powder, it exploded, and she became irresponsible." This was not the moral insanity that had afflicted Amelia Norman or Mary Harris—although the Hyde defense attorneys quoted at length from both those precedent-setting cases; this was something new called *transitoria mania* which, luckily for the sufferer, came and went in a flash. A definitive description of the disease written by the noted authority Dr. William Hammond was read to the jury: "There is a form of insanity, which, in its culminating act is extremely temporary in its character, and which, in all its manifestations, from beginning to end, is of that duration. . . . By authors it has been variously designated as transitoria mania, ephemeral mania, temporary insanity and morbid impulse. It may be exhibited in the perceptional, intellectual, emotional or volitional form, or as general mania." The exciting causes of the disease, according to Hammond, included almost everything from "hasheesh" to air pollution and dampness and, certainly, menstruation. Dr. John Byrne, clinical professor of uterine disease at Long Island Medical College, testified that during perfectly normal menstrual periods, teenaged girls were "affected mentally to the extent of hysterical paroxysms."

What chance was there for poor Fanny Hyde, seduced, aborted, abused, "afflicted with a disease" (dysmenorrhea), and also with "the peculiar condition of woman at stated periods," and attacked again by George Watson? A parade of medical experts—in person and in print—discussed insanity; and Hyde herself took the stand to speak quite collectedly of Watson's harassment and abuse. Reporters covering the case couldn't figure out whether the defense was insanity or simply "fearful provocation." The tearful and thoroughly confused jury wrangled for hours and announced that it could not reach a verdict; nine men voted for acquittal, but two held firm for a manslaughter conviction and one even voted for murder. The jury was dismissed and Fanny Hyde was released on $2,500 bail.

That was in April 1872. In January 1873 her case was called for retrial in the King's County Court of Oyer and Terminer; Hyde failed to answer, her bail was forfeited, and on March 24, 1873, she was arrested in Washington, D.C., and returned to Brooklyn's Raymond Street jail to await a new trial. There she met Kate Stoddart, under arrest for the murder of Charles Goodrich. The police had been a long time catching up with Stoddart, although she still lived in the neighborhood, worked at hat making in Manhattan, and attended Charley's funeral; and during that time the police had created a great muddle of imaginary suspects and accomplices, paid informers, and outlandish theories. Kate Stoddart, who according to some reports had once been confined in the asylum at Taunton, Massachusetts, added to the confusion by repeatedly changing her story; a reporter noted that although she was a woman of "remarkable intellect, . . . her mind frequently drifted from the channel of good, sound reasoning."

The district attorney, trying to build a case for conviction in the new trial of Fanny Hyde, now had another case on his hands of the vile seducer called to account. Commentators were already describing "her once plump and shapely form . . . gone away to a skeleton; her round, rosy cheeks . . . hollow and wan." Reporters who had headlined FANNY HYDE'S SAD LIFE would do sentimental wonders with the tale of Kate Stoddart. Her landlady was prepared to testify that she was a perfect lady. Letters of sympathy began to pour into the jail, offering help and support. Perhaps the district attorney caught the drift of public opinion. On September 4, 1873, Fanny Hyde was released from jail on $2,500 bail pending a new trial. Some time after that Kate Stoddart must have been released, for she was never called to trial; like Fanny Hyde, who was never called again, she simply disappears from history.

There wasn't much a prosecutor could do against an insanity defense in cases of this sort, even though almost everyone acknowledged that the insanity was trumped up. In the case of Fanny Hyde, District Attorney Winchester Britton said flatly that the insanity defense was a "sham." It was not the "real" defense in the case but rather a fake defense "interposed for the purpose of ringing the changes on what is claimed to be the wrongs of this young girl." Prosecutors in the case of Mary Harris similarly charged that the insanity defense was merely a ruse to permit introduction of the sort of evidence that brought tears to the jurors' eyes. Since the ruination of all these young women took place well before they murdered, testimony about their seduction and betrayal was technically inadmissible as evidence *except* insofar as it went to prove insanity. In the Harris case, Judge Wylie initially ruled Burroughs's letters to Harris inadmissible, then ruled to admit them since they tended to establish her shock of disappointed love, a cause of her insanity; and those letters, which conclusively displayed the dalliance of the grown man with the preadolescent girl (today we would call it child molesting), more than any other evidence provoked the jurors' sympathy. District Attorney Carrington told the Harris jurors: "You know that this woman is not insane. If you acquit her upon the ground of insanity, it will be a pretext only."

Probably he was right. The reporter for the New York *Tribune* commented after the acquittal that "the plea of insanity is almost universally considered invalid," but "the popular verdict coincides with that of the jury." During the trial the press was sympathetic to her, and Mrs. Abraham Lincoln, recently widowed, sent her flowers. When the verdict was announced, the spectators in the courtroom cheered, as they cheered the acquittals of Norman, Moriarty, and Hyde. Men threw their hats in the air; women waved their handkerchiefs. The defendant fainted and was carried from the courtroom by her gallant attorney. Jurors rushed to congratulate her. Judge Wylie and his wife stood on the street corner to see a carriage pass by, carrying Mary Harris to the depot for her trip to Baltimore, where she would recuperate. So it came as a surprise to many that Mary Harris failed to recuperate and had to be returned to Washington to the asylum where she spent the rest of her life.

3.

Cases of seduction, betrayal, and revenge had to be decided on the basis of sentiment rather than law because the law, quite simply, did not fit the community. It seemed clear to everyone—even to those outraged newspaper editors who weren't able to put their finger on the problem—that enforcing the letter of the law in these cases would contradict the very principles on which those laws were based. Theoretically, law serves several purposes in a society. For one thing, punishment of criminals is popularly supposed to provide an example and deter crime. Defense attorney Daniel Voorhees argued in the Harris case, however, that if the jurors sought to make "examples for the correction of vice and the preservation of morality," they ought not "to commence with the humblest, the feeblest, and the most helpless." These women, after all, were ruined for life. Unlike men who avenged wrongs to their honor, these women did not become heroes and they did not reclaim their good names. They remained fallen women, publicly humiliated by a criminal trial, permanently stained in mind and body. What woman could want to follow their example? To punish these women further as a deterrent to others seemed redundant and cruel.

The law also is supposed to protect society by providing that dangerous persons will be removed from its midst, but scarcely anyone could think that society was in imminent danger from these despoiled maidens. Prostitution was generally thought to pose a threat to society, but these vengeful women had attempted homicide precisely because they were unwilling to become prostitutes. And they were unlikely to repeat their crimes; since they could not, by definition, be ruined again (they were already ruined once and for all), they would have no reason to retaliate again. Besides, women who blamed certain individuals rather than society for their grievances and who sought redress through personal revenge rather than political action did not threaten the social structure but, in effect, affirmed it.

If anyone threatened society then, it was not the despoiled maidens but their vile seducers. It was the "poison and mildew of licentiousness" that were "corrupting the heart of society." Milton Haynes, defending Mary Moriarty, argued that "he, who seduces a maid, upon the most solemn vow of marriage, hath committed a worse crime than that of *murder*." Professor Fowler echoed the sentiment: "Compared with this crime," he said, "murder is innocence." Attorney I. B. Catlin, representing Fanny Hyde, went further: "Men whose base lust will spur them to such acts of violence are a disgrace to humanity," he maintained, "and their destruction by the victims of their lust is a proper doom."

That, perhaps, was going a bit far; but it did seem that these victims of the seducer's lust were only trying to do what society prescribed for them. They seemed to regard nothing so highly as what they had been taught. They seemed to want nothing more than to become respectable wives and mothers. But that destiny necessarily involved placing their unquestioning trust in some man—and they chose the wrong ones. For the right men, they might have made exemplary wives. Milton Haynes raved about the unfailing love and unselfish devotion of women in general and Mary Moriarty in particular. Kate Stoddart was described as "a woman who loves with an affection amounting to idolatry." And Mary Harris, her defenders argued, would have been a "respected wife" but for the defection of Burroughs; then "the world would have applauded her sublime devotion to him." Lydia Maria Child described Amelia Norman's nature as nearly perfect: she was "a girl of strong feelings, but quiet, reserved, and docile to the influence of those she loves." "A proper education," Child said, "would have made her a noble woman." Mary Harris's attorneys claimed too that "she did no more than what the proudest, the purest, and the best have done in all countries and at all times." And attorney Haynes frankly compared Mary Moriarty's defense of her virtue to the saintly doings of Lucretia and Virginia. These women, even when insane, were not "unnatural" in the least; they were, in fact, models of femininity. They killed only to defend that virtue (and the social position it entitled them to) which society itself had taught them to overrate.

They killed to defend that stolen honor for which society neither offered protection nor exacted punishment from the thief. They went outside the law because the law seemed unable or unwilling to protect them, even though the state is morally obliged to protect all of its citizens. The state contracts that obligation when it denies individual citizens the right to retaliate against others in their own behalf and undertakes instead to defend the interests of all citizens alike. But in the case of seduction the state sat on its hands, and the betrayed maidens took the law into their own.

Despite the public outcry against seduction, society did nothing to alter legal or social arrangements to protect women from predatory men. The state, in effect, violated the social contract with its women citizens (who weren't full citizens anyway); and though it retained the legal right to punish them for retaliating for themselves, that law was without moral foundation. Its irrelevance was exposed—when women did retaliate for themselves and were put to trial—in the paradoxes of the proceedings: the killer was a victim; the victim was a criminal, perhaps worse than a killer; the state was a villain; the jurors were to protect the confessed killer from punishment at law; and so on. Attorney Haynes actually was quite right when he argued in the Moriarty case that there was "not much law in it." And somehow it seemed to a confused public perfectly proper that the President's widow should send a bouquet to a young woman on trial for gunning down a government employee in the halls of a federal office building. As usual, men called their response chivalry and declined to look too closely at what was really going on.

For it was men whom the law served, and the real issue in these cases had little to do with women. Acquitting the woman who killed her seducer was merely a way of ratifying *his* punishment for, as Professor Fowler said, female chastity was just as valuable to men as to women; a woman lost her virtue through seduction, but a man lost his *property*. The only law punishing seduction on the books in Tennessee when Mary Moriarty was tried entitled the father to sue the seducer for the loss of his daughter's services during her confinement.

The contempt for women that underlay the fine talk showed through from time to time as it does in this report to the New York State Assembly from the committee on the judiciary concerning the great number of petitions "signed extensively by females" calling for laws to punish seduction:

> It is not to be disguised that the female sex are the principal sufferers by the prevalence of the crimes alluded to; and however some may deem them trenching upon matters from which female modesty ought to recoil, we cannot shut our eyes to the obvious fact, that while *they* endure the anguish of broken hearts and cancelled hopes, *we* claim of right, and rightfully or not, we exercise all the power. If they suffer then, they have no means of redress but this; and whatever may be our views of the policy of granting their prayer, none will deny their right to petition.

Let the women suffer, they said, and let them petition. We are obliged to do nothing but make a report now and then.

Women did continue to petition; and the judiciary committee continued to receive the petitions and to write reports to the Assembly in which they discussed the injuries that the wily seducer inflicted upon *men*. It was true, they said in their 1842 report, that through the "crime of adultery or seduction" (neither adultery nor seduction *was* a crime in New York as it was the purpose of the petitions to point out) the "*weaker* party is ruined in fortune and prospects, consigned to poverty and disgrace [and] expelled from respectable society," but "*a still greater injury is perpetrated upon the mental happiness and moral feelings of her friends.*" In the case of adultery, they asked, "Who would not feel a relief from the grief that weighs down the spirits under such circumstances, if he could be permitted to *exchange* this scene for the funeral of his wife or his daughter?" No one suggested that the wives and daughters—the very women who were signing all those petitions—might take a somewhat different view.

And all those legislators who would just as soon have seen their wives and daughters dead certainly did not want to see them equal. In a final ironic turn of the historic screw the argument for punishing seduction became an argument against women's rights. Demands rooted in woman's desire for equal justice—a single sexual standard of conduct for all—were construed to mean that women were naturally bad creatures who had to be saved from themselves by men. The whole issue made Tennessee Claflin hot under the collar. Women who joined in the "clamour about seduction," she argued, merely conceded to the false notion "that women are weaklings and ninnies, and that they have no opinion, no character, no power of self-defense, but simply the liability to be influenced to their ruin by men." The fight for antiseduction laws *was* an admission of inequality, for women *were* unequal; and the antiseduction argument was not taken to mean that the hindrances to woman's achieving equality should be removed, but rather that she—inferior as she was—should be protected by the "romantic paternalism" of the social fathers. Claflin argued that any talk of seducers must cut both ways, for a woman whose only career was marriage necessarily made the seduction of some man the business of life. In her unorthodox view, women more than held their own: "They not only have the cunning to beguile the men, in the majority of cases," she observed, "but the astuteness also to throw the blame on the men for betraying them." And if that was "sharp practice" it was only what women had learned from men, the "natural and necessary" result of trying to survive in man-made society. Consequently, any law to protect women from male seducers should be accompanied by "an Act for the Protection of [male] Ninnies against Designing Women," Claflin argued. "If law is to regulate the matter," she said, "let the whole ground be effectually covered." But Claflin's sophisticated spoofing of the social comedy went beyond the immediate issue. The good wives and daughters continued to sign petitions for antiseduction legislation; and in complaining of injustice, they invited more. Men would indeed protect women from seduction—though on an informal, one-to-one basis; and they would also protect women from education, fair wages, entry into the professions, and the vote.

In political and sexual transactions the women were mere counters in the man-to-man game. That inescapable fact is illustrated by the case of the Honorable Daniel E. Sickles, United States congressman from New York, and defendant in one of the century's most celebrated murder trials—the trial that established the insanity defense later borrowed by Mary Harris's attorneys. In 1859 Sickles learned from an anonymous informer that his wife, Teresa, a beautiful woman fifteen years his junior whom he had "fondled" from childhood and married when she was sixteen, was secretly meeting a lover at a Washington house hired for that purpose. Sickles, a notorious "connoisseur of women," had enjoyed a scandalous affair with a New York prostitute, and he firmly believed in the double standard. He investigated, found the allegation true, confronted his wife, and forced her to confess everything (in lurid detail) in writing. He cut off her wedding ring and made her sleep on the floor. The next day in Lafayette Square he shot down her lover, the debonair widower Philip Barton Key (son of the author of "The Star-Spangled Banner"), although Key tried valiantly to defend himself with his opera glass. Sickles was tried for murder and defended by a phalanx of famous lawyers, headed by Edwin Stanton, who later became Lincoln's secretary of war. President Buchanan himself paid an eyewitness to leave town. Women were excluded from the courtroom. On the plea of temporary insanity, Sickles was acquitted and returned to his seat in the House of Representatives.

Teresa Sickles, immediately after Key's murder, was shipped back to her father in New York like damaged goods. The public supported Sickles through it all until a few months later he "forgave" his wife and attempted a reconciliation. Public opinion was solidly against Sickles's climb back into the defiled marriage bed, for it made Key's death seem less a matter of honor than of simple butchery. So they didn't live together, and Teresa Sickles almost never left her house until she died in 1867 at age thirty-one of a "cold." Sickles, on the other hand, went on to serve as an incompetent Union general during the Civil War, losing a leg and more men than any other commanding officer: more than four thousand at Gettysburg alone. For half a century after the trial Sickles remained active in public life and (as people joked) "private affairs," including a notorious liaison with Queen Isabella II when he was ambassador to Spain. When he died in 1914 at the age of ninety-five, he was accorded a full military funeral. His body was borne through the streets of the capital on a caisson followed by a riderless horse and buried amid salvos at Arlington National Cemetery.

But that grand funeral procession took place half a century after a hot day in July 1865 when—with the war over and the talk about his disobeying General MacLean's orders at Gettysburg quieting down—the one-legged General Sickles returned to Washington after a prolonged "inspection tour" of Central and South America. The newspapers announced his return, but the big news in Washington concerned Mary Harris: acquitted of murder. Her attorneys had followed the lead of the famous Sickles defense team in arguing that their client was insane. (Perhaps they did not realize that Harris actually was mad, while Sickles had been merely angry.) In any event, it would have been graceless to deny them the right to enter on behalf of a young woman the same plea that had proved so effective in the case of a prominent man. But unlike the Sickles case, which was a deadly serious though sensational affair, the Harris case was often treated lightly by the press. *The New York Times,* in an editorial on the acquittal, observed that "the course of the trial, from its beginning to its close, has been followed with very great interest throughout the country," but "not because the incidents of the crime were of any very extraordinary character . . . or that there was any expectation that any new principle would be settled by it, or that the verdict would be other than what it has been." *The Times* speculated that "the popular interest manifested in the case arose mainly . . . from the fact that the times are rather dull, and an episode of this kind furnishes a lively subject of gossip amid the grave public questions now before the country." During the "rather dull" times between Mary Harris's arrest at the end of January and her trial in July, General Sherman marched to the sea, the Confederacy surrendered, President Abraham Lincoln was assassinated at a popular local theater, President Andrew Johnson was inaugurated, and on the very day Harris's trial began Mrs. Mary Surratt and three male conspirators in Lincoln's assassination were publicly hanged at the Washington arsenal.

Yet *The Times* found in the Harris case only diversion and "a new illustration of what must be regarded as a settled principle in American law—that any woman who considers herself agrieved [*sic*] in any way by a member of the other sex, may kill him with impunity, and with an assured immunity from the prescribed penalties of law." The man, said the editorial, need be guilty of no offense whatsoever; a woman "seized by a fancy" could simply murder him and "escape, not only the extreme penalty of the law, but any penalty whatever.'' If that broad allegation were true (as clearly it was not), it should have struck editorial sparks; but *The Times* was complacent: "It were useless to find fault with this state of things. It is peculiar to America, and people in general are decidedly proud of it."

Feminists were not. They found fault with the man-made legal system. They campaigned for woman suffrage specifically so that women would have a say in formulating the laws under which they were forced to live. They argued that women should be tried by a jury of *their* peers. They worked toward better education, better job opportunities, and fair wages for women so that they would be wiser and less dependent upon men and marriage. They repudiated the "chivalry" extended to a few women and called for equal justice for all women and men under the law. The Ohio Woman's Rights Convention in 1850 resolved "that all rights are *human* rights, and pertain to human beings, without distinction of sex; therefore justice demands that all laws shall be made, not for man, or for woman, but for mankind, and that the same legal protection be afforded to the one sex as to the other."

This plea for justice, for the most part, was ignored or ridiculed. It was one thing for men to excuse the occasional remorseful woman for her crimes, and quite another for women en masse to demand legal rights. When some radical feminists, such as Elizabeth Cady Stanton, began to discuss these random cases of shooting "paramours" along with divorce cases as part of a concerted assertion of "new womanhood," men grew angry. Laura Fair made them angrier still. Twice married and shady at best, she shot her lover, the Honorable A. P. Crittenden, a prominent San Francisco judge and respectable family man, on the Oakland ferry in 1870. She was convicted and sentenced to death (Laura Fair was not, by any stretch of the imagination, a despoiled maiden and Judge Crittenden was a prominent man), but the decision was reversed on a technicality. Always looking for the main chance, Mrs. Fair proposed to tour, lecturing on the subject of American morals. General Sickles, she claimed, and other male avengers of adultery like him, had "done more for true morality than have all the sermons preached by the servants of the Most High." But in her view, a woman should stand up for herself: when "an American woman in justice avenges her outraged name, the act will strike a terror to the hearts of sensualists and libertines a thousand times more telling than . . . the acts of a thousand Sickles. . . . By her act, her sex throughout the world will glory in the name of American women. . . ." Mrs. Fair intended to set forth these views inciting wronged women to murder in a lecture at Platt's Hotel in San Francisco on November 21, 1872; but when a crowd of two thousand gathered outside the hotel and another crowd of equal size surrounded her residence on Kearney Street, she called for police protection. The police declined, saying that the situation was too dangerous. (So much for protection.) She stayed at home, publishing her lecture later in pamphlet form, but the crowd outside— all men—"hooted and yelled and some of the men tried to force their way upstairs" to attack her.

Women were supposed to be grateful and quiet, content with the "chivalry" men substituted for justice. Above all, they were not to notice that the "vile seducers" were not a species apart from the chivalrous patriarchs who pretended to protect women. In fact, the seducers seemed to be very ordinary men indeed. And they came from all walks of life: poor workingmen like Johnny Shehan; successful businessmen and merchants like George Watson, Charles Goodrich, Henry Ballard; rising civil servants like Adoniram Burroughs. Some, like Burroughs, were highly connected; his brother, a clergyman, was president of the University of Chicago. The brother of Charley Goodrich was a well-known Brooklyn attorney. Others were prominent in themselves, like the adulterous Judge A. P. Crittenden. They might be unmarried, like Burroughs and Shehan; widowed like Goodrich; or firm family men like Judge Crittenden and George Watson. In some carefully separate compartments of their lives they might even seem to be quite admirable—perhaps exemplary. The widow of George Watson, the man who coerced fifteen-year-old Fanny Hyde, took the witness stand to say that he was "the kindest and best of husbands."

Only the New York *Tribune* came close to the truth in its editorial on the acquittal of Mary Harris. The *Trib* noted the implicit unfairness of the verdict: "Had *she* jilted *him,* and *he* had therefore shot *her,* nobody would have adjudged him guilty of insanity." Nevertheless, the editors said, there was "a rough, 'wild justice' in this and kindred verdicts" because the law did nothing to protect women. "Every one who conspires or aids to deprive a girl of her virtue should be punished at least as severely as a burglar, a forger, or a highway robber," the *Trib* maintained. Yet "they are not so punished, because it is to many magnates inconvenient that they should be. . . . the wrong is felt, though not redressed."

So it all came down again to the simplest possible terms. Men chose to keep women ignorant, dependent, and dedicated to "purity" so they could not protect themselves. And men chose not to give women laws to protect them from seducers because men wished to protect themselves from charges of seduction, and they wished to retain for themselves the privileges of dealing with seducers (by violence if necessary) and of *becoming* seducers. "Our laws are made by men," said the *Tribune,* "and they are not just to woman. They ought to punish the conspirator against female purity severely; but they do not, because too many of our legislators and jurists are libertines." That was a bald and simple equation that no feminist could have got away with, but the *Tribune* was armed with righteousness and money. "That is a rather blunt way of stating it," the *Trib* admitted, "but it is the fact."

LAYING DOWN
THE LAW

1.

"You have granted that woman may be hung," said Wendell Phillips to his fellowmen, and "therefore you must grant that woman may vote." It was as simple as that. Either women were the peers and equals of men, and in that case should enjoy all civil and political rights equally with them, or women were (as men repeatedly maintained) an inferior caste; and in that case, any woman tried by a jury of men was automatically deprived of the right to trial by a jury of her peers. Feminists argued that men simply could not have it both ways.

For the men the choice was no choice at all, for to concede either point was to lose ground—and that would never do. The inconsistency of their position was rather embarrassing, but certainly not unbearably so—considering what there was to lose to those implacable women so relentlessly consistent in their demands. The New York State Woman's Rights Committee laid out the agenda at the Tenth National Woman's Rights Convention in 1860: "We now demand the ballot, trial by jury of our peers, and an equal right to the joint earnings of the marriage copartnership. And, until the Constitution be so changed as to give us a voice in the government, we demand that man shall make all his laws on property, marriage, and divorce, to bear equally on man and woman." "A citizen can not be said to have a right to life," the feminists argued, "who may be deprived of it for the violation of laws to which she has never consented—who is denied the right of trial by a jury of her peers—who has no voice in the election of judges who are to decide her fate."

As things were, women could not get simple justice. "It is not to be denied," Elizabeth Cady Stanton argued to the New York legislature in 1854, "that the interests of man and woman in the present undeveloped state of the race, and under the existing social arrangements, are and must be antagonistic. The nobleman can not make just laws for the peasant; the slaveholder for the slave; neither can man make and execute just laws for woman, because in each case, the one in power fails to apply the immutable principles of right to any grade but his own." In the courts of law in particular, how could a woman receive just treatment from "men who, by their own admission, are so coarse that women could not meet them even at the polls without contamination?" Feminists demanded "in criminal cases that most sacred of all rights, trial by jury of our own peers. The establishment of trial by jury is of so early a date," Cady Stanton explained with that reasonableness so maddening to her opponents, "that its beginning is lost in antiquity; but the right of trial by a jury of one's own peers is a great progressive step of advanced civilization. . . . Hence, all along the pages of history, we find the king, the noble, the peasant, the cardinal, the priest, the layman, each in turn protesting against the authority of the tribunal before which they were summoned to appear. Charles the First refused to recognize the competency of the tribunal which condemned him: For how, said he, can subjects judge a king? The stern descendants of our Pilgrim Fathers refused to answer for their crimes before an English Parliament. For how, they said, can a king judge rebels? And shall woman here consent to be tried by her liege lord, who has dubbed himself law-maker, judge, juror, and sheriff too?—whose power, though sanctioned by Church and State, has no foundation in justice and equity, and is a bold assumption of our inalienable rights."

The embattled social fathers would not give way. Some of them undoubtedly came to believe their own propaganda. By the latter half of the nineteenth century, the excuses that originally justified confining woman to her sphere had taken on the authority of scripture. Men insisted that woman must be secluded from the world because she was by nature more delicate, more sensitive—all in all a finer creature. And after a time, convinced by their own florid rhetoric, some believed that woman was indeed the better half. (Women, for reasons of their own, tended to agree.) Men began to fall all over themselves in the scramble to transform popular ideology to public policy, to codify the legend as law.

It is impossible to say now whether the men who spoke out—in courtroom arguments, legislative debates, and newspaper editorials—sincerely believed the doctrines of chivalry and true womanhood, routinely spouted the platitudes, or consciously used them to suppress women. Even at the time many an anxious man must have found it hard to figure out the extent of his own sincerity. But in any case, going by the myth instead of by the book always produced the same result: increasingly unequal justice erratically enforced. On paper the criminal law for women and men was substantially the same (except that a husband was legally responsible for any crimes his wife committed in his presence); in practice, it was not. Popular ideology—not law—was the guideline in women's cases; so there was no telling where the sentiments of judges and jurors might lead them. When women were acquitted—whether the decision seemed justified or not—newspapers complained that women could get away with murder. In fact, in the capricious criminal justice system, the wind often blew the other way.

On one hand, the social fathers hastened to protect some women (as we have seen) and in the process set at liberty women who were guilty of capital crimes. On the other hand, they sometimes handed down stiff sentences to prove that they were not unfairly lenient; they called that unwarranted severity "justice." Cady Stanton, with her irritating sense of history, pointed out: "No rank of men have ever been satisfied with being tried by jurors higher or lower in the civil or political scale than themselves; for jealousy on the one hand, and contempt on the other, has ever effectually blinded the eyes of justice." Certainly, as case after case indicated, jealousy and contempt were never far from any courtroom where a woman was on trial. And as feminist demands and the anxiety they provoked increased, the lawgivers—judges, jurors, legislators, politicians—stumbled over the fundamental inconsistency (not to say immorality) of their position. Torn between protection and punishment—and sometimes at odds about strategies for retaining power—they improvised plea and statute as they went along and learned to turn on a phrase. Legal and legislative wrangles were prolonged, confusing, and thoroughly unpredictable. Only a society truly dedicated to unequal justice would have set itself such a course.

In St. Paul, Minnesota, Stanislaus Bilansky fell ill with indigestion on March 2, 1859, and, despite the constant attendance of his wife, Ann, and of Rosa Sharf, a young woman hired to nurse him, he died nine days later. His death was scarcely surprising. Bilansky, who had come from Poland in 1842 as one of the first settlers of St. Paul, was well into middle age. Everyone knew him to be a cantankerous, moody man, given to bouts of hard drinking and violence. His personal physician of many years, Dr. Alfred Berthier, who thought he had "a gloomy . . . hypochondriacal disposition," examined Bilansky during his last illness and diagnosed a severely aggravated case of indigestion. A coroner's jury attributed the death to natural causes, and Bilansky was buried. After the funeral, Ann Bilansky returned to her home with John Walker, a young man who claimed to be her nephew; and there, two days later, they were arrested on suspicion of the murder of Stanislaus. Someone had gone to the police with highly incriminating evidence omitted from the inquest. A friend of Stanislaus's said that Ann refused to call a doctor as his condition worsened. Rosa Sharf said that Ann undressed right in front of her nephew and slept in the same room with him. A neighbor, Lucinda Kilpatrick, who went shopping with Ann Bilansky on February 28, said that Ann bought arsenic to kill the rats in her house and commented offhandedly that she wouldn't mind giving Stanislaus "a pill." Officials ordered an autopsy, but bumbling frontier physicians found neither poison nor a natural cause of death. Their subsequent chemical tests were muddled and inconclusive, their evidence—according to the St. Paul *Pioneer and Democrat*—"about as unsatisfactory as it was possible to make it." Nevertheless, it was convincing enough to persuade a second coroner's jury that "the deceased came to his death by the effects of arsenic administered by the hands of Mrs. Bilansky." John Walker was released on March 15 for lack of evidence implicating him in Bilansky's death, but Ann Bilansky, after a preliminary hearing, was bound over for trial in May 1859 on a charge of first-degree murder.

The evidence brought against Ann Bilansky at the trial was substantially the same as that of the inquest, with one very important addition: the local physician who took some of the dead man's stomach to Chicago for chemical analysis now testified authoritatively that Bilansky died of arsenic poisoning. The case against the widow was strong, but a couple of doubts nagged. For one thing, Ann Bilansky seemed to have no motive either to marry Stanislaus or to murder him. As Ann Evards Wright—a tall, good-looking, thirty-three-year-old widow—she came to St. Paul from Fayetteville, North Carolina, in May 1858, to nurse her young nephew during an illness. Through Walker she met Bilansky and married him in September 1858. Six months later she was a widow again, this time, allegedly, of her own making. The two classic motives suggested themselves: money and love. Yet no one seriously maintained that she had done it for the money because Stanislaus didn't have any. For a long time he had lived off "the accumulations of former years" and at the time of his death he was heavily in debt. His friends said he brooded about it. So even if Ann mistakenly married Stanislaus for his money (it was hard to imagine another reason for marrying the notoriously abusive man) she clearly didn't *murder* him for a purse she knew to be empty. The prosecution claimed that the motive was love—her adulterous love for John Walker. First the district attorney, then the newspapers, then even the governor himself talked about their love affair as a universally known fact; but Ann Bilansky and Walker always denied it, and the only witness to an "impropriety" between them was Rosa Sharf, who knew that they slept in the same bedchamber after Bilansky's funeral because she too slept in that room. In fact the main "evidence" that Ann and Walker were having an affair seems to have come from Stanislaus himself, who complained of it to several of his friends but did nothing to stop it.

Certainly it was easy enough to imagine that any wife would want to be rid of the evil-tempered Stanislaus, and Ann made no secret of the fact that she hated him. She said quite openly that his fatal illness started after he ate a voracious meal, then grew violently angry with her for refusing to sleep with him. In an extraordinary moment of sisterhood, Bilansky's first wife, Mary Ellen, came forward to testify in Ann's defense. She had lived with Bilansky for ten years and had borne four children. She knew him to be a very heavy eater and hard drinker who was "always sick after his sprees." He was a "morose and jealous man," she said, "and cruel as a husband." What's more, he was very superstitious; he believed that he would die in March, and every year in March he got sick. After ten years of abuse, Mary Ellen Bilansky walked out. Wife number two and wife number three, in their turn, followed her. And Ann Bilansky, apparently, was planning to do the same thing. Six weeks before Stanislaus fell ill Ann showed him a letter requiring her to return to North Carolina to be a witness in a trial. Bilansky asked Dr. Berthier and some other friends to help him find a housekeeper. His wife, he said, was going to North Carolina with Walker, and he did not expect her to come back. But if she could just walk out with Walker, why would she kill Bilansky? All in all, the question of motive was troubling. So, too, was the fact that the two most damaging prosecution witnesses, Rosa Sharf and Lucinda Kilpatrick, both seemed to be enamored of the irresistible John Walker; and Lucinda, a respectable married woman, had written him some compromising letters.

There were other holes in the prosecution's case. The contradictory toxicological tests left doubt about the cause of death. Admittedly Ann Bilansky prepared her husband's food and drink during his last illness, but no one saw anything suspicious in the way she went about it. Bilansky was doctoring himself with patent medicines of unknown contents, despite Dr. Berthier's warning that his system was far too upset to tolerate medicines. And Bilansky, always a moody man given to frequent attacks of the blues, was worried about his debts, about the supposed infidelity and imminent departure of his fourth wife, and about March—the month in which he knew he would sicken and die. Perhaps, as Ann Bilansky suggested, Stanislaus had taken the poison himself. The loopholes were just big enough to admit some doubt of Ann Bilansky's guilt. But she had bought arsenic; and what had become of it?

The brand-new state of Minnesota was chiefly concerned with cleaning up its own image. The area had always had an unsavory reputation for lawlessness; in fact, the very first recorded death in St. Paul was that of a murder victim. In the two years just before Minnesota was admitted to the Union there were four reported murders in St. Paul, a fast-growing frontier town of almost ten thousand people; in three cases the murderer was never found, and in the fourth case he escaped.

St. Paul was a wide-open town, and lusty—a man's world. (Cities, like ships, are traditionally referred to as feminine, but Mark Twain in *Life on the Mississippi* quite deliberately called St. Paul "he.") Rape was a frequent crime, usually prosecuted (if at all) as assault and battery, an offense that carried a modest fine. The next case on Judge Palmer's docket, after he got the unsavory Bilansky business out of the way, was that of James Murphy, a man who had "heretofore borne a good character in the community" and who received only a small fine for attempting, while "very intoxicated" to rape a ten-year-old girl. Men understood that sort of thing. At the Bilansky trial the prosecutor, defense attorneys, and witnesses joked about which of them had made the greatest public spectacle of himself; honors went to defense attorney (and former mayor) John Brisbin, habitually drunk "down on Jackson Street." For the leading men of St. Paul, drunkenness was simply a way of life.

In 1858, the year Minnesota became a state (and the year Ann Evards Wright and Stanislaus Bilansky got married), the crunch came: a land speculation bubble burst and one bank after another closed its doors. Something had to be done to restore confidence in the future of the state. Still drunkenness, robberies, murders, and lynchings continued to give the place a bad name. Only a few months before Stanislaus Bilansky's death, a man in nearby Wright County, acquitted of murdering a neighbor, was lynched by his fellow citizens in a general ruckus known as the "Wright County War." But while lynch law was harsh, the official courts of law often were amazingly lenient. Two months before Ann Bilansky's arrest, a man charged with murdering his wife and burying her under the ice house was convicted of second-degree murder and given a "short term" in the penitentiary. And on the very day Ann Bilansky's sentence was pronounced, a man convicted of manslaughter after he beat, clubbed, stomped, and kicked his wife to death was sentenced to five years in the Stillwater prison. Clearly a crackdown for law and order was long overdue. And Ann Bilansky, the vivacious stranger from the South who married one of St. Paul's first settlers, supposedly cuckolded him, mocked him, and at last apparently did him in, was a convenient target. On June 3, 1859, the trial jury found her guilty of murder in the first degree.

The St. Paul *Pioneer and Democrat* evaluated the case as a "repetition of a tragedy, which has been enacted all the world over, wherever a woman, bad enough to be a harlot and bold enough to be a murderer, has wished to get rid of a husband whom she disliked, for a paramour whom she preferred." But having analyzed the motive as adulterous love—the prosecution's theory—the newspaper went on to say in the same editorial that this perfectly "cold-blooded" murder was "apparently without any adequate motive. . . . It could not have been for money for the man was poor; nor to get rid of matrimonial chains which were no restraint on the inclinations of the murderess." But the paper resolved the issue of the lack of motive once and for all by turning it *against* Ann Bilansky: "It is this very absence of any explainable human motive which gives to the deed its most hideous features, and compels us to seek its explanation in the attributes of fiends."

As soon as Ann Bilansky was convicted, efforts began to save her; for first-degree murder carried the penalty of death by hanging, and Minnesota had never before hanged a woman—or, for that matter, a white man. Fiend or not, it seemed out of step with the times to do so now.

The defense motion for a new trial was denied on June 22, but only a few days later the troubled judge certified the case to the Minnesota Supreme Court for review. Arguing the case before the three Supreme Court justices, defense attorney Brisbin tried to talk his way around the death penalty. Mrs. Bilansky, he argued, could write and was therefore entitled to have her life spared by benefit of clergy, an antique legal loophole never open to women and, in any case, plugged long before. Furthermore, he argued, hearkening back to earlier times, a wife who killed her husband was guilty of petit treason, not murder, and since Minnesota had abolished the crime of petit treason it must also have abolished the death penalty for that crime. The judges, unimpressed, refused to interfere and sent the case back to the district court for sentencing. At the end of July Ann Bilansky acted in her own defense; she squeezed over the top of the window bars at the jail and disappeared. But in August she was recaptured as she tried to leave the state, dressed in men's clothing, with her nephew; and on December 2, Judge Edward C. Palmer, who had presided at her trial, pronounced the death sentence.

The case then fell squarely into the lap of Governor Henry Sibley, for under Minnesota law the governor alone was empowered to order the execution and set the date. Sibley was immediately swamped with letters and petitions calling for commutation of the Bilansky death sentence. Even Supreme Court Justice Charles Flandrau, on the day his court affirmed Bilansky's conviction, sent an extraordinary personal message to Sibley: "It is my firm conviction that a strict adherence to the penal code will have a salutary influence in checking crime in the State, but it rather shocks my private sense of humanity to commence by inflicting the extreme penalty on a woman. I believe she was guilty, but nevertheless hope that if you can consistently with your view of Justice and duty, you will commute the sentence which will be pronounced, to imprisonment." Under the same public pressure the Minnesota House of Representatives told its judiciary committee to investigate the advisability of doing away with capital punishment, then sat on its hands and waited for the governor to act. Governor Sibley, always the politician, did nothing. On December 31, 1859, Democrat Sibley passed on to Republican Alexander Ramsey the office of governor and the problem of Ann Bilansky.

Ramsey was not squeamish. He had long been the appointed governor of the unruly territory; now it was up to him to civilize the state with some strict application of the law. The Bilansky defense motion for a new trial had been denied in the courts. So even when Rosa Sharf died of an overdose of laudanum, raising some embarrassing questions about her role in the "murder" and the prosecution, Ramsey did not reconsider the case. He ordered the sheriff to hang Ann Bilansky between the hours of 10:00 A.M. and 2:00 P.M. on Friday, March 23, 1860.

Her supporters redoubled their efforts. They brought up again in the Senate the bill to abolish capital punishment, but it was sent back to committee. They followed with a bill "to commute the sentence of Mrs. Anna [*sic*] Bilansky to imprisonment for life"; it dragged through both houses of the legislature and went to Governor Ramsey for signature on March 5. He immediately vetoed the bill on the grounds that it was unconstitutional; it represented a legislative incursion upon the powers of the executive, specifically the power to pardon, which the state constitution invested exclusively in the state executive. Besides, Ramsey added, the circumstances of the case hardly called for clemency. Ann Bilansky, he reminded the legislators, was guilty of the most vile and insidious form of murder: the murder of a husband by poison. In cases of this sort, he said, "The husband will not suspect that she who has sworn to love and cherish will betray and destroy; and it shocks the moral sense of the whole community to believe it. And so, against the wife with murder in her heart, no man has any protection, except in the certainty of the punishment which the law affixes to the crime." (Against the husband with murder in his heart, no wife had protection either; and the husband's punishment was likely to be five years, two years, a year in the state prison. But that was another problem not addressed in Governor Ramsey's message to the legislature.)

Having discussed the constitutional grounds for his veto and the

Bilansky case itself, Governor Ramsey added almost as an after-thought a brief account of "the history of the administration of criminal justice in capital cases in Minnesota." Ever since the territory was organized, he said, there had been great "remissness in punishing murderers: murders are committed, and no one apprehended, no one hardly suspected of the deed. Or, the accused is apprehended, but escapes. Or, witnesses are spirited away, and no indictment is found. Or, the jury, through sympathy, or misapprehending the instruction of the bench, aquit. [*sic*] Or, the Court having misapprehended the law, a new trial is had . . . people throughout the State have almost despaired of obtaining the protection of life from the Courts, which the laws and the Courts were established to secure." The law against murder prescribed the penalty of death, he said; and he asked the legislators: "What feature of the case under consideration entitles it to be made a special exception?"

On March 23, 1860, while a detachment of the Pioneer Guard kept back the crowd clamoring for a better view, Ann Bilansky was hanged upon a scaffold in the courtyard of the Ramsey County jail—the first white person and the first and last woman to be hanged by the state of Minnesota. Just before the trap was released, she made a little speech: "I die without having had any mercy shown me, or justice. I die for the good of my soul, and not for murder. May you all profit by my death. Your courts of justice are *not* courts of justice—but I will yet get justice in Heaven. I am a guilty woman, I know, but not of this murder, which was committed by another. I forgive everybody who did me wrong. I die a sacrifice to the law. I hope you all may be judged better than I have been, and by a more righteous judge. I die prepared to meet my God."

Governor Ramsey, with obstinacy that passed for political courage, had not allowed "the mob spirit" to interfere with "the regular course of Justice." Even the opposition *Pioneer and Democrat* pronounced Republican Ramsey's conduct "manly." While wife murderers went to jail for a few years, Ann Bilansky was hanged to prove to the country that Minnesota, bastion of law and order, would not be unduly lenient to women but would impartially enforce the letter of the law—just like any other civilized state.

Unfortunately for Ann Bilansky, word had not yet reached Minnesota that truly civilized societies did not execute ladies. Supreme Court Justice Flandrau's "sense of humanity" may have been rather shocked at the prospect of hanging a woman, but his judicial decision was not altered. Elsewhere, particularly in the more highly "civilized" eastern states, men went to great lengths to avoid putting the noose around a pretty neck, for the status of woman had become the measure of civilization: the more idle and useless the women, the more prosperous must be their husbands and the more fully evolved their society. In a highly civilized society woman was an exquisitely refined decoration. (In a perfect society she might simply evanesce.) So while the people of Minnesota fought unsuccessfully to save Ann Bilansky from the gallows, the people of New York State fought to save the neck of Mary Hartung; the strategies were the same, but the results were far different.

On March 3, 1859, while Stanislaus Bilansky struggled with his final illness in St. Paul, a judge in Albany, New York, sentenced twenty-three-year-old Mary Koehler Hartung to be hanged. She had been convicted in February of the murder of her husband, Emil Hartung, and her attorney's motion for a new trial was denied. The story of the marriage and the murder has a familiar ring.

In 1852, Emil Hartung, twenty-seven-year-old deliveryman for Schindler's Brewery, married sixteen-year-old Mary Koehler; like Emil, Mary was an immigrant from Germany. By 1858 Emil earned and borrowed enough money to buy a saloon and boardinghouse that he put into the charge of Mary—by then the mother of two children—while he continued to work as a deliveryman. Overburdened, Mary found consolation with boarder William Rheimann, and by the end of April Emil Hartung, the taskmaster, was dead of a long, painful illness—and buried. The servant girl talked too loudly about Mary Hartung's arsenic purchases; and the boarders gossiped about her intimacy with Rheimann. When the talk turned to digging Emil up again, Mary and Rheimann disappeared. On May 21, 1858, examiners from the Albany Medical College found arsenic in the exhumed body of Emil Hartung. Three days later the police found William Rheimann in a saloon and charged him as an accessory before the fact in the murder of Emil Hartung. Mary Hartung fled to Gottenburgh, New Jersey, and found work as a servant, using the name Elizabeth Shulz, but William Rheimann was still on her mind; in July she wrote to him at Albany, addressing the letter by a prearranged code to Ferdinand Shulz, but by an unlucky coincidence there was living in Albany at the time a *real* Ferdinand Shulz, who claimed the letter and took it to the police. By mid-July Mary Hartung had joined her lover in jail, charged as the principal in the murder of her husband.

At her trial in February 1859 the evidence against her was conclusive. The medical men said that Hartung had died of phosphorus
and arsenic poisoning. The servant, the boarders, and the druggist said
that Mary Hartung kept a little yellow pot of rat poison containing
phosphorus on a kitchen shelf although there were no rats in the
house, and she bought arsenic twice—once just before her husband
took sick and again just before he died. The Hartung boarders and the
keepers of hotels where Rheimann and Mary Hartung stayed together
testified to their adultery. And Rheimann himself told the police that
Mary confessed the murder to him. Mary's attorney, on the other
hand, blamed Rheimann and cast Mary Hartung as the innocent who
bought arsenic for him without suspecting what he wanted it for, but
as the snarl of Mary Hartung's lies unwound in the courtroom, that
version grew harder to believe.

Still the jury spent the entire weekend in deliberation, not wanting to come to the obvious verdict. Some jurors who thought that
Rheimann may have instigated the crime asked the judge if it were
possible to compromise on the verdict—perhaps to find her guilty of
some lesser type of homicide. The judge advised them that compromise was impossible; so, on February 7, 1859, they bowed to necessity
and pronounced her guilty of murder.

Some newspapers, equally reluctant to think the worst of a woman—particularly a pretty one—denounced the verdict; others reassured the public that means were at hand to redress it. Even when
Hartung was sentenced to hang, press and public generally seemed to
believe that the sentence would be commuted. The expectation was
reasonable. In the first place, the sentence was severe. During the previous decade in Albany County many defendants convicted of taking
life received much lighter sentences. Some, like James Moore, who
killed his wife, Elizabeth, in 1852, pled guilty to manslaughter and got
off lightly; Moore was sentenced to only two years while a half-dozen
other defendants received sentences of from two to seven years. Four
men convicted of the more serious charge of murder, including Barney
Leddy, who kicked his wife to death in 1849, were sentenced to life;
but one, John Jackson, who killed his mother-in-law in 1850, got only
four years. And of the seven people—all men—sentenced to death in
Albany County in the preceding decade, four—including two wife
murderers—had their sentences commuted to life imprisonment and
one was pardoned. The only two condemned men actually hanged
were guilty of particularly reprehensible crimes: one murdered two
small boys and the other murdered his wife—significantly—by poison.

The Albany *Atlas and Argus* said of Mary Hartung that "the penitent woman still clings to the idea that a pardon will be obtained to save her from the gallows and this seems to be the hope of the community." Taking no chances, Mary Hartung's supporters circulated a petition calling for commutation of her sentence to life imprisonment, and by the time it was presented to Governor Edwin D. Morgan late in March it had been signed by the attorney general who prosecuted the case, the district attorney, seventeen state senators and eighty assemblymen, the secretary of state, the state treasurer, state comptroller, the adjutant general, several court commissioners, most of Albany's leading businessmen and nine hundred merchants, many reporters, the sheriff, under sheriff, and all the deputy sheriffs of the county, the surrogate and clerk of the county, the mayor and the recorder of Albany, the chief of police and all but one of his captains, and almost all the lawyers in town. Governor Morgan, however, also had on his hands the case of James Stephens of New York City, convicted of poisoning his wife, Sophia, in a particularly cold-blooded and grisly manner, so that he might propose to her niece. Stephens was also awaiting execution, and it seemed to Morgan, a new governor who was given to fairness rather than chivalry, that he could not save Hartung's neck without saving Stephens's as well—and only the most dedicated opponents of capital punishment suggested that Stephens should not be hanged. Arguing that poisoning was the "worst sort of murder," Morgan refused to intervene in either case.

Many people who had the governor's ear urged him to make a special exception of Mary Hartung solely because she was a woman. They contended that "even though she were guilty, public opinion would revolt at her execution, and the practical effect of such as event would be that hereafter no conviction of a woman charged with a capital offence could be procured from a jury." Certainly that had been the practical effect in Massachusetts of hanging pregnant Bathsheba Spooner. There the public had never recovered from the nasty experience, and juries simply would not convict any woman of murder while the crime carried a mandatory sentence of death. Faced with that unbridgeable gap between legal prescription and popular opinion, Massachusetts had only recently been forced to change its homicide law. In 1857 after a Plymouth County jury was unable to reach a verdict in the case of a woman charged with poisoning her husband, despite incontrovertible evidence against her, the state legislature enacted a new statute distinguishing a new category of homicide: murder in the second degree, carrying a mandatory sentence of life imprisonment. Under the new statute the Plymouth County woman was brought to trial again, and this time convicted of the lesser charge—murder in the second degree. Yet it was one thing to change the law itself, as Massachusetts had done, and quite another for a governor to make a special exception to the law. Governor Morgan would not be moved.

Hartung's execution was postponed as her attorneys appealed to the state Supreme Court; and in April her supporters took the extraordinary measure of introducing a bill in the state legislature to commute her sentence. *The New York Times,* which had been partial to Mrs. Hartung throughout the trial, called this step "a decided novelty in the disposition of criminal cases." The paper continued, "So far as we are aware it is the first instance in which a Legislative body has attempted to exercise the pardoning power." That power was vested in the governor, and *The Times* conceded that it was "at least doubtful" whether the legislature could "step in." If the legislature passed the bill the governor might sign it and all would be well. If the governor vetoed the bill and the legislature voted to override his veto the state would be caught in a major constitutional crisis—or as *The Times* blandly put it, "a nice question of law." Other papers were less sanguine. The New York *Post* stormed: "Let the Legislature consider that the question of MRS. HARTUNG'S *guilt or innocence,* and the question whether women should be hung or not, constitute no reason at all for the inauguration of such a monstrous and subversive principle as that implied in the bill." Embarrassed, the legislature backed down, but when in December 1859 the state Supreme Court affirmed the conviction of Mary Hartung, the legislature set about work that *was* within its constitutional power: changing the law.

Much depended upon general efforts to abolish capital punishment in the state. For two decades opponents of the death penalty had been arguing for repeal; in 1841 a repeal bill was defeated in the Assembly by only five votes, and in 1851 it lost in the Senate by only one vote. Now, with Mary Hartung on death row, long-standing opponents of capital punishment were joined by her sympathizers in petitioning the legislature. The Assembly designated a select committee to respond to the issue, and on February 16, 1860, the committee hurriedly brought in its report "On the Petitions for a Repeal of the Death Penalty." The committee came out emphatically for repeal with arguments drawn from scripture, history, reason, and the experience of Michigan, Wisconsin, and Rhode Island, which had already eliminated the death penalty without suffering an increase in capital crime. They urged upon the legislature "the importance of as early action as possible" but never mentioned the worrisome case of Mary Hartung. The legislature took up the issue, but despite the persuasive arguments of the Assembly committee, it did not abolish the death penalty. Instead, on April 14, 1860, it passed "An Act in relation to capital punishment, and to provide for the more certain punishment of the crime of murder," an incredibly inept piece of legislation that made it doubtful whether the crime of murder could be punished in New York State at all. That impasse may very well have been the unspoken intention of the bill, however, for it was introduced by A. J. Colvin, a newly elected state senator who had assisted attorney William Hadley in the defense of Mary Hartung.

The act of 1860 provided that only treason and murder in the first degree would be punishable by death. Every person sentenced to death, however, was also to be sentenced to "confinement at hard labor in the state prison until such punishment of death shall be inflicted." After the prisoner spent one year in confinement—and not before—she or he could be executed at the governor's order, a curious provision that dumped all the responsibility upon the chief executive. Even more unusual was section 10 of the bill, which made it apply retroactively to prisoners then under sentence of death, and section 11, which repealed certain other sections (designated only by number) of the existing state statutes, among them the section that prescribed hanging as the method of carrying out sentences of death. Under the terms of the act of 1860, then, even if the governor should order the execution of a condemned prisoner, there was no way to carry out the sentence—no means to inflict death.

With the new law in hand, attorney Hadley carried the Hartung case to the Court of Appeals and got the ruling he wanted. According to the court, since the new law voided the old law under which Mary Hartung had been tried, her conviction—valid at the time—was now void. Moreover, although the new law said that those convicted under the old law should be punished as if convicted under the new, that procedure was impossible for it would constitute an unconstitutional ex post facto punishment; people simply could not be punished in terms of a law that didn't exist at the time they committed their offenses. Mary Hartung could not now be punished under *either* law. She would have to be tried again.

When Hartung came up for trial again on the charge of murdering Emil, Hadley entered a plea of double jeopardy; she had already been tried once for this offense, he argued, and she could not be tried again. The lower courts ruled against Hadley, but when he carried the case again to the Court of Appeals, the court agreed. It ruled on March 25, 1863, that the act of 1860 amounted to a legislative pardon for Mary Hartung; just as if she had been acquitted by a jury, she could not be tried again. The legislature had hastily redressed its blunder in 1861 by reinstating all the statutory provisions eliminated by the act of 1860. But Mary Hartung, after four years of legal maneuvering, slipped through the loophole, a free woman. Along with her went four male murderers under sentence of death—including one man who poisoned his wife and another who burned his up—the incidental beneficiaries of the campaign to spare Mary Hartung.

Even Mary Hartung's supporters had to admit that the whole affair was an expensive and embarrassing legal muddle. How could such a debacle be prevented in the future? Many people supported the position *The New York Times* had been advancing for years: abolition of capital punishment *for women only.* Other influential people and newspapers—such as the Albany *Courier,* which had covered the Hartung case and saw absolutely no reason not to hang a woman—were troubled by the blatant sexual discrimination of that proposal. *The Times* tried repeatedly to explain why it thought that hanging was not a "decent or proper punishment for a woman under any circumstances"—even if she were guilty—but the position was hard to defend with reason, particularly since the paper so strongly supported capital punishment for men. "It would be difficult, doubtless, to give any very cogent reasons why we should not hang a woman as well as a man, if equally guilty of murder—but it would be equally difficult to give any good reason for not striking a woman, as well as a man, under equal provocation. The reason for the distinction lies in the *feeling* that it exists and should be observed. There are cases where feeling must take the place, and do the work, of reason, and this is one of them."

It is odd to find this sort of "feeling"—usually thought to be the mark of feminine intellectual inferiority—passed off as argument; but how else were the guardians of society to defend an increasingly indefensible position? After all, the feminists and their supporters were so inexorably logical. Wendell Phillips told a little story about Madame de Staël: asked by Napoleon why women kept meddling in politics, she replied, "Sire, so long as you will hang us, we must ask the reason." Phillips observed, "The whole political philosophy of the subject is in that. The instant you say 'Woman is not competent to go to the ballot-box,' I reply: 'She is not competent to go to the gallows or the State

prison. If she is competent to go to the State prison, then she is competent to go to the ballot-box, and tell how thieves should be punished.' "
All the social fathers who worked so hard, and at times so clumsily, to free Mary Hartung, spoke of chivalry, decency, propriety, civilization; but implicitly they replied to Phillips: "If we do not make woman go to the gallows and the state prison, then we need not let her go to the ballot-box." Sometimes they almost said as much—and gave the whole game away. As *The New York Times* put it: "The same feelings which make civilized men shrink from the spectacle of womanhood unsexed by woman herself on the platform or in the field, make them shudder at the thought of womanhood unsexed by man at the whipping-post, or on the gallows."

Some simple souls, like the editor of the Albany *Courier and Enquirer,* held that "if men and women have both been guilty of one crime they should both suffer the same punishment." But *The Times* warned: "The same logic would require men and women, having the same wants, to meet them the same way. Both men and women need clothes to protect them from the cold. Why should not both wear the same garments? Both men and women need maintenance and a livelihood. Why should not both do the same kinds of business? . . . Why should we not all bring up our daughters to follow the sea, seek situations for our wives in the police force, set our female poor to dredging the docks or to quarrying stone?" Why not indeed?

2.

Plausibility counted. Not logic. The myths the fathers built to shore up their position did not have to be reasonable; they only had to be believable—and you could make people believe almost anything if you repeated it often enough. Thorstein Veblen described the process of self-delusion in *The Theory of the Leisure Class.* First, upper-class men gussied up their wives in elaborate and expensive clothing that made all "useful effort" impossible. The wife became "useless and expensive, and . . . consequently valuable as evidence of pecuniary strength." And finally men came to find "the resulting artificially induced pathological features" (the lady's deformed rib cage and misshapen feet) "attractive," although to the "untrained sense," Veblen said, these were "mutilations of unquestioned repulsiveness." The myth of the lady—her beauty, her nature, her sphere—was stronger than the eye and certainly stronger than reason.

The myth did not have to match up with the facts of life. *The New York Times* was genuinely appalled at the notion of women working, and even as the lady-ideal began to fade at the turn of the century, Veblen noted sarcastically: "It grates painfully on our nerves to contemplate the necessity of any well-bred woman's earning a livelihood by useful work. It is not 'woman's sphere.'" Yet at the time, and throughout the nineteenth century, the greater number of women worked in one capacity or another; for most women were not "ladies."

They called themselves "ladies." Early in the century the English travelers, so accustomed to titles of social distinction, complained that the word "woman" had all but disappeared from the language on this side of the water. Just as every American man called himself "mister," every woman—maid and mistress alike—called herself a lady. And for a time, in fact, all that talk of woman's sphere and woman's special nature was applied more or less indiscriminately, at least to white women. In the criminal courts the rhetoric of true femininity could be rolled out in defense of almost any white woman, no matter where she stood in society. Chivalry could save the neck of an Irish servant girl like Mary Moriarty in 1855 or a German boardinghouse keeper like Mary Hartung in 1860. At least until mid-century juries could be persuaded to find true femininity even in an uncorseted woman with calloused hands.

Some time after mid-century, things changed in ways that historians who have believed in the myth of a classless America are just beginning to examine. (These slow reshufflings of social practice can't be marked off, like battles or elections, by precise dates.) Perhaps the upheaval of the Civil War made people more anxious to assign a fixed order to people and things. Certainly the economic gap between rich and poor widened as the century went on, with more and more of the country's wealth coming into the hands of fewer and fewer men. And contrary to the cherished belief in the self-made man, the herditary "haves" spun patterns of living far glossier than those of the "have nots." Manners, not just money, marked off one class from another.

And subtly the definition of woman's sphere changed. It had been a place where woman performed all those domestic duties—from washing clothes to teaching numbers—for the greater good of her hus-

band, her family, and hence (so the story went) of the whole society
and of God himself. It became instead a place in which the true lady
did *nothing*. At least by 1857 when Mrs. C. S. Hilborn, a former mill-
worker, took up her pen to denounce the useless "modern aristocracy," the difference between the woman and the lady was clear. On the
one hand was the "poor mother, who takes in washing, and scrubs and
toils and sweats, until she looks like the skeleton of a perpetual motion." On the other was the lady "who arrays herself for a street prom-
enade as though for a shop window exhibition, with consequential airs
and robes spanning the sidewalks, and an expression of arrogant con-
ceit which says to every passer by 'did you *ever* see anything half so
magnificently beautiful as I am?'" The outward differences between
the lady and the woman had always been there, but they grew more
apparent as time went on. The narrow upper class grew richer, more
ostentatious, more conspicuous, while the lower classes, augmented by
hordes of immigrants, spread around them. At the turn of the century,
even as Veblen coined the term *conspicuous consumption* to describe
the chief activity of the rich, Lester Ward, the leading sociologist of
his day, estimated the poor at 80 percent of the population.

At the time, the chief difference between the upper and the lower
classes was thought to lie not in the pocketbook but in the heart and
mind. As Ward put it, the idea that "there exists a fundamental difference based on inherent qualities and belonging to the nature of things
. . . clings to the mind of man, and modern social classes are conceived
to be marked off from one another by nature." At its simplest the fundamental difference between the classes was this: the rich were physically, intellectually, and morally superior; the poor physically,
intellectually, and morally inferior, and indeed often depraved. As
William Graham Sumner, another of sociology's founding fathers put
it: "Only a small fraction of the human race have as yet, by thousands
of years of struggle, been partially emancipated from poverty, ignorance, and brutishness." That small portion, "naturally," was the ruling class. What made Mrs. Hilborn (a member of the lower 80
percent) so angry was that the ladies of the ruling class were not only
useless but were praised as morally superior beings on that account.
As Veblen described the beliefs of the ruling class: "Abstention from
labour is not only a honorific or meritorious act, but it presently comes
to be a requisite of decency. . . . Prescription ends by making labour
not only disreputable in the eyes of the community, but morally impossible to the noble freeborn man [and his lady], and incompatible
with a worthy life."

When men dragged this doctrine, along with their other mythical baggage, into the courtroom, they compounded inequity. The true lady—idle, respectable, proper, and useless—could do no wrong. The woman, however, might be capable of almost anything; she could not be punished too severely. So "justice" for women in the criminal court shook down—as had so many other aspects of American life—to the basis of social class.

For black women there was no justice at all. There are few cases of black women in this book because as often as not they were punished—even hanged or burned—without legal proceeding. Sometimes their executions—legal or illegal—were mentioned in a line or two in a newspaper. A "female slave" was hanged, they reported, or "a colored female." Rarely was her name given, and almost never her story. And never was there any talk of protecting a delicate female, of saving a pretty neck. Nothing was said of refinement and sensibility and true womanhood. On the same day that Ann Evards Wright Bilansky was hanged in Minnesota—March 23, 1860—two black women, speedily arrested and convicted for the murder of one Dr. Croxton, were hanged in Essex County, Virginia. There was no talk of commuting their sentences, no talk even of preparing their immortal souls for death. Their names—the only names the white world allowed them— were Ann and Eliza.

The next lowest thing to a black woman in the American hierarchy was an Irishwoman of the servant class. Around mid-century, with famine and unrest in Ireland, the Irish came to America by the thousands. Some, like Mary Moriarty and John Shehan, found their way south. The family of Mary Harris went to the Midwest. But many more landed in the Northeast and stuck, the women filling the kitchens of the Eastern Seaboard and moving on, in time, to the carding and spinning rooms of the mills. On the whole, they were thought to be stupid, sluggish, thoroughly undependable. "Every one knows what kind of servants they commonly are," said Harriet Martineau (who usually thought for herself), repeating the popular prejudice. "Some few of them are the best domestics in America: those who know how to value a respectable home . . . but too many of them are unsettled, reckless, slovenly; some dishonest, and some intemperate."

In the industrial Northeast the competition of factories and mills for cheap female labor created a "servant problem." Ladies looking for domestic help had to take what they could get. They could get Irish.

As a rule (or so the ladies said) the Irish servants were too coarse to wait on table, too clumsy for fine ironing, but they were well suited to scrubbing, heavy cleaning, fetching and carrying. To the upper-middle-class families of the Eastern Seaboard, the Irish domestic came to be a necessary fixture, but one that could be replaced, if the need arose, by her duplicate.

In 1867 the household of Dr. William Coriell in New Market, New Jersey, employed a domestic named Bridget Durgan. In 1892 the household of Mr. Andrew Borden in Fall River, Massachusetts, employed a domestic named Bridget Sullivan. (She, however, was known as Maggie, for Mr. Borden's daughter, Lizzie, found it so much simpler to call all the Irish servants who passed, one after another, through the household, by the same name.) The Coriell house and the Borden house came to have one other thing in common: each became the scene of an extraordinarily brutal and vicious murder. In both cases the killing took place within the house. No one saw it. In both cases the suspected murderer told confused and contradictory stories of what happened and tried to pin the crime on someone else. In both cases the suspect willfully destroyed physical evidence. In both cases, on the basis of highly incriminating circumstantial evidence, the suspected woman was charged with murder and brought to trial. And there all resemblance stops. For one alleged killer was an Irish servant. And the other was Miss Lizzie Borden.

Bridget Durgan at twenty-two was such a plain, ordinary woman that no one really noticed her. Employers in whose houses she had worked for months couldn't remember what she looked like. Even after she careened to the center of public attention, a *New York Times* reporter could write no more colorful description than that she was "an ordinary-looking Irish girl, with plain features" and "plainly clad." No one who knew her had anything particularly bad to say of her—nor anything particularly good either. She was quiet, they said. Ordinary.

Bridget was born in Ireland, in County Sligo, and she came to the United States as a teenager. It was typical of Bridget that she remembered arriving in New York two weeks before Christmas but didn't remember the year. She found work as a domestic in Brooklyn and in Manhattan; and then in a Manhattan domestic employment agency she met a man from Middlesex County, New Jersey, who took her home as a servant. She spent a year with the Dayton family, and then began moving around the county from one position to another—a month here, two months there. The work was hard, the life unsettled, the future all of a piece.

On October 22, 1866, Bridget Durgan went to work in the household of William Coriell, a forty-year-old physician. The household was small—just the doctor, his thirty-one-year-old wife, Mary Ellen, and their only living child, two-year-old Mamie. Asa Bush, the hired man, took his meals there, but he slept at his mother's house up the road. Mary Ellen Coriell was well enough, but she wasn't strong. She had lost some babies over the years, and at a little more than a hundred pounds, she was too thin for her five-feet-four-inch frame. Bridget took over all the heavy work and helped look after Mamie during the day. She told everyone how kind Dr. and Mrs. Coriell were to her, and because she hadn't known kindness before, she grew greedy for it and fearful that what had just fallen into her life could fall out again. Dr. Coriell observed only that she was a quiet, peaceable girl who treated his wife with respect.

But she was not altogether a satisfactory servant. She wasn't quite as neat as Mary Ellen Coriell could have wished. And she was so often sick. She had first met Dr. Coriell when he was called to the Daytons' to treat her for amenorrhea; and he was called in again when her eyes went bad while she was working for the Winsteads. And then there were her fits: "slumbers," she called them, but Dr. Coriell diagnosed cataleptic seizures closely related to epilepsy, and a second physician named the problem "hysterico-epilepsy." When the slumbers came on, drowsiness crept upon her, then shook off in a convulsive rigor as she fell, with her eyes rolling sideways to catch and stare for five minutes or fifteen or more. Sometimes she slid for an hour into an insensibility that Dr. Coriell called "hysterical coma" or deeper into the heavy sleep of a body racked and exhausted. Sometimes the muscle spasms riveted her again but without rousing her. Dr. Coriell was interested in her disease, but he must have thought that it could go on in much the same way for decades, since at the heart of the problem, as he saw it, was the first cause familiar to all up-to-date physicians: faulty menstruation. When the fits were upon her every two or three weeks, Bridget couldn't be relied on to work; and Dr. Coriell was sometimes put to the additional expense of hiring a woman to watch her through the night. (He already paid Bridget eight dollars a month, a sum that his wife considered extravagant for their small household.)

In February 1867, when Bridget had spent almost four months

with the Coriells, Mrs. Coriell made the appalling discovery that Bridget had "filthy habits." These habits were never more specifically described, but they went far beyond appeal. Bridget's time was extended slightly because she was sick again—she had her menstrual period—and must be allowed some days to recuperate, but Mrs. Coriell was firm: Bridget must go. Bridget told acquaintances that she hated to leave and feared she wouldn't get another position—certainly not with anyone as kind as the doctor and his wife. She had no place to go, though she spoke vaguely of going back to New York; but it was a bad time to travel—cold and snowing heavily. Still, on Monday, February 25, the day before her departure, she washed all her own clothing along with the family's laundry. When Dr. Coriell left home in the late afternoon to deliver a child in Piscataway, she was contentedly ironing her skirts. It seemed that she intended to start out fresh in the morning. Instead, in the middle of the night, she murdered Mary Ellen Coriell.

Afterward it was Bridget herself who gave the alarm. She snatched up the baby and ran down the road to the house of Dr. Coriell's cousin; but Israel Coriell was an old man and frightened. He told her to go on to the Reverend Mr. Little's house, and there, when she pounded on the door, the minister let her in. He could see at a glance that she had had a terrible fright; her hair was coming down, she had not taken time to put a skirt over her white underskirt, and she had run through the snow in her stocking feet. Two burglars were at the Coriell house, she blurted. They went upstairs and upset the bureau, and right now, for all Bridget knew, they might be murdering Mrs. Coriell. The Reverend Mr. Little, thinking she had been frightened by someone coming to fetch the doctor in the middle on the night, was only concerned about the child being carried through the cold. He led Bridget to the bedroom so she could turn Mamie over to his wife, and there when he lit the lamp he first saw the patch of fresh red blood, as wide as his palm, on Bridget's white skirt. She followed his eye, saw the stain, carefully folded it under her, and sat down. She told her story again, adding that she didn't know whether the house was on fire or not. The Reverend Mr. Little hurried to fetch his carbine; and Mrs. Little, taking Mamie into the bed to warm her, noticed that her hair was singed and that her clothing smelled of kerosene.

The Coriell house was quiet, but in the sitting room chairs had been overturned and broken, and on the wall near the bedroom door was the clear print of a bloody hand. The bed was smoldering, and near it, adrift in feathers from the slashed bed-tick and blanketed by smoke, lay Mary Ellen Coriell. When the Reverend Mr. Little dragged her out, he and the other neighbors he had roused could see that she had indeed been murdered. Her face was bruised and badly swollen, her neck gashed and bloody. But only when the body was more closely examined would they see how hard Mary Ellen Coriell had fought for her life. The list of her wounds took up half a column in the newspaper. The woman who laid out the body counted twenty-six gashes, not including those on her hand which had been slashed to the bone, apparently as she grasped the blade of the knife her assailant wielded. There were "scratches and just cuts" all over the body, two dozen stab wounds up and down the spine, deep wounds in the thighs and shoulders, a dozen jagged tearing wounds in the neck from unsuccessful attempts to cut the throat, scratches and teeth marks on the face. Her hair was torn in clumps from her scalp. Her face, both arms, and her right leg were terribly bruised and swollen—a grim detail of great importance, for swelling does not occur after death. Mary Ellen Coriell's struggle with her attacker had been fierce—and long.

On the night of the murder, after the rescuers dragged Mrs. Coriell's body out of the bedroom and put out the fire, they found Bridget on the porch, calmly changing her skirt. Everyone asked her what had happened, and she had a story ready. Two men came to the house at about 8:30 (sometimes she said 7:30) asking for the doctor; and Mrs. Coriell told them he was at Piscataway. At 10:30 the men returned; Mrs. Coriell let them in (or in another version told Bridget to let them in, thinking they were her husband); and then she told Bridget to run and fetch the doctor. Bridget grabbed the child and ran for help. And who were the mysterious men? One was tall, one was short. One was fair, one was dark. One had a mustache. Bridget had never seen them before and couldn't recognize them again. She would recognize one of them. She would recognize them both.

Dr. Coriell suspected her almost at once. She told him the story of the two men, and he thought it odd that his wife would direct the men to Piscataway without telling them exactly which house he was visiting. Certainly, he thought, his wife could not have mistaken two men at the kitchen door for himself coming home, since he always let himself in through the sitting room. And what, he asked, was Bridget doing with the child, who was always in her mother's care during the night? Bridget grew confused and stopped talking. Once, when the doctor asked her a difficult question, she simply picked up the lamp—

the only one in the room—and left. Then word came from the physician examining the body that the marks of teeth had been found—absolute proof, according to the biases of the time, that the murderer was a woman. Dr. Coriell accused Bridget of the murder.

No, she said, she hadn't done it. But she knew who had. The killers were Barney Doyle, whose child had died under the doctor's care, and a man named Hunt. Both men, as time and testimony would prove, were home in their beds, and not alone, when Mary Ellen Coriell was murdered. But when it dawned, belatedly, on Bridget that the investigators were looking for a woman, she changed her story. It was her friend Anne Linen, another servant, who had done it. She came to the house to steal some money and attacked Mrs. Coriell. And what of the men Bridget had accused before? Oh, they were there too, but only as onlookers. But Anne Linen, at the time of the murder, also was fast asleep in the house of her employer. Well, Bridget said, she *did* know who killed Mrs. Coriell but her questioners had made her so angry that she wouldn't tell. And she never did. Even at her trial she kept looking around as if she expected someone else to walk in and confess.

Circumstantial evidence went against her. That night, after the murder, Bridget washed the bloodstain out of her white skirt. The next morning she went out to the garden shed, and when searchers followed her they found the Coriells' meat-slicing knife badly bent. No one could find any trace in the snow of the mysterious night visitors. And none of Bridget's stories tallied with the sequence of events established by other witnesses who had passed by the quiet house during the evening or been awakened by cries or the sound of "pounding." Bridget still insisted that she ran for help when the men arrived about 10:30, but she arrived at the Reverend Mr. Little's house, 345 feet away, about two hours later. Bridget's suggestion to the Littles that the house might be on fire counted against her, too, for if she had been on hand when Mrs. Coriell's assailant threw the kerosene lamp on the mattress—clearly the last round of the fight—then she must have been present during the whole death struggle, a struggle that had lasted, to judge from Mary Ellen Coriell's bruises, at least half an hour and probably longer. As the prosecutor reconstructed events: Mary Ellen Coriell, already in bed for the night, was alarmed by something she heard Bridget doing—possibly overturning the bureau upstairs. She threw on a dress and confronted Bridget, who attacked her with the knife, dragged her back into the bedroom, clubbed her with a chair and the child's chair, and left her for dead. But Mary Ellen Coriell got up again and Bridget returned to the bedroom to beat her again with a round from the shattered chair. By that time Harriet Hillyer, roused from sleep in the next house, was looking out her window; she saw the shadows against the wall and heard the pounding in the Coriell house, but Mary Ellen Coriell was too near death to cry out. Bridget threw the lamp onto the bed and left the house.

But why did she do it? After the trial one opportunist who wrote and hawked Bridget's "confession" said that she killed Mrs. Coriell in hopes of taking her place with the doctor; but that is precisely the sort of motive a man would invent—one woman killing another on the off chance of getting a man. At the time of the investigation and trial, no one paid any attention to a remark Bridget made to Mrs. Little as the minister went to find his carbine. Now, she said, she could get on with the preparations she had been making—before she was interrupted by the "rogues"—to take Mamie to Boston. Bridget, everyone agreed, had no motive whatsoever to murder Mary Ellen Coriell. And since there was no motive, the lawyers reasoned—as lawyers had reasoned in the cases of wives who poisoned their husbands—the murder could only have been committed by a fiend. The difference was that in this case everyone was eager to believe that Bridget Durgan was indeed a fiend. After all, she was Irish.

Attorney Garnett R. Adrain, one of two lawyers appointed by the court to defend Bridget Durgan, warned the jurors—men with names like Vanderwenter, Van Dyke, Grant, Scudder, and Messler—that there was "prejudice in this community" and they "must be careful lest it reach them." But that prejudice, coupled with the fact that Bridget was a friendless woman, had already given everyone license to disregard such small rights as she had against self-incrimination. Law officers (and the merely curious) questioned her endlessly; and they coerced her into making a "tooth print" in wax which a dentist then claimed to match exactly to his drawings of the tooth marks in Mary Ellen Coriell's neck. And only at the last moment did the court appoint counsel to represent her—attorney Adrain and attorney William H. Leupp—whose case was a slapdash affair.

In fact, the defense had no case at all except to claim that Bridget was innocent and to refute bit by bit each piece of circumstantial evidence advanced by the prosecution, saying usually that it came to "nothing." Occasionally defense counsel hinted at another plea. Bridget must be innocent, they said, because a guilty person would have tried to run away or at least to hide her bloodstained clothing. Either she was innocent—or she was crazy. A guilty person, attorney Adrain argued, wouldn't have named as the murderers two men who lived in the neighborhood and whose whereabouts could easily be checked. "Either she was innocent in this," he said, "or she was not of sound mind." And certainly Bridget didn't bite Mrs. Coriell on the neck—or "if she did bite her it was the act of an insane person." The defense even produced two physicians to testify that Bridget's fits were "hysterico-epileptic" and that "about four-fifths of these epileptic cases in the end result in some kind of mental alienation." Even one fit of epilepsy, said an expert witness, could produce insanity and cause "the patient to commit acts that otherwise might not have been committed." Nevertheless, the defense attorneys stated flatly in their summation that they entered no plea of insanity for Bridget. Instead they foolishly rested their case upon her entire innocence.

Meanwhile, Bridget continued to have her fits. On the morning after the murder, Dr. Coriell testified, she fell down in a fit and remained insensible on the floor for two or three hours. (He did not say why no one bothered to pick her up.) Her jailers testified that she had fits all the time. Jailer Archibald Allen described the seizures, saying that if she was "sitting on a box she would fall off, be senseless a few moments, then open her eyes, and then sometimes say her head pained, and sometimes that she felt well." Jailer William Cox had "seen her fall over and remain for hours in a fit." Both men testified that when the fits were upon her "froth and blood ran from her mouth . . . as if she had bit her tongue," but when she was "herself" she "generally had a sleepy look." Neither man was concerned about her strange behavior, though Allen admitted that he had been worried enough at first to send for a doctor who assured him that the fits were "nothing." After that, he testified, "When she had a fit I would say, 'She'll get over it; let her alone'; and she always did get over it." Sometimes, when she had been insensible for a long time, they stuck pins in her to try to bring her around, but mostly they left her alone.

Bridget Durgan was a sick woman. And according to the popular novelist Mrs. Elizabeth Oakes Smith, who visited Bridget in jail, her "human intelligence" was "on the very lowest level." It seems clear in retrospect that she suffered from frequent, severe grand mal epileptic seizures, and that she probably killed Mary Ellen Coriell while suffering what modern medicine calls a seizure of psychomotor or temporal lobe epilepsy—a type of seizure often characterized by rage, physical violence, and amnesia. Even at the time her attorneys might have entered on her behalf a plea that reflected her diminished responsibility—a plea of not guilty by reason of insanity, or guilty of a lesser charge of homicide or manslaughter—for medical jurisprudence already knew something of epilepsy. The relationship of epilepsy to insanity and hence to legal responsibility had been energetically disputed by experts since the first interposition of an epileptic insanity defense in the case of one Fyler, tried at Syracuse, New York, in 1855 for the murder of his wife. Like Bridget Durgan, Fyler murdered at midnight, ran half-clothed through the snow to summon help, and insisted that two men had done the killing. But in his case, a curious compromise led to an unforeseen result. Convicted of murder largely by the testimony of the renowned Dr. William Hammond, who found him sane, Fyler was institutionalized for treatment of his epilepsy and sentencing was deferred until a "cure" could be effected. By the time the doctors pronounced him ready for sentencing, the law under which he was convicted had been repealed for the benefit of Mary Hartung, so Fyler too had to be released. Years later, the experts were still debating the actual degree of Fyler's legal responsibility.

Opinions of epilepsy varied widely from Hammond's notion of momentary "mental aberration" to the unqualified assertion of French expert Delasiauve, "It is certain that on passing by an epileptic we elbow one who might be an assassin. . . ." The eminent Isaac Ray announced in 1867, just after the Durgan trial, his view that epilepsy automatically "annulled" legal "liabilities" in its sufferers; but he admitted that his view was too advanced for his age. Reviewing the international debate on the topic for the *American Journal of Insanity*, Dr. Manuel Gonzales Echeverria observed that epileptic insanity in any particular case was rarely determined by scientific expertise. Instead it was "left entirely dependent on the eloquence displayed in its advocacy, and above all on the degree of public feeling concerning the prisoner."

In the Durgan case public feeling ran strongly against the defendant, and the most effective "advocacy" came from Dr. Coriell, who must have carried great weight with the jury when he testified in his triple capacity as husband of the deceased, personal physician of the defendant, and impartial expert witness. Dr. Coriell regarded Bridget's illness as strictly physical in nature; and although leading experts on epilepsy at the time placed the "seat" of the disease "in the head," Dr. Coriell placed it in the uterus. "Her fits were caused by amenorrhea," he testified flatly. To cure them he had once prescribed a diuretic, and at another time croton oil, which acts as a powerful cathartic when taken internally, and when applied externally raises blisters and pustules. Dr. Coriell did not specify which of these procedures he had prescribed to cure Bridget Durgan's abnormal menstruation and hence her epilepsy; but he clearly did not worry that her amenorrhea would lead to insanity. And Durgan's lawyers, who at least hinted at the possibility of epileptic insanity, never suggested that she suffered from the far more common female complaint, insanity caused by abnormal menstruation. That plea seems to have been considered a plea for delicate ladies only, or at the very least for ex-ladies in a delicate condition, such as the seduced-and-abandoned maidens. Coarse Irish girls like Bridget Durgan might have "fits" as a result of abnormal menstruation, but they lacked the delicate sensibilities to go insane in a fashion picturesque enough to capture the heart of a jury. So all the pleas of diminished responsibility that might have worked in another case—in the case of a man or a woman of a higher class—were denied to Bridget Durgan.

There was only one lady involved in this case, and she was the victim. Even the defense attorneys professed boundless admiration for the "lovely, accomplished" Mary Ellen Coriell, a lady who, according to the prosecution, rushed to the defense of her child with a courage unrivaled on any battlefield of history. "What heroism" asked the prosecutor, "could compare with that of this gentle woman, who, bleeding with half a hundred wounds, tottered in the stillness of the night to confront her murderess for the sake of her poor baby!" Mary Ellen Coriell's brave fight made Bridget seem a beast indeed; one commentator claimed that Bridget had not "one spark of womanhood" and Elizabeth Oakes Smith, visiting the jail, found Bridget scarcely more than an animal. Bridget had "cunning and ability to conceal her real actions," said Mrs. Smith, just like "the fox, the panther, and many inferior animals." Her eye was "the eye of a reptile in shape and expression." Her jaws were "large and heavy," her mouth small, the gums narrow and "cat-like in shape, with pointed teeth. . . . The whole person is heavy," said Mrs. Smith, "inclined to fulness, and the hands are large, coarse, and somehow have a dangerous look. . . . There is not one character of beauty, even in the lowest degree, about the girl; not one ray of sentiment, nothing genuine, hardly human, except a weak, sometimes a bitter, smile." Even science contributed to the diagnosis of Bridget's subhuman character: "She is large in the base of the brain, and swells out over the ears, where destructiveness and secretiveness are located by phrenologists, while the whole region of intellect, ideality and moral sentiment is small. Her texture, temperament, all are coarse; hair coarse and scanty, forehead naturally corrugated and low, nose concave and square at the nostrils, leaving a very long upper lip."

But if Bridget were a beast, as the prosecutors maintained and as Mrs. Smith described her—a beast "born without moral responsibility, just as much as the tiger or the wolf is so born"—then the question of her culpability remained open. Mrs. Smith readily agreed that Bridget was a danger to society and should not be at large, but she put a "question for our advanced civilization to consider": "whether it is right to take an irresponsible morally idiotic creature, and she a woman, whose sex had no voice in making the laws under which she will suffer, and hang her by the neck till she is dead."

That question was not considered in the courtroom. Judge Vrendenburgh, charging the jury, reviewed the physical evidence so incriminating to Bridget Durgan and dismissed altogether the issue of her responsibility, saying that he "knew of no evidence that Bridget was insane beyond the atrocious wickedness of the deed." As to her motive, he asked rhetorically: "Was not cruelty sufficient motive for the cruel?" Nor need the jury fret about premeditation—though there was plenty of evidence to show that Bridget had intended to leave the Coriells in peace—for only an instant's impulse was enough to constitute premeditation and first-degree murder. And as to Bridget's sex, the jury should think nothing of it. The prosecutor had already eliminated the issue of sex by claiming that Bridget had "unsexed herself" through her "monstrous crime" and so could "claim no sympathy." The judge's charge directed conviction. The jury took less than an hour to follow instructions and find her guilty as charged.

On June 17, 1867, Judge Vrendenburgh summarized the circumstances of Bridget's crime, which he considered to be one of the most horrible in the history of the world, praised the fairness of her trial, and sentenced her to be hanged on August 30. He warned her to prepare to die, for no mercy would be shown her in this world. And then the ordinarily taciturn Bridget, who sat through most of the trial with her face buried in her handkerchief, did a most remarkable thing. "The prisoner sat down as soon as the sentence was pronounced and commenced to cry aloud, rocking herself to and fro and uttering screams that could be heard far beyond the Court-house. After some delay she was removed, still screaming, from the Court-house and carried to the jail, where for some time she continued to utter screams that were heard by the crowd without."

The crowd was unmoved. Everyone had been against Bridget all along. On the second day of the trial a reporter for *The New York Times* noticed that "the guilt of the accused seems to be a foregone conclusion among outsiders, and when the counsel for the prosecution makes a good point there is a sympathetic buzz and flutter throughout the court-room." A month later, when Judge Vrendenburgh pronounced the death sentence, the courtroom audience applauded. The philanthropic and the curious flocked to the jail to get a glimpse of the fiend, and the jailers, who soon wearied of trying to discriminate between them, let them all in. Thousands applied to the sheriff for tickets to the hanging, since executions, out of deference to the anticapital punishment political forces, were no longer public events but private showings. The sheriff seems to have been generous to his friends, for on the morning of August 30, 1867, some two thousand turned up within the prison compound—including hundreds of newly sworn "deputies." Women filled the upper windows of the jail and perched on the roof. Men covered the roof of a nearby barn and clambered so thickly onto an improvised platform outside the jail enclosure that it broke down under their weight. Outside the walls spectators—mostly men—vied for a glimpse of the condemned fiend. *The New York Times* called them "the roughest, rudest and most ungentlemanly crowd of men we ever saw"—a crowd made up of "many hundreds of profane, indecent and ungentlemanly persons who pushed and hauled, and swore and fought." Although the influential newspaper had all along subscribed to the view that Bridget should be hanged, the rather fastidious reporter sent to cover the execution was outraged by the conduct of the crowd. They "surged to and fro," he reported. "Every man pushed for position. Oaths and profane ejaculations of the most outrageous nature, mingled with cries and calls, such as one may hear at a circus. For five minutes," said the journalist, "we stood in the midst of these brutes, and wondered of what stuff and refuse they were made."

Through that crowd to the scaffold the sheriff led Bridget Durgan, dressed in a plain brown suit, a white collar and gloves, and supported on the arms of two priests. She was drunk. Afraid that she would be too distraught to walk to the scaffold or that she would fall down in a seizure, the sheriff had awakened her at five o'clock in the morning and begun administering "appropriate stimulants" under the direction of the prison physician. And once the ceremony was under way, the sheriff rushed things along, not knowing how long Bridget could keep on her feet without passing out or having a fit. So even while the prayers were being said, the cap was fitted over her face; and then she was "jerked into eternity."

The device used in the execution was no proper gallows, for the professional executioner had refused to lend his skill to the occasion, saying that he hanged "men, not women." The rig improvised by amateurs didn't drop the condemned woman through a trap and break her neck. Rather, when a weight was released, it jerked her some three feet off the ground and held her there, convulsed and struggling, while slowly she choked to death. *The Times* reporter noted that the jostling crowd of men, who might just as well have attended a race or a prizefight, were "afforded amplest gratification" by the last "contortions" of Bridget Durgan.

After she hung for half an hour, they took her down and buried her, but that was not the end of the story of Bridget Durgan. For the men who had investigated her, arrested her, tried her, convicted her, and turned out in their Sunday best to see her hanged—or some of them anyway—had to go home and remember. And as the reporter found, it is one thing to urge capital punishment from the safety of a Manhattan editorial office and another thing altogether to shoulder into the crowd beside the scaffold. With some understanding of the relationship between a guilty public and its pocketbook, the city recorder, one of the jailers, and even Bridget's attorney Adrain offered her "true confessions" for sale among the crowd.

These pamphlets went straight to the heart of nagging doubts about the justice of Bridget's sentence and dispelled them, so it is easy to see why the execution crowd would pay good money for a copy to take away. It was like buying absolution. And the crowd particularly needed the written word in this case because the clergymen who attended Bridget at the end were Catholic priests, prevented by their vows of office from blabbing what they knew or didn't know (as Protestant clergy all too often did) and thus thoroughly worthless at mitigating public guilt. One written confession purported to be handwritten by Bridget herself (though the real Bridget was illiterate), and it said that Bridget planned the crime for a long time (leaving no doubt about premeditation), received no encouragement whatsoever from Dr. Coriell (leaving no doubt of his honor), and was for most of her life a hardened prostitute and criminal with other attempted murders to her credit (putting aside once and for all the suggestion of insanity or moral irresponsibility). She was impelled to this particular murder, she "confessed," by seeing the picture of one woman stabbing another in a newspaper. She too wanted her picture in the rotogravure. As a little psychological bonus to the purchasers of the confession, Bridget emphatically forgave everyone. Although she was to be hanged "like an old cat," the confession said, that was strictly her own fault.

In addition, the commentary accompanying the confession made clear that Bridget was not a human being in the first place. It offered this description of her behavior when she was first imprisoned: "She exhibited exactly the same traits that a wild beast would have done. Her eyes glared wildly; she would clutch her hands in the air, tug furiously at her straggling hair, rush from one side of the cell to the other, throw herself on her straw bed and bite it with her teeth. The last act was a favorite one of hers and it proved very conclusively her guilt, at least circumstantially; for the neck of her victim *was bitten* nearly through on one side." The account also repeated the rumor that Bridget was secretly the wife of one Antoine Probst, another notorious murderer known, like Bridget, for "the most depraved animal instincts" and "the greatest blood thirstiness." The confession and commentary concluded with the assessment of a "gentleman" who was an expert criminologist: Bridget Durgan, he is reported to have said, "is the most perfect combination of the wolf, the tiger, the hog and the hyena, that I ever came across." Hanging Bridget—or the passel of wild animals that went under that name—became a virtuous act of public service.

For more sophisticated people, another pamphlet published after the hanging offered another version of Bridget's story, differing from other accounts in two important respects. In the first place, the rowdy circus of Bridget's execution was erased; a little boisterousness admittedly had occurred, but that was all—and in Bridget's presence every gentleman was on his best behavior. Secondly, Bridget herself was no fiendishly ugly monster; she was a "not ill looking" girl of respectable family background. The hanging crowd and Bridget seem to have behaved quite decorously; only Dr. Coriell had behaved unbecomingly by indicating to Bridget that he would welcome his wife's death and so inciting Bridget to murder. In the view of the more sophisticated author of this confession, Bridget was no monster. His most damning diagnosis was this: "That she was exceedingly ambitious, is beyond all manner of doubt; and that she constantly endeavored to rise above her condition is equally certain."

Public attitudes toward Bridget Durgan's crime were extreme and complicated. At the time of the murder of Mary Ellen Coriell, Bridget was both powerless and threatening; she had no family or friends capable of assisting her in any way or of protesting if she were treated badly, yet as only one among thousands of Irish servants who might turn homicidal she was scary. So the way was clear to treat her as the public mind wished: to make of her a summary example for all rebellious servants. And most people seemed quite able either to disregard the very real mitigating circumstances of her poverty and sickness or to consider them only as further evidence of her brutish, subhuman nature. Others, perhaps discomforted by Mrs. Smith's suggestion that hanging an "animal" might be less than noble, preferred to rehabilitate Bridget—to make her out to be not a social victim but a woman who had been given an even break and turned to crime anyway for that most intelligible of all motives—the love of an irresistible man. The most remarkable aspect of this view, presented in the second "confession," is that Bridget is nowhere seen as what she was: a poor, homely, illiterate, epileptic servant. And it was this upgraded version of the Bridget Durgan story that was reprinted and recirculated fifteen years later. In that final authoritative account, all the real circumstances of Bridget's life fell away in the vision of a happier America. Her only remaining problem then was this—"she constantly endeavored to rise above her condition." And odd as it may seem in a country where men were thought to catapult from log cabin to White House, such ambition in a lower-class woman was still grounds for hanging.

3.

Lizzie Andrew Borden, thirty-two-year-old spinster, of Fall River, Massachusetts, might have understood that ambition, for she felt it herself. Miss Borden, however, was entitled to it. Bordens were among the very first settlers of Fall River. Wisely, they grabbed up the water rights in what was destined to be a mill town; and God rewarded their foresight with riches and power. By the late nineteenth century, when Fall River had become the largest cotton manufacturing center in the United States, the mills and banks and shipping lines were all Borden.

And one of those Bordens was Andrew Jackson, Miss Lizzie's father. His father, Abraham, was one of the poor relations who attach remotely to even the best of families—a fish peddler at the end of the Borden coattail. But Andrew, by dint of hard work and parsimony and an impeccably dour face, had won his rightful Borden place in the town. He sat on boards of directors at some of the Borden mills and the new Fall River street railway, he officiated at several local banks, and he owned a good deal of real estate, including the new, massive red-brick "Borden Block." He was worth more than a quarter of a million dollars.

You wouldn't have known it, for Andrew Jackson Borden was the perfect capitalist. He made money—lots of it—for the sake of making money. Yet, as a Christian, Andrew Borden knew that money could be the root of all evil—if one took pleasure in money and used it as a source of enjoyment. The trick then, for a good Christian capitalist, was to make money but to enjoy it not at all. And that skill Andrew Borden had perfected.

His second daughter, Lizzie, had not. She complained a good deal, mostly about money. But there was more to it than that. Since Andrew Borden, held back by his meager beginnings, had taken longer than his luckier cousins to make his mark, his every move seemed, by the standards of his fellow entrepreneurs, just a little late, a little short, perhaps flawed by the unshakable caution of a man who started poor and didn't want to finish that way. Andrew's success was impressive, if imperfect, and it apparently pleased him; but it left his daughter mired in might-have-beens. Lizzie Borden might have lived, as her name and money entitled her to, among the society people on the hill, but Andrew, when he left his father's homestead, moved only a few blocks to "the flats" near the business district, below the hill. And the house he bought was not even a proper house, but two apartments gerrymandered into a one-family residence. Miss Borden might have visited on the hill, but for that a proper lady needed a private carriage, a luxury Andrew Borden had no use for. And a proper lady needed a chaperone, a position that Andrew's second wife, Abby, for all her grand old Durfee blood, could never fill, for she too was a poor relation, the daughter of a blacksmith, and for a time herself a "tailoress." Lizzie was acquainted on the hill; most of her cousins lived there. She had even persuaded Andrew to send her with some of them on a European grand tour, but Lizzie was no Consuela Vanderbilt or Jennie Jerome; she returned reluctantly without a lord.

At the time, thanks to a half-century battle for woman's rights, women could do more than marry or go into society. The Fall River *Daily Globe*, which Lizzie read every day, reported that women were graduating from medical school in New York, running for public office in Wyoming, voting—at least in school elections—right there in Fall River. And Lizzie had several friends (she planned to go off to a house party at Marion with them soon) who were single, self-supporting, working women: teachers, school principals, bookkeepers. But Lizzie herself, born just a little too soon to join the fashionable Fall River daughters going off to the new women's colleges, was not trained for any work. She taught some classes in the Sunday school now and again, but mostly she stayed at home. With her stepmother, her older sister, Emma, and the Irish servant all keeping house for one old man, there wasn't much to do in that small house. She tidied up her own bedroom, mended her own dresses, ironed her own hankies. She kept the treasurer's records for her church group. She read magazines and the newspaper and sometimes a letter from a friend.

Perhaps staying at home wouldn't have been quite so tiresome if home had included any of those amenities one might reasonably expect in the household of a man who was well on his way to becoming a millionaire: a piano perhaps, a stereopticon, some new furniture to replace the ugly horsehair parlor fittings fashionable forty years before, electric lighting, or perhaps even a toilet. Other people with far less money had such conveniences. Many families on the hill indulged in luxuries: garden parties with an orchestra imported from Boston and a cold collation on the lawn. But Andrew Borden, content to accumulate the wealth that his labor and God's grace allowed him, remained adamantly, righteously above enjoying the comforts his money could buy him. So daughter Lizzie, neither career woman nor society matron, had none of the joys of work—or of ostentation. She had only leisure. Like Bridget Durgan, who could look forward only to endless work in the kitchens of others, Lizzie Borden's life was all of a piece; for she was nothing but Andrew Borden's daughter, a woman whose life was apparently without the possibility of an event.

On the morning of August 4, 1892, just before eleven o'clock, widow Adelaide Buffinton Churchill, returning from market to her home on Second Street, saw the Borden family's servant Bridget Sullivan "walking fast" toward the house of Dr. Seabury Bowen across the street. It was not a day for hurrying; the heat wave continued and already the temperature was in the nineties. "Someone at the Bordens' must be sick," Mrs. Churchill thought. She went into her house, put down her bundles, and looked out at the Borden house next door from her kitchen window. Later, in court, Adelaide Churchill described what she saw and what she did:

> Miss Lizzie Borden was standing inside their screen door, at the side of their house. I opened the window and said, "Lizzie, what is the matter?" She replied, "Oh, Mrs. Churchill, do come over. Someone has killed father." I went over and stepped inside the screen door. She was sitting on the stair. I put my hand on her arm and said "Oh, Lizzie!" Then I said, "Where is your father?" She said, "In the sitting room."

Mrs. Churchill went through the kitchen to the sitting room. There on the horsehair sofa lay Andrew Jackson Borden, apparently stretched out for a nap, except that where his face should have been was only blood and pulp. The coroner would find the marks of ten hatchet blows.

Before running to summon help, Mrs. Churchill put two more questions to Lizzie Borden. The second—"Where is your mother?"—was answered later when Mrs. Churchill and Bridget Sullivan, searching upstairs at Lizzie's suggestion, found Mrs. Borden huddled on the guest-room floor, her skull battered in. But the first question—"Where were you when it happened?"—has never been satisfactorily answered, although Lizzie Borden, like Bridget Durgan before her, pulled a story together. Sometimes she had to shave it here or puff it out there to make it fit; but finally, unlike Bridget Durgan, she drew the line and held it.

She had been in the barn behind the house, she said, for ten minutes or fifteen or twenty—in any case, just long enough to miss her father's murder. She had been looking for lead to make some sinkers for her fishline, although she hadn't gone fishing for five years; or she was looking for a piece of screen to repair a window. And she had eaten some windfall pears, perhaps two or three, while standing up in the hayloft looking out the window, or perhaps not looking out the window. In any case, after some time she walked the few yards back to the house and heard a grating noise, or her father groaning, or nothing at all. The kitchen screen door was wide open, and her father lay dead upon the sofa. As for her stepmother, Lizzie had not seen her since shortly after nine o'clock when the old woman went upstairs to make the bed in the guest room. Lizzie, who spent the entire morning in the kitchen reading an old magazine and perhaps eating a cookie, thought that her stepmother had gone out in response to a note from a sick friend. Lizzie had told that story earlier to the servant; she had told it to her father when he returned from the morning round of his business interests and prepared for a nap on the sofa before midday dinner; and she repeated it again and again although, curiously enough, all the investigators on the case were unable to find the note, the woman who sent it, or the boy who delivered it.

Later, as the police questioned the family and friends, Miss Lizzie told of her father's quarrels with laborers at his farm and with a prospective tenant. She told of mysterious men she had seen lurking about the house, of vandals breaking into the barn, of family sickness that Abby Borden feared to be poisoning, of a strange ransacking of Abby's desk the year before, a robbery that Andrew had reported to the police and then asked them to forget. All the murder suspects Lizzie suggested either had sound alibis or proved to be phantoms; but Lizzie clearly had been worried all along. On the evening before the murders she recounted her fears to her best friend, Miss Alice Russell, who repeated them in court: "I feel depressed," Lizzie had said. "I feel as if something was hanging over me that I cannot throw off, and it comes over me at times, no matter where I am. . . . I feel as if I wanted to sleep with my eyes half open—with one eye open half the time—for fear they will burn the house down over us. . . . I am afraid somebody will do something; I don't know but what somebody will do something." The next day somebody did something, and it seemed strange that Miss Lizzie should so clearly have seen it coming.

The murders took place on Thursday morning. Saturday morning, while Lizzie attended her parents' funeral, the police vainly searched her closet for a bloodstained dress. That evening the mayor, paying a condolence call, told Lizzie that she was suspected. On Sunday morning, when Lizzie's friend Alice Russell entered the Borden kitchen, she found Lizzie, in Emma's presence, burning a dress in the stove. "I'm going to burn this old thing up," she said. "It is covered with paint."

On the following Tuesday, Wednesday, and Thursday, Lizzie testified at the inquest—circling, evading, contradicting, revising her story as she went along, scorning the badgering of District Attorney Hosea Knowlton. Accounting for some twenty minutes spent in the barn loft, Lizzie told of slowly eating two or three pears. But Knowlton remembered that she, like her parents and Bridget Sullivan, had been nauseated the day before and unable to eat breakfast that morning. The story of her eating pears in the barn loft—improbable on the face of it—became doubly suspect, and Knowlton tried to pin her down.

Q. You were feeling better than you did in the morning?
A. Better than I did the night before.
Q. You were feeling better than you were in the morning?
A. I felt better in the morning than I did the night before.
Q. That is not what I asked you. You were then, when you were in that hot loft, looking out of the window and eating three pears, feeling better, were you not, than you were in the morning when you could not eat breakfast?
A. I never eat any breakfast.
Q. You did not answer my question, and you will, if I have to put it all day. Were you then, when you were eating those three pears in that hot loft, looking out of that closed window, feeling better than you were in the morning when you ate no breakfast?
A. I was feeling well enough to eat the pears.
Q. Were you feeling better than you were in the morning?
A. I don't think I felt very sick in the morning only—Yes, I don't know but I did feel better. As I say, I don't know whether I ate any breakfast or not, or whether I ate a cookie.
Q. Were you then feeling better than you did in the morning?
A. I don't know how to answer you, because I told you I felt better in the morning anyway.
Q. Do you understand the question? My question is whether, when you were in the loft of the barn, you were feeling better than you were in the morning when you got up?
A. No, I felt about the same.

Lizzie Borden was not easily pushed around. When she claimed not to know whether Bridget had actually been washing windows that morning, Knowlton asked in exasperation, "Do you think she might have gone to work and washed all the windows in the dining room and the sitting room and you not know it?"

"I don't know, I am sure," replied Miss Lizzie, "whether I should or not. I might have seen her, and not know it."

That was too much for Hosea Knowlton. "Miss Borden," he said, "I am trying in good faith to get all the doings that morning of yourself and Miss Sullivan, and I have not succeeded in doing it." He asked her directly, "Do you desire to give me any information or not?"

"I don't know," said Miss Lizzie. "I don't know what your name is." Miss Lizzie, after all, was a Borden. But Hosea Knowlton—who was he? On Thursday afternoon, August 11, one week after the murders, Lizzie Andrew Borden was arrested for the murder of Andrew Jackson Borden. But she never weakened. And by the time her trial was all over, unknown Hosea Knowlton, prosecuting attorney, would seem to be—like the judges—on the side of Miss Lizzie Borden.

When Miss Lizzie took her seat in the middle of the courtroom, just in front of the railing that separated the public section at the rear from the judicial bench, she was wearing a simple black crepe dress trimmed with rows of black velvet piping. Her new black snubnosed shoes were more practical than stylish. Her hat, a black straw "poke shaped" style featuring a blue plume and blue rosettes, was "of no existing fashion." Black cotton gloves concealed her hands. Halfway through the trial, Miss Borden appeared in a new dress—a dress that even to the untrained eyes of male crime reporters was obviously expensive: black silk overlaid with black lace in a cape effect, much more stylish than the old-fashioned shirred basque in which she made her courtroom debut. But with the new dress appeared the old hat and the old black cotton gloves—an ensemble distinctly out of the contemporary fashion, which called for a medley of colors in the costume. Of course, she was in mourning, but at her throat she wore a large enameled pansy pin, which even reporter Julian Ralph of the New York *Sun*, who so admired Miss Borden, considered "rather loud." Her ignorance or defiance of the rules of fashion marked her as no mere fashion plate but a true lady. Indeed she had about her, as reporter Ralph put it, "that indefinable quality which we call ladyhood."

Her face, "like her dress," according to Ralph, "was that of a lady." She had "large brown eyes, and a fine high forehead, but her nose," he wrote, "is a tilting one, and her cheek bones are so prominent that the lower part of her countenance is greatly overweighted. Her head is broadest at the ears. Her cheeks are very plump, and her jaws are strong and conspicuous. Her thick, protruding lips are pallid from sickness, and her mouth is drawn down into two very deep creases that denote either a melancholy or an irritable disposition." Curiously enough, this face "of a lady"—with its irregular nose, heavy jaws, thick lips, and prominent creases—corresponds closely to Elizabeth Oakes Smith's description of the fiendish Bridget Durgan. But Ralph interprets these features differently. "She is no Medusa or Gorgon," he writes. "There is nothing wicked, criminal, or hard in her features."

Only one thing troubled the reporters, most of whom were, like

Ralph, sympathetic to Miss Borden. Her calm self-possession, appropriate to a lady, seemed too tightly controlled. Shortly after the murders, the Fall River *Daily Globe* observed that Lizzie showed "no other feeling than that of a disinterested party."

For the first two days of the trial she scarcely altered the posture she assumed on first taking her seat. In the morning she rested her chin on her left hand, in the afternoon on her right. The journalists, who described her as "a graven image," agreed that Miss Borden was possessed of an extremely "phlegmatic and undemonstrative" nature. And everyone knew, for it was widely reported, that she had not been seen to shed a tear since the death of her father and stepmother—and a woman who did not cry was surely an unnatural creature. Then, after a long, tense debate among the attorneys, a crucial point of law was decided in Lizzie's favor—and she began to cry. To reporters like Ralph, it made all the difference. "Miss Borden's womanhood," he wrote, "was fully established when she burst into tears. . . ." During the following days of the trial Lizzie was sometimes in great distress: she called for water, she asked to be excused, she leaned heavily for support upon the railings behind and in front of her, she sniffed her smelling salts, she wept, and more than once she fainted dead away. The sympathetic journalists reported these incidents with detailed flourishes. Miss Borden, it seemed, was not only a lady, but a true womanly woman.

As such, she was conspicuously out of place in the courtroom that resembled nothing so much as an old boys' club. Ralph reported that "the Judges, the lawyers, the Sheriff, and most of the attendants were in the main a white-haired, aged lot of citizens." All three judges were thin-lipped "grey beards." The jurors, all men, were chosen deliberately by the defense because they were at middle age or beyond. The foreman was a prosperous landowner, and another juror managed an iron works; the rest were farmers or artisans of modest means. Miss Borden was represented by a panel of attorneys well respected among the "grey beards." Andrew Jennings was a prominent citizen who for many years had been Andrew Borden's attorney. Melvin O. Adams, an experienced Boston trial lawyer, impressed the jury with his big-city manners and waxed mustache. And George D. Robinson, at fifty-nine, a stately, imposing gentleman of the old school, had served three times as governor of the Commonwealth.

The attorneys for the prosecution were somewhat less impressive. Arthur Pillsbury, attorney general of the Commonwealth, whose duty it was to prosecute, dropped out pleading ill health rather than face the undignified work of prosecuting a lady. "No lawyer who could have his choice would care to try a woman for her life," commented the Fall River *Daily Globe*. The task fell to Hosea Knowlton, district attorney of Bristol County, who had already had enough of Miss Borden at the inquest. He too tried to get out of the job—a thankless one politically—and when he couldn't shirk the task, he performed it with conspicuous lethargy. He was assisted by William Moody, district attorney for the eastern district of Essex County, at thirty-eight the youngest man in the courtroom and thoroughly eclipsed by the posturings of his elders.

Not long before, Moody had argued an eminent domain case with Robinson and split a very large fee. That was just one of the many professional and political associations that bound together the law officers of the Borden court. Defense attorneys Jennings and Adams were graduates of Boston Law School; defense attorney Robinson and prosecutors Knowlton and Moody were Harvard men. Jennings, Knowlton, and Robinson had served as state representatives and state senators, as had Albert Mason, now chief justice of the court; Robinson and Mason had served together on legislative committees. And as governor, Robinson had appointed to lifetime tenure on the Superior Court Justice Justin Dewey, before whom he now appeared to argue Miss Borden's case. Those attorneys, judges, and jurors who were not old friends quickly seemed to be. *The New York Times* noted that "Judges and attorneys are alike interested in securing celerity"; and after witnessing four days of the trial, Ralph wrote, "The temper of the lawyers is peculiar. They work in almost unbroken harmony, each side treating the other side in a friendly, polite, and respectful manner. They have a common understanding as to the conduct of the case. . . ."

In this courtroom, thickly carpeted and amply furnished with spittoons, Lizzie Borden, a lady in sensible shoes, fanned herself while William H. Moody delivered the opening arguments for the prosecution.

The government's case, as Moody presented it, was based upon three propositions: that Lizzie was predisposed to commit the murders, that she did in fact commit them, and that her behavior since the murders indicated her guilt. Many witnesses testified to the hostility within the

Borden household: to locked doors and silences and squabbles over property and Lizzie's persistence in addressing her stepmother of twenty-five years as "Mrs. Borden." Medical experts agreed that the murderous blows were well within a woman's capability. Other witnesses established that Lizzie had the opportunity to commit the murders while other possible suspects, such as her uncle John Morse, her sister Emma (who was away), and Bridget Sullivan, did not.

Miss Lizzie's defense team offered no opposing theory of the crime but attacked the prosecution's case by discrediting witnesses, casting doubt on their memory or credibility. Then they effectively created a smoke screen, ignoring real issues as if they had never been raised, arguing as central issues points that were at best tangential. It was a clever if devious defense. As prosecutor Moody said of one of Governor Robinson's torrents of irrelevant oratory, "It is magnificent, but it is not law." Central to the defense was the sanctity of Lizzie's relationship with her father, as described by Governor Robinson.

> He [Andrew Borden] was a man that wore nothing in the way of ornament, of jewelry but one ring, and that ring was Lizzie's. It had been put on many years ago when Lizzie was a little girl, and the old man wore it and it lies buried with him in the cemetery. He liked Lizzie, did he not? He loved her as his child; and the ring that stands as the pledge of plighted faith and love, that typifies and symbolizes the dearest relation that is ever created in life, that ring was the bond of union between the father and the daughter. No man should be heard to say that she murdered the man that so loved her.

This evidence that Andrew was fond of Lizzie was construed by both sides to mean that Lizzie was fond of Andrew.

That a woman should kill her father, to whom she was attached even in a pre-Freudian era by so many Freudian strings, was simply *unthinkable*. Particularly must it have been so to Chief Justice Mason, who had three daughters, all about Lizzie's age; to Judge Dewey, whose three daughters were only a few years younger; and to several of the jurors who had been carefully chosen by the defense especially *because* they had daughters of nearly Lizzie's age. In his summation Governor Robinson reminded them: "You are out of families, you come from firesides, you are members of households, you have wives and daughters and sisters and you have had mothers. . . ." When the trial was over these men would go home, as Andrew Borden had, to be greeted by their daughters. A jacket would be hung, a pair of slippers fetched, a pillow puffed and placed beneath the head—if Lizzie Borden were guilty as charged who among them would ever feel the same about such domesticities?

The defense asked, "Where is the motive for this crime?" as though coming into a half-share of a quarter of a million dollars is not motive enough for murder. To prove that Miss Lizzie was a well-to-do young woman who could not have wanted for money the defense asked her older sister, Emma, to testify to Lizzie's holdings at the time of her father's death. Two thousand dollars in one bank, $500 in another, $172.75 in a third bank, $141 in a fourth. In addition she held two shares of the Fall River National Bank and nine shares of the Merchants' Manufacturing Company. That Miss Lizzie, at the age of thirty-two, possessed almost $3,000 in her own name was considered evidence that she had all a woman could want. "What is the use of talking about that?" Governor Robinson asked the jury. "Did she want any more to live on in comfort?" If she *did* wish for more, it was ever so tactfully suggested, she had only to wait a few years until her father died. The Fall River *Daily Globe* pointed out that, according to Massachusetts law, if her father died before her stepmother, Abby would inherit at least one-third of Andrew's estate as her widow's dower, but nothing whatsoever was made of this point at the trial by either the prosecution or the defense who got on so curiously well with one another. And no one alluded to those intangible things a woman with enough money might buy: independence, self-determination, a larger life.

Everyone pretended that women do not care about money. On the Sunday following the murders the Reverend W. Walker Jubb, Lizzie's minister and supporter, asked the Central Congregational Church: "Where is the motive? When men resort to crime it is for plunder, for gain, from enmity, in sudden anger or for revenge. Strangely, nothing of this nature enters into this case, and again I ask—what was the motive?" Interviewed a few days later by the *Daily Globe*, Jubb quoted Emma Borden as saying to him: "Lizzie is innocent. . . . I cannot see the slightest motive she might have, either in the way of money or revenge, for of the first she had all she needed, and of the latter there was no reason." And in an early interview granted the *Daily Globe* two days after the murders, Andrew Jennings, referred to in the article as Andrew Borden's attorney, said, "A most outrageous, brutal crime . . . and absolutely motiveless—absolutely motiveless." Months later, at the trial, Jennings was still of the same opinion.

Opening for the defense, he said: "The Government's . . . claim . . . is that whoever killed Abby Durfee Borden killed Andrew J. Borden; and even if they furnish you with a motive on her part to kill the stepmother they have shown you absolutely none to kill the father."

The defense also made a good deal of Miss Lizzie's godliness—calling various ministers and wizened ladies to testify to her character—and of her cleanliness immediately after the discovery of the bodies. Mrs. Churchill, Miss Russell, Bridget Sullivan, Dr. Bowen, Mrs. Bowen—all testified that immediately following the murders, as they comforted and fanned Miss Lizzie, they saw no sign of blood upon her; but the defense argued that the killer must have been drenched in the blood of *his* victims. In fact, all the medical experts agreed that the assailant need *not* have been spattered with blood. Reporters who first viewed the bodies had found the absence of blood one of the most remarkable features of the case; and the first doctors who examined Abby Borden's body concluded from the lack of spattered blood that she had merely fainted. By the time of the trial, however, when Governor Robinson ranted on about the "blood flying all over the walls and the furniture, on the bed and everywhere," the tidy scene of the Borden murders and the person of the "unknown assailant" were thought to be awash in a "sea of blood." But not Miss Borden. Except for a tiny blood spot near the hem of her white petticoat—a spot which at the inquest she attributed to fleas—she was immaculately clean. That single speck of blood was discussed briefly at the trial. Professor Wood, who examined it, swore that it came from the outside, but the defense quickly, delicately, and improbably explained it away as a trace of Miss Borden's "monthly sickness" which had ended Wednesday evening before the murders. And that was the end of it. Because she was a woman, Lizzie Borden was used to disposing of bloody cloths; but because she was a lady, it could not be discussed.

During menstrual periods, women of the time, in the days before disposables, wore fairly heavy cloth napkins or towels, which could be laundered and reused. That is what Lizzie did; and she kept the used, blood-soaked napkins in a pail under the sink in the cellar. Thursday night—after the murders and presumably twenty-four hours after Lizzie stopped menstruating—she made two trips to the cellar, both observed by Officer Joseph Hyde stationed outside. She went down first with her friend Alice Russell, who was staying with her, to empty a slop pail in the water closet. Miss Russell, obviously nervous, held the lamp with a trembling hand. Later Lizzie came down again alone, carrying a lamp, and for about a minute stooped over the sink. Officer Hyde couldn't see what she was doing.

Governor Robinson quickly dismissed Hyde's testimony as meaningless; and Julian Ralph wrote that it was off-limits. "That is, it was without significance," he wrote, "as it seemed that the prisoner's second visit to the cellar had to do with a certain pailful of towels that was in the cellar and which *both sides have agreed not to discuss during this trial.*" The gentlemen in the courtroom had little choice; menstruation had been discussed in earlier courtrooms—at the trial of Mary Harris, for example—but creeping prudery had since made it no fit subject for gentlemen to discuss in the presence of ladies. The men of the Borden court could not discuss menstruation without inviting the charge of indelicacy and the argument that women must be judged by their peers to protect them from such offenses to their sensibilities. So the Borden prosecutors, who might have made *something* of spotless Lizzie's pail full of bloody towels, used Hyde's testimony only to argue that Lizzie's midnight solo trip to the spooky cellar of the murder house required extraordinary nerve of a naturally timid female. "I do not care to allude to the visit to the cellar," said prosecutor Knowlton as he summarized the case for the jury. "And all the use I propose to make of that incident is to emphasize from it the almost stoical nerve of a woman, who ... should have the nerve to go down there alone, ... and calmly enter the room *for some purpose that had I know not what connection with this case.*"

4.

Connections often seemed obscure or missing because behind the conduct of the Borden trial was another level of meaning so powerful that it became more decisive than mere physical evidence. Even as the attorneys debated and the judges and jurors decided, all of them seemed caught up in a drama far more encompassing and profound than the facts of the case would suggest. They played their parts as surely as if each had been handed a script, acting—as Julian Ralph noted—in curious concert. It is no wonder that Lizzie became a legend to subsequent generations, for her trial itself was the ritual reenactment of a very old legend: the embarrassingly trite tale of the damsel in distress.

It is true that at age thirty-two the stolid, plain-faced Lizzie was miscast as a fair damsel. But the habitual practice in the United States of referring to adult women as "girls" distorted perceptions then just as it does today. Throughout the trial, Lizzie—a full-grown, ablebodied woman—was referred to by prosecution and defense alike as "this poor girl." Often she was "this poor *defenseless* girl" for she had no parents (particularly no father) to protect her from harm. That she probably was, as Alexander Woollcott quipped, a "self-made orphan" was beside the point. The force of legend is not to be deterred by facts.

At least Lizzie *was* a lady. No one champions a lower-class woman; and many commentators on the case, then and now, would pin the crime on Bridget Sullivan with the same alacrity that made the hanging of Bridget Durgan such a festive event.

District Attorney Knowlton spoke directly of these class differences in his summation:

> One [woman, namely Bridget] is poor and friendless, a domestic, a servant, uneducated and without friends, and the other [Lizzie] is buttressed by all that social rank and wealth and friends and counsel can do for her protection. . . . supposing those things that have been suggested against Lizzie Borden had been found against Bridget Sullivan, poor, friendless girl. Supposing she had told wrong stories; supposing she had put up an impossible alibi; supposing she had put up a dress that never was worn that morning at all, and when the coils were tightening around her had burned a dress up that it should not be seen, what would you think of Bridget? Is there one law for Bridget and another for Lizzie?

The answer, of course, was and still is "Yes." During the inquest Bridget trudged more than a mile every day to the hearing from the house of the friend who had taken her in, while Miss Lizzie was driven the few short blocks from her house in a closed carriage dispatched at public expense. The Fall River *Daily Globe* commented on town gossip: "Open statements are made that if Lizzie Borden were a poor and unfortunate woman, she would not be treated as she has been."

Once Lizzie caught on to the role expected of her as a lady, she played it to the hilt. The tears that dissolved her sullen immobility of the first two days may have been genuine, but at times alert reporters caught her playacting. Julian Ralph noticed that whenever the prosecutors mentioned blood, Lizzie hid her face in her hands, but when her attorneys talked of it, she listened brightly. Oddly enough, this artifice counted in Lizzie's favor; like her tears, her dissembling—one of the "arts and ways of femininity"—was proof of her feminine nature. Later in the trial—about the time she donned her new, more fashionable dress—Lizzie began carrying flowers into the courtroom: one day a little nosegay of pansies, another day a single white rose.

How convincing it must have been when Robinson, falling back heavily and comfortably on old notions men shared about ladies, exhorted the jury: ". . . you *must* say such acts are physically and morally impossible for this young woman. It is a wreck of human morals to say this of her."

The role of villain in the courtroom drama fell naturally to the Fall River police department, and although most officers seemed more bumbling than sinister, they all finally appeared to be persecutors of Miss Lizzie. Three months before the Borden murders, the Fall River *Daily Globe* reported as "a matter of common notoriety that the police force is in a more or less demoralized condition." Individual officers were accused of dereliction of duty and indifference to discipline; and the whole department was charged with "rottenness." And on the very day of the murders, when the alarm came into headquarters, most of the officers were out of town, attending the annual department picnic. Within days of Lizzie's arrest, the *Daily Globe* reported that "three-fourths of the New England papers were sneering at the police and expressing a belief in Lizzie Borden's innocence."

Then, in October, after Lizzie had been bound over to the grand jury but before she was indicted for the murders, there occurred the notorious "Trickey-McHenry Affair" which thoroughly discredited the police *and* the prosecution, and brought the two most powerful newspapers in New England, the Boston *Globe* and the Boston *Herald*, into the lists for Lizzie. Since the Fall River police department had no detectives—there being usually little to detect in Fall River—Marshal Rufus Hilliard hired Edwin D. McHenry, a private detective from Providence, Rhode Island, and a thoroughly unscrupulous character. After working two months with the Fall River police, McHenry struck a secret bargain with a young Boston *Globe* reporter, Henry G. Trickey. In exchange for five hundred dollars Detective McHenry provided Trickey with the entire prosecution case against Miss Borden, a document that filled column after column of the *Globe*'s morning edition on October 10, 1892. The story charged, among other things, that

Lizzie was pregnant and had quarreled violently with her father, who disinherited her and threatened to throw her out of the house. The evening edition of the paper repeated the story, adding that "all New England" had read the story in the morning paper "bought by thousands." The story was convincing and damning—but it had been fabricated by the inventive Detective McHenry.

By the next day, the *Globe* knew it had been duped and issued a complete retraction. "The Globe, being thus misled," said the front-page editorial, "has innocently added to the terrible burdens of Miss Lizzie Borden. So far as lies in our power to repair the wrong, we are anxious to do so, and hereby tender her our heartfelt apology for the inhuman reflection upon her honor as a woman, and for any injustice the publication of Monday inflicted upon her." The whole affair generated enormous sympathy for poor Miss Lizzie throughout New England and placed the repentant Boston *Globe* firmly in her corner. And it did not escape notice that the scheming Detective McHenry, who slandered a lady and brought a great newspaper near to ruin, was in the pay of the Fall River police department.

In his summation at the trial, Governor Robinson reminded the jurors that "you do not get the greatest ability in the world inside a policeman's coat." He was being charitable; and he could afford to be, for he had earlier made fools and worse of the Fall River officers. "When they come upon the witness stand," he remarked, "they reveal their weakness. . . . They knock their own heads together. They make themselves, as a body of men, ridiculous. . . ." Indeed they did.

State Police Officer George Seaver, giving physical evidence for the prosecution, read off a list of the bloodstains: five spots on the mopboard, eighty-six above the head of the lounge, forty on a picture over the lounge, the highest spot six feet one inch from the floor, the most distant spot nine feet seven and one-half inches from the lounge—and so on, listing the tiniest pinpoints of blood in both murder rooms. Then in cross-examination Robinson forced him to admit that after taking the measurements he had lost his notebook and had written down all the data again *from memory*. Officer Harrington testified that the window in the barn loft was shut; Robinson read his previous inquest testimony, saying that it was open. Some officers who searched the Borden closet said the dresses were covered with a sheet; others said they were not. Several officers saw the head of the so-called handleless hatchet, the suspected murder weapon, but only one said that the handle was found right along with it. One officer said he wrapped the hatchet head in a pocket-sized package; another said he wrapped it in a large bundle. And some officers seemed to have learned their testimony by rote.

Governor Robinson played the discrepancies in the officers' testimony for full theatrical effect, and he began to interpret such carelessness and bungling as signs of sinister conspiracy. Commenting on the case later in the *American Law Review*, Professor John H. Wigmore, one of the country's foremost legal scholars, noted the defense's suggestions throughout the trial that "the testimony of *all* the officers was *wilfully* false." Robinson cast even standard police procedures in a bad light. Although it is hard to imagine how the police could have proceeded without looking over the Borden premises and interviewing the person who discovered the crime, Robinson denounced their harassment of Lizzie: "And there [Assistant Marshal Fleet] was, up in this young woman's room in the afternoon [on the day of the murders], attended with some other officers, plying her with all sorts of questions in a pretty direct and peremptory way. . . . Is that the way for an officer of the law to deal with a woman in her own house? What would you do with a man—I don't care if he had blue on him—that got into your house and was talking to your wife or your daughter in that way?" Reporters lamented that the "unfortunate maiden" had been "ten months in the custody of [these] witch burners."

Dr. Dolan, the chief medical examiner, explained in court that before the Bordens were buried, their stomachs were removed for chemical analysis and their heads were cut off and stripped of tissue so that the skulls might be exhibited and the wounds examined. He testified that this grisly procedure was carried out under police order and without notifying the Borden daughters. At that moment, wrote Julian Ralph, "nearly all eyes were turned upon the lonely girl in deep black as she sat listening with her calm face. A new bond of sympathy was created for her in every sympathetic heart, and for her sister also, who had not been told what dismemberment followed the mutilation of the bodies of their father and stepmother." No matter who was guilty of the murders, it was the police who had dismembered the bodies.

Luckily for Miss Borden, the unfortunate damsel beset by this squad of villains, she had her champions. Ralph described Andrew Jennings's opening argument for the defense in these terms: "For an hour he championed her cause with an ancient knight's consideration for her sex and herself. It must have been a strange sensation to that girl to hear, for the first time in ten months of agony, a bold and defiant voice ringing out in her defense. She wiped her eyes furtively a few times, but the tears came so fast that she had to put up her handkerchief." Strange indeed that the "girl" should be both the accused and the romantic heroine.

But Jennings and Robinson were more than simply knightserrant impaling police dragons in defense of a fair maiden; for both men also stood as surrogate fathers to her—Jennings by reason of his long friendship with her father, and Robinson by reason of his age and public position as a leader of the Commonwealth. The newspapers commented again and again that her attorneys treated Lizzie in the manner of "kindly fathers." The ritual courtroom drama was complicated by this dual role of Lizzie's attorneys, for they were both patriarchs and champions, both fathers and lovers. This double role of the father/protector to the young woman, with all its incestuous implications, runs as a sinister undercurrent throughout the trial and surfaces only rarely, as in Robinson's maudlin references to Lizzie's ring that Andrew wore at his death and that was buried with him, as though he were not father but spectral groom.

Since Miss Lizzie was accused of slaying the patriarch, her defense had to rest with other patriarchs, traditionally with those who both guarded her chastity and controlled access to her, the role symbolically filled by her attorneys. Only they could vindicate her, and they *did* vindicate her because an attack upon the patriarch is an attack upon the patriarchy itself. Robinson contended:

> It is not impossible that a good person may go wrong. One heretofore good may go wrong and a good reputation be blasted by a wrongful act, but our human experience teaches us that if a daughter grows up in one of our homes to be 32 years old, educated in our schools, walking in our streets, associating with the best people and devoted to the service of God and man, binding up the wounds of the unfortunate, teaching the ignorant and down-trodden, spending her life for others, it is not within human experience to find her suddenly come out into the rankest and baldest murderess. That would be a condition of things so contrary to all that our human life has taught us that our hearts and feelings revolt at the conception.

Robinson's argument has absolutely nothing to do with the evidence presented at the trial and everything to do with patriarchal prejudice. Thus, it is not surprising to hear the same argument in the mouth of another patriarch, alderman Beattie, president of the Fall

River board of aldermen, months *before* the trial—in fact, just after Lizzie's arrest. "I am sorry that it was found necessary to arrest Lizzie Borden," he said. "We hate to believe, we find it hard to think, that a girl brought up as well and with the intellectual associations she has had would commit such a crime as this." ("I have always wondered," he added, with his class prejudices showing, "why the servant girl was not arrested. . . .") Surely it is preferable in such circumstances not to punish the offender but to pretend there has been no offense. Paradoxically, then, the defense of Miss Borden becomes the defense of the patriarchy itself.

Ritual drama is always oversimplified, for its purpose is to reduce human ambiguity to unitary, straightforward statements that can be acted out. So in this courtroom drama of the distressed maiden, there are only two male parts: champion-*cum*-lover played by Lizzie's attorneys, and villain played by the police. But other men were intimately involved with the case—the prosecuting attorneys, the judges, and the jurors. As discreetly as possible, they aligned themselves with Miss Borden's champions; and in doing so these "grey beards" carried out the task entrusted them by the "public" (that is, other men), the defense of the patriarchy and of themselves. They could scarcely have been expected to do otherwise. Julian Ralph, who saw mythic symbols everywhere, described the flowers on the judges' bench: ". . . the deep red carnations that typify bloody guilt and the gentle pink ones that stand for maidenly suffering. A change in the carnations was noticed. The guilty ones were drooping and their heads hung down around their vase. The others, emblematic of distressed maidenhood, were erect." How was a mere man to remain disinterested in a drama in which even the flowers were thought to take sides?

Prosecutor Hosea Knowlton, unfortunately, found himself on the wrong side; and from the time of Lizzie's arrest, he explained every time he got a chance that he was only doing his duty as district attorney. Apparently he was convincing, for the Fall River *Daily Globe* stated with approval that "District Attorney Knowlton was prejudiced On Miss Borden's Side from the first. It did not devolve on him to support the local police in their views. . . . he never performed a harder duty than when he was forced to order Miss Borden's arrest." Knowlton had good reason to try to protect himself; Judge Josiah Blaisdell, when he bound Lizzie over for the grand jury, was heavily criticized for the harsh words he spoke against her—words that had served as the standard form of criminal complaint in Massachusetts for 150 years. But in the last stages of the trial, in his summation to the jury, Knowlton was still going on about his "painful duty." He said, "The prisoner at the bar is a woman and a Christian woman . . . of the rank of lady, the equal of your wife and mine, of your friends and mine, of whom such things had never been suspected or dreamed before. I hope I may never forget, nor in anything that I say here today lose sight of the terrible significance of that fact."

Nevertheless, it remained Knowlton's duty as district attorney to prosecute, and he cautioned the jury to "face this case as men, not as gallants"; judgment must be based strictly on facts, not on "fealty to the [female] sex," he said—after agreeing with the defense attorneys not to discuss the delicate topic of Lizzie's bloody towels. He simply couldn't bring himself to judge her in the same terms that he would apply to men. Labeling her resentment of her stepmother as "petty," he continued: "Nay, if it was a man sitting in that dock instead of a woman, I would characterize it in more opprobrious terms than those. I trust that in none of the discussion that I engage in today shall I forget the courtesy due from a man to a woman; and although it is my horrible and painful duty to point to the fact of this woman being a murderess, I trust I shall not forget that she is a woman, and I hope I never have." He never did—and he never let anyone else forget it either.

For Lizzie had committed patricide. There lay the "terrible significance" Knowlton saw in the case. The murder of Mrs. Borden hardly counted. Verbally re-creating the crime, Knowlton said: "I have left the dead body of that aged woman upon the guest-chamber floor in the room where she was last at work, and am now asking you to come down with me to a far sadder tragedy, to the most horrible word that the English language knows, to a parricide." Strictly speaking, the murder of Abby Borden was also a case of parricide—that is, the killing of a father, mother, or other revered person. But to Knowlton, Abby was simply an old woman who had "served her husband for thirty years for her room and board." Andrew's death was what mattered. Knowlton continued:

> There may be that in this case which *saves us* from the idea that Lizzie Andrew Borden planned to kill her father. *I hope she did not. I should be slow to believe she did.* But Lizzie Andrew Borden, the daughter of Andrew Jackson Borden, never came down those stairs. It was not Lizzie Andrew Borden that came down those stairs, but a murderess, transformed from all the thirty-three [*sic*] years of an honest life, transformed

from the daughter, transformed from the ties of affection, to the most consummate criminal we have read of in all our history or works of fiction.

Knowlton argued that Lizzie, the daughter, hated Mrs. Borden, planned to kill her, and carried out that plan; but when Lizzie, the murderess, came downstairs and saw her father, it occurred to her that he probably would discover what she had done and disapprove of it. So, on the spur of the moment, she had to kill him too, even though she hated to do it. "But it is a *grateful relief* to our conceptions of human nature," he said, "to be able to find reasons to believe that the murder of Andrew Borden was not planned by his youngest daughter, but was done as a wicked and dreadful necessity, which *if she could have foreseen she never would have followed that mother* up those stairs. . . ."

Knowlton's argument gave the jurors an out. They could convict this "consummate criminal," for she was not a lady after all, and not a *real* patricide. And if the jury returned a conviction, Knowlton's argument provided rationalizations for the patriarchy which otherwise would have to deal with a certified female father-killer. Significantly, Knowlton's argument rests on the assumption that a woman who could plan and carry out a murder couldn't think ahead to what she would do next. If that notion of female intelligence was taken seriously by the men in the courtroom, it is no wonder Lizzie Borden terrified them. "And so I leave that [argument] there," Knowlton said, "not as a matter of proof—oh, no, oh, no—but to relieve my mind of the dreadful necessity of believing that there is a deliberate parricide yet living in America." The jury didn't want to believe it either.

Neither did the judges. In earlier rulings on the admissibility of evidence, the three justices had given a decided advantage to the defense. First, in the most important evidentiary decision of the trial, the court ruled that testimony Lizzie gave at the inquest could not be read in court and entered as evidence. Three days later the justices ruled out the testimony of Eli Bence and two other clerks from Smith's Pharmacy who were prepared to swear that Lizzie Borden had attempted to purchase prussic acid from Bence on the morning before the murders. This testimony, which the prosecution hoped would clinch its argument that Lizzie was predisposed to murder, was ruled out largely on the grounds that the attempt to purchase poison was not relevant to murders committed with a hatchet. All the precedents cited by prosecutor Moody in his thoroughly documented argument—

including the most authoritative works of Wigmore on *Evidence* and Warren on *Homicide*—were defied by the court; what the justices and Robinson kept referring to as "common sense" prevailed over the law. The renowned Professor Wigmore himself later attacked both these evidentiary decisions, but the immediate damage to the prosecution's case had been done. And as the trial neared its end, *The New York Times* noted: "On every legal point the prosecution has been defeated, and this has greatly lessened the strength of their case."

After Robinson's final four-hour theatrical performance for the jury and Knowlton's apologetic summary, Justice Dewey dealt the final blow to the prosecution's case: his charge to the jury amounted to a directive for acquittal. He began by explaining that state statute required him to instruct the jury on certain matters of applying the law, but not on matters of fact. The statute, he explained, "was intended to prevent the judges . . . from expressing any opinion as to the credibility of witnesses or the strength of evidence." Dewey then proceeded to do exactly what the statute forbade. He discredited prosecution witnesses, including one woman whose testimony he discounted altogether because she had used "the language of a young woman" instead of what he considered to be the "real meaning" of words. He suggested that the five medical-expert witnesses had been irreconcilably at odds with one another when in fact they had agreed unanimously on every substantive point. He raised issues that had not been brought up in the testimony, and he ignored matters—such as the dress burning—which the prosecution considered significant.

Justice Dewey overstepped the bounds of his authority at every turn, but the most remarkable passage of his address occurred as he cautioned the jury not to count Lizzie's failure to take the stand against her.

It is a matter which the law submits to her own discretion and to that alone. You can see, gentlemen, that there may be cases where this right to testify would be valuable to a defendant. It may be able to afford the jury some further information or give some explanation that would help the defense. In another case where there was no doubt that an offense had been committed by someone, he might have no knowledge as to how or by whom it was done, and could only affirm under oath his innocence, which is already presumed. The defendant may say, "I have already told to the officers all that I know about this case, and my statements have been put in evidence; whatever is mysterious to others is also a mystery to me. I have no knowledge more than others have. I have never professed to be able to explain how or by whom these homicides were committed."

Lizzie had never said anything of the sort. In effect, the judge was testifying *for* her. "As you have the right to reason from what you know of the laws and properties of matter," he advised the jurors, "so you have a right to reason and judge from what you know of the laws and property of human nature and action." Dewey said, in effect, that if the evidence in the case conflicted with the jurors' preconceived notions about the nature of ladies, the jurors were free to vote their preconceptions. Certainly Judge Dewey had made his own preconceptions clear. The Boston *Globe* headlined its report of his address: JUDGE'S CHARGE A PLEA FOR THE INNOCENT.

Judge Blaisdell, in announcing his verdict of "probably guilty" at the preliminary hearing, had said, "Suppose for a single moment that *a man* was standing there [in the dock]. He was found close by the guest chamber which to Mrs. Borden was a chamber of death. Suppose that *a man* had been found in the vicinity of Mr. Borden and the only account he could give of himself was the unreasonable one that he was out in the barn looking for sinkers, that he was in the yard, that he was looking for something else. Would there be any question in the minds of men what should be done with such a man?" But the prisoner was not a man; the prisoner was, as even prosecutor Knowlton said, "a woman, one of that sex that all high-minded men revere, that all generous men love, that all wise men acknowledge their indebtedness to. It is hard, it is hard," said the district attorney to the gentlemen of the jury, "to *conceive* that woman can be guilty of crime." What's more, she was a lady; and that made all the difference. For the men of the Borden court shared—in addition to a common host of fears—a body of beliefs about true womanhood. Lizzie Borden owed her life largely to those tacit assumptions: ladies aren't strong enough to swing a two-pound hatchet hard enough to break a brittle substance one-sixteenth of an inch thick. Ladies cry a lot. Ladies love to stay home all the time. Ladies are ceaselessly grateful to the men—fathers or husbands—who support them. Ladies never stand with their legs apart. Ladies cannot plan more than a few minutes ahead. Ladies' conversation arises from ignorance, hysteria, overenthusiasm, or the inability to use language properly, and in any case, is not to be taken seriously.

None of these generalities about "women" applied to Irish servants. No one ever suggested that Bridget Durgan was too weak to slash and beat Mary Ellen Coriell. And had Bridget Sullivan been tried for the Borden murders on evidence similar to that raised against Miss Lizzie, the result would certainly have been different. As lower-class women, the Bridgets were thought ignorant and sluggish, prone to filthy habits, petty thievery, and perhaps more serious crime; they were almost never suspected of giddiness, physical weakness, gratitude, or innocence.

The twelve "stout-hearted men" of the Borden jury who shared the assumptions of the attorneys and the justices marched off to the jury room, voted Lizzie's acquittal on the first ballot, sat for an hour to avoid the appearance of undue haste, and returned to the courtroom. Before he was asked the question, the eager foreman blurted out, "Not guilty."

Lizzie dropped into her seat like a stone and wept as loud cheers went up in the courtroom. Mr. Jennings, almost in tears, shook Mr. Adams's hand, saying in a breaking voice, "Thank God." Mr. Adams was unable to speak. Governor Robinson turned to the jury and "gleamed on them with a fatherly interest in his kindly eyes. . . ." District attorneys Moody and Knowlton crossed the room to shake hands with the defense counselors—and with Miss Borden. Judge Dewey's eyes flooded with tears, and "Judge Blodgett's face contorted with the violence of his effort to repress his strong emotion." Sheriff Wright, whose duty it was to maintain order, was crying too much to try. His daughter Isabel had been a childhood playmate of Lizzie Borden.

As the cheers continued, Lizzie retired to an adjoining room and sent for Julian Ralph and other reporters to thank them for their support. But the journalists were not quite finished. *The New York Times*, which had been relatively restrained in its trial coverage, printed a long editorial condemning the villainy of the police—"of the usual inept and stupid and muddle-headed sort that such [small] towns manage to get for themselves"—and "the legal officers who secured the indictment and have conducted the trial." *The Times* took the acquittal of "this most unfortunate and cruelly persecuted woman" as "a declaration, not only that the prisoner was guiltless, but *that there never was any serious reason to suppose that she was guilty. . . .* We do not remember a case in a long time in which the prosecution has so completely broken down, or in which the evidence has shown so clearly, not merely that the prisoner should not be convicted, but *that there never should have been an indictment.*" The editor fell back on the

myth of the distressed damsel: "The Fall River police needed a victim
. . . and the daughter was the nearest and most helpless." Fortunately
for Miss Borden, as a jubilant Julian Ralph wrote: ". . . it took only an
hour for the jury to decide that witches are out of fashion in Massachusetts and that no one is to be executed there on suspicion and on
parrot-like police testimony." The Boston *Globe* even printed an interview with Judge Dewey. Although it was highly irregular for a trial
judge to publish his opinions, Dewey professed to be "perfectly satisfied" with the verdict. "I was satisfied when I made my charge to the
jury," he said, "that the verdict would be not guilty, although one cannot always tell what a jury will do."

Just before the preliminary hearing, the Reverend Dr. Mason, visiting
from Brunswick, Maine, had reassured the congregation of the Fall
River Central Congregational Church that God the Father was "with
that poor, tried tempest-tossed girl" and would "make her glad. . . .
The Father is over all," he intoned. "He will vindicate, and raise and
glorify." And sure enough, he did.

Banker Charles Holmes, his daughter Anna, and Emma Borden
took Lizzie by train to Fall River and arrived in a carriage at the
Holmes Pine Street residence about eight-fifteen that evening, Wednesday, June 20, 1893. Several friends called during the evening to offer
congratulations; and Lizzie told a United Press reporter that she was
"the happiest woman in the world." Her friends, she said, had agreed
not to discuss "the subject." Just before ten o'clock a band stopped in
front of the Borden house on Second Street and played "Auld Lang
Syne." But Lizzie and Emma, not long afterward, sold that house and
bought a much finer one, a spacious Victorian with indoor plumbing,
on the hill; they had the name *Maplecroft* carved into the stone steps
out front. Lizzie changed her name to Lisbeth, bought a horse and carriage, and hired a coachman who drove her about, mostly alone. After
the grand charade of the trial, most of her townspeople—who knew
she had got away with murder—turned against her; though perhaps
they would have been kinder if she had not flaunted her victory so.
Years later even Emma left her in what was rumored to be a quarrel
over property. Miss Lisbeth Borden continued to live in the big house
on the hill, taking occasional excursions to Boston, until she died in
1927 at the age of sixty-six, leaving a good bit of the legacy she had received from her father to the Animal Rescue League. Then she passed
into legend.

Lizzie Borden haunts America largely because Edmund Lester Pearson, the popular true-crime writer, dragged her stage center for one curtain call after another. Even before Lizzie Borden's death, Pearson had begun writing essays on the case and preparing an abridged version of the trial transcript for publication. Like a dog with a bone, Pearson couldn't quit worrying the case; and the reason is implied in his very first essay. Almost paraphrasing Hosea Knowlton and Andrew Jennings, he wrote: ". . . to suggest that a woman of good family, of blameless life and hitherto unimpeachable character, could possibly commit two such murders, is to suggest something so rare as to be almost unknown to criminology. . . . When, in modern times, the attack has taken a more brutal form," he continued, "the murderess has usually been a woman of base antecedents, one from the criminal class, and acting in concert with a man. There is that about the act of battering in the skulls of an elderly man and woman which suggests the male butcher, not the more subtle though equally malicious methods of the murderess." Pearson always argued, on the basis of the trial evidence, that Lizzie Borden was guilty as charged; but some nagging issues of sex and class—of subtlety and base antecedents—kept him from accepting that verdict and letting go.

Pearson started the revival, and from the 1920s on, books, essays, and articles appeared every few years, spading up again the familiar ground. Lizzie's story has been reinterpreted on the stage, in several plays, a ballet, and an opera, and on television in at least one feature-length film. Lizzie has been portrayed by actresses from Lillian Gish to Elizabeth Montgomery; she has been discussed on radio by attorney Robert Welch, actor Robert Preston, and perennial host Alistair Cooke. She dies hard, and she sprouts theories like dandelions.

Most of the latter-day versions of the Borden story, like the trial itself, try to get society (that is, men) off the hook. Many contend that the killer was someone else: a farm laborer, a mutinous seaman, Bridget Sullivan, Emma Borden, or (in a most peculiar version) Andrew Borden himself in the grip of "male menopause." Other versions that ascribe the murder to Lizzie find a credible motive in "true love"; either Lizzie wants a man but can't get him, or has a man but (thanks to Andrew) can't keep him, or—in suggestive Freudian scripts—has a taboo yen for Andrew himself. In one such tale she nerves herself for murder by imagining herself in the "hungry arms" of her forbidden suitor, "his full lips seeking and finding her quivering mouth." In another tale circulated just after the murders to explain the absence of a bloodstained dress and picked up by Freudians as a titillating theory,

Lizzie strips naked to butcher her father. In other stories—predictably—Lizzie, though guilty, is not a "normal" woman. She is a lesbian, or in the most recent apocryphal tale, a sufferer of psychomotor epilepsy. (Needless to say, no one has written a defense of epileptic Bridget Durgan.)

But the wildest—and the most predictable—reincarnation of Lizzie Borden was created by a husband-and-wife writing team who rehashed the case as melodrama in 1953 for Fawcett's popular paperback "Gold Medal Series of Classic Murder Trials." They mistook Lizzie for a feminist "doing her bit to free her sex from its traditionally inferior position." They based this theory on the coincidence that "the old double standard started to disappear" at the time of the Borden trial; and they concluded, "If today woman has come out of the kitchen, she is only following Lizzie, who came out of it with a bloody ax and helped start the rights-for-women bandwagon rolling." Lizzie certainly was no feminist; her aspirations ran to carriages and indoor plumbing. But just as certainly, society's anxiety about feminism and its extraordinary response to Lizzie Borden's trial are profoundly connected.

Other American women have murdered their fathers without passing into folklore. Who today remembers the name of Alice Christiana Abbott, who poisoned her stepfather in 1867 because he repeatedly raped her and threatened to commit her to an asylum if she told? Even at the time her charges were regarded as "singular" and best forgotten. And there have been many other ax murders. Right there in Fall River, even as the Borden jury was being selected, José Corierro struck down a woman with an ax; but he was a man and a lower-class Portuguese immigrant—just the sort of person to commit brutal homicide. But Lizzie's crime, with its "masculine" motive (money and independence) and its "masculine" weapon, raised all sorts of anxious questions that cluster about the difficult issue of woman's place.

Lizzie Borden herself was connected with women's groups, including the prosuffrage Woman's Christian Temperance Union, but her affiliation with women was mainly social and religious rather than political; and it was, at best, sporadic. Still, women rallied to her support. Shortly after Lizzie's arrest the Fall River Woman's Union, a philanthropic social club, passed a resolution of support:

> We offer our profound sympathy to Miss Lizzie A. Borden in the sad and painful bereavement which has befallen her in the recent tragic deaths of her parents. We would also declare our unshaken faith in her

as a fellow-worker and sister tenderly beloved, and would assure her of our constant and earnest prayers that she may be supported under the unprecedented trials and sorrows now resting upon her.

The Christian Endeavor Society and the Fruit and Flower Mission of the Congregational Church—Lizzie's chief interests—passed similar resolutions; and Henry Brown Blackwell, husband of Lucy Stone, reprinted them in *The Woman's Journal*, the organ of the American Woman Suffrage Association. Lucy Stone used the occasion to write again about the need for women jurors (without voicing any opinion in Lizzie's case); and Mary Livermore, the abolitionist and suffragist then in her seventies—the same Mary Livermore who had argued in *What Shall We Do with Our Daughters?* that all young women should be trained for jobs so they would not be dependent upon men for their happiness—went to visit "the girl" in Taunton jail and wrote a passionate, misguided article on her innocence for the Boston *Post*. Feminists were concerned, quite correctly, that Lizzie Borden would not get a fair trial from a jury of men—although they did not foresee that the unfairness would swing in her favor. Suffragists must also have been somewhat embarrassed by the possibility of her guilt, for they had won supporters to the cause of suffrage recently with the elitist argument that votes of well-educated, morally superior ladies were needed to offset the votes of ignorant, lower-class men. A lady ax murderer could do the cause no good.

The support Lizzie Borden received from religious and social women's clubs and from people like Stone, Livermore, and Blackwell, who had been leaders of the suffrage campaign for so long, must have amplified the fears men already felt as husbands, fathers, patriarchs. Society seemed to be coming unglued. And all this talk of woman's rights—where would it lead? Only a few years later an analysis of New York City crime rates provided an answer at once alarming in its implications and comforting in its foolish conventionality: women's emancipation produces women criminals. The rate of women's crimes seemed to be increasing even faster than that of men's crimes. Overall arrests of women were up from 412 in 1886 to 722 in 1896. Only 8 female burglars had been arrested in 1886; a decade later the number had doubled. In 1886 only 8 women were arraigned for homicide; in 1895 the number was 19, an increase of over 100 percent. Like the 1690s, which produced the Salem witch trials, and the 1840s, which produced both the Seneca Falls Convention and a whole body of literature about evil women, this was an anxious time. And it is hardly surprising that in another anxious time, just after World War II, when women liberated by wartime jobs and independence were shoved back into the sculleries and bedrooms of America, antifeminists should pry Lizzie Borden free of her own history and resurrect her as a "feminine vigilante," a lesbian marching out of the kitchen with a bloody ax, a sort of Nat Turner of the women's movement.

Of all the latter-day revisionists of the Borden story, however, Agnes DeMille came closest to the bone of Lizzie Borden's existence when she created her ballet *Fall River Legend*. "Lizzie's life," she wrote, "consisted mainly in things . . . that didn't happen. And how does one put inaction, lack of dynamics, the maintenance of status quo into dance? . . . How does one express boredom on stage?" Like the courtroom myth of true womanhood, the modern theories—whether of true love, lesbianism, violent "feminism," repressed sexuality, or incestuous desires—constrict woman's life, a life already passed in too narrow a house. Lizzie Borden the lady was pronounced innocent and sent home; Bridget Durgan the maid was hauled drunk into the street and hanged in the middle of a prayer. At the time, according to the social fathers, these two women had nothing in common. And today the laws and the continuing legends of a man-made society are still unwilling to acknowledge that they were both women, that they shared a life consisting mainly in things that didn't happen.

LET THAT BE A LESSON

1.

The Reverend Edward Wheeler Hall was found on September 16, 1922, lying on his back under a crab apple tree in DeRussey's Lane on the outskirts of New Brunswick, New Jersey. He was stretched out in apparent comfort with his Panama hat over his face and his calling card propped against his foot. On his right lay Eleanor Mills, with her head resting on the minister's right hand, and her hand in turn resting on his knee. The Reverend Mr. Hall had been shot once through the head and Mrs. Mills three times; her throat had been cut so deeply that her head was almost detached. Word of the double murder spread quickly in New Brunswick, for the victims were highly respectable citizens, though lately linked scandalously together. The Reverend Edward Hall was minister of the fashionable Episcopal Church of St. John the Evangelist, and Eleanor Mills was the leading singer in the church choir. Hall's wife, the former Frances Noel Stevens, was the only daughter of one of New Brunswick's wealthiest families, and

James Mills, Eleanor's husband, though he hadn't amounted to much, was sexton of the Reverend Mr. Hall's church.

In the next four years everyone in America would come to know all about Edward Wheeler Hall and Eleanor Mills. Their names and faces became as familiar as those of Clara Bow or Charles Lindbergh. Every bit of the prolonged investigation was reported in the papers— then the proceedings before the grand jury that failed to indict anyone, and finally, almost four years later on the basis of new evidence unearthed by the tabloid New York *Mirror*, the arrest, trial, and acquittal of Mrs. Frances Stevens Hall and her two brothers, charged with the murder of her husband and his mistress. To keep on top of the case eight daily newspapers rented houses in New Brunswick for their staffs of reporters and photographers. The world's largest portable telegraph switchboard—formerly used at the Dempsey-Tunney fight—was set up at press headquarters. Before it was all over, more words had been written about the Hall-Mills case than about any other single topic in the history of the world—enough words to fill nine volumes of the *Encyclopaedia Britannica*. Everyone wrote about the case, reporters and novices alike: Damon Runyon, Louella Parsons, Dorothy Dix, Billy Sunday, and even Charlotte Mills, the teenaged daughter of one of the victims. In the papers America could read every intimate detail of the Hall-Mills affair, including the letters the philandering minister had sent to his choir singer: "Dear, dear, darling heart of mine: . . . I wanted to get away to dreamland, Heavenland. Can I meet you tomorrow, our road, at two P.M.? . . . Dearest, love me hard, harder than ever, for your babykins is longing for his mother."

The whole sordid business was exposed: secret notes hidden in the minister's bookshelf, groping sexual encounters in the darkened church, torrid letters from babykins. And the newspaper-buying public couldn't get enough. According to Bruce Bliven, writing in the *New Republic*, that intense public curiosity grew as the case stripped the wraps off one "fairly typical respectable American town." As witness after witness came forward, they fleshed out a picture not only of the errant couple but of New Brunswick as well. On the night that Hall and Mills were murdered, Bliven wrote with some exaggeration, half the townspeople were in rustic DeRussey's Lane, and all of them were up to no good: theft, assault, incest, adultery, murder. The idyllic country lane came to seem as sinister as any urban alley. And the reading public believed that "there are ten thousand DeRussey's Lanes" and that "the pathetic missives between the enamored cleric and his love could be duplicated in every mail sack. . . ." Social scientists who began earnestly surveying American sexual behavior in the twenties confirmed that the Reverend Mr. Hall was not alone in his hypocrisy. From all accounts, the disillusioned hangover of World War I stimulated sexual activity already on the rise at the end of the nineteenth century. Apparently more and more upstanding citizens, including a good many preachers and devout parishioners, were slipping over the back fence, both before and after marriage. What made the Reverend Mr. Hall and Mrs. Mills so endlessly fascinating, then, was their very ordinariness and banality. They were just like the adulterers next door—or nearer.

While sexual practice was changing rapidly, official moral teaching was not. The Reverend Mr. Hall, up to the time of his death, probably preached the same sort of sermons about sexual morality that he had delivered twenty years before. But the wider the gap between such official preaching and private sexual practice grew, the more anxious and confused people became. Anxiety drove them to desperate means—either to evade or to enforce the old morality. Hall and Mills, on one hand, planned to scorn proprieties and run off together. But all across the country, members of the Ku Klux Klan, under orders to "clean up their towns," bludgeoned, tarred and feathered, branded, and murdered violaters of what they called "*the* moral code." Four decades after the still unsolved Hall-Mills murders, attorney William Kunstler advanced the plausible theory that New Jersey Klansmen, acting as moral enforcers, were the killers. In the shadow of that old moral code, popular rumor at the time of the murders maintained that Hall's penis had been cut off and left in Mrs. Mills's mouth. Official records indicate that the rumor wasn't true, but people believed it because to the dark side of the Victorian imagination the mutilation seemed symbolically appropriate.

Throughout the Hall-Mills notoriety, the old moral code and the new conduct squared off against each other in the persons of Mrs. Frances Hall, the bereaved and suspected widow, and Charlotte Mills, a self-styled flapper who was sixteen at the time of her mother's death and grew up during the years of investigation and trial. Frances Stevens Hall still lived in the same big Victorian house in which she had been born to an old family and old money. One of her first acts after she learned of the discovery of the bodies was to send some articles of her wardrobe to Philadelphia to be dyed black for her mourning period; even in the midst of scandal—*particularly* in the midst of scandal—the proprieties must be observed. Even when she was accused of his murder she remained steadfastly loyal to her husband; if he could be here, she said, he could explain everything. Young Charlotte Mills, on the other hand, seemed a brash girl, prematurely jaded by her mother's confidences. She knew all about the affair, she said. She knew in what book the vapid love notes were hidden, how the clandestine meetings were arranged. She held press conferences about the case, wrote letters to the governor, and worked as a journalist during the trial, though some said she didn't write the stories she signed. She wore short skirts, rolled her stockings, and was photographed on the arm of a chair with her legs crossed. "I'm a flapper," she said, in an appeal for public sympathy. "Mrs. Hall doesn't like flappers." But the public generally supported the proper, dowdy widow Hall, even though she was the prime murder suspect, and looked askance at the nervy, uncertain girl who had lost her mother to a murderer and a curious public.

The smoking, drinking flapper, freed from corsets and sexual repression, became the role model for young Charlotte Mills and the symbol for the Jazz Age. But like that other legendary character of the early twenties, the bearded Bolshevik, the naughty flapper who tantalized in the headlines was not likely to be welcomed home. The lure of flapperdom on the one hand was matched by the persistent need to guard one's reputation. Young women were caught between the old code and the new conduct. For the all-American girls of Muncie, Indiana, the choice was to pet or to be unpopular; by 1930, a girl could be either a "hot number" or a "flat tire." More and more women complained that men were taking advantage of them and of the new "behavior." But most women, in the perhaps wishful opinion of Mrs. Henry W. Peabody, president of the Federation of Women's Boards of Foreign Missions of North America, did not succumb to pressure. "The women who transgress," Mrs. Peabody wrote in 1924, "are still, I believe, a very small minority." Most American women were still, as they had always been, "pure-minded, clean-living, self-sacrificing" and engaged in "disinterested and weariless activities for the physical welfare and moral uplift of the whole community." Sociologists Phyllis Blanchard and Carlyn Manasses, who were systematically studying young women, confirmed that only a "relatively small number" of "girls" practiced "free behavior."

Since most "new" women were still very much like the old, all the talk of free conduct and emancipated female sexuality seems to have been something of a tempest in a teapot. Despite some measurable changes in illicit sexual conduct, the old moral code was still in force. The woman who was too "emancipated" in her sexual conduct crossed the fine line between "free" and "loose" and lost her reputation and her marriageability. The bad woman and the "oversexed" woman were, as they had always been, one and the same. But the big difference for women under the dispensation of the new sexuality was this: the good woman too—after she became a wife—was now supposed to be sexual.

The "new" notion that woman could and should experience pleasure in the sexual relationship ought not to have been astonishing. America had a long history of radicals, reformers, utopianists, and "crackpot" philosophers who advocated drastic changes in marital relations—usually in the direction of sexual equality—and sometimes the abolition of the marriage institution altogether. Certainly many of these free thinkers—from Robert Dale Owen and Frances Wright to John Humphrey Noyes and Elizabeth Cady Stanton—were arguing for social, legal, or spiritual parity rather than erotic liberation, but there was nothing particularly spiritual or vague about the brand of free love practiced and publicized by the Claflin sisters before they dwindled into wedded monogamy. Polite society, however, didn't discuss such matters; so it was rather shocked when, toward the end of the century, the new sexologists began speaking out and finding an audience eager to learn.

Dr. Alice Stockham, writing in 1896 with a pen "dipped in the fire of love," advocated "Karezza," a method of sexual intercourse without "crisis," which not only prevented pregnancy but led to "deep spiritual love." Ellen Key, the Swedish writer whose romantic new "feminism" swept America in the decade of World War I, preached that love was a new religion; woman was its priestess and the "sex relation . . . invested with an all-pervasive, all-decisive significance and sanctity. . . ." Havelock Ellis, the most prolific and influential of the new sexologists, found that woman's "sex impulse," repressed for half a century, was actually "larger" than man's and more "diffuse." It was time, he said, for women to assert their "erotic rights." By 1925 Margaret Sanger, leader of the American birth control movement, could announce that woman was not just woman anymore; she was a "warmly pulsating personality."

Woman owed it to herself, said the new sexologists, to take up the religion of love, to find sexual fulfillment. Better yet, woman owed it to the future of the race to fulfill herself sexually. And certainly the future of the race seemed to hinge upon calling in some obligations. Already staggering, the American family appeared to be on its last legs. For decades the steadily falling birth rate had been more than matched by sharply increasing divorce rates. Between 1870 and 1920, while the population increased three times, the divorce rate increased fifteen times over; and the number of married couples who had no children at all rose to almost one-third of all families. The Great War slaughtered men, Progressive ideals, and optimism. It also enlisted in the labor force women who afterward had to be persuaded to return to housewifery, an occupation stripped by industrial technology of all but the most menial drudgery. On top of all these blows to the family came woman suffrage, which even some of its supporters feared would be "disintegrating." Socialists argued that the industrial system itself struck at the family: it used up "hands," paid them too little to feed their children, maimed and killed them at an appalling rate, and cast them out unemployed, or dead. Popular opinion tended to blame women—especially flappers and feminists—for the decline in family life. Even the experts could not pin down all the causes, but everyone knew that the future of the race was an increasingly speculative proposition. It seemed a tragic irony that this uncertainty should occur just as evolutionary social theory announced that perfection of the race was not only a possibility but a moral obligation.

Happily, the sexologists came forward to assure women that they could fulfill themselves sexually *only* by fulfilling their moral obligations to the future of the race. In fact, woman's two obligations—to herself and to posterity—were merely one, for her greatest sexual fulfillment came, said the experts, from having babies. To Ellen Key "the bearing and rearing of the new generation" was woman's "*most exalted task.*" A woman who did not wish to undertake the duty suffered from a dark, perverse instinct. Havelock Ellis maintained that because "reproduction is the end and aim of all life everywhere . . . every healthy woman should have, not sexual relationships only, but the exercise at least once in her life of the supreme function of maternity. . . ." Unless she became a mother, no woman could have a "completely human life." (The prescribed number of children kept rising: Ellen Key urged three or four; psychiatrist Joseph Collins, in 1927, recommended five to ten.) In 1939 Hannah and Abraham Stone, in their popular marriage manual, defined marriage as "not merely a sexual relationship, but a parental association," while other sociologists debated whether a husband and wife without children could properly be called a "family." Even the leaders of the birth control movement, who felt that fewer children meant better ones, agreed that motherhood was woman's highest calling. Margaret Sanger argued that marriage was merely an "apprenticeship" to motherhood. Her English counterpart, Marie Stopes, contemplating passionate conception in the heady early days of the new sexology, simply lost her grip:

> When two who are mated in every respect burn with the fire of the innumerable forces within them, which set their bodies longing towards each other with the desire to interpenetrate and to encompass one another, the fusion of joy and rapture is not purely physical. The half-swooning sense of flux which overtakes the spirit in that eternal moment at the apex of rapture sweeps into its flaming tides the whole essence of the man and woman, and as it were, the heat of the contact vapourises their consciousness so that it fills the whole of cosmic space. For the moment they are identified with the divine thoughts, the waves of eternal force, which to the Mystic often appear in terms of golden light.
>
> From their mutual penetration into the realms of supreme joy the two lovers bring back with them a spark of that light which we call life.
> And unto them a child is born.
> This is the supreme purpose of nature. . . .

Couched in such prose, the new sexology was irresistible: poetic yet thoroughly scientific, romantic yet up to date, morally purposeful, idealistic, socially responsible, thrilling, and just a bit naughty. Shocking at first, the new doctrines were quickly domesticated; and their message—the message of the great sexual revolution—came down to this: the truly emancipated woman is the one who marries, has babies, and stays ever so quietly at home. After a century of struggle, women came back to square one.

Most women didn't recognize the old neighborhood. Plenty of suffragists triumphantly went home with their ballots, their limited goal achieved. And plenty of eager young women took their places in the lower levels of Washington bureaucracy, in professorial ranks of the women's colleges, in the leftist bohemian circles of Greenwich Village. They called themselves "new women" or "modern women." They called themselves "new feminists," and they were very clear about how they differed from the "old feminists" now so hopelessly old hat. As Havelock Ellis pointed out, the old feminists had "propagandised" for the "now rather antiquated notion of the 'equality' of the sexes"—a feminist "fetish" that had some application to the social and political relations of women and men but none whatsoever to biology. Early in the twentieth century, however, all those old "superficial" differences between the sexes had been wiped out: any woman, it was said, could go to college, take up a profession or a job, go out without a chaperone, vote, show her ankles. Opportunities abounded. But with the superficial social and political differences supposedly "eliminated," sexology rushed in to identify the *real* differences between the sexes. Soon the new sex experts were preaching "discoveries" women had heard before: that women are more infantile, men more savage; that women are inward-turning, while men are naturally outward-turning; that men have a genius for intellect, women for love; that men are active, women passive; and that woman's destiny is maternity.

The old feminists, according to Ellis, had known nothing of these "new" biological truths; so, unhappily, they made the mistake of trying to "imitate" men, demanding the same work and civic responsibilities. Although their intentions were good, their efforts were hopelessly misguided by ignorance. Ellis maintained that the natural and scientific relation of the sexes was a certain biological balance—not equality but "equivalence." The new "feminists," informed at last by the "truth," would be first and foremost women—of the new sexual/maternal style so recently unearthed by the scientists.

Old feminists had fought for "the privilege of self-support"; new feminists knew that work was only "part of life," and not a particularly glamorous part at that. The truly "modern girl," said sociologists Blanchard and Manasses, who had studied and surveyed the type, saw "the loneliness of older, unmarried friends" and was "beginning to discount the rewards from a material success that must be accomplished at the expense of love." A few of the most "advanced" modern women talked and wrote endlessly about the marriage and/or career dilemma that burned out their own energy, but in fact very few married women were able to maintain professional careers, and married women in the work force—only 9 percent of all married women in 1920—generally clustered at the lowest levels of industrial and menial labor, pushed there by the desertion or unemployment of their husbands. Most women in the labor force were very young and unmarried; and ironically their "emancipation" in work gave them the money to marry earlier, quit working, and "start a family" right away. Blanchard reported in 1930 that the average "modern girl" wanted more than anything in life to be married and to have at least two or three children.

In that she was exactly like the new "feminist" who, with the help of the sexologists, had discovered herself at last. As Floyd Dell, the novelist and self-styled feminist, portrayed her, the new "feminist" was adventurous, good-natured, fun-loving, a pal. But Dell's heroine Janet March, the prototypical new "feminist" in American literature, has some curiously traditional ideas. When she discovers she is pregnant, she and her lover, who have been living together, decide to marry to make their relationship "real." "One has to risk something—create something!" Janet says exultingly. "All my life I've wanted to *do* something with myself. Something exciting. And this is one thing I *can* do. . . . I can help create a breed of fierce and athletic girls, new artists, musicians, and singers. . . ." In the context of the sexual revolution, that was feminism.

After a century of contrariness, woman had been lured back to the heart of woman's sphere—to the dead center of domesticity. She was encouraged, sometimes forcibly, to remain there by a system of public rewards and punishments. The good wife and mother, besides enjoying the esteem of her family and community, was honored by the federal government, although she was not accorded the full rights of citizenship. By act of Congress the nation celebrated its first Mother's Day on May 8, 1914, with white carnations—signifying "sweetness, purity and endurance"—for those who earned them. Mothers who gave up their sons to be killed in the Great War were awarded little banners with gold stars emblazoned on them. In later decades, some experts, citing the excellent example of Nazi Germany, proposed that mothers of "well balanced" families should receive honorary college degrees. The good mother, and the good woman, as the experts defined them, were one and the same; and that ideal image, the product of man's theorizing, was held up to women as a model.

Recalcitrant old-line feminists protested against the model. They wanted no part of the blissful return to domesticity; they entered marriage apprehensively or not at all. Economist and feminist theoretician Charlotte Perkins Gilman warned quite correctly that "the ingenious mind of man" had simply thought up "a new theory to retain what the old ones no longer assured him"—his control of women. "Whereas in the past women were taught that they had no such 'imperative instincts' as men," she wrote in 1930, ". . . now it is quite otherwise. All that elaborate theory of feminine chastity, that worship of virginity, goes by the board, and women are given a reversed theory—that they are just the same as men, if not more so; our 'double standard' is undoubled and ironed flat—to the level of masculine desire." Theoretician Suzanne LaFollette warned that woman's "destined" maternity, unless "committed" according to man's proprietary rules, was simply sin. Feminists such as Crystal Eastman and Henrietta Rodman who saw, like Gilman, that women needed more than what the experts called "sex adjustment," were fired and blacklisted for preaching feminist ideas that seemed increasingly radical as more and more "modern women" succumbed to orthodoxy.

The new sexual doctrine was an astonishingly powerful instrument for social control. It supplanted religion, which clearly had lost its ability to keep woman under Adam's rule. And it supplemented the law, so significantly weakened by feminist attacks and in any case so hard to square with a Constitution that ranted inconveniently about equal rights. In place of external rules the new sexual doctrine pressed woman's own desire for "self-fulfillment" into service as policeman. It enlisted her in individual, isolated search for "sex adjustment"—obscuring the common social and political concerns all women shared. As an instrument of social control sex was powerful, and it worked.

By 1929, when sociologists Robert and Helen Lynd went to Muncie, Indiana, to study a typical American town, they found housewives isolated in their homes, troubled about their sex adjustment, worried about bringing up their children properly, vaguely dissatisfied, and generally unhappy because their husbands didn't talk to them. Many women, who said they had no friends and no companionship in marriage, asked the interviewers to come back; they liked having someone to talk to. Like the foreign travelers who visited America a century before, the sociologists who visited Indiana found at the heart of American domestic life a profound and lonely silence.

But isolation and silence were not as bad as the punishments awaiting the woman who strayed outside her sphere. If the rewards of being a good wife and mother—the illusory vaginal orgasm, gold stars, flowers once a year on Mother's Day—seemed paltry, the penalties for being a bad woman were not. As an example to others—a kind of negative model—"bad" women were punished by guilt, ridicule, ostracism, and death. Assertive women and feminists in particular were derided and damned. Said one male psychiatrist in a liberal publication in 1923: "Most of the terrible women one must meet, women with the blatant views and voices, women who have to be noticed, who shoulder one about, who can't take life quietly, belong to this large percentage of women who have never made a sex adjustment." Since the sexually "adjusted" woman was by definition a quiet stay-at-home, a woman who took the slightest interest in social or political affairs opened herself to mockery and contempt, to the charge of being neurotic, infantile, frigid, or lesbian.

The modern psychological perspective was also applied retroactively to deform the great feminist leaders of the past to grotesques. Neo-Freudians discovered that the leaders of the nineteenth-century feminist movement had suffered from sexual repression and were obsessed by a "deep desire to engage in lecherous and sensual activities." Profoundly "sadistic" women such as Susan B. Anthony and Elizabeth Cady Stanton wanted only to emulate a particular "imaginary" male: "a rake and a roué, a Don Juan, a Casanova, a roving impregnator" who "raped, seduced and enslaved women, treated them like dirt." The modern feminist could not follow her great predecessors without being tarred by the same brush. After the "sexual revolution" and the rise of psychotherapy there could be no *issues*, only *neuroses*. Questions of equal wages, access to jobs and professions, education—everything came down in the end to a question of "adult" sexual adjustment to the vaginal orgasm and, incidentally, its attendant domestic obligations. Under such coercion, "new feminists" dropped out of public life to work out their "emancipation" at home; and all feminist social, political, and economic concerns fell to that dead level of personal mental pathology.

Even within the home women were not safe from punishment. They could always be reached through their children. And the child, at the turn of the century, had become the center of everyone's attention. Sexologists proclaimed woman's supreme maternal destiny; social Darwinists announced that the child held the key to the future of the "race"; and busy humanitarian reformers came across "juvenile delinquents"—the strayed chicks of bad mothers—and brought them home to roost. Their notion was that twigs bend; and the child suffering from bad mothering or none at all could be reformed by joining the "family" of an institutional "home." The reformers who devised "juvenile justice" to look after homeless and criminal children alike professed concern for the welfare of the children and the future of society; but the system they created turned out to be—incidentally—a powerful enforcer of "right" motherhood. Locking up junior let the mother know that she was a failure at the one and only job that could justify her existence; when the police took him away, it was the mother who had to ask, "Where did I go wrong?"

Perhaps because it was such an effective system for imposing the old moral code on children, women, blacks, immigrants, and the poor, the juvenile-justice system grew like quack grass. The first juvenile courts were established in Illinois and Colorado in 1899; by 1917 all but three states had passed juvenile-court legislation, and by 1932 more than six hundred juvenile courts were in operation. Youngsters were carted off to institutional homes for such offenses as truancy and playing ball in the street. Throughout the early decades of the twentieth century the juvenile-justice system continued to grow right along with the shocking increase in the number of juvenile delinquents; but it was hard to tell which came first—the court or the criminal, the punishment or the crime.

One thing was clear: Mother was to blame. And as the juvenile-justice system grew, so did the charges against "Mom." By mid-century psychiatrist Marynia Farnham and writer Ferdinand Lundberg, warning readers that Hitler was his mother's son, could identify four kinds of bad mothers: the rejecting, the overprotective, the dominating, and the overaffectionate. All of them ruined their sons. (The experts were never much concerned with the fate of the daughters.) The overaffectionate mother produced "sissies" or "passive-homosexual males," while the rejecting, overprotective, and dominating mothers "produced the delinquents, the difficult behavior problem children" and "some substantial percentage of criminals." "Momism" had become a major social problem, and Mom, when not a criminal herself, the mother of criminals.

By far the most direct and dramatic public punishments of this century, however, were reserved for women who exercised their "erotic rights" in their own behalf; for the so-called sexual emancipation of women had never been intended to set women free but merely to enlist their sexuality in the service of men. In fact, one of the most distinctive features of the new sexuality—just like the old sexuality—was its exclusivity. The good woman was to be sexually emancipated only in the master bedroom. The Finnish anthropologist Edward Wester- marck announced in 1891 his scientific discovery that the traditional Western family—patriarchal, monogamous—was a primeval human institution; and luckily enough the new sexology fit right in. All the experts agreed that while woman was surprisingly sexual, her ardor was a "slumbering" thing. Waking this sleeping giant was a long pro- cess. A woman might not be aroused until after she had given birth to at least one child; in any given case, it might take years. And since woman's sexuality was so intimately connected with "love" it could be elicited, in most cases, only by one man—her husband. So, the natu- rally active man must go on practicing the art of love on his naturally passive wife, and perhaps after a few years her dormant desires would spring to life and fix themselves gratefully, permanently, on him. For her part, the woman who had waited for marriage had only to contin- ue to wait for orgasm. Waiting and praying, as religion counseled, was her lot in life; she scarcely needed science to tell her it was also her "nature." So passivity engendered passivity—and perhaps children. And maybe after the next child or the one after that she would experi- ence the "new womanhood." If not, she had only herself to blame for her failure to make an adequate sex adjustment.

Instead of sexually freeing woman, as it pretended to do, the new sexology bound her to one man and to a life of watching for orgasm as earlier generations of women had watched for signs of their own salva- tion. To woman's traditional duties as wife and mother, sexology add- ed the duty of "developing" passion. Later sex experts encouraged the woman who did not experience orgasm to fake it for the sake of her husband's ego; but the early sexologists required her to develop the genuine article.

An American doctor wrote to Havelock Ellis about the case of a "fine womanly young woman with splendid figure" who, try as she might, simply could not "develop desire and passion" for her husband. The doctor was afraid that "the man will someday appear who will be able to develop the latent feelings," but Ellis passed over that subver- sive possibility. Although men, throughout the twenties, belatedly dis- covered their pretty "spiritual affinities" only after contracting wives, woman's desire had to be constant or slumber on. Every woman, said Margaret Sanger, is a Cinderella at heart; she could be transformed, presumably, only by the fit of the right shoe.

The social fathers, profoundly uneasy about this tricky business of female sexual "liberation" from the outset, understood that a promiscuous Cinderella mocked the whole patriarchal fairy tale. They were fully prepared to make a bad example of the princess if she dared to run off with the coachman. And, thanks to the growth of news media, they had the means to do it. Radio was a new craze; and newspapers, which had proliferated and added pages of plentiful wartime news, now searched for any new sensation to fill space and keep up circulation. But the Hall-Mills case that sustained more than one paper for half a decade was ultimately disappointing; for the guilty princess was already dead, her paunchy Prince Charming beside her. And if she had been killed by her husband, or her lover's wife and family, or the Klan, so much the better. However serviceable it might be as moral exemplum, as public spectacle a corpse was not very gratifying. But almost before the ink had dried on the last of the Hall-Mills stories, another Cinderella named Ruth Snyder took up with a salesman—a corset and brassiere salesman to be exact—and together they murdered her husband in his bed. In its own way her crime was as subversive of American domesticity as the anarchism of Nicola Sacco and Bartolomeo Vanzetti was of the American political and economic order. Like Sacco and Vanzetti, Ruth Snyder died in the electric chair while the whole country watched the clock. The limits of acceptable American behavior in the twenties were drawn by these highly publicized punishments: the electrocution of two "Bolsheviks" and a "flapper"—two immigrant workingmen and a suburban Long Island housewife. But while the execution of political wrongdoers Sacco and Vanzetti prompted outraged demonstrations, the execution of sexual transgressor Snyder gratified the public. Almost everyone agreed that Ruth Snyder had to die.

2.

Ruth Brown was born on 125th Street in Manhattan in 1895, the daughter of a working-class Scandinavian family. She left school after the eighth grade and got a job with the telephone company; at night she took business classes in shorthand and typing. She was a hard worker and determined to get ahead, but like most young women of her time, she said that she "thought more of marriage than [of] a business career." So when at nineteen she landed a secretarial job with *Motor Boating* magazine and handsome thirty-two-year-old Albert Snyder, an art editor, took an interest in her, she didn't discourage him. Albert Snyder was Ruth Brown's first real "gentleman friend" and after keeping company with him for a few months, she married him in 1915.

The couple lived first in Brooklyn; after their daughter, Lorraine, was born in 1918 they moved to a larger apartment in the Bronx. And as Albert advanced with the magazine, he moved his family to an eight-room house in Queens Village on Long Island. For Albert the move to Queens was a mark of success. For Ruth it was a lonely step into the isolation of suburban life, but she worked hard at housekeeping, sewing curtains and slipcovers and clothing for herself and Lorraine. By 1925 Ruth Brown Snyder had achieved "everything that most women wish for." The newspapers, telling her story after she came to public attention, reported that "she had a house of her own, an automobile, a radio, good furniture, money in the bank, protection and an athlete for a husband." Albert Snyder was not actually an "athlete" but he kept a motorboat for weekend outings and often had a tan. He was also, according to the papers, "a good man, a faithful husband. He took pride in his wife, his child and his home. Made little things to ornament the house. Was thrifty. Worked hard and late. Bought a home, an automobile, a radio and turned in most of his money at home. A model husband."

Unfortunately, he was also gloomy and evil-tempered. His mother-in-law, Josephine Brown, who moved into the Queens Village house with the Snyders when she was widowed, told reporters that while Ruth was gay and fun-loving, Albert was almost always "glum." Ruth liked people and parties; her friends nicknamed her "Tommy" because she was such a good sport—like one of the boys. Albert liked to stay at home. Ruth enjoyed restaurants, the theater, bridge. Albert's hobbies were tinkering with his car and puttering in his garden. Ruth loved animals and would have filled the house with them; Albert grimly tolerated a lone canary and filled the house instead with inanimate "artistic knickknacks" of his own devising. Ruth loved children and was devoted to her daughter, Lorraine. Albert, who hadn't wanted children at all, was doubly disappointed at being stuck with a girl. On the whole, Albert found Ruth too young and giddy for him; he often told her about his previous, more "serious" fiancée Jessie Guischard, who had died before the wedding. It was a pity, he said, that Ruth couldn't be more like her. The unfortunate Snyder alliance probably was no more badly mismatched than any of hundreds of others behind the drawn curtains of Queens communities, but it was unhappy enough that Josephine Brown advised her daughter to seek a divorce, and that Ruth Snyder found a lover, and that little Lorraine Snyder mentioned to a policeman, after her father had been found dead in bed, that her mama and daddy fought all the time.

That remark coupled with the peculiarly amateurish look of the burglary of the Snyder house and the ferocity of Albert's murder kept the police questioning Ruth Snyder long after she first told them of the swarthy intruder—"a tall man with a dark mustache"—who struck her on the head and left her bound hand and foot. They questioned her through the day and night while they searched the Snyder home and found her "stolen" jewelry under the mattress, the five-pound sash-weight—with which Albert had been struck three times—in the basement, and her address book listing the names of twenty-eight men. On the floor in the bedroom where Albert had been clubbed, chloroformed, and finally strangled with picture wire, the police found a small pin bearing the initials *J.G.* for Jessie Guischard. Albert Snyder had carried it as a memento of his former sweetheart, but the police, thinking it might have been dropped by the murderer, matched the initials to a name in Ruth Snyder's address book and asked her: "What about Judd Gray?" Exhausted and surprised, Ruth asked, "Has he confessed?" The police said he had. Then it was only a matter of hours before Henry Judd Gray, Ruth's lover, was arrested at his hotel in Syracuse and returned to New York to confess his part in the killing. Both Snyder and Gray admitted they had conspired together, but each blamed the other for the murder.

Albert Snyder was murdered shortly after he returned from a party at 2:00 Sunday morning and went to bed. By Tuesday morning, all the daily papers carried photographs of the illicit lovers and the text of their confessions of murder. The papers were delighted to have another big case to replace the Hall-Mills affair in their columns. The tabloid *Daily Mirror*, which had dug up so much of the evidence in the New Jersey case, immediately reassigned its top reporters to the Snyder story and began recruiting celebrities to write about the upcoming trial. Even Charlotte Mills, who made her name reporting on the murder of her own mother, was reassigned to the Snyder case. But what was to be said of it? Unlike the Hall-Mills case, there was no mystery, no element of the whodunit about the Snyder story. The murderers had confessed their conspiracy, and the question of which one twisted the lethal wire around Albert Snyder's neck seemed inconsequential. Certainly the people involved in the Snyder affair were, if anything, even more drearily ordinary than those associated with the Hall-Mills case. But there, according to the popular magazine *Outlook*, was the real mystery of the Snyder case. For if Ruth Snyder and Judd Gray were no different from their neighbors, what was to deter those neighbors from committing similar adulteries and murders?

The question was not an idle one. Certainly infidelity and murder of the sort made notorious by the Hall-Mills case seemed epidemic. Only the year before, in 1926, Fanny Soper was convicted of killing her husband, Harry, a deputy sheriff in Blauvelt, New York, and very narrowly escaped the death penalty. In 1924 the notorious Risteen-Plummer triangle and in 1921 the Hemming-Eberhardt affair left husbands murdered in both cases. In 1922, right beside the lurid Hall-Mills letters, newspapers reported the intimate correspondence between Harold GaNun and Ivy Giberson, whose husband, William, supposedly was murdered, like Albert Snyder, by intruders. Mrs. Giberson was sentenced to life. As prosecutors prepared for the Snyder trial, Sadie Raser confessed that she and her lover Frank Van Sickle had murdered her husband, Edward, in Newton, New Jersey, two years before. And during the Snyder trial, Ruth Snyder sometimes shared headlines with Lucy Baxter Earley, on trial in Newburgh, New York, for allegedly murdering her husband with the help of her lover William Wegley. Overworked medical experts dashed between Newburgh and Queens, testifying in both trials at once. The adulterous mate-slaying was certainly nothing new, and whether it occurred any more often during the twenties than it had in the past is impossible to say. But there is no doubt that mate-slaying, like the extramarital relations that led to it, *seemed* to be increasing dramatically. The New York *Post* noted alarmingly that "if even a small percentage of irregular love affairs should lead to killings, the streets of our great cities would resemble the battle of Gettysburg." There was good reason then to ask, as the *Outlook* did of Ruth Snyder and Judd Gray, "If these two could commit such a murder, why not any of countless thousands of others?"

It was more than just a question of deterring murder, for these killings seemed, to contemporary commentators, to reflect a profound

social malaise; the New York *Herald Tribune* called it "a social cancer" or "psychopathia suburbis." Murder was only the last act in a
long, sordid history of family obligations betrayed and common decen-
cies violated. In the Snyder case, the rather commonplace, shabby
affair between the two lovers had been going on for a year and a half—
months of lies and coded notes and bribed postmen and clandestine
afternoon sex at the Waldorf, while Lorraine entertained herself by
riding the elevators. And there was an even more mundane motive in
three insurance policies which Albert Snyder did not know he held;
they would have paid his widow, who secretly met the premiums,
about $100,000. The Snyder murder, like so many others at the time,
seemed to have been prompted by "the pettiest, the most ignoble, kind
of self-indulgence." And that self-indulgence was thought to be the besetting sin of a society that had lost track altogether of the boundaries
of right conduct.

The newspapers, then, in cooperation with the court, took up the
task of excising that social cancer, of reestablishing old standards, of
ensuring, as the *Herald Tribune* put it, that the "slightly pale yellow
dawn of a new decadence, which rose after the lurid sunsets of the
war," would deepen "into the clear blue of another, an almost Victorian earnestness." The more respectable dailies tended to serious reflections upon the case while the tabloids went in for sensational, and
often wholly fictitious, sidelights. Among them all, they turned the
Snyder case into one of the top media events of the decade—and its
most important morality play, designed like medieval moral drama to
point the way to heaven. By the time it was over, all of the papers had
written volumes and, incidentally, sold more newspapers than ever
before.

The hundreds of thousands of words written about the case at the
time repeatedly sounded two refrains. In the first place, as one reporter
coolly noted, everyone is interested in things that are "sexy" and
"vile." The tabloids increased their circulation by reporting every little
kink in the Snyder-Gray love affair, so that every reader could indulge
vicariously in the forbidden; it was a heyday for voyeurs, at least until
Gray was called upon to enumerate from the stand every drink he had
ever drunk at every lunch he had ever eaten with Ruth Snyder—and
the thrilling affair became so tedious that bored spectators left the
courtroom. But this exposure of every detail of the adulterers' conduct
appealed to the readers' prurient interest and also served to define precisely what conduct was bad and what was permissible. Before it was

all over, avid readers knew that respectable women did not smoke, drink, dye their hair, cross their legs, lunch out with strange men, or feel ingratitude toward their husbands. Still, despite the obvious lessons of the Snyder case, the notion of slipping off to the Waldorf for an afternoon of clandestine sex did have a certain sinister appeal to bored wives and husbands; so the newspapers carefully stressed that Snyder and Gray were *not* ordinary folks. They might *appear* ordinary to reflective publications like the *Outlook*, given to raising ponderous questions better left alone; but at heart they were very different. Gray was not truly a man, and Snyder was certainly no woman. As the trial went on, more and more reporters noticed that Snyder didn't even *look* like a woman anymore. Luckily, the reassurance that Snyder and Gray were not, after all, ordinary people made it easier for newspaper readers to indulge vicariously in their crimes without fear of falling into such sin. And the inescapable conclusion, by the end of the trial, that Ruth Snyder was scarcely human at all made it that much easier to send her to the electric chair.

These two themes of the trial coverage—establishing the standards of right conduct and setting apart the evildoers from the great mass of upstanding citizens who supposedly followed those standards—came together in the public presentation of Ruth Snyder: a bad woman, a bad wife, a bad mother, and at the same time an utterly cold, inhuman vampire completely unlike those good, warm, self-sacrificing wives and mothers who represented the best of American womanhood.

In the first reports of the Snyder murder, Ruth Snyder was described as the "beautiful wife" of the slain art director; but the newspapers quickly realized their mistake. After her confession the *Mirror* made one attempt to point up the contrast between Ruth's lovely appearance and hideous crimes; on March 24, just after she confessed, the paper ran a full-page studio portrait with instructions to "study this face, pretty, soft, smiling, with curling hair and delicate features. One of a loving wife and a devoted mother, you would say. Yet it is that of Mrs. Ruth Brown Snyder. . . ." But that line was quickly abandoned. Ruth Snyder became instead the "Fiend Wife," the "faithless wife," the "blonde fiend," the "marble woman" encased from head to toe in a "mask of marble," "flaming Ruth," a "vampire," and "Ruthless Ruth, the Viking Ice Matron of Queens Village." The more sober New York *Post* found her to be a "hard-faced woman" probably "oversexed" and certainly overly interested in "power and authority."

Physically, the *Post* said, she was "heavy and coarse." The New York *Herald Tribune*, apparently casting about for the right approach to the story, called her a "woman of steel" and then criticized her for having rough skin, straight hair, and a wrinkled dress, concluding its report of the first press interview given by the confessed conspirator in murder with the apparently damning judgment: "She is not well groomed."

But it was to the tabloid *Mirror* that readers turned for murder news, and in its pages Ruth Snyder was compared to Lucretia Borgia, Messalina, and Lady Macbeth. The paper hired Dr. Edgar C. Beall, a well-known phrenologist, to study three photographs of Snyder and prepare an analysis that guided the subsequent observations of many celebrity reporters. Dr. Beall noted that Snyder had "flattened" eyelids, "especially on the left side," a configuration "very pronounced in Brigham Young" and clearly indicating a "polygamous disposition." Her other distinctive feature—which everyone was to notice—was her mouth: "as cold, hard, and unsympathetic as a crack in a dried lemon." Although some reporters commented on her square "masculine" jaw, Dr. Beall thought that her chin tapered "like the lower face of a cat," suggesting her "treachery" and "ingratitude." All in all, Dr. Beall judged that it was easy to see in her face "the character of a shallow-brained pleasure seeker, accustomed to unlimited self-indulgence, which at last ends in an orgie [*sic*] of murderous passion and lust, seemingly without a parallel in the criminal history of modern times." Thanks to such pseudoscientific clues, celebrity-reporter Natacha Rambova, second wife of Rudolph Valentino, was able to conclude after watching Ruth Snyder for one hour in the courtroom: "There is lacking in her character that real thing, selflessness. She apparently doesn't possess it and never will. Her fault is that she has no heart." By the time novelist Thyra Samter Winslow visited the courtroom on May 6, there was little left to say, but she mentioned all the telltale features. Snyder, she said, has "cold, mean eyes, and her slit of a mouth is even crueler than I had been led to suppose. Her determined jaw is all that the papers have said it is." "If Ruth Snyder is a woman," thundered playwright Willard Mack in a highly acclaimed article, "then, by God! you must find some other name for my mother, wife or sister. . . ."

On the other hand, Henry Judd Gray, Snyder's lover and co-defendant, was thought to be an awfully nice fellow. Even the detective who arrested him commented, "He's as nice appearing a gentleman as you'd want to meet." Married for eleven years to his childhood sweetheart and, like Snyder, the parent of a nine-year-old daughter, he was regarded in his community—East Orange, New Jersey—as a "model" citizen. As the *Herald Tribune* reported, "He was a Red Cross worker in the World War, was an assiduous worker for the Sunday school of the First Methodist Church, was quiet mannered in the home and a local country club man. He golfed and bridged and motored. He was a member of the Orange Lodge of Elks." In short, a regular fellow. But he also seemed to be a murderer. How could that be explained?

His defense team first followed up the suggestion of Gray's shocked wife: "He must be insane!" Four "alienists" tapped Gray's spinal fluid, X-rayed his head, and interviewed him for days; but they could not find him insane. In fact, he seemed to Dr. Sylvester Lahey, spokesman for the group, a "fine cultured fellow" and "very affable." So the alienists reverted to a theory first advanced by the police on the very day that Gray confessed. As the *Herald Tribune* reported at the time: "All facts now adduced point to a love-mad man completely in the sway of the woman whose will was steel, and brain active and intelligent. She dominated him, police said, and forced her will upon him, even when he desired to back out on some of her proposals." The alienists took up the notion and repeated it to the press before the trial began: "A strange charm of Mrs. Snyder made him do it. . . . Her personality dominated him—he was helpless." At 5 feet 5 inches and 120 pounds, Gray suited the part of the cringing weakling. So by the time attorney William J. Millard summed up the case for the defense of Henry Judd Gray the theory had become gospel. "That woman," he said to the jury and the ranks of reporters who copied down every word, "like a poisonous snake, drew Judd Gray into her glistening coils, and there was no escape. It was a peculiarly alluring seduction. Just as a piece of steel jumps and clings to the powerful magnet, so Judd Gray came within the powerful, compelling, attractive force of that woman. She held him fast. This woman, this peculiar venomous species of humanity, was abnormal, possessed of an all-consuming, all-absorbing passion, an animal lust, which seemingly was never satiated." In the updated Eden of attorney Millard's imagination, Ruth Snyder became the temptress Eve and the serpent too; while poor Judd Gray, like Adam, unwisely but helplessly succumbed. Judd Gray became a pathetic figure, a "putty man" malleable to the will of the Viking woman of steel, as much her victim as was poor deceived Albert Snyder. Fortunately, the very weakness that made Gray a creature to be pitied also distinguished him from ordinary men, for the true *manly* man retained the power to dominate and control women.

It was the detectives—all men—who first found Gray such a likable fellow and passed on to the public as fact his story that he had been bewitched and dominated. As it happened, in their initial confessions both Snyder and Gray lied and with increasingly bitter recriminations each blamed the other for the actual killing, but the police believed Gray; and even when he later changed his story, neither he nor they gave up the theory that he had been the woman's puppet. The male alienists, too, accepted Gray's interpretation of himself as victim and never interviewed Snyder at all. In court the jurors were still by law in New York all men, all at mid-life, married, with children—men very much like the dead Albert Snyder, or Judd Gray. Women, for their part, judged Ruth Snyder no more generously; she repeatedly appealed for the sympathy of wives and mothers, and apparently received none. Women journalists unanimously found her "unfeminine" and unsympathetic, and the wife of one of the jurors publicly expressed her hope that her husband could not be swayed by such a "brazen woman." Snyder thought that women jurors would see her "side of the case better than a crowd of men" because they would "know the complications and cross-currents of domestic life," but an informal press jury made up of six female and six male reporters condemned her to death. Women, like men, accepted the officially sanctioned version of the case.

That version was firmly grounded in the old double sexual standard, which had not, after all, been "ironed flat." Snyder and Gray had to be judged differently because they were not weighed in the same scales of justice. Ruth Snyder was marked as a "bad woman" from the moment she first met Judd Gray. It was bad to send him a note, bad to visit his office for a "corset fitting," bad to have sex with him. And as the *Post* noted, when Snyder took the stand to face the prosecutor she seemed to be on trial "for adultery instead of murder."

Judd Gray, on the other hand, until he participated in killing Albert Snyder, had done nothing wrong. Officially adultery was frowned upon for both sexes, and Cornelius Vanderbilt, Jr., touted a single sexual standard—including marital fidelity for all—in an editorial for the *Mirror*; but off the record, men knew better. As Havelock Ellis put it: "Promiscuous women, who were not professional prostitutes, or feeble-minded, or insane, have always been rare, while many men who seem practically promiscuous have cut a figure in the world." That is why playwright and *Post* columnist W. E. Woodward could approve Gray's assessment of himself—"I have always been a gentleman and I have always been on the level with everybody"—although "everybody" obviously did not include Gray's wife.

Gray had established his alibi for the murder with the help of an old friend, Haddon Gray (no relation), who posted two letters to Judd's wife, rumpled his bed in the hotel, and hung out a Do Not Disturb sign to make it appear that Judd was still in Syracuse when in fact, so far as Haddon knew, he was really visiting a girl friend. Haddon even lied to the police, maintaining his friend's alibi, until he learned that Judd had confessed to murder. When Haddon Gray took the stand at the trial to tell the truth, he was described in the press as a loyal friend and a true gentleman who had bravely done what any man would do for a good pal: lie so the man could visit his girl friend without his wife's knowledge. To some commentators even Judd Gray's elaborate plans for the murder seemed a harmless amusement. Columnist Woodward speculated in the *Post* that "this mild corset salesman" probably was entertained on "his lonely trips" by the thought "of crushing a rival, of being a strong, brutal caveman." And just before the murder Gray had wrapped the sashweight in paper so it wouldn't hurt Snyder quite so much—a "humane" gesture which showed that Gray was a "kindhearted man at bottom." Playwright Willard Mack echoed in the *Mirror* that Gray had "never been a murderer in his heart." He was simply, to one courtroom observer, the admirable "kind of fellow who'd do anything in the world for somebody he liked." Because of the double sexual standard that still persisted after the so-called sexual revolution, Snyder and Gray, who had sinned together, could not be judged alike. If they had stopped short of murder, Ruth Snyder would still have been a "bad" woman while Judd Gray would have been merely a regular fellow. As it was Gray seemed to be no worse than what the papers called him: a poor boob, a weakling, a puppet, a sap. He was simply "a bunch of dough that somebody forgot to knead," a man who couldn't "put up a croquet set without help."

The Snyder case as media event—the great morality play of the decade—was meant almost exclusively for the edification of women. Gray's sister, Margaret Logan, touched upon the need for the lesson in her prepared statement to the press during the trial: "I never before realized how much tragedy is concealed in houses all around us. This is created by evil women. Most of their depredations upon happy domestic life don't become public. Few come to such a dreadful pass as the catastrophe in our own family." With woman cast as the source of evil, as Eve in league with Satan, all the old-fashioned notions of chivalry were turned inside out. Ruth Snyder became a fiend "unworthy of the chivalry, protection and consideration which right thinking men have always accorded decent womanhood." So when one of Snyder's attorneys, summing up her case, made a misguided plea for chivalry, he was answered by titters from the audience. As the *Post* reporter described it: "He was a knight fighting a battle of terrific odds for a golden damozel disguised as a blonde, fattish and ice-hard housewife."

True femininity in this case was represented by the loyal, grieving mothers of the defendants, Josephine Brown and Margaret Gray. Judd's mother, in particular, was a woman so dignified in her relations with the press that rumors she had made Judd a mamma's boy quickly were squelched. She was not blamed for his crime but left to wonder aloud, "Wherein did I fail?" Little was said during the trial about Gray's wife, Isabel, who had gone into seclusion, but when she visited the prison after his conviction to forgive him, she was praised for displaying the loyalty of a "good little wife." The daughters, Lorraine Snyder and Jane Gray, were greatly pitied because both had been deprived of a father's love.

If there was to be a hero of the drama, amid this chorus of weeping women, it could only be Judd Gray; and curiously enough, with the old chivalric code upended, he was able to fill that role not by protecting his ladylove but by ratting on her. In the final days of the trial, Gray took the stand to redeem his manliness by telling "the truth": Ruth Snyder committed the murder. Judd was there, of course. He never denied that. But, he said, he had tried to talk her out of it, tried to leave the house; he was powerless against her. So, incited by Ruth and a bottle of whiskey, he struck the first blow with the sashweight only to have Albert wake up and fight back. Unable to carry on, Gray called out "Help me, Momsie." And Momsie finished the job. At the end of his testimony Gray broke into tears that swept all skepticism away. As the *Mirror* put it, Gray "emerged from the mire into which he slipped wearing a crown that few achieve—the crown of truth." Even the district attorney, summing up the state's case against Snyder and Gray, called Gray "a decent, red-blooded, upstanding American citizen."

Ruth had her own story to tell, but no one wanted to hear it. In court the attorneys and the judge kept telling her to answer yes or no and stop trying to explain. The papers said she "lied like a dog to save her own cheap hide." There were things she never got a chance to say, so later, on death row, she wrote out her story for the *Mirror*—an erratic jumble of painful remembering, rage, religious platitudes, and grief. She had been a respectable and faithful wife, she said, until she met Gray, a sweet-talking commercial traveler accustomed to "selling" women. She fell in love with him, though she knew he saw other women: Alice in Rochester and someone called "Snooks." But he started asking her for money—ninety dollars here, a hundred dollars there—and suggesting that he might have to speak to Albert if she didn't come up with it. She did as he asked—even though she wanted to break off the affair—for fear that in a showdown with Albert, she would lose her daughter. The insurance policies and the murder, she claimed, were Gray's idea; he talked about it whenever he was "liquor-logged" as he was almost all the time, but Ruth thought she could talk him out of it as she had done before. On the night of the murder she set out the bottle of bootleg whiskey he demanded, but Gray, instead of taking the bottle and leaving, as she expected him to do, drank it and stayed. He was still there hiding when she and Albert came home from the party. After Albert went to sleep, she tried to persuade Judd to leave; and just when she thought she had succeeded, he went upstairs while she was in the bathroom and murdered Albert. And ever since, the "lying, cringing jackal" had been hiding behind her skirts.

On the face of it, Ruth Snyder's story was no less plausible than Judd Gray's. And while witnesses established that Gray had bought the murder weapons and set up an alibi well in advance, the only evidence that Ruth Snyder had participated in the murder was the testimony of Gray himself. Still, no one believed any part of her story. Even when she converted to Catholicism in jail, most New Yorkers who spoke to the *Mirror*'s inquiring reporter about it thought she had converted only in hopes of winning a commutation from Catholic Governor Al Smith. Writing her final story, Ruth Snyder asked, "Don't the 'outside' believe ANYTHING I tell?" But she already knew the answer.

The newspaper-reading public, which doubted Ruth Snyder and condemned her, eagerly supported her right to die in the electric chair. Even before the trial began, a female social worker argued in the *Mirror*, "Any woman who commits a man's crime should be given a man's punishment." And State Senator William Lathrop Love of Brooklyn urged "equal 'rights' for Women Criminals. . . . Women should suffer the same penalties that are meted out to men for the crimes they commit," he maintained. "If a woman enters the competition with men she has a chance to gain the same ends, and I see no reason why she should not suffer the same penalties." While the verdict was being awaited in the Snyder case, several papers published accounts of the death in 1899 of Martha Place, the last woman to die in the electric chair in New York; and the *Mirror* quoted approvingly from then Governor Theodore Roosevelt's decision denying clemency: "In the commission of a crime, a woman is deserving of the same blame as a man in a similar case. I would deal with the woman as with the man—no whit differently." On January 10, 1928, while Snyder and Gray waited on death row at Sing Sing, Governor Al Smith issued a similar statement denying their application for executive clemency. "The execution of this judgment on a woman is so distressing," he said, "that I had hoped that the appeal to me for executive clemency would disclose some fact which would justify my interference with the processes of the law. But this did not happen." It was widely predicted that Smith's firm stand would do him good in his campaign for the presidency; certainly Roosevelt's firmness in the Place appeal had not harmed his political future. Pleased with Smith's decision, *The New York Times* said in an editorial: "Equal suffrage has put women in a new position. If they are equal with men before the law, they must pay the same penalties as men for transgressing it."

Feminists could scarcely quarrel with the argument for equal rights, yet in this case it smacked unmistakably of expediency rather than justice. No one could claim that Snyder and Gray had been treated "no whit differently" in the courtroom where Snyder had been tried for adultery and murder, Gray for murder alone. And as a spokeswoman for the American Association of Labor Legislation pointed out in another context: "Equal treatment of unequals is the greatest inequality." But Ruth Snyder had claimed for herself sexual prerogatives that belonged only to men; through her execution the full implications of "equality" could be brought home to feminists and flappers alike. Arguing that both Gray and Snyder should be executed, Willard Mack gave away the vindictiveness behind the equal rights argument. Ruth Snyder had wanted "ONE BED" with her lover, Mack said. Let her have "ONE CHAIR."

In the last act of the drama, both Snyder and Gray did go to the chair on the night of January 12, 1928. And even then Snyder got a bad press. When the sentence was passed on May 9, 1927, the "stone woman" became hysterical, and afterward in her cell she suffered from "nervous paralysis" and "epileptic spasms" that the papers called "the forerunners of insanity." Gray, on the other hand, received the sentence "with calmness and prayer." "Gray finds enough of traditional manhood in him to take his medicine without whining," reported the *Mirror*. But "Ruth Snyder—woman—turns to the immemorial device of her sex to wring pity from male hearts. Already she is ill and suffering. Expect her to grow worse and worse as the hour of her atonement nears." No change in their behavior could change the opinion the press had already formed of Snyder and Gray; and by the night set for execution Ruth Snyder had indeed grown worse. In keeping with a Sing Sing tradition of executing the more distraught prisoner first, she went first to the electric chair. She was "a disheveled wreck" in a drab prison shirtwaist and smock; her blonde hair had gone almost gray. She entered the death chamber murmuring prayers, but she cried out and collapsed when she saw the electric chair and had to be lifted into it by the two matrons who accompanied her. Quickly the executioners strapped her in; the matrons retired; Warden Lewis Lawes, who opposed capital punishment, turned away; and while the priest intoned prayers and Snyder, sobbing, cried out "Father, forgive them for they know not what they do," chief executioner Robert Elliott threw the switch. An imaginative reporter for the New York *World* wrote that as the current passed through her body "her left hand twisted back and upward as if trying to escape the imprisoning strap and the index finger of this hand stiffened in a pointed accusation at herself." And an imaginative photographer from the Chicago *Tribune*, smuggled in by the New York *Daily News* in a last attempt to one-up its competitor, the *Mirror*, raised his trouser leg and snapped her picture with a miniature camera strapped to his ankle. She died under the eyes of thirty reporters, doctors, and prison officials—all men—wearing a regulation football helmet wired to 2,000 volts.

A few minutes later Judd Gray, wearing a well-pressed dark gray suit "with invisible stripe," entered the room with the prison chaplain. "Here was a man," said the New York *Sun*, "who was going to his death with a controlled spirit. He crossed the threshold without the need of a supporting hand. His step was firm and assured. He walked upright, with shoulders thrown back slightly. There was no weakening of the knees, no trembling of hands or lips." The chaplain recited the beatitudes, and until the switch was thrown, Gray followed them inaudibly: "Blessed are the poor in spirit; for theirs is the kingdom of Heaven."

Then it was all over. Judd Gray had repeatedly urged young men to stay away from bad liquor and bad women; and in the end he had died like a man. On the front page of the *Mirror* Ruth Snyder's portrait was replaced by the smiling face of Charles Lindbergh. The show-business celebrities who had haunted the trial went back to Hollywood and the Great White Way: D. W. Griffiths to the movies, Evelyn Law to the Ziegfeld Follies, and David Belasco—who had attended the trial to gather material for a new play—went back to Broadway, where lesser shows had folded while thousands were turned away from the Queens courthouse. *The New York Times* hoped the execution of a husband-slayer—the first such execution in New York in forty years—would have a much-needed deterrent effect, while the *Mirror* congratulated itself that the "impressive lesson of the Snyder case—more effective than a thousand sermons"—would save countless people from their own "follies." The morality play was over. After the executions, which the *Post* termed the "Finale of Queens Pageant," columnist Nunnally Johnson summed up the "drama of violence": "That was the end. It was a grand show. It never failed once. It had no surprises, no Theatre Guild stuff, no modernisms. It was the good old stuff done well and fiercely. It was grim and grand. It moved slowly and inevitably like Dreiser. And it came at last, last night, to the magnificent, the tremendous, the incomparable curtain that the audience was counting on. Everybody walked out with a satisfied feeling. It was regular."

And well might everyone feel satisfied, for the moral could not have been more clear. The final lesson of the Snyder-Gray drama was the lesson that had been taught to Ruth Snyder herself. In her last interview and in her final story for the *Mirror* she, in turn, restated the lesson for the public. "If I were to live over again," she said, "I would be what I want my child to be—a good girl, really making the fear of God a guide to a straight life." Again she wrote: "I said before 'Go Straight' and I mean it more than ever. And I wish a lot of women who may be sinning could come here and see what I have done for myself through sinning and maybe they would do some of the thinking I have done for months and they would be satisfied with their homes and would stop wishing for things they should try to get along without when they can't have them.

"Maybe there are women who have nice homes (and husbands who do the best they can for them) even if they don't like their husbands and they could bear it if they would only make up their minds everything can't be just perfect.

"Some husbands don't make enough money to get their wives the things they wish they had and if the wives have any brains they will just take what they can get and try to make the best of it."

And again she wrote: "OH, GOD, HOW A LOT OF WOMEN WOULD CHANGE IF THEY COULD COME HERE AND SEE MY PUNISHMENT."

3.

Some women wouldn't learn. Only the night before thirty-three-year-old Ruth Snyder walked into the death chamber at Sing Sing, thirty-three-year-old Fannie Krelich in New York City hit her husband, John, over the head with an ax; and when she and her lover were arrested, she only wanted to know whether she would be able to collect the $1,000 insurance. And the day after Snyder's execution the papers reported that Velma West, age twenty-one, had been indicted in Painesville, Ohio, for beating her husband to death with a hammer in their "honeymoon bungalow" at Perry in December 1927. Velma West's husband had forbidden her to go to an evening bridge party in Cleveland, so she killed him, took the car, drove to Cleveland, and played bridge. The papers christened her "the split-mind flapper slayer" and prepared to make an example of her, but her lawyers made a deal after "pressure had been brought to bear on the case from an unrevealed source." She pled guilty to the reduced charge of murder in the second degree and accepted a life sentence so that the state would not disclose in court her "attachment for another woman." Leaving for Marysville Reformatory, from which she would be eligible for parole in ten years, Velma West was pleased to have escaped the death penalty. "I love life and I want to live it," she said. "That's the way of youth, I guess."

No wonder that more "old-fashioned" folks marveled at what the world was coming to. Dr. Frederick L. Hoffman, a consulting statistician for the Prudential Insurance Company, lamented the rising rates of homicide in 51 of the 122 American cities in which people bothered to keep score. All this murder, he said—particularly the "atrocious" Snyder-Gray case—indicated that the American school, church, and state were not succeeding in that "development of character" so essential to crime prevention. Frederick Hoffman's alarm may not have been disinterested; at the time his company was entering litigation to avoid paying insurance benefits on the death of their client Albert Snyder. But when Ida Austin and her lover Arthur Abadore offered a "thug" (who turned out to be a deputy sheriff) one hundred dollars to murder her husband, Fred, the whole newspaper-reading public knew that a husband's life didn't count for much. Fred Austin, though he "had never spoken a kind word" to his wife in nine years of marriage, forgave her and brought her two canaries to jail. Still the reading public was uneasy.

Insurance statistician Hoffman thought that capital punishment did not help to deter crime, but the social fathers did not share his opinion. When the need arose, they invoked the death penalty again to teach a lesson. So Anna Antonio, a twenty-eight-year-old mother of three children, walked to the electric chair at Sing Sing on August 9, 1934. After her came Vincent Saetta and Samuel Feraci, the two men who shot and stabbed her husband on a highway near Albany. They had told Anna Antonio that they intended to kill her husband and wanted a share of his insurance money. She had replied, "I don't care what you do. I am only interested in the children." So when Saetta and Feraci killed her husband, Anna Antonio was also indicted, tried, and convicted of murder.

On July 16, 1936, Mary Frances Creighton, age thirty-six, became the first person ever transferred to the electric chair at Sing Sing by wheelchair. Some of the doctors on the special examining team appointed by the governor said that Mrs. Creighton was suffering from hysterical paralysis, others that she was malingering; but in any case, she couldn't walk. The officials wheeled her in, strapped her to the chair, and executed her anyway for the arsenic murder of Mrs. Ada Appelgate, age thirty-six, in September 1935. She was followed to the chair by Everett Appelgate, about thirty-six, a past commander of the Nassau County, Second Department, American Legion. Appelgate, by his own admission, was the lover of Mrs. Creighton's fifteen-year-old daughter, and according to Mrs. Creighton, her own lover as well. Appelgate, a fat, gray, balding man, wanted to marry Mrs. Creighton's daughter, but he denied that he had had a hand in killing his wife. Mrs. Creighton freely admitted poisoning Ada Appelgate because Ada had been circulating stories damaging to her daughter's reputation; but in the murder, she said, she had been helped by Everett Appelgate.

So the two alleged conspirators were executed, but without the lip-smacking satisfaction that attended the killing of Snyder and Gray. There was about the Creighton-Appelgate affair something a little too seamy and a little too drab. For seven years John and Mary Frances Creighton and their two children had shared a five-room bungalow with Everett and Ada Appelgate and their thirteen-year-old daughter because it was the only way for two World War I veterans, employed at best only part-time, to make ends meet. If they were somehow thrown into explosive intimacies not of their own choosing, a reading public scraping through the Depression could understand it. Mrs. Creighton was one thing—perhaps a crazy woman. Years before, in 1923, she had been tried and acquitted in New Jersey, first for the arsenic murder of her brother, and second for the arsenic murder of her mother-in-law. But Everett Appelgate had served in the war and become a respected officer of the American Legion. The whole thing left a bad taste.

Besides, people had other things to think about. The late years of the Depression were no time to worry about the sins of one's neighbors; and then a place called Pearl Harbor filled the moral map. Men went to war, and in unprecedented numbers women went to work. Whatever needed doing on the home front—from driving trains to assembling munitions—women did. Afterward, the social fathers congratulated them for their outstanding war effort—and told them to go home. So men came home from war and went to work. And many women came home from work and went to the suburbs. After almost a generation of Depression and war, prosperity and peace returned, and with them domestic bliss. Fifteen fat years succeeded fifteen lean. Everything seemed as rosy as an Eisenhower smile until Betty Friedan identified "the Problem that has no name"—the profound disaffection of housewives who know that something is wrong. Anger had been festering and swelling since the end of the war, when many married women flatly refused to leave the labor force; now even the woman who had been "just a housewife" all these years wanted something to do. She took off her apron and went, timorously at first, back to school, out to work, and, before many years had passed, into a women's consciousness-raising group where vague yearnings clicked into rebellion. All at once "togetherness" became claustrophobic, and complacency gave way to unease. The first whispers of a renewed women's movement rustled across the country, stirring old fears of women on the loose. It was an anxious time. Time for a new sensation.

The newspapers thought they had found it in July 1965 when a Dade County, Florida, grand jury indicted Candace Mossler and her lover Melvin Lane Powers for the 1964 murder of her husband, Jacques Mossler, at his Key Biscayne apartment. By the time the pair came to trial in Miami in January 1966, more than forty reporters from around the country were waiting to pounce. The Chicago *Daily News* reported that the trial "gives every sign of being one of the most lurid and bloodstained among latter-day criminal cases." The Houston *Chronicle* noted that the case was laced with "threads of love, hate, greed, savage passion, intrigue, incest and perversion." Certainly the case had all the ingredients of a tabloid hit, yet despite all the column-inches of reportage it never achieved the stature as moral drama that the Snyder-Gray case enjoyed. The Mossler-Powers trial was not a morality play but a Hollywood extravaganza starring a bleached blonde, a parade of disreputable witnesses, and the flamboyant Texan Percy Foreman, who boyishly admitted to the press that he was the greatest lawyer of the twentieth century. Newspaper readers were not drawn into a battle of good and evil as they had been in the Snyder-Gray drama; instead they were content to sit back and watch. As one courtroom spectator said, "It was better than a movie." But it was equally unreal.

The press tried hard enough to turn the trial into a drama of good and evil. The Chicago *Tribune* attempted to make the garrulous widow a sympathetic figure: "She is remarkable for an outgoing disposition that makes it appear she seeks friends for friendship only and neither needs nor wants sympathy. She is remarkable for her gaiety, her effervescence, and for an underlying intelligence that is her ultimate armor." Jim Bishop of the Hearst papers tried to make her a figure of evil on the model of Ruth Snyder: "The lady is 60 inches of wrought iron. It is blonde and pale and unyielding. It isn't something that God wrought. Candace did it. From the day long ago, when the little Georgia belle found out females have an earthy attraction for males, Candace has coated that little body with so many veneers of honey and passion that if the real Candace stood up, Mrs. Mossler would probably disown her." But the old formulas didn't work. As the trial progressed the Associated Press surveyed sixty of its papers and found that twenty-one of them weren't even running the story, while on a day of particularly seamy testimony, only seven ran the story on the front page. The AP general-news editor noted, "These trials don't have the impact they used to have. More significant things go on in the world today." When the managing editor of United Press Internationalal learned that only three of twenty-five member newspapers he questioned had the story on page one, he speculated that "Candy just couldn't compete with the Viet Nam war." *Newsweek* referred to the trial news as "Stale Candy."

But the real trouble with the Mossler-Powers case was that it was at once too predictable and too bizarre. On the one hand the Mossler marriage and murder was the oldest story in the book. When Jacques and Candace met in New Orleans, he was a millionaire Houston bank tycoon and she a young beautiful divorcée with two children, making ends meet with a modeling agency. After sixteen years of marriage Jacques was a sixty-nine-year-old man who slept in his undershirt in a Florida apartment and threatened to divorce the forty-five-year-old blonde described in the press as an "earthy" and "lissome" Houston socialite. The old, rich man who gets taken for his money or his life by a lusty young woman is part of the folklore of marriage; at first envied for his youthful bride, he becomes the fool, the butt of the joke—never a figure of compassion. Mossler's killer had overdone the attack, clubbing him over the head and then stabbing him thirty-nine times, but what else could you expect?

On the other hand, the people involved in the Mossler case were *not* just like the folks next door. (Asked to comment on the charges of murder and incest against her, Candace said, "Well, sir, nobody's perfect.") To most Americans, the rich are different; and the Mosslers were very rich indeed. And Candace, who was often described as a spunkier version of Lana Turner, was glamorous. The Miami *Herald* said that she was "like her name—all pretty colors and sweet voice. Pink lips, pale-green eye-shadow, silver hair. And her life and her habits . . . nocturnal rides . . . a good-morning kiss on the cheek of a child as she herself tumbles into bed, apartments strung like beads across a continent, four, five, six cars . . . are a little like the stuff they sell on sticks at fairs. Airy-fairy." She wrote to her lover on stationery from the Mexico City Continental Hilton: "I'd like you to keep me ever so warm." And that lover, big, hulking twenty-four-year-old Mel Powers—the man charged with doing the actual killing while Candy established an alibi for herself with a migraine headache at a hospital emergency room—differed from the predictable young lover of the folktales in one important respect. He was her nephew, the son of her younger sister. And he bragged a lot to a whole string of unsavory men who showed up in court to testify to Mel's sexual virtuosity, specifying acts that could only be designated in the newspapers as "certain erotic activities." The UPI managing editor complained that many papers didn't cover the case because "there was just too much sex." But it was the sexual exploits of Candy and Mel that most excited the interest of readers; and those exploits, for decency's sake, could not be reported. What good was newspaper coverage of the trial if you had to *be* there?

The trial itself scarcely got around to the murder. The prosecution brought plenty of evidence about the illicit relationship between Mrs. Mossler and her nephew, and it produced a lineup of convicts who testified one after another that Powers or Mrs. Mossler or both had offered them money for a "hit." There were witnesses who placed Powers, a Houston resident, on a plane to Miami. There were his fingerprints in the car left at the Miami airport, his bloody palm print on Jacques Mossler's kitchen counter. It had not been a tidy job. But Powers's defense lawyer Foreman preferred to talk about Jacques Mossler's alleged homosexuality and about certain other young men who might have turned against him. Foreman produced his own string of convicts to impugn the character of the convicts brought forward by the prosecution; and in two cases he brought on the convicts' wives to say that they were notorious liars. It went on for seven weeks although Candace Mossler and Powers never took the stand. Foreman called no witnesses to the defense of Powers, and he never let his client say a word to anyone during the trial. It took days for the nine attorneys to finish their summations; Foreman alone addressed the jury for five hours. Then it took the all-male jury three more days of deadlock and card playing to decide on acquittal. Only then did Candace and Mel embrace. Candy kissed all the jurymen, too, and Mel admitted that he had been in Miami after all. At a press conference Candace said, in answer to a reporter's question, that they had no immediate plans to marry—overlooking the fact that aunt and nephew cannot legally marry anywhere in the United States. They drove away in attorney Clyde Woody's convertible with the top down, smiling and waving to the crowd like the king and queen of the prom. Then Candace went back to her Houston mansion, $28 million the richer. The prosecutor was disappointed but philosophical: "That is the American system of justice," he said. "The case is closed."

The New York *Daily News* called the finish "a Hollywood-style ending to one of the most sensational and lurid murder cases of our time," and indeed the movie was over. Candy turned up from time to time in later reels—when she sued Foreman for return of collateral and the *Saturday Evening Post* for libel, when she married a thirty-four-year-old man in 1971, and again when he mysteriously fell off the roof in 1972 and when they divorced in 1974. She died in 1975 of suffocation during a drug-induced sleep in a Miami hotel room, and a few months later 650 people turned up at the auction of her estate in Houston, seeking some souvenir of the "infamous" woman. But despite her own best efforts and those of attorney Foreman and a squad of forty reporters, she had never really captured the imagination or touched the fears of middle America. She remained too "airy-fairy." Her exploits were no more real than was the killing in the family of Lana Turner herself, the killing of the star's abusive lover by her teen-aged daughter. It was all Hollywood. Froth and flimflam. Readers were titillated by these goings-on, but nobody seemed morally outraged anymore by the extramarital sexual adventures of women like Mossler and Turner. Only Turner herself was outraged when she was asked to portray Mossler in a film exploiting the notoriety of the case. Society seemed willing to wink a leering eye as long as the lady-adventurer kept her transgressions confined to Hollywood, or to her own family.

The result of the Mossler case was deceptive, however; for what was thrilling in Hollywood became threatening on Main Street. The sexual standards loosened for the rich and glamorous wrapped the everyday housewife as tightly as ever. That was made clear by a case that broke at the same time as the Mossler-Powers affair. In July 1965, just as the grand jury indicted Mossler and Powers for murder in Florida, a man in Queens phoned New York's 107th Precinct to report that his children were missing.

When the police arrived at the apartment in Kew Gardens, Queens, they found Edmund Crimmins, a husky aircraft mechanic thickened by too much beer-drinking, and his twenty-six-year-old wife, Alice. Eddie, separated from his wife, had been summoned by her frantic 9:00 A.M. phone call: the children, five-year-old Eddie and four-year-old Alice Marie, called Missy, had disappeared from their bedroom. Detective Gerard Piering, in the absence of senior detectives, fell into command of his first major case; and according to all reports, he took one look at Alice Crimmins and disliked her. Alice Crimmins was what the newspapers called a "shapely" woman in toreador pants, her strawberry blonde hair carefully teased and lacquered, her makeup perfectly applied. She cast herself in the same mold as Candy Mossler and Lana Turner, but she was a working-class housewife. To Jerry Piering, Catholic father of six, she did not look like "Mother." When he gave orders to question Eddie and Alice Crimmins separately, he announced to his partner, "I'll take the bitch." That afternoon he took Alice Crimmins to a vacant lot half a mile away to look at her dead daughter. Missy was lying on her side in the sun, her pajama top knotted around her neck, her body swarming with flies. Alice Crimmins staggered, swooned, and fell into the arms of a detective; but she didn't cry. To Piering her reaction was too theatrical—not like a real mother; he was sure he had his murderer. That evening when reporter Kenneth Gross went on assignment to the Crimmins apartment, other reporters and photographers popping flashbulbs in Alice Crimmins's face told him what the police had told them: "The bitch killed her kids."

The police continued to question Eddie Crimmins and to check out tips on prowlers and known sex offenders, but they focused on Alice Crimmins. They tapped her telephone and bugged the new apartment that she and Eddie, temporarily reconciled by crisis, shared; but in three years of listening in on the life of Alice Crimmins, they found no bit of incriminating evidence to use against her. Perhaps that's why they turned nasty and began to harass her in other ways. When she went to bed with another man in her apartment, the listening police phoned Eddie and told him to go home. Whenever she got a new job under her maiden name—she was an executive secretary and reportedly an excellent one—the police visited her employer and told him who she was. They leaked word to the press that although their bugging tapes wouldn't be admissible in court, they proved that Alice had killed her children. Soon it was "common knowledge" among the police and the press that Alice Crimmins was guilty of murder, though so far there wasn't any evidence to prove it. There was plenty of evidence, however, on the tapes and off, that Alice Crimmins had had sexual relations with several different men. What's more, she never denied it, never was ashamed of it, and even when she knew the police were watching her constantly, she never made the slightest effort to change her ways. "If she were my wife," said Detective Piering, "I'd kill her." Instead, on September 13, 1967, he arrested Alice Crimmins for the murder of her daughter. She was tried and convicted of manslaughter.

During the trial there was scarcely a fact that was not in dispute. A good deal of what should have constituted the physical evidence in this case existed only in the memory of Detective Piering. Whether the children could have been taken or enticed through the bedroom window and whether they had eaten veal or manicotti for supper became issues of crucial significance, but only Piering had seen the layer of dust on the bureau under the window and the manicotti carton in the trash. He had made no note at the time, no photographic record. He just remembered. The testimony of the star witnesses for the prosecution, Joseph Rorech and Sophie Earomirski, was equally problematical. Rorech, once a high-rolling contractor rapidly going bankrupt and an ex-boyfriend of Alice Crimmins, testified that she had confessed killing Missy in anger, and through the help of another boyfriend, summoned a hit man to silence little Eddie, who had witnessed the killing. Alice screamed that Rorech was lying.

There was no incontrovertible proof on either side; everything depended on whose word was believed. Could one believe the testimony of star witness Sophie Earomirski, the middle-aged housewife who came forward eighteen months after the children's disappearance to say that at 2:00 A.M. on July 14, 1965, she had seen Alice Crimmins, a little boy, a dog, and a big man throwing a bundle into the back of a car? The defense pointed out that Sophie Earomirski had filed a workman's compensation claim for brain damage—she had jumped and struck her head at work when a "yellow mouse" ran up her arm—had attempted suicide with an overdose of tranquilizers, and had once been found with her head in the oven. (She was checking on dinner, she said.) Sophie Earomirski marched into court like a soldier, and after telling her improbable tale, she marched out again with her fist raised in triumph while the appreciative courtroom crowd cheered her on. She was photographed like that—the moment's hero—for all the papers. Nothing made it quite so clear that what was going on was not a search for justice but a war on Alice Crimmins.

Crimmins reacted accordingly: scornful, unashamed, hurt, and defiant. Outside the courtroom she masked the grief she refused to share with the public behind a desperate, brittle gaiety. Inside the courtroom, she was angry; and when she took the stand her cold anger told against her. Later she told reporter Gross that when she reread her own testimony she thought she sounded like a bitch. "But the thing is," she explained, "I was angry. I just wanted to get to the point. That man, the prosecutor, he kept asking me those questions about sex. I wanted to get to the point. He only wanted to know about sex." Her own attorneys wanted her to change her hairdo, her dress, her style; they wanted her to break down and cry for the jury, but she would not. The prosecution took her angry composure for hardness and worse.

To the press she was a sexy swinger. The pulp *Front Page Detective* featured the story of "Sexpot on Trial," calling her an "erring wife, a Circe, an amoral woman whose many affairs appeared symptomatic of America's Sex Revolution." The New York *Daily News* called her "the Queens housewife with hamster morals." Her name was rarely mentioned without some descriptive swipe: curvy, comely, shapely, flame-haired, blonde. And always she was identified by an occupation she had filled for only six months: the ex-cocktail waitress—a term used pejoratively to sneer at Alice Crimmins and a whole category of women workers at once. Before long the terms lost their meaning and became merely slurs so that on a single page of a newspaper she might be identified as a "sllekly [*sic*] attractive redhead" in one column and a "shapely blonde" in the next. But they all added up to bitch and the capacity to kill. A Queens housewife who attended several sessions of the trial told *New York Times* reporter Lacey Fosburgh that she found it hard to believe that any woman could kill her children, but "a woman like that . . . well . . . it makes it easier to understand." One of the jurors agreed: "A tramp like that is capable of anything." There was no question that Alice Crimmins was a woman "like that"; her own attorney said she was "amoral" and acknowledged that the jury had been forced to listen to a lot of "filth."

But Alice Crimmins, who thought the prosecution never did get to the point, got a new defense team and fought back. In May 1968 the Appellate Division reversed her conviction and ordered a new trial because three of the jurors admitted visiting the scene without permission. The prosecution retaliated by carrying the case before a second grand jury which, in July 1970, returned indictments charging Alice Crimmins with manslaughter in the death of her daughter and murder in the death of her son. (Indicting her a second time for murder in her daughter's death would have constituted double jeopardy.) On March 15, 1971, she went on trial again.

The court heard the same conflicting, inconclusive evidence that had filled the newspapers before; and a few additional witnesses added to the confusion. The alleged hit man identified by Crimmins's ex-boyfriend Joseph Rorech took the stand for the defense; Vincent Colabella, serving a twenty-year sentence in Atlanta penitentiary on drug charges, testified that he had never seen Alice Crimmins before but that a former Queens assistant district attorney had offered to let him "go home free" if he would say that he had gone to the Crimmins apartment and found both children already dead. A woman testified that she had seen the same group—woman, boy, dog, and man with bundle—that Sophie Earomirski claimed to have spotted from her window. Marvin Weinstein testified that he and his family, leaving a friend's Kew Gardens apartment at 2:00 A.M., may well have been the group that Earomirski saw. The friend, Anthony King, said the Weinstein family hadn't been at his house. Mrs. Weinstein came in to court to say that they had so; and another of King's acquaintances testified that King was a notorious liar.

So it went, back and forth, until Dr. Milton Helpern, New York City's chief medical examiner and undoubtedly the world's most famous "coroner," testified unequivocally that Missy Crimmins had died within two hours of eating her last meal, which consisted in part of "macaroni." Somehow, in that snarl of charge and countercharge, Helpern's testimony seemed a decisive scientific fact that pinned the murder on Alice Crimmins and the vanished manicotti carton—despite her own insistence that she had fed the children veal at 7:30 and seen them alive at midnight. Meanwhile, the press raked over Alice Crimmins's sex life again, and there was nothing to prevent twelve graying, middle-aged male jurors, who were never sequestered, from taking it all in. The judge instructed them to use their common sense, and on April 23, 1971, they announced their verdict: guilty of murder in the first degree—the most severe judgment they could have reached. Crimmins was sentenced to life imprisonment on the murder charge and five to twenty years for manslaughter; bail was denied as attorney Herbert Lyon, who always maintained that she had been tried for her morals and not for murder, began the complicated legal battle to free her.

Two years later, on May 7, 1973, the Appellate Division overturned both convictions because of various "errors and improprieties" by the prosecution prejudicial to the defendant. The court threw out the murder conviction altogether and ordered that Crimmins be retried on the manslaughter charge. Having served two years in prison, Crimmins was released, but in February 1975 the State Court of Appeals reversed the decision of the Appellate Court. (The Appeals Court did agree to throw out the murder conviction because the state could not prove beyond reasonable doubt that little Eddie Crimmins, found five days after his disappearance and too badly decomposed for autopsy, had in fact been murdered.) But it upheld the manslaughter conviction—although in order to do so it had to establish a new interpretation of the law. Formerly errors in trial procedure had been considered prejudicial to the defendant if there was a "rational possibility" that the jury would have acquitted the defendant if the error had not occurred. The Appeals Court now maintained that an error was prejudicial only if there was "significant probability" that without it the case would have gone the other way. Two dissenting justices argued that by accepting the new standard the court was "dangerously diluting the time-honored standard of proof beyond a reasonable doubt, cornerstone of Anglo-Saxon criminal jurisprudence," but the majority bounced the case back to the Appellate Division judges with orders that they look at it again; and, in light of the new standard applied by the higher court, the Appellate Division reversed its own reversal and declared that Alice Crimmins was indeed guilty of manslaughter. On May 16, 1975, she was returned to prison to continue serving out her five- to twenty-year term; and in December the Court of Appeals ruled that she could not appeal any further. It took a succession of district attorneys, a flock of underlings, thousands of police man-hours, three grand juries, two trials, a reinterpretation of appellate law, and ten years, but at last Alice Crimmins was put away.

Perhaps Alice Crimmins was guilty. Perhaps not. Certainly the fragmentary evidence did not prove her guilt beyond a reasonable doubt; but she was granted no presumption of innocence. It is not that anyone deliberately set out to convict an innocent woman, but that so many people—beginning with Detective Piering—almost immediately assumed she was guilty because she was "like that." That assumption skewed the initial investigation—the police had hours of tape recordings of Alice Crimmins in bed and no photographs of the window through which her children may have been abducted—and that assumption, picked up by an almost all-male press corps, colored everything that followed. Alice Crimmins touched a raw nerve not just in Detective Piering but in a troubled society just beginning to recoil from too much domestic togetherness. Even if Crimmins hadn't killed her children, said one reporter, she had plenty to feel guilty about. "*IF* she had been a faithful wife—and mother—whose primary concern was her home, her husband, and her children, there probably would have been no estrangement from her husband. *IF* there had been no estrangement, her husband would very likely have been at home on that fateful night. . . . *IF* her husband had been at home that night, the children might never have been abducted, might never have been murdered." But as they had in the twenties, women seemed to be seizing sexual prerogatives reserved for men. If Alice Crimmins had been the only nice Catholic housewife "sleeping around" in Queens, there would have been no need to make her a public example. But of course she was not.

Prosecutors, reporters, police, and jurors alike condemned her morals and never questioned those of the married men who were her partners in sex. Nor did they seem to find anything particularly odd in the behavior of husband Eddie Crimmins, who during their separation tapped Alice's phone, went to her apartment when she was away just to be around her "things," hid in the basement under her bedroom to listen to her have sex with other men, and by his own admission, exposed himself to little girls in the park. To women, Alice Crimmins was a home wrecker—a threatening woman freer than those traditional wives who clung, whether happily or not, to the security of house and husband. And to mothers—"good" and "bad"—she was sinister. Following up the prosecution theory that Crimmins had strangled Missy in momentary anger, the press asked over and over: "What kind of woman could do a thing like that?" A high school classmate said Alice couldn't have done it because she was "no different from the rest of us." But the press quickly found an answer in "that kind" of woman: a bleached blonde, a promiscuous ex-cocktail waitress—a woman totally unlike "the rest of us." Yet any mother, isolated day after day with her children, would know—if she could bear to think about it— that maybe, just maybe, she could do it too. Several more years passed before the statistics began to appear regularly in the newspapers: the figures on how many children had been beaten, burned, scalded, strangled, broken, and killed by mothers and fathers behind closed doors. But there were then thousands of women and men who did not need the statistics to know.

Only the New York Radical Feminists offered to support Alice Crimmins, and their offer was turned down by her attorneys. Crimmins was already under attack precisely because she was under no man's control or protection. Sexually, at least, she was a free agent, a threat to society. The last thing the Crimmins defense attorneys wanted was to have her identified with equally subversive feminists, although paradoxically the anxiety that provoked the war on Alice

Crimmins was undoubtedly riled by the renewed women's movement. Reporter Gross concluded: "The Alice Crimmins case . . . was perceived as frightening because the women's movement was just coming into existence when the case broke, and the implications—a housewife grown rebellious and out of control—terrified those who felt a stake in maintaining the status quo." Certainly Crimmins herself was no feminist. "Oh, I'm for equal pay for equal work," she said in 1971. "But not for all the far-out things. I don't hate men. I believe that women are put on this earth to serve men. A man should be dominant. I believe in women's liberation, but not at the price of my femininity." Only the Radical Feminists with their simple slogan, "Free Alice Crimmins," suggested the real problem: that "feminine" Alice Crimmins was, in effect, a prisoner of sexual politics.

In January 1976 Alice Crimmins became eligible for a work-release program and began work in a secretarial job. In March 1977 she became eligible for parole, but her application was denied because "taking into account the extreme seriousness of the offense," the parole board feared that "release at this time could promote disrespect for the law." In addition, the board doubted that she could "live and remain at liberty without violating the law." Then in August 1977 the New York *Post* in a front-page photo story broke the news that Alice Crimmins had spent Sunday—"as she has spent many balmy summer Sundays of her prison term—on a luxury cruiser at City Island." Crimmins, it seemed, like other prisoners in the work-release program, had every other weekend to herself; and she had been spending many of those weekends with Anthony Grace, a wealthy sixty-six-year-old contractor, the boyfriend who allegedly had sent her Colabella, the hit man. Grace testified for the defense at both trials, visited Crimmins regularly during her imprisonment, and as the *Post* soon discovered, married her in July 1977—with the requisite permission of correction officials. In a full page of telephoto shots of Crimmins in bikini and T-shirt "looking remarkably attractive for her 37 years," the *Post* tried to rake up the public anger that had sold so many papers over the years. The *Post* followed up the next day with a front-page story headlining the opinion of Queens District Attorney John Santucci: ALICE SHOULD BE BEHIND BARS. Beside a picture of Crimmins (now officially Mrs. Grace) about to enter her husband's white Cadillac, the paper quoted a juror who had helped convict her: "They should lock her up and throw away the key." Santucci announced his opposition to Crimmins's parole request, claiming that "this defendant has not served adequate time for the crime of which she was convicted." Over at the

Daily News, columnist Pete Hamill denounced that "smarmy" little story and jeered: "Santucci is running for reelection; he knows a great irrelevant issue when he sees one."

Then, at last, the newspapers gave it up. For the Alice Crimmins case, dredged up and recycled, was an embarrassment of history. Even the *Post* knew that the issue was no longer sex but class. Nobody cared anymore about Crimmins's bed partners; she was attacked not for sleeping with Anthony Grace (who cared whether they were married or not?) but for driving in a Cadillac, relaxing on board a "yacht." The Crimmins case had gone on too long. After twelve years even the most faithful tabloid reader began to ask: "Why do they keep picking on her?"

So, on September 7, 1977, Alice Crimmins Grace was paroled. The board delayed it as long as they could. They sent her for a psychiatric examination. Then they "exercised a seldom used option" and sent her for another psychiatric examination. Then, on September 9, 1977, they had to let her go. District Attorney Santucci tried to block the parole; a Queens assemblyman, who had been one of the prosecutors at the second Crimmins trial, blasted the decision. But it was perfectly legal; Crimmins, after thirty months in prison and nine months in the work-release facility, was free. Ironically, if she had never appealed her first conviction, she would have been eligible for parole six years earlier.

Alice Crimmins still wanted vindication, but her petition for a new trial was denied on November 1, 1977. So she remains a woman smashed in a society's shifting gears—too far ahead of her time for people to think her innocent, then too far behind for people to care if she were guilty. Many men made a lesson of her, and when they found (like John Santucci) that continuing the war on Alice Crimmins wouldn't win votes or promotions, they gave it up. But Alice Crimmins, unlike Ruth Snyder, never gave up; and she never lost track of what it had all been about. Before she was sentenced at her second trial she turned to the two prosecuting attorneys and said, "Anything you people have done to me in the past . . . anything you are doing to me now . . . and anything you may do to me in the future can't be worse than what was done to me six years ago when my children were taken from me and killed. And I just hope and pray the world will see all your lying and scheming against me. And I just hope and pray to have the chance to put you all down some day for what you are. . . ."

TOTALING WOMEN

1.

On March 9, 1977, Francine Hughes returned from business college to her Dansville, Michigan, home and put a frozen dinner in the oven for her husband, James. He didn't like it. Francine, he said, should be at home preparing meals for him, not running off to school. He beat her up, as he had done many times before; and to drive home his point he tore up her schoolbooks and term papers and forced her to burn them in the trash barrel. Twelve-year-old Christy Hughes called the police, who came to the house long enough to calm James down but declined, as they had many times before, to arrest him. They left James, tired from beating Francine, asleep in his bedroom. Determined to "just drive away," Francine piled the children into the family car. "Let's not come back this time, Mommy," they said. She carried a gasoline can to the bedroom, poured the contents around the bed where James lay asleep, backed out of the room, and set a match to it. The rush of flame sucked the door shut.

Francine Hughes drove immediately to the Ingham County sheriff's office, crying hysterically, "I did it. I did it." She was charged with first-degree murder.

Dansville adjoins East Lansing, home of Michigan State University and consequently of many social-action groups. Within two months feminists and other interested people in the Lansing area had formed the Francine Hughes Defense Committee to raise money and public awareness for her defense. They were careful to say that they neither advocated nor condoned murder, but they held that women confronted with violence have a right to defend themselves. They argued that "Francine Hughes—and many other women facing similar charges—should be free from the threat of punishment," for Francine Hughes was a battered woman.

At the time wife-beating was a growing feminist issue, following close on the heels of feminist attacks upon rape, a crime it resembles in many ways. Both rape and wife-beating are crimes of violence against women. Both are widespread, underreported, trivialized, and inadequately punished by the legal system. Both are acts of terrorism intended to keep all women in their place through intimidation. In fact, rape is often part of wife abuse, though so far only a few states acknowledge even the possibility of rape within marriage. The chief difference between the two crimes is that while the victim of nonmarital rape must live with a terrifying memory, the abused wife lives with her assailant. Rapists are, in Susan Brownmiller's phrase, the "shock troops" of male supremacy. Wife-beaters are the home guard.

American feminists took up the issue of wife-beating when they learned in 1971 of the work of Erin Pizzey, founder of Chiswick Women's Aid, the first shelter house in England exclusively for battered women and their children. Rainbow Retreat, the first American shelter for abused families of alcoholics opened in Phoenix, Arizona, on November 1, 1973; and in St. Paul, Minnesota, Women's Advocates, a collective that began with a phone service in 1972, opened Women's House to battered women and their children in October 1974. Rainbow Retreat, during its first two and a half years, sheltered more than six hundred women and children. In St. Paul the five-bedroom Women's House sheltered twenty-two women and fifteen children during its first month of operation; less than a year later Women's Advocates were negotiating to buy a second house. Across the country the shelter movement spread to Pasadena, San Francisco, Seattle, Boise, Albuquerque, Pittsburgh, Ann Arbor, Boston, New York. To open a shelter was to fill it beyond capacity almost overnight. Suddenly it seemed that battered women were everywhere.

While activists opened shelters, researchers and writers set about documenting the problem of wife-beating or, as it came to be called more euphemistically in the academic literature, "domestic violence." The records showed that 60 percent of night calls in Atlanta concerned domestic disputes. In Fairfax County, Virginia, one of the nation's wealthiest counties, police received 4,073 disturbance calls in 1974. During ten months in 1975–76 the Dade County Florida Citizens Dispute Settlement Center handled nearly 1,000 wife-beating cases. Seventy percent of all assault cases received in the emergency room at hospitals in Boston and Omaha were women who had been attacked in their homes. Eighty percent of divorce cases in Wayne County, Michigan, involved charges of abuse. Ninety-nine percent of female Legal Aid clients in Milwaukee were abused by men.

The FBI guessed that a million women each year—women of every race and social class—would be victims of wife-beating. Journalists Roger Langley and Richard C. Levy put the figure at more than 28 million. Some said that one in four women married to or cohabiting with a man would become a victim; others said one in three. In some areas the incidence seemed even greater. In California the experts said one of every two women would be beaten. And in Omaha, the Mayor's Commission on the Status of Women estimated that 95 percent of women would be abused at some time. There scarcely seemed need of additional evidence, so the same statistics began to turn up in every new account, but repetitious as they were, they showed all too clearly that wife-beating is a social problem of astounding dimensions.

It may always have been so. English Common Law gave husbands the right to chastise their wives, but the precarious Puritan colonies of New England assigned that right to the civil authorities. Individual husbands were forbidden to administer "stripes," while the state, which depended for its continued existence upon stable family life, took upon itself the task of mediating family disputes and meting out punishment. American reversion to a Common Law standard after the Revolution put the stick back in the husband's hand so that each man might keep his own house in order. In 1824 the Mississippi Supreme Court ruled that a man had the right to chastise his wife moderately "without subjecting himself to vexatious prosecutions for assault and battery, resulting in the discredit and shame of all parties concerned." By the mid-nineteenth century the ideal of domesticity brought further modification of the chastisement rule in the courts. A North Carolina court ruled not only that chastisement was the husband's right but that the state had no business interfering unless "some permanent injury be inflicted or there be an excess of violence." Otherwise the law was not to "invade the domestic forum or go behind the curtain" but rather to "leave the parties to themselves, as the best mode of inducing them to make the matter up and live together as man and wife should." Toward the end of the century, however, states began to repudiate the "revolting precedent," and by the second decade of the twentieth century courts found that society had progressed so much since Blackstone's "rude" age that a husband no longer needed a rod "to teach the wife her duty and subjection. . . . And the privilege, ancient though it be, to beat her with a stick, to pull her hair, choke her, spit in her face or kick her about the floor, or to inflict upon her other like indignities," was no longer "acknowledged by our law."

That change in the law was brought about partly through the unrelenting efforts of nineteenth-century feminists, for wife-beating is not a "new" issue. Behind all the women's movement struggles for temperance, married women's property rights, liberalized divorce, child custody, and suffrage lay the grim fact that dependent women and children were subject to physical and sexual assault. Behind the veiled nineteenth-century references to "indignities" and "brutality" stood the battering, sexually abusive husband. By the early twentieth century high rates of domestic violence and homicide impelled Dorothy Dix's argument for liberalized divorce laws.

But changing the law did not mean that the law would be enforced. When feminist agitation subsided after women got the vote, the issue was buried. And despite laws on the books specifically designating wife-beating as an assault like any other, the state unofficially continued its policy of noninterference simply by looking the other way. Throughout most of the twentieth century, wife-beating has been against the law, but the police, the courts, and public officials have winked at it.

Information about the problem, newly unearthed again in the seventies, began to turn up here and there. In June 1974 *Ms.* magazine reported on England's Women's Aid, and Karen Durbin discussed wife-beating in the *Ladies' Home Journal*; and in July, *Newsweek* opened a report on crisis-intervention training for police with an anecdote about a wife-beater who shot his wife moments after the police had "settled" the dispute and left the house. In the same year Betsy Warrior, a former battered wife who became a one-woman information clearinghouse on wife-beating, printed a pamphlet called *Battered Lives* that reached women's centers and women's bookstores around the country. In 1975 "The Assaulted Wife: 'Catch 22' Revisited," a report prepared for the Ann Arbor, Michigan, chapter of the National Organization for Women by two University of Michigan law students was widely circulated. The June issue of *McCall's*, citing that study, called wife-beating a major social problem requiring "public awareness"; and the New York *Daily News* noted that the problem of battered women was beginning to surface in New York City.

Public awareness should have increased dramatically in 1976. *Newsweek* reported on wife-beating in February, *Woman's Day* in March, *People* in May, *Do It Now* (a publication of the National Organization for Women) in June, and *Good Housekeeping* in July. By August *Ms.* could put a decorously battered face on its cover and devote the entire Gazette section of the magazine to a list of services and shelters. *Ms.* received so many letters in response to this issue that in December it published several of them along with additional notes on new projects. At the same time, *Ms.* editor Gloria Steinem was working with producer Joan Shigekawa of public television's "Woman Alive!" series on a show about battered wives, first aired in April 1977. San Francisco's small Glide Publications brought out Del Martin's *Battered Wives*, still the best book on the subject; and in November 1977, as Francine Hughes went to trial, Pocket Books republished it as an inexpensive paperback for national distribution.

Word had spread fast. So when the Hughes trial opened, Michigan feminists were prepared to make an issue of it. The issue would be self-defense.

In fact the issue already had been fought out in other contexts. After long and expensive litigation, Inez Garcia, the California woman who shot and killed a man who helped to rape her, was exonerated of murder charges in March 1977. Joan Little, the black North Carolina woman jailed for burglary, was cleared of murder charges in 1975 after stabbing the jailer who sexually abused her. And Yvonne Wanrow, a Washington State Colville Indian woman sentenced in 1974 to two twenty-year terms and one five-year term for wounding one attacker and killing another she believed to be a child molester and rapist, was finally granted a new trial in January 1977; she entered a guilty plea to reduced charges of manslaughter and second-degree assault and was sentenced to five years on probation. Both Garcia and Wanrow were convicted at their first trials despite their claims of impaired mental state and, in Wanrow's case, self-defense; but Garcia's second trial—like Joan Little's—was argued successfully on the basis of self-defense, and Wanrow's initial conviction was reversed partly on grounds that the jury had not been properly instructed on self-defense.

In that landmark decision the Washington State Supreme Court held that the jury instruction, drawn to the standard of a "reasonable man" (and incidentally couched in masculine pronouns), did not adequately represent a woman's perspective and consequently threatened to deny women equal protection under the law. Since the court's decision "made" law and established the "Wanrow jury instruction" in legal procedure, it is worth quoting at length.

> [The instruction as given by the trial court] leaves the jury with the impression the objective standard to be applied is that applicable to an altercation between two men. The impression created—that a 5'4" woman with a cast on her leg and using a crutch must, under the law, somehow repel an assault by a 6'2" intoxicated man without employing weapons in her defense, unless the jury finds her determination of the degree of danger to be objectively reasonable—constitutes a separate and distinct misstatement of the law and, in the context of this case, violates the respondent's right to equal protection of the law. The respondent was entitled to have the jury consider her actions in the light of her own perceptions of the situation, including those perceptions which were the product of our nation's "long and unfortunate history of sex discrimination." ... Until such time as the effects of that history are eradicated, care must be taken to assure that our self-defense instructions afford women the right to have their conduct judged in light of the individual physical handicaps which are the product of sex discrimination. To fail to do so is to deny the right of the individual woman involved to trial by the same rules which are applicable to male defendants.

Traditionally women who killed had been seen as insane, unnatural, or aberrant; but the Wanrow instruction made it possible to argue—as the Little, Garcia, and Wanrow defense teams did—that a woman who killed to save herself or her children from imminent danger of death or great bodily injury might be acting in a *reasonable* and *justifiable* manner.

In the trial of Joan Little and the second trial of Inez Garcia, jurors acquitted the women apparently because they were convinced that Little and Garcia did no more than any reasonable woman would do to defend herself under the circumstances. Now it seemed time to test whether jurors could be convinced that women had a right to defend themselves against the men who—according to the statistics— were most likely to murder them: their own husbands and lovers.

Even before the Wanrow appeal was won by Elizabeth Schneider and Nancy Stearns, attorneys from the Center for Constitutional Rights, it was clear to women working on wife-beating that the issue would eventually find its way to the courts. So in December 1976 when Roxanne Gay, a diminutive black woman from Camden, New Jersey, stuck a knife in the throat of her sleeping husband, 225-pound Philadelphia Eagles defensive lineman Blenda Gay, feminists thought they had a test case. Records showed that Roxanne Gay had phoned for police assistance at least twenty times during her three-and-a-half-year marriage, and neighbors told the press that whenever the Eagles lost a game Blenda Gay literally bounced his wife off the walls. She was once hospitalized with injuries and once signed and then dropped a complaint against him. A defense committee rallied to her support and at a benefit Gloria Steinem was photographed for *People* with Roxanne's attorney and her brother. In November, as Francine Hughes went to trial, *Ms.* published a brief account of the facts of the Gay case and an appeal for funds. But Roxanne Gay's trial was put off again and again as she underwent psychiatric testing. Blenda Gay's family claimed that Roxanne had always been a disturbed and violent woman; other observers believed that years of beatings and isolation brought on her severe suicidal depression. In any case, a sanity hearing in March 1978 found insufficient evidence that she had been, as she still maintained, a battered wife. Instead, four psychiatrists, all male, determined that she was a "nervous" and "suspicious" woman and that she "suffered from delusions that her husband, her family and police were plotting to kill her." The Camden police testified that she often complained of beatings, but her own attorney said there was "no evidence" that Blenda Gay beat his wife. Murder charges against her were dropped and Roxanne Gay was shuffled off to a New Jersey state hospital for the insane, officially listed as a paranoid schizophrenic.

While Roxanne Gay slipped into the oblivion of a state asylum, Francine Hughes took her place as a test case, championed by a feminist defense committee prepared to argue that she had acted reasonably in defense of herself.

There could be no doubt of Francine Hughes's credentials as a battered woman. In 1963 at age sixteen she married James, her high school sweetheart, and dropped out of high school in Jackson, Michigan. They moved to nearby Dansville, where James went to work as a bricklayer and Francine bore four children during six years of beatings and psychological abuse. At last in 1971 she divorced him and took the children back to Jackson. About six months later while James was visiting the children he argued bitterly with Francine, slammed out of the house, and drove straight into a near-fatal car crash that left him apparently ablebodied but unable to work and supposedly in need of care. His parents and Francine's own guilty conscience brought her back to Dansville to a house next door to the Hughes family. James, now permanently unemployed, spent time in both houses, letting both his mother and his former wife look after him, and the beatings began again. In 1976 Francine decided to get some job skills and then a job so that she could leave both James and the welfare rolls behind. James swore that if she left him he would track her down and kill her, but she enrolled in business college and confided to a classmate that she wanted to leave James and support her children herself.

Then on the evening of March 9, 1977, James tore up her books and told her he wouldn't allow her to return to school. And while the police summoned by the child were still in the house, he told her that he was going to kill her that very night. But the police, thinking it an "idle threat," left; and Francine killed James instead. Later a neighbor who described James as "a mean SOB" advanced the theory that "she got him before he got her."

Nevertheless, the method of the murder made the plea of self-defense problematical. Traditionally, deadly force in self-defense is supposed to be exerted against comparable deadly force. One man lunges at another with a knife. The second clubs the first with a tire iron he happens to have in hand, killing him. That's self-defense. But sneaking up on a sleeping man to set his room on fire seems to be another kind of move altogether, unless you see it clearly and fairly from the perspective of Francine Hughes, taking into consideration (as the law stipulates) all she knew and all she had learned to expect from this man who threatened to kill her. Yet the notion of the "preventative strike" so widely used in international conflicts seems unsporting and downright cowardly when applied to a battered woman who sneaks up on a man. Thus, Hughes's attorney, taking no chances, hedged on the self-defense principle so clear to feminists and argued instead, much like the attorneys of seduced-and-abandoned maidens a century ago, that the woman was temporarily insane. He argued further, however, that Hughes suffered temporary insanity not for any reasons familiar to legal tradition but *because* she was a battered woman. Evidence that she was battered was admitted in that it went to show her state of mind; and in the end the jury acquitted her on grounds of temporary insanity. She went through some routine psychiatric tests and was freed.

For feminists it was a hollow victory, and even presiding Judge Ray C. Hotchkiss told reporters that the real issue in the trial had never been joined. "All of a sudden," he said, "we realize that we have thousands of people who have had no recourse under the law. Where are we when these people are crying out for help? Self-defense is a real issue, but it was never really covered in the trial." But the Hughes case was to have far greater repercussions than Judge Hotchkiss or the defense committee could have guessed.

Even before the trial began, the defense committee brought the case to national attention. In September, ABC's Sylvia Chase, covering the story for the Saturday network news, said that Michigan feminists hoped to make Francine Hughes "a symbol for battered women, the way Joan Little became a symbol for rape victims," but that the case was still "a legal longshot." A week after the trial Francine Hughes and her attorney Aryon Greydanus appeared on a talk show originating from WABC in New York and hosted by Stanley Siegel. (Siegel went bluntly to the point: "All right, when I come back [from a commercial break], I'm going to ask you a very important question. After thirteen years of public humiliation, beatings, kicking the baby, causing your dog to freeze to death, I'm going to ask you what you felt when you realized that you had set fire to your husband. . . .") Siegel mistakenly thought that the Hughes case was "precedent shattering" and would make "legal history"; but attorney Greydanus, who had chosen the temporary insanity defense precisely because it is the oldest and safest defense for a woman, told him that the only significance of the Hughes case lay in the social conditions surrounding it, in the "enormous amount of women who are undergoing this type of abuse in the United States." Unless local authorities and the federal government did "something" for battered women, Greydanus warned, "The same thing is going to happen, and . . . a jury again will acquit a woman for doing the same thing."

Greydanus's warning was meant to enlist public support for battered women, but it corroborated the worst fears of some men. A neighbor who had once pulled James off Francine when he was beating her in the yard nevertheless thought that Francine "should sit in prison the rest of her life. . . . If she gets out of this," he told reporters, "there'll be a lot of dead guys lying around." A friend of James Hughes told reporters that Francine Hughes's acquittal "means open season on men." If Francine Hughes could get away with murder, what was to deter other women from trying the same thing?

That question bothered the national press. Columnist Richard Cohen of the Washington *Post* headlined: VIGILANTE JUSTICE BACK IN WOMEN'S MOVEMENT. *Time*, in an article entitled "A Killing Excuse," noted that "an array of women have managed to walk away unpunished after killing their husbands or even former husbands." *Time* cited three women as members of this "array," including Hughes and Gloria Maldonado of Chicago, whose shooting of her drunken husband in the presence of witnesses while he was attacking their eight-year-old son with a shoe was so clearly an act of self-defense that the state's attorney did not even prosecute. But the issue for *Time*, as it had been for James Hughes's friends and neighbors, was not punishment but deterrence of others. Sheriff Lawrence Schmies of Waupaca, Wisconsin, where Jennifer Patri was about to stand trial for the murder of her husband, was quoted as saying, "I wonder if these people [feminists] know what they're doing. If they get their way, there's going to be a lot of killings." By January 1978 *Newsweek* was able to discern in the cases of "Wives Who Batter Back" a "trend" that might well create "a new legitimacy for violent retaliation," a trend that "smacks uncomfortably of frontier justice."

Curiously enough the old frontier town of Bismarck, North Dakota, took the acquittal of Francine Hughes calmly. In fact District Judge Benny Graff, who presided in Steele, North Dakota, at the 1975 trial of Katherine Rohrich, told the Bismarck *Tribune* that he thought the Rohrich case provided the very precedent the feminists failed to get in the Hughes case. Katherine Rohrich shot her husband four times as he slept, but only after she and her eleven children had endured years of battering, and only after she had been denied the help of local law-enforcement personnel several times. "Insanity was never pled in our case," said Judge Graff. Instead he submitted the case to the jury on grounds of self-defense and compulsion, defined as "a force that would render a person of reasonable firmness incapable of resisting the pressure." To Judge Graff it seemed perfectly reasonable that Katherine Rohrich, whom he described as a woman "pushed to the wall," would shoot her husband under the circumstances; and so it must have seemed to the jurors who acquitted her. Commenting in an editorial on the cases of Hughes and Rohrich and another young Bismarck woman denied police protection from a threatening man who subsequently murdered her, the Bismarck *Tribune* speculated that there must be some way to protect threatened and abused women without waiting for them to kill or be killed.

But the *Tribune* was almost alone in its concern for women's right to equal protection under the law. Other publications joined the influential *Time* and *Newsweek* in their concern that the lives of men might be imperiled if women, claiming an equal right to self-defense, could "get away with murder." The backlash was under way, and in retrospect it became clear that the real significance of the Francine Hughes case was this: it marked the turning point in the development of a feminist issue, the beginning of the backlash, the moment at which the anxious social fathers said "Enough!" and closed ranks to turn it all around.

A county prosecutor in Cleveland, Ohio, where Kathy Thomas was awaiting trial for shooting her common-law husband, stated that he didn't want the law "to give a woman a license to kill someone." (Thomas was convicted of murder and sentenced to fifteen years; in nearby Painesville, Patricia Hale, convicted of murdering her husband, drew fifteen to twenty-five years.) A Berkeley law school professor claimed that juries were "stretching the law to exonerate battered wives" and that acquittals might "herald an open hunting season on husbands." During 1978 a few women writers—notably Andrea Dworkin in *Mother Jones* and Karen Lindsey in *Viva*—continued to explain the plight of the battered woman, but such informative articles designed to raise public awareness were out. Press coverage was devoted instead to frightening summaries of cases—invariably numbered as "at least a dozen" though usually only two or three were specified—in which murderous women had "got off scot free."

Before long, even some women who had worked on behalf of battered wives were subscribing to the backlash argument that the potential risks to men from findings of justifiable homicide far outweighed the actual present jeopardy of women and children. Maria Roy, founder of New York City's Abused Women's Aid in Crisis and editor of a source book on battered women, told *New York Times* reporter Anna Quindlen that "the publicity the acquittals have received presents a danger because of the tendency some women may have to see that as a solution." Quindlen herself noted that the acquittals "confirmed some men's worst notions about the women's movement." The real danger, however, was not that some women might turn to murder to solve their problems but that frightened men would assuage their "worst notions about the women's movement" by further depriving women of equal protection under the law, and wasting the lives of thousands of women and men in violence.

By 1979 the controversy seemed to have subsided, but the anxiety remained. Acquittals of women who killed their husbands were still news. In March *New West* ran the story of "Chano & Blanche," romantically subtitled "A Ballad of love, death and the law in Tulare County." It was not a ballad at all, but the grim story of battered and sexually abused Idalia Mejia, who shot and killed her husband, Ralph, in December 1977, and after three trials was cleared of murder charges. In April *Family Circle* printed "The Case of Patricia Gross," the story of a battered Port Huron, Michigan, woman who shot her husband during an attack in May 1978 and was acquitted in September. Ironically, such articles sympathetic to the women driven to defend themselves contributed to the general—and mistaken—impression that more and more women were walking away from murder.

Nationally circulated newspapers, such as *The New York Times* and the Washington *Post*, also reported the outcome of cases that seemed to be of national significance, and for the moment at least, that meant cases of women acquitted of murder. So when Jeanette Smith was acquitted in Gaylord, Michigan, in April 1979, of the second-degree murder of her abusive husband, both *The Times* and the *Post* reported the story. The *Post* opened its account with word that "for the third time in two years, a Michigan jury has acquitted a defendant who claimed spouse abuse as her defense against charges she killed her husband." That was news. But neither paper mentioned the Michigan convictions of Elsie Monick in 1975 or of Violet Mae Allen or Hazel Morris in 1977. Nor did they cover a case much closer to home: the murder conviction in Ithaca, New York, of Bernadette Powell, less than a month before the acquittal in Michigan of Jeanette Smith. Those women who did *not* walk away from murder were not newsworthy.

Acquitted women, on the other hand, were news precisely because they were the exception and not the rule; but reporting only acquittals left the reading public with the mistaken notion that women were "getting off" with increasing frequency and were rarely if ever convicted of murder. Newspaper accounts listing women acquitted often mentioned Evelyn Ware and Sharon McNearney, tried and acquitted of murdering their husbands in Orange County, California, and Marquette, Michigan, respectively, during November 1977. The accounts did not mention results of some other trials that took place during the same month: Sharon Crigler, convicted of manslaughter in Tacoma, Washington, for shooting her ex-boyfriend and sentenced to ten years; Carolyn McKendrick, convicted of third-degree murder in Philadelphia for shooting her live-in boyfriend and sentenced to five to ten years; Claudia Thacker, convicted in Port Orchard, Washington, of second-degree murder in the death of her husband and sentenced to five to twenty years; Carol Ann Wilds, convicted in Evansville, Indiana, of second-degree murder in the shooting death of her husband and sentenced to fifteen to twenty-five years.

Other press reports noted the case of Marlene Roan Eagle, acquitted in South Dakota in July 1976 on grounds of self-defense and defense of her unborn child (she was in the seventh month of pregnancy at the time), although her battering husband was armed "only" with a broken broom handle. In the same month, the first-degree murder conviction of Barbara Jean Gilbert in Maryland went virtually unnoticed. (First sentenced to life plus five years on a concealed-weapon charge, Gilbert was granted a new trial on grounds of her attorney's incompetence, and in July 1978 she was retried, convicted of involuntary manslaughter, and handed the maximum sentence: eight years.) Along with Francine Hughes, Evelyn Ware, Sharon McNearney, and Marlene Roan Eagle, Bernestine Taylor of Rockford, Illinois, was often listed among the "array of women" more or less routinely acquitted of murder. Both Bernestine Taylor and Idalia Mejia, the subject of the *New West* article, were acquitted in December 1977. In that same month Hazel Kontos was convicted of first-degree murder in Alabama and sentenced to life imprisonment. In Chattanooga, Tennessee, Lillian Quarles was convicted of second-degree murder and sentenced to ten years. And in Waupaca, Wisconsin, Jennifer Patri was convicted of manslaughter. Many other women were already in prison: Shirley Garcia, Shirley Martin, Jenna Kelsie. The list kept lengthening. In March 1979 twenty-year-old Martha Hutchinson was sentenced to fifteen years after vigorous prosecution by a district attorney who feared "open season on the men of Marion County" (Florida) if Hutchinson were not severely punished. The national "trend" toward acquitting "wives who batter back" was not quite as definitive as the public was led to believe.

The case of Jennifer Patri illustrates quite clearly how the public was misled by selective journalism. On March 26, 1977—just two weeks after Francine Hughes set fire to her husband's bedroom—Jennifer Patri killed her estranged husband, Robert, with two blasts from a .12 gauge shotgun. Then she got rid of his car, wrapped up the body, buried it in a shallow grave, cleaned up the bloodstains, and set the house on fire. When the fire marshal spotted a human hand sticking out of a pile of debris, he called the sheriff. Jennifer Patri was charged with first-degree murder and held in jail on $100,000 bond for three months before her brother and her dead husband's brother found an attorney—a big-city lawyer from Milwaukee named Alan Eisenberg— to effect her release and represent her. Eisenberg enlisted the support of Wisconsin NOW chapters, hoping that the case might "do as much for the battered woman as the Joanne [*sic*] Little case did for the rape victim." Perhaps hoping that it might also do something for the career of Alan Eisenberg, he encouraged publicity. And since the Patri trial was to open only a month after the acquittal of Francine Hughes, he got it.

The *Time* article on women who "managed to walk away unpunished after killing their husbands," printed just after the Hughes acquittal, discussed the upcoming Patri case, describing Jennifer Patri as a thirty-two-year-old "happily active" farm wife who "taught Lutheran Sunday school, presided over a local P.T.A. and supervised a busy hog farm." It described husband Robert as a hard-drinking man who slapped her around, "subjected her to agonizing sexual abuse," and molested her twelve-year-old daughter. The article omitted only one fact that gained significance during the trial: when Jennifer Patri shot her husband—during a quarrel over his right to "visit" his daughters—Robert Patri, armed with a butcher knife, was threatening to shut her mouth, once and for all. Instead, the article noted that when Robert Patri (who had been living in town with another woman) showed up to "take the girls on a day's outing—only Jennifer was waiting—with the loaded shotgun nearby." In the accompanying photo Jennifer Patri smiles coolly with attorney Eisenberg smirking behind her.

The trial itself, which was not covered in the national press, was not an easy one. Officials to whom Jennifer had confessed testified that she told them her husband never hit her, and the Milwaukee *Journal* reporter noted snidely that "feminist groups *had* campaigned in support of Mrs. Patri"—as though their discredited efforts were ended. Robert Patri's mother and brother testified in Jennifer's defense, but Jennifer herself changed her story of where the shooting took place; and she couldn't remember anything that happened between the time she shot her husband and the time she was arrested. The defense case didn't seem to go according to expectations, and in the end the jury reached a verdict of guilty of manslaughter. NOW representatives who attended the trial called the verdict a great defeat, for it found neither premeditated murder nor self-defense but a kind of half-baked compromise that made little sense of the facts of the case.

In January Jennifer Patri made the national press again, this time in the *Newsweek* article on "Wives Who Batter Back," which featured another photo of the defendant and her smiling attorney. Eisenberg called the manslaughter conviction "a complete and total victory," though an unnamed Waupaca resident claimed that Patri probably would have "gotten off" altogether if the city-slickers had kept out of it. A publisher advanced $50,000 for the story of her life, and both Joanne Woodward and Cloris Leachman reportedly professed interest in playing Jennifer Patri in a movie. Then Jennifer Patri passed from the national press. To the readership of *Time* and *Newsweek* she remains a cool woman who shot her husband in the back after an "argument," hid the body, and later enjoyed a complete and total victory in the courtroom.

For Jennifer Patri the story continued. She was sentenced to ten years in prison and began serving her sentence at the Taycheedah Correctional Institution. Then, in December 1978, a year after her murder trial, the prosecutor brought her to trial on an arson charge for having set fire to her house after the shooting. The jury found her guilty as charged; but the following day, in a second phase of the trial to determine sanity, they found her *not* guilty by reason of insanity. Defense psychiatrists testified that indeed Patri had been temporarily insane when she set the fire after the shooting, but the jury went the experts one better; they decided that she was still insane and should be transferred from prison to a state mental hospital. And there Jennifer Patri, having won "a complete and total victory," remains.

2.

The anxious reaction against women who apparently got away with murder took many forms. It showed up in the familiar phenomenon known as blaming the victim. Freud's theory of masochism, popularly believed to refer simply to the enjoyment of pain, offered a ready formula for turning the tables on the battered woman. So battered women reported the same remarks at every stage of the legal process: "What did you do to provoke him?" "C'mon, you know you like those love taps." And always they heard the challenge: "If you don't like it, why don't you just leave?" Every popular article on battered women contained a compulsory section entitled "Why Does She Stay?" and academic sociologists studied the same question. Supporters of battered women spent an inordinate amount of time responding to that question with all the obvious answers. Women are likely to be both emotionally and economically dependent upon their husbands. Often they have no marketable job skills, and even an employed woman can expect to make only fifty-seven cents to a man's dollar on the present market. She may still love her husband who, in the periods between beatings, may be a perfectly nice guy. She probably has been brought up to believe that making a marriage work is her duty as a woman; a failed marriage is her fault. She probably has several children and no place to go. She may realize that in leaving home she can lose all legal claim to her property and even to her children. She may be terrified of her husband who perhaps threatens, as James Hughes did, to track her down and kill her.

Psychologist Lenore Walker, an expert witness at the homicide trials of several battered women, devised a theory of "learned helplessness" to explain the failure of many battered women to effect change in their lives. According to Walker, battered women facing their husbands' random, unpredictable violence, soon learn that there is no necessary connection between what they do and what happens to them. A husband may beat his wife for overcooking an egg, or for undercooking it, for turning on the TV or for turning it off, for talking or for keeping still. Many battered women report that they are attacked while they sleep. The battered woman who seeks help will relearn the lessons of helplessness: the police won't arrest, the prosecutor won't prosecute, the judge won't sentence, and too often even family and friends will not help or even believe her. Under these circumstances the woman finds that whatever she does to help herself may boomerang or at best come to nothing. Why go on trying? Andrea Dworkin, once a battered wife, described the descent into passivity:

> I remember withdrawing further and further into that open grave where so many women hide waiting to die—the house. I went out to shop only when I had to; I walked my dogs; I ran out screaming, looking for help and shelter when I had the strength to escape, with no money, often no coat, nothing but terror and tears. I met only averted eyes, cold stares

and the vulgar sexual aggression of lone, laughing men that sent me running home to a danger that was at least familiar and familial. Home, mine as well as his. Home, the only place I had. Finally, everything inside crumbled. I gave up. I sat, I stared, I waited, passive and paralyzed, speaking to no one, minimally maintaining myself and my animals, as my husband stayed away for longer and longer periods of time, slamming in only to thrash and leave. No one misses the wife who disappears. . . . Wives, after all, belong in the home. Nothing outside it depends on them.

Andrea Dworkin, however, is no longer a battered wife but a feminist writer; and the mass of research on why battered women accept abuse obscures the most obvious answer: they don't. In a study unduplicated in the United States, English psychiatrist J. J. Gayford, interviewing a group of women who left home and returned, found that twenty-seven women went back because their husbands promised to reform and eight because they felt love or sorrow for their husbands; seventeen returned because of threats and further violence, thirteen because their children were still in the home, and fourteen returned to the home (a common shelter not to be confused with the man) because they had no other refuge. In Gayford's study, then, thirty-five women returned to their husbands for wishful reasons, while the other forty-four cannot be said to "stay" willingly with the men. In this country researchers from the Western Michigan University School of Social Work reported that "most" of the battered women they studied in Kalamazoo, Michigan, had "called the police for physical protection. Over two-thirds had received counselling. . . . Over one-half had consulted with attorneys and almost half turned to divorce" and in addition "two-thirds of the victims reported relying on family and friends for emotional support or to provide emergency shelter." The surprised researchers noted that "the victims in the sample reported here do not fit the popular conception of people who do not really want help." Another study of battered wives found that 80 percent of them were divorced or divorcing. Many women, fearing marriage failure and led on by husbands' promises to reform, endure battering situations for years, but the popular image of the beaten wife who passively stays and stays and stays is not borne out by rising divorce rates, jammed police switchboards, overcrowded shelters, and husbands shot, stabbed, and burned to death.

Battering husbands, on the other hand, are usually described by their wives as extremely possessive people. Usually they persuade or force their wives to stop working or going to school. They are cool or rude to family and friends, gradually cutting their wives off from social contacts. Some keep the car keys; some permanently sabotage their wives' cars. Others make sure their wives never have enough cash to go out. Some won't let their wives use the telephone; James Hughes used to rip the wires out of the wall if he thought Francine had used the phone, and another husband beat the telephone to splinters on the concrete floor. Some lock their wives in; others follow them when they leave the house. Some make their wives literal prisoners. During a five-month marriage, Gary Bartosh of Charlotte, North Carolina, never let his wife, Eileen, out of his sight except for some "monitored trips to the bathroom." When he finally turned his back, she shot him. A study that analyzed how victims and offenders in marital homicide perceived their sex roles found that men were more than ten times as likely as women to define their spouse as "an object of personal property" and to treat her accordingly. And it is hardly surprising that men who do so may be killed.

Homicide is a last resort, and it most often occurs when men simply will not quit. As one woman testified at her murder trial, "It seemed like the more I tried to get away, the harder he beat me." Gloria Timmons left her husband, but he kept tracking her down, raping and beating her; finally when he attacked her with a screwdriver, she shot him. Patricia Evans filed for divorce, but her husband kept coming back to beat her with a dog chain, pistol-whip her, and shoot at her. At last, after she had been hospitalized seven times, she shot him. Sharon Crigler evicted her live-in boyfriend, but he insisted on getting back into the apartment, even when she threatened to shoot. Jennifer Patri filed for divorce, but her husband kept coming back to threaten her and to visit his daughters, at least one of whom he had sexually molested. Ruth Childers was divorced and her husband had remarried, but he would not stop arguing and threatening her about property. Bernadette Powell was divorced, but her ex-husband decided to terrorize her one more time. Janice Strand was forced to return to her husband when he threatened her parents' lives. Patricia Gross's husband tracked her from Michigan to Mississippi and threatened to kill her relatives there to force her to return to him. Judy Austin's live-in boyfriend chased her from California to Arizona to Wyoming. Kathy Thomas's boyfriend forced her to come home at gunpoint. Mary McGuire's husband, teaching submission, made her watch him dig her grave, kill the family cat, and decapitate a pet horse. When she fled he brought her back with a gun held to her child's head. Martha Hutchinson's Klansman husband threatened to kill her if she left him, burned a cross on her lawn when she did, and chased her through the woods, shooting at her with a pistol and a shotgun. Agnes Scott's husband found her and cut her up seven years after she left him. There are cases on record of men still harassing and beating their wives twenty-five years after the wives left them and tried to go into hiding. If researchers were not quite so intent upon assigning the pathological behavior to the women, they might see that the more telling question is not "Why do the women stay?" but "Why don't the men let them go?" But mired in reactionary anxiety, even feminists carry on valiantly, pointlessly, asking and answering the wrong question.

That anxiety—which exaggerates what women are "getting away with" and blames them for creating the problem in the first place— also rallies the forces of reaction around the bright, deceptive flag of "equality." Feminists who call for equal protection under the law are accused of seeking special favors. "Why are women now claiming more lenient laws in self-defense, when they are claiming equality in every other area?" asks a female prosecutor. A public defender objects to any change in the concept of self-defense which he describes as "basic to civilized society": "It allows for *a man* to preserve his own life and only to take the life of another when *his* own life is in imminent danger." Attorneys for the Women's Self-Defense Law Project, formed in April 1978 under joint sponsorship of the Center for Constitutional Rights and the National Jury Project to develop legal strategies and assist defense attorneys throughout the country, counter that self-defense law has always been shaped by men to reflect male experience, and as the Wanrow decision recognized, the experience of women in a country with a history of sex discrimination is certain to take a very different shape.

Little boys are taught to be physically aggressive; little girls are taught to be demure. Most boys, like it or not, receive athletic training, while women have been barred from sports programs until very recently, and they still are "channeled" away from contact sports. And for thousands of men the armed forces provide a kind of finishing school in violence. (Many battered women complain that their husbands learned in the service how to inflict great pain without leaving visible marks.) This difference in physical and psychological training, coupled with the usual differences in size and strength between marriage partners, makes self-defense a different matter for women. When one man attacks another with his fists, the court assumes that they are more or less evenly matched and generally does not allow the man attacked to counter with a weapon. To acknowledge that a 110-pound woman might need a weapon against her 255-pound husband, or that she might try to catch him off-guard is not special pleading but facing facts. To a small woman untrained in physical combat, a man's fists and feet appear to be deadly weapons, and in fact they are: many women miscarry after a beating, and most women killed by their husbands are not shot or stabbed but simply beaten and kicked to death. The woman who counters her husband's fists with a gun may *in fact* be doing no more than meeting deadly force with deadly force.

The standard-bearers of equality, however, contend not only that women and men are evenly matched in physical combat, but that men might in fact be getting the worst of it. Perhaps the most ludicrous part of the backlash against battered wives was the discovery of yet another social problem of staggering proportions: battered husbands. It was a phony issue from the outset, and although some community-based wife-abuse centers decided to offer services to men too, the "movement" for battered men produced not a single shelter or program; it recruited not a single volunteer. But in the media it got a big play.

The sociologists who first published research on household violence—Richard J. Gelles, Murray Straus, and Suzanne Steinmetz—were concerned with overall levels of violence within the family. The first book on the subject, written by Gelles and published in 1974, was called simply *The Violent Home*. Although his data indicated that violence was far more often used *against* women than *by* them, Gelles was not primarily concerned with who was beating up whom or why. So it was left to Suzanne Steinmetz to publicize the fact that wives sometimes physically abuse their husbands. Her academic paper on "The Battered Husband Syndrome," prepared with funding from the National Institute of Mental Health and scheduled for publication early in 1978 in *Victimology*, a scholarly publication, was released to the press in the fall of 1977 and turned up in a UPI wire service story headlined: STUDY BACKS UP SUSPICIONS HUSBAND IS MORE BATTERED SPOUSE.

Steinmetz supported her contention that "husband-beating constitutes a sizeable proportion of marital violence" by citing all those old comic strips (drawn by men) in which Maggie greets Jiggs at the door with a rolling pin. In her own research studies she recorded roughly equal numbers of occasions when wives and husbands hit, pushed, and threw things; but she overlooked the context of the events and left out altogether the types of physical attack battered women most often experience: kicking, stomping on, biting, choking, pulling out hair, burning, cutting, bashing the head into a solid stationary object.

Steinmetz's speculative paper drew the immediate fire of four other scholars (Elizabeth and Joseph Pleck, Marlyn Grossman, and Pauline Bart), who pointed out in a paper titled "The Battered Data Syndrome" that Steinmetz was not above actually twisting data to match her thesis. As proof that husbands are equally victimized, for example, Steinmetz cited criminologist Marvin Wolfgang's classic Philadelphia study finding that wives killed their husbands almost as often as husbands killed their wives; but she neglected to mention Wolfgang's corollary finding that the women were seven times more likely than the men to be acting in self-defense. Her critics concluded that Steinmetz's work posed "a most serious ethical issue for our profession," but the damage had already been done. Workers for battered women suddenly found themselves running up against the Steinmetz report at every turn. Battering, they were told, is not a women's problem. Support for aid to battered women fell off.

The media, ever mindful of a good diversionary issue, jumped on the battered-husband bandwagon; and so did Suzanne Steinmetz's colleagues, who must have noticed that she had become a minor celebrity. So in March 1978 when *Time* devoted a full page to the plight of "The Battered Husbands," Murray Straus joined Steinmetz in asserting that "women are as prone as men to use violence on their mates." And Richard Gelles, in another distortion of the Wolfgang study, jumped in to state, "Men and women have always been equal victims in family violence. Fifty percent of the killings are men. Fifty percent are women. That hasn't changed in at least 50 years." (The *Time* article concluded with the erroneous report that England's Erin Pizzey had established a house for battered men, when in fact the Chiswick Men's Aid house served *battering* men.) But by this time, Steinmetz had come up with some figures: each year "at least 250,000 American husbands are severely thrashed by their wives. . . . The most unreported crime is not wife beating—it's husband beating." Writers Langley and Levy picked up the Steinmetz exaggerations and added a few of their own for a chapter on "Battered Men" in their 1977 book *Wife Beating: The Silent Crisis.* Soon they joined Steinmetz on the talk-show circuit, and in July Langley wrote an article on "Battered Husbands" for the Sunday magazine of the New York *Daily News,* which featured on the cover a handsome male model bruised in five colors. Langley and Levy upped the number of battered men to 20 percent of American husbands, and Dr. Joyce Brothers reported their "amazing conclusion" in her syndicated column. When Langley and Levy kicked the number up to 12 million, even Steinmetz quit the field, calling the figure "preposterous" and leaving Langley to do the David Susskind show on his own.

That show, first aired in February 1978 and still periodically re-run, was perhaps the apex of the battered-husband crusade. But viewers who had read Langley's magazine article or Langley and Levy's book must have been somewhat disappointed to hear the carefully masked battered husbands tell the same familiar personal experiences. Did the "movement" actually consist only of the same three guys? And how was one to account for the changes in their stories? One guest recounted the same incident of husband-beating Langley had quoted in the book: without provocation his wife slapped him and scratched his face with her fingernails, drawing blood. "My reaction was more bafflement and hurt than anger," he had told Langley. But on television he described his reaction differently: "I picked her up by her string tie and blouse and lifted her three feet off the ground, shoved her into the bathroom wall, and said, 'If you do that again, you will be annihilated. Literally annihilated. I will knock you from here to Thursday.'"

The battered-husband bandwagon passed, dragging casualties behind it. Sociologists Steinmetz, Straus, and Gelles, all of whom had done reputable work before, looked foolish. The legitimate needs of those men who actually are physically abused by their wives were discredited. And most important, the battered-husband hype which equated husband-beating with wife-beating obscured and trivialized the massive problem of wife abuse. Yet, in the midst of the reactionary brouhaha, feminists found levelheaded support in an unexpected quarter. In response to a letter urging establishment of shelters for the countless battered husbands who had no recourse but suicide, Ann Landers, the most widely read advice columnist in the country, said flatly: "I'm sure more men beat up their wives than the other way around, but if you think there is a need for a Shelter for Battered Husbands, gather together those of like mind and get one going. I'm working the other side of the street, Mister."

Despite the backlash, feminists continued to work for battered women. The shelter movement grew although many women began to wonder why women and children should be forced to exile themselves to refuges while their assailants remained at liberty. Why not lock up the battering men and let the women and children remain in their own homes? To this end, New York City battered wives filed suit accusing police and courts of denying them their right to equal protection under the law. The suit, which eventually was joined by more than seventy women, charged police with unlawfully refusing to arrest assailants, and court personnel with unlawfully denying the women access to a judge in order to seek a court order of protection. The State Supreme Court refused to dismiss the case, and in June 1978 the police department settled out of court, agreeing to arrest men who committed felonious assault against their wives. The police also agreed to notify complaining wives of their rights and help them get medical aid; and if the husband had left the scene, they agreed to search for him as they would any other suspect. This landmark case, the result of three years' work by six attorneys and twenty-five law students, paralegal workers, and secretaries, is being duplicated in other cities.

In the end, New York police simply agreed to perform the duties prescribed by their own professional leadership. A 1976 directive of the International Association of Chiefs of Police specifically differentiated common family disturbances that involve no physical violence from wife-beating. Crisis-intervention skills would be required in both cases, the chiefs' directive explained, but when a wife-beating attack takes place, the police officer is supposed to be "prepared to conduct an assault investigation." The directive continued: " 'Family disturbances' and 'wife beatings' should not be viewed synonymously; nor should wife abuse be considered a victimless crime or solely a manifestation of a poor marriage. A wife beating is foremost an assault—a crime that must be investigated."

Nevertheless, programs to train police in crisis intervention, rather than assault investigation, have proliferated since the sixties under the leadership of New York psychology professor (and former policeman) Morton Bard, who believes that police should no longer be simply "enforcers of the law" but should become "managers of human crisis and conflict." That training is undoubtedly useful to officers in responding to the estimated 50 to 71 percent of family disturbance calls that do not involve physical violence. In practice, however, police have applied their new intervention skills across the board, treating the crime of assault as just another family argument. Standard police-training manuals counsel officers to avoid arrest at all costs and to discourage the woman complainant by telling her (often erroneously) how difficult and expensive it would be for her to follow through on prosecution. A Michigan police bulletin cautions officers to smooth things over by appealing to the woman's "vanity" and reminds them that "the officer should never create a police problem when there is only a family problem."

This policy of not arresting men clearly discriminates against women, but the police offer various excuses. Officers often claim—and advise wives—that arresting the battering husband will only make him angrier and more dangerous, but since the police have never made it a practice to arrest wife-beaters, they have no data to verify or disprove this opinion. (Law-enforcement data on wife-beating are conspicuously missing or mixed up; in one Indiana county, the sheriff records wife assaults, if at all, along with complaints of dogs barking.) Battered wives often report that when police leave the decision to press charges up to the wife, the husband grows angrier and more threatening, for he holds her solely responsible for his arrest; but on the other hand, when police officers themselves make the arrest, wives report that husbands sometimes are cowed, and at least for a short time, maintain good behavior.

Secondly, the police claim that their nonarrest policy saves lives—police lives. Ever since Bard first began developing his crisis-intervention training programs, the estimates of police casualties on domestic calls have grown. Bard himself claimed that about "22 percent of police deaths occurred while intervening . . . in disputes *often* between family members" and that "about 40 percent of police injuries occurred in the same way." It struck many women as odd that the police should be excused from doing their job on grounds that it was too dangerous, but now it seems that the danger to police has been exaggerated all along.

It is hard to determine from the FBI statistics just how many officers have been killed or injured on domestic disturbance calls because those calls fall under the general heading of "Disturbance," a category that also includes street-corner fights and highly dangerous "man-with-a-gun" calls. During the period 1968–77, however, FBI statistics indicate that most officers were killed responding to robbery and burglary calls (287) or in attempting other arrests (241). Almost as many officers lost their lives in traffic pursuits (121) as in disturbances of all kinds (175). A 1979 study by Lieutenant James J. Fyfe of the New York City police department suggested that the false belief of many officers that family quarrels are the most dangerous assignment—a belief originally developed to justify the nonarrest policy and fostered by intensive training in domestic crisis intervention—has led the police into greater danger by leaving them unprepared to deal with "routine" robberies which in fact are far more dangerous. During the five years covered in Fyfe's study (1970–75) nearly one-third of the incidents in which police fired their guns were robberies. By contrast, only 12 percent of firings were precipitated by disputes of all kinds, from barroom brawls to wife assaults. And the single most frequent cause of police officers' deaths was not domestic-dispute calls but suicide.

Nevertheless, many women are reluctant to push for arrest and prosecution of wife-beaters. To white middle-class liberal women, the position smacks uncomfortably of law and order. They don't know whether arrest actually deters battering, but they do know that the impact of arrest falls disproportionately on poor and nonwhite men. Yet the number of poor and nonwhite women who joined in the suit against New York police and courts indicated that they want legal protection from "their men." Those women, often seen as "natural" and even willing victims of ghetto violence or the "ethic" of machismo, are least likely to receive police protection and most likely to suffer under the law if they act in self-defense. To such women the change in policy of the NYPD was heartening, not only because it might have an immediate effect upon the lives of thousands of battered women of all classes in New York City, but also because "New York's Finest" might set an example for other police departments to follow. Yet few women would argue that locking men up is a final solution.

Other agencies seem even more reluctant than the police to aid battered women. In Congress, the Domestic Violence Act of 1978, sponsored by representatives Barbara Mikulski, Lindy Boggs, and Newton Steers, and senators Wendall Anderson and Edward Kennedy, was killed off in the House. Wary of taxpayer rebellion, some congressmen were unwilling to start another federal program to deal with a "local problem," while other poorly informed legislators thought that the bill's euphemistic title, "The Domestic Violence Act," referred to political terrorism within the United States. The bill, which would have provided $15 million in its first year for abused "spouses" of both sexes—just about the same amount of money Congress had earmarked for the 1980 Olympics—failed to get even a simple majority.

Other agencies of government masked their inaction behind new liberal programs. The generously funded Law Enforcement Assistance Administration of the Justice Department, for example, continued through its grants program to foster police training in crisis intervention. Critics pointed out that the process of dispute mediation, adopted from labor negotiations, works only when the parties enter the proceedings willingly and from roughly equivalent positions of power. Urging a bruised and bleeding woman who wants to make an assault complaint to "negotiate" with her assailant is both ridiculous and unlawful in that it effectively denies the woman her right to protection from bodily harm. Many police officers themselves objected to the programs, saying they would rather be cops than social workers. An Oakland, California, patrolman argued that if the policeman's role in an assault was only to recommend a marriage counselor, he "might as well give the guy a gun to shoot his wife." And his view is borne out by the Kansas City police department study which showed that in 85 percent of spouse murders, the police had "intervened" at least once before; and in 50 percent of the cases police had "mediated" disputes at least five times before. Supporters of police crisis intervention, on the other hand, claimed that women who were treated once to crisis intervention hardly ever required it again, especially if the police were accompanied (as they are in some "advanced" programs) by social workers or clergymen prepared to offer marriage counseling, whether or not it is requested. Indeed, it is hard to imagine that a beaten woman who called the cops and got a preacher would ever call them up again.

In 1979, LEAA, which had funded shelters and other programs for battered women in the past, decided instead to encourage programs for batter*ing* men. The rationale for this change in emphasis was that the "problem" of wife-beating could best be eliminated by attacking it at the source: men. Women's advocates who favored arrest and prosecution of wife-beaters agreed that the heart of the problem lay in male violence; but the new programs for batterers were to aim not at punishment but at understanding and rehabilitation. What the law defined as a crime, LEAA redefined as a "problem."

Unfortunately, programs to reform batterers promised little success. All earlier studies indicated that battering men "communicated" with their fists and couldn't voice their feelings, a hitch that made them unlikely to succeed in the verbal process of counseling. Secondly, the preliminary studies indicated that battering men—who come from all social classes and walks of life—are not "sick" in any recognized clinical sense; for the most part their friends, their employers, and their counselors describe them as regular guys. And while counseling might prove helpful in individual cases, the number of wife-beating men in the country—estimates ran as high as 50 percent of the male population—made it unlikely that any definitive character structure or pathology would be found among them.

To many women the therapeutic approach is itself suspect, since psychology tends to look at "problems" from the perspective of the men who invented the field. Typically, a 1964 Freudian study of battered wives in Framingham, Massachusetts, who charged their husbands with assault, found that the wives were aggressive, masculine, frigid, and masochistic, and that a husband's assaultive behavior serves "to fill a wife's need even though she protests it." Too often, it seems, psychology overrules the "protests" of women. In December 1978 twenty-six-year-old Lynn Ditter charged her estranged husband, David, with two counts of sexual assault and one of assault and battery in what would have been a landmark case in Nebraska law, testing whether it is illegal for a husband to rape his wife. The case was never brought to trial, for in January 1979 David Ditter, free on bond, shot and killed his wife. Even after Lynn Ditter went into court on January 5 to report that her husband was constantly following and threatening her and to ask that his bond be revoked, the judge continued bond on the strength of a report from a psychiatrist at the Nebraska Mental Health Clinic: "Our investigation has not revealed any indication that Mr. Ditter should be considered assaultive or dangerous to be at large at this time. He presents every evidence of good emotional and physical self-control at this time."

By far the biggest obstacle to curing men of their problem is that most wife-beaters think they have no problem. Invariably it is the wife in a violent household who seeks out marriage counseling or therapy; and invariably it is the husband who quits after one or two sessions or refuses counseling in the first place. Ray Lee, who supervised the short-lived Men's Aid house in London, reported that some men came to the house only as a ploy to coax their wives to come home, while others pronounced themselves "cured" and left after a week or two. The three psychiatrists who made the 1964 study of battered wives in

Framingham actually had set out to study battering husbands. They staffed a court-affiliated clinic established by the Massachusetts Division of Legal Medicine to provide psychiatric evaluation and treatment for assaultive men; but the thirty-seven batterers referred to the clinic during its five years of operation refused to cooperate. It was their wives who had problems, the batterers said; and the psychiatrists—for lack of anything else to do—studied the cooperative wives and agreed. In 1978 an Indiana prosecutor, James Kizer, refused to prosecute for murder a man who beat and kicked his ex-wife to death in the presence of a witness and raped her as she lay dying. Filing a manslaughter charge instead, Kizer commented, "He didn't mean to kill her. He just meant to give her a good thumping." And in Florida a fifty-nine-year-old man who kidnapped, beat, raped, and sodomized a fourteen-year-old girl sought to clear up the criminal charges against him by offering to marry her. Clearly the hardest part of any program for batterers was going to be convincing them that they had done something wrong. But any program for batterers—like the earlier attention to battered husbands—would divert money and concern from the countless battered women who every day were being kicked and punched and beaten to death, and from those few on the edge of despair who saw no way out but to defend themselves.

Some few concerned observers call for "an absolute prohibition of violence" in any form. Others are pessimistic. Some charge that the criminal-justice system itself fosters domestic assault as a "primary source" of violence and crime in the next generation; after all, without violence and crime, criminal justice would be out of business. Marxists argue that domestic violence always will be promoted by capitalism because wife-bashing provides an emotional outlet for the exploited workers. Feminists know that open violence against women, urged on by pornographic propaganda, is the last weapon, as it was the first, of male supremacy.

Scholars continue research into the causes of violence. Sociobiologists look to the genes and testosterone; psychologists blame castrating wives and overprotective mothers; social psychologists talk of environmental stress; and sociologists go on counting the gross numbers of pushes, punches, and swats. Marxists name capitalism, clergymen the loss of faith, and conservatives maintain that whatever the cause of violence, we must not interfere with the sanctity of the family. On one point everyone agrees: violence is learned by example and bequeathed from one generation to the next. Therefore it seems imperative that society do something. The testosterone people are resigned, but other researchers speak hopefully of full employment, the elimination of poverty, and the rehabilitation of 30 million wife-beaters. And in the meantime, women who kill their husbands come into court to face the backlash.

3.

Ruth Childers ran up against that backlash when she went on trial for murder in December 1978 in Benton County, Indiana. She was charged with shooting her former husband, Clifford. All the witnesses to the shooting, whether they testified for the prosecution or for the defense, agreed almost entirely in their descriptions of what happened at the Childers farm on August 18, 1978. Ruth and her teenaged sons, preparing to move to a new home, were loading odds and ends of furniture and farm equipment onto a rented truck when the man who had recently purchased the farm from Clifford Childers claimed that some of that property belonged to him. Ruth thought that under the terms of the divorce agreement the property belonged to her, as in fact it did, but she was willing to wait for an authoritative opinion before removing it; the new owner contacted Clifford Childers and the sheriff. Clifford arrived near-drunk and arguing. Ruth told him to wait for the sheriff and went into the house to phone her lawyer. She got a busy signal, and while she waited to try again, her daughter reported that Clifford was unloading the truck. Ruth reached for a shotgun kept over the door and walked to the truck to confront Clifford. "You've interfered once too often," she told him. "Now get out of that truck and wait for the sheriff." But Clifford lunged toward her and she stepped backward and stumbled. The gun went off. The ambulance was slow in coming, and the hospital miles away. Clifford Childers died on the operating table.

Against the murder charge, Ruth Childers's attorneys raised two defenses: first, that Ruth Childers, who feared her ex-husband after eighteen years of battering, acted in self-defense in taking up the gun to hold him off, and second, that the gun then discharged by accident. Her attorneys hoped that the accident defense would reduce Ruth's culpability to involuntary manslaughter, and that the plea of self-defense would then cancel out all criminal liability. Since the gun went off by accident, she wasn't guilty of murder, they argued; and since she had picked up the gun in self-defense, she wasn't guilty of manslaughter either. The case was well prepared and presented, the self-defense argument a model of women's self-defense law. But the jury didn't buy it.

They apparently accepted the expert testimony of English gunsmith David Trevallion that the "murder weapon"—a discount-store shotgun, the equivalent among long guns of a "Saturday-night special"—was defective in several respects and had a hair trigger. Trevallion was able to make the gun fire by tapping it on the floor and witnesses testified that it had discharged of its own accord while it was being carried away from the scene of the shooting. But the jury apparently did not accept the expert testimony of psychiatrist Elisa Benedek, who explained why Ruth Childers, suffering from "battered-woman's syndrome," picked up the gun to defend herself. Women might get away with that sort of thing elsewhere, but not in Benton County. The jury found Childers guilty of involuntary manslaughter, and Judge R. Perry Shipman handed down the sentence prescribed by statute: five years.

Judge Shipman could have reduced the term to two years or suspended it altogether, but he didn't—even though Ruth Childers, as the mother of four minor children who would suffer during her imprisonment and as a previously law-abiding citizen highly unlikely to repeat her offense, qualified for a suspended sentence under every provision of the Indiana statute. The last two people charged with murder in Benton County, both men, seemed in comparison to have gotten off rather easily: one who shot his wife was convicted of voluntary manslaughter and given the minimum sentence of one to ten years, while the other, the man who beat his wife to death and raped her while giving her "a good thumping," was never tried for murder (despite what the sheriff called "a lot of evidence") but allowed to plead guilty to manslaughter and given a six-year sentence.

The problem for Ruth Childers, as it is for most battered women, is that at every step of the legal process the prevailing standard of justice is male. As attorneys Elizabeth Schneider and Susan Jordan have written:

> Standards of justifiable homicide have been based on male models and
> expectations. Familiar images of self-defense are a soldier, a man pro-

tecting his home, family, or the chastity of his wife, or a man fighting off an assailant. Society, through its prosecutors, juries, and judges, has more readily excused a man for killing his wife's lover than a woman for killing a rapist. The acts of men and women are subject to a different set of legal expectations and standards. The man's act, while not always legally condoned, is viewed sympathetically. He is not forgiven, but his motivation is understood by those sitting in judgment upon his act since his conduct conforms to the expectation that a real man would fight to the death to protect his pride and property.

The body of law, made by men, for men, and amassed down through history on their behalf, codifies masculine bias and systematically discriminates against women by ignoring the woman's point of view. Today the law still is largely enforced, interpreted, and administered by men; so it still works in the interests of men as a group. Women, schooled like men to good citizenship, accept the law's male bias as objective justice; women lawyers, judges, and jurors, taught the same rules, usually uphold the same male standard. And whether that male standard constitutes conscious sex discrimination or the innocent side effect of a shared male point of view, the result for women is the same: they are deprived at every step of equal protection under the law; and even those women who receive fair and equal treatment are likely to be thought of as having gotten away with something.

Often that male bias shows up at one stage or another of the legal process in the exercise of "discretion." That built-in flexibility which allows a judge or a prosecutor or a police officer to use "better judgment" is essential, experts agree, to a legal system that tries to deal fairly with individual cases. But since discretion usually is exercised *by* men (or by women trained to the male standard), it is usually exercised *for* men, for the male standard. Judicial discretion, repeatedly exercised to protect the same male interests, becomes a mask for the law's underlying systematic discrimination against women. The characteristic male slant of legal discretion tilts every case of homicide committed by battered women.

Bias may begin with the police, most often as a matter of departmental policy. Police chose not to arrest Jeanette Smith's husband for beating her; they were still in front of the house when he turned on her again and she defended herself with a kitchen knife. Police chose not to arrest James Hughes, despite his threat to kill Francine on the very night that she killed him instead. The Benton County sheriff took almost half an hour to respond to the last call to the Childers farm, perhaps to give the couple time to battle it out and cool off; and Ruth Childers, waiting for help, tried to hold off her ex-husband with a defective gun.

Even when the male assailant is arrested, most cases of wife assault never get as far as the prosecutor's office. Criminal-court officers tell complaining women that they belong in family or civil court; civil-court officials direct them to the criminal court. And in most jurisdictions, the prosecutor's policy of nonprosecution parallels the police policy of nonarrest. Prosecutors argue that the cases are a waste of time because women habitually drop charges, although there is no evidence that battered women drop charges any more frequently than do other complainants who know their assailants. On the other hand, there is plenty of evidence that women who want to press charges are discouraged or actually prevented from doing so. And many women, like Lynn Ditter, have been killed by the men they have tried unsuccessfully to prosecute. Some officials, such as prosecutor John Meyers of Tippecanoe County, Indiana, believe that whether women want to press charges or not is irrelevant. Since it is generally agreed that violence is harmful to society and that it is learned at home, prosecutors have a duty to prosecute in the interest of the people, no matter what the woman wishes. Adopting a "tough policy" toward wife-beating and child abuse, Meyers argues that "we have to start somewhere if we're to do anything about the patterns of violence that are passed on from generation to generation."

But few prosecutors are as zealous as Meyers, except when a battered woman resorts to homicide. In one extraordinary case, a prosecutor responded sensibly, if belatedly, to redress old grievances. The New Orleans district attorney's office in July 1978 dropped charges against Viola Williams, who shot her common-law husband, Harold Randolph, twice in the head and neck and eleven times in the back. Pretrial investigation determined that Randolph had beaten her for ten years, shoved her face into an anthill, and once pled guilty to a simple battery charge after clubbing her with a baseball bat; at the time she shot him, he was attacking her with a knife. She shot twice in self-defense, she said, and then eleven times more for what he had done to her. Assistant District Attorney Sheila Myers, announcing the decision not to prosecute, acknowledged that Williams had "a valid self-defense claim. . . . I'm sorry the system didn't help her sooner," she said. "We have evidence that she sought help many times before."

Far more often prosecutors respond by enforcing what they take to be a blanket prohibition on homicide. An eager Brooklyn assistant district attorney, Edward McNew, obtained a 1978 manslaughter indictment against Agnes Scott by withholding information from the grand jury. Jurors wanted to know why Agnes Scott plunged a kitchen knife into her estranged husband, but when Scott's thirteen-year-old daughter testified that her father was "getting ready" to hit her and her younger brother at the time (having already beaten Agnes with a leather belt) the assistant district attorney instructed the jurors to disregard the girl's perception. When jurors asked if the apartment in which the killing took place was Agnes Scott's legal residence, he told them the question was irrelevant. He didn't tell them that Agnes Scott had started criminal proceedings against her husband six months earlier when he broke into her apartment; nor did he mention that four months before the killing, Richard Scott attacked Agnes in the street with a knife, and that he was under a court order to keep away from his family. The assistant district attorney commented on her failure to appear before the grand jury in terms that made her silence suspect, when in fact he had not notified her of her right to give testimony.

Luckily for Agnes Scott, her attorney, Margaret Ratner, moved to have the indictment quashed; and the New York State Supreme Court dismissed it, ruling that the prosecutor's instructions to the grand jury were "patently and fatally defective." Justice Julius Helenbrand ruled that the grand jury had received "little, if any, enlightenment" from the prosecutor. He called McNew's failure to explain the law concerning the justifiable use of deadly force "not a mere irregularity or a harmless procedural defect" but "a substantive prejudicial denial of due process."

Sometimes the woman's own attorney, applying the male standard of justice, acts against her interest. One woman drew an attorney whose confidence in winning her release was undimmed by any previous experience with criminal law. Without bothering to inform his client, he rejected the prosecutor's offer to let her plead guilty to manslaughter in exchange for a short sentence, a bargain she would have accepted. The attorney lost the case, and his client served eight years for an accident. In Seattle, Gloria Timmons at nineteen had been raped, beaten, and burned with scalding water by her estranged husband. In January 1973 while she was hospitalized with injuries sustained when he threw her down a flight of stairs, he came to the hospital and beat her up again. Restrained by hospital personnel, he was arrested and released to await trial; he came after her again with a screwdriver and she shot him once with a .22 pistol. She was charged with murder, and despite ample evidence of self-defense, her attorney convinced her to plead guilty to manslaughter. She served five and a half years of a one to twenty-year sentence for a "crime" that never should have been brought to trial.

The law itself, which varies from state to state, may be even harder on women in some jurisdictions. In Massachusetts Roberta Shaffer was convicted of manslaughter for the 1971 shooting of her fiancé, John Ferruzzo, who was threatening to beat her and her little boy, as he had done before. She fled to the basement of her house to join her son and daughter, and when Ferruzzo kept coming, she shot him. Massachusetts law, however, requires that the defendant retreat as far as possible to avoid violence; and Roberta Shaffer had only retreated as far as the basement. Shaffer argued that she could not retreat farther with her young children, and she would not leave them behind; but in 1976 the Massachusetts Supreme Court upheld her conviction. Ironically, in almost any other state Roberta Shaffer could have been acquitted. Most states find no duty to retreat from one's own lawful residence; and in Michigan a wife's conviction for murdering her husband was reversed because the judge had failed to instruct the jury that the defendant was not required to retreat from an attack in her own home.

Often it is the judge who feels that the jury has been unduly sympathetic to the defendant and exercises his discretion on the side of "law and order." One woman was convicted in a midwestern state of involuntary manslaughter after shooting her husband during a beating. He had beaten her repeatedly, and on the night of his death he locked her in the house, smashed the telephone into fragments, and beat her severely. When she thought he was going to attack the baby, she shot him. The jury's verdict was not unsympathetic; they had been moved by the testimony of the dead man's mother who asked that her daughter-in-law not be punished. She was an exemplary wife and mother, the older woman said, while since his return from the army her own son had been violent and "not himself." Nevertheless, in January 1972 the judge handed down the maximum sentence: ten years. Subsequently the public defender appealed for a reduced sentence, citing the defendant's excellent record of employment and community service and the fact that she had two small children at home. The state's assistant attorney general asked the Supreme Court not to reduce the sentence on the grounds that "sympathy should not stand in the way of justice," but the court found the sentence excessive and ordered it cut in half. That made her eligible for parole after one year, but the parole board—another body with discretionary power—ruled that her community was "not ready" for her return and although she was an exemplary prisoner she was held for another year.

In Tacoma, Washington, Sharon Crigler, a twenty-year-old unmarried mother, was sentenced to ten years after being convicted of first-degree manslaughter for fatally shooting her ex-boyfriend through her apartment door, which he was trying to enter. In sentencing her, Judge James Ramsdell announced that it was impossible for him to find any sympathy for her because she "desired" to remain on welfare instead of going to work. The heavy sentence meant that she must serve at least five years before becoming eligible to apply for parole.

In Maryland Barbara Jean Gilbert, after two trials, was finally convicted of involuntary manslaughter in the death of her husband, who had beaten her for fifteen years. Although the parole and probation board, which kept tabs on her through the long ordeal of two trials and an appeal, pronounced her conduct as citizen and mother of four "exemplary" and asked for probation, and the prosecuting attorney declined to ask for a jail sentence, Judge Samuel Meloy handed down the maximum sentence: eight years. "You have snuffed out a life," he said. "Therefore the court has the right to inflict pain and deprivation on you." The district attorney, greatly upset, observed that since Gilbert didn't need to be rehabilitated and didn't need to be deterred from further criminal behavior, "it comes down to punishment."

In Chattanooga, Tennessee, in December 1977, in the first aftermath of the Francine Hughes case, a judge warned the jury that they would be setting a "dangerous precedent" if they acquitted Lillian Quarles of the murder of her husband. Dutifully, the jury convicted her of second-degree murder and the judge sentenced her to ten years. Quarles claimed to have acted in self-defense as her husband beat her with a chair, the last attack in fifteen years of marital brutality. During those years Lillian Quarles suffered broken vertebrae, broken ribs, premature childbirth induced by beatings during pregnancy, and the loss of sight in one eye; her husband had no recorded injuries. Nevertheless, the judge, in pronouncing sentence, observed: "This battered wife syndrome is just another cause, just a new word for your old fighting couple. . . . I think she was a battered wife, but he was a battered husband."

In the case of Ruth Childers the judge chose to exercise his discretion by not exercising it. Despite many possibilities open to him under the statutes to temper her sentence, he simply prescribed the basic term. In sentencing her, Judge Shipman observed that a judge often will explain why he decides to assign a particular sentence. And sometimes he won't. A judge, he said, does not have to explain himself if he doesn't want to. He didn't.

The discretion of law-enforcement officials is influenced by other considerations besides sex. Class is a factor, and race. So if middle-class white women like Jennifer Patri, Ruth Childers, and Barbara Jean Gilbert are treated unfairly, poor women of color haven't a prayer. In fact, the success of the self-defense argument often rests not on the facts of the case but on the color of the "criminal." Sharon Crigler, Agnes Scott, Patricia Evans, Carolyn McKendrick, Gloria Timmons, Bernadette Powell, Mattie Bryant, Beverly Ibn-Tamas, and Kathy Thomas are all black. Black women have less claim to self-defense because in the eyes of white jurors they are not real "ladies" whom men should refrain from hitting. Simply by being black they assume the risk of being targets of black male violence; and in racist minds that assumption of risk seems to relieve the police of any responsibility to protect them or the court to consider their perceptions. So the black woman who kills in self-defense is likely to be seen as just another violent black person, shooting it out. In New Jersey, in May 1979, Bulesa Gibbs was convicted of atrocious assault and battery (which carries a possible sentence of seventeen years) for shooting her husband, even though he survived and testified that she had acted in self-defense when he moved to drench her with boiling water. Ironically, the criminal-justice system, which often is eager to believe that black men are naturally violent and threatening, is willing to give them the benefit of the doubt *only* when the people they attack are their black wives and girl friends.

The male standard pertains at every level from the precinct to the Supreme Court. It is manifest in discriminatory laws and in discriminatory exercise of discretion by police, prosecutors, judges, and jurors alike. It makes criminal justice for women whimsical, punitive, divisive, and unjust.

Bernadette Powell had a hard time from the beginning with her husband, Herman Smith. He drank too much and often beat her up, but people did come to her aid now and then. Her younger brother Guy-dell, when he stayed with her, heard the beatings and ran to call the police. Her big brother Oscar intervened and slugged it out with Herman. A sympathetic female attorney helped Powell obtain orders of protection from the Family Court and finally a divorce. The police in the community of Vestal, New York, came to the house whenever they were called. Lieutenant Richard Fundis, who suffered two cracked ribs trying (and succeeding) to arrest Smith, testified for Bernadette Powell.

Even after the divorce, Bernadette and Herman quarreled because Bernadette, who had custody of their seven-year-old son, and Herman, who had visitation rights, did not see eye to eye on how the child should be brought up. The resentment grew until the night of July 8, 1978, when she went to pick up the boy at a house where Herman Smith was drinking and playing cards. Smith came away with her, saying he'd drive her back home; then he pulled out a gun, the same kind he had been known to use in street fights. He drove for several hours, threatening to have her "pumped full of heroin" so he could get custody of the child; then he registered at a motel on the outskirts of Ithaca, New York, harangued her for another hour at gunpoint, and fell asleep. Bernadette Powell said that she was trying to take the gun from her ex-husband's pants so she could flee, when he started up and she pulled the trigger. He died almost instantly of a single .22 caliber bullet through the heart.

Despite the murder charges filed against her, Bernadette Powell seemed confident. Neither she nor her nonchalant attorney was quite prepared for the case the prosecutor presented against her. District Attorney Joseph Joch produced a string of incriminating witnesses to testify to the animosity between Bernadette and her former husband; but most damaging was the testimony of one man who said he had sold the murder weapon to Bernadette Powell and another who placed the salesman (though not Powell) at the scene of the alleged transaction. Trial proceedings, sometimes out of the presence of the jury, indicated that the first man once battered his wife into the hospital, while the second was charged with a series of assaults upon women, including two charges of rape then pending against him. Bernadette Powell, who had known that someone was scheduled to give such evidence against her, fled the courtroom in hysterics because she had been expecting to see an old enemy whose animosity and lies she could discredit; instead, the chief witness against her, the supposed gun salesman, was a man she had never seen before, and she had no defense against his allegations. The defense attorney hinted to the jury that the cooperation of the men who testified against Powell might have been secured in exchange for some "consideration."

In the end it came down to their word against Bernadette Powell's. The jury would have to choose whom to believe. To help them in making that choice, District Attorney Joch set out with enormous vigor to discredit the character of Bernadette Powell.

The defense, to show the jury that Powell was too terrified for herself and her child to escape from her ex-husband during the long night's drive, brought in evidence of the beatings she suffered during her marriage; but prosecutor Joch counterattacked with innuendo. Powell, he suggested, enjoyed being tied up and beaten; she got her sexual kicks that way. "Do you know what a masochist is?" he asked her. "Are you a person that likes to be hurt?" "No, sir," she said. "I am not." When Powell's brother described an attack he had broken up, Joch asked about Herman Smith: "Was his penis out?" Joch argued that no man would do the damage attributed to Herman Smith— he once destroyed $5,000 worth of property—if he were not provoked. He portrayed Powell as a nagging wife, always after Smith for more money, always manipulating him by threatening to withhold either sex or his son—or both. As the trial went on the attacks grew more and more vicious. The character assassination of Bernadette Powell went far beyond the evidence and far beyond the interest of the people in securing justice. Herman Smith, as District Attorney Joe Joch portrayed him, was a man who never got an even break from the castrating, manipulative wife who alone provoked him so unmercifully that he retaliated with violence. Yet there on the stand sat Powell's divorce attorney with records of all the orders of protection issued by the Family Court and her own memory of the bruises. And there sat burly Lieutenant Fundis, an experienced police officer and former amateur wrestler, to describe how his ribs were cracked by poor victimized Herman Smith.

All the while, locked in the files of the New York Supreme Court, was a private and apparently unrelated document: a transcript of proceedings only a month before when complainant Marie de Jong-Joch obtained a divorce from District Attorney Joseph Joch after almost nine years of marriage. In the uncontested proceedings the district attorney's wife alleged that

in or about November 1974 . . . December 6, 1974 . . . March 8, 1975 . . . May 1975 . . . April 15, 1975 . . . May 1976 . . . August 1976 . . . October

1976 ... December 1976 ... March 5, 1977 ... June 7, 1977 ... June 18, 1977 ... August 17, 1977 ... at the marital home ... at the marital home ... in the bedroom ... at the marital home ... at the marital home ... at the marital home ... in the bedroom ... in the den ... in the bedroom ... in the driveway ... in the bedroom ... at the marital home ... at the marital home ... in the automobile ... at the marital home ... at the marital home ... defendant hit and beat the plaintiff about the head with his fists and hands, causing plaintiff to fall to the floor while holding her young child ... brutally and violently pushed the plaintiff ... brutally and violently beat the plaintiff about her head and face ... repeatedly hit and beat the plaintiff about the face and body ... struck the plaintiff and struck the son of the parties ... violently grabbed and pushed the plaintiff ... brutally struck the plaintiff ... maliciously directed his automobile toward the plaintiff ... repeatedly pushed ... repeatedly hit ... pushed ... hit ... struck ... punched ... dragged ... hit. ....

Beaten-wife Bernadette Powell, zealously prosecuted by the same Joe Joch, was convicted of second-degree murder and sentenced to fifteen years to life in prison.

Downstate the influential *New York Times* did not report Powell's case, but in April the paper reported the acquittal of Jeanette Smith in Michigan; and in May 1979 in a story headlined RIGHT OF WOMEN TO SELF-DEFENSE GAINING IN "BATTERED WIFE" CASES: POWERFUL STRATEGY FOR BATTERED WIVES it reported the acquittals of Diane Barson (who also tried to kill herself) in Houston, and Cynthia Hutto in Charleston, South Carolina. Toward the bottom of the page the writer quoted Detroit attorney Marjory Cohen as saying: "There's a real backlash ... on the part of the public. People think any woman can kill her husband and get away with it." But *The Times* article itself could only have the effect of adding to the backlash. What was becoming known as "the Francine Hughes syndrome" seemed—in the newspapers at least—epidemic.

In fact, homicides committed by women declined somewhat in the last twenty years, while a woman's chances of becoming a murder *victim* steadily increased. In 1960 one white woman and eleven black women in each one hundred thousand became homicide victims. By 1973 the numbers had risen to three white women and sixteen black women—and they were still going up. One of every four murder victims is a woman. Nine out of ten murdered women are murdered by men. Four out of five are murdered at home. Almost three out of four are murdered by husbands or lovers. Almost none are killed by strangers.

On the other hand, studies suggest that at least 40 percent of women who commit murder do so in self-defense. And most women who kill, whatever their reason, are punished, though women sometimes receive seemingly short sentences in recognition of the great provocation that caused them to defend themselves. Much less publicized is the fact that men sometimes get away with murder. Battering husbands who kill their wives often are allowed to plead guilty to manslaughter and given short sentences. In Prince Georges County, Maryland, a man who shot his wife in the face with a .20 gauge shotgun because she forgot to lock the door pled guilty to second-degree murder and was given a suspended sentence by Judge Audrey E. Melbourne because the murder was "a singular act—out of character."

In New Hampshire the State Commission on the Status of Women, a group whose sole recorded achievement is the designation of the *lady*bug as the official state insect, turned down a proposal to shelter battered wives on the grounds that wife-beating was *caused* by feminism. One of the commissioners said, "Those women libbers irritate the hell out of their husbands." In fact, the battered woman who kills her husband is likely to ignore feminism or oppose it. Battering may happen to any woman at any time, but many battered women marry in their teens and give up their own education or work. When marriage is not the perfect haven they've been led to expect they blame themselves; many battered women report studying Marabel Morgan's influential *The Total Woman*, the bible of self-abnegation, to learn how to please their husbands or boyfriends and stop the beatings. Then they learn that their behavior has little influence on his self-triggering violence; and in desperation they reach for the butcher knife.

Women who kill their battering husbands or lovers almost always express great remorse and sorrow. They say they still love the dead man and grieve at his loss. Some feel so guilty and depressed that they try to take their own lives, or say that they would if they did not have children to care for. But at the same time, many of them experience an exhilarating sense of release. "Even when I knew I would have to go to prison," said one woman, "I felt as if a stone hand had been lifted off my head." Another said, "Suddenly I knew that I could take a walk, call my mother, laugh—and it would be all right. For the first time in eleven years, I wasn't afraid." Another said, "While I was out on bail waiting for trial, even though I'd done such a terrible thing, the kids and I had fun for the first time in years." Some women experience a new sense of themselves when people begin to treat them with a certain deference. "Even the sheriff, who laughed off the beatings for fifteen years, suddenly can't do enough to help me," one woman reported. Many of them use their painfully acquired self-respect to aid others through programs for battered women. Their message is always the same: "Get out—you don't have to take it." And some women use their power directly. One woman, who served eight years for shooting her husband to death, was asked what she would do if she found out that her daughter was being battered by a husband or boyfriend. "I think I'd just take the man aside and have a little talk with him about nonviolence," she said. "And then I'd tell him who I am."

SEVEN

WOMEN'S RIGHTS AND WRONGS

1.

On March 10, 1980, when Jean Harris pulled the trigger of her .32 caliber Harrington & Richardson in the bedroom of Dr. Herman Tarnower in Purchase, New York, I was on vacation.

Friends sent me the initial reports of the shooting, saying the case was right up my alley. When taken into police custody, Harris reportedly had "severe bruises on her face and arm"; and her attorney, Joel Aurnou, implied that she might have killed in self-defense. "We have not ruled out the possibility that Jean Harris might be a victim," he said. But those early reports also described a "new girl in the ball park": Lynne Tryforos, the "young, exotic-looking and beautiful assistant" at the Scarsdale Medical Center, long "involved" with her boss, the society cardiologist whose 1979 diet book made him a multimillionaire.

The killing rated headlines because the victim was a famous man. Who hadn't delivered at least two weeks of her/his life into the hands of the Scarsdale Diet Doctor? And the alleged murderer was an upper-middle-class lady (Smith '45), headmistress of Virginia's ritzy Madeira School for girls. The press, assuming that whatever happens to "important" people must be important, seemed obliged to give it significance. When Tarnower's neighbors hinted that the killing capped a lovers' triangle, reporters began to call it a "classic case."

Yet it seemed to me almost from the outset that the case was at once far too predictable and far too unusual to be significant. "Now," I thought, "we'll hear endlessly about woman's helpless passion for her man, about slavish devotion and jealousy and unrequited love." That was the predictable part; but because jealousy is in fact a motive that seldom impels women to murder, the Harris case seemed atypical of women's homicides and therefore unlikely to reveal much beyond itself.

In January 1981, while Jean Harris took the stand in a Westchester courtroom to tell her story to a jury of eight women and four men and to a regiment of reporters and eminent female authors, I sat on the edge of an uncomfortable plastic chair in the overheated officers' lounge of a prison in Indianapolis, Indiana, and listened to the stories of women confined to that stark compound for ten years or fifteen or more. These women had helped me by sending information for this book, and because no woman in prison ever has enough visitors, I went to see them. All of them were killers.

Some killed by accident; meaning merely to prevent or to stop a beating, they delivered death instead through a chance blow or a hair trigger. Others, like Carol Ann Wilds, struck quickly in self-defense. "Fuck that baby," Gary Wilds had shouted, punching his wife's belly, distended by pregnancy. "I'll kill that baby, too!" Then she snatched his gun and pulled the trigger again and again until the bullets were spent. Some few women painstakingly planned ahead. Tiny, gaunt Joyce DeVillez, wrapped in a soft plaid shawl against some invisible cold, told me about her twenty-three years as a hostage to her husband Bernard; unable to escape and afraid that her battered teenaged son would kill Bernard if she didn't, she hired a hit man. (Today, after seven years in prison, she says that given the choice between life with Bernard and life behind bars, she would choose prison.)

In all these cases—from accident to justifiable homicide to premeditated murder—the women were impelled not by passionate, possessive love for their men but by deadly fear. "When I get out of here," said Ruth Childers, whose shotgun went off by accident, "I'll never have a gun around the house again." "If I ever get out of here," countered Joyce DeVillez, "I'll never have a *man* around the house again." It is not Jean Harris but these women, battered and sexually abused, turning at last against their assailants, who are the "classic" homicides of our time.

In November 1980, as Jean Harris went to trial, a jury in Atkinson County, Georgia, found Elaine Mullis, a battered wife for thirteen years, guilty of murdering her husband Connie and sent her to prison for life. Her twelve-year-old son, who witnessed the killing, testified that Connie Mullis, drunk and stoned, had attacked Elaine earlier that day. Late in the evening, while she stood in the kitchen slicing to-matoes, he came after her again. As Mullis mauled and choked her, he stumbled drunkenly and fell against the paring knife she held. The four-inch blade left a tiny wound requiring only four stitches in his chest, but it struck arteries. Medical help, delayed and inadequate, failed to save his life. The jury discounted these chance elements in the killing of Connie Mullis just as they disregarded the eyewitness testi-mony of the boy, suspected of favoring his battered mother because Mullis battered him too. "We couldn't let her go," said one juror after the trial. "It would have been open season on husbands in Atkinson County." (Law and order in the county is maintained by the sheriff, Connie Mullis's stepfather.) Now that was a case so familiar I could almost have written the record myself. *That* is a classic.

But what I hadn't counted on in the Harris case is how much so many people would be fascinated by the thing itself, how much they seemed to want to hear and tell about the obsession of this particular woman—who appeared outwardly so self-possessed—for this particu-lar man. First the journalists were drawn into the case and through their efforts the rest of us, until it became impossible to avoid. People I scarcely knew invited me to dinner in hopes that, as an authority on homicide, I might bring new gambits for conversation which, as the trial dragged on, grew somewhat repetitive. Almost every woman, it seemed, knew a loathsome "Tarnower type," while many men could speak of career "girls" they knew who couldn't quite pull their weight or drank on the sly. Those interminable conversations circled relent-lessly around ourselves, feeding on old anxieties about "women's lib" and equal rights and the uncertain future of the mythic "American fam-ily." Having heard it all before, I decided not to attend the trial or, for the time being, any more dinner parties. But in the end, I found myself buying every paper.

Sixty-nine-year-old Herman Tarnower summoned his servants near midnight. They found him crouched between the beds in his room, his blue pajamas soaked with blood from four bullet wounds. Jean Harris, driving away, met a police officer and returned to the house to say, "I did it." At her trial, which stretched over four months, the prosecution argued that the killing was intentional, that Jean Harris, thrown over at age fifty-seven after fourteen years as Tarnower's mistress and enraged by jealousy of the "other woman" young enough to be her daughter (young enough at thirty-seven to be Tarnower's granddaughter), had driven five hours from the Madeira School to Tarnower's house, intent upon murdering him. The prosecutor, George Bolen, produced a patient of Dr. Tarnower to say that on the very day of the shooting she inadvertently overheard portions of a phone call during which the doctor said, "Goddamit, Jean, I want you to stop bothering me." And most tellingly, the prosecutor brought on a medical expert whose arcane testimony went to show that tissue from Tarnower's hand was imbedded in his chest, that two of his wounds came from a single bullet which passed through his defensively upraised hand and, fatally, into his chest. That was the kind of technical "fact" that a jury adrift on a sea of emotion and conjecture can grab hold of.

The defense, on the other hand, maintained that the killing happened by accident, that as a result of unlucky circumstances Dr. Tarnower (in Anita Loos's memorable phrase) "became shot." Depressed and unable to handle her work, Harris wanted only to die. First reports held that she drove to Purchase to get Tarnower to kill her. By trial time she claimed to have intended to kill herself; but she wanted to do it near Tarnower's pond where daffodils bloom in the spring, and she wanted first to have one last comforting talk with the man she had loved for so long, or as her lawyer put it in a tactless allusion to another murdered man, to "say goodnight to her sweet prince."

Unfortunately, the prince in this case had already taken his nightly laxative and gone to bed. He wanted to sleep. "Jesus," he said when she came in clutching a bouquet and a pocketbook containing her .32, "It's the middle of the night." He rolled over, hugging a pillow. To get his "attention" Harris began to throw things, including Tryforos's nightgown and a box of hair curlers which broke a window. (This was not customary behavior; Tarnower's housekeeper said she had seen Harris express anger to Tarnower twice in fourteen years, and Harris herself said they quarreled only about the use of the subjunctive.) Tarnower got out of bed and hit her; she put the gun to her head; they struggled. She shot him once through his hand, she said, and again during the struggle when she thought the gun muzzle was touching her own belly. Another shot, apparently fired to check the gun after it clicked on an empty chamber when she aimed it again at her head, went through the headboard of the bed. Two other shots—the fatal ones—she couldn't remember. She put her gun to her head again and "shot and shot and shot" but it was empty. And Tarnower was dying. In Jean Harris's storybook ending to her storybook romance, Herman Tarnower died trying to save her life.

The defense mustered a parade of medical and ballistics experts to affirm that the struggle could have happened as Harris claimed; six experts found no palm tissue in the chest wound. Yet the jurors, trying to reenact the script Harris provided, couldn't simulate the right wounds in the right place in the right sequence. So they didn't believe Harris's experts. And worse, they didn't believe Harris when she became the star witness in her own defense.

The truth as Harris saw it and told it during eight days on the stand often didn't match up to the truth as others saw it. Under oath she insisted she was not jealous of Lynne Tryforos. Then the prosecutor demanded the notorious Scarsdale letter, a certified letter from Harris to Tarnower mailed just before she left Virginia, a whiny self-pitying letter which, in a phone call, she asked him to destroy without reading, a letter her attorneys fought unsuccessfully to keep out of evidence. (Harris, for all her propriety, overlooked Emily Post's stern advice to "silly girls" and "foolish women" who "feel impelled to pour out their emotions in letters to men . . . : *don't!*" Post warned that "The Letter No Woman Should Ever Write" turns up "in evidence in courtrooms every day.") In this letter Harris repeatedly called Tryforos a "whore" and worse, and she insisted she would attend Tarnower's birthday celebration even if Tryforos were present, even if Tryforos "pops naked out of a cake with her tits frosted with chocolate." Jurors thought the letter was penned in jealous rage; by denying her jealousy, Harris lost all credibility.

Denial, it seems, was how Jean Harris customarily got by. Denial and projection. Thinking that Tryforos had destroyed some of her clothing, Harris destroyed gifts Tryforos had given Tarnower. Thinking that Tryforos phoned her in the middle of the night to torment her, Harris repeatedly phoned Tryforos in the middle of the night to tell her to stop. Addicted to the methamphetamine Desoxyn (speed), barbiturates, and half a dozen other mood-changing drugs prescribed by Tarnower over a decade, Harris denied her addiction, but in the Madeira School crisis that precipitated her final distraction, expelled four seniors for smoking marijuana. (Speaking euphemistically of her addiction, Harris testified: "I never thought of it as a dependency. It was something I used and I didn't do without it . . . I felt better when I took it." She ran out of speed only two days before the incident she referred to as "when Hi died.") Knowing that Tarnower collected women, mostly slim blondes, Harris thought of the others as sluts and of herself as "the only decent one" in the lot. The Scarsdale letter, with its vicious references to "your psychotic whore," left a particularly bad taste because, as one juror asked, "Wasn't Mrs. Harris doing the same thing with Dr. Tarnower that Lynne Tryforos was doing?" One columnist concluded that Harris couldn't tell herself the truth, another that she couldn't tell others a lie. Probably both were right. A woman on the jury put it simply: "She couldn't see herself."

The story that unraveled from her testimony was this: Harris and Tarnower met in 1966 at the home of friends. They dated and danced at the Pierre. In 1967 he gave her a large diamond and asked her to marry him. A few months later, when she pressed him to name the date, he backed out. She, quite properly, offered to return the ring and received other gifts: Desoxyn, Valium, Nembutal, Percodan, Plexonal, Percobarb. ("I trusted Hi," she said. "I took what he gave me.") Columnist Mary McGrory thought drugs a dubious prescription for a broken heart, but it was the same prescription thousands of Dr. Feelgoods nationwide routinely dispense to women for marital afflictions ranging from silence to felonious assault. Jean Harris obediently swallowed her rage with her pills, and as Hi Tarnower turned to other women, she wrote bitterly amusing doggerel about his philandering: " 'Twas the Night before Christmas . . ./In the guestroom lay Herman/Who trying to sleep/Was counting the broads in his life/Instead of his sheep."

In the end, the same mechanism of denial probably cushioned her psyche from the grim fact of killing and invited her conviction. It often happens that a person who under extreme circumstances performs an act completely out of character represses or denies or "forgets" the event; anyone subjected to the profound psychic stress of a fatal struggle is likely to "forget" exactly how it happened or even to forget the event altogether. But Harris's jury, which had come to expect more from her by way of accounting (wasn't she a schoolmistress?), held it against her that she could not recall the two shots fatal to Tarnower. They leaned toward acquittal on the murder charge until the foreman donned Tarnower's blood-stained pajama top and they took turns grappling with him for the gun. "We tried every which way," one said later. "It just couldn't have gone the way Mrs. Harris said."

On February 24, after deliberating eight days, the jury returned a verdict of guilty of murder in the second degree, the most serious charge which could have been brought against her in a state that reserves Murder One for killings of police officers and prison guards, and the only charge the jury ever considered. On March 20, Judge Russell Leggett, undoubtedly considering Harris's previously respectable social position and peaceable record, handed down the lightest possible sentence: fifteen years to life. She was transferred immediately from the county jail to Bedford Hills Correctional Facility, the New York State prison for women.

By that time, the Harris case had indeed become a kind of classic— not that it was representative of women's homicides but that it matched so neatly the traditional male "Frankie and Johnny" fantasy of the vengeful woman. Appallingly old-fashioned notions of the feelings and behavior proper to "ladies" shaped arguments on both sides of the courtroom, leaving many puzzled feminists with the sense of having pushed forward boldly into the past. The prosecutor argued that Harris was murderously jealous, the defense attorney that she was suicidally depressed by overwhelming problems at work. Both views came down to the tough, inescapable conclusion that Jean Harris—intelligent, attractive, well-educated, successful, apparently independent— simply could not live and work without the man she loved, that for his sake she willingly endured years of humiliation and insult, and then, finding the man indifferent and the pills gone, went haywire. Jurors said they would have acquitted her happily on grounds of temporary insanity, but defense attorney Aurnou's tactics prevented such considerations. To Aurnou, Harris's groveling dependence and suicidal depression amounted to a noble passion. "This is a story of love," he told the jury, summing up. "Love gone wrong, love of a woman who had more to give than a man could accept or a man could handle. . . . This was a tragedy because he was incapable of accepting the greatest gift a woman has to give."

Whether that puppy dog dependence of woman upon man can endure is doubtful. But certainly it is an old tradition. And certainly in the Harris case it is the point. It is reassuring to men to know that women, no matter how seemingly independent, simply cannot live without them. It is reassuring to housewives, bedeviled by "women's lib," to know that the real career of the career woman is a cutthroat battle to snare a man of her own. And it is a chastening and timely lesson to feminists, who seem to have seduced women away from love and marriage and devotion to men, that for all their talk of equality and independence, the age-old bondage of woman to man—like murder—will out. Like the other great tabloid trials of this century—those of Ruth Snyder and Alice Crimmins—the trial of Jean Harris gave substance to popular fears about woman's changing roles. Finding its themes in the sexist preconceptions of the lawyers, the press, and the defendant herself, the trial became a morality play in the guise of a soap opera, teaching—just as prim schoolmistress Harris had done for years—good conduct to "good girls." The Harris case became the anti-feminist lecture of our day.

This reassurance that good girls still love even bad boys was doubly welcome to a nervous public coming as it did after the highly publicized trials of raped and battered women who killed their assailants and, in a few notorious cases, were acquitted on grounds of temporary insanity or found to have committed justifiable homicide in self-defense. National publications which only two years before predicted an "open season on husbands" thanks to the "vigilante justice in the women's movement" now reaffirmed that real women—including the most accomplished ladies—still go wild for men. And even a singularly unattractive, balding sixty-nine-year-old philanderer, if he played his cards right, could have many young, beautiful women fighting tooth and fingernail for the privilege of sharing his bed.

These comforting notions do not mark the failure of feminism. In fact, if feminism had not altered a few social practices and the attitudes of many women and men, the public would not need such reassurance. It is precisely at those stressful moments in history when everything seems to be changing that we worry most about woman's proper place. Ruth Snyder was executed in the wake of World War I, woman suffrage, and the sexual revolution of the Roaring Twenties, a time if ever there was one when woman needed to be put in her place and kept there. The ordeal of Alice Crimmins followed upon another so-called sexual revolution and the awakening of a renewed women's movement. A glance backward into the recurring cycles of history could have told us that the 1970s' wave of feminism and the imagined "open season on men" would stir anxiety and impel a new morality play for the instruction of uppity women.

The Harris trial did have one new twist. It was customary in these exemplary cases to depict the woman's fate as a consequence of her bad character. The simple moral taught that if she had been a good girl she would not have come to a bad end. If Ruth Snyder had not committed adultery, she would not have fallen to murder and the electric chair. If Alice Crimmins had not been promiscuous, her husband would not have left home, her children would not have been killed, and she never would have gone to jail. So the lessons go.

All the accounts tell us, however, that Jean Harris, aside from being a confirmed snob, was an estimable lady. It is true that "Integrity Jean" clung to a lover without benefit of clergy and felt humiliated by that compromising situation, but the public seemed to take the affair as a matter of course. Her fault lay not in being unfaithful to a man but in trying too hard to be faithful—a fault men can pity. With her good manners, her propriety, her medicated composure, she is all that a lady should be. No wonder that attorneys and reporters alike wept for convicted Jean Harris, a woman who in her inability to find satisfaction in the life she made for herself, her abject dependence on a man who mistreated her, and her animosity toward her rival represented the antithesis of that respect for self and for other women that feminists espouse and who became instead a curious model of how a real lady behaves—until she runs amok.

"I was a person, and nobody ever knew," Jean Harris wrote in a last pathetic note before she drove off to the final meeting with her lover. It was hard to *see* the person for the lady. Tarnower didn't see. Harris herself didn't see. Defense attorney Aurnou didn't see beyond his own decidedly male assumptions and consequently placed his client in jeopardy. A woman's passion—all that unbounded love Aurnou said she had to give away—is supposed to serve male privilege, not challenge it. So observers in and out of the jury box who were willing to believe all her weeping confessions of love and desperation balked at her narration of how the killing occurred. And all the evidence of her life and all the strung-out paranoia of that last weekend when she was (as she would have been called if of another class or color) a speed freak undergoing detox, hungry for a fix—all that faded before some trajectories crudely calculated in the jury room with a foreman in bloody pajamas as target.

Nevertheless, since the defendant—carefully wrapped in cashmere and good tweeds and mink collar—was so conspicuously an upper-middle-class lady, many commentators hinted all along that she would get off easy. Radical attorney William Kunstler, for one, thought the trial was "such a middle-class soap opera" that the jury, following its "script," would reach some compromise verdict or no verdict at all. Misled by their left-wing analysis, such commentators did not understand—or at least they didn't admit—that when a woman is tried for murder in troubled times like these, the overriding issue is not class but gender. (One male attorney, fiercely clutching his class analysis despite the verdict, concluded foolishly that the law discriminates against the rich.) And if the killing of Tarnower was not an accident, as Harris claimed it was, then perhaps she was as vengeful as all those homicidal battered women appeared to be. Luckily for nervous men, as a man on the street interviewed by New York City's Channel Four put it, a Harris conviction would serve as a lesson to all women that they can't shoot men just because the men cheat on them. (That lesson, he added, was urgently needed, for without it, "all men would get shot.") That lesson also was remarkably similar to the "moral" of the convictions of battered women of all social classes: women can't shoot men just because the men beat them up. Earlier in this century the social fathers feared and punished the sexual outlawry of women like Ruth Snyder and Alice Crimmins. Today they seem to fear nothing so much as simple revenge.

In shops, elevators, buses, and at the newsstand, one heard: "Well, she killed a man. You can't just kill a man." But in fact you can. Taking life is universally regarded as morally wrong, but the law always has recognized that under certain circumstances a life may be taken with impunity. Killing in self-defense is justifiable homicide, and accidental killing (as Harris claimed Tarnower's death to be) is not punishable unless some degree of recklessness or negligence is found. In every criminal case, whatever the charge, the defendant is to be considered innocent until proven guilty. Nevertheless, when a man lies dead and a woman holds the gun, we conclude automatically that a murder has been committed. She must pay for it. In the context of the Harris case, "You can't kill a man" means "A woman can't kill a man, no matter what he has done to her, and get away with it."

Cesare Lombroso, father of modern criminology, told us almost a century ago that a woman abandoned by her man would find her only honorable course in suicide. "Good girls," after all, are trained to inflict their disappointments upon themselves, to become not angry and aggressive but depressed and self-destructive. According to that tradition, Jean Harris should have chosen suicide. If only she had succeeded in killing herself there by the pond where the daffodils grow in the spring, she would have retained unblemished her record of seemliness and spared the criminal justice system the embarrassment of packing a lady off to prison usually reserved for poor, nonwhite women. Certainly she would have set a much tidier example of how a lady should behave.

But instead she walked in and he rolled over, embracing the pillow, and said something like, "Oh, shut up, Jean. I'm trying to sleep." And then everything went wrong.

Looking back on the Harris case, it seems just about as unusual and as predictable as I anticipated. Once again the courtroom became didactic theater, the show publicized by the same old tabloid reporting and celebrity writers—right down to the fuzzy blow-up front page photo of the woman behind bars under the headline: GUILTY! The Snyder and Crimmins trials had gone into reruns. But for all the hoopla, the lessons of the Harris case—love your man and know your place—were lost on a great many women everywhere who were too busy getting on with their lives to tune in again to old programs.

In a final puff of authority, some prominent male attorneys blamed Harris's conviction on the women jurors (most of whom, in fact, professed great sympathy for Harris and one of whom held out until the end). Percy Foreman, who got Candy Mossler off with an all-male jury, repeated the truism that women are always hardest on each other. "Man's inhumanity to man," he said, "is exceeded only by woman's inhumanity to woman." Melvin Belli agreed: "I wouldn't have women judging the Venus de Milo." On the other hand, Belli said, digging out another chestnut, "Men just can't bring themselves to put a woman in the bucket." (Defense attorney Aurnou apparently thought otherwise; in a pretrial interview he said that the chief quality he would look for in jurors was "nice legs.")

As Judge Leggett, with apologies for the painful necessity of sentencing a woman, put Harris in the bucket for fifteen years to life, he too made a little speech, stressing again the distinctions of class and caste between one sort of woman and another, distinctions that fogged his courtroom just as they fouled the mind of Jean Harris. Leggett commended her as a "brilliant woman" who had "so much to offer women." She could be most useful in prison, he thought, "by bringing some light into *those other women's* lives." To deny her the opportunity to teach those other women would be "to deprive society and other inmates of a great blessing." (Jean Harris, who dutifully abides by this old system for distinguishing decent women from other women, confided to Shana Alexander that if she had intended to kill anyone it should have been Lynne Tryforos.)

Then Judge Leggett dispatched Harris—middle-aged, white, upper-middle class—to the same prison that confines Bernadette Powell—young, black, poor. Jean Harris reportedly was terrified of going to prison; terrified of the other women, vicious women, lesbian women, poor women, uneducated women, Hispanic women, black women, women like Bernadette Powell. Bernadette would understand that fear because when she first entered prison, it so struck her that she lost the power to speak. Silent, she slept on the floor of her cell, her face pressed to the crack of light beneath the door.

For all the barriers of race and caste and class, these women now share a common prison, just as all women from the outset are confined to the same social boxes by religious dogma, scientific "fact," political institutions, economic systems, social custom, psychological theory, biological "destiny," sexual practices, popular philosophy, media imagery, liberal education, patriarchal attitudes, brute force, family structure, tradition, manners, fashion, pornography, language, habit, ignorance, inertia, fear, misogyny, and the law. Jean Harris thought she was "different," but when she came squarely up against the law, she found that what mattered most was not her white skin or her pearls or her college degree. What mattered most was her sex. In a women's prison, all the inmates are "ladies."

2.

Jean Harris became #81-G-98. That is, she was the ninety-eighth prisoner to arrive at Bedford Hills Correctional Facility in 1981. In the ten years that have elapsed since she entered prison, all her appeals and applications for clemency have failed, she has had a heart attack, she has written two books (one of them titled *They Always Call Us Ladies*), and she has changed. Fear and snobbery have fallen away, and she has become an eloquent voice for women behind bars.

Her books are the only first-hand reports we have of life in women's prison, and of the life-before-prison that brings women there. Most of the inmates are young and poor and black. Most are mothers. Few are married. Many are in very poor health. Many have had no medical or dental care before entering prison. Many are illiterate. Some don't speak English. A great many are mentally ill. More than 60 percent of them were abused as children, "physically, sexually, emotionally, or all three." More than half of them were "sexually abused at one time in their lives." Many behave like the children they never got a chance to be, yet they are hardened and pathologically detached. Of the average prisoner, Harris writes to her white middle-class readers: "You probably wouldn't like [her] very much. She has habits and qualities that would make you turn away. . . . One of the least just things about justice is that its decisions are colored not only by the deeds done, but by the fact that deeds are often done by people who are unattractive, even disgusting to us." But in Harris's impassioned account of "the devious, funny, brave, obscene, tragic" lives of these hapless women, they have names and human faces. They are her neighbors.

They are decidedly not feminists. (So much for the dire warnings of criminologists that women's liberation would produce a new breed of female criminals.) "They fear men, even despise men," Harris reports. Yet they hold to "the myth of happily ever after" and, according to Harris, the average prisoner "associates feminism, if she thinks about it at all, with white middle class. . . . She also associates feminism with man-hating, and however badly she has been treated by men, she doesn't hate them. Her fondest wish is to find a good one to support her and her children." Poverty, not male violence and irresponsibility, is "the bogy man in her life."

The average female prisoner at Bedford Hills, sentenced for property or drug offenses, stays in prison two years and seven months. But women convicted of manslaughter and murder serve much longer terms. Consequently, about 40 percent of Harris's neighbors are serving time for homicide. Most of them, Harris says, were battered women. She reports:

> It is one of the many ironies of this prison that many of the women with the longest terms are the least dangerous, and led the most useful lives before coming here. . . . They were good daughters, good wives, good mothers and good citizens until the day or night the final straw of cruelty was piled on top of all the other straws. . . . Depending upon the attitude of the judge and district attorney, they have been given anywhere from three to twenty-five years to life. Sonia's husband had a habit of breaking her arm. She finally killed him and got three years, was out in two. Garnell found her husband raping her daughter. She killed him and got eight and one-third to twenty-five. She's still here. Penny's husband was a policeman before he was fired from the force. She supported him for three more years while he threw dinner at her because he didn't like it and beat her brutally. She asked repeatedly for police protection from him, but you don't arrest an old buddy even if he did get fired for cause. She killed him and got eight and a third to twenty-five, too. Claudine's husband tried to kill her with acid and an ice pick. The top half of her body and face are horribly scarred and she must carry one arm up against her body, almost in a gesture of supplication. In the struggle, she threw some acid on him. He died of a heart attack. She has six to eighteen. These are women who are victims as surely as anyone is a victim. And now they are twice victims.

During the ten years that Jean Harris has been confined in prison, stories such as these became familiar. During that time, women in the US have killed an average of 800 husbands every year, and half as many boyfriends. And each year more than 1500 wives have died at the hands of their husbands, while another 500 women were murdered by boyfriends. During the decade, the battered women's movement in the United States carried on its strenuous efforts to heighten public awareness, gain community support, and effect changes in the response of the state and its agencies, particularly the criminal justice system. In 1985 the Surgeon General, noting that domestic violence had reached "epidemic" proportions, described it as a "public health menace." In 1991 the Senate Judiciary Committee held hearings on "a bill to combat violence and crimes against women in the streets and in homes." If passed, the bill would (among other things) encourage arrest and prosecution of an assaultive "spouse," make it a crime for him to track his wife across state lines, and recognize gender crimes in the street and home as civil rights violations with civil rights remedies.

Nevertheless, men go on beating women. Conservative estimates hold that two million women in the US will be "severely assaulted" by their "partners" in the next year. Researchers in the field place the number at four million. As I reflect on the last decade of massive work and remarkable achievements on behalf of abused women, I am struck by the obvious: The more things change, the more they remain the same.

A decade of struggle has made it easier to see *why*. First of all, the nature of abuse has become clearer, and the purpose it serves in society and in the lives of individual men. The work of feminist researchers and activists bears out the thesis sociologists R. Emerson Dobash and Russell Dobash developed in 1979 after studying violence against wives in Scotland; namely, that violence between husbands and wives is an extension of the historic domination and control of husbands over their wives and "should be understood primarily as coercive control." In other words, domestic violence is *not* just a series of isolated blow ups, the result of anger or stress or too much to drink, though it often looks that way to the woman who is its target. Rather, domestic violence is *a process of deliberate intimidation intended to coerce the victim to do the will of the victimizer*.

That process of coercion involves more than physical abuse. Emerge, a Boston counseling program for men who batter, uses this working definition of violence: it is "any act that causes the victim to do something she does not want to do, prevents her from doing something she wants to do, or causes her to be afraid." They note that "violence *need not involve physical contact with the victim*, since intimidating acts like punching walls, verbal threats, and psychological abuse can achieve the same results." Psychological abuse, which they define as "behavior that directly undermines . . . self-determination or self-esteem," becomes "particularly powerful" when mixed with physical violence. Behavior such as "yelling, swearing, sulking, and angry accusations" *is* violence if it coerces or frightens another person, as it is very likely to do if it is "reinforced by periodic or even occasional [physical] violence." At its most proficient, male coercion resembles the intimidation, terrorizing, brainwashing, and torture of hostages and prisoners of war. Yet it is insidious precisely because it aims to enforce "normal" power relationships. After studying 247 battered women, 42 of whom killed or tried to kill their batterers, social psychologist Angela Browne concluded: "Abuse by male partners and responses by female victims are extensions of our cultural *expectations* of romance and relating," instances of boy gets girl carried to the extreme. What women are up against then, in trying to combat violence against women, is the task of *re*constructing "manhood," power, and "normal" relations between women and men.

Secondly, because law functions to maintain traditional power relationships (not to mention its *own* power), the law itself and law enforcement are far more resistant than women could have anticipated to appeals to reason, fairness, equality, and justice. The battered women's movement in the United States has focused on the law, legal reform, and individual rights, while theorists of the similar movement in England, notably Carol Smart, have cautioned feminists against empowering the law. I focus on this issue here because I believe that the American experience of the last decade bears out the wisdom of English warnings. Indeed, the law in the United States seems vulnerable only to a quick blow to the pocketbook. At least that seems to be the moral of the unfinished story of Tracey Thurman.

Taking her young son with her, Tracey Thurman left her assaultive husband Charles in 1982 after a brief violent marriage. Charles Thurman refused to divorce her. Instead, for eight months, he harassed her by phone and in person, and he threatened publicly to kill her. He smashed in the windshield of her car—when she was in the car—and the court put him on probation. He violated the probation, threatening to shoot her and the child, but the police refused to arrest him. She got a restraining order, but the police declined to enforce it. She later told a reporter: "I went as far as, if my ex-husband would call me on the telephone and threaten me, I would call the police department immediately and tell them, 'I want this put down on record,' because I figured that if they heard Charles Thurman's name enough times, they're going to finally pick him up." But the police didn't pick him up.

On June 10, 1983, Tracey Thurman called the police again and asked them to arrest Charles who once again was outside her house, threatening her. The officer dispatched stopped by the police station first to use the toilet, and when he arrived at Tracey Thurman's house twenty-five minutes later, he found that Charles had already cut her face with a buck knife and stabbed her repeatedly in the chest, neck, and throat. The officer stood by while Charles attacked Tracey again as she lay on the ground. Charles jumped on her face and broke her neck. Then the police arrested him.

Tracey Thurman survived—permanently disfigured and partially paralyzed. Charles Thurman was convicted of assault and sentenced to fifteen years in prison. (He is now eligible for parole and has promised to "finish the job.") Tracey Thurman sued the City of Torrington, Connecticut, and twenty-four individual police officers on behalf of herself and her son. She brought suit in federal court under the provision of the Fourteenth Amendment to the Constitution, which says in part that "No state shall . . . deny to any person within its jurisdiction the equal protection of the laws." She argued that the City of Torrington and its police had denied her equal protection of the laws as an abused spouse. By following a policy of not arresting assaultive husbands, she said, the Torrington police failed to provide the same protection to abused spouses and children as they afforded the victim of similar assault outside a domestic relationship.

The Federal District Court agreed. It held, in part:

> A man is not allowed to physically abuse or endanger a woman merely because he is her husband. Concomitantly, a police officer may not knowingly refrain from interference in such violence, and, may not automatically decline to make an arrest simply because the assaulter and the victim are married to each other. . . . City officials and police officers are under an affirmative duty to preserve law and order, and to protect the personal safety of persons in the community. . . . If officials have notice of the possibility of attacks on women in domestic relationships . . . they are under an affirmative duty to take reasonable measures to protect the personal safety of such persons in the community. Failure to perform this duty would constitute a denial of equal protection of the laws.

The jury awarded Tracey Thurman $2.3 million in compensatory damages. Then things began to change. Insurance companies, facing the prospect of paying out millions in damage claims, pressured police to arrest assaultive men. Municipalities and state legislatures, looking at higher insurance costs, higher taxes, crippling lawsuits, and bankrupt city treasuries, responded with stiffer law enforcement policies. Almost overnight the State of Connecticut adopted a new comprehensive domestic violence law calling for mandatory arrest for assaultive "spouses." Men went to jail. In a single year the number of arrests in Connecticut for domestic assault rose from roughly 5,000 to more than 25,000. And once it was clear that assaultive men would be arrested, the number of battered women seeking additional help from the Connecticut domestic abuse hotline jumped from 14,000 a year to more than 20,000. Many callers got the hotline number from an information card they received—as required by the new law—when they called the police.

For a few months after the Thurman decision, it seemed that the criminal justice system cared about the rights of women. But of course it was the dollar that mattered. Throughout the eighties, all across the country, in California and Kansas and Pennsylvania and Texas, women brought suits similar to Tracey Thurman's. As case after case alleged the same pattern of facts, it was plain to see that the battered woman denied protection is not the exception but the rule. But the courts acted quickly to plug the loophole through which Tracey Thurman had reached for safety and justice and money. In case after case, women lost. In case after case, police and public officials won immunity from prosecution for their failure to protect battered women. Finally, in 1989, in a case involving a child battered by his father into permanent brain damage, the United States Supreme Court ruled that the "state's failure to protect an individual against private violence does not constitute a violation" of the individual's constitutional rights. The worst that could be said of public officials in such "tragic" circumstances, the court ruled, was that they "stood by and did nothing," a description of precisely what the Torrington police did during the deconstruction of Tracey Thurman. So much for their "affirmative duty."

This was the hard lesson of the decade: for all its fine liberal rhetoric, the law has no interest in safeguarding the rights of women. It does not even acknowledge what one might have supposed to be a fundamental right to live free from bodily harm. What else should women expect? The law stands in relation to advocates for battered women just as the batterer stands in relation to the battered woman herself. It speaks in the same voice: the voice of the dominant male. Rather than uphold the civil rights of women, the law creates wrongs.

Consider the instance of women who kill in self-defense. For fifteen years feminist lawyers have tried to persuade courts to acknowledge that women have a right to assert a self-defense claim, just as men do. But as law professor Elizabeth Schneider (the attorney who argued the landmark appeal of Yvonne Wanrow described in chapter six) observes, "When you push the law, you can't control the forms the law is going to take." In 1980 she discussed in the *Harvard Civil Rights–Civil Liberties Law Review* the theoretical difficulties of asserting woman's right to self-defense. She noted that "the male assumptions contained in legal doctrine and the manifestation of those assumptions in court rulings . . . deny to women an opportunity equal to that of male defendants to present their claims of self-defense." She concluded optimistically that an "approach, which permits consideration . . . of the particular circumstances and perceptions under which a battered woman kills her assailant, will correct the sex bias in the law that disadvantages such women defendants."

But what's wrong with the law is not a superficial sex bias, easily peeled away to reveal an egalitarian core. There is no more reason to believe that the law, at heart, is not biased than there is to believe that a batterer, at heart, is not violent. The law itself is gendered, as many feminist legal scholars have pointed out, and that gender is essential to the law's power. With male dominance at stake, the law—or more conspicuously a judge who speaks in its name—can turn deaf or strident or surly. The law flexes its muscles.

The law reserves to itself the power to decide what's relevant and what's not. In any given case, it's up to attorneys and presiding judges to determine what's heard and what's ruled out of bounds. (Or to put it in the intellectual jargon of our day, it is the law, not feminism, that constructs the law's discourse.) More often than not, what lawyers omit or trial judges exclude is precisely what a woman has to say in her own defense. They may consider evidence of past abuse and threats too remote in time, evidence of the deceased's violent behavior not germane. Prevented from putting before the jury what she sees as relevant facts, a woman cannot make her plea of self-defense understood. Some defense attorneys, sharing the law's bias, simply leave the woman's story out. Others, who don't see that a battered woman's history of abuse *should* come into a trial under the standard rules of evidence, can't figure out how to get her story before the jury. Their answer: Get someone else to tell it. Enter the Expert Witness.

Usually the expert is a psychologist or psychiatrist armed with the theory of "learned helplessness," first promulgated by Lenore Walker, to explain the questions uppermost in the jury's mind: "Why did she kill him?" and "Why didn't she just leave?" Often the expert is Dr. Walker herself, explicating what has come to be known as "the battered woman's syndrome"—a pattern that includes the loss of a sense of control over life, the lack of real or perceived options, and a fearful, paralyzing depression. The expert presents no *legal* defense. Rather, the expert is supposed to help the jurors understand the defendant's *state of mind* at the time of the killing. The expert does so by talking about what psychology says of battered women in general (the "syndrome") and the history of the abused defendant in particular—the history that led the woman to think she had to defend herself. The defendant's *legal* defense, presented by her attorney, is that she acted in self-defense, but in case after case it is the expert who catches the attention of press and public. So it has come to seem to lawyers, courts, and the public alike that the "battered woman's syndrome" is in fact the legal defense.

The original intention of expert testimony, as feminist legal theorists saw it, was to answer questions in the minds of judge and jury so that they could see the defendant's "crime," in the particular situation she faced, as a *reasonable* and *justifiable* act. And sometimes it seems to have worked. Defendants who could afford the services of an expert, however, also could afford the most savvy lawyers—it's the lawyer who hires the expert—so in the end there was no way to tell whether it was the expert witness or the clever lawyer or simply the deep pockets of the defendant that won the day. (Partial studies indicate that only a small percentage of battered women who kill are acquitted, but the studies don't report whether expert testimony helped or hindered, or even if it was offered.)

The courts, however, recognized the expert's potential to change outcomes for women defendants. Not surprisingly, many courts excluded not only the defendant's story but the expert's testimony as well. When that happened and the defendant was convicted, the exclusion of expert testimony often became an important issue in appeal proceedings. Consequently, the struggle to overturn particular convictions was enacted all across the country as a struggle to get expert testimony admitted into evidence. Today, expert testimony is admissible in some states and not in others, and to get around the issue, some courts are now building in *separate* standards of admissibility for battered women. The long struggle for equal treatment, then, produces both what it aims for—and what it aims to overcome.

The battered woman's syndrome describes a "victim" of battering, paralyzed by "learned helplessness," who suddenly kills in a moment of desperate fear. But this emphasis on victimization is problematic at every level. Theorist Susan Schechter writes: "The focus on victimization helps to blur the insight that the struggle for battered women's rights is linked to the more general fight for women's liberation," and the corollary insight that battering is collective oppression as well as individual victimization. In the courtroom the emphasis on victimization sets the battered woman apart, in a special class. And it raises divisive questions.

In the first place, if this battered woman is so helpless, how can her decisive *action* be explained? And how is the jury to reconcile her supposed "helplessness" with the facts of her life? What about the battered woman who takes care of her kids or holds down a job or starts divorce proceedings or manages to obtain welfare? What about the battered woman who has been standing up to her husband all along—who called the police or took him to court? What about the battered woman who is not depressed but fed up and angry? About 85 percent of killings in which women claim self-defense take place in the midst of violent, life-or-death confrontations, but what about that rare battered woman who, like Francine Hughes, kills a sleeping man, or like Joyce DeVillez, hires a hit man? Is this "helplessness"? These women, by definition, don't seem to qualify as "real" battered women. And if "battered woman's syndrome" is essential to the plea of self-defense, then such women seem to have no right to make the claim.

Yet as more and more battered women told their stories, "learned helplessness" came to seem a particularly unfortunate misnomer. The alleged passivity and helplessness of battered women is better understood as lying low—an active, venerable, temporary, and smart survival strategy. Walker herself observed that "women develop survival or coping skills that keep them alive with minimal injuries." In short, few women actually match the only story the courts became willing to hear. But the courts increasingly found experts useful, as Elizabeth Schneider warned, "not as a complement to, but as a substitute for, women's voices."

In courtroom proceedings, in misguided trial reportage, and in the popular mind, the "battered woman's syndrome" gave rise to a new stereotype. Those women who don't measure up seem to be even more vulnerable to conviction than they were before the advent of the expert. Those women who *do,* seem to be presenting not a justification, but an *excuse.* They may be acquitted, but not because reasonable women, like reasonable men, are *justified* in defending themselves from attack. Rather, like women acquitted of husband-killing in the nineteenth century by reason of insanity, women supposedly afflicted with the battered woman's syndrome may be "let off" because they're "sick." Their "crime" is psychologized and their defense becomes a kind of special pleading centered not in their social conditions but in their impaired psyche and their sex. Psychology and law join forces in an old enterprise: distinguishing worthy defendants from cold-blooded killers, setting apart the "good" girls (relatively speaking) from the bad.

This is just one more example, if more were needed, of the peculiar imperviousness of the law to feminist discourse, and of the power of those who act in the name of the law to distort and delay feminist claims. Nevertheless, feminist legal theorists engaged today in "pushing" the law through "battered women's work" reflect upon how they came to this pass, ponder the dark heart of the law—so rigidly gendered, so punitive toward women—and plot new strategies to reassert the argument for equal rights with which they began long ago.

Meanwhile, battered women continue to invoke the law because, like any other citizens, they need the protection of law and law enforcement. Feminist activists continue to confront police, prosecutors, and judges, trying to make them more responsive to the needs of abused women. And they continue to urge abused women, as I have done, to use the criminal justice system to protect themselves. In Duluth, Minnesota, a city of 92,000 people, the model Domestic Abuse Intervention Project unites police, prosecutors, judges, probation officers, batterers' educators, women's advocates, feminist political activists, mental health agencies, substance abuse counselors, and leaders of the native American community in a single concerted effort to protect women and children. In Duluth, one of every twenty-four male citizens has been found by the courts to have committed acts of domestic abuse. In consequence, one of every twenty-four male citizens has been through a batterers' reeducation course, designed to alter not only his behavior but his views on men, women, and power. Ellen Pence, who founded the program in 1980, can now say with confidence: "There are women and men walking around in Duluth today who would be dead if it weren't for this program." But in other communities a battered woman protected by one segment of the system may be betrayed by another. The result is deadly.

On December 27, 1988, Joseph Grohoski kicked down a locked door at the home of his estranged twenty-four-year-old wife Lydia and shot her in the face with a 12-gauge shotgun. Then he shot himself.

Two days later William Croff rammed a car driven by his estranged wife Elizabeth, age thirty, fired a rifle at her, and chased her down in his car as she fled on foot, carrying her two-year-old daughter. He shot her in the head, wounded the child, then shot himself. A week later Anthony LaSalata shot his former wife April, age thirty-four, on her own doorstep when she returned from work. Police found him several days later in a car parked at a rest stop on the Long Island Expressway. He had shot himself. All three murder–suicides took place in Suffolk County (Long Island), New York. All three women murder victims died in possession of a legal restraining order—an order of protection—requiring her murderer to keep away.

Elizabeth Croff's mother, with whom she lived, told reporters: "She wanted him arrested, but the police wouldn't do anything." Three days before her death she went to court, reported that her husband had violated her order of protection, and asked for a warrant for his arrest. When she was murdered, the warrant had not yet been typed. (She didn't know, and the judge didn't tell her, that she didn't *need* a warrant. By law, police can, and should, make an arrest on the strength of a protected victim's verbal complaint.) Lydia Grohoski planned to testify against her husband when he went on trial for reckless endangerment, assault, and menacing—charges brought against him when he assaulted her three weeks earlier. He was free on $10,500 bail when he killed her. Anthony LaSalata was awaiting trial too, for attempted murder. He had broken into April's home eleven months earlier, in February 1988, armed with a rifle and a knife, and stabbed her many times in the chest. He was released in August on $25,000 bail. Prosecutors and April LaSalata herself appealed to the judge to increase bail and jail LaSalata, but the judge refused. April LaSalata was also denied a permit for a gun with which she might have protected herself. In the past two years, twelve women with orders of protection have been murdered in Suffolk County alone, while others, like Cecilia Eagleston, stabbed twenty-three times, came close to death. ("Many times I saw him, and I called the police," she says, "but they never showed up.")

Such stories appear in the press with remarkable regularity. Yet no one in the criminal justice system ever admits to having made a mistake. In Westminster, Colorado, in 1987, David Gunther—a man who had already established a reputation for violence by killing a neighbor with a .357 magnum—broke into the home of his estranged wife Pamela, took her hostage, and held off the police for five hours. Pamela Gunther too had a restraining order, and she too had called the cops many times. When David Gunther finally surrendered, police confiscated his gun and turned him loose on $10,000 bail. He bought another gun, using his wife's credit card, and killed her. Afterwards, District Attorney James Smith told reporters: "I didn't feel the system let Pamela Gunther down." And commenting on David Gunther's subsequent conviction for murder, he added: "We learned from the Gunther case that at some point in time most criminals are held accountable for their actions."

Lisa Bianco of Mishawaka, Indiana, was another battered woman who used the criminal justice system and as a shelter staff-member counseled other battered women to do the same. When she divorced Alan Matheney, he kidnapped the children and fled the state. Arrested and released on bond, he broke into her house, raped her, and tried to strangle her. Sentenced to prison for five years, Matheney continued to harass Bianco by telephone, threatening to kill her. Prison officials, pleased that Matheney "relates well" and appeared to have "no mental impairments that would hinder his ability to function in society," gave him a day's furlough on March 4, 1989. He drove directly to Mishawaka, stole a shotgun, and used it to club Lisa Bianco to death. Interviewed two years later in prison, where he is now serving time for Bianco's murder, Matheney said with a smile that he had "no regrets."

And what about the state of Indiana? A spokesman for the state department of corrections allowed at the time of Bianco's murder that someone may have exercised "poor judgment." Two years later, in February 1991, another Indiana woman, identified only as "Bonnie," told a reporter that her ex-husband, serving time for battery, was soon to be released. The prosecutor warned her to buy a gun or "relocate." With her child, she went into hiding. She said: "The prosecutor's people read the files and told me, 'I'm scared to death for you.' So, help me. I don't want to be another media 'tragedy' like Lisa just to wake more people up. They say that Lisa's death helped so much. What did it do? It didn't do nothing for me."

When "media tragedies" like these hit the news, battered women get the message: the system that fails to protect them from assault at home will not protect them when they leave. When David Gunther killed Pamela Gunther, battered women at a shelter she had used were reportedly "very, very scared." One advocate said: "We had women go back to their batterers because they would rather stay alive and live with being beaten periodically and verbally abused periodically than wind up dead." An advocate in Suffolk County, New York, said that

after the murders of Lydia Grohoski, Elizabeth Croff, and April La-
Salata, battered women in her shelter felt "like it's open season on
women." Another woman hiding out in a shelter there with her child
and her order of protection said: "I see what happened to these women
with their orders and I think that I could be any one of them, that I
could be next." Advocates at shelters in Colorado said that they received "an avalanche of calls" from frightened women in 1985 after
fifty-one-year-old Jane Campbell was shot to death by her second husband Blond Cole Hunter. Women said that their husbands were "deliberately leaving newspaper accounts of the murder around the house"
and warning them to "pay careful attention to what had happened to
Jane Campbell." Lisa Bianco's mother says, "People are always trying
to turn the blame on women, saying 'Why don't they leave?' That's
why they don't leave. They get killed."

Since 1974 violent crimes committed by men against women in
the United States have increased 50 percent. A rape now occurs every
six minutes, a domestic assault every twelve seconds. Domestic violence is now the leading cause of injury to American women, causing
more injuries annually than automobile accidents, rape, and muggings
combined. And the sharpest increase is in violent crimes—rape, gang
rape, battery, homicide—against young and single women.

On the other hand, violent crimes committed by women against
men have declined by 12 percent. Most dramatic is the decline in homicides. Angela Browne reported to the Senate Committee on the Judiciary in December 1990 that from 1976 through 1987 the number of
women killing male partners decreased by 25 percent. In fact, murder
of men by women is the *only* kind of homicide that is not on the rise
in violence-prone America. This decline is especially marked in lo-
calities that provide shelters and services for abused women, leading
researchers like Browne to conclude that women will not resort to homicide if they have other ways to escape assailants.

Similarly, Sue Osthoff, cofounder and director since 1987 of the
National Clearinghouse for the Defense of Battered Women, notes that
few battered women attempt to kill their husbands and boyfriends. She
credits "all the hard work of the battered women's movement over the
last fifteen years" with creating more opportunities for women to leave
abusive men. Having worked on cases of more than 350 battered
women facing criminal charges for defending themselves, Osthoff says:
"I've met only one woman who *wanted* to kill her husband. Battered
women don't want to do it. And they *won't* do it if they don't abso-

lutely have to." But like many women in the battered women's movement, Osthoff is appalled at the rising tide of violence against women in the United States. "I went into this work to help women," she says. "Now it seems like we've all been working very hard all these years to save the lives of *men*. It's not what I had in mind."

As Lisa Bianco's mother observed, it is *because women leave,* or try to, that they are killed. One researcher suggests that at least half of all women who leave abusers are followed and harassed or assaulted again, many of them fatally. Women murdered in the United States and Great Britain are far more likely to be killed by a husband or boyfriend than by any other person; and a great many of those murders occur when women are on their way out.

It is significant too that while women sometimes kill men, men "normally" *over*kill women. Men commonly try to kill wives and girlfriends by clubbing them twenty times (Lisa Bianco), stabbing them twenty-three times (Cecilia Eagleston), or beating them beyond recognition. This superfluous evidence of woman-hating comes as no surprise to feminists, but precisely why men go on beating and raping and killing women with such ferocity is a question the research establishment has yet to face. The eminent sociologists and psychologists who gave us "battered husbands" and compiled so many faulty statistics over the years at public expense have still not addressed the question raised in chapter six: "Why don't men let women go?" Like law and psychology, the academic establishment seems able to turn a tidy profit on feminist issues while remaining impervious to feminist claims. It too speaks in the voice of male dominance. Recently, however, after reviewing the "standard literature" in the field, two male "experts" noted: "What is surprising is the enormous effort to explain male behavior by examining characteristics of women. It is hoped that future research will show more about the factors that promote violent male behavior and that stronger theory will be developed to explain it." The identity of those who hope is not yet specified.

It is a custom in the United States to conclude any discussion of "social problems" on just such a positive note. Time for an upbeat story, then, from the recent press: On January 10, 1991, outgoing Ohio Governor Richard F. Celeste commuted the sentences of four women on death row in the Ohio State Prison to life imprisonment. All four women were convicted of murder. All four are black. (Of the people who live in Ohio, 10 percent are black; of the people who live on Ohio's death row, 50 percent.) One of the women—one of two women also given the possibility of future parole—is Beatrice Lampkin, a battered woman who hired a hit man to kill her husband. (The three other women, two of whom seem to be mentally retarded, are known to have been abused as children.) Governor Celeste's action left thirty-three women on death row in American prisons. *At least* fourteen of them were convicted of murdering husbands or boyfriends. It's likely that some or all of them were battered women, who perhaps killed in self-defense; but in most cases *the defense attorney who represented the woman at her trial does not know whether she was battered or not.*

A month earlier, on December 21, 1990, Governor Celeste announced that he would free twenty-five inmates in the first mass release of women inmates ever in the United States. He told reporters that all the women to whom he granted clemency had been "convicted of killing or assaulting husbands or companions who . . . had physically abused them." After reviewing the cases of more than one hundred women in the Ohio prison, Celeste concluded that these twenty-five had been "victims of violence . . . entrapped emotionally and physically." They had defended themselves against the men who assaulted them, but they had been prevented from defending themselves in court because prior to 1990, Ohio courts refused to admit the testimony of expert witnesses about the "battered women's syndrome."

The irony that women who committed justifiable homicide should be freed from prison because a sex-biased system had deprived them of a sex-biased defense was not lost on feminists. Nevertheless, they had to admire Governor Celeste for redressing judicial wrongs—as all governors could do if they had a scrap of courage. He took a lot of heat from the conservative press. But feminists felt good. For a day or two, it felt almost like justice.

3.

Justice is represented by a female figure wearing a blindfold. Some say the blindfold represents the fairness of justice, uninfluenced by irrelevant concerns. Some say the blindfold suggests that female Justice can not bear to look at what male Law does in her name. Consider the circumstances under which women live today—in the United States, and all around the world. And consider justice.

During the past fifteen years in the United States reported crimes of all kinds against women have risen at a significantly higher rate than total crimes. The number of reported rapes is currently rising four times faster than that of any other crime. (Most rapes occur within the home and are never reported.) The rate of reported rape in the United States is thirteen times higher than England's, four times higher than Germany's, twenty times higher than Japan's. Other physical assaults against women between the ages of twenty and twenty-four are up 50 percent in the last fifteen years. (Assaults against men of the same age group decreased.) Reports of domestic assault increase every year. By every indication, violence against women in the United States is now at an all-time high, and going up.

Some of the offenses against women that feminists have addressed during the last fifteen years are wife abuse, child abuse, incest, rape, the commonplace practice of tranquilizing women who complain (as Herman Tarnower did Jean Harris), and the consequent widespread problem among women of substance abuse, addiction, drug induced psychosis, and suicide. All of these offenses come together in the life of Margie Velma Bullard Burke Barfield. And the ultimate offense, the ultimate violence, of law.

Between 1978 and 1984, Margie Velma Bullard Burke Barfield was one of the women on death row. Like Jean Harris, she was white. Like Jean Harris, she did *not* kill in self-defense. Like Jean Harris, she took too many drugs and couldn't quite explain why things happened the way they did. But Velma, as she was called, wasn't well off or educated like Jean Harris. She started and finished poor. She started—on October 29, 1932, in Sampson County, North Carolina—to live an ordinary American life. Considering that *three out of four* American women are victims of *at least one* violent crime committed by men, you could say that her life was "normal." She finished in 1984 when the state of North Carolina put her to death. She was the first woman executed in the United States since 1962, the first woman executed in almost a quarter century. Why the state killed her is even less clear than why Velma killed her victims.

Velma was born into a family of nine children. Her father Murphy Bullard worked at the Burlington Mills fixing looms. The family lived from one paycheck to the next. Murphy Bullard was known outside the family as a good man, but he was a hard man at home. Not long before her death at age fifty-two, Velma described her childhood in Murphy Bullard's household: "My dad was very, very hot tempered. He had no patience at all with us, and he could be very abusive at times, physically and verbally. He hit me many times . . . but I have seen him hit Olive [an older brother] and wonder if Olive would live from it, and I wondered if I was going to get the same thing. He would be worse when he was drinking . . . And my mother was so afraid of him . . . I have seen her cry many times. I have seen her trembling from him, from my dad, from his cursing and threatening her . . . I have been woke up many times . . . after he would come home at night from her own screams. He was twisting her arm, you know . . . he had her in the kitchen with the gun, threatening to kill her . . . And I always felt bad because mama never protected us, and I felt bitter about it . . . I know she was just as afraid of him as any of the rest of us was. But I did feel angry at her. I could not understand why she would not protect us. Mama was a good person, patient, very patient, the most patient one human I think maybe that I have ever known in my life."

Murphy Bullard took to molesting Velma, and when she was thirteen, he raped her. Velma was too frightened to tell anyone until, near the end of her life, she confided in a clergyman. At sixteen Velma started dating Thomas Burke who was a year ahead of her in high school. When she was just seventeen, they eloped. There followed, by Velma's description, the best fifteen years of her life. She said: "I think I went into it saying that I would never permit anybody to beat on me any longer, you know, or let a man ever beat on my kids like I had seen my daddy do. . . . For two children to be married, we got along pretty good." Thomas worked a delivery route for Pepsi Cola. Velma worked the night shift at Burlington Mills. At nineteen she had a son, at twenty-one a daughter. Velma's daughter says of those years, "We were just a normal American family."

Then a series of misfortunes occurred. Thomas Burke's father died, leaving him depressed. Thomas had a car accident and suffered afterwards from blinding headaches. He started drinking heavily. He lost his job. He became violent and abusive. Velma said that Thomas never hit her, but he tried; and she became afraid of him. Once, when he was jailed for drunk driving, she signed papers to have him hospitalized for treatment. The hospital released him after only three days, but according to Velma's son, "It embarrassed him . . . and he never forgave her for that." Her son also says that when Thomas took to drinking, Velma raised the two children "by herself" and worked two jobs to support them. She lost a lot of weight, and one day she collapsed. A doctor in the emergency room sent her home with tranquilizers. She too was involved in a car accident and began to suffer from back problems and headaches. The pills seemed to help.

In 1968 Thomas went to bed drunk, passed out while smoking a cigarette, and suffocated in the fire that ensued. By that time Velma was already making the rounds of doctors, collecting prescriptions for tranquilizers and sedatives. For the next ten years, her brother reports, "She was always on that medication." Velma described herself, in southern vernacular, as "always fearful of what might could happen." She said: "I was fearful of people finding out about the medication. . . . I felt really afraid when my medication got really low, if I was gonna make it to get some more." But she continued to work at a department store in Fayetteville. A young man who worked there introduced Velma to his father, Jennings Barfield, a retired civil servant and a widower.

In August 1970, Velma married Barfield, although he was afflicted with emphysema and heart disease. She says of the marriage: "I know that I was addicted to drugs then, and there was no way possible that I could have loved him. But I just felt sympathy for him, something, I don't know. . . . But he was good to me. He was a good man." Eight months later, in March 1971, Barfield died of a heart attack. Velma slid deeper into drugs and depression.

Early in January 1972, Velma was rushed to the hospital suffering from a deliberate drug overdose. In mid-January she was back in the hospital, heavily drugged and bruised from a fall. The diagnosis: "depressive reaction," suicide attempt, and "drug abuse." She was treated with more drugs: Dalmane, Elavil, Librium. In April Velma's father died, and five months later she attempted suicide again. This time the hospital held her for twenty-one days, treating her with more drugs: Dilantin, Dalmane, Librium. She lost her job at the department store and went back to work in the mills. Soon she overdosed again. "Many times," she said, "to be honest, I really didn't care if I lived or died. I felt that way many times."

In March 1973, Velma was arrested for passing "worthless checks." She was put on probation. A month later she was arrested for "obtaining drugs on false pretenses." She moved in with her mother, Lillie Bullard, took out a loan to support her drug habit, and then started forging Lillie's signature on checks drawn against Lillie's account. In December 1974, Lillie Bullard died after what seemed to be a bad bout with flu.

Soon after, in February 1975, Velma was hospitalized again for "Drug dependence and abuse and Depressive Neurosis." Ten days later she was back in the hospital for "Overdose . . . Chronic drug abuse, Endogenous depression, and Fracture of left clavicle." In her drugged state, Velma had fallen again. She was given more medication: antidepressants and, because she was in pain, sedatives. According to the attending psychiatrist's report, the sedatives made "meaningful therapy" impossible. She was discharged, although the psychiatrist recorded: ". . . the patient herself admitted that she still had depressive thoughts, some of them quite morbid, in that she felt that she had not been able to ventilate her problems adequately." Velma herself said: "They would always take me into the hospital, and the longest I ever stayed was three weeks, and I would come home with as much medication as . . . I went into the hospital with."

Soon after this hospitalization, early in 1975, Velma was convicted of passing bad checks, a misdemeanor, and imprisoned for six months in the North Carolina Correctional Facility for Women. In prison, she said, she remained on "some medication"—Elavil, a mood elevating psychotropic drug originally prescribed to counteract her depression and the depressive effects of the tranquilizers she obtained by shopping from doctor to doctor. She said she felt "safer" in prison.

When she was released, Velma began working as a live-in nurse's aide for elderly people. In September 1976, while she was working for eighty-five-year-old Dollie Taylor Edwards, she met Ms. Edwards's nephew. Stewart Taylor was a tobacco farmer, ten years older than Velma, with what Velma described as "a bad alcohol problem." Velma said, "He could get abusive. He was violent. He put himself into it. Very dictating. I was with him sometimes when he was drinking, and I would leave. I can't even comprehend why I wanted to be with him, except sometimes we're just lonely. Somebody to talk to, you know." They planned to marry in the summer of 1978. But on February 3, 1978, Taylor died.

A routine autopsy revealed arsenic. One thing led detectives to another. When they checked death certificates of four other people close to Velma, they found gastrointestinal symptoms, typical of arsenic poisoning, in three cases. The day they arrested Velma for the murder of Stewart Taylor, she had taken two Elavils and a double dose of four different kinds of tranquilizers. She confessed that she had put ant poison in Taylor's beer and tea. She hadn't meant to kill him, she said, but only to make him sick and nurse him back to health so he wouldn't be angry with her for forging checks against his account. She admitted that she also poisoned Dollie Taylor Edwards and another octogenarian in her care, John Henry Lee. She said she poisoned Lee for the same reason she poisoned Taylor; he and his wife discovered that Velma had forged a $50 check in his name. As for Dollie Edwards, Velma said, "I didn't have any reason. My mind was real fuzzy at the time." To give herself time to repay the loan she'd taken out to buy drugs, Velma said, she also poisoned her mother.

Velma went on trial for the murder of Stewart Taylor on November 27, 1978. Some evidence was found in a pre-trial psychological evaluation that she might be suffering from paranoid schizophrenia, but her court-appointed attorney didn't bring it up. It was his first capital case. The prosecution was handled by Joe Freeman Britt, listed in the *Guiness Book of World Records* as "the world's deadliest prosecutor" for bringing in twenty-three death verdicts in twenty-eight months and for once having thirteen "offenders" on death row, all at the same time. In six days the trial was all over and Velma was sentenced to death.

Then began a series of appeals, conducted largely by attorneys who oppose the death penalty, and carried all the way to the United States Supreme Court. The appeals were based on a substantial list of legal issues, including the ineffective assistance of Velma's trial attorney and the severity of her drug addiction—under North Carolina law, a circumstance that may mitigate capital punishment. As the legal process dragged on, Velma withdrew from drugs in the Women's Prison and emerged from what she called the "dark period" of her life. Prison officials, who described her as "a deeply religious person," credited her with being a model prisoner and providing support and counseling to many young women inmates. She told a reporter: "There were days during those ten years that I knew everything that was going on and days I didn't know anything. The first time everything cleared up was when I was in here." Her sisters and brothers, her children, and her two young granddaughters visited her regularly in prison.

In 1984, Velma Barfield exhausted her legal appeals and petitioned Governor James B. Hunt, Jr. to commute her sentence to life in prison. Hunt met with Velma's family, who urged commutation, and with relatives of Stewart Taylor and John Henry Lee, who urged that commutation be denied. Velma's execution was scheduled to take place four days before the election in which Hunt was trying to unseat the reactionary Republican incumbent Senator Jesse Helms. A newspaper editor in the state capital observed: "If Gov. Hunt grants clemency to Velma Barfield, it could very well cost him votes . . . and this is a very tight election." Noting that 78 percent of North Carolinians favored the death penalty, he observed that "Hunt would be politically safer to deny clemency." Historically the death penalty has been "overwhelmingly applied against black men," as Barfield's attorney noted, so Velma Barfield, being white and a woman, was "statistically okay to kill." In September Governor Hunt announced that he would not commute Velma Barfield's sentence. That was the kind of "tough decision," he said, that he "often had to make as governor."

On November 2, 1984, Velma Barfield was put to death, the first woman executed in the United States in twenty-two years. (On November 6 Jesse Helms was reelected to the Senate.) Before the execution, Velma issued a brief statement, saying in part: "I know that everybody has gone through a lot of pain, all the families connected, and I am sorry, and I want to thank everybody who have been supporting me all these years." She declined the offer of a last meal and had a Coke and some Cheez Doodles instead. Her attorney said that she wanted to die "with as much dignity as the state of North Carolina will allow."

She wore for the occasion pink pajamas and blue house slippers. Representatives of the state of North Carolina strapped her to a gurney, drugged her, and plugged her in to an IV. They wheeled her in to the execution chamber, the old gas chamber at Central Prison in Raleigh. Sixteen observers watched through glass panels. Five cc's of the powerful muscle relaxant pancuronium bromide, triggered by concealed correction officials, dripped through the IV tube into Velma Barfield to stop her heart. "She just seemed to relax," said one official observer. "I didn't notice any type of suffering."

NOTES

A NOTE ON SOURCES

Research into murder is not easy because murder (except political assassination) normally is omitted from history. No one wants to admit that homicide goes on in "our town." Consequently, I have had to take my information where I could find it: in everything from tabloids to stenographic trial transcripts, from nineteenth-century medical textbooks on insanity to law reports, from crumbling penny pamphlets to monitored prison visits. Striking out into untested sources is always risky, especially with a topic so often exploited for sensational purposes. I can say only that I entered armed with years of research experience and a healthy skepticism, and I did the best I could. For information on the colonial period I relied chiefly on Massachusetts and Virginia sources both because they are more abundant (Massachusetts Puritans were particularly diligent in recording crimes *and* sins) and because they had the most lasting effect on American jurisprudence. Colonial execution sermons, as listed in Charles Evans's *American Bibliography,* were invaluable. For the nineteenth century, Thomas McDade's *The Annals of Murder: A Bibliography of Books and Pamphlets on American Murders from Colonial Times to 1900* (Norman, Okla.: University of Oklahoma Press, 1961)—particularly the continually updated copy in possession of the New York Historical Society—is indispensable. And in all periods no source is richer in ephemeral history than the newspapers. I abbreviate some often cited sources as follows: *UCR*: U.S. Department of Justice, Federal Bureau of Investigation, *Uniform Crime Reports for the United States* (Washington, D.C.: U.S. Government Printing

Office, annual editions); *AST: American State Trials,* 17 vols., John D. Lawson, ed. (St. Louis: Charles C. Thomas, 1914–1937); *HWS: History of Woman Suffrage,* 6 vols., ed. Elizabeth Cady Stanton, Susan B. Anthony, and Matilda Joslyn Gage (New York: Fowler & Wells, 1881).

INTRODUCTION

page

1–2 On Peachie Wiggins: Harrisburg *Patriot,* June 4, 1969, p. 31; Dec. 3, 1968, pp. 1–2; Pittsburgh *Courier,* June 14, 1969, p. 1; Sharon "Peachie" Wiggins, interview, March 6–7, 1979. I am indebted to Jane Alpert for putting me in contact with Sharon Wiggins.

2 "shady aspect of liberation": Freda Adler, *Sisters in Crime: The Rise of the New Female Criminal* (New York: McGraw-Hill, 1975), pp. 13, 15. See also "The Hand That Rocks the Cradle Increasingly Holds a Gun, Warns a Woman Criminologist," *People,* Oct. 13, 1975, pp. 20–22; Lucinda Franks, "Who did what, how and where, but not why," *New York Times Book Review,* July 6, 1975, p. 7; Freda Adler, "Sisters in Crime," Pennsylvania *Gazette,* Nov. 1975, pp. 32–37; Lois DeFleur Nelson, "Will Changing Roles Have an Impact on Women in Crime and on the Way They Are Treated?" Washington *Post,* Oct. 13, 1977, p. D.C.5; and Judy Klemesrud, "A Criminologist's View of Women Terrorists," *New York Times,* Jan. 9, 1978, p. A24, in which Adler sees female "terrorist activity as deviant expression of feminism." Her views also were widely disseminated by official news releases from Professor Gerhard O. W. Mueller, chief of the United Nations crime prevention and criminal justice section, and Adler's husband. See, for example, Kathleen Teltsch, "The Women in Crime," *New York Times,* May 18, 1975, p. 56.

2–3 On Adler's misleading figures: Tom Buckley, "Critics Assail Linking Feminism with Women in Crime," *New York Times,* March 14, 1976, p. 48; Adler, p. 16; *UCR,* 1973, pp. 126, 131.

3 The greatest increases in women's crimes: Buckley, p. 48; Judy P. Hansen, "Women's Rights, and Wrongs," *New York Times,* March 17, 1975, p. 29; Harold M. Schmeck, Jr., "Crime Rise Tied to Heroin Price Rise," *New York Times,* April 25, 1976, p. 36; Nancy Hicks, "U.S. Study Links Rise in Jobless to Deaths, Murders and Suicides," *New York Times,* Oct. 31, 1976, pp. 1, 23.

3 "Women criminals today . . .": Robert Shannon, "Equality on the Wanted List," *Oui,* April 1975, p. 122.

3–4 That overreaction to an imaginary wave: See Kai T. Erikson, *Wayward Puritans: A Study in the Sociology of Deviance* (New York: John Wiley & Sons, 1966) and Stephen Nissenbaum and Paul Boyer, *Salem Possessed: The Social Origins of Witchcraft* (Cambridge, Mass.: Harvard University Press, 1974). On European witch hunts as a means to protect the social order, see George Rosen, *Madness in Society: Chapters in the Historical Sociology of Mental Ill-*

ness (New York: Harper & Row, 1968), p. 17, passim. For a modern instance, see Ann Jones, "Nurse Hunting in Michigan: The Narciso-Perez Case," *The Nation,* Dec. 3, 1977, pp. 584–88.

4 The rate of murders: Lee H. Bowker, *Women, Crime, and the Criminal Justice System* (Lexington, Mass.: D. C. Heath, 1978), pp. 4, 10; Rita James Simon, *Women and Crime* (Lexington, Mass.: D. C. Heath, 1975), p. 36; Laura Crites, ed., *The Female Offender* (Lexington, Mass.: D. C. Heath, 1976), pp. 33–35.

4 But the rate of arrests: Bowker, p. 6. More recently arrest rates leveled off; between 1976 and 1977 arrests of women increased only one percent for Crime Index offenses, 3 percent overall. Juvenile arrests were up 3 percent for both girls and boys. *UCR,* 1977, p. 171.

4 Researchers for the National Prison Project: " 'Violent' Women's Unit to Close at Kentucky Prison," *Women's Agenda,* Jan. 1979, p. 12.

4 "If it's equality these women want . . .": Simon, p. 18.

5 That focus is quite legitimate: Edwin H. Sutherland and Donald R. Cressey, *Principles of Criminology,* 6th ed. (Philadelphia: J.B. Lippincott, 1960), p. 111. Men still account for 80 percent of people arrested, 90 percent of people arrested for violent crimes. *UCR,* 1977, p. 171.

5–8 On modern criminology: Caesar Lombroso and William Ferrero, *The Female Offender* (New York: D. Appleton, 1897), trans. from *La Donna Delinquente, La Prostituta E La Donna Normale* (1893); William I. Thomas, *Sex and Society: Studies in the Social Psychology of Sex* (Chicago: University of Chicago Press, 1907); Thomas, *The Unadjusted Girl* (1923; rpt. Montclair, N.J.: Patterson Smith, 1969); Otto Pollak, *The Criminality of Women* (Philadelphia: University of Pennsylvania Press, 1950). For a feminist commentary see Dorie Klein, "The Etiology of Female Crime: A Review of the Literature," *Issues in Criminology,* vol. 8, no. 2 (Fall 1973), pp. 3–30.

6 For the good woman: Lombroso, pp. 274, 28.

6 On the case of Louise C.: Lombroso, p. 99; the photograph follows p. 100.

7 "Men crave excitement": Thomas, *Unadjusted Girl,* pp. 4, 17, 109.

7 "the adjustment of her person . . .": Thomas, *Sex and Society,* pp. 172, 241.

8 "their hope ever to become a man": Pollak, p. 127. Most of Pollak's notions can be found in Erich Wulffen, *Woman as a Sexual Criminal,* trans. David Berger (New York: American Ethnological, 1934). Wulffen's work, prompted by his concern for "woman's . . . independent spirit" and his fear (borne out by statistics) that "female criminality" was "suddenly leaping up" (pp. 156–57), corresponded nicely with the *kinder, küche und kirche* drive of Nazi Germany.

8 He picked up the popular nineteenth-century notion: Yet even Pollak's data confirm that women are more likely than men to be convicted of homicide, pp. 4–5. For a popular retailing of Pollak's chivalry thesis, see Janet Kole, "Women Who Murder," *New Times,* Jan. 24, 1975, pp. 34–39.

8 Arrest rates are climbing: Bowker, p. 213.

8 Between 1970 and 1975: Ronald G. Iacovetta, "Corrections and the Female Offender," *Resolution of Correctional Problems and Issues,* Summer 1975, p. 25.

9 women tend to receive *heavier* sentences: Bowker, p. 211.

9 In many states the law itself: Carolyn Engel Temin, "Discriminatory Sentencing of Women Offenders: The Argument for ERA in a Nutshell," rpt. from 11/355/ *American Criminal Law Review,* (1973), in Crites, pp. 51–58.

10 offenses . . . that would not be considered crimes: Gisela Konopka, *The Adolescent Girl in Conflict* (Englewood Cliffs, N.J.: Prentice-Hall, 1966), pp. 18–19; Karen DeCrow, *Sexist Justice* (New York: Random House, 1974), pp. 215–17.

10 A classic criminological study: Sheldon Glueck and Eleanor T. Glueck, *Five Hundred Delinquent Women* (New York: Alfred A. Knopf, 1934), p. 300.

10 A 1920 study: Mabel Ruth Fernald, et al. *A Study of Women Delinquents in New York State* (New York: Bureau of Social Hygiene, 1920), pp. 380–82.

10 In 1923 Thomas found: *Unadjusted Girl,* p. 101; see also Sophonisba P. Breckenridge and Edith Abbott, *The Delinquent Child and the Home* (New York: Russell Sage, 1917), pp. 106–107.

10 In 1966, criminologist Gisela Konopka: p. 51; Susan Reed, interview, April 24, 1979. Criminologists view the "delinquent" girl's charge of rape or incest as a "false accusation" typical of the lying, manipulative behavior which characterizes criminal women. See Pollak, pp. 24–26; Wulffen, p. 182; Lombroso, pp. 226–30. The false accusation can be traced at least as far back as Potiphar's wife. Susan Brownmiller reports the interesting fact that cases of "false accusation" of rape, when investigated by policewomen instead of policemen, turn out not to be false after all. Brownmiller concludes: "Women believe the word of other women. Men do not." *Against Our Will: Men, Women and Rape* (New York: Simon and Schuster, 1975), p. 387. The same would hold true for incest.

10–11 Lombroso inveighed: Lombroso, pp. 204–206; Thomas, *Unadjusted Girl,* passim; Pollak, p. 149.

11 as one feminist critic has noted, it is "retarded": Carol Smart, *Women, Crime and Criminology: A Feminist Critique* (London: Routledge & Kegan Paul, 1976), p. 52. The low intellectual level of American criminology is indicated by its continued regard, in spite of Smart's work, for Pollak's book as the very last word on women criminals. See Joy Pollock, "Early Theories of Female Criminality," in Bowker, pp. 25–55. American contributions to the criminology of women include "the Lady Macbeth Factor" advanced by Walter C. Reckless and "the Feline Syndrome" propounded by Barbara Kay. Reckless and Kay, *The Female Offender,* Paper submitted to the President's Commission on Law Enforcement and Administration of Justice, 1967, pp. 13, 15; Reckless and Charles L. Newman, eds., *Interdisciplinary Problems in Criminology: Papers of the American Society of Criminology, 1964* (Columbus, Ohio: Ohio State University Press, 1965), p. 212.

11 A twentieth-century psychiatrist: Ferdinand Lundberg and Marynia F. Farnham, *Modern Woman: The Lost Sex* (New York: Harper & Bros., 1947), pp. 197–98, 167.

12 There have always been some female armed robbers: "Life, Last Words and Dying Confession of Rachel Wall" (Boston: a broadside, 1789), rpt. Linda Grant DePauw and Conover Hunt, *Remember the Ladies: Women in America, 1750–1815* (New York: The Viking Press, 1976), p. 64.

12–13 Description of a typical woman in prison: Susan Reed, interview, April 24, 1979.

13 After her last commutation application: Sharon Wiggins, interview, March 6, 1979.

14 Enid Bagnold wrote: *Call Me Jacky* (1968) in *Four Plays* (London: Heinemann, 1970), pp. 330–31.

14 "they are just average, every-day sort . . .": Florence Monahan, *Women in Crime* (New York: Ives Washburn, 1941), p. 260.

ONE: FOREMOTHERS: DIVERS LEWD WOMEN

15–16 On Margaret Nicholson: Hampshire *Gazette,* Oct. 4, 1786, p. 1.

16 "fitt to be ymploied in forraine discoveries . . .": Abbot Emerson Smith, *Colonists in Bondage: White Servitude and Convict Labor in America, 1607–1776* (New York: W. W. Norton, 1971), pp. 92–93.

16 "Many of the Poor who had been useless . . .": Smith, p. 300.

16–17 Colonial court records, strewn with cases: Cheesman A. Herrick, *White Servitude in Pennsylvania: Indentured and Redemption Labor in Colony and Commonwealth* (Philadelphia: J. J. McVey, 1926), p. 141.

17 "When we see our Papers fill'd continually . . .": Pennsylvania *Gazette,* April 11, 1751, p. 2; rpt. Virginia *Gazette,* May 24, 1751, p. 3.

17 And Benjamin Franklin, petitioning: Edith Abbott, *Historical Aspects of the Immigration Problem, Select Documents* (Chicago: University of Chicago Press, 1926), pp. 544–45.

17 On Connecticut, Virginia, and Maryland restricting immigration: Emberson Edward Proper, "Colonial Immigration Laws: A Study of the Regulation of Immigration by the English Colonies in America," *Studies in History, Economics and Public Law,* vol. XII, no. 2 (1900), p. 33; Abbott, pp. 542–44.

17 In 1717 Parliament passed "An act . . .": Smith, pp. 110–111.

18 crisis in England as jails overflowed: Frederick Howard Wines, *Punishment and Reformation: A Study of the Penitentiary System,* rev. ed. (New York: Thomas Y. Crowell, 1919), p. 169.

18 "the Importations of Germans . . .": Abbott, p. 703.

18 France had taken to exporting convicts: James D. Hardy, Jr., "The Transportation of Convicts to Colonial Louisiana," *Louisiana History,* vol. VII, no. 3 (1966), pp. 207–20.

18 Perhaps one-third of them were women: Estimates vary and early records are fragmentary. Smith (pp. 116–17) established that 30,000 convicts (about

70 percent of those convicted at the Old Bailey) reached America in the eighteenth century. Considering that thousands came from Great Britain in the seventeenth century as well, and that numberless felons came from German and French jails, 50,000 seems a conservative figure. Smith estimates that about one-quarter of transported felons were women. Walter Hart Blumenthal puts the figure at one-third. *Brides from Bridewell: Female Felons Sent to Colonial America* (Westport, Conn.: Greenwood Press, 1962), pp. 17, 36.

18 Such shipments continued: Blumenthal, pp. 15–25; James Davie Butler, "British Convicts Shipped to American Colonies," *American Historical Review*, vol. II, no. 1 (Oct. 1896), pp. 24–25.

18 Mrs. Elizabeth Grieve: Butler, p. 30.

19 On Englishwomen hanged and burned: Blumenthal, p. 61.

19 "young and fitted for labor": Smith, p. 105.

19 "the market is against our sex . . .": Daniel Defoe, *The Fortunes and Misfortunes of the Famous Moll Flanders* (1722; rpt. New York: Modern Library, 1950), p. 14.

19 The problem throughout the seventeenth: Lawrence Stone, *The Family, Sex and Marriage in England 1500–1800* (London: Weidenfeld & Nicolson, 1977), p. 380; see also Arthur W. Calhoun, *A Social History of the American Family from Colonial Times to the Present* (1917; rpt. New York: Barnes and Noble, 1945), vol. I, p. 34.

19 "There is no proportion . . .": Defoe, p. 66.

20 "with a small stipend . . .": Mary Wollstonecraft, *A Vindication of the Rights of Women* (1792; rpt. New York: W. W. Norton, 1975), p. 65.

20 ". . . it was requisite to a whore to be handsome . . .": Defoe, p. 60.

20 the arduous crossing: Blumenthal, p. 23.

20 Like Iphigenia, women were sometimes killed: Raphael Semmes, *Crime and Punishment in Early Maryland* (Baltimore: Johns Hopkins Press, 1938), pp. 172–73; Julia Cherry Spruill, *Women's Life and Work in the Southern Colonies* (1938; rpt. New York: W. W. Norton, 1972), p. 327.

20 "a villainous and demoralized lot": Charles Bateson, *The Convict Ships, 1787–1868* (Glasgow: Brown, Son & Ferguson, 1959), pp. 96, 101–02, 105–06. On the transportation of women to Australia, see Anne Summers, *Damned Whores and God's Police: The Colonization of Women in Australia* (Ringwood, Victoria: Penguin, 1975).

21 On runaway indentured servants: Linda Grant DePauw and Conover Hunt, *Remember the Ladies: Women in America, 1750–1815* (New York: The Viking Press, 1976), p. 68; Blumenthal, pp. 46–47.

22 The first consignment of ninety single women: Spruill, pp. 8–9. See also the report to the Quarter Court in London, Nov. 21, 1621: ". . . whereby the Planters minds may be the faster tyed to Virginia by the bonds of Wyves and Children care hath bin taken to provide them young, handsome and honestly educated mayds. . . ." in Edward D. Neill, *History of the Virginia Company*

of London (1869; rpt. New York: Burt Franklin, 1968), pp. 262, 566. Records indicate that ninety women arrived in 1620 aboard the *Jonathan* and the *London Merchant;* fifty-seven more came in 1621, thirty-eight of them in the *Tiger,* eleven in the *Marmaduke,* and the rest in the *Warwick.* The company announced plans to send another hundred and another sixty, but the plans probably fell through.

22 On William Robinson and Owen Evans: Carl Bridenbaugh, *Vexed and Troubled Englishmen, 1590–1642* (New York: Oxford University Press, 1968), p. 419.

22–23 Superfluous daughters were the price: Stone, p. 382, quoting Milton's "Animadversions Upon the Remonstrant's Defence" (Columbia Ed., vol. III, p. 160). Calhoun states flatly that "unmarried daughters were undesirable members of the household," vol. I, p. 34.

23 "Women were transported to America . . .": Bridenbaugh, *Vexed,* pp. 419–20; see also Blumenthal, pp. 64–78; Richard Hofstadter, *America at 1750: A Social Portrait* (New York: Vintage Books, 1973), pp. 34–37.

23 Women shipped to Louisiana to become wives: Blumenthal, pp. 86, 82.

23 "The poor creatures who have been induced . . .": Abbott, p. 28.

23–24 "What we unfortunat English People . . .": Isabel M. Calder, *Colonial Captivities, Marches and Journeys* (New York: Macmillan, 1935), p. 151.

24 On Anne Vaughan and Ann Beetle: Semmes, p. 139.

24 ". . . the Misfortune of wanting Wives.": Roger Thompson, *Women in Stuart England and America, A Comparative Study* (London: Routledge & Kegan Paul, 1974), p. 36.

24 "The Women that go over into this Province . . .": Thompson, p. 36.

25 "Yesterday was married, in Henrico . . .": Spruill, p. 161.

25–26 On Ellinor Spinke: Semmes, pp. 222–23.

26 On servants who ran off in their mistresses' clothing: Spruill, p. 134.

26 On Sarah Wilson: Butler, p. 29.

27 "a paradise on Earth . . .": Thompson, p. 42.

27 "Whereas Dorethy the wyfe of John Talbie . . .": George Elliott Howard, *A History of Matrimonial Institutions, Chiefly in England and the United States* (Chicago: University of Chicago Press, 1904), vol. II, pp. 161–62; see also *Historical Collections of the Essex Institute* (Salem: Essex Institute, 1865), vol. VII, p. 129.

28 "Whereupon she grew worse": John Winthrop, *Winthrop's Journal: "History of New England," 1630–1649,* James Kendall Hosmer, ed. (New York: Charles Scribner's Sons, 1908; rpt. as *Original Narratives of Early American History,* vols. 18–19), vol. I, p. 282.

28 In July 1638: *Historical Collections of the Essex Institute,* vol. VII, p. 187; see also *Records and Files of the Quarterly Courts of Essex County, Massachusetts* (Salem: Essex Institute, 1911), vol. I (1636–1656), p. 9.

28 When they hanged her: Winthrop, vol. I, p. 283. Modern sexist bias against aggressive women, whatever the source of their aggression, infests historian

Henry W. Lawrence's description of Dorothy Talbye as "unsubmissive and brutally mannish" and a "vixen." *The Not Quite Puritans* (Boston: Little, Brown, 1928), pp. 162–63. Primary sources indicate that she indeed was unsubmissive; the other value-laden terms are Lawrence's own.

28   When John Talbye died: *Courts of Essex County,* vol. I, p. 73.

28–29   On colonial law and punishment for murder: George Lee Haskins, *Law and Authority in Early Massachusetts: A Study in Tradition and Design* (New York: Macmillan, 1960), p. 149; Edwin Powers, *Crime and Punishment in Early Massachusetts, 1620–1692: A Documentary History* (Boston: Beacon Press, 1966), pp. 258–59; see also Daniel J. Boorstin, *The Americans: The Colonial Experience* (New York: Random House, 1958), pp. 20–28, and Julius Goebel, Jr., "King's Law and Local Custom in Seventeenth Century New England," 31 *Columbia Law Review* 416 (1931).

29   "found the said Allice Bishope . . .": *Records of the Colony of New Plymouth in New England,* Nathaniel B. Shurtleff, ed. (Boston: White, 1855), vol. II, p. 134.

30   "much better [than] any husband can": Samuel Eliot Morison, *Builders of the Bay Colony* (Boston: Houghton Mifflin, 1930), p. 75. Winthrop, who came to Massachusetts as an adult, bringing English attitudes full-blown, thought less of women than did subsequent colonial leaders.

30   "this act shall not be construed . . .": Edith Abbott, *Women in Industry: A Study in American Economic History* (New York: D. Appleton, 1913), p. 33.

30   On women engaged in work: Abbott, pp. 11, 34; DePauw, pp. 61–62; Elisabeth Anthony Dexter, *Colonial Women of Affairs: Women in Business and the Professions in America Before 1776,* 2nd ed. (Boston: Houghton Mifflin, 1931), passim; Eugenie Andruss Leonard, Sophie Hutchinson Drinker, and Miriam Young Holden, *The American Woman in Colonial and Revolutionary Times, 1565–1800* (Philadelphia: University of Pennsylvania Press, 1962), pp. 36, 76–80, 88, 94–97, passim, Boorstin, pp. 186–87; Thompson, passim.

31   ". . . *bad ones are better than none*": Edmund S. Morgan, *The Puritan Family: Religion and Domestic Relations in Seventeenth-Century New England* (New York: Harper & Row, 1966), p. 29.

31   On equity law: Thompson, pp. 135, 161–69; Mary R. Beard, *Woman as Force in History: A Study in Traditions and Realities* (1946; rpt. New York: Collier, 1962), pp. 87–105.

31   opportunities unknown in the Old World: Semmes, pp. 91–92; Thompson, p. 76.

31   antenuptial and postnuptial contracts: In 1675 John Hurst of Virginia was forbidden to "meddle" with the property of Elizabeth Alford, his prospective wife. Such agreements were customary in the case of widows with children and property inherited from a deceased husband. Philip Alexander Bruce, *Social Life of Virginia in the Seventeenth Century,* 2nd ed. (Lynchburg, Va.: J. P. Bell, 1927), p. 236. See also Thompson, pp. 165–66.

31 women could vote: Leonard, pp. 33–35. The number of women granted suffrage was small, but so was the number of men.

31 "... whether man or woman be the most necessary": Spruill, p. 9.

32 On James Britton and Mary Latham: Winthrop, vol. II, pp. 161–63. Following biblical precedent, adultery was not equitably defined; legally adultery was an act committed by a "Married or Espoused Wife" and "any Person." Powers, p. 261; Haskins, p. 149. Nevertheless, husbandly adultery was grounds for divorce in Plymouth Colony. Thompson, p. 176.

32 On the execution of Nepaupuck: Rollin G. Osterweis, *Three Centuries of New Haven, 1638–1938* (New Haven: Yale University Press, 1953), pp. 18–19.

32 On Hannah Occuish: Frances Manwaring Caulkins, *History of New London Connecticut from the First Survey of the Coast in 1612, to 1852* (New London: author, 1860), pp. 576–77; Thomas M. McDade, *The Annals of Murder: A Bibliography of Books and Pamphlets on American Murders from Colonial Times to 1900* (Norman, Okla.: University of Oklahoma Press, 1961), p. 216; Henry Channing, *God Admonishing His People of Their Duty, As Parents and Masters, A Sermon Preached at New-London, December 20th, 1786* (New London: T. Green, 1787), pp. 29–31; Hampshire *Gazette,* Jan. 10, 1787, p. 3. By the beginning of the nineteenth century, children and teenagers usually were not executed. Anthony M. Platt cites two exceptions: Guild, a twelve-year-old boy executed in New Jersey in 1828 for beating an old woman to death, and Godfrey, an eleven-year-old boy executed in Alabama in 1858 for murdering a four-year-old boy who had broken his kite. Both Guild and Godfrey were black slaves and almost certainly would not have been executed had they been white. *The Child Savers: The Invention of Delinquency* (Chicago: University of Chicago Press, 1969), pp. 194–202.

32 "God Almighty in His most...": John Winthrop, "A Model of Christian Charity," in *The American Puritans: Their Prose and Poetry,* Perry Miller, ed. (1938; rpt. New York: Doubleday, 1956), p. 79.

33 "to show forth the glory of His wisdom...": Winthrop, "A Model," p. 79.

33 *"Who are ... meant by Father...":* Morgan, p. 19.

33 "There are *Parents* in the *Common-Wealth*...": Cotton Mather, *A Family Well-Ordered, or an Essay to Render Parents and Children Happy in One Another* (Boston: B. Green & J. Allen 1699), p. 66.

33 "There is a strain in a man's heart": John Cotton, "Limitation of Government," in Miller, p. 86.

33 "the more occasion to manifest...": Winthrop, "A Model," p. 79.

33–34 Husbands were forbidden: Powers, p. 542. The same law forbade wives to strike their husbands. It was for violating this law that Dorothy Talbye was first arraigned.

34 On annulment and divorce: Howard, vol. II, pp. 328–33.

34 Similar laws protected servants: Haskins, pp. 154–57.

34 "... worst of all forms of government": Morison, p. 92.

34 "The woman's own choice . . .": John Winthrop, "Speech to the General Court," in Miller, pp. 92–93.

34 ". . . it is good for the wife . . .": Cotton, p. 87.

35 On Joan Miller: Calhoun, vol. I, p. 144.

35 On Mrs. Cornish: Winthrop, *Journal,* vol. II, pp. 218–19.

36 On law of petit treason: William Blackstone, *Commentaries on the Laws of England* (Philadelphia: Robert Bell, 1771; rpt. from 4th London ed.), vol. IV, p. 75.

36 ". . . Other offences are injurious . . .": Hugh F. Rankin, *Criminal Trial Proceedings in the General Court of Colonial Virginia* (Williamsburg: Colonial Williamsburg, 1965), p. 222.

36 "as the natural modesty . . .": Blackstone, vol. IV, p. 93.

36–38 On Catherine Bevan: Pennsylvania *Gazette,* June 17–24, 1731, p. 493; Sept. 9–23, 1731, p. 540.

37–38 "The 'judgments of God' . . .": Cotton Mather, *Magnalia Christi, or, The Ecclesiastical History of New-England* (1702; rpt. from 1852 ed., New York: Russell, 1967), vol. II, p. 385.

38 On 1639 murder at Hartford: John Hope Franklin, *From Slavery to Freedom: A History of Negro Americans,* 3rd ed. (New York: Vintage Books, 1969), p. 101.

38 "I am flesh and blood . . .": Mather, *Magnalia,* vol. II, p. 408. The other attributed his fall to disobedience to parents.

38 "The Proud hearts of many *Servants* . . .": Mather, *Family Well-Ordered,* pp. 66–67.

38 ". . . whatever ye do . . .": Mather, *Family Well-Ordered,* p. 67.

38–39 On slave codes: John Hope Franklin, pp. 105–106; Douglas Greenberg, "Patterns of Criminal Prosecution in Eighteenth Century New York," *New York History,* vol. LVI, no. 2 (April 1975), p. 139.

39 ". . . at Wallingford in Connecticut . . .": Pennsylvania *Gazette,* July 22–29, 1731, p. 513.

39 "The Negro Woman who lately kill'd . . .": Virginia *Gazette,* Feb. 18–25, 1737, p. 4.

39 "On Friday last a Negro man . . .": Virginia *Gazette* (Pardie & Dixon), Aug. 24, 1769 (no. 953), p. 2. The two reportedly poisoned the woman's master, one James Sands, and his wife and child. The child died. Albert Matthews, "Burning Criminals," *Virginia Magazine of History and Biography,* vol. IV (1896–1897), p. 341.

39 "on the high hills of Orange County . . .": Arthur P. Scott, *Criminal Law in Colonial Virginia* (Chicago: University of Chicago Press, 1930), pp. 196–97; A. G. Grinan, "The Burning of Eve in Virginia," *Virginia Magazine of History and Biography,* vol. III (1895–1896), pp. 308–10.

39 Crimes such as these poisonings: In Virginia alone incomplete records indicate that between 1774 and 1864 slaves were convicted of at least 1,418 capital crimes, including 346 known murders. Of the 286 murder cases in which

the victim was identified by race, more than two-thirds of the victims were white. Ulrich B. Phillips, "Slave Crime in Virginia," *American Historical Review*, vol. XX (1914–1915), pp. 336–40.

40–41 On Phillis and Mark: Abner C. Goodell, Jr., "The Murder of Captain Codman," *Proceedings of the Massachusetts Historical Society*, vol. XX (1882–1883), pp. 122–57; Boston Evening *Post*, Sept. 22, 1755, p. 4; "The Trial of MARK and PHILLIS (Negro Slaves) for Petit Treason, in the Murder of Captain John Codman, their Master, Cambridge, Massachusetts, 1755," *AST*, vol. XI (1919), pp. 511–27.

40 On Maria: Maria was burned at Boston, Sept. 22, 1681. Executed with her was a black male slave, Chessaleer Jack, who had been convicted in a separate case of arson at Northampton. Jack was condemned to be hanged until dead and then burned in the fire that consumed Maria alive. The legal basis for burning Maria is not clear since her case does not seem to be petit treason, unless one construes the law to include (as some commentators do) any injury to the master in his person or property. Increase Mather writes in his diary for Sept. 22, 1681, that a child was burned to death in one of the houses Maria set on fire, but unless the child were Maria's mistress, the charges against Maria should have been arson and manslaughter, both punishable by hanging. See *Records of the (Massachusetts) Court of Assistants*, vol. I, pp. 198–99; John Noble, "The Case of Maria in the Court of Assistants in 1681," *Publications of the Colonial Society of Massachusetts*, vol. VI (1904), pp. 323–36. Bridenbaugh mentions the case of a black woman burned in New Amsterdam in 1664 for setting fire to her master's house. *Cities in the Wilderness: The First Century of Urban Life in America, 1625–1742* (New York: Ronald Press, 1938), p. 69.

41 On gibbeting Mark: Goodell, p. 148. Blackstone points out that gibbeting is quite contrary to the express command of the "Mosaical law" which orders that "the body of a malefactor shall not remain all night upon the tree; but thou shalt in any wise bury him in that day, that the land be not defiled" (Deuteronomy 21:23). He observes that the practice "seems to have been borrowed from the civil law; which, besides the terror of the example, gives another reason for this practice, *viz.* that it is a comfortable sight to the relations and friends of the deceased"—that is, presumably, the murderer's victim. Vol. IV, p. 202. Revere's letter of Jan. 1, 1798, is in *1 Massachusetts Historical Collections*, vol. V, p. 107.

42 Bastardy itself was everywhere a crime: Henry Bamford Parkes reports that "bastardies doubled or even tripled or quadrupled" between 1730 and 1770. "Morals and Law Enforcement in Colonial New England," *The New England Quarterly*, vol. V (1932), p. 443.

42 Cities grew too rapidly: Bridenbaugh, *Cities in the Wilderness*, p. 226.

43 "abandon'd Morals and profligate Principles": Bridenbaugh, *Myths and Realities, Societies of the Colonial South* (Baton Rouge, La.: Louisiana State University Press, 1952), pp. 173–74.

43 That law made servants' pregnancies: Thompson, p. 251.

43–44 On bastardy law and punishment: Semmes, pp. 187–97; Arthur Scott, pp. 279–81; Betty B. Rosenbaum, "The Sociological Basis of the Laws Relating to Women Sex Offenders in Massachusetts (1620–1860)," *Journal of American Institute of Criminal Law and Criminology,* vol. 28 (May-June, 1937–Mar.-Apr., 1938) pp. 832–33; Susies M. Ames, *Studies of the Virginia Eastern Shore in the Seventeenth Century* (Richmond: Dietz Press, 1940), pp. 186–87; Boorstin, p. 130.

43 On Eve Sewell: Nelson Manfred Blake, *The Road to Reno: A History of Divorce in the United States* (New York: Macmillan, 1962), p. 51.

44 "In the Southern Parts of this Country": Cotton Mather, *Warnings from the Dead, or, Solemn Admonitions Unto All People* (Boston: Bartholomew Green, 1693), p. 44.

44 "the only crime which good society . . .": *Report of the Trial of Susanna, A Coloured Woman* (Troy, New York: Ryer Schermerhorn, 1810), p. 29.

45 "Act to prevent the Destroying . . .": Thomas Foxcroft, *Lessons of Caution to Young Sinners, A sermon Preach'd on Lord's-Day Sept. 23, 1733* (Boston: Kneeland & Green, 1733), from the Preface "by Mr. Cooper" citing *Province Laws,* chapter 11 (1696).

45 "People determined upon the commission . . .": *The Trial of Alice Clifton for the Murder of her Bastard-Child* (n.p., n.d.), p. 13.

46 "Take heed . . . that you do not *dishonour* . . .": Foxcroft, p. 50.

46 "They who have Committed folly of this Kind . . .": Eliphalet Adams, *A Sermon Preached on the Occasion of the Execution of Katherine Garret, An Indian-Servant Who was Condemned for the Murder of her Spurious Child* (New London: T. Green, 1738), p. 30.

46–47 On Mary Martin: Winthrop, *Journal,* vol. II, pp. 317–18; Mather, *Magnalia,* vol. II, pp. 404–05.

47–48 "And let our young Women be admonish'd": Foxcroft, p. 36.

48 "to hide her misfortune": Hampshire *Gazette,* April 16, 1788, p. 3; Charles Allen Converse, *Some of the Ancestors and Descendants of Samuel Converse, Jr., Major James Convers, Hon. Heman Allen, M.C., Captain Jonathan Bixby, Sr.* (Boston: Eben Putnam, 1905), vol. I, p. 79. Abiel Converse is wrongly identified in the Converse genealogy as male.

48 "with intent to conceal her Lewdness . . .": *Records of the Court of Assize and General Gaol Delivery,* Hampshire County (Massachusetts), 1698, vol. II, p. 193.

48 On the servant Susanna: *Trial of Susanna,* pp. 45, 15.

48 black women deprived their masters of slaves: Eleanor Flexner, *Century of Struggle: The Woman's Rights Movement in the United States* (Cambridge, Mass.: Harvard University Press, 1973), p. 95. Black slaves, if detected in infanticide, often were punished by their masters; consequently public records of such cases are rare. Undoubtedly the women were severely punished, but because they were valued as property they probably were not killed.

48–49 *"And all the people shall hear...":* Adams, p. 25. Given the total population of these areas in the eighteenth century, these crowds are astonishing. There is no present-day equivalent, for it would have to be a gathering of many millions.

48 "so many Thousands" gathered: John Rogers, *Death the Certain Wages of Sin to the Impenitent... Occasioned by the Imprisonment, Condemnation and Execution of a Young Woman, Who was Guilty of Murdering her Infant begotten in Whoredom* (Boston: B. Green & J. Allen, 1701), pp. 2, 153.

48 "surrounded with a Vast Circle of people...": Adams, p. 42.

48–49 On hanging Sarah Bramble: Caulkins, p. 468.

49 Esther Rodgers was the first person sentenced: Rogers, p. 3.

49 The double hanging: William Shurtleff, *The Faith and Prayer: A Sermon Preached December 27, 1739 On Occasion of the Execution of two Criminals* (Boston: J. Draper for D. Henchman, 1740), from the preface by Jabez Fitch, p. i.

49 Simeon Clapp: Judd Manuscript, Collections of the Forbes Library, Northampton, Massachusetts, Misc. vol. X, p. 108.

49 "Beware the Sin of *Pride* . . .": Foxcroft, p. 35.

49 Undoubtedly there are many more forgotten names: Rankin has determined that twelve of the fifty-nine murder trials reported in the Virginia *Gazette* are cases of women charged with killing their bastards.

49 Women . . . do not have to be restrained: Glanville Williams writes: ". . . there are forms of murder, or near-murder, the prohibition of which is rather the expression of a philosophical attitude than the outcome of social necessity. These are infanticide, abortion, and suicide. . . . The prohibition of killing imposed by these three crimes does not rest upon considerations of public security. If it can be justified at all, this must be either on ethico-religious or on racial grounds." *The Sanctity of Life and the Criminal Law* (New York: Alfred A. Knopf, 1957), p. x.

50 When Robert Thompson was convicted: Judd MS, Misc. vol. I, p. 321.

50 "In many if not most instances of murder...": Aaron Bascom, *A Sermon Preached at the Execution of Abiel Converse* (Northampton, Mass.: William Butler, 1788), p. 19.

50 ". . . the evil of sinners . . .": Bascom, p. 6.

51 ". . . what malice or revenge . . .": *Trial of Susanna,* p. 23.

51 The women who killed their children: Bascom, p. 19.

51 birth control after the fact: Linda Gordon observes, "If infanticide is not suitable in most of today's societies, it is because we have found better methods of birth control, not because we are morally superior." *Woman's Body, Woman's Right: A Social History of Birth Control in America* (New York: Grossman, 1976), p. 35.

51 Such statements challenge civil: Many societies have practiced systematic infanticide to control population, but Gordon points out that "where infanticide was legal, men almost always governed its application. To give women

the right to decide the fate of babies would have meant that men would give up a key part of their patriarchal power." P. 33.

52 "an unclean and whorish woman . . .": Hampshire *Gazette,* April 30, 1788, p. 3; Bascom, p. 22. It is curious that even the best modern historians uncritically accept the judgment of the colonial ministers. On the basis of Rev. Rogers's denunciation of Esther Rodgers as a whorish woman, historian David J. Rothman identifies her as a "prostitute." *The Discovery of the Asylum: Social Order and Disorder in the New Republic* (Boston: Little, Brown, 1971), p. 15.

52 "The Apostle wou'd have the young women taught . . .": Foxcroft, p. 48.

52 Franklin's satiric essay: Benjamin Franklin, "What Are the Poor Young Women to Do? The Speech of Polly Baker," *The Writings of Benjamin Franklin,* Albert Henry Smyth, ed. (New York: Macmillan, 1905), vol. II, pp. 463–67.

52 By 1780 the Marquis: Marquis de Chastellux, *Travels in North America, in the Years 1780, 1781 and 1782,* trans. Howard C. Rice, Jr. (1786; rpt. Chapel Hill: University of North Carolina Press, 1963), vol. I, pp. 67, 253–54.

52–53 At the Court of General Sessions: Records of the Court of General Sessions of the Peace, Hampshire County, Mass., May Term, 1785. *Sessions Records,* Book No. 14 (May 1776–Jan. 1790), pp. 184–85.

53 Esther Rodgers went out to the field: *The Declaration & Confession of Esther Rodgers,* appended to Rogers, p. 124.

53 Susanna Andrews left her parents' house: *Records of Plymouth County Court,* 1696, vol. II, p. 49.

53 Katherine Garret gave birth in the barn: "brief account" of Katherine Garret appended to Adams, p. 38; *Records of the Superiour Court of Judicature Court of Assize and General Gaol Delivery of Suffolk County,* 1698, vol. II, p. 199; *Trial of Alice Clifton,* p.3.

53 Esther Rodgers, sentenced to die: Rogers, p. 122.

53 On Sarah Simpson and Penelope Kenny: William Shurtleff, pp. ii–iii.

53 "to make proper and pertinent Reflections . . .": "A Brief Narrative Concerning the Criminals," appended to William Shurtleff, p. 25.

54 *"her miserable and perishing Estate"*: William Shurtleff, pp. 26, 29.

54 Mather concentrated his efforts: Mather, *Warnings from the Dead,* p. 74.

54 After the ministers "prepared": *The Declaration, Dying Warning and Advice of Rebekah Chamblit* (Boston: Kneeland & Green, 1733), a broadside.

54 Esther Rodgers said that God: Rogers, p. 122.

54 Sarah Simpson said: William Shurtleff, pp. 27–28.

54 "I am a Miserable Sinner . . .": Mather, *Warnings from the Dead,* pp. 70–71; also in *Magnalia,* vol. II, pp. 418–19.

54–55 "Here I am come to Dy . . .": Rogers, pp. 147–48.

55 Sarah Simpson advised young people: William Shurtleff, p. 28.

55 At first Esther Rodgers refused to speak: Rogers, pp. 127–28.

55 Rebekah Chamblit also kept: Foxcroft, p. ii; *The Declaration . . . of Rebekah Chamblit.*

55 Sarah Smith told nothing: Mather, *Magnalia,* vol. II, p. 420.

55 "Bloody *Murderer*": Mather, *Warnings from the Dead,* pp. 72–74.

55 Simpson and Kenny denounced: William Shurtleff, p. 26.

55 Eleanor White: Harry B. Weiss and Grace M. Weiss, *An Introduction to Crime and Punishment in Colonial New Jersey* (Trenton: Past Times, 1960), p. 55.

55 "Stupid & Obstinate and Insensible . . .": Adams, pp. 32, 39.

55–56 Yet even Elizabeth Wilson blamed: *A Faithful Narrative of Elizabeth Wilson; Who Was Executed at Chester, January 3d, 1786* (Philadelphia: n.p., 1786), p. 11.

56 Simpson and Kenny also: William Shurtleff, p. iii.

56 "I find . . . a willingness in me . . .": Rogers, pp. 131, 126.

56 Some few condemned women held out: Caulkins, p. 468; Mather, *Magnalia,* vol. II, p. 420; *The Declaration . . . of Rebekah Chamblit.*

56 Each was preached a sermon: John Williams, *Warnings to the Unclean: in a Discourse From Rev. XXI.8 Preacht at Springfield Lecture, August 25th, 1698. At the Execution of Sarah Smith* (Boston: B. Green & J. Allen, 1699), title page; Foxcroft, title page, p. 19.

56 Then the condemned woman walked: Rogers, p. 144.

57 "made apt and pertinent remarks . . .": Adams, p. 41.

57 Sarah Simpson displayed: William Shurtleff, p. 26; Rogers, p. 153.

57 Katherine Garret delivered: Adams, p. 42.

57 Rebekah Chamblit, responding: Foxcroft, p. 63.

57 On the purpose of punishment: Thomas Hobbes, *Leviathan* (1651; rpt. London: J. M. Dent, 1965), p. 166; John Locke, *Of Civil Government* (1690; rpt. London: J. M. Dent, 1924), vol. II, p. 120. Compare Montesquieu's opinion that "the excessive severity of laws hinders their execution: when the punishment surpasses all measure, the public will frequently out of humanity prefer impunity to it."

57 public capital and corporal punishments: Michel Foucault, *Discipline & Punish: The Birth of the Prison,* trans. Alan Sheridan (New York: Vintage, 1979), pp. 8–11.

57 The number of religious sects: See Hofstadter, pp. 187–94.

58 One of the "privileges" of some: Judd MS, Misc. vol. X, p. 108; Parkes, pp. 446–47.

58 On Mrs. Thompson: Virginia *Gazette,* July 6, 1769, p. 3.

58–59 Three years after the slave Eve: Grinan, p. 310.

59 On Sarah Kirk: Delaware Federal Writers' Project (U.S. Works Progress Administration), *New Castle on the Delaware* (New Castle, Del.: New Castle Historical Society, 1936), p. 103.

59 In colonial Pennsylvania: Herbert William Keith Fitzroy, "The Punishment of Crime in Provincial Pennsylvania," *Pennsylvania Magazine of History and Biography,* vol. LX, no. 3 (July 1936), pp. 256–57.

59–62 On Bathsheba Spooner: Peleg W. Chandler, *American Criminal Trials* (Boston: Little, Brown; T. H. Carter, 1841–1844), vol. II, pp. 1–58; pp. 375–83; See also "The Trial of Bathsheba Spooner, William Brooks, James Buchanan and Ezra Ross for the Murder of Joshua Spooner, Massachusetts, 1778," *AST,* vol. II (1914), pp. 175–201.

61 "The loud shouts of the officers . . .": Chandler, vol. II, p. 52.

62 In 1837 the Edgefield: Jack Kenny Williams, *Vogues in Villainy: Crime and Retribution in Ante-Bellum South Carolina* (Columbia, S.C.: University of South Carolina Press, 1959), p. 22.

TWO: DOMESTIC ATROCITY

62 Everyone noticed the odd silence: Historians often discount the observations of nineteenth-century foreign travelers as biased and superficial. Foreign opinion critical of American society produced vigorous denunciations at the time, however, precisely because it so often struck accurately at raw nerves. In the matter of the relations between the sexes, the travelers' views are too often unanimous to be ignored. And if descriptions of American society often seem superficial, that—as Dickens pointed out—is precisely the point; society *was* superficial and relationships between women and men strained.

63 One could always spot: Charles Joseph LaTrobe, *The Rambler in North America* (London: Seeley & Burnside, 1836), vol. II, p. 143.

63 In the 1820s: Frances Trollope, *Domestic Manners of the Americans* (London: Whittaker, Treacher, 1832), vol. I, pp. 82–83; vol. II, p. 101.

64 According to Englishman: Edward Augustus Kendall, *Travels Through the Northern Parts of the United States in the Years 1807 and 1808* (New York: I. Riley, 1809), vol. I, p. 327.

64 Ladies were relegated: Basil Hall, *Travels in North America in the Years 1827 and 1828* (Philadelphia: Carey, Lea & Carey, 1829), vol. I, pp. 259–60; Richard Weston, *The United States and Canada in 1833 with the View of Settling in America* (Edinburgh: Weston, 1836), pp. 86–87; Morris Birkbeck, *Notes on a Journey in America From the Coast of Virginia to the Territory of Illinois* (Dublin: T. Larkin, 1818), pp. 88–89.

64 In New York City: Thomas Hamilton, *Men and Manners in America* (Philadelphia: Carey, Lea & Blanchard, 1833), vol. I, pp. 69–70, 131.

64 From Cincinnati: Trollope, vol. II, pp. 161, 100.

64 Kendall reported a fact: vol. I, pp. 327–28.

64 It was the "want of . . .": Henry Duhring, *Remarks on the United States of America, With Regard to the Actual State of Europe* (London: Simpkin & Marshall, 1833), p. 78.

64 "Young women of the respectable . . .": James Edward Alexander, *Transatlantic Sketches* (London: R. Bentley, 1833), vol. II, p. 311.

65 tobacco-spitting drunkards: See John Fowler, *Journal of a Tour in the State of New York in the Year 1830* (London: Whittaker, Treacher, Arnot, 1831), p. 217 on "that disgusting habit of *smoking* and *chewing* tobacco, and of nearly *indiscriminate spitting*." For an American woman's view, see Cather-

ine Maria Sedgwick, *Morals of Manners, or Hints for our Young People* (New York: G. P. Putnam, 1846), pp. 25–30.

65 In 1800 there were only five cities: Russel Blaine Nye, *The Cultural Life of the New Nation, 1776–1830* (New York: Harper & Row, 1960), p. 124; see also Charles Dickens, *American Notes for General Circulation,* eds. John S. Whitley and Arnold Goldman (1842; rpt. London: Penguin, 1972), pp. 136–39.

65 On the surplus of women: In 1845 Catherine Beecher reported, "By the census, it appears that the excess of female population in New England over that of the other sex is more than 14,000." This surplus female population led to the exploitation of women workers, particularly in factories and in the needle trades, while in the West, where women were scarce, the traditionally female job of teaching young children was assumed by men. Alarmed by the "impropriety" of both situations, Beecher proposed to move eastern single women west as missionary teachers. *The Duty of American Women to their Country* (New York: Harper & Bros., 1845), p. 119, and *The Evils Suffered by American Women and American Children: the Causes and Remedy ... Also, An Address to the Protestant Clergy of the United States* (New York: Harper & Bros., 1846), pp. 6, 12. In 1858 the St. Paul *Pioneer and Democrat* claimed that Minnesota had 25,000 more men than women because of "the desire ... of henpecked husbands and others to escape from [Massachusetts] women." March 18, 1858, p. 2. By 1883, when Mary Livermore lectured on "superfluous women," women outnumbered men in Massachusetts by 60,000. *What Shall We Do with Our Daughters? Superfluous Women and Other Lectures* (Boston: Lee & Shepard, 1883), p. 138. Many women left behind were married. Speaking to the New England Convention for Woman's Rights in 1859, Rev. John T. Sargent of Boston said, "Hundreds of poor, desolate, forsaken women, especially in the winter months, have come ... with the same pitiable tale of poverty, desertion, and tyranny on the part of their worthless and drunken husbands, who had gone off to California, Kansas, or the West, taking away from their wives and children every possible means of support, and leaving them the pauper dependents on a public charity." *HWS,* vol. I, pp. 270–71.

65–66 Women had to stay at home: William Alexander Alcott, *The Young Woman's Guide to Excellence* (New York: Clark, Austin & Smith, 1852), p. 175; Duhring, p. 74. On the definition of woman's sphere, see Nancy F. Cott, *The Bonds of Womanhood: "Woman's Sphere" in New England, 1780–1835* (New Haven: Yale University Press, 1977), pp. 63–100.

66 Woman's sphere and its intrinsic rewards: Trollope, vol. II, pp. 71–75; Harriet Martineau, *Society in America* (London: Saunders & Otley, 1839), vol. III, p. 47.

66 Society ladies were not: Birkbeck, p. 128; Alexander, vol. II, pp. 114–15; Anna Howard Shaw, "The Story of a Pioneer" (1915), in Mary R. Beard, *America Through Women's Eyes* (New York: Macmillan, 1933), p. 105;

Michael Lesy, *Wisconsin Death Trip* (New York: Pantheon, 1973), entry for the year 1893.

66–67 In every class: Arthur W. Calhoun, *A Social History of the American Family from Colonial Times to the Present* (1917; rpt. New York: Barnes & Noble, 1945), vol. II, p. 133. Recent scholarship bears out the observation. See Caroll Smith-Rosenberg: "American society [between the mid-eighteenth and mid-nineteenth centuries] was characterized in large part by rigid gender-role differentiation within the family and within society as a whole, leading to the emotional segregation of women and men." "The Female World of Love and Ritual: Relations Between Women in Nineteenth-Century America," *Signs*, vol. I, no. 1 (Autumn 1975), p. 9. In *The Angel Makers: A Study in the Psychological Origins of Historical Change, 1750–1850*, Gordon Rattray Taylor is "struck by certain signs of the existence of very powerful overt resentments between the sexes." (New York: E. P. Dutton, 1974), p. 13. Taylor studies English society, but many of the psychological elements he discusses apply to America as well; and America was heavily influenced during the period by all things English.

67 It was commonplace to excuse: Francis J. Grund, *The Americans, in Their Moral, Social, and Political Relations* (London: Longman, Rees, 1837), vol. II, p. 1 ff; Fowler, p. 215; Henry Adams, *History of the United States of America During the Administration of Thomas Jefferson* (1891–1896; rpt. New York: Antiquarian, 1962), pp. 174–75. (Adams, however, thought American avarice no worse than European and even touched with certain noble aspects.) Thomas L. Nichols, *Forty Years of American Life* (1864; rpt. New York: Johnson Reprint, 1969), vol. I, pp. 403–404.

67 Women, then, were not so much: Duhring, pp. 65–66; Trollope, vol. I, pp. 215–16. The New York celebration of Robert Owen's eighty-third birthday in 1854 was memorable because the ladies—including Lucy Stone and Ernestine Rose—"did not sit in the galleries, as the custom then was, to look at the gentlemen eat . . . but enjoyed an equal share in the whole entertainment." *HWS*, vol. I, p. 619. Historian Page Smith, who studied the reports of foreign travelers, concluded: "American men accorded their women more deference, lavished more money on them, regarded them with more respect than was accorded the women of any other country. But they did not particularly like them. They did not enjoy their company; they did not find them interesting or rewarding as people and as women in themselves. They valued them as wives and mothers; they sentimentalized over them; they congratulated themselves on their enlightened attitude toward them. *But they did not (and they do not) particularly like them.*" *Daughters of the Promised Land: Women in American History* (Boston: Little, Brown, 1970), p. 92. For the implications of this behavior in southern society, see William R. Taylor, *Cavalier and Yankee: The Old South and American National Character* (New York: Doubleday Anchor, 1961), pp. 123–55. Taylor notes that the growth of southern "plantation fiction," which is heavily concerned with the roles of

women, coincides with the "first stirrings of the movement for women's rights. . . ." P. 144.

67–68 Harriet Martineau granted: vol. I, p. 206.

68 Sarah Grimké dissented: *Letters on the Equality of the Sexes and the Condition of Woman* (Boston: Isaac Knapp, 1838), p. 15. See also her judgment that "As *they* [men] have determined that Jehovah has placed woman on a lower platform than man, they of course wish to keep her there." P. 61.

68 "vain question of equality": Maria J. McIntosh, *Woman in America: Her Work and Her Reward* (New York: D. Appleton, 1850), pp. 22–23.

68 Martineau noticed it: vol. III, p. 115. Sarah Grimké also argued against "the unscriptural notion . . . that there is a distinction between the duties of men and women as moral beings." *Letters,* p. 20. Lydia Sigourney, on the other hand, accepted it wholly. The "passive and enduring virtues" are feminine, she said, although the love of children, which is a virtue in men, is merely natural in women. *Letters to Mothers* (Hartford, Conn.: Hudson & Skinner, 1838), pp. 198, 48.

68 Duhring listed the manly virtues: pp. 64–65.

68 The thoroughly American author: James Fenimore Cooper, *The Travelling Bachelor; Or, Notions of the Americans* (New York: W. A. Townsend, 1859), p. 199.

68–69 Luckily, as the century progressed: Albert Mathews (Paul Siegvolk), *Ruminations: The Ideal American Lady and Other Essays,* 2nd ed. (New York: G. P. Putnam's, 1894), pp. 74–75.

69 When Frances Trollope visited New York: vol. II, p. 170; vol. I, p. 103. Literary historian Ann Douglas suggests that women conspired to get influence and power. *The Feminization of American Culture* (New York: Alfred A. Knopf, 1977). Contemporary observers like Trollope saw it the other way round: the church was the refuge of neglected and powerless women, and almost the only place they were sent. Historian Barbara Welter argues that women moved into a "power vacuum," but through church work they gained confidence, skills, and social concerns that led them to reform movements and an expansion of woman's sphere. "The Feminization of American Religion: 1800–1860," *Clio's Consciousness Raised: New Perspectives on the History of Women,* eds. Mary S. Hartman and Lois Banner (New York: Harper & Row, 1974), pp. 137–57.

69 Still, many girls dwindled: Peter Neilson, *Recollections of a Six Years' Residence in the United States of America* (Glasgow: David Robertson, 1830), p. 265; Frederick Marryat, *A Diary in America, with Remarks on its Institutions* (New York: D. Appleton, 1839), vol. II, p. 225; Frances Wright (D'Arusmont), *Views of Society and Manners in America* (New York: Bliss & White, 1821), p. 28; Axel Klinkowström, *Baron Klinkowström's America, 1818–1820,* trans. Franklin D. Scott, ed. (Evanston, Ill.: Northwestern University, 1952), pp. 124, 133; Frances Anne Kemble (Butler), *Journal* (Philadelphia: Carey, Lea & Blanchard, 1835), vol. I, p. 160. Similar remarks occur in sev-

eral unpublished diaries quoted in Cott, *Bonds of Womanhood,* pp. 53–54. See also Anne Firor Scott, *The Southern Lady, From Pedestal to Politics, 1830–1930* (Chicago: University of Chicago Press, 1970), p. 27

69–70 With her spirit went her looks: Wright, p. 24; Hamilton, vol. I, p. 149; Trollope, vol. I, p. 166; Martineau, vol. III, p. 131. See also Neilson, p. 265; Grund, vol. I, pp. 35–36; Beecher, *Evils Suffered,* p. 14.

70 With overwork and too much childbearing: William Alexander Alcott, *The Young Wife, Or Duties of Woman in the Marriage Relation* (Boston: G. W. Light, 1838), p. 229; Beecher, *Letters to the People on Health and Happiness* (1855; rpt. in part in Nancy F. Cott, ed. *Root of Bitterness: Documents of the Social History of American Women* (New York: E. P. Dutton, 1972), pp. 263–70; Abba Gould Woolson, *Woman in American Society* (Boston: Roberts Bros., 1873), pp. 189–90; Martineau, vol. III, pp. 154–56. See also Wright, pp. 314–16; Frances Anne Kemble, *Records of Later Life* (New York: H. Holt, 1884), pp. 23–24. On "Corsetitis" as a nineteenth-century medical and social problem, see John S. Haller, Jr., and Robin M. Haller, *The Physician and Sexuality in Victorian America* (New York: W. W. Norton, 1974), pp. 146–74; Woolson, pp. 192, 194.

70–71 There were psychological symptoms: Martineau, vol. III, pp. 159–60. Some early temperance societies, such as the Female Temperance Society of West Bradford, Massachusetts, tried specifically to stop *woman's* drinking. See Cott, *Bonds of Womanhood,* p. 180. On the growing problem of female alcoholism and opium addiction in Victorian America, see Haller and Haller, pp. 273–303.

71 In exchange for their cloistered lives: Martineau, vol. III, pp. 89–90. See also Sedgwick, pp. 20–22 (she counsels the young ladies to profess gratitude); Grimké, p. 127; Hall, vol. II, p. 156; Nichols, vol. II, p. 15; Martineau, vol. III, p. 106; see also James Stuart, *Three Years in North America* (New York: J. J. Harper, 1833), vol. I, p. 60; Patrick Shirreff, *A Tour Through North America; Together with a Comprehensive View of the Canadas and the United States* (Edinburgh: Oliver & Boyd, 1835), p. 76.

71 . . . vain, harsh, despotic, and tyrannical: Klinkowström, p. 133; Wright, pp. 315–16; Martineau, vol. III, pp. 117–18.

71 "In no country has such constant care . . .": Alexis de Tocqueville, *Democracy in America* (1838), trans. Henry Reeve, 4th ed. (New York: Henry G. Langley, 1845), vol. II, p. 225. For discussion of the peculiar new division of labor by gender that comes with industrial capitalism see Ann Oakley, *Woman's Work: The Housewife, Past and Present* (New York: Vintage Books, 1976), pp. 1–59; see also Frederick Engels, *The Origin of the Family, Private Property and the State,* (1891) Introd. Eleanor Burke Leacock (rpt. New York: International, 1972).

72 Jane Swisshelm, publisher: *Letters to Country Girls* (1853) in Gerda Lerner, *The Female Experience: An American Documentary* (Indianapolis: Bobbs-Merrill, 1977), pp. 117–18. See also Eliza W. Farnham, *California, In-Doors and Out* (New York: Dix, Edwards, 1856).

72 Timothy Dwight: *Travels; in New-England and New-York* (New Haven: T. Dwight, 1821–22), vol. IV, p. 474.

72 At that time, *thousands* of women: Calhoun, vol. II, pp. 91–92; Shirreff, p. 45.

72 Yet Dwight's false notion: Martineau, vol. III, p. 131; Sigourney, *Letters to Mothers,* p. 9; "The Women of Philadelphia," *Public Ledger and Daily Transcript,* in Calhoun, vol. II, pp. 84–85.

72–73 The married woman's "quiet circle . . .": On the specific tasks of women, see Anne Firor Scott, pp. 31–35; Julia Cherry Spruill, *Women's Life and Work in the Southern Colonies* (1938; rpt. New York: W. W. Norton, 1972), passim; Lydia Maria Child, "Employments in 1864" in Lerner, pp. 125–26. Mary Livermore observed that women performed the heaviest sorts of "hard manual work, to which, indeed, in many instances, they seemed adapted physically." She noted: "Women have always been toilers from a time coincident with the beginning of history, and, undoubtedly, anterior to that; but no tears have been shed for them, save what they have wept themselves, until they began to enter higher fields of labor, and to receive better compensation. Lo! then the floodgates of grief are hoisted, and there is mourning that will not be comforted." *What Shall We Do with Our Daughters?,* pp. 134, 136.

73 The advice books all agreed: Sigourney, *Letters to Young Ladies* (Hartford, Conn.: William Watson, 1835), p. 29, quoting from Lydia Maria Child. It is surely no coincidence that so many noteworthy nineteenth-century women came from families of sisters—the Peabodys, the Alcotts, the Blackwells—who could share the domestic labor and so find time for learning.

73 Those other changes also made: See Gerda Lerner, "The Lady and the Mill Girl: Changes in the Status of Women in the Age of Jackson, 1800–1840," *The Majority Finds Its Past: Placing Women in History* (New York: Oxford University Press, 1979), pp. 15–30, also rpt. in Nancy F. Cott and Elizabeth H. Pleck, eds., *A Heritage of Her Own: Toward a New Social History of American Women* (New York: Simon & Schuster, 1980). See also Cott, *Bonds of Womanhood,* pp. 5–6, 58, et passim. On the decline in woman's status see also Page Smith, pp. 57–59 and William O'Neill, ed. *The Woman Movement: Feminism in the United States and England* (New York: Barnes & Noble, 1969), pp. 15–19; Charlotte Perkins Gilman, *The Home: Its Work and Influence* (New York: McClure Phillips, 1903).

73–74 That dependent state: Mary R. Beard, *Woman as Force in History* (New York: Macmillan, 1946), pp. 117–55. See also Grimké, *Letters,* pp. 74–83. On woman's better position at law in colonial America, see Richard B. Morris, *Studies in the History of American Law,* 2nd ed. (Philadelphia: J. M. Mitchell, 1959), pp. 126–200.

74 After studying the law, Sarah Grimké: *Letters,* p. 81.

74 There were only two alternatives: Sigourney, *Letters to Young Ladies,* p. 37; Tocqueville, vol. II, 225–26; Grimké, *Letters,* p. 10.

75 Emily Collins reported: *HWS,* vol. I, p. 88. See also Margaret Fuller, *Woman in the Nineteenth Century* (1845; rpt. New York: W. W. Norton, 1971), pp. 32–33.

75 On the basis of her work: Grimké, *Letters,* pp. 88, 78.

75 One murderer, Guy Clark: New York *Spectator,* Feb. 17, 1832, p. 3. One indicator that domestic violence was accepted is an inspirational vignette by popular writer Fanny Fern (Sara Payson Willis Parton): a brutal, violent father beats his son, and when the boy subsequently dies of head injuries the father is very sorry and never loses his temper again. That the repentant father is morally and legally guilty of homicide is never suggested. "The Passionate Father," *Fern Leaves from Fanny's Portfolio* (Auburn: Derby & Miller, 1853), pp. 135–38.

75 Yet it was not until 1871: *Commonwealth* v. *Hugh McAfee,* 108 Mass 458 (1871).

75 And not until 1879: *Commonwealth* v. *William H. Devlin,* 126 Mass 253 (1879).

75 An 1860 cartoon: in E. Douglas Branch, *The Sentimental Years, 1836–1860* (New York: D. Appleton, 1934), pp. 40, 215.

75–76 William Lloyd Garrison: *HWS,* vol. I, p. 138.

76 On Patrick Doherty's wife: *New York Times,* Sept. 3, 1873, p. 5.

76 In Massachusetts in 1857: Calhoun, vol. II, pp. 125–26.

76 "Your service is very, very, very often involuntary . . .": Calhoun, vol. II, p. 96. Ads for runaway wives often appeared in newspapers beside ads for runaway slaves.

76 "fitted by nature to cheer . . .": Jonathan F. Stearns, "Female Influence and the True Christian Mode of its Exercise" (1837) in Aileen Kraditor, *Up From the Pedestal: Selected Writings in the History of American Feminism* (Chicago: Quadrangle, 1968), p. 47.

77–90 On Lucretia Chapman: *Trial of Lucretia Chapman, Otherwise Called Lucretia Espos y Mina, Who was Jointly Indicted With Lino Amalia Espos y Mina, for the Murder of William Chapman, Esq. Late of Andalusia, County of Bucks, Pennsylvania, In the Court of Oyer and Terminer, Held at Doylestown, for Bucks, December Term, 1831, Continued to February Term, 1832.* Prepared by William E. DuBois (Philadelphia: G. W. Mentz, 1832). Some copies of this volume include "Supplement: Trial of Lino Amalio Espos y Mina for the Murder of William Chapman, Court of Oyer and Terminer, holden at Doylestown, for the County of Bucks, April Session, 1832." See also "The Trial of Lucretia Chapman for the Murder of William Chapman, Andalusia, Pennsylvania, 1832," *AST,* vol. VI (1916), pp. 99–396, and "The Trial of Carolino DeMina for the Murder of William Chapman, Andalusia, Pennsylvania, 1832," *AST,* vol. VI (1916), pp. 397–410. See also *Trial and Execution of Mina, the Murderer Who was executed at Doylestown, Bucks County Pennsylvania June 21, 1832, for poisoning Doctor Chapman* (New York: C. Brown, 1832). I have also used newspaper accounts in the *National Gazette* (Philadelphia) and the New York *Spectator.*

80 ". . . no, Lino . . . I do not believe . . .": *Trial of . . . Chapman,* p. 48.

81 "the facts of the poisoning . . .": rpt. in *National Gazette,* Oct. 1, 1831, p. 1.

81–82 On the separation of trials of conspirators: Another Pennsylvania case in 1847 went very differently when Judge Gaylord Church and his associates ruled that Mary Myers and John Parker, indicted for the arsenic murder of her husband, John Myers, had no right to be tried separately. Mary Myers, a respectable, fortyish mother of eleven, might have won the jury's sympathy. Myers was a very intemperate man, and the only evidence against her was her frequent statement that she would like to divorce him, the fact that she was pregnant although she admittedly had not slept with her husband in twenty months, and the fact that she nursed him during his last illness. Parker, on the other hand, had shown an inordinate curiosity about poison and about what the neighbors thought of his relationship with Mrs. Myers. He bought arsenic surreptitiously twice, prepared drinks for Myers during his last illness, insisted on sitting up with him, and showed a guilty knowledge of the crime. One can only imagine how the jury heard the evidence, but on the face of it, the case against Mary Myers seems much less convincing than that against Lucretia Chapman. But the evidence against Parker was strong, and both he and Myers were found guilty and sentenced to hang. The jury had the option of finding one guilty and the other not guilty; but when a man and a woman are tried together, particularly when adultery is proved against them, they are far more likely to be tarred with the same brush. *The Trial and Conviction of Mary Myers and John Parker, for the Murder of John Myers (The Husband of Mary Myers) Late of Rockland Township, Venango County, Penn'a, By Administering Arsenic,* Reported by E. S. Durban (Franklin, Pa.: E. S. Durban, 1847).

82 "So long as [woman] is nervous . . .": *Sociology for the South, or the Failure of Free Society* (Richmond: Morris, 1854), pp. 214–15. Fitzhugh expresses the popular notion. Compare the view of the Congregational clergy: "The power of woman is in her dependence, flowing from the consciousness of that weakness which God has given her for her protection. . . . But when she assumes the place and tone of man . . . our care and protection of her seem unnecessary; we put ourselves in self-defense against her; she yields the power which God has given her for protection, and her character becomes unnatural." "Pastoral Letter of the General Association of Massachusetts (Orthodox) to the Churches Under Their Care," *The Liberator,* August 11, 1837, in Kraditor, p. 51. See also the view of a popular woman writer: "There is, indeed, something unfeminine in independence. It is contrary to nature, and therefore it offends. . . . A really sensible woman feels her dependence. . . . she is conscious of inferiority, and therefore grateful for support. . . . Women, in this respect, are something like children; the more they show their need of support, the more engaging they are." Mrs. John Sandford (Elizabeth Poole), *Woman in her Social and Domestic Character,* 6th ed. (Boston: Otis, Broaders, 1842), pp. 15–16.

83 "If the death had been caused by cholera . . .": *Trial of . . . Chapman,* p. 188. The question was rarely resolved conclusively. In the notorious case of Eliza-

beth Wharton, accused of poisoning General W. S. Ketchum, to whom she owed money, with tartar emetic (Baltimore, 1871), a little army of medical experts appeared for each side; and even after Mrs. Wharton was acquitted, the medical evidence continued under review in medical journals. After summarizing all the evidence in an article for the *American Journal of Medical Sciences,* April 1872, John J. Reese, Professor of Medical Jurisprudence and Toxicology at the University of Pennsylvania, concluded: "As is generally the case in such trials, there was a considerable conflict of professional opinions, both medical and chemical, among the experts; . . . we must be content to leave the decision with the intelligent reader." *A Review of the Recent Trial of Mrs. Elizabeth G. Wharton on the Charge of Poisoning General W. S. Ketchum* (rpt. Philadelphia: n.p., 1872), p. 27. Toxicologist Donald Hoffman of the New York Medical Examiner's Office finds the medical evidence in the Chapman case unreliable and inconclusive.

84   "it is not a common thing for ducks . . .": *Trial of . . . Chapman,* p. 35.

84   "a passing tear of pity": *Trial of . . . Chapman,* p. 172.

85   "Here it has been supposed . . .": *Trial of . . . Chapman,* p. 212.

85   "MY DEAR LENA . . .": *Trial of . . . Chapman,* p. 41.

85   "It seems a long time . . .": *Trial of . . . Chapman,* p. 42.

85–86   "When I left Baltimore . . .": *Trial of . . . Chapman,* p. 45.

86   ". . . no, Lino, when I pause . . .": *Trial of . . . Chapman,* p. 48

86   On the very day of his release: Both the date of Mina's release and the date of his first appearance at the Chapmans' are given variously as May 9 and May 19, but the two events seem to have happened on the same day: May 19 probably is the correct date, May 9 a typographical error repeated as fact.

86–87   "most horrible and atrocious": *Trial of . . . Chapman,* pp. 180–81.

87   "compel" a man "to make the bed . . .": *Trial of . . . Chapman,* pp. 192–93.

87   "teach the wife in whose bosom . . .": *Trial of Chapman,* p. 99.

87   "malignity of the crime . . .": *Trial of . . . Chapman,* p. 71.

87   "a *female,* with whose character . . .": *Trial of . . . Chapman,* p. 155.

87–88   Proof of her womanhood: *Trial of . . . Chapman,* pp. 149–51.

88   "Ah! from what a height . . .": *Trial of . . . Chapman,* pp. 84–85. The long letter is not wholly romantic; its purpose is to persuade Cuesta to get her a lawyer.

89   "It is indeed painful": *Trial of . . . Chapman,* p. 195.

89   But there she sat: *National Gazette,* Feb. 28, 1832, p. 3; New York *Spectator,* Feb. 24, 1832, p. 4.

89   "generally displayed levity . . .": *National Gazette,* May 1, 1832, p. 2.

89   He asked for a stay: *Trial of . . . Espos y Mina,* p. 9.

90   Finally, he "made a confession . . .": *National Gazette,* May 1, 1832, p. 2; *The Life and Confession of Carolino Estradas De Mina, Executed at Doylestown, June 21, 1832, for Poisoning with Arsenic, William Chapman, Written By Himself in the Spanish Language While under Sentence of Death in the Jail at Doylestown, and Delivered by Him to the Sheriff of Bucks County, with*

a Request to have the same Translated into English, trans. C. G. (Philadelphia: Robert DeSilver, 1832). Mina's disturbed fantasies reveal a good deal about the hidden side of male-female relationships. The psychological theme of rebellion against the father, who nevertheless remains beloved and loving, was acted out in Mina's friendly, murderous rivalry with his "adopted father" William Chapman, for whose murder he clearly did not expect to be punished. More significant in the context of this discussion is the central psychological motif of the *Confession*: fear and hatred of women as the source of all evil, and an overwhelming desire to humiliate them.

90 "Here began the ruin . . .": *Life . . . of . . . De Mina,* p. 31.

90 So in the end they hanged: The swift merciless retaliation of men against Mina speaks of the same masculine anxieties which underlie Bram Stoker's story of *Dracula* (1897). Like the Transylvanian count, Mina was a bizarre foreigner of inexplicable origin who by means unknown to the civilized community aroused the sexuality of an otherwise respectable woman, making her fatally dangerous to her legal master and to the community at large. All the forces of male society—science, religion, and law—are brought to bear against the corrupting invader. Oddly enough, Mina seems to have looked the part: he "displayed a low but extended forehead; his eyes are sunk within their spheres; his lips are thin; his complexion is sallow, tinctured with a hue of livid blue, giving a shade which might be, perhaps, best described as a sickly green, and the lower part of his countenance is disproportionately smaller than the upper." *Trial and Execution of Mina,* p. 2.

91 When a man and woman: The same generalization does not apply to black women or to others who were perceived as more threat than lady. When Tony Nellum killed Henry Harris with an ax in Louisiana in 1874, Alcee Harris said "she was glad of her husband's death, because he had beaten her and threatened to take her life." Apparently Alcee Harris conspired with Nellum in the murder plot, for Harris was killed in his own bed; she and Nellum were hanged in Monroe on Nov. 26, 1875, before a crowd of five thousand people "mostly colored." The three principals were black; Alcee Harris was twenty-four. *New York Times,* Nov. 27, 1875, p. 1.

92 The case of Ann Baker: *The Trials of Richard Smith, and Ann Carson, Alias Ann Smith, As Accessary for the Murder of Captain John Carson on the 20th Day of January, 1816, at a Court of Oyer and Terminer Held at Philadelphia, May, 1816, By the Judges of the Court of Common Pleas, Judge Rush. . . . President; Together with the Arguments of Counsel, the Charges and Sentence of the President* (Philadelphia: Thomas DeSilver, 1816); see also "The Trial of Richard Smith for the Murder of John Carson, Philadelphia 1816," *AST,* vol. V (1916), pp. 713–25.

91 The judge instructed the jury: The judge's instruction certainly was open to question. Pennsylvania divorce law held that a married person of either sex could marry again if a spouse had been absent without word for two years *and* some evidence of the spouse's death existed. The judge ruled that a ru-

mor of John Carson's death did not constitute sufficient evidence that he was, in fact, dead.

91–92 She did not even have the right: The law held that a married person of either sex who returned to find a spouse remarried could apply to the courts within six months to have his or her marriage restored. So Ann Carson did not lose her right of choice simply because she was a woman; had she returned to find John remarried, the decision to take or leave the first marriage would have been hers. In practice, since women were less likely to roam the world, the right of choice usually fell to a returning man.

92 The indictment charged that she: *Trials of Smith and Carson,* Appendix, p. iii.

92 "certainly the prisoner . . .": *Trials of Smith and Carson,* p. 247.

92 At Albany, New York: *Trial of Elsie D. Whipple, Charged with being Accessary to the Murder of her Husband John Whipple, at a Special Court of Oyer and Terminer, Holden in Albany, July, 1827* (n.p., n.d.). See also *The Trial of Jesse Strang, for the Murder of John Whipple* (Albany: n.p., 1827).

92 In Harpswell, Maine: *Celebrated Murders, as Shown in Remarkable Capital Trials,* By a Member of the Massachusetts Bar (Chicago: Belfords, Clarke, 1879), pp. 327–31.

92–93 And in Rochester, New York: *"The Last Writing" of Marion Ira Stout, Containing His Confession, Revelations, and also his "so Called" Principles of Philosophy and Religion. He was Executed at Rochester, N.Y., Oct. 22, 1858, for the Murder of his Brother-in-Law, Charles W. Littles, on the 19th Dec., 1857* (Rochester, N.Y.: H. Sellick Merrill, 1858), p. 14. See also *Confession of Sarah E. Littles, of the Murder of her Husband, by Marion Ira Stout. A True Statement, Made at Sing Sing, Saturday, October 30th, 1858* (Rochester, N.Y.: Curtis, Butts, 1858).

93 Criminal Marion Stout might:.At a Rochester, New York, meeting to oppose capital punishment and to save Marion Ira Stout from hanging, the "principal personage" was Susan B. Anthony. *New York Times,* Oct. 11, 1858, p. 5.

93 Properly understood . . . a motive: See Hyman Gross, *A Theory of Criminal Justice* (New York: Oxford University Press, 1978), pp. 102–106.

93–98 On the case of Hannah Kinney: *Trial of Mrs. Hannah Kinney for the Alleged Murder of her Husband, George T. Kinney, By Poison. Before the Supreme Court of Massachusetts, Judges Shaw, Putnam, and Wilde, Present; Sitting at Boston, from Dec. 21st to Dec. 26th, with the Arguments of Counsel, and the Charge of the Chief Justice Fully Reported,* By a Member of the Bar (Boston: Times & Notion, 1840). See also "The Trial of Hannah Kinney for the Murder of George T. Kinney, Boston, Massachusetts, 1840," *AST,* vol. XVII (1936), pp. 535–649.

94 "a total absence of motive": *Trial of . . . Kinney,* p. 27.

94 "was spoken of very highly . . .": *A Review of the Principal Events of the Last Ten Years in the Life of Mrs. Hannah Kinney: Together with Some Comments Upon the Late Trial, Written by Herself* (Boston: J. N. Bradley, 1841), p. 8.

94–95 For the next two years: *A Review,* pp. 38, 53.

95 "He often appeared singular . . .": *A Review,* p. 66.

95 William Alcott expressed: *The Young Wife,* pp. 25, 33. Emphasis mine. In an 1851 letter to *The Liberator* Henry C. Wright discussed the same "Biblical" argument: "Man is to rule woman by violence; woman must rule man by love, kindness, and long-suffering." *HWS,* vol. I, p. 310.

95 ". . . we must allow men . . .": Mrs. Farley Emerson, *Woman in America: Her Character and Position as Indicated by Newspaper Editorials and Sustained by American Social Life* (Cincinnati: author, 1857), p. 21.

96 Kinney might have taken the poison himself: This plea sometimes worked. A Chicago jury, convinced that the alleged murder victim had committed suicide, acquitted Anna Adair of poisoning her husband in Lorraine, Illinois, in Jan. 1873. *New York Times,* April 11, 1873, p. 1. In 1866 eighteen-year-old Sarah Henry Rubens was acquitted of murdering her husband, James Rubens, a Lockport, New York, laborer, thought to have killed himself because he was a confirmed Millerite, believing that the world would be purged of wickedness by the end of the month, and had recently received a letter charging that because of infidelity to a previous Millerite fiancée he would not "share in the felicity of the millennium." *New York Times,* Oct. 1, 1866, p.5.

96 The second theory: Lawson, editor of *American State Trials,* thinks that the medical evidence is inadequate and that "the chances are infinitely greater that the poisoning, if any, was done for a fee by the quack practitioner." Vol. 17, p. xxix. Dr. Donald Hoffman of the New York Medical Examiner's Office thinks the tests do demonstrate the presence of arsenic, but of course, they do not indicate *who* was giving the arsenic to Kinney.

97 So in the end it came down: *Trial of . . . Kinney,* pp. 47, 53.

97 But was Hannah Kinney: *Trial of . . . Kinney,* pp. 44, 3, 5.

97–98 but that prompted Witham: Ward Witham, *A Brief Notice of the Life of Mrs. Hannah Kinney, for Twenty Years* (n.p.: author, 1840), p. 106.

98 The prosecutor spoke early: *Trial of . . . Kinney,* p. 5. I have found no other record of the cases of Norton and Floor.

98 On the day that Mina: *Life and Confession of . . . Mina,* pp. 49–50.

98–102 On the case of Ann Simpson: *The Trial of Mrs. Ann K. Simpson Charged with the Murder of her Husband, Alexander C. Simpson, By Poisoning with Arsenic. Before His Honor, Judge William H. Battle, At the Fall Term of the Superior Court of Law for the County of Cumberland, Holden at Fayetteville, North Carolina, on Thursday and Friday, Nov. 14th and 15th, A.D. 1850,* Reported by William H. Haigh (Fayetteville, N.C.: Edward J. Hale, 1851). See also "The Trial of Ann K. Simpson for the Murder of Alexander C. Simpson, Fayetteville, North Carolina, 1850," *AST,* vol. V (1916), pp. 369–527.

100 "A wife is arraigned . . .": *Trial of . . . Simpson,* pp. 95–96.

100 Only a "monster": *Trial of . . . Simpson,* p. 121.

100 She was "giddy, and thoughtless . . .": *Trial of . . . Simpson,* p. 98.

100–01 some "busy Iago": *Trial of . . . Simpson,* pp. 182–83.

101 his "own daughter pursued . . .": *Trial of . . . Simpson,* pp. 187–88.

101 "Hitherto we have been wont . . .": *Trial of . . . Simpson,* p. 144.

101 "If the secret poisoner . . .": *Trial of . . . Kinney,* p. 53.

101 "cast her forth . . .": *Trial of . . . Simpson,* p. 153.

102 "weak and fragile woman . . .": *Trial of . . . Simpson,* p. 59.

102 "any notions of expediency . . .": *Trial of . . . Simpson,* pp. 146–47.

102–03 William L. Sayer, a reporter: "The Thyng Case," New Bedford *Sunday Standard,* Feb. 7, 1909. See also *Trial of Rosalie A. Thyng at New Bedford for the Murder of Her Husband, George H. Thyng,* by B.F.H. Reed (New Bedford: n.p., 1876).

103 The prosecutor at Ann Simpson's trial: *Trial of . . . Simpson,* p. 72.

103–04 "This method of causing death . . .": J. E. Butler, "Introduction," *Trial of Jane M. Swett, of Kennebunk, for Homicide. S.J.C., Jan. Term, 1867, Hon. R. P. Tapley, J. Presiding.* J. E. Butler, ed. (Biddeford, Maine: Butler & Place, 1867), pp. 3–4.

104 "When we see a wretch . . .": *Trial of . . . Simpson,* p. 87.

104–07 On the case of Jane Swett: See *Trial of . . . Swett.*

106–07 "ill starred marriage": *Trial of . . . Swett,* pp. 60–62. Emphasis mine.

107 The prosecutor complained: *Trial of . . . Swett,* pp. 80–81.

107–09 On the case of Elizabeth Van Valkenburgh: *The Confession of Elizabeth Van Valkenburgh, Who was Executed for the Murder of her Husband, John Van Valkenburgh, January 24, 1846; Comprising a History of her Life, in which Some Awful Disclosures are Made; Together with the Sentence of the Judge, and the Letter of the Governor Refusing to Interfere with the Execution of the Law* (Johnstown, N. Y.: G. Henry & W. N. Clark, n.d.). See also *Confession and Awful Disclosures of Elizabeth Van Valkenburgh, . . . Who Was Executed for the Murder of her Husband on the afternoon of Jan. 24, 1846, in Fulton County, New York* (New York: n.p., n.d.).

108 "There is no foundation . . .": *Confession of . . . Van Valkenburgh,* p. 11.

108–09 Elizabeth Van Valkenburgh said in her confession: *Confession of . . . Van Valkenburgh,* pp. 12–13, 15–16.

109 Many women enjoyed the kindness: The law also enabled a husband to spend or dispose of family property without regard to his wife's wishes. Rebecca Peake, who had been married to Jonathan Peake for about thirty years and had brought up his nine children as well as two of her own, poisoned his eldest son Ephraim when her husband decided to give him *all* his property. She was sentenced to hang in Orange County, Vermont, in 1835 but died in prison while awaiting execution. *Trial of Mrs. Rebecca Peake, Indicted for the Murder of Ephraim Peake, Tried at Orange County Court, Dec. Term, 1835. Embracing the Evidence, Arguments of Counsel, Charge, and Sentence* (Montpelier, Vermont: E. P. Walton, 1836).

109 Margaret Fuller countered: p. 32. See also *HWS,* vol. I, pp. 212–15. Concurring in an 1873 Supreme Court decision upholding the state of Illinois in barring women from the practice of law, Justice Bradley wrote: "It is true that

many women are unmarried and not affected by any of the duties, complications, and incapacities arising out of the married state, but these are exceptions to the general rule. The paramount destiny and mission of woman are to fulfil the noble and benign offices of wife and mother. This is the law of the Creator. And the rules of civil society must be adapted to the general constitution of things and cannot be based upon exceptional cases." *Bradwell* v. *Illinois,* 38 U.S. (16 Wall) 130, 141–42 (1873). For commentary on this argument at law, see Susan Cary Nicholas, Alice M. Price, Rachel Rubin, *Rights and Wrongs: Women's Struggle for Legal Equality* (Old Westbury, N.Y.: Feminist Press, 1979), pp. 6–7.

109 Sarah Grimké said: *Letters,* p. 21.

109 And Susan B. Anthony: "Social Purity" (1875), in Kraditor, p. 159. For the case of Anthony's rescue of a woman wrongfully confined by her husband to an insane asylum for eighteen months, see *HWS,* vol. I, p. 469.

110 "if married, in the eye . . .": *HWS,* vol. I, p. 70.

110 "those laws which confer . . .": in Lerner, *The Female Experience,* pp. 345–46.

110 "We do not seek to protect . . .": in Kraditor, p. 220.

110 "mannish" and "unsexed women . . ." : Page Smith, 120; see also the New York *Herald* editorial, Sept. 12, 1852, in *HWS,* vol. I, pp. 853–54 and Kraditor, pp. 189–91.

110 "regard home as her appropriate . . .": *Woman in America,* excerpted in Cott, *Root of Bitterness,* p. 145.

110 By the end of the 1830s: See Barbara J. Berg, *The Remembered Gate: Origins of American Feminism: The Woman and the City, 1800–1860* (New York: Oxford University Press, 1978), and William O'Neill's introduction to *The Woman Movement,* pp. 19–21.

111 fictional accounts of women murderers: American literature during the 1840s was strikingly concerned with a consciousness of evil in woman, as David Brion Davis has pointed out. He argues that "the concern with adultery and feminine evil was clearly a result of the progressive uncertainty over woman's status and of the ever-widening gap between the ideal and reality." The "portrait of the wicked woman undoubtedly represented a growing fear of adultery, which, in turn, reflected a general anxiety over the changing status of women. . . . Social disorganization could be represented in its ultimate form in the union of sex and death." *Homicide in American Fiction, 1798–1860* (Ithaca, New York: Cornell University Press, 1957), pp. 201–02, 209. In the cautionary tales, adultery is the least of woman's crimes; women are the direct agents of death. Perhaps the last refinement of the theme is Hawthorne's "Rappacini's Daughter" in which the woman herself is poisonous. Hawthorne undoubtedly had other themes in mind, but the choice of metaphor is no accident.

111 Their authors publicized them: *Life and Confession of Ann Walters, the Female Murderess!* (Boston: Skinner's, 1850), p. 3.

111–13 On fictional murderesses: *Life and Confession of Mary Jane Gordon, Who was Tried, Condemned, and Hung, on the 24th Day of February, 1847, for the Murder of Jane Anderson, A Native of Vassalboro, Maine . . . Carefully Collected by the Author, J. S. Calhoun, Attorney at Law, Augusta, Maine* (Augusta: author, 1847); this pamphlet reappears as *Life and Confession of Mary Jane Gordon, Who was Tried, Condemned, and Hung, on the Twenty-Fourth Day of February, 1849, for the Murder of Jane Anderson, A Native of Covington, Kentucky . . . Carefully Collected by the Author, J. S. Calhoun, Attorney at Law, Covington, Kentucky* (Covington, Ky.: author, 1849); *Ellen Irving, The Female Victimizer, Who Cruelly Murdered Sixteen Persons in Cool Blood, for Revenge on Her First Love, William Shannon, Who Had Betrayed Her. Also, An Account of Her Association with Charles Dorian, An Italian Murderer,* ed. Rev. Robert B. Russel (Baltimore: Arthur R. Orton, 1856); *Private History and Confession of Pamela Lee, Who Was Convicted at Pittsburgh, Pa., December 19th, 1851, for the Wilful Murder of Her Husband and Sentenced to be Hanged on the 30th Day of January, A.D. 1852. Written at her Request and According to her Dictation, and Prepared by the Rev. Augustus Dimick* (Pittsburgh, Pa.: n.p., 1852); *Trial, Conviction, and Confession of Mary B. Thorn, Who Was Sentenced to be Hanged at Portsmouth, Va., December 22d, 1854, for the Murder of Thos. Brady and Family. Written at Her Request, and According to Her Dictation, and Prepared by the Publisher, William C. Murdock* (Norfolk, Va.: William C. Murdock, 1854); *Life and Confession of Ann Walters, the Female Murderess!* (Boston: Skinner's, 1850), reprinted as *Confession of Ann Walters, the Murderess* (Boston: Skinner, 1856). The two versions of the Ann Walters story are revised forms of *Narrative and Confessions of Lucretia P. Cannon, Who Was Tried, Convicted, and Sentenced to be Hung at Georgetown, Delaware, with Two of Her Accomplices, Containing an Account of Some of the Most Horrible and Shocking Murders and Daring Robberies Ever Committed By One of the Female Sex* (New York: n.p., 1841).

111–12 The meanest of the lot: *Life and Confession of Ann Walters,* pp. 17–18, 14–15.

112 "doubly shocking and attrocious [*sic*] . . .": *Life and Confession of Ann Walters,* P. 3; *Narrative and Confession of Lucretia P. Cannon,* p. 1.

112 But the authors "reported": *Trial . . . of . . . Thorn,* p. 31; *Private History of . . . Lee,* p. 32.

112 Had they been content with domesticity: *Private History of . . . Lee,* pp. 5, 16–17.

112 "warning to all [men] . . .": *Life and Confession of . . . Gordon,* 1849 edition, p. 4.

112 After all, Mary Thorn is "beautiful": *Trial . . . of . . . Thorn,* p. 14; *Private History of . . . Lee,* p. 5; *Life and Confession of . . . Gordon,* 1849 edition, p. 7; *Life and Confession of Ann Walters,* pp. 9, 14.

113 "in the female character . . .": Nathaniel W. Chittenden, *Influence of Women*

Upon the Destinies of a People: Being an Oration of Salutory Addresses—Delivered at the Annual Commencement of Columbia College, Oct. 3, 1837, in Berg, p. 70.

113 Thirty years earlier, Parson Mason Locke Weems: *The Bad Wife's Looking Glass Or, God's Revenge Against Cruelty to Husbands. Exemplified in the Awful History of the Beautiful, But Depraved Mrs. Rebecca Cotton, Who Most Inhumanly Murdered Her Husband John Cotton, Esq. for Which Horrid Act God Permitted Her, in the Prime of Life and Bloom of Beauty, to be Cut Off by her Brother Stephen Kannady, May 5th 1807. With a Number of Incidents and Anecdotes, Most Extraordinary and Instructive.* Second Edition Improved (Charleston: Author, 1823), pp. 26–27.

114 "The ballot is not even half . . .": Laura Bullard, "What Flag Shall We Fly?" *The Revolution,* Oct. 27, 1870, p. 264, in O'Neill, *Everyone Was Brave: A History of Feminism in America* (Chicago: Quadrangle, 1969), pp. 19–20.

114–15 "The institution of marriage . . .": "What Justifies Marriage?" *The Revolution,* Aug. 18, 1870, p. 104. The argument had been made by other social critics. Marriage reformers Thomas Nichols and his wife, Mary Gove Nichols, wrote in 1854: "There is a hopelessness in indissoluble marriage that is one of its greatest evils. . . . Husband and wife feel that their fate is irrevocable. . . . I cannot idealize about the dignity of manhood, when men beat their wives because they are property, or kill them in the drunkenness of rum, anger or jealousy; when wives poison their husbands, and women, married and single, murder their babes. *Marriage* (Cincinnati: V. Nicholson, 1854), pp. 240–41.

115 Conservatives counterattacked: Orestes A. Brownson, "The Woman Question" (1869 and 1873), in Kraditor, pp. 192–93.

115 And when social anthropologists proclaimed: See Elizabeth Fee, "The Sexual Politics of Victorian Social Anthropology," in Hartman and Banner, pp. 86–102.

115–16 One holdout was Dorothy Dix: "Dorothy Dix on the Great Poison Mystery," New York *Evening Journal,* June 4, 1906, p. 2; see also her column, "Things Worse Than Divorce: If it Were Abolished, Would Not the Number of Wife Murders be Increased?" New York *Evening Journal,* March 29, 1911, p. 19. While many women killed to get out of marriage, it is only fair to say that a few killed to get in. Libbie Garrabrant, age sixteen, for example, poisoned Ransom Burroughs, owner of the Paterson, New Jersey, saloon in which she was employed, in order to get the furniture to set up housekeeping with her sixteen-year-old sweetheart, Van Winkle Bogert. She was sentenced to be hanged in Passaic on July 19, 1872. New York *Sun,* April 23, 1872, p. 1; May 20, 1872, p.3.

116–21 On Lydia Sherman: *The Poison Fiend! Life, Crimes, and Conviction of Lydia Sherman, (The Modern Lucretia Borgia,) Recently Tried in New Haven, Conn., for Poisoning Three Husbands and Eight of Her Children* (Philadelphia: Barclay, 1873); *"Truth Stranger Than Fiction." A Thrilling History.*

Lydia Sherman. Confession of the Arch Murderess of Connecticut . . . (Philadelphia: T. R. Callender, n.d.).

119 "I thought that I could not get along . . .": *"Truth Stranger Than Fiction,"* pp. 10–11.

119 George kept "continually growing worse": *"Truth Stranger Than Fiction,"* pp. 11–12.

119 Lydia, "downhearted and much discouraged": *"Truth Stranger Than Fiction,"* p. 12.

120 "I felt so bad": *"Truth Stranger Than Fiction,"* p. 25.

120 "I was alone in the world": *"Truth Stranger Than Fiction,"* p. 14.

120 Having blundered into that marriage: Studying Englishwomen who kill, Patrick Wilson found similar patterns. In rural areas, where survival depended upon the family unit, women killed in jockeying for a secure position within the family, just as Lydia Sherman did in trying to secure her place in Horatio Sherman's household. Rebecca Peake, who poisoned her stepson to get her husband's farm for her own children, follows that pattern. *Trial of Rebecca Peake.* So does the second wife of Henry Miller of Montville Township, New Jersey, who poisoned her husband "to obtain possession of the old man's farm for herself and the children of her first husband." New York *Tribune,* Nov. 4, 1870, p. 5. In cities, on the other hand, where survival depended upon supporting oneself, women killed to remove useless dependents, as both Sarah Jane Robinson and Lydia Struck Sherman did. Among the Englishwomen who killed several members of their own families, Wilson identifies one common characteristic: "A desire for assertion and freedom, a need to sweep away everyone in the home in the hope of some ill-defined, better future."*Murderess* (London: Michael Joseph, 1971), pp. 46, 172.

120 "a neat black alpaca dress . . .": *The Poison Fiend!,* p. 30.

120 "not exactly prepossessing": *New York Times,* April 17, 1872, p. 1.

120 When her sister and brother-in-law: *The Poison Fiend!,* pp. 30–31.

121–28 On Sarah Jane Robinson: *The Official Report of the Trial of Sarah Jane Robinson for the Murder of Prince Arthur Freeman in the Supreme Judicial Court of Massachusetts* (Boston: Wright & Potter, 1888). My account of the case is based also on press coverage in the New York *Sun* and the Boston *Globe.*

121 arrested for the murder of her son: New York *Sun,* Dec. 12, 1887, p. 5. See also Boston *Globe,* Evening Edition, Aug. 12, 1886, p. 1, which reports that Robinson was arrested August 11 for "administering poison" and did not know of William's death on August 12 until she was formally arraigned on that day and charged with his murder.

122 "took them pretty much all up" : *Trial of . . . Robinson,* p. 135.

122 "slow, rambling, and . . . pointless": New York *Sun,* Dec. 16, 1887, p. 3.

122 After six days of hearing testimony: Edmund Pearson, *More Studies in Murder* (New York: Harrison Smith & Robert Haas, 1936), p. 34.

123 But Mrs. Robinson had a premonition: Although arsenic was found in Annie Freeman's body, poisoning could not definitely be established as the cause of

death because the body had been embalmed, possibly with arsenic. The undertaker could not remember what he had used.

123 "give him a dose...": Trial of... Robinson, p. 37.

124 a ten-cent concoction of strawberry syrup: Boston Globe, Aug. 22, 1886, p. 4.

125 "a woman of tears...": Boston Globe, Evening Edition, Aug. 12, 1886, p. 1.

125 Dr. Charles Follen Folsom: Studies of Criminal Responsibility and Limited Responsibility (n.p.: author, 1909), p. 99.

125 "Mrs. Robinson's Ordeal": New York Sun, Feb. 8, 1888, p. 2. Sentiment turned against the insurance companies which tempted the poor. In 1873 a New York Evening Post editorial denounced the rivalry between insurance agents which led them to sell policies to people who had "no visible means to pay the premiums and support themselves besides." The result was scandalous abuse and murder, said the Post, citing two notorious cases of insurance fraud in which the insured staged his own death with someone else's body. The paper did not comment on the method Mrs. Robinson and others used to bilk the insurance companies: murder of the insured. "Murder and Life Insurance," June 6, 1873, p. 2.

127 "Mother always seemed to like us": Boston Globe, Aug. 15, 1886, p. 2.

128 "Polish Borgia" and "Mrs. Bluebeard": Chicago Tribune, Nov. 20, 1922, p. 6.

128 But like Robinson and Sherman—and their English counterparts: For accounts of the English multiple murderers see Patrick Wilson. The pattern still pertains. Janie Lou Gibbs, who married a Cordele, Georgia, farmer when she was fifteen, is currently serving five consecutive life sentences for the arsenic murders of her husband, three sons, and grandson, insured for a total of $31,000.

129 Her sister said she was "money mad": Chicago Tribune, May 7, 1908, p. 3. My account of the Belle Gunness case is drawn primarily from coverage in this paper. Her profit was estimated by the Chicago Tribune, May 18, 1908, p. 6. Lillian De la Torre places the figure at $30,000. The Truth About Belle Gunness (New York: Fawcett, 1955), p. 174. In terms of equivalent purchasing power today the figures would be $375,000 or $200,000.

129 "deep affection for her own...": Chicago Tribune, May 8, 1908, p. 3.

130 his two life insurance policies: De la Torre, p. 171.

130 "the prettiest and happiest country home...": Letter from Belle Gunness to Andrew Helgelein, in Chicago Tribune, May 9, 1908, p. 2.

130 With his young daughter Svenveld: Writers of popular crime stories repeat the claim that Peter Gunness also brought with him an infant who died five days after arrival and that the attending doctor suspected the child had been deliberately suffocated. See De la Torre, p. 41. I find no evidence of this. Peter did have an infant who died before he met Belle; presumably both the infant and Peter's first wife died during or soon after childbirth.

131 "to see the King crowned": Chicago Tribune, May 9, 1908, p. 2. He is identified as Olaf Lindbom.

131 "WANTED—A WOMAN WHO OWNS . . . ": Chicago *Tribune,* May 9, 1908, p. 2. This ad is translated and reprinted from the Norwegian-language *Scandinaven* in which it ran in March 1908. It's Gunness's last-known ad.

131 Apparently the victims had first been poisoned: Testimony on this point conflicted. A medical examiner found arsenic in the bodies, but an undertaker had embalmed them with arsenic *before* the autopsies. There is some indication that the examiner found strychnine as well. The arrangement of the bodies clearly indicated that they were dead before the fire, but the cause of death could not be determined.

132 Just at first no one could accept: The greater the atrocity of a woman's crime, the less credible was her guilt. On the other hand, even the most ordinary man was thought capable of any enormity. In Trenton, New Jersey, in 1893, Mattie C. Shann was tried for murdering by mercury poisoning her syphilitic son John, whose life she had insured for $2,000. After his death John's body was disemboweled within a few hours of Mattie Shann's learning that the insurance company was demanding an autopsy. The viscera could not be found. Mattie Shann's story was that three men had rung her doorbell in the middle of the night, shouldered past her when she opened the door, run upstairs to eviscerate her son, and disappeared. Her defense attorney found it impossible to believe that "a human being bearing the name of woman could have contemplated the mutilation in this horrible manner of her own offspring." He blamed Mr. Goff, an insurance investigator sent from New York City to look into the crime. Goff, the defense charged, stole John Shann's viscera to perform his own autopsy, then realized he had committed a crime and became afraid to return the missing organs. Chauncy H. Beasley, *Closing Argument On the Part of the Defense in the Case of the State vs. Mattie C. Shann Under Indictment of Murder* (Trenton, N.J.: MacCrellish & Quigley, 1893), pp. 28–31.

133 The watches of at least eleven men: De la Torre, pp. 55–56. *The Mrs. Gunness Mystery,* a sensational pamphlet at the time, credited her with forty-two murders, but there is no factual basis for this estimate. My own rough guess is sixteen.

135 Lamphere boasted to the bartenders: Chicago *Tribune,* May 9, 1908, p. 2.

135 "I thought Belle Gunness . . .": Chicago *Tribune,* Nov. 27, 1908, p. 1.

135 Even a minister's tale: The same minister coerced Lamphere to let him serve as a confidential spiritual "confessor" after Lamphere's arrest, then published the confidences in the newspapers. To see him as an unreliable opportunist seems generous.

136 "women in smartly tailored gowns . . .": Chicago *Tribune,* May 11, 1908, p. 1.

137 "the appearance of a fair . . .": Chicago *Tribune,* May 10, 1908, p. 2.

137 "an organized feast of the morbid . . .": Chicago *Tribune,* May 11, 1908, p. 1.

137 "I never saw folks . . .": Chicago *Tribune,* May 11, 1908, p. 2.

137 "My dear Andrew . . .": Chicago *Tribune,* May 9, 1908, p. 2. Another multi-

ple murderer who killed in the line of work, Jane Toppan, also was successful largely because she played the superficial role expected of her so well.
Toppan, who worked in private families following a job at Massachusetts
General Hospital and a post as head nurse at Cambridge Hospital, was widely known as the best nurse in Cambridge. Yet she stole a good deal of money
here and there; she was addicted to morphine; and in the course of about six
years, she poisoned a great many people (she confessed to thirty-one murders) from most of whom she had borrowed substantial sums of money. She
was found to be insane and committed for life to Taunton asylum. An interesting contemporary assessment of this unusual woman—who like Belle
Gunness was exceedingly clever, convincing, and ambitious—is in Folsom,
pp. 102–53.

139 The Reverend Mr. M. H. Garrard: Chicago *Tribune,* Nov. 21, 1908, p. 20.
139 On Sunday, November 23, 1908: Chicago *Tribune,* Nov. 23, 1908, p. 2.

THREE: SPOILING MAIDENS

140–41 Thanks to Darwin: John S. Haller, Jr., and Robin M. Haller, *The Physician
and Sexuality in Victorian America* (New York: W. W. Norton, 1974), p. 50.
141 "simply a lesser man . . .": Thomas Wentworth Higginson summarizing Darwin and Huxley in *Common Sense About Women,* 4th ed. (London: Swan
Sonnenschein, 1891), p. 14.
141 Not that men complained: O. S. Fowler, *Sexual Science; Including Manhood, Womanhood, and their Mutual Interrelations; Love Its Laws, Power,
etc.* (Cincinnati: National, 1870), p. 134; Jules Michelet, *Love,* trans. from
4th Paris ed. by J. W. Palmer (New York: Rudd & Carleton, 1859), p. 76.
141–42 Professor Fowler explained: pp. 134–35. A literary case in point is Henry
James's *Washington Square.*
142 "Behold her clinging . . .": Fowler, pp. 322–23.
143 "It is time to consider . . .": *HWS,* vol. I, pp. 144–45. How decisively women
were "ruined" and "cast out" is illustrated by the case of Edith Wilson of Ot-
sego County, New York, who in 1873–74 was repeatedly forced into intercourse and finally impregnated by Charles S. Smith, a forty-year-old married
man who was superintendent of the Presbyterian Sunday school and a trust-
ee of the school district. Edith Wilson was a semi-invalid, and at the time her
pregnancy was discovered she was eleven years old. Her many friends "suddenly dropped off; they appear to lay all the sin at the child's door. Those
who sought her companionship now shun it, and those who formerly
thought nothing too good to say of Edith Wilson, can now hardly find words
to express their bad opinion of her. Even those whose duty it is to succor the
weak and console the afflicted, have now to all intents and purposes, abandoned the child to her fate." Her father also abandoned her. *The Trial and
Conviction of Charles S. Smith of Otego, N.Y. . . . for Bastardy. . . .* (Otego,
N.Y.: Otego, 1874), p. 12.
143–44 Only the Claflin sisters: Lady Cook (Tennessee Claflin), "Virtue," *Essays on*

Social Topics (London: Roxburghe, n.d.), pp. 5–9, rpt. from *Woodhull & Clafllin Weekly,* Dec. 23, 1871.

144 Professor Fowler condemned seducers: pp. 326–27.

144 On one hand, as Fowler reminded men: pp. 326–27. Emphasis mine.

144 the working life of a prostitute: "Report of the Committee on the Judiciary, for laws to suppress licentiousness," State of New York Assembly Documents, No. 333 (April 23, 1840) 5. In an 1875 speech on "Social Purity" Susan B. Anthony noted that "the ranks of professional prostitution [are] continually replenished by discouraged, seduced, deserted unfortunates, who can no longer hide the terrible secret of their lives" in Ida Husted Harper, *The Life and Work of Susan B. Anthony* (Indianapolis: Bowen Merrill, 1899–1908), p. 1005.

144–45 George Lippard: *The Midnight Queen; Or, Leaves from New York Life* (New York: Garrett, 1853), p. 100.

145 Some argued even then: "Report of the committee on the judiciary, on petitions praying for the suppression of licentiousness," State of New York Assembly Documents, No. 159 (March 30, 1842) 2, 10.

145 It was seduction that was the sticking: State of New York Assembly Documents, No. 159 (March 30, 1842), "An Act to prevent licentiousness," 3, articles 4 and 3.

145 "Does the noble lion pounce . . .": Fowler, pp. 323, 326.

146 To relieve them, women did: Barbara J. Berg, *The Remembered Gate: Origins of American Feminism: The Woman and the City, 1800–1860* (New York: Oxford University Press, 1978), p. 175. For a full discussion see pp. 161–80.

146 The best thinkers among the moral reformers: See Mary Livermore, *What Shall We Do with Our Daughters? Superfluous Women and Other Lectures* (Boston: Lee & Shepard, 1883). The feminist position on seduction and its consequences is summed up in the 1868 campaign of the Working Women's Association to free Hester Vaughn, an English immigrant servant girl seduced by her employer and subsequently convicted of infanticide in the death of her illegitimate baby, sentenced to death, and finally pardoned and deported. Feminists decried the lack of job opportunities for women, low wages, sexual vulnerability resulting from economic dependency, the double sexual standard, ostracism of unwed mothers, and exclusion of women from juries. See *The Revolution,* Nov. 19, 1868, p. 312; Dec. 10, 1868, p. 361; and Aug. 19, 1869, p. 105. See also "A Struggle for Life," *New York Times,* Nov. 6, 1868, p. 5; Ellen Carol DuBois, *Feminism and Suffrage: The Emergence of an Independent Women's Movement in America, 1848–1869* (Ithaca, N.Y.: Cornell University Press, 1978), pp. 145–47; Lois W. Banner, *Elizabeth Cady Stanton: A Radical for Woman's Rights* (Boston: Little, Brown, 1979), pp. 106–108.

146 They found an ally: Brooklyn *Daily Eagle,* Nov. 9, 1846, in Clifton Joseph Furness, ed. *The Genteel Female, An Anthology* (New York: Alfred A. Knopf, 1931), pp. 98–99.

146 Lucy Stone put the issue: Speech at National Woman's Rights Convention, Cincinnati, Ohio, Oct. 17–18, 1855, in *HWS*, vol. I, p. 166. Compare this item from the Portland *Tribune*: "Some one in Philadelphia advertised for females to make shirts at the rate of twelve and a half cents a piece, and about eight hundred females applied for the work." Rpt. *Advocate of Moral Reform*, Jan. 1, 1844, p. 7. Despite agitation for higher wages for women, the wages for shirt making in Philadelphia did not budge in the decade between this editorial and Lucy Stone's speech. Compare Susan B. Anthony's challenge: "If the plea that poverty is the cause of woman's prostitution be not true, perfect equality of chances to earn honest bread will demonstrate the falsehood by removing that pretext and placing her on the same plane with man. Then, if she is found in the ranks of vice and crime, she will be there for the same reason that man is and, from an object of pity, she, like him, will become a fit subject of contempt." Harper, p. 1007.

146 Still they were not deterred: A Queens (New York) district attorney caused a sensation by ordering police to arrest male "johns" along with female prostitutes in 1977. The Female Moral Reform Society called for such a practice in the 1830s. For evidence that the interstate and international traffic in women still flourishes, see Kathleen Barry, *Female Sexual Slavery* (Englewood Cliffs, N.J.: Prentice-Hall, 1979).

146–47 Meanwhile Professor Fowler noted that men: pp. 324–26. (Fowler's racism is apparent in his frequent references to "Indians.") Oddly enough, the doctrine of woman's natural frailty was construed by many reformers, such as the conservative moralist Mrs. Sandford, as a latter-day Calvinist argument for a sisterhood of sorts. "The same passions exist, in embryo, in every heart, and need only liberty and provacative [*sic*]. The mild, and amiable, and gentle woman may bless God for his restraining grace; and the better she becomes acquainted with herself, the more apt will she be to commiserate those who have given way to evil." *Woman in Her Social and Domestic Character*, 6th ed. (Boston: Otis, Broaders, 1842), p. 75.

147–52 On Amelia Norman: "Trial and Acquittal of Amelia Norman," *Advocate of Moral Reform*, Feb. 1, 1844, pp. 21–23. My account of this case is based also on coverage in the New York *Post*. I am indebted to Susan Brownmiller for bringing this case to my attention.

147 When she became pregnant: At the trial these incidents were referred to as stillbirths, the abortionist as a midwife; but few women "give birth" to two stillborn babies within six months.

147–48 "committed a premeditated assault . . .": "Trial and Acquittal of . . . Norman," p. 23.

148 Up in Concord: Margaret Fuller, *Woman in the Nineteenth Century* (1845; rpt. New York: W. W. Norton, 1971), pp. 148–49.

148 The moral reformers stated flatly: "Trial and Acquittal of . . . Norman," p. 21.

149 The same issue of the *Advocate*: "Why Do You Ask a Law?" *Advocate of Moral Reform*, Feb. 1, 1844, p. 20.

149–50 "A youth fascinating in person . . .": *Advocate of Moral Reform*, Feb. 1, 1844, pp. 20–21. Another common fate of seduced and abandoned maidens is illustrated in *The Victim of Seduction: An Affecting Narrative of the Tragical Death of Miss Fanny Salisbury, A Native of New Jersey, Who, Having Been Enticed From Her Widowed Parents and Basely Seduced By a Young Man of the City of New York, After Enduring Incredible Hardships in That City, Terminated Her Own Existence By Hanging Herself In a Forest Near Newark, on the 23d of January Last* (Boston: Artumus Belcrey, 1820).

150 The Philadelphia *North American*: rpt. New York *Post*, March 5, 1844.

150 The *Advocate* noted acidly: "Unpunished Crime," *Advocate of Moral Reform*, July 15, 1843, p. 108.

151 At the trial of Amelia Norman: "Trial and Acquittal of . . . Norman," pp. 22–23.

151 Yet he hastened to add: New York *Post*, Jan. 20, 1844, p. 1.

151 "occasional triumph of the moral sentiments . . .": New York *Post*, Feb. 8, 1844, p. 1.

152 "When the poor girl returned . . .": "L.M.C." (Lydia Maria Child) in a letter to the Boston *Courier*, rpt. New York *Post*, Feb. 8, 1844, p. 1.

152–53 When Virgil Knapp seduced: "The Last Death by Seduction," rpt. *Advocate of Moral Reform*, Oct. 15, 1845, p. 160; See also "Sarah Decker and Her Destroyer," *Advocate*, Nov. 1, 1845, pp. 165–66.

153–58 passim On the case of Mary Moriarty: *Trial of Mary Moriarty, for the Murder of John Shehan, Her Seducer, Also, the Speech of Milton A. Haynes, Esq. in Her Defense. Before the Criminal Court of Memphis, Tenn., 1855* (Memphis: Memphis Typographical Association, 1855).

153–66 passim On the case of Mary Harris: "The Trial of Mary Harris for the Murder of Adoniram J. Burroughs, Washington, D.C., 1865," *AST*, vol. XVII (1936), pp. 233–373; *Official Report of the Trial of Mary Harris, Indicted for the Murder of Adoniram J. Burroughs, Before the Supreme Court of the District of Columbia, (Sitting As A Criminal Court.) Monday, July 3, 1865. Prepared by James O. Clephane, Official Reporter* (Washington, D.C.: W. H. & O. H. Morrison, 1865).

153–66 passim On the case of Fanny Hyde: *Official Report of the Trial of Fanny Hyde, for the Murder of Geo. W. Watson, Including the Testimony, the Arguments of Counsel, and the Charge of the Court, Reported Verbatim. With Portraits of the Defendant and the Deceased. From the Short-hand Notes of William Helmstreet, Official Reporter of the Court* (New York: J. R. McDivitt, 1872).

153–65 passim On the case of Kate Stoddart: *The Goodrich Horror Being the Full Confession of Kate Stoddart, or Lizzie King. Why She Killed Charles Goodrich. Showing A Deserted Woman's Vengeance* (Philadelphia: Franklin, 1873).

154 "he proposed to mold and fashion . . .": "Trial of . . . Harris," p. 295.

157–58 At the trial of Mary Moriarty: *Trial of Mary Moriarty*, pp. 7, 10–11. On sex discrimination today in applying the "unwritten law" defense see Leo Kanowitz, *Women and the Law: The Unfinished Revolution* (Albuquerque: University of New Mexico Press, 1969), pp. 92–93.

158 The unwritten law provided that men: A century later when Joan Little and Inez Garcia killed their rapists their right to self-defense was supported only by some radical feminists; and they did not enjoy popular sympathy. In society as it is constituted killing a rapist is a more serious offense than killing a seducer, for while seducers threaten society by injuring men in their property, rapists serve society by terrorizing women and keeping them in their place. See Brownmiller, *Against Our Will: Men, Women and Rape* (New York: Simon & Schuster, 1975), pp. 1–5 et passim.

158 The prosecutor in the case of Amelia Norman: New York *Post,* Jan. 20, 1844, p. 2.

158–59 Then, as now, neither lawyers nor doctors: James Hendrie Lloyd, "The Claim of Moral Insanity in its Medico-Legal Aspects," *The Medical Record,* May 14, 1887 (rpt. New York: Trow's, 1887), p. 15. See also David Brion Davis, *Homicide in American Fiction, 1798–1860: A Study in Social Values* (Ithaca, N.Y.: Cornell University Press, 1957), pp. 60–76.

159 In the eyes of the law: Herbert Fingarette, *The Meaning of Criminal Insanity* (Berkeley: University of California Press, 1972), pp. 11–12.

159 Other experts, like Isaac Ray: *A Treatise on the Medical Jurisprudence of Insanity,* ed. Winfred Overholser (1838; rpt. Cambridge, Mass.: Harvard/Belknap, 1962), pp. 127–72; see also C. H. Hughes, "Moral (Affective) Insanity: A Plea for its Retention in Medical Nomenclature," Abstract of a paper presented to the International Congress at London, August 1881 (n.p., n.d.). On the reception of Ray's theories, see Norman Dain, *Concepts of Insanity in the United States, 1789–1865* (New Brunswick, N.J.: Rutgers University Press, 1964), pp. 71–83.

159 The term *moral mania*: Edward C. Mann, *Insanity; Its Etiology, Diagnosis, Pathology, and Treatment, With Cases Illustrating Pathology, Morbid Histology, and Treatment* (New York: G. P. Putnam's Sons, 1875), p. 16; William A. Hammond, *Insanity in Its Relations to Crime. A Text and A Commentary* (New York: D. Appleton, 1873), p. 74.

159 Trying to clarify the options: Lloyd, p. 4.

159–60 Where women were concerned: Fowler, p. 72; Ray, *Contributions to Mental Pathology* (1873; rpt. Delmar, N.Y.: Scholars' Facsimiles, 1973), p. 286.

160 On some points, the psychological experts: Mann, pp. 7–8; Ray, *Contributions,* p. 286.

160–61 Of all the causes of insanity in women: Michelet, p. 48; Henry Putnam Stearns, *Insanity: Its Causes and Prevention* (New York: G. P. Putnam's, 1883), pp. 188–89; T. S. Clouston, *Clinical Lectures on Mental Diseases* (Philadelphia: Henry C. Lea's, 1884), p. 336.

161 The horrors of *abnormal* menstruation: Stearns, pp. 190–91, 196. The leading exponent today of menstruation as disease is Katherina Dalton, an English physician, who concludes on the basis of scanty samples that five to eight of every ten women suffer from abnormal menstruation—a figure which leaves one wondering how the "normal" is determined. Like her nineteenth-century counterparts, Dalton is chiefly concerned with the impact of

women's abnormal menstruation upon their husbands and sons (no mention of daughters) as though the sole purpose of woman's life was to make the lives of adjacent males ripple free. *The Menstrual Cycle* (New York: Pantheon, 1969).

161 Physicians generally agreed: Clouston, p. 336; Hughes, p. 1.

161–62 Clouston was convinced: p. 237. See also Stearns, p. 196.

162 Dr. Halliday Croom: Clouston, p. 336.

162 Isaac Ray thought menstruating women: *Treatise,* pp. 154–58.

162 From the moment Harris read: "The Trial of Mary Harris," pp. 246, 243.

162–63 Such was her appearance: "Trial of . . . Harris," pp. 270, 321. An illustration in Paula Weideger's *Menstruation and Menopause: The Physiology and Psychology, the Myth and the Reality* (New York: Dell, 1975), p. 152, depicts a cursory gynecological examination performed by a kneeling physician with one hand up under the skirts of a standing, fully clothed patient. Dr. Fitch might have performed such an exam during his flying visits, but he wouldn't have learned much.

163 If that was not enough: "Trial of . . . Harris," pp. 270–71.

163 That double insanity: "Trial of . . . Harris," p. 251.

163–64 When Fanny Hyde came to trial: *Official Report of the Trial of Fanny Hyde,* pp. 28–29.

164 Summing up for the defense: *Official Report of the Trial of Fanny Hyde,* p. 102.

164 A definitive description of the disease: *Official Report of the Trial of Fanny Hyde,* p. 31.

164 Dr. John Byrne: *Official Report of the Trial of Fanny Hyde,* p. 74.

164–65 "afflicted with a disease": *Official Report of the Trial of Fanny Hyde,* p. 150.

165 Reporters covering the case: New York *Sun,* April 17, 1872, p. 1.

165 The tearful and thoroughly confused jury: *New York Times,* Jan. 21, 1873, p. 2.

165 ". . . her mind frequently drifted . . .": *Goodrich Horror,* p. 8.

165 "her once plump and shapely form . . .": *Goodrich Horror,* p. 4.

165 "FANNY HYDE'S SAD LIFE": New York *Sun,* April 18, 1872, p. 3.

165 Her landlady was prepared to testify: *Goodrich Horror,* p. 24.

166 In the case of Fanny Hyde: *Official Report of the Trial of Fanny Hyde,* p. 143.

166 District Attorney Carrington: "Trial of . . . Harris," p. 365.

166 The reporter for the New York *Tribune*: July 20, 1865, p. 5.

166 When the verdict was announced: New York *Herald,* July 20, 1865, p. 1.

167 Defense attorney Daniel Voorhees: "Trial of . . . Harris," p. 339.

167 "poison and mildew . . .": *Official Report of the Trial of Fanny Hyde,* p. 37.

167–68 Milton Haynes, defending Mary: *Trial of Mary Moriarty,* p. 11.

168 Professor Fowler echoed the sentiment: p. 326.

168 Attorney I. B. Catlin: *Official Report of the Trial of Fanny Hyde,* p. 29.

168 "a woman who loves . . .": *Goodrich Horror,* p. 18.

168 "respected wife": "Trial of . . . Harris," p. 298.

168 "a girl of strong feelings . . .": New York *Post,* Feb. 8, 1844, p. 1.

168 "she did no more . . .": "Trial of . . . Harris," p. 298.

168 They went outside the law: See Hyman Gross, *A Theory of Criminal Justice* (New York: Oxford University Press, 1978), p. 17.

169 The only law punishing seduction: *Trial of Mary Moriarity,* p. 10.

169 "It is not to be disguised . . .": State of New York Assembly Documents, No. 333 (April 23, 1840), 1–2.

170 Women did continue to petition: State of New York Assembly Documents, No. 159 (March 30, 1842), 4–5.

170–71 The whole issue made Tennessee Claflin hot: Lady Cook, "Which Is to Blame?" *Essays on Social Topics,* pp. 123–31. Rpt. from *Woodhull & Claflin Weekly,* Jan. 6, 1872. This same double bind was repeated early in the twentieth century when reformers' demands for better working conditions for *all* workers brought protective legislation for women who, as Brandeis argued in the landmark *Muller* v. *Oregon* case (1908), are a class apart because of their biological function of reproduction. Only a few feminists could foresee that this protective legislation would then be used to exclude women from jobs and advancement. See Albie Sachs and Joan Hoff Wilson, *Sexism and the Law: A Study of Male Beliefs and Legal Bias in Britain and the United States* (New York: Free Press, 1978), pp. 111–16.

171–72 On the Sickles case: W. A. Swanberg, *Sickles the Incredible* (New York: Charles Scribner's Sons, 1956), pp. 57–76; "The Trial of Daniel E. Sickles for the Murder of Philip Barton Key. Washington, D.C., 1859," *AST,* vol. XII (1919), pp. 494–762.

172 When he died in 1914: *New York Times,* May 10, 1914, IV, p. 7; Swanberg, p. 390.

172 the one-legged General Sickles returned: *National Intelligencer,* July 11, 1865, p. 1; July 20, 1865, p. 3.

172 *The New York Times,* in an editorial on the acquittal: July 20, 1865, p. 4.

173 Yet *The Times* found in the Harris case: July 20, 1865, p. 4.

173 The Ohio Woman's Rights Convention: in Gerda Lerner, *The Female Experience: An American Documentary* (Indianapolis: Bobbs-Merrill, 1977), p. 345.

173 When some radical feminists: *The Revolution,* May 19, 1870, pp. 306–307.

173–74 On Laura Fair: "The Trial of Laura D. Fair for the Murder of Alexander P. Crittenden, San Francisco, California, 1871," *AST,* vol. XV (1926), pp. 197–464.

174 Always looking for the main chance: "Wolves in the Fold," in William Seagle, *Acquitted of Murder* (Chicago: Henry Regnery, 1958), pp. 99–100.

174 Mrs. Fair intended to set forth: *New York Times,* Nov. 22, 1872, p. 1.

174–75 Only the New York *Tribune*: July 21, 1865, p. 4.

175 "Our laws are made by men": New York *Tribune,* July 21, 1865, p. 4.

FOUR: LAYING DOWN THE LAW

176 "You have granted . . .": *HWS*, vol. I, p. 701.

176–77 The New York State Woman's Rights Committee: *HWS*, vol. I, p. 744. The committee consisted of Cady Stanton, Anthony, Ernestine Rose, Lydia Mott, and Martha Wright.

177 "A citizen can not be said . . .": *HWS*, vol. I, p. 675.

177 As things were, women could not get: *HWS*, vol. I, p. 597. Jury service for women was a long time coming. The Civil Rights Act of 1957 ensured the right of women to serve on federal juries, but as late as 1962 twenty-one states still did not permit women to serve equally with men. By 1973 women were permitted on juries in all states, but nineteen still imposed special qualifications or exemptions. Not until 1975 did the Supreme Court invalidate laws limiting jury service on the basis of sex in *Taylor* v. *Louisiana*, 419 U.S. 522 (1975). As of this writing Missouri and Tennessee still automatically exempt women, but the Missouri method of jury selection is being challenged in the courts by the American Civil Liberties Union on behalf of a criminal defendant (*Duren* v. *Missouri*). See Albie Sachs and Joan Hoff Wilson, *Sexism and the Law: A Study of Male Beliefs and Legal Bias in Britain and the United States* (New York: Free Press, 1978), pp. 123, 213; *Civil Liberties*, Nov. 1978, p. 5.

178 "No rank of men have ever been satisfied . . .": *HWS*, vol. I, p. 597.

179 His personal physician: St. Paul *Pioneer and Democrat*, May 26, 1859, p. 3. My account of the Bilansky case is based mainly on coverage in this paper.

179 "about as unsatisfactory . . .": March 17, 1859, p. 3. Toxicologist Donald Hoffmann of the New York Medical Examiner's Office finds the medical evidence in the Bilansky case unsatisfactory and inconclusive, and these belated tests open to question.

180 As Ann Evards Wright: Manly Wade Wellman suggests that Ann Bilansky and Ann Simpson of Fayetteville, acquitted in 1850 of poisoning husband Alexander, are one and the same. *Dead and Gone: Classic Crimes of North Carolina* (Chapel Hill: University of North Carolina Press, 1954), pp. 40–41. Walter Trenerry points out that the physical descriptions of the two women don't tally. *Murder in Minnesota: A Collection of True Cases* (St. Paul: Minnesota Historical Society, 1962), pp. 230–31. Wellman's suggestion is an instance of the popular notion that fearsome criminals are identical or at least related to one another—in other words, of limited number and clearly set apart from the rest of the human family.

180 their love affair as a universally known fact: *Pioneer and Democrat*, May 25, 1859, p. 3. Trenerry writes of the case as though they were lovers.

180–81 Bilansky's first wife, Mary Ellen: *Pioneer and Democrat*, March 19, 1859, p. 3.

182 The next case on Judge Palmer's docket: *Pioneer and Democrat*, June 7, 1859, p. 3.

182 "down on Jackson Street": *Pioneer and Democrat,* May 28, 1859, p. 3.

182 "Wright County War": J. Fletcher Williams, *A History of the City of Saint Paul and the County of Ramsey, Minnesota* (St. Paul: Minnesota Historical Society, 1876), pp. 389–90.

182 Two months before Ann Bilansky's arrest: Williams, p. 388.

182 And on the very day: Williams, p. 392; *Pioneer and Democrat,* Jan. 28, 1860, p. 3.

182–83 The St. Paul *Pioneer and Democrat* evaluated: June 5, 1859, p. 2.

183–84 Even Supreme Court Justice Charles Flandrau: Trenerry, p. 38.

184 He immediately vetoed the bill: *Pioneer and Democrat,* March 9, 1860, p. 2.

184–85 Having discussed the constitutional grounds: *Pioneer and Democrat,* March 9, 1860, p. 2.

185 On March 23, 1860: *Pioneer and Democrat,* March 24, 1860, p. 3.

185 Governor Ramsey, with obstinacy: *Pioneer and Democrat,* March 9, 1860, p. 2; March 24, 1860, p. 3.

186–92 On the case of Mary Hartung: I base my account on coverage in the Albany, New York, newspapers (the *Journal,* the *Atlas and Argus,* and the *Courier*), *New York Times* and other New York City dailies. See also "The Case of the Susceptible Solons" in William Seagle, *Acquitted of Murder* (Chicago: Henry Regnery, 1958), pp. 47–79.

187 During the previous decade in Albany: George R. Howell and Jonathan Tenney, *Bi-Centennial History of Albany. History of the County of Albany, N.Y., from 1609 to 1886* (New York: W. W. Munsell, 1886), pp. 305–306.

188 The Albany *Atlas and Argus* said: Seagle, p. 67.

188 "worst sort of murder": *New York Times,* April 8, 1859, p. 8.

188 "even though she were guilty . . .": New York *Post,* April 8, 1859, p. 2.

188–89 In 1857 after a Plymouth County jury: Robert Sullivan, *Goodbye, Lizzie Borden* (Brattleboro, Vt.: Stephen Greene, 1974), p. 193.

189 Hartung's execution was postponed: *New York Times,* April 9, 1859, p. 4.

189 The New York *Post* stormed: in *New York Times,* April 11, 1859, p. 4.

189 For two decades opponents: "Report of the Select Committee on the Petitions for a Repeal of the Death Penalty in this State," State of New York Assembly Documents, No. 82 (Feb. 16, 1860) 20.

189–90 The Assembly designated a select committee: State of New York Assembly Documents, No. 82, (Feb. 16, 1860) 1, 3.

190 The act of 1860 provided: Laws of the State of New York, 83rd Session, Chapter 410, Section 1, 4, 5, 10, 11, pp. 712–14. Massachusetts had passed a similar law in 1852 as a sort of de facto way of abolishing capital punishment; but Massachusetts did not make the law retroactive, as New York did.

191 The legislature hastily redressed: Laws of the State of New York, 84th Session, Chapter 303, pp. 693–94, passed April 17, 1861.

191 Along with her went four male murderers: Seagle, p. 78. Wife-murderer Stephens was not among them. He was executed Feb. 3, 1860, just before the act of 1860 was passed. *New York Times,* Feb. 4, 1860, p. 2.

191 Even Mary Hartung's supporters: *New York Times,* April 9, 1859, p. 4.

191–92 Wendell Phillips: Address to the New England Convention, May 27, 1859, *HWS,* vol. I, p. 275.

192 As *The New York Times* put it: April 15, 1859, p. 4.

192–93 Thorstein Veblen described: *The Theory of the Leisure Class: An Economic Study of Institutions* (1899; rpt. New York: The Viking Press, 1965), pp. 148–49.

193 "It grates painfully . . .": Veblen, p. 179.

193 Some time after mid-century, things changed: The popular belief that America has always been a mobile society has been refuted by the consensus of recent mobility studies. See Edward Pessen, ed., *Three Centuries of Social Mobility in America* (Lexington, Mass.: D. C. Heath, 1974), especially Pessen, "The Myth of Antebellum Social Mobility and Equality of Opportunity," pp. 110–21.

194 At least by 1857: Mrs. C. S. Hilborn, *Modern Aristocracy, Or Money Worship* (Providence: Knowles, Anthony, 1857), p. 9.

194 The narrow upper class: Veblen, p. 68; Lester F. Ward, "Social Classes in the Light of Modern Sociological Theory," *The American Journal of Sociology,* vol. XIII, no. 5 (March 1908), p. 627.

194 At the time, the chief difference: Ward, p. 619. He might have said the same thing about the differences between women and men. William Graham Sumner, *What Social Classes Owe to Each Other* (1883; rpt. Caldwell, Idaho: Caxton, 1952), p. 62; Veblen, p. 41.

195 On the same day that Ann: St. Paul *Pioneer and Democrat,* March 8, 1860, p. 2.

195 "Every one knows what kind of servants . . .": Harriet Martineau, *Society in America* (London: Saunders & Otley, 1839), vol. III, p. 136.

196–209 On Bridget Durgan: My account is based largely on coverage in *The New York Times.*

196 "an ordinary-looking Irish girl . . .": *New York Times,* May 21, 1867, p. 1.

197 And then there were her fits: *New York Times,* May 28, 1867, p. 1.

199 The list of her wounds: *New York Times,* May 23, 1867, p. 1.

201 "prejudice in this community": *New York Times,* May 29, 1867, p. 1.

201–02 it came to "nothing": *New York Times,* May 29, 1867, p. 1.

202 The defense even produced two physicians: *New York Times,* May 28, 1867, p. 1.

202 Her jailers testified: *New York Times,* May 28, 1867, p. 1.

202 And according to the popular novelist: *New York Times,* Aug. 25, 1867, p. 6.

203 The relationship of epilepsy to insanity: Isaac Ray, *Contributions to Mental Pathology* (1873; rpt. Delmar, N.Y.: Scholars' Facsimiles, 1973), pp. 278–79.

203 Opinions of epilepsy varied widely: Ray, *Contributions,* pp. 280–81; M. G. Echeverria, "Criminal Responsibility of Epileptics, as Illustrated by the Case of David Montgomery," *American Journal of Insanity,* Jan. 1873, p. 414. Echeverria quotes Delasiauve, p. 412.

203 the "seat" of the disease "in the head": Ray, *A Treatise on the Medical Juris-prudence of Insanity,* ed. Winfred Overholser (1838; rpt. Cambridge, Mass.: Harvard/Belknap, 1962), p. 95. Coriell also confused epilepsy with catalepsy as he should not have done had he kept up on his medical authorities; Sir John Russell Reynolds wrote in 1861: "The features of CATALEPSY are so peculiar that they can not well be mistaken for epilepsy." *Epilepsy: Its Symptoms. Treatment, and Relation to Other Chronic Convulsive Diseases* (London: John Churchill, 1861), p. 288.

203 "Her fits were caused . . .": *New York Times,* May 28, 1867, p. 1.

204 So all the pleas of diminished responsibility: The plea of epileptic insanity or the suggestion of epilepsy as mitigating circumstance did not always work for men either. George Winnemore, previously an inoffensive young man, was tried in May 1867 at Philadelphia for killing a woman with a razor under circumstances very similar to the Fyler and Durgan cases; he was executed the day before Bridget Durgan, August 29, 1867, but quietly, within the prison, in the presence of only a few officials. Dr. Isaac Ray and other leading psychiatrists tried to intervene on Winnemore's behalf, asking executive clemency or delay; and when that effort failed, Ray subsequently wrote about the case, suggesting that Winnemore had been too hastily and unjustly dispatched. The Fyler and Winnemore cases are often mentioned in volumes of medical jurisprudence—the Durgan case, so far as I know, never. Yet the chief differences between the Winnemore and Durgan cases are the sex of the defendant and the unusual cruelty of Durgan's punishment. For the Winnemore case and a brief account of the Fyler case see "Trial of Winnemore," in Ray, *Contributions,* pp. 264–81.

204 There was only one lady: *New York Times,* May 29, 1867, p. 1; June 1, 1867, p. 2.

204 not "one spark of womanhood": *Life, Crimes, and Confession of Bridget Durgan, The Fiendish Murderess of Mrs. Coriel: Whom She Butchered, Hoping to Take Her Place in the Affections of the Husband of Her Innocent and Lovely Victim. The Only Authentic and Hitherto Unpublished History of Her Whole Life; And the Hideous Crime for Which She Was Executed at New Brunswick, N.J.,* by Rev. Mr. Brendan (Philadelphia: C. W. Alexander, 1867), p. 21.

204–05 Elizabeth Oakes Smith: *New York Times,* Aug. 25, 1867, p. 6.

205 But if Bridget were a beast: *New York Times,* Aug. 25, 1867, p. 6.

205 Judge Vrendenburgh, charging the jury: *New York Times,* June 1, 1867, p. 2.

205–06 On June 17, 1867: *New York Times,* June 18, 1867, p. 8.

206 On the second day of the trial: *New York Times,* May 23, 1867, p. 1.

206–07 The sheriff seems to have been generous: *New York Times,* Aug. 31, 1867, p. 8.

207 The device used in the execution. *New York Times,* Aug. 31, 1867, p. 8. By 1930 when the New Brunswick Sunday *Times* recalled the case of "The First Woman to be Executed in New Jersey" Bridget's death scene had been com-

pletely rehabilitated. "Bridget," the paper said, "showed fine courage to the bitter end. There is a kind of heaven-sent strength that supports frail humanity in moments of awful strain, and it seemed the same kind of buoyancy that made Marie Antoinette so brave on the eve of the guillotine came also to the Irish servant girl as she faced the quick and horrible death among strange people." June 22, 1930.

208 It offered this description of her: *Life, Crimes, and Confession,* p. 43.

208 The account also repeated the rumor: *Life, Crimes, and Confession,* p. 47.

208 His most damning diagnosis: *The Life and Confession of Bridget Dergan [sic], Who Murdered Mrs. Ellen Coriell, the Lovely Wife of Dr. Coriell, of New Market, N.J., to Which is Added Her Full Confession, and An Account of Her Execution at New Brunswick* (Philadelphia: Barclay, 1867), p. 46. This pamphlet was reprinted in 1881.

209–33 On Lizzie Andrew Borden: There is a mass of information on the United States' most famous woman killer. I base my account largely on Frank H. Burt's official transcript—*Trial of Lizzie Andrew Borden: upon an indictment charging her with the murder of Abby Durfee Borden and Andrew Jackson Borden; before the Superior Court for the County of Bristol: Mason, C. J., and Blodgett and Dewey, J. J. Official stenographic report.* (New Bedford, Mass.: 1893)—a microfilm copy of which is deposited at the University of Massachusetts at Amherst; but whenever possible my citations and pagination are to the more accessible: Edmund Lester Pearson, ed. *Trial of Lizzie Borden: Edited, with a History of the Case* (Garden City, N.Y.: Doubleday, Doran, 1937).

212 "Miss Lizzie Borden was standing . . .": Pearson, p. 153.

213 "I feel depressed": Pearson, pp. 156–58.

214 "Q. You were feeling better . . .": Pearson, p. 418.

214 "I don't know," said Miss Lizzie: Pearson, p. 413.

215 When Miss Lizzie took her seat: New York *Sun,* June 6, 1893, p. 1; June 13, 1893, p. 1.

215 "that indefinable quality . . .": New York *Sun,* June 14, 1893, p. 3.

215 Her face, "like her dress": New York *Sun,* June 6, 1893, p. 1. See also Caesar Lombroso and William Ferrero, *The Female Offender* (New York: D. Appleton, 1897), pp. 147–91. The famous criminologist describes such features as typical of the "born criminal" woman.

216 "no other feeling . . .": Aug. 5, 1892, p. 7.

216 "a graven image": New York *Sun,* June 13, 1893, pp. 1–2.

216 "Miss Borden's womanhood": New York *Sun,* June 13, 1893, p. 2.

216 "the Judges, the lawyers, the Sheriff . . .": New York *Sun,* June 6, 1893, p. 1.

217 "No lawyer who could have his choice . . .": May 13, 1893, p. 8.

217 "Judges and attorneys are alike . . .": June 8, 1893, p. 8.

217 "The temper of the lawyers . . .": New York *Sun,* June 10, 1893, p. 2.

218 "It is magnificent . . .": Pearson, p. 194.

218 "He [Andrew Borden] was a man . . .": Pearson, pp. 306–307.

218 "You are out of families . . .": Transcript of the trial of Lizzie Borden, p. 1,620.

219 "What is the use of talking . . .": Transcript, p. 1,680.

219 "Where is the motive? When men . . .": Fall River *Daily Globe,* Aug. 8, 1892, p. 7.

219 "Lizzie is innocent . . .": Aug. 16, 1892, p. 8.

219 "A most outrageous, brutal crime . . .": Aug. 6, 1892, p. 8.

220 "The Government's . . . claim . . .": Pearson, p. 255.

220 "blood flying all over the walls . . .": Pearson, p. 312.

221 "That is, it was without significance": New York *Sun,* June 13, 1893, p. 2. Emphasis mine.

221 "I do not care to allude . . .": Pearson, pp. 356–57. Emphasis mine.

222 "One [woman, namely Bridget]": Transcript, pp. 1,856–57.

222 "Open statements are made . . .": Aug. 29, 1892, p. 8.

223 "arts and ways of femininity": New York *Sun,* June 13, 1893, p. 2.

223 ". . . you *must* say such acts . . .": *New York Times,* June 20, 1893, p. 9. Emphasis mine. *The New York Times* paraphrases a longer statement found in Pearson, p. 286.

223 "a matter of common notoriety . . .": April 20, 1892, p. 4.

223 "three-fourths of the New England papers . . .": Aug. 15, 1892, p. 7; see also Aug. 12, 1892, p. 1.

224 "The Globe, being thus misled . . .": Evening edition, Oct. 11, 1892, p. 1.

224 "you do not get the greatest ability . . .": Pearson, p. 286.

224 "When they come upon the witness stand": Transcript, pp. 1,618–19.

225 Commenting on the case later: "The Borden Case," 27 *American Law Review* 819 (1893) 833. Emphasis mine.

225 "And there [Assistant Marshal Fleet] . . .": Pearson, pp. 297–98.

225 "unfortunate maiden": New York *Sun,* June 21, 1893, p. 1.

225 "nearly all eyes were turned . . .": New York *Sun,* June 13, 1893, p. 2.

225–26 "For an hour he championed . . .": New York *Sun,* June 16, 1893, p. 1.

226 "It is not impossible that a good person . . .": Transcript, p. 1,743.

227 "I am sorry that it was found necessary . . .": Fall River *Daily Globe,* Aug. 13, 1892, p. 7.

227 ". . . the deep red carnations . . .": New York *Sun,* June 11, 1893, p. 1.

227 "District Attorney Knowlton was prejudiced . . .": Aug. 16, 1892, p. 7.

228 "The prisoner at the bar . . .": Pearson, p. 326.

228 "face this case as men . . .": Pearson, p. 327; Transcript, pp. 1,757–58.

228 "Nay, if it was a man . . .": Transcript, pp. 1,776–77.

228 "I have left the dead body . . .": Pearson, p. 344.

228–29 "There may be that in this case . . .": Pearson, pp. 344–45. Emphasis mine.

229 "But it is a *grateful relief* . . .": Pearson, p. 345. Emphasis mine.

229 "And so I leave that [argument] . . .": Transcript, p. 1,809.

230 "On every legal point . . .": *New York Times,* June 16, 1893, p. 8.

230 Justice Dewey dealt the final blow: Sullivan, pp. 218–34.

230–31 Justice Dewey overstepped: Transcript, p. 1,917; Sullivan, pp. 231, 227; Boston *Globe*, June 21, 1893, p. 4. Dewey's comments violate Borden's Fifth Amendment protection against self-incrimination. His charge was attacked at the time by Professor Wigmore and by Charles G. Davis, *The Conduct of Law in the Borden Case, with Suggestions of Changes in Criminal Law and Practice* (Boston: Boston *Daily Advertiser*, 1894), and recently by former Massachusetts Superior Court Judge Robert Sullivan. Despite his criticism of the conduct of the trial, Wigmore improbably pronounced it "a model of what trials should be." 27 *American Law Review* 819 (1893) 835.

231 "Suppose for a single moment . . .": Victoria Lincoln, *A Private Disgrace: Lizzie Borden By Daylight* (New York: G. P. Putnam's Sons, 1967), pp. 219–20.

231 "a woman, one of that sex . . .": Pearson, p. 327. Emphasis mine.

232 Lizzie dropped into her seat: *New York Times*, June 21, 1893, p. 1.

232 "Judge Blodgett's face contorted . . .": New York *Sun*, June 21, 1893, p. 2.

232–33 "of the usual inept and stupid . . .": *New York Times*, June 21, 1893, p. 4.

233 ". . . it took only an hour for the jury . . .": New York *Sun*, June 21, 1893, p. 1.

233 The Boston *Globe* even printed an interview: June 21, 1893, p. 5.

233 "with that poor, tried . . .": Edwin H. Porter, *The Fall River Tragedy. A History of the Borden Murders* (Fall River, Mass.: author, 1893), p. 80.

233 "the happiest woman in the world": *New York Times*, June 21, 1893, p. 2.

234 ". . . to suggest that a woman of good family . . .": Pearson, *Studies in Murder* (New York: Macmillan, 1924), p. 32.

234 in the grip of "male menopause": Q. Patrick, "The Case for Lizzie, or A Theoretical Reconstruction of the Borden Murders," *The Pocket Book of True Crime Stories*, ed. Anthony Boucher (New York: Pocket Books, 1943), p. 254.

234 "his full lips seeking and finding . . .": Marie Belloc Lowndes, *Lizzie Borden: A Study in Conjecture* (New York: Longmans, Green, 1939), p. 178.

235 She is a lesbian, or: Charles and Louise Samuels, *The Girl in the House of Hate* (New York: Fawcett, 1953), pp. 8–9; Lincoln, pp. 41–48 et passim.

235 "doing her bit to free her sex . . .": Samuels, p. 144.

235 On Alice Christiana Abbott: *New York Times*, May 25, 1867, p. 1.

235–36 "We offer our profound sympathy . . .": "Lizzie Borden Believed Innocent," *The Woman's Journal*, Aug. 20, 1892, p. 270.

236 Lucy Stone used the occasion: "A Flaw in the Jury System," *The Woman's Journal*, June 17, 1893, p. 188; Livermore, "A Talk with Lizzie Borden," rpt. *The Woman's Journal*, May 27, 1893, pp. 162–63.

236 The rate of women's crimes: J. Sanderson Christison, *Crime and Criminals*, 2nd ed. (Chicago: author, 1899), pp. 12–13.

237 "feminine vigilante": Samuels, p. 18.

237 "Lizzie's life," she wrote: Agnes DeMille, *Lizzie Borden: A Dance of Death* (Boston: Little, Brown, 1968), p. 134.

FIVE: LET THAT BE A LESSON

239 Everyone wrote about the case: Silas Bent, "The Hall-Mills Case in the Newspapers," *The Nation,* Dec. 8, 1926, pp. 580–81; Bruce Bliven, "The Hall-Press-Mills Case," *The New Republic,* Dec. 1, 1926, pp. 39–40.

239 "Dear, dear, darling heart . . .": Charles Boswell and Lewis Thompson, *The Girl in Lover's Lane* (New York: Fawcett, 1953), p. 96.

239–40 According to Bruce Bliven: p. 40.

240 members of the Ku Klux Klan: William M. Kunstler, *The Minister and the Choir Singer: The Hall-Mills Murder Case* (New York: William Morrow, 1964), pp. 317–34.

241 "I'm a flapper": The photograph and the remark are reprinted in Kunstler, following p. 168.

241 For the all-American girls: Robert S. Lynd and Helen Merrell Lynd, *Middletown: A Study in Contemporary American Culture* (New York: Harcourt Brace, 1929), pp. 138–39; Phyllis Blanchard and Carlyn Manasses, *New Girls for Old* (New York: Macaulay, 1930), p. 3.

241 More and more women complained: Ernest R. Groves, *The American Woman: The Feminine Side of A Masculine Civilization* (New York: Greenberg, 1937), p. 390.

241 "The women who transgress": Mrs. Henry W. Peabody, "Woman's Morality A Light Through the Ages," *Current History,* vol. 19, no. 4 (Jan. 1924), pp. 588–89.

241 "a relatively small number" of "girls": Blanchard & Manasses, p. 13.

242 Dr. Alice Stockham, writing in 1896: Alice B. Stockham, *Karezza: Ethics of Marriage* (New York: R. F. Fenno, 1896); Ellen Key, *Love and Ethics* (New York: B. W. Huebsch, 1911), pp. 30–31; Havelock Ellis, *Studies in the Psychology of Sex* (1901; rpt. New York: Random House, 1936), vol. I, part 2, pp. 250–51; *On Life and Sex: Essays of Love and Virtue* (1922 and 1931; rpt. Garden City, New York: Garden City, 1937), vol. I, p. 112; Margaret Sanger, *Happiness in Marriage* (New York: Brentano's, 1926), p. 100.

243 Between 1870 and 1920: William Fielding Ogburn, "Eleven Questions Concerning American Marriages," *Social Forces,* vol. VI, no. 1 (Sept. 1927), p. 7; "The Family and Its Functions," *Recent Social Trends in the United States: Report of the President's Research Committee on Social Trends* (New York: McGraw-Hill, 1933), vol. II, p. 687. The sudden discovery of female sexuality and maternal (i.e., heterosexual) destiny may have occurred partly in response to increased female bonding in the later nineteenth century as indicated by declining marriage and birth rates, especially among educated women, and increasing association of women. See Nancy F. Cott, *The Bonds of Womanhood: "Woman's Sphere" in New England, 1780–1835* (New Haven: Yale University Press, 1977), pp. 160–96, and William R. Taylor and Christopher Lasch, "Two 'Kindred Spirits': Sorority and Family in New England, 1839–1846," *New England Quarterly,* vol. XXXVI (1963), pp. 23–41.

243 It also enlisted in the labor force: Edward A. Ross, *The Social Trend* (1922) in *The American Woman: Who Was She?* ed. Anne Firor Scott (Englewood Cliffs, N.J.: Prentice-Hall, 1971), pp. 130–31.

243 On top of all these blows: Charles Franklin Thwing, "The Family at the Parting of the Ways," *Current History,* vol. 19, no. 4 (Jan. 1924), p. 591.

243 Happily, the sexologists came forward: Ellen Key, *The Woman Movement,* trans. M. B. Barthwick (New York: G. P. Putnam's Sons, 1912), p. 187; *The Century of the Child* (New York: G. P. Putnam's Sons, 1909), p. 71; Havelock Ellis, *The Task of Social Hygiene* (Boston: Houghton Mifflin, 1912), pp. 65–66; *These Modern Women: Autobiographical Essays from the Twenties,* ed. Elaine Showalter (Old Westbury, N.Y.: Feminist Press, 1978), p. 145.

243–44 In 1939 Hannah and Abraham Stone: *A Marriage Manual: A Practical Guide-book to Sex and Marriage* (New York: Simon & Schuster, 1939), p. 3; Robert C. Binkley and Frances Williams Binkley, *What Is Right with Marriage: An Outline of Domestic Theory* (New York: D. Appleton, 1929), p. 52.

244 "apprenticeship" to motherhood: Sanger, p. 196.

244 "When two who are mated . . .": Marie Carmichael Stopes, *Married Love: A New Contribution to the Solution of Sex Difficulties,* 7th ed. (London: G. P. Putnam's Sons, 1919), pp. 127–28.

245 the old feminists had "propagandised": Havelock Ellis, *Man and Woman: A Study of Secondary and Tertiary Sexual Characters* (Boston: Houghton Mifflin, 1929), pp. v, 25, 461–69; Ellis, *Social Hygiene,* pp. 101, 131.

245 The old feminists, according to Ellis: *Social Hygiene,* p. 127.

245–46 Old feminists had fought for: Blanchard & Manasses, pp. 237, 175–84.

246 "All my life I've wanted . . .": Floyd Dell, *Janet March* (New York: Alfred A. Knopf, 1923), p. 456.

246 In later decades, some experts: Ferdinand Lundberg and Marynia F. Farnham, *Modern Woman: The Lost Sex* (New York: Harper & Bros., 1947), p. 361.

246–47 Charlotte Perkins Gilman warned: "Toward Monogamy," *Our Changing Morality: A Symposium,* ed. Freda Kirchwey (New York: A. & C. Boni, 1930), p. 58.

247 Theoretician Suzanne LaFollette warned: *Concerning Women* (New York: A. & C. Boni, 1926), p. 96.

247 Feminists such as Crystal Eastman: June Sochen, *The New Woman: Feminism in Greenwich Village, 1910–1920* (New York: Quadrangle, 1972), pp. 52–60; Blanche Wiesen Cook, ed. *Crystal Eastman on Women and Revolution* (New York: Oxford University Press, 1978), pp. 29–30. For an analysis of the "red smear" used to discredit even moderate social feminists, see J. Stanley Lemons, *The Woman Citizen: Social Feminism in the 1920s* (Urbana: Illinois University Press, 1975), pp. 209–27.

248 "Most of the terrible women . . .": Showalter, p. 143.

248 The modern psychological perspective: Lundberg and Farnham, p. 196. I use this 1947 statement as illustration because it best represents the full-blown

neo-Freudian interpretation; but its germ can be found in Ellis's patronizing dismissal of ignorant feminists and their peculiar fetishes. The remarkable myth of the nineteenth-century repressed spinster suffragists still persists even among people who should know better. See Showalter's remark: "Nineteenth-century feminists did not see marriage and public life in conflict for women; they recognized them as mutually *exclusive,* and accepted the necessity of choosing between them." p. 5. In fact, the acknowledged leaders of the nineteenth-century women's movement—Elizabeth Cady Stanton, Susan B. Anthony, Lucretia Coffin Mott, Martha Coffin Pelham Wright, Lucy Stone Blackwell, Antoinette Brown Blackwell, Olympia Brown, Carrie Chapman Catt, Ernestine Rose, Matilda Joslyn Gage, Mrs. C.I.H. Nichols, Harriet Stanton Blatch—all (except Anthony) married at least once. All but Anthony and Rose had children; and Anthony spent a good deal of time looking after Cady Stanton's.

249 The first juvenile courts: Anthony M. Platt, *The Child Savers: The Invention of Delinquency* (Chicago: University of Chicago Press, 1969), pp. 9–10. For a detailed analysis of the juvenile justice system, see Platt. In a final turn of the screw, however, he largely blames women for devising the system of "maternal justice." Many women found jobs within the juvenile justice system by default because social work, like nursing, teaching, and other nurturing jobs, was regarded as a legitimate extension of woman's sphere. Platt sees that children and lower-class families were not beneficiaries but victims of the system; he does not understand that women of all classes were also victimized by it.

249 One thing was clear: Lundberg and Farnham, p. 305; The most popular and influential indictment of "momism" was Philip Wylie, *Generation of Vipers* (New York: Holt, Rinehart and Winston, 1942).

250 a "slumbering" thing: William J. Fielding, "The Art of Love," *Sex in Civilization,* ed. V. F. Calverton and S. D. Schmalhausen (New York: Macaulay, 1929), p. 652; Sanger, p. 125; Ellis, *Studies,* vol. I, part 2, pp. 239–46; Ellis, *Sex in Relation to Society* (London: W. Heinemann, 1937), p. 419; Stone, p. 227.

250 An American doctor wrote: Ellis, *Studies,* vol. I, part 2, p. 239*n.*

251–66 On the case of Ruth Snyder: This case was big news. I base my account on the New York tabloids' coverage supplemented by coverage in the major New York papers, which cared more about facts.

252 "thought more of marriage...": New York *Hearld Tribune,* March 24, 1927, p. 10.

252 "everything that most women wish for": New York *Mirror,* March 24, 1927, p. 4.

254 in 1926, Fanny Soper: *Herald Tribune,* March 25, 1927, p. 15.

254 In 1924 the notorious Risteen-Plummer: New York *Post,* March 23, 1927, p. 7.

254 In 1922, right beside the lurid: *New York Times,* Oct. 19, 1922, p. 2.

254 As prosecutors prepared: *Herald Tribune,* April 13, 1927, p. 2.

254 And during the Snyder trial: *Mirror,* April 21, 1927, p. 6.

254 "if even a small percentage . . .": May 3, 1927, p. 8.

254 "If these two could commit such a murder . . .": *Outlook,* May 18, 1927, p. 75.

255 "a social cancer": *Herald Tribune,* March 24, 1927, p. 10.

255 "the pettiest, the most ignoble . . .": *Outlook,* May 18, 1927, p. 75.

255 "slightly pale yellow dawn . . .": *Herald Tribune,* March 24, 1927, p. 16.

255 "sexy" and "vile": *Mirror,* May 6, 1927, p. 18.

256 In the first reports of the Snyder murder: *Mirror,* March 21, 1927, p. 3; March 24, 1927, back cover. All these terms are used repeatedly; the last is from Irene Kuhn's column, May 3, 1927, p. 6.

256–57 The more sober New York *Post:* April 27, 1927, pp. 1, 10; April 28, 1927, p. 1.

257 The New York *Herald Tribune:* March 24, 1927, p. 10.

257 The paper hired Dr. Edgar C. Beall: *Mirror,* March 26, 1927, p. 4.

257 "There is lacking in her character . . .": *Mirror,* April 23, 1927, p. 3.

257 "cold, mean eyes . . .": *Mirror,* May 7, 1927, p. 7.

257 "If Ruth Snyder is a woman": *Mirror,* May 10, 1927, p. 4.

257 "He's as nice appearing a gentleman . . .": *Herald Tribune,* March 22, 1927, p. 12.

258 "He was a Red Cross worker . . .": March 23, 1927, p. 12.

258 a "fine cultured fellow": *Herald Tribune,* April 16, 1927, p. 2.

258 "All facts now adduced . . .": March 23, 1927, p. 12.
"A strange charm of Mrs. Snyder . . . ": *Herald Tribune,* April 17, 1927, p. 13.

258 "That woman," he said to the jury: *Mirror,* May 10, 1927, p. 9. This is the accepted version of the story in every later account of the case I have seen. Rupert Furneaux's "story of a suburban housewife who forced a harmless little man to become a vicious murderer" is typical. *Courtroom USA 2* (Baltimore: Penguin, 1963), p. 82.

259 "brazen woman": *Mirror,* April 22, 1927, p. 4; *Herald Tribune,* April 21, 1927, p. 12.

259 Snyder thought that women jurors: *Mirror,* March 26, 1927, p. 4; May 7, 1927, p. 3.

259 "for adultery instead of murder": *Post,* May 3, 1927, p. 8.

259 Officially adultery was frowned upon: *Mirror,* April 15, 1927, p. 19.

259 "Promiscuous women . . .": "Woman's Sexual Nature," *Woman's Coming of Age: A Symposium,* ed. Samuel D. Schmalhausen and V. F. Calverton (New York: Horace Liveright, 1931), p. 232.

260 "I have always been a gentleman . . .": *Post,* April 28, 1927, p. 19.

260 "this mild corset salesman": *Post,* April 28, 1927, p. 19.

260 "never been a murderer . . .": *Mirror,* May 5, 1927, p. 11.

260 "kind of fellow who'd do anything . . .": *Mirror,* May 7, 1927, p. 6.

260 "a bunch of dough . . .": *Mirror,* April 29, 1927, p. 31; May 2, 1927, p. 3.

260–61 "I never before realized . . .": *Post,* April 22, 1927, p. 6.

261 "unworthy of the chivalry . . .": *Mirror,* May 2, 1927, p. 3.

261 "He was a knight . . .": *Post,* May 9, 1927, p. 1.

261 "Wherein did I fail?": *Mirror,* April 22, 1927, p. 35. In the same issue of the *Mirror,* readers could find similar guilt-ridden lamentations from the mother of Clyde Griffiths in Dreiser's *American Tragedy* running as a cartoon serial, p. 37.

261 "emerged from the mire . . .": *Mirror,* May 5, 1927, p. 12.

261 "a decent, red-blooded . . .": *Mirror,* May 10, 1927, p. 9.

261–62 "lied like a dog . . .": *Mirror,* May 5, 1927, p. 11.

262 There were things she never got a chance to say: "Ruth's Last Story" was serialized in the *Mirror,* Jan. 6–12, 1928, with each installment beginning on the front page.

262 "Don't the 'outside' believe . . .": *Mirror,* Jan. 6, 1928, p. 3; for the inquiring reporter see May 18, 1927, p. 4.

262 "Any woman who commits . . .": *Mirror,* March 30, 1927, p. 4.

262–63 "equal 'rights' for Women Criminals . . .": *Herald Tribune,* April 13, 1927, p. 2.

263 "In the commission of a crime . . .": *Mirror,* May 9, 1927, p. 6.

263 "The execution of this judgment . . .": New York *World,* Jan. 11, 1928, p. 1.

263 "Equal suffrage has put women . . .": Jan. 14, 1928, p. 16.

263 "Equal treatment of unequals . . .": Irene Osgood Andrews mobilizing opposition to the Equal Rights Amendment, 1922, quoted in *Mary Ritter Beard: A Sourcebook,* ed. Ann J. Lane (New York: Schocken Books, 1977), p. 25.

263 Arguing that both Gray and Snyder: *Mirror,* May 5, 1927, p. 11.

263–64 When the sentence was passed: *Mirror,* May 10, 1927, p. 1; May 11, 1927, p. 15.

264 An imaginative reporter for the New York *World*: Jan. 13, 1928, p. 1.

264 And an imaginative photographer: *Daily News,* Jan. 13, 1928, extra edition, p. 1. See also New York *Sun,* Jan. 13, 1928, p. 16.

264 "Here was a man": Jan. 13, 1928, p. 16.

265 The show-business celebrities: *Mirror,* April 29, 1927, p. 27.

265 "impressive lesson of the Snyder case . . .": *Mirror,* May 13, 1927, p. 21.

265 "That was the end . . .": *Post,* Jan. 13, 1928, p. 3.

265 "If I were to live over again": *Herald Tribune,* Jan. 13, 1928, p. 10.

265–66 "I said before 'Go Straight' . . .": *Mirror,* Jan. 11, 1928, p. 10.

266 Only the night before: *Times,* Jan. 12, 1928, p. 29.

266 And the day after Snyder's execution: *Mirror,* Jan. 13, 1928, p. 2, back page; *Times,* March 6, 1928, p. 9.

266 Leaving for Marysville: *New York Times,* March 7, 1928, p. 2.

266–67 Dr. Frederick L. Hoffman: *New York Times,* March 29, 1928, p. 21.

267 But when Ida Austin: *New York Times,* May 14, 1928, p. 23; May 15, 1928, p. 16; May 16, 1928, p. 8. She is also identified as Iva Austin, her lover as Arthur Bedore or Badour.

267   So Anna Antonio: *New York Times,* Aug. 10, 1934, p. 1.

267-68   On Mary Frances Creighton: My account is based on coverage in *The New York Times.* See especially Oct. 7, 1935, p. 1; July 16, 1936, p. 8; July 17, 1936, pp. 1, 18.

268   "the Problem that has no name": Betty Friedan, *The Feminine Mystique* (New York: Dell, 1963), pp. 11–27 et passim.

269   The newspapers thought they had found it: "The Armored Lady," *Time,* Feb. 4, 1966, p. 43.

269   "It was better than a movie": "Crime: The Candy Trial," *Newsweek,* March 14, 1966, p. 35.

269-70   The press tried hard enough: *Time,* Feb. 4, 1966, p. 43; "Press: Stale Candy," *Newsweek,* March 14, 1966, p. 64.

270   "like her name—all pretty colors . . .": Miami *Herald,* July 2, 1964, p. 1.

270   "I'd like you to keep me . . .": Miami *Herald,* July 8, 1964, p. 1.

271   "there was just too much sex": *Newsweek,* March 14, 1966, p. 64.

271   "That is the American system . . .": L. H. Lapham, "The Trials of Candy and Mel," *Saturday Evening Post,* Sept. 10, 1966, p. 46. Lerves Lapham's coverage of the trial is reprinted in *Fortune's Child* (New York: Doubleday, 1980), pp. 31–69.

271   "a Hollywood-style ending . . .": New York *Daily News,* March 7, 1966, p. 3.

272   "infamous" woman: "Memories of Murder Case Draw Many to Sale," *New York Times,* April 5, 1977, p. 20.

272   the killing in the family of Lana Turner: Joe Morella and Edward Z. Epstein, *Lana* (New York: Dell, 1971), pp. 166–206. Cheryl Crane stabbed Johnny Stompanato in her mother's bedroom on April 4, 1958. A coroner's jury ruled Stompanato's death justifiable homicide and the district attorney did not bring criminal charges, p. 201.

272   Only Turner herself: Morella and Epstein, pp. 247–48.

273   "I'll take the bitch": Kenneth Gross, *The Alice Crimmins Case* (New York: Alfred A. Knopf, 1975), p. 17.

273   "The bitch killed her kids": Gross, p. ix.

273   "common knowledge" among the police: Gross, p. viii.

273   "If she were my wife": Gross, p. 122.

274   A good deal of what should have constituted: Gross, pp. 29, 69–70.

274-75   Later she told reporter Gross: Kenneth Gross, "Crimmins," *Newsday,* April 10, 1971, p. 14W.

275   To the press she was a sexy: West Peterson, "Sexpot on Trial," *Front Page Detective* (Sept. 1968), p. 44; Files of the New York *Daily News; Daily News,* April 24, 1971, p. 3; *New York Times,* March 29, 1971, p. 54. *Times* reporter Lacey Fosburgh was the only print journalist who never used the familiar pejorative terms in her accounts. When she left the *Times* and a male journalist took over the case, Crimmins became, for the first time in the paper, a "former cocktail-waitress." Feb. 26, 1975, p. 34.

275   One of the jurors: Gross, p. 230.

275   a lot of "filth": *Newsday,* April 10, 1971, p. 13W; Gross, p. 259.

276 "go home free": *Times,* April 24, 1971, p. 30.

276 So it went, back and forth: For a summary of the trial see *Times,* April 24, 1971, pp. 1, 30. *Daily News,* April 24, 1971, pp. 3, 10. In his book on the case, Gross charges that Helpern changed his initial conclusion, narrowing down the possible time of death under pressure from the prosecutor's office, pp. 65, 124–25. Helpern, claiming scientific detachment, termed the charge "nonsense." Milton Helpern with Bernard Knight, *Autopsy: The Memoirs of Milton Helpern, the World's Greatest Medical Detective* (New York: St. Martin's Press, 1977), pp. 120–21.

276–77 the State Court of Appeals reversed the decision: *Times,* Feb. 26, 1975, p. 34.

277–78 "*IF* she had been a faithful wife . . .": George Carpozi, Jr., *Ordeal By Trial: The Alice Crimmins Case* (New York: Walker, 1972), p. 79.

278 "What kind of woman could do a thing . . .": *Daily News,* Aug. 11, 1968, M1.

278 Only the New York Radical Feminists: Susan Brownmiller, of New York Radical Feminists, interview, Feb. 1, 1979.

279 "The Alice Crimmins case . . . was perceived . . .": Gross, p. x.

279 "Oh, I'm for equal pay . . .": *Newsday,* April 10, 1971, p. 14W.

279 "taking into account the extreme seriousness . . .": *Times,* March 20, 1977, p. 45.

279 "live and remain at liberty . . .": *Times,* Sept. 8, 1977, p. A1.

279 Then in August 1977: *Post,* Aug. 22, 1977, pp. 1–7; Aug. 23, 1977, p. 1.

280 columnist Pete Hamill: *Daily News,* Aug. 24, 1977, p. 4.

280 So, on September 7, 1977: *Daily News,* Sept. 8, 1977, p. 3.

280 "Anything you people have done . . .": Carpozi, p. 323. It is likely that she will be remembered as guilty. Of the two reporters who wrote books about the case, Kenneth Gross found her not guilty and George Carpozi found the charges against her not proven: "I am not convinced that Alice Crimmins killed her children. Nor am I convinced that she didn't," p. 330. A made-for-TV movie starring Tuesday Weld is sympathetic to the Crimmins figure. But the most popular version of the case, Dorothy Uhnak's *The Investigation* (New York: Simon & Schuster, 1977), a thinly veiled fictionalized account, depicts protagonist Kitty Keeler as guilty. The book was a best-seller in hardcover, the main selection of three major book clubs, and when the paperback rights sold for $1,585,000, a softcover best-seller as well. (New York: Pocket Books, 1977). See New York *Post,* April 18, 1977, p. 6. It is through this account that most people "know" Alice Crimmins.

SIX: TOTALING WOMEN

281 for her husband, James: At the time, James and Francine were divorced but living together.

282 "I did it . . .": Michael Hirsley, "Battered ex-wife becomes new murder trial cause," Chicago *Tribune,* Sept. 11, 1977, sec. 1, p. 22.

282 "Francine Hughes—and many other women ...": "Newsletter of the Francine Hughes Defense Committee," n.d., p. 1.

282 only a few states acknowledge even the possibility of rape: Arkansas, Delaware, Iowa, Hawaii, and Oregon have removed provisions exempting marital rape from rape statutes, and New Jersey has amended its rape law to include spousal rape. The rape conviction in Massachusetts, September 21, 1979, of James K. Chretien was the first spousal rape conviction in the United States. See *Response to Violence in the Family* (newsletter of the Center for Women Policy Studies), November 1979, p. 4.

282 "shock troops" of male supremacy: *Against Our Will: Men, Women and Rape* (New York: Simon & Schuster, 1975), p. 209.

282–83 American feminists took up the issue: Del Martin, *Battered Wives* (New York: Pocket Books, 1977), pp. 197–254, gives the fullest account of the shelter movement and how to join it.

283 The records showed that 60 percent: "Cops and Couples," *Newsweek,* July 8, 1974, p. 79.

283 In Fairfax County: Martin, p. 20.

283 During ten months in 1975–76: "Battered Women," *Newsweek,* Feb. 2, 1976, p. 47.

283 Seventy percent of all assault cases: Betsy Warrior, "Battered Lives," *The Second Wave,* vol. 4, no. 2 (Fall 1975), p. 8; Louan Moody, "Legal Control of Discrimination," Unpublished report for the Lincoln-Lancaster (Nebraska) Commission on the Status of Women, Task Force on Abused Women, Dec. 8, 1976, p. 3.

283 Eighty percent of divorce cases: Martin, pp. 15–16.

283 Ninety-nine percent of female: Margo Huston, "Abused Women: Who's at Fault," Milwaukee *Journal,* Jan. 26, 1976, part 2, p. 4.

283 Journalists Roger Langley and Richard C. Levy: *Wife Beating: The Silent Crisis* (New York: Pocket Books, 1977), cover.

283 And in Omaha: Moody, p. 2.

283–84 American reversion to a Common Law standard: *Bradley* v. *State,* 2 Miss. (Walker) 156, 158 (1824); *State* v. *Black,* 60 N.C. 162, 163, 86 Am. Dec. 436 (1864); *Harris* v. *State,* 71 Miss. 462, 464, 14 So. 266 (1894); Stedman, *Right of Husband to Chastise Wife,* 3 Va. L. Reg. (n.s.) 241 (1917); cited in Sue E. Eisenberg and Patricia L. Micklow, "The Assaulted Wife: 'Catch 22 Revisited,'" 3 *Women's Rights Law Reporter* 138 (1977) 138–39.

284 not a "new" issue: See, for example, *HWS,* vol. I, p. 730, which argues that "want of a Divorce" directly results in domestic homicide. An old story following a familiar present-day pattern is this: in 1847 Mary Runkle, about age fifty, of Whitesboro, New York, fought back with her fists in the middle of the night against her husband, who had been punching, kicking, and choking her since tea time, and killed him. She claimed "that she did not intend to murder him, but did so in defending herself from his assault" (p. 30). She was hanged. *Life and Confession of Mary Runkle Who Was Condemned and Sentenced to be Executed at Whitesboro, Oneida Co., N.Y. on the 9th day of*

November 1847, for the Murder of her Husband, John Runkle (Troy, N.Y.: J. C. Kneeland, 1847).

284–85 Information about the problem: Gay Search, "London: Battered Wives," *Ms.,* June 1974, pp. 24–26; Karen Durbin, "Wife-Beating," *Ladies' Home Journal,* June 1974, pp. 62–72; *Newsweek,* July 8, 1974, p. 79; Eisenberg and Micklow; Marj Jackson Levin, "The Wife Beaters," *McCall's,* June 1975, p. 37; Ricki Fulman, "Wife Abuse," New York *Daily News,* June 10, 1975, p. 44.

285 Public awareness should have increased: *Newsweek,* Feb. 2, 1976, p. 47; Susan Edmiston, "The Wife Beaters," *Woman's Day,* March 1976, pp. 61, 110–11; "The Battered Wife, an Expert Says, Can Be Found in Millions of American Homes, Rich and Poor," *People,* May 3, 1976, pp. 35–38; Joseph N. Bell, "New Hope for the Battered Wife," *Good Housekeeping,* July 1976, pp. 94–95, 133–38; Judith Gingold, "One of These Days—POW Right in the Kisser" and "*Ms.* Gazette," *Ms.,* Aug. 1976, pp. 51–52, 95–98; "Unforgettable Letters From Battered Wives," *Ms.,* Dec. 1976, pp. 97–100.

285–86 In fact the issue already had been fought: *People* v. *Garcia,* Cr. No. 4259 (Superior Court, Monterey County, Cal. 1977); *State* v. *Little,* 74 Cr. No. 4176 (Superior Court, Beaufort County, N.C. 1975); *State* v. *Wanrow,* 88 Wash. 2d 221, 559 P. 2d 548 (1977). These cases and many others in which women defendants plead self-defense are discussed in Elizabeth M. Schneider and Susan B. Jordan, "Representation of Women Who Defend Themselves in Response to Physical or Sexual Assault," 4 *Women's Rights Law Reporter* 149 (1978). (Reprints of this essential article are available from the Women's Self-Defense Law Project, Center for Constitutional Rights, 853 Broadway, 14th Floor, New York. N.Y. 10003.) See also Women's Self-Defense Law Project, *Representation and Support of Women Who Defend Themselves Against Physical or Sexual Assault* (Charlottesville, Va.: Michie, 1980).

286 "[The instruction as given by the trial court]": *State* v. *Wanrow, supra* 559 P. 2d 548 (1977) 558–59. See also Jennifer Marsh, "Women's Self-Defense Under Washington Law—*State* v. *Wanrow,* 88 Wn. 2d 221, 559 P. 2d 548 (1977)," 54 *Washington Law Review* 221 (1978). Simply using female terms in stating the law alters one's perspective. In *South Carolina* v. *Cynthia Hutto* on a charge of first-degree murder, the judge instructed the jury that "a woman's home is her castle." She was acquitted. But in *Florida* v. *Martha Hutchinson* the judge declined to interpret the self-defense statute as suggested by the Wanrow court and consequently ruled the substantial evidence of wife abuse inadmissible. Hutchinson was convicted of second-degree murder and sentenced to fifteen years. (Responses to defense attorney questionnaires, Files of the Women's Self-Defense Law Project.)

287 So in December 1976 when Roxanne Gay: Lynne Baranski, "A Pro Football Player is Stabbed to Death, and Wife Abuse is Roxanne Gay's Defense," *People,* Oct. 24, 1977, pp. 34–35; "The Case of Roxanne Gay," *Ms.,* Nov. 1977, p. 19.

287 a sanity hearing in March 1978: "Murder charges dropped against gridder's

wife," Bergen (New Jersey) *Record*, March 12, 1978, p. A16.

287–88 Francine Hughes's credentials as a battered woman: "Francine Hughes Defense Committee Newsletter"; Linda Grant, "Self Defense Standard at Stake in Michigan Trial," *In These Times*, Aug. 10–16, 1977, p. 6.

288 "a mean SOB": Hirsley.

288 Traditionally, deadly force: Courts have consistently ruled that a misdemeanor assault must be suffered without resort to deadly force; and in several homicide cases, resisting a felonious wife-beating assault was refused as a defense because "the felony contemplated by the statute on justifiable homicide . . . is one that is more dangerous than a personal assault, and . . . the legislative purpose in making the beating of a wife by her husband a felony was to reduce domestic conflict, not promote resort to violence in the household." *People* v. *Jones*, 191 Cal. App. 2d 478, 12 Cal. Rep. 777 (1961). See also *State* v. *Copley*, 101 Ariz. 242, 418 P. 2d 579 (1966). In both these cases battered women who acted in self-defense were convicted—Theresa Jones of manslaughter and Mildred Copley of first-degree murder.

289 Judge Ray C. Hotchkiss: "Fems Hail Her Acquittal for Slaying Ex-Husband," New York *Daily News*, Nov. 5, 1977, p. 4.

289 In September, ABC's: "ABC Saturday News" with Sylvia Chase and Tom Jarriel, Sept. 3, 1977.

289 hosted by Stanley Siegel: Transcript of "The Stanley Siegel Show," WABC-TV, New York, Nov. 11, 1977, pp. 15, 22–23.

289–90 A neighbor who had once pulled James: Hirsley.

290 "means open season on men": "Wife Cleared in Ex-Mate's Death," Bergen (New Jersey) *Record*, Nov. 4, 1977.

290 That question bothered the national press: Washington *Post*, Dec. 4, 1977, pp. B1–2; "A Killing Excuse," *Time*, Nov. 28, 1977, p. 108; "Wives Who Batter Back," *Newsweek*, Jan. 30, 1978, p. 54. It also bothered the law; see Marilyn Hall Mitchell, "Does Wife Abuse Justify Homicide?" 24 *Wayne Law Review* 1,705 (1978). Mitchell argues that "To establish a 'battered wife' defense comparable to self-defense . . . would not only validate a kind of vigilante justice . . . but would also establish a virtual sex discrimination classification . . ." p. 1,731.

290 District Judge Benny Graff: "Judge Reflects on Steele Case: State Ruling 'Clearer Landmark,' " Bismarck (North Dakota) *Tribune*, Nov. 4, 1977.

290–91 Commenting in an editorial: John O. Hjelle, "The Abused and Threatened," Bismarck *Tribune*, Nov. 5, 1977.

291 A county prosecutor in Cleveland: Katherine L. Hatton. " 'A right to defend myself,' " Cleveland *Plain Dealer*, May 15, 1978, p. 11A. For disposition of the Thomas case, see "Battering-defense fails; Ms. Thomas is guilty of murder," *Plain Dealer*, June 21, 1978, pp. 1, 9A. For Hale conviction see *Plain Dealer*, June 18, 1978, p. 6.

291 A Berkeley law school professor: Nadine Joseph, "When battered wife turns killer juries often sympathize," Bergen (New Jersey) *Record*, p. A1. Undated clip in files of Women's Action Alliance.

291 During 1978 a few women: Andrea Dworkin, "The Bruise that Doesn't Heal," *Mother Jones,* July 1978, pp. 31–36; Karen Lindsey, "When Battered Women Strike Back: Murder or Self-Defense," *Viva,* Sept. 1978, pp. 58–59, 91–94.

291 Press coverage was devoted: Joseph; Peter S. Greenberg, "Thirteen Ways to Leave Your Lover," *New Times,* Feb. 6, 1978, p. 6; "Battered Wives and Self-Defense Pleas," Washington *Post,* Dec. 4, 1977, pp. A1, A14; Laura Meyers, "Battered Wives, Dead Husbands," *Student Lawyer,* March 1978, pp. 47–51; Anna Quindlen, "Women Who Kill Their Spouses: The Causes, the Legal Defenses," *New York Times,* March 10, 1978, p. B4. See also Mitchell, a law review article that purports to be balanced but deals only with acquittals.

291 Maria Roy: Quindlen.

292 By 1979 the controversy: Tom DeVries, *New West,* March 12, 1979, pp. 48–66; Bonnie and Charles Remsberg, *Family Circle,* April 24, 1979, pp. 58–60, 152–55.

292 Nationally circulated newspapers: "Abused Spouse Acquitted," Washington *Post,* April 12, 1979, p. A7; see also "Woman in Michigan is Freed in Slaying," *New York Times,* April 15, 1979, p. 28. Convictions of Monick, Allen, Morris, and Powell are cited respectively in Jane Myers, "The Beaten Wife," Ann Arbor (Michigan) *News,* Sept. 18, 1975; Lindsey, p. 93; Files of the Women's Self-Defense Law Project; Fred Gaskins, "Jury finds Powell guilty of murder," Ithaca (New York) *Journal,* March 22, 1979.

292–93 The accounts did not mention results: Richard Sypher, "Woman handed 10 years for slaying boyfriend, 24," Tacoma (Washington) *News-Tribune,* Nov. 29, 1977; Murray Dubin, "Mrs. McKendrick found guilty," Philadelphia *Inquirer,* Dec. 3, 1977, p. 1; Deborah McBride, "Thatcher [*sic*] case raises questions," *The Spokesman Review* (Spokane, Wash.), Jan. 15, 1978; letter to author from Carol Ann Wilds, April 13, 1979. Sharon Crigler's conviction was overturned by the Court of Appeals (State of Washington) on July 13, 1979. 23 Wash. App. 716, 598 P. 2d 739 (1979).

293 the case of Marlene Roan Eagle: *Newsweek* commented that Roan Eagle was acquitted "although she was in little danger of being killed by a broomhandle blow." Jan. 30, 1978, p. 54. Note the assumption that the husband would strike only a *single* blow.

293 murder conviction of Barbara Jean Gilbert: "Battered Woman: Vindictive Sentence in Md," *The Guardian,* July 26, 1978.

293 In that same month Hazel Kontos: Convictions of Kontos, Quarles, Patri, and Hutchinson are cited respectively in Lindsey, p. 93; "Killed Husband: Jury Convicts 'Beaten Wife,' " *Tennessean,* Dec. 11, 1977; Pat Hensel, "Patri Defense Claims Victory," Milwaukee *Journal,* Dec. 16, 1977, p. 1; Files of the Women's Self-Defense Law Project.

293 Many other women were already in prison: Files of the Women's Action Alliance and the Women's Self-Defense Law Project. Jane Totman found that twenty-eight of thirty women in California prisons for killing their

mates had been "subject to what they defined as undeserved and unreasonable amounts of physical and/or verbal humiliation from the victim." *The Murderess: A Psychosocial Study of Criminal Homicide* (San Francisco: R and E Research Associates, 1978), p. 48.

293–95 On the case of Jennifer Patri: "Jennifer Patri Defense Committee Fact Sheet," n.d.; Alan Eisenberg, telephone interview, June 4, 1979. My account is based also on coverage in the Milwaukee *Journal* and the Waupaca (Wisconsin) *Post.*

294 "do as much for the battered woman . . .": Annie Laurie Gaylor, "Battered woman fights fears," *Daily Cardinal* (Madison, Wis.), Sept. 28, 1977, p. 1.

294 The *Time* article on women: Nov. 28, 1977, p. 108.

294 "feminist groups *had* campaigned . . .": Hensel, "Sheriff Says Patri Never Hit Wife," Milwaukee *Journal,* Dec. 9, 1977, p. 18. Emphasis mine.

294 she couldn't remember anything: Hensel, "Patri Was a Violent Man Jury Told," Milwaukee *Journal,* Dec. 11, 1977, p. 25; "Mrs. Patri Veers From Earlier Stories," Milwaukee *Journal,* Dec. 13, 1977, p. 14. Often women don't remember for they pass into a dissociated state which psychologists term *episodic dysfunction.* After shooting her husband in self-defense, Diane Barson dismembered his body, packed it in trash bags in the trunk of her car, and drove from Texas to California, where she attempted suicide. This bizarre conduct, which stems from the woman's inability to entertain the unthinkable fact of murder, *looks* like cold-blooded butchery. (Barson, who clearly had acted in self-defense in an extreme situation, was acquitted.) Files of the Women's Self-Defense Law Project.

295 Eisenberg called the manslaughter conviction: *Newsweek,* Jan. 30, 1978, p. 54. Attorney Eisenberg publicly professed optimism because of the results of two similar Wisconsin cases: in 1974 the charge against Betty Jean Carter was reduced from murder to manslaughter with probation, and in 1975 Eva May Heygood was acquitted. Patri's conviction may have been a reaction to those earlier "new-fangled" decisions rather than to "city-slickers." See also Myra MacPherson, "Battered Wives and Self-Defense Pleas," Washington *Post,* Dec. 4, 1977, pp. A1, A14.

295 Then, in December 1978: "Jury Finds Mrs. Patri Guilty of Arson Charge," Milwaukee *Journal,* Dec. 11, 1978, p. 15; "Mrs. Patri Mentally Ill and Needs Care, Jury Says," Milwaukee *Journal,* Dec. 12, 1978, p. 11.

296 "Why Does She Stay?": For example, Richard J. Gelles, "Abused Wives: Why Do They Stay?" *Journal of Marriage and the Family,* vol. 38 (Nov. 1976), pp. 659–68, rpt. in *Family Violence* (Beverly Hills, Ca.: Sage, 1979).

296 "learned helplessness": Lenore E. Walker, *The Battered Woman* (New York: Harper & Row, 1979). See also Seymour L. Halleck, *Psychiatry and the Dilemmas of Crime: A Study of Causes, Punishment & Treatment* (Berkeley: University of California Press, 1971), p. 69.

296–97 "I remember withdrawing . . .": Dworkin, p. 36.

297 In a study unduplicated: J. J. Gayford, "Wife Battering: A Preliminary Sur-

vey of 100 Cases," *British Medical Journal,* Jan. 25, 1975, rpt. as "Battered
Wives" in *Violence and the Family,* ed. J. P. Martin (New York: John Wiley,
1978), p. 25. Totman's study of thirty women imprisoned for mate-killing in
California indicated that nine had left home, twelve wanted to but either had
no place to go or feared reprisals, and one had attempted suicide as a way
out. Pp. 52–53.

297 In this country researchers: John P. Flynn, "Recent findings related to wife
abuse," *Social Casework,* Jan. 1977, p. 18.

297 Another study of battered wives: Eisenberg and Micklow, p. 143.

297–98 extremely possessive people: Francine Hughes and her attorney reported on
"The Stanley Siegel Show" James Hughes's habit of ripping out the phone;
the other behaviors have all been reported to me by battered women who
killed their batterers. On the Eileen Bartosh case, see Marilyn LeVine,
"Beaten Wife Free in Husband's Death," Charlotte (North Carolina) *News,*
Oct. 7, 1977, pp. 1B, 6B.

298 A study that analyzed how victims: Study by G. Marie Wilt and James Ban-
non, cited in Marjory D. Fields, "Wife Beating: Government Intervention
Policies and Practices," unpublished paper, Dec. 29, 1977, p. 65.

298 "It seemed like the more . . .": Testimony of Ruth Childers, *State of Indiana*
v. *Lois Ruth Childers,* Benton County Circuit Court, Cause No. 578–69
(1978).

298 Gloria Timmons: Juana Brown, "Battered Women—2: In prison for self-defense," *The Guardian,* June 1, 1979, p. 9.

298 Patricia Evans: Bob Greene, "Free battered woman who killed?" Chicago
Sun-Times, Oct. 11, 1977, p. 3.

298 Sharon Crigler: Sypher, "Victim warned to stay away before fatal shot," Tacoma *News-Tribune,* Sept. 20, 1977.

298 Jennifer Patri: "The Battered Woman—A Classic Example," *Common
Ground: The Women's Coalition Monthly Newsletter* (Milwaukee), Sept.
1977.

298 Ruth Childers: Testimony of Ruth Childers.

298 Bernadette Powell: Testimony of Bernadette Powell, *People of the State of
New York* v. *Bernadette Powell,* Indictment No. 78–63, State of New York,
County Court, County of Tompkins (1979). See also Edward Hower, "From
Inside Tompkins County Jail: Bernadette Powell Tells Her Story," Ithaca
Times, Aug. 16–22, 1979, pp. 1, 3, 5.

298 Janice Strand: interview, April 13, 1979. Real name withheld.

298 Patricia Gross's husband: Remsberg, p. 152.

298 Judy Austin's live-in boyfriend: Files of the Women's Self-Defense Law Project.

298 Kathy Thomas's boyfriend: "Report from the Gold Flower Committee: The
Right to Self-Defense?" *What She Wants,* June 1978, p. 5.

298–99 Mary McGuire's husband: Lindsey, pp. 91–92. Mary McGuire, interview,
Feb. 2–3, 1980.

299   Martha Hutchinson's Klansman husband: Files of the Women's Self-Defense Law Project.
299   Agnes Scott's husband: "Agnes Scott Defense Committee Fact Sheet," n.d.
299   There are cases on record: Lindsey, p. 92.
299   Feminists who call for equal protection: Meyers, p. 48. Emphasis mine.
300   most women killed by their husbands: Marvin E. Wolfgang, *Patterns in Criminal Homicide* (Philadelphia: University of Pennsylvania Press, 1958), p. 162; "A Sociological Analysis of Criminal Homicide," *Studies in Homicide*, Wolfgang, ed. (New York: Harper & Row, 1967), p. 15. See also Lee H. Bowker, *Women, Crime, and the Criminal Justice System* (Lexington, Mass.: D. C. Heath, 1978), p. 123.
300   The first book: Gelles, *The Violent Home: A Study of Physical Aggression Between Husbands and Wives* (Beverly Hills, Ca.: Sage, 1974).
300   "STUDY BACKS UP SUSPICIONS . . .": Chicago *Daily News*, Aug. 31, 1977, cited in Elizabeth Pleck, Joseph H. Pleck, Marlyn Grossman, and Pauline B. Bart, "The Battered Data Syndrome: A Comment on Steinmetz's Article," *Victimology*, vol. 2, nos. 3–4 (1977–78), p. 682; see also "A reply to Suzanne K. Steinmetz, 'The Battered Husband Syndrome,' " *Victimology*, vol. 2, nos. 3–4, pp. 499–508.
301   but she overlooked the context: The same limitations affect her study, *The Cycle of Violence: Assertive, Aggressive, and Abusive Family Interaction* (New York: Praeger, 1977).
301   Her critics concluded: Pleck, et al., p. 683.
301   So in March 1978: "The Battered Husbands," *Time*, March 20, 1978, p. 69. In fact the Wolfgang study of a hundred mate slayings in Philadelphia during 1948–52 found that fifty-three victims were wives, forty-seven were husbands. "The number of wives killed by their husbands constitutes 41 percent of all women killed, whereas husbands slain by their wives make up only 11 percent of all men killed." (*Studies in Homicide*, p. 23) Wolfgang concluded that twenty-eight of the forty-seven male victims had precipitated their own deaths, while only five of the fifty-three wives had done so (p. 82). That significant finding has been lost in the bowlderizing of Wolfgang's concept of victim precipitation. Thus psychiatrist David Abrahamsen asserts flatly that women are most often the victims of domestic homicide because "the victim herself unconsciously provokes her husband to murder." *The Murdering Mind* (New York: Harper & Row, 1973), p. 39.
301   Writers Langley and Levy: pp. 198–208.
302   in July Langley wrote an article: "Battered Husbands," New York *Sunday News Magazine*, July 2, 1978, pp. 7, 21, 28.
302   "amazing conclusion": Joyce Brothers, "Husbands can be battered," Bergen *Record*, July 13, 1978.
302   "preposterous": Susan Abrams, "The Battered Husband Bandwagon," *Seven Days*, Sept. 28, 1978, p. 20.
302   "I'm sure more men . . .": Ann Landers, "Arise, battered husbands!" undated clipping in files of Lincoln (Nebraska) Task Force on Abused Women.

303 To this end, New York City: "Police Will Arrest Wife Beaters in Reversal of New York Policy," *New York Times,* June 27, 1978, pp. A1, A16; Barbara Miner, "Cops Ordered to Arrest Wife-Beaters," *The Guardian,* July 12, 1978, p. 7. The women complainants in *Bruno* v. *Codd, et al.* were represented by attorneys from MFY Legal Services, Brooklyn Legal Services, the Legal Aid Society, and the Center for Constitutional Rights. A federal suit in Oakland, California, charging that police nonarrest policy violated federal civil rights guarantees of battered women illustrates another legal approach to forcing law enforcement officers to provide women equal protection from bodily harm.

303 A 1976 directive: "Training Key #245: Wife Beating," published by the Police Management and Operations Divisions of the International Association of Chiefs of Police, Inc. 1976, p. 3; see also "Training Key #246."

303 "enforcers of the law": Morton Bard, "The Police and Family Violence: Practice and Policy," in *Battered Women: Issues of Public Policy,* A Consultation Sponsored by the United States Commission on Civil Rights, Washington, D.C., Jan. 30–31, 1978, p. 49.

304 A Michigan police bulletin: Eisenberg and Micklow, p. 156; Cynthia Krolik, "Study says no legal protection from husband assault," *Michigan Free Press,* April 14, 1975.

304 Law-enforcement data: Attorneys John Gambs and Jay Seeger, interview, April 10, 1979.

304 "22 percent of police deaths . . .": Bard, p. 49. Emphasis mine. The word "often" got lost, and the figures are quoted as referring only to domestic disturbances.

304 During the period 1968–77: *UCR,* 1977, p. 291.

305 A 1979 study: Leonard Buder, "A Police Study Challenges Belief Family Fights Are Riskiest Duty," *New York Times,* Feb. 11, 1979, p. 50.

305 "New York's Finest" might set an example: Changes in police arrest policy along the lines suggested by *Bruno* v. *Codd* have been successfully negotiated by attorneys in Chicago and New Haven, Conn. See Laurie Woods, "Litigation on Behalf of Battered Women," 5 *Women's Rights Law Reporter* 7, (1978) 31, n. 156.

305 In Congress: see Virginia Wheaton, "What Happened to the Domestic Violence Act of 1978?" *The Grantsmanship Center News,* Jan./Feb. 1979, pp. 13–18, 83. Modified domestic violence bills (S. 1843 and H.R. 2977) were reintroduced late in 1979 but not acted upon.

306 "might as well give the guy . . .": *Time,* July 8, 1974, p. 79. Morton Bard, the crisis intervention advocate, told the U.S. Commission on Civil Rights in Orwellian Newspeak terms: "Many police officers long for . . . the simple solution that arrest offers." It is difficult, Bard said, to prevent police who perceive "misconduct and injustice" from "resorting to the law." *Battered Women: Issues of Public Policy,* p. 51.

306 And his view is borne out: Warrior, p. 9.

306 Supporters of police crisis intervention: On LEAA funded programs to train

clergymen to deal with "domestic abuse" see "FVP Grantees Train Clergy," *Response to Violence in the Family* (newsletter of the Center for Women Policy Studies), July 1979, p. 3.

307 Typically, a 1964 Freudian study: John E. Snell, Richard J. Rosenwald, and Ames Robey, "The Wifebeater's Wife: A Study of Family Interaction," *Archives of General Psychiatry*, 11 (Aug. 1964), pp. 110–11.

307 On Lynn Ditter: "Man accused of murdering wife was free despite intimidation reports," (AP dispatch, Columbus, Nebraska) unidentified clipping in files of the Lincoln (Nebraska) Task Force on Abused Women. Ironically, that report coincides with what almost all battered women report of their husbands: that to the outside world they present "every evidence of good emotional and physical self-control." If such men behaved outside the home as they do in it, they'd have been jailed long ago. See also the murder of Ewa Berwid reported by Teresa Carpenter, "Murder on a Day Pass," *The Village Voice*, Feb. 25, 1980, pp. 1, 23–27.

307 Ray Lee: Joy Melville, "A Note on 'Men's Aid,' " in Martin, pp. 311–12.

307–08 The three psychiatrists: Snell, et al., pp. 107–12.

308 In 1978 an Indiana prosecutor: Ken Rains, "Cops a Plea to Manslaughter," Lafayette (Indiana) *Journal and Courier*, June 13, 1978.

308 And in Florida: unidentified newspaper clipping in files of Lincoln (Nebraska) Task Force on Abused Women.

308 "an absolute prohibition . . .": Attorney Marjory Fields appearing on "Wife-beating Update," "The MacNeil-Lehrer Report," PBS, Dec. 22, 1978.

308 Some charge that the criminal-justice system: Assistant District Attorney Charles Schudson of Milwaukee, Wisconsin, headed a battered women's project which LEAA funded, named best project of the year, and dropped. Schudson testified before the U.S. Commission on Civil Rights (Jan. 30–31, 1978) that the criminal-justice system serves to maintain domestic violence as a "primary source" of further violence and crime. *Battered Women: Issues of Public Policy*, p. 81.

309–16 On Ruth Childers: Sherry Brown, " 'I'm sorry,' wife said over husband's
passim body," Lafayette (Indiana) *Journal and Courier*, Dec. 7, 1978. My account is based largely on Sherry Brown's articles in this paper and on personal interviews with Ruth Childers, her family and friends, two of her attorneys— John Gambs and Jay Seeger—and expert witness David Trevallion in April 1979. I am indebted to Betsy Warrior for putting me in contact with Ruth Childers.

309–10 Against the murder charge: Gambs and Seeger, interview.

310 The last two people charged: Rich Linden, "Grammer guilty: charge cut," Lafayette *Journal and Courier*, May 27, 1978, p. 1; Rains, *Journal and Courier*, June 13, 1978.

310 the prevailing standard of justice is male: As recently as 1961 the U.S. Supreme Court found constitutional a state law that automatically exempted women from jury service. *Hoyt* v. *Florida*, 368 U.S. 57 (1961). The decision

was not overruled until 1975 in *Taylor* v. *Louisiana,* 419 U.S. 522 (1975). The female defendant in the Hoyt case, who argued that she was entitled to have both women and men on her jury, had been convicted by an all-male jury of murdering her abusive husband with a baseball bat. See Albie Sachs and Joan Hoff Wilson, *Sexism and the Law: A Study of Male Beliefs and Legal Bias in Britain and the United States* (New York: The Free Press, 1979), pp. 123–24.

310–11   Standards of justifiable homicide: Schneider and Jordan, p. 153.

312   And many women, like Lynn Ditter: The murder of Lynn Ditter in Nebraska is a case in point. See also Martin, p. 100, on the murder of Ruth Bunnell in San Jose, California, and p. 117 on the murder of "Loretta" in New York City. See also " 'Battered' Wife Murdered," *The Guardian,* Oct. 4, 1978, p. 11, on the murder of Beverly Carter in Philadelphia. The murders of Jacqueline Hughes, Alicha Warren, Diane Hallman, and Geraldine Williams by abusive husbands against whom they were instituting legal proceedings have been widely reported. Cases of this type are commonplace.

312   prosecutor John Meyers: Rains, "Law to get tougher on child, wife beaters," Lafayette *Journal and Courier,* Feb. 15, 1979. On the transmission of violent behavior see Wolfgang and Franco Ferracuti, *The Subculture of Violence: Towards an Integrated Theory in Criminology* (London: Tavistock, 1967), pp. 147–48.

312   The New Orleans district attorney's: Clancy DuBos, "Battered Woman Freed, Slay Charges Dropped," New Orleans *Times-Picayune,* July 25, 1978, sec. 1, p. 2.

313   An eager Brooklyn assistant district attorney: "The Agnes Scott Case Before the Grand Jury: A Case History of Prosecutorial Misconduct and Control of Grand Jury Proceedings," *Quash,* Jan./Feb. 1979, pp. 9–10.

313   Luckily for Agnes Scott: Jerry Capeci, "Slew mate to save kids; she's freed," New York *Post,* June 21, 1978, p. 24. This decision later was modified by the Appellate Division, but when the prosecutor moved to indict Scott again, a second grand jury, before which she testified, refused to do so. See William Kunstler, "Jury Refuses to Indict Agnes Scott: People v. Scott—A Primer in Grand Jury Procedure," *Quash,* June/July 1979, pp. 1–2.

313   One woman drew an attorney: interview, April 15, 1979; name withheld.

313–14   In Seattle, Gloria Timmons: Juana Brown, p. 9; Lindsey, p. 91.

314   In Massachusetts Roberta Shaffer: "The Right To Kill," *Newsweek,* Sept. 1, 1975, p. 69; "Parole board to consider woman's commutation," *Hampshire Gazette* (Northampton, Mass.) June 2, 1975, p. 9.

314   in Michigan a wife's conviction: *People* v. *Paxton,* 47 Mich. App. 144, 149, 209 N.W. 2d 251, 253–54 (1973), cited in Eisenberg and Micklow, p. 147.

314   Often it is the judge: Thomas Cannon, chief staff attorney of the Milwaukee, Wisconsin, Legal Aid Society, underscores the result of excluding women from the judiciary: "I am convinced that if women were exercising more of this discretion, it would be exercised in different ways." Huston. That sug-

gests why the judiciary remains a male bastion; more women drive locomo-
tives in the United States than sit on the federal bench. See Susan Ness, "A
Sexist Selection Process Keeps Qualified Women Off the Bench," Washington *Post,* March 26, 1978, p. C8.

314–15   One woman was convicted: interview, April 13, 1979; name withheld. I am
indebted to Del Martin for putting me in contact wtih this woman.

315   In Tacoma: Sypher, Tacoma *News-Tribune,* Nov. 29, 1977. Crigler's conviction was overturned by the Court of Appeals July 13, 1979. 23 Wash. App.
716, 598 P. 2d 739 (1979).

315   In Maryland: John Feinstein, " 'Exemplary' Woman Receives Top Sentence," Washington *Post,* July 13, 1978, pp. C1, C3; "Vindictive Sentence,"
The Guardian, July 26, 1978.

315   In Chattanooga: "Killed Husband," *Tennessean,* Dec. 11, 1977.

316   In New Jersey, in May 1979: After a strong display of feminist and community support, Gibbs, the mother of eleven children and regularly employed as
a school bus driver, was sentenced to five years on probation. Files of the
Women's Self-Defense Law Project.

316–19   On Bernadette Powell: My account is based on my own notes of the trial,
daily articles by Fred Gaskins in the Ithaca *Journal,* March 10–20, 1979, and
personal interviews.

318–19   All the while, locked: *Marie de Jong-Joch* v. *Joseph Joch,* Index No. 78-1293,
Supreme Court, County of Tompkins, New York (1979).

319   Downstate the influential *New York Times*: "Woman in Michigan is Freed in
Slaying," April 15, 1979, p. 28; Wayne King, "Right of Women to Self-Defense Gaining in 'Battered Wife' Cases," May 7, 1979, pp. A1, A18.

319–20   In fact, homicides committed: "A Statistical Portrait of Women in the Unit-
ed States," *Current Population Reports, Special Studies Series,* P-23, no. 58,
U.S. Department of Commerce, Bureau of the Census, April 1976, p. 64;
Bowker, pp. 122–29.

320   at least 40 percent: "Study of Female Killers Finds 40 Percent Were
Abused," *New York Times,* Dec. 20, 1977, p. 20. See also Wolfgang, ed.
Studies in Homicide, pp. 23–24, 82–83. In a study of English women murderers, Patrick Wilson found they most often killed husbands in self-defense:
"The typical husband-murderess . . . is not a Suburban Messalina, but the
middle-aged mother of a large family in an industrial town who has stuck a
carving knife into her drunken husband when he has thrashed her on Saturday night once too often." *Murderess* (London: Michael Joseph, 1971), p. 25.

320   In Prince Georges County: *Shelter Network News,* Newsletter No. 7, 1978, p.
23.

320   In New Hampshire: "New Hampshire Panel Rejects Proposal to Aid 'Battered Wives,' " Washington *Post,* Sept. 14, 1977, p. A12.

320   In fact, the battered woman who kills: personal interviews. See also Lindsey.
In her study of thirty California women, Totman arrived at the following description of women at the end of the tether: "Women murder their mates

when their relationship with the mate is felt to be directly and overtly destructive to them and their sense of identity as a woman, when they feel they cannot share their concerns and thus get adequate support and help from other significant relationships or community resources, when they have exhausted all other alternative courses of action either actually or in fantasy and find them not viable, and finally when they have redefined and reinterpreted their negative situation so it calls for action not previously considered possible." p. 94.

320–21 Women who kill their battering husbands: personal interviews, names withheld.

SEVEN: WOMEN'S RIGHTS AND WRONGS

322   "We have not ruled out . . .": "The Lady and the Doctor," *Newsweek*, March 24, 1980, p. 41.

322   But those early reports: Lally Weymouth, "The Trial and Trials of Jean Harris," *New York*, Dec. 15, 1980, p. 24; "The Lady and the Doctor," p. 42.

323   Some killed by accident: interviews, Jan. 23–27, 1981.

324   On Elaine Mullis: Carole Ashkinaze, "Holiday Brings Little Cheer for Elaine," Atlanta *Journal and Constitution*, Nov. 29, 1980, p. 4B; Rhonda Cook, "Abused Wife in Prison for Killing Husband," Savannah *Press*, Dec. 22, 1980, p. 36; Bill Boyd, "The Mullis Case," Macon *Telegraph and News*, Dec. 27, 1980, p. 1B; Ron Taylor, "Elaine and her man: a sad tale of rural love, abuse, ending in death," Atlanta *Journal*, Jan. 18, 1981, pp. 1B, 3B; Carol C. Preston (representing Committee to Free Elaine), telephone interviews, March 20, 23, 1981.

325   "Goddamit, Jean . . .": Theo Wilson, "Jury told of angry phone talk," *Daily News*, Feb. 10, 1981, pp. 3, 20. My account of the killing and the trial is based largely on coverage in the *Daily News*, the *New York Post*, and *The New York Times*, March 1980, Nov. 1980–March 1981.

325   "became shot": *Gentlemen Prefer Blondes* (New York: Popular Library, 1963), p. 46.

325   ". . . her sweet prince": Weymouth, p. 23. The line, of course, is Horatio's farewell to the dead Hamlet.

325   "It's the middle of the night": Wilson, "Jean tells of Doc's death night," *Daily News*, Jan. 30, 1981, p. 22.

326   "THE LETTER NO WOMAN SHOULD EVER WRITE": *Etiquette*, 10th ed. (New York: Funk & Wagnalls, 1960), pp. 533–34.

326   "pops naked out of a cake . . .": The Scarsdale letter is printed in full in the *Daily News*, Feb. 5, 1981, pp. 40–41.

327   "I never thought of it . . .": Wilson, "Harris—the defense rests," *Daily News*, Feb. 7, 1981, p. 18.

327   "Wasn't Mrs. Harris doing the same . . .": Lisa Zumar, "A juror's diary," *Daily News*, Feb. 27, 1981, p. 21.

327 One columnist concluded: Murray Kempton, "Pros in center stage create a lull," *New York Post*, Feb. 11, 1981, p. 47; Shana Alexander, "A Matter of Integrity," *People*, March 9, 1981, p. 91.

327 "She couldn't see herself": Lally Weymouth, "Was Jean Harris's Defense Bungled?" *New York*, March 16, 1981, p. 33.

327 "I trusted Hi": Charles Lachman and Joe Nicholson, "I became a drug addict on the diet doctor's pill," *New York Post*, Feb. 6, 1981, p. 5.

327 "'Twas the Night before Christmas . . .": "Jean Harris: the ultimate unliberated woman," *New York Post*, Feb. 9, 1981, p. 31; "Jean Harris' Amazing Sex Poem," *New York Post*, Jan. 28, 1981, pp. 1, 3.

328 "We tried it every which way": Zumar, "A juror's diary," *Daily News*, Feb. 28, 1981, p. 9.

328–29 "This is a story of love": Wilson, "Harris trial: Defense, prosecutor go for broke," *Daily News*, Feb. 17, 1981, p. 22. In opening argument Aurnou said his case would prove "that a woman is capable of having her own life, her own feelings, her own emotions, independent of a man." Weymouth, "The Trial and Trials," p. 23. This early hint of Harris as feminist hero could not be sustained.

331 ". . . middle-class soap opera": Mike Hurewitz and Pat Smith, "Defense made big mistakes, say top lawyers," *New York Post*, Feb. 25, 1981, p. 4.

331 Misled by their left-wing analysis: That violence is lower class is a widespread belief, a belief for which poor and nonwhite men as well as women pay dearly in the criminal-justice system. In fact all the available statistics in the world indicate that violence is overwhelmingly male. In recent years male violence aimed particularly at women and children—in wife and child assault, rape, and incest as well as murder—has increased so dramatically that feminists in Berkeley and Oakland, California, are now planning the first international conference on "femicide."

331 law discriminates against the rich: James J. Duggan, "a well-regarded defense lawyer," quoted by Weymouth, "Was Jean Harris's Defense Bungled?" p. 30.

332 Cesare Lombroso: and William Ferrero, *The Female Offender* (New York: D. Appleton, 1897), trans. from *La Donna Delinquente, La Prostituta E La Donna Normale* (1893), p. 274. Compare attorney Aurnou's view of passionate love to this from Lombroso: "This predominance among women of suicide over homicide is in perfect harmony with our view of the nature of love in women. We saw that in women love is a species of slavery, a sacrifice gladly made of the entire personality. These elements . . . are so exaggerated in passionate natures that ill-treatment on the part of their lover only increases their fury of self-sacrifice." p. 274. "Pure, strong passion, when existing in a woman, drives her to suicide rather than to crime. . . . [To] a capacity for murderous assaults, . . . the true woman, the finished woman, is a stranger. The true crime of love—if such it can be called—in a woman is suicide. . . ." p. 276.

332–33 some prominent male attorneys blamed: Richard Rosen, "Say female jurors did Jean in," *Daily News*, Feb. 25, 1981, p. 5. Shana Alexander also blamed the jurors, but for reasons of class, not sex. p. 90.

333   "nice legs": Lindsay Van Gelder, "The Scarsdale-Diet-Doctor Murder Case," *MS*, Aug. 1980, p. 70. The apparent resemblance between Aurnou's attitude toward women and Tarnower's would be remarkable if this attitude were not so commonplace.

333   Leggett commended her: James Feron, "Defiant Jean Harris Sentenced to Mandatory 15 Years," *New York Times*, March 21, 1981, pp. 1, 26. Emphasis mine.

333   Jean Harris, who dutifully abides: Alexander, p. 100.

334   she has written two books: Jean Harris, *Stranger in Two Worlds* (New York: Macmillan, 1986), and *"They Always Call Us Ladies": Stories from Prison* (New York: Charles Scribner's Sons, 1988).

334   More than 60 percent: *Stranger in Two Worlds*, p. 223.

334   More than half of them were "sexually abused": *"They Always Call Us Ladies,"* p. 116.

334   "You probably wouldn't like [her]": *Stranger in Two Worlds*, p. 224.

334   But in Harris's impassioned account: *"They Always Call Us Ladies,"* p. 7.

334   "They fear men": *Ibid.*, p. 116.

334   Yet they hold to "the myth . . .": *Stranger in Two Worlds*, pp. 229–230.

335   about 40 percent of Harris's neighbors: *Ibid.*, pp. 235–236.

335   "It is one of the many ironies": *"They Always Call Us Ladies,"* p. 219.

335   During that time, women have killed: Angela Browne and Kirk R. Williams, "Trends in Partner Homicide By Relationship Type and Gender: 1976–87," unpublished paper; Browne and Williams, interviews, Feb. 12, 1991. Between 1976 and 1987, 38,648 American women and men were killed in what statisticians call "partner homicide." Browne, testimony before the United States Senate Committee on the Judiciary, Dec. 11, 1990. In the United States firearms are the weapon of choice for both men and women in slightly more than 70 percent of homicides, but 11.8 percent of female victims (as compared to 1.6 percent of male victims) are bludgeoned to death. See James A. Mercy and Linda E. Saltzman, "Fatal Violence among Spouses in the United States, 1976–85," *American Journal of Public Health*, vol. 79, no. 5 (May 1989), p. 596.

335   During the same period in England: Official Criminal Statistics, Home Office, 1990. Because firearms are not in common use, as they are in the United States, most male victims are killed with a sharp instrument. Female victims are killed by sharp instruments in 32 percent of homicides, but in most cases females are killed without a weapon, just as they were in the United States before the widespread distribution of handguns. Of female victims in England, 26 percent are strangled, 12 percent bludgeoned with a blunt instrument, and 11 percent bludgeoned by hand. "Crime: The facts, the figures, the fears," *Observer*, Feb. 17, 1991. I am grateful to Sue Lees and Octavia Wiseman for providing homicide data for England and Wales.

335 During the decade, the battered women's movement: See R. Emerson Dobash and Russell P. Dobash, "The Response of the British and American Women's Movements to Violence Against Women," in *Women, Violence and Social Control*, ed. Jalna Hanmer and Mary Maynard (Atlantic Highlands, NJ: Humanities Press International, 1987), pp. 169–179.

335 In 1985 the Surgeon General: "Wife Abuse: An Opportunity for Prevention," *Injury Prevention Network Newsletter*, vol. 5, no. 1 (Spring/Summer 1988), pp. 2–3.

335–36 "A bill to combat violence and crimes": Hearings were conducted on Senate Bill 2754 on June 20, Aug. 29, and Dec. 11, 1990. The bill died along with the 101st Congress but should reappear in 1991 in the 102nd Congress as Senate Bill 15.

336 Conservative estimates hold: Browne, Senate testimony, Dec. 11, 1990.

336 Researchers in the field: *Ibid.*

336 The work of feminist researchers: R. Emerson Dobash and Russell Dobash, *Violence Against Wives: A Case Against the Patriarchy* (New York: The Free Press, 1979), p. 15.

336 Emerge, a Boston counseling program: David Adams, "Treatment Models of Men Who Batter: A Profeminist Analysis," *Feminist Perspectives on Wife Abuse*, ed., Kersti Yllo and Michele Bograd (Newbury Park, CA: SAGE, 1988), p. 191.

337 "Abuse by male partners": *When Battered Women Kill* (New York: The Free Press, 1987), p. 3.

337 while English theorists . . . have cautioned: The most thorough and persuasive cautionary analysis is Carol Smart, *Feminism and the Power of Law* (London: Routledge, 1989).

337 She later told a reporter: "Hitting Home," *48 Hours*, CBS TV, June 18, 1988.

337–38 On June 10, 1983: Amy Eppler, "Battered Women and the Equal Protection Clause: Will the Constitution Help Them When the Police Won't," *Yale Law Journal*, 95 (1986), p. 788.

338 "A man is not allowed to physically abuse": *Thurman* v. *City of Torrington*, 595 F. Supp. 1521 (1984); *Thurman* v. *City of Torrington*, USDC DConn, No. H-84-120, June 25, 1985.

338 The jury awarded Tracey Thurman: The decision was appealed, and Thurman settled out of court for $1.9 million. The jury also awarded her son $300,000.

339 In a single year the number of arrests: Anne Menard, Connecticut Coalition Against Domestic Violence, interview, Feb. 14, 1991.

339 Throughout the eighties, all across the country: See for example *Balistreri* v. *Pacifica Police Dept.*, 855 F. 2d 1421 (9th Cir. 1988); *Watson* v. *City of Kansas City, Kan.*, 857 F. 2d 690 (10th Cir. 1988); *Hynson* v. *City of Chester Legal Dept.*, 864 F. 2d 1026 (3rd Cir. 1988); *McKee* v. *City of Rockwall, Tex.*, 877 F. 2d 409 (5th Cir. 1989).

339 Finally, in 1989, in a case involving a child: *DeShaney* v. *Winnebago County DSS*, 109 S. Ct. 988 (1989) 1007.

340   "When you push the law": interview, Feb. 14, 1991.

340   In 1980 she discussed: "Equal Rights to Trial for Women: Sex Bias in the Law of Self-Defense," *Harvard Civil Rights–Civil Liberties Law Review*, vol. 15, no. 3 (Winter 1980), pp. 623–647.

340   "The male assumptions contained": *Ibid.*, p. 647.

340   Some defense attorneys, sharing the law's bias: see Ann Jones, "When Battered Women Fight Back," *Barrister*, vol. 9, no. 4 (Fall 1982), pp. 48, 51.

340   the theory of "learned helplessness": Lenore E. Walker, *The Battered Woman* (New York: Harper & Row, 1979), pp. 42–54.

340–41   the "battered woman's syndrome": Walker, *The Battered Woman Syndrome* (New York: Springer, 1984), and *Terrifying Love: Why Battered Women Kill And How Society Responds* (New York: Harper & Row, 1989).

341   Partial studies indicate: Charles Patrick Ewing, *Battered Women Who Kill: Psychological Self-Defense as Legal Justification* (New York: Lexington, 1987), pp. 41–43; Sue Osthoff, National Clearinghouse for the Defense of Battered Women, interview, Feb. 11, 1991. Lenore Walker discusses outcomes of cases she worked on in "A Response to Elizabeth M. Schneider's *Describing and Changing: Women's Self-Defense Work and the Problem of Expert Testimony on Battering,*" *Women's Rights Law Reporter*, vol. 9, nos. 3 & 4 (Fall 1986), p. 224.

341   The battered woman's syndrome describes a "victim": for analysis of the theory, use, and misuse of expert testimony in battered women's cases see Elizabeth M. Schneider, "Describing and Changing: Women's Self-Defense Work and the Problem of Expert Testimony on Battery," *Women's Rights Law Reporter*, vol. 9, nos. 3 & 4 (Fall 1986), pp. 195–222.

341–42   Theorist Susan Schechter writes: *Women and Male Violence: The Visions and Struggles of the Battered Women's Movement* (Boston: South End Press, 1982), p. 252.

342   The alleged passivity and helplessness: See the Uncle Remus stories of Joel Chandler Harris, allegories of the black experience in the United States, for illustration of "lying low" and various other survival strategies of the oppressed.

342   Walker herself observed: *The Battered Woman Syndrome*, p. 33.

343   In Duluth, Minnesota: Ellen Pence, Domestic Abuse Intervention Project, interview, Feb. 12, 1991.

343   On December 27, 1988, Joseph Grohoski: "L.I. Man Kills Estranged Wife; Commits Suicide," *New York Times*, Dec. 28, 1988, B2.

344   Two days later William Croff: Eric Schmitt, "L.I. Man Fatally Shoots Wife, Then Himself," *New York Times*, Dec. 30, 1988, B1.

344   A week later Anthony LaSalata: Dan Fagin and Phil Mintz, "Stabbing Survivor Shot to Death on LI; Ex-Spouse Sought," *Newsday*, Jan. 4, 1989, p. 7; Eric Schmitt, "Suffolk Woman Being Protected Is Shot to Death," *New York Times*, Jan. 5, 1989.

344   Police found him: Kinsey Wilson and Joshua Quittner, "Wife-Slay Suspect

Found Dead," *Newsday*, Jan. 7, 1989, p. 5; "Man Found Dead in His Car Was Wanted in L.I. Killing," *New York Times*, Jan. 7, 1989, p. 30.

344   Elizabeth Croff's mother: "Husband Slays Wife in LI Murder–Suicide," *Newsday*, Dec. 30, 1988, p. 25.

344   Anthony LaSalata was awaiting trial: Sheila Weller, ". . . til death do us part," *Redbook*, Aug. 1989, p. 137.

344   In the past two years, twelve women: Frank Bruni, "Court-'protected' women fear for their lives," New York *Post*, Jan. 9, 1989.

344–45   In Westminster, Colorado, in 1987: "'My Husband Is Going to Kill Me,'" *Frontline*, PBS TV, 1988.

345   Afterwards, District Attorney James Smith: *Ibid*.

345   Lisa Bianco: Dick Polman, "In the shadow of violence," Philadelphia *Inquirer*, April 9, 1989, K1.

345   Interviewed two years later in prison: "Til Death Do Us Part," *48 Hours*, CBS TV, Feb. 6, 1991.

345   A spokesman for the state: Polman, K1.

345   another Indiana woman, identified only as "Bonnie": "Til Death Do Us Part," *48 Hours*.

345   When David Gunther killed Pamela: "'My Husband Is Going to Kill Me.'"

345–46   An advocate in Suffolk County: Bruni.

346   Another woman hiding out in a shelter: *Ibid*.

346   Advocates at shelters in Colorado: Jan Hoffman, "By Her Husband's Hand," *The Village Voice*, Aug. 13, 1985, p. 92.

346   Lisa Bianco's mother: "Til Death Do Us Part," *48 Hours*.

346   Since 1974 violent crimes: "Federal Government Increasing Focus on Violence Against Women," *NCJA Justice Research*, Sept./Oct. 1990, p. 3; Victoria A. Brownworth, "Violence Against Women on the Rise," *Philadelphia Gay News*, Aug. 17–24, 1990, p. 1.

346   Angela Browne reported: Senate testimony, Dec. 11, 1990. See also Browne and Kirk R. Williams, "Exploring the Effect of Resource Availability and the Likelihood of Female-Perpetrated Homicides," *Law & Society Review*, vol. 23, no. 1 (1989), pp. 76–94.

346–47   Similarly, Sue Osthoff: interview.

347   One researcher suggests that at least half: Browne, *When Battered Women Kill*, p. 110, citing D. M. Moore, *Battered Women* (Beverly Hills, CA: SAGE, 1979).

347   Women murdered in the United States: Browne and Williams report that from 1980 to 1984, 52 percent of women murdered in the United States were killed by male partners. British homicide data for the period 1984–1988 indicate that 44 percent of female homicide victims in England and Wales are killed by male partners.

347   men "normally" overkill women: I am indebted to law professor Holly Maguigan for reminding me that crimonologist Marvin Wolfgang, in his well-known 1958 study of Philadelphia homicide, took note of the remarkably bru-

tal ways men murder women. To describe it, he coined the seemingly redundant term "violent homicide."

347 "What is surprising is the enormous effort": Gerald T. Hotaling and David B. Sugarman, "An Analysis of Risk Markers in Husband to Wife Violence: The Current State of Knowledge," *Violence and Victims*, vol. 1, no. 2 (1986), p. 120.

347–48 four women on death row: Adele Shank, General Counsel to the Ohio Public Defender, interview, Feb. 14, 1991.

348 *At least* fourteen of them: Leigh Dingerson, National Coalition to Abolish the Death Penalty, interview, Feb. 12, 1991.

348 A month earlier, on December 21, 1990: Isabel Wilkerson, "Clemency Granted to 25 Women Convicted for Assault or Murder," *New York Times*, Dec. 22, 1990, p. 1.

349 During the past fifteen years: all data from "Women and Violence," transcript of the Hearing before the Committee on the Judiciary, United States Senate, June 20, 1990, Serial No. J-101-80 (Washington: U.S. Government Printing Office, 1990), p. 12.

349 On Margie Velma Bullard Burke Barfield: The most complete account of her life and death is Elin Schoen, "Does This Woman Deserve To Die?" *The Village Voice*, vol. XXIX no. 17 (June 5, 1984), pp.. 1, 10–20.

350 "My dad was very, very hot tempered": Schoen, p. 12.

350 "I think I went into it . . .": Schoen, p. 13.

350 "We were just a normal . . .": Schoen, p. 13.

350 "It embarrassed him . . .": Schoen, p. 14.

351 "She was always on that medication": Schoen, p. 14.

351 "always fearful of what might . . .": Schoen, p. 14.

351 "I know that I was addicted . . .": Schoen, p. 14.

351 "Many times," she said: Schoen, p. 15.

352 ". . . the patient herself . . ." Schoen, p. 15.

352 "They would always take me . . .": Schoen, p. 15.

352 "He could get abusive": Schoen, p. 15.

353 "I didn't have any reason": Schoen, p. 16.

353 Prison officials, who described her: William E. Schmidt, "Woman Executed in United States for First Time Since 1962," *New York Times*, Nov. 3, 1984.

353 "There were days . . .": Michael Hirsley, "Female killer stirs life-or-death debate," *Chicago Tribune*, Sept. 9, 1984, p. 14.

354 "If Gov. Hunt grants clemency . . .": Hirsley, p. 14, quoting Claude Sifton, editor of the *Raleigh News & Observer*.

354 Historically the death penalty: Schoen, p. 20.

354 "tough decision": Schmidt.

354 "I know that everybody . . .": Schmidt.

354 "with as much dignity . . .": Schmidt.

354 "She just seemed to relax": Schmidt.

INDEX